THE 1912 OLYMPIC GAMES

In memory of the thousands
of brave and proud Americans
who lost their lives on September 11, 2001.

THE 1912 OLYMPIC GAMES

Results for All Competitors in All Events, with Commentary

by Bill Mallon
and Ture Widlund

RESULTS OF THE EARLY MODERN OLYMPICS, 6

McFarland & Company, Inc., Publishers
Jefferson, North Carolina, and London

Library of Congress Cataloguing-in-Publication Data

Mallon, Bill.
    The 1912 Olympic Games : results for all competitors in all
events, with commentary / by Bill Mallon and Ture Widlund.
       p. cm. — (Results of the early modern Olympics ; 6)
    Includes index.
    ISBN 0-7864-1047-7 (library binding : 50# alkaline paper) ∞
    1. Olympic Games (6th : 1912 : Stockholm, Sweden)
    2. Olympics — Records.   I. Widlund, Ture.   II. Title.
    III. Series : Mallon, Bill. Results of the early modern Olympics ; 6
    GV721.8.M35   2002 vol. 6
    [GV722 1912]
    796.48 — dc21   2001044619

British Library Cataloguing-in-Publication data are available

Manufactured in the United States of America

McFarland & Company, Inc., Publishers
  Box 611, Jefferson, North Carolina 28640
   www.mcfarlandpub.com

Table of Contents

Introduction

This is the 6th in a series of seven books giving complete summaries of the earliest Olympic Games. The series has run chronologically and the earlier books covered, in order, the 1896, 1900, 1904, 1906, and 1908 Olympic Games. The 1896 book was coauthored by Bill Mallon and Ture Widlund, the 1900–1906 books were the sole work of Bill Mallon, and the 1908 book was coauthored by Bill Mallon and Ian Buchanan. The final book in the series will deal with the 1920 Olympic Games, and will again be solely attributed to Mallon. This book, covering the 1912 Olympic Games, is coauthored again by Mallon and Widlund. The 1912 Olympic Games took place in Stockholm, Sweden, and Ture Widlund was an obvious choice as coauthor, as he is one of Sweden's best-known Olympic historians and researchers. (Note from Mallon: This book would not have been possible in anywhere near its present form without Ture's contribution. His efforts in researching all of the original 1912 sources were inestimable.)

This series of books covers the earliest Olympics because these are the Olympic Games for which results were not well recorded. Currently, at the end of each Olympic Games, the Organizing Committee is required by the International Olympic Committee to produce a detailed "Official Report" of the Olympic Games. At the end of the first century of the Modern Olympic Movement, these Official Reports are often exhaustive, covering in great detail every aspect of the organization and the results of the Olympics. This was not the case in the early years.

Official Reports did exist for all the Olympic Games between 1896 and 1920 but they were of varying quality. Some of them barely contained results at all — the medalists were usually mentioned, but often nothing further. Thus, this series is an attempt to complete and re-create the Olympic Record, as it were, by filling in the many gaps left by several of the less than complete early Official Reports.

Having said that, it should be stated that the 1912 Official Report was by far the best of that era. Nonetheless, we have expanded on the results listed in that book, whose actual title (in English) is *The Fifth Olympiad. The Official Report of the Olympic Games of Stockholm 1912.* To do so, we have used many of the other contemporary sources published in Sweden in 1912, notably newspapers and especially *Olympiska Spelen Tidning/The Olympic News*, which was published especially to cover the Olympic Games in Stockholm.

Finally, please note that students of Olympic history will not find the 1912 report or any of the early reports with ease. Copies are rare and few libraries have it. It does show up for sale in certain Olympic auctions of memorabilia from time to time, but expect to pay at least $1,000 (US) for the 1912 report.

The study of Olympic history has undergone a renaissance in the past decade, partly sparked by the formation of the International Society of Olympic Historians (ISOH). ISOH was formed on 5 December 1991 at a meeting at a pub called the "Duke of Clarence" in the Kensington section of London. We were both present as founding members of ISOH.

We would like to give thanks to the following sports and Olympic historians, many of them members of ISOH, who have helped us with the compilation of this book: Paulo Barbosa (POR), Tony Bijkerk (NED), Gherardo Bonini (ITA), Ian Buchanan (GBR), Pete Cava (USA/Jim Thorpe/ Baseball), Bob Clotworthy (USA/Diving), Herman De Wael (BEL), Þorstein Einarsson (ISL/ Glíma Wrestling), Heiner Gillmeister (TEN), Arild Gjerde (NOR), Harry Gordon (AUS), Pavel Hladík (CZE), Líney R. Halldórsdóttir (ISL), Rupert Kaiser (GER), Ove Karlsson (SWE), Gabor Kobzos (HUN), Cuneyt Koryurek (TUR), Jiří Kössl (BOH), Henry Landress (USA), Hans Agersnap Larsen (DEN/ISL), Lappe Laubscher (RSA), Jos Luypaers (BEL), Wolf Lyberg (SWE), John Mallon (USA/Jim Thorpe), Bob Miyakawa (JPN), Ray Nemec (USA/Jim Thorpe), Giuseppe Odello (ITA), Ingrid O'Neil (USA), Ruud Paauw (NED/Fencing), Ron Palenski (NZL), Jaroslav Pruner (BOH), Florence Ridlon (USA/Jim Thorpe), Daniel Schamps (FRA), Markku Siukonen (FIN), Gabriel Szabó (HUN), Athanassios Tarasouleas (GRE), Magne Teigen (NOR), Oleg Vorontsov (RUS), David Wallechinsky (USA/FRA), Bob Wheeler (USA/Jim Thorpe), and Ekkehard zur Megede (ATH)

Bill Mallon
Durham, NC, USA
September 2000

Ture Widlund
Stockholm, SWE
September 2000

Abbreviations

General Abbreviations

1B	first base	km.	kilometer(s)
2B	second base	L	lost
3B	third base	lbs.	pounds
A:	athletes competing	LF	leftfield
AB	abandoned	m.	meter(s)
AC	also competed (place not known)	mi.	mile(s)
AE	also entered	ML	matches lost
B.C.E.	before common era (aka B.C.)	MW	matches won
bh	behind	NH	no-height
C	catcher	NM	no mark
C:	countries competing	NP	not placed
C.E.	common era (aka A.D.)	OR/or	Olympic Record
CF	centerfield	P	pitcher
d.	defeated	Q	automatic qualifier for the next round
D:	date(s) of competition		
dec	decision	q	conditional qualifier for the next round
DNF	did not finish		
DNS	did not start	r	round
DQ	disqualified	RF	rightfield
E	entered	S:	site of competition
e	estimate(d)	SS	shortstop
f	final	T:	time of competition starting
F/f	foul	TF	touches for (fencing)
F:	format of competition	TR	touches received (fencing)
h	heat	v.	versus
HA	hits against (fencing)	wo	walkover (won by forfeit)
HF	hits for (fencing)	W	won
IAAF	International Amateur Athletic Federation	WR	World Record
		yd(s).	yard(s)
kg.	kilogram(s)		

National Abbreviations

AUS	Australia/Australasia (Australia and New Zealand)	ISL	Iceland
		ITA	Italy
AUT	Austria	JPN	Japan
BEL	Belgium	LUX	Luxembourg
BOH	Bohemia	NED	The Netherlands
CAN	Canada	NOR	Norway
CHI	Chile	NZL	New Zealand
DEN	Denmark	POR	Portugal
EGY	Egypt	RSA	South Africa
ENG	England	RUS	Russia
FIN	Finland	SCO	Scotland
FRA	France	SRB	Serbia
GBR	Great Britain and Ireland	SUI	Switzerland
GER	Germany	SWE	Sweden
GRE	Greece	TUR	Turkey
HUN	Hungary	USA	United States
IRL	Ireland	WLS	Wales

Sports Abbreviations

ATH	Athletics (Track and Field)	ROW	Rowing and Sculling
CYC	Cycling	SHO	Shooting
DIV	Diving	SWI	Swimming
EQU	Equestrian Events	TEN	Tennis (Lawn and Covered Courts)
FEN	Fencing		
FTB	Football (Association) [Soccer]	WAP	Water Polo
GYM	Gymnastics	WRE	Wrestling
MOP	Modern Pentathlon	YAC	Yachting

References

with Their Abbreviations as Cited in Text

Primary Sources from Circa 1912

12OR	"Official Report," proper title in English is *The Fifth Olympiad. The Official Report of the Olympic Games of Stockholm 1912*, edited by Erik Bergvall, Esquire, translated by Edward Adams-Ray. Stockholm: Wahlström & Widstrand, 1913. Proper title in Swedish is *V. Olympiaden. Officiell Redogörelse Olympiska Spelen i Stockholm 1912*.
ASZ	*Allgemeine Sport-Zeitung*, daily Austrian sporting newspaper, 1912.
BWMR	*The Bicycling World and Motorcycling Review*, weekly American cycling magazine, New York, 1912.
Diem	Diem, Carl. *Die olympischen Spiele 1912*. Berlin: Bürger, 1912.
FenPro	*Programme, Tournoi d'Escrime*. Stockholm: 1912.
Frick	Frick, Eric, ed. *Reglaer och allmanna bestammelser for allman idrott vid Olympiska Spelen i Stockholm 1912*. Stockholm: 1911.
Herczeg	Herczeg, István. *Impresszionim a stockholmi olimpiadrol*. Budapest: Stephaneum nyomda, 1912.
HorseProg	*Hästtäflingar. Dagsprogram. 13–17 July. Daily Equestrian Program*. Stockholm.
Lindroth	Lindroth, Elis, ed. *Segraren. Resultat vid 5. Olympiaden Stockholm 1912*. Stockholm: 1912.
Marathon	Bergvall, Erik. *Marathon vid Olympiska Spelen 1912*. Stockholm: Nordiskt Idrottslif, 1912.
Nordiskt	*Nordiskt Idrottslif*, weekly Swedish sporting newspaper, Stockholm, 1912.
NTFI	*Ny Tidning för Idrott*, weekly Swedish sporting newspaper, Stockholm, 1912.
NYT	The *New York Times*, daily American newspaper, New York, 1912.
Ofen	Fick, Emil. *Les Escrimeurs à la Véme Olympiade a Stockholm 1912*. Stockholm: Imprimérie A.-B. Hasse-W. Tullberg, 1913.
OlyCyc	*Generalprotokoll m. Fl. Uppgifter ofver Olympiska Spelens cykeltäfaling Mälaren rundt*. Stockholm: Centraltryckeriet, 1912.
Olympiaden	Hermelin, [Colonel,] Baron Sven [D. A.]; Peterson, Erik. *Den Femte Olympiaden. Olympiska Spelen i Stockholm 1912 i Bild och Ord*. Göteburg: Åhlén & Åkerlund, 1912; and Stockholm: Åhlén & Åkerlund, 1954.

Onews   *Olympiska Spelen Tidning/The Olympic News*, eds. Viktor Gustaf Balck and Erik
            Bergvall, Esquire. 33 issues. 31 May (No. 1A), 17 June–27 July 1912 (25 June–20
            July daily) (Nos. 1–32). This was a coalescence of the three Swedish sporting news-
            papers, *Nordiskt Idrottslif, Idrottsbladet,* and *Ny Tidning för Idrott.*
ORes   *Official Results.* Typewritten results, loosely translated as "Official Protocol," held
            at the Riksarkivet in Stockholm in their archives concerning the 1912 Olympic
            Games.
Paasivirta Paasivirta, Juhani. *Finland och de Olympiska Spelen i Stockholm.* Helsinki: Ekenäs
            Tryckeri Aktiebolags Förlag, 1963.
Prog   *Fifth Olympiad. Olympic Games of Stockholm, Sweden. 1912. (June 29th–July 22nd)—
            Programme and General Regulations.* Stockholm: Swedish Olympic Committee,
            1912.
Rau   Rau, Gustav. *Die Konkurrensen zu Pferde an den Olympischen Spielen zu Stockholm.*
            Stuttgart: Verlag von Schickhardt & Ebner (Konrad Wittwer), 1913.
SAR   *Svenska arméns rulla.* Stockholm, 1912.
Seybold   Seybold, Eugen. *Olympischen Spiele 1912. Stockholm.* München: author, 1912.
Spalding   Sullivan, James E[dward]. *The Olympic Games Stockholm 1912.* New York: Amer-
            ican Sports Publishing Company, 1912.
Spiedl   Spiedl, Zoltán. *A stockholmig olympiai jatekok.* Budapest: Rozsavolgyi es tarsa
            kiadasa, 1912.
Stadion   *Dagens Nyheter Stadion.* Stockholm. 36 editions. 5 June 1912–27 July 1912. This was
            a special Olympic newspaper which preceded, and was replaced by, *Olympiska
            Spelen Tidning/Olympic News* (see above).
StadProg   *Stadion-Program.* 6–15 July 1912. Daily Program. Stockholm, 1912.
SwimProg   *Dagsprogram för Simtäflingarna.* 6–16 July. Daily Swimming Program. Stockholm,
            1912.
TF   *The Field,* weekly British sporting magazine, London, 1912.
Times   *The Times,* daily British newspaper, London, 1912.
Uggla   Uggla, Gustaf G:son. *Olympiska Spelen i Stockholm 1912.* Stockholm: Svenska Bok-
            förlaget, 1912.
Wagner   Wagner, Julius and Guido Eichenberger. *Olympische Spiele Stockholm 1912.* Zurich/
            München: J. Wagner Verlag, 1913.
Webster   Webster, Frederick A. M. *The Evolution of the Olympic Games 1829 B.C.–1914 A.D.*
            London: Heath, Cranton & Ouseley, Ltd., circa 1914.

Olympic and Sporting Historical and Statistical Works after 1912

AG/MT   Gjerde, Arild and Teigen, Magne. *Index of Participants of Olympic Athletics 1896–
            1988. Part 1: 1896–1912 Men.* Skedsmokorset, NOR: Norske Olympiahistorikere,
            1992.
Andersen   Andersen, Per Christian; Wold, Ragnar. *Sport i navn og tal.* Oslo: 1950.
Balck1   Balck, Viktor. *Minnen. I Ungdomen.* Stockholm: 1929.
Balck2   Balck, Viktor. *Minnen. II Mannaåren.* Stockholm: 1931.
Barcs   Barcs, Sándor. *The Modern Olympics Story.* Budapest: Corvina Press, 1964.
Bergvall1   Bergvall, Erik. *Stadion 25 år.* Stockholm: 1937.
Bergvall2   Bergvall, Erik. *Boken om simning.* Stockholm: 1948.
Björkman   Björkman, Ingmar. *Med idrotten i blodet.* Helsingfors: 1995.
Bland   Bland, Ernest. *Olympic Story.* London: Rockfliff, 1948.

Bratt1   Bratt, K. A. J. *Sigfrid Edström En levnadsteckning. Förra delen.* Stockholm: 1950.

Bratt2   Bratt, K. A. J. *Sigfrid Edström En levnadsteckning. Senare delen.* Stockholm: 1953.

Campaign   Coubertin, Pierre de. *Une campagne de vingt-et-un ans (1887–1908).* Paris: Librairie de l'Education Physique, 1909.

Coubertin   Coubertin, Pierre de. *Mémoires olympiques.* Lausanne: Bureau international de pédagogie sportive, 1931. English translation by Geoffrey de Navacelle published in 1979 for the IOC — page numbers in footnotes refer to this version.

Dansk   *Dansk Sportsleksikon.* København: 1945.

Durry   Durry, Jean. "'Hohrod and Eschbach' A Mystery Finally Solved." In: *Olympic Review,* 32: 26–28, April-May 2000.

DW   Wallechinsky, David. *The Complete Book of the Olympics.* 4th edition. New York: Little Brown, 1996.

EK   Kamper, Erich. *Enzyklopädie der Olympischen Spiele.* Dortmund: Harenberg, 1972. Parallel texts in German, French, and English. American edition issued as *Encyclopaedia of the Olympic Games* by McGraw-Hill (New York) in 1972.

Ekegren   Ekegren, Lars, et. al. (eds.) *Idrottskamrater minns.* Stockholm: 1977.

EL   Laitinen, Esa. *10 000 m Tulokset ja Tilastot Results and Statistics.* Pihkala, Finland: np, 1986.

EzM   zur Megede, Ekkehard. *The Modern Olympic Century 1896–1936.* Berlin: Deutsche Gesellschaft für Leichtathletik-Dokumentation, 1999.

FIFA   *Fédération Internationale de Football Association 1904–1929.* Amsterdam: no year given.

FJGVDM   Van Der Merwe, Floris J. G. "Formation of the South African National Olympic Association." In: *The Olympic Games Through the Ages: Greek Antiquity and its Impact on Modern Sport.* R Renson, M Lämmer, J Riordan, D Chassiotis, eds. Athens: Hellenic Sports Research Institute, 1991. pp. 251–259.

FM   Mező, Ferenc. *The Modern Olympic Games.* Budapest: Pannonia Press, 1956. English edition.

FW   Wasner, Fritz. *Olympia-Lexikon.* Bielefeld, Germany: Verlag E. Gunglach Aktiengesellschaft, 1939.

Gandil   Gandil, Johannes. *Dansk fodbold.* København: 1937.

Ganebro   Ganebro, Lennart (ed.). *Arosidrotten 1000 år.* Västerås: 1989.

Gärdin   Gärdin, Gösta (ed.). *Den Olympiska Rörelson.* Stockholm: 1992.

Gillmeister   Gillmeister, Heiner. *Olympisches Tennis. Die Geschichte der olympischen Tennisturniere (1896–1992).* Sankt Augustin, GER: Academia Verlag, 1993.

Guiney   Guiney, David. *Ireland's Olympic Heroes.* Dublin: David Roderick, 1969.

Gynn   Gynn, Roger. *The Guinness Book of the Marathon.* London: Guinness, 1984.

G/M   Gynn, Roger and David Martin. *The Olympic Marathon: The History and Drama of Sport's Most Challenging Event.* Champaign, IL: Human Kinetics, 2000.

Haglind   Haglind, Henning; Pallin, Erik. *Kungl Svenska Segel Sällskapet 1830–1930.* Stockholm: 1930.

Hansen   Hansen, Jørn; Skovgaard, Thomas (eds.). *Folkekultur of Finkultur.* Odense: 2000.

Henry   Henry, Bill. *An Approved History of the Olympic Games.* 1st edition. New York: G. P. Putnam, 1948.

H/A   Hugman, Barry J. and Peter Arnold. *The Olympic Games: Complete Track & Field Results 1896–1988.* London: The Arena Press, 1988.

ICOSH   *ICOSH Seminar 1988. The Olympic Movement: Past, Present and Future.* Sarajevo, 1988.

IFFHS   "Die olympischen Fußball-Turniere (1900–1920)." In: *IFFHS Fußball-Weltzeitschrift,* 16, (Jan/June 1989), pp. 4–37.

Jatekok   Szerelemhegyi, Ervin and Béla Szabó. *A Modern Olimpiai Játékok.* 2nd ed. Buda-
               pest: Légrády Nyomda és Könyvkiadó R.-T. Kiadása, 1932.
Johnson   Johnson, William Oscar. *All That Glitters is Not Gold.* New York: Putnam, 1972.
Karaki   Karaki, Kunihiko. "The first Japanese Olympic delegation in 1912." In: *The Olympic
               Games Through the Ages: Greek Antiquity and its Impact on Modern Sport. Proceed-
               ings of the 13th International HISPA Congress, Olympia/Greece, May 22–28, 1989.*
               eds. Roland Renson, Manfred Lämmer, James Riordan, Dimitrios Chassiotis.
               Athens: Hellenic Sports Research Institute, 1991; pp. 261–265.
Kossl   Kössl, Jiří. "Origin and Development of the Czech and Czechoslovak Olympic
               Committee." In *Citius, Altius, Fortius*, 2(3), (Autumn 1994), 11–26.
Krüger   Krüger, Arnd. "Coubertin's Ruskianism." In: *Olympic Perspectives: Third Interna-
               tional Symposium for Olympic Research*, London, Ontario, CAN: Centre for Olym-
               pic Studies, October 1996, pp. 31–43.
Larsson   Larsson, Mats. *Svitjod. Resor till Sveriges ursprung.* Stockholm: 1998.
Libero   *Libero International.* Wiesbaden. Nos. 10–14, 1993–1994.
Lignell   Lignell, Ivar, et. al. (eds.). *Svensk Tennis.* Stockholm: 1938.
Lilliehöök   Lilliehöök, Gösta, et. al. (eds.). *Svenska folkrörelser III Idrott.* Stockholm: 1992.
Lindhagen1   Lindhagen, Sven. *Mina 13 olympiader.* Stockholm: 1952.
Lindhagen2   Lindhagen, Sven. *Rekordmän på kolstybb.* Stockholm: 1954.
Lindqvist   Lindqvist, Herman. *Historien om Sverige. Från islossning till kungarike.* Stockholm:
               1992.
Löwgren   Löwgren, Göran (ed.). *Stadion 75 år.* Stockholm: 1987.
Lucas   Lucas, John A. *The Modern Olympic Games.* South Brunswick, NJ: A. S. Barnes,
               1980.
Lyberg   Lyberg, Wolf. *The History of the IOC Sessions. I. 1894–1939.* Lausanne: Interna-
               tional Olympic Committee, October 1994.
Lyberg2   Lyberg, Wolf. *Fabulous 100 Years of the IOC.* Lausanne: IOC, 1996.
MacAloon   MacAloon, John. *This Great Symbol: Pierre de Coubertin and the Origins of the Mod-
               ern Olympic Games.* Chicago: Univ. of Chicago Press, 1981.
Mezo   Mező, Ferenc. *A stockholmig olympiai jatekok.* Budapest: 1955.
Müller   Müller, Norbert. *One Hundred Years of Olympic Congresses 1894–1994.* Lausanne:
               International Olympic Committee, 1994.
NordFam   *Nordisk Familjeboks Sportlexikon.* Stockholm, 1938–1949.
NQ   Nelson, Cordner and Roberto Quercetani. *The Milers.* Los Altos, CA: TAFNews
               Press, 1985.
Olympiadebogen   Andersen, Peder Christian and Vagn Hansen. *Olympiadebogen. De Olymp-
               iske Lege 1896–1948.* København: np, 1948.
O'Neill   O'Neill, Terry. *European Football Line-ups 1872 to 1919.* Daventry: date uncertain.
OS   Crossman, Colonel Jim. *Olympic Shooting.* Washington: National Rifle Associa-
               tion, 1978.
OSVK   Kluge, Volker. *Olympische Sommerspiele. Die Chronik I: Athen 1896 — Berlin 1936.*
               Berlin: Sport Verlag, 1997.
OTAF   Editors of Track & Field News. *Olympic Track and Field.* Los Altos, CA: Tafnews
               Press, 1979.
Oxenstierna   Oxenstierna, Eric. *Så levde vikingarna.* Stockholm: 1959.
Phillips   Phillips, Bob. *100 Years of the Olympic Marathon.* London: National Union of Track
               Statisticians, 1996.
POE   Associated Press and Grolier. *Pursuit of Excellence: The Olympic Story.* New York:
               Franklin Watts, 1979.

Psilander   Psilander, Nils Georg. *Svenska skyttar.* Uppsala: 1939.
QK   Quercetani, Roberto L. and Nejat Kök. *Wizards of the Middle Distances: A History of the 800 Metres.* Milan: Vallardi & Associati, 1992.
Quercetani   Quercetani, Roberto L. *A World History of Track and Field Athletics.* London: 1964.
Robinson   Robinson, Michael, ed., Colin José (Statistics and Write-Ups). *Soccer: The International Line-ups & Statistics Series — Olympic Football Part 1 1900–1964.* Humberside, England: Soccer Book Publishing, Ltd., 1996.
Schaap   Schaap, Richard. *An Illustrated History of the Olympics.* New York: Knopf, 1963.
Schödl   Schödl, Gottfried. *The Lost Past.* Budapest: 1992.
Scot   Scot, Alan. "Gångsport i Olympiska Spel." In: *SOF-Bulletinen,* S-35, (1997).
SG   Greenberg, Stan. *The Guinness Olympics Fact Book.* 3rd edition. Enfield, Middlesex, England: Guinness, 1983.
Sheridan   Sheridan, Michael. *Good Reasons: 100 Years of Olympic Marathon Races.* Somerset, England: author, 1996.
Siukonen   Siukonen, Markku; Pulakka, Martti; Ahola, Matti. *Urheilutieto. 14.* Jyväskylä: Gummerus Kirjapaino Oy, 1996.
Svahn   Svahn, Åke; Thunvik, Sten. *En bok om rodd.* Stockholm: 1944.
Svensson   Svensson, Sten (ed.). *Svensk Idrott 1903–1953.* Malmö: 1953.
TMF   Martin, David E., Gynn, Roger W. H. *The Marathon Footrace.* Champaign, IL, USA: CC Thomas, 1979.
Ueberhorst   Ueberhorst, Horst. "Stockholm 1912: The Games of the Vth Olympiad." In: *Historical Dictionary of the Modern Olympic Movement,* eds. John E. Findling and Kimberley D. Pelle. Westport, CT: Greenwood Press, 1996.
VK   Kluge, Volker. *Die olympischen spiele von 1896 bis 1980.* Berlin: Sportverlag, 1981.
Wahlqvist1   Wahlqvist, Bertil. *Vikingarnas lekar. Vikingen som idrottare.* Stockholm: 1993.
Wahlqvist2   Wahlqvist, Bertil. *Vikingarnas öar.* Stockholm: 1996.
Webster   Webster, Frederick A. M. *The Evolution of the Olympic Games 1829 B.C.–1914 A.D.* London: Heath, Cranton & Ouseley, Ltd., circa 1914.
Weyand   Weyand, Alexander. *The Olympic Pageant.* New York: Macmillan, 1952.
Widlund   Widlund, Ture. *Seglingstävlingarna i Paris 1900.* Stockholm: 1996.
Wigley   Wigley, Jon (ed.). *70 Golden Years IAAF 1912–1982.* Lausanne: 1982.
WW   Maritchev, Gennadi. *Who is Who at the Summer Olympics: 1896–1992.* Riga: Demarko Sport Publishing, 1996.

National Olympic and Sporting Histories

Bijkerk, Ton. and Paauw, Ruud. *Gouden Boek van de Nederlandse Olympiers.* Haarlem, NED: Uitgeverij de Vrieseborch, 1996.

Buchanan, Ian. *British Olympians: A Hundred Years of Gold Medallists.* London: Guinness, 1991.

Český Olympijský Výbor. *Dokumentace k dějinám českého olympismu. 1. díl: 1891–1918.* Praha: author, 1998.

Charpentier, Henri. *La Grande Histoire des Médaillés Olympiques Français de 1896 à 1988.* Paris: Editions Robert Laffont, 1993.

Colasante, Gianfranco. *La nascita del Movimento Olimpico in Italia. 1894–1914.* Rome: CONI, 1996.

Coqs et Centurions. Paris: Fédération Française d'Athletisme, 1986.

Cosentino, Frank and Leyshon, Glynn. *Olympic Gold: Canadian Winners of the Summer Games.* Toronto: Holt, Rinehart, and Winston, 1975.

1888–1988: Un Siecle d'Athletisme Français. Paris: Fédération Française d'Athletisme, 1989.

Glanell, Tomas, Huldtén, Gösta, et al., (eds.). *Sverige och OS*. Stockholm: Brunnhages Förlag AB, 1987.

Gordon, Harry. *Australia and the Olympic Games*. St. Lucia, Queensland: University of Queensland Press, 1994.

Guiney, David. *Gold Silver Bronze*. Dublin: Sportsworld, circa 1991.

Howell, Reet, and Howell, Max. *Aussie Gold: The Story of Australia at the Olympics*. South Melbourne: Brooks Waterloo, 1988.

Hungarian Olympic Committee. *Az Olimpiai Játékokon Indult Magyar Versenyzők Névsora 1896–1980*.

Klír M., Kössl J., Martínkovi, AaM. *Almanach Ceskoslovenskych Olympioniku*. Prague: 1987.

Koryürek, Cüneyt E. *Atina Atlanta 1896–1996: 28 Asrlk Olimpiyadlar Tarihi*. Istanbul: Arcelik Gururla Sunar, 1996.

Kössl, Jiří; Kroutil, František, et. al. *Malá encyclopedie olympijských her*. Prague: 1981.

Kristensen, Preben and Larsen, Hans Agersnap. *De Olympiske. Biografi af danske OL-deltagere 1896–1996*. København: Danmarks Idræts-Forbund, 1996.

Lester, Gary. *Australians at the Olympics: A Definitive History*. Sydney: Lester-Townsend Publishing, 1984.

Mallon, Bill, and Buchanan, Ian. *Quest for Gold: The Encyclopaedia of American Olympians*. New York: Leisure, 1984.

Matthews, Peter and Ian Buchanan. *Guinness All-Time Greats of British and Irish Sport*. London: Guinness, 1995.

Mező, Ferenc. *Golden Book of Hungarian Olympic Champions/Livre d'Or des Champions Olympiques Hongrois*. Budapest: Sport Lap. És Könyvkiadö, 1955. Parallel texts in English and French.

Naughton, Lindie and Watterson, Johnny. *Irish Olympians*. Dublin: Blackwater Press, 1992.

"Norske deltakere i olympiske leker 1900–1980." In: *Norges Olympiske Komité, 1977–80: XIII vinterleker Lake Placid 1980— XXII sommerleker Moskva 1980*. Aage Møst, editor. Oslo: Norges Olympiske Komité, 1980.

Palenski, Ron and Maddaford, Terry. *The Pride and Drama of New Zealanders at Olympic & Commonwealth Games: The Games*. Auckland: MOA Publications, 1983.

Pellissard-Darrigrand, Nicole. *La Galaxie Olympique*. Paris: J & D Editions, 1997.

Pettersson, Ulf, editor. *1896–1980 Guldboken om alla Våra Olympiamästare*. Stockholm: Brunnhages Förlag AB, 1980.

Roxborough, Henry. *Canada at the Olympics*. 3rd edition. Toronto: Ryerson Press, 1975.

Siukonen, Markku; Pulakka, Martti; Ahola, Matti. *Urheilutieto. 14*. Jyväskylä: Gummerus Kirjapaino Oy, 1996.

Tarasouleas, At[hanassios]. *Helliniki Simmetokhi Stis Sinkhrones Olympiades*. [Transliterated title from the Greek] Athens: author, 1990.

Other Sources

D'Este, Carlo. *Patton: A Genius for War*. New York: Harper Collins, 1995.

Gibson, Richard Lee. "Avery Brundage: Professional Amateur," Ph.D. Thesis, Kent State University, August 1976.

Goksøyr, Matti; von der Lippe, Gerd; and Mo, Kristen, eds. *Winter Games Warm Traditions*. Selected papers from the 2nd International ISHPES Seminar, Lillehammer, 25–30 January 1993. Oslo: Falch Hurtigtrykk, 1994.

Guttmann, Allen. *The Games Must Go On: Avery Brundage and the Olympic Movement.* New York: Columbia University Press, 1984.

Hannus, Matti. *The Flying Finns: Story of the Great Tradition of Finnish Distance Running and Cross Country Skiing.* Helsinki: Tietosanoma, 1990.

Krüger, Arnd. "The History of the Olympic Winter Games: The Invention of a Tradition." Presented at the ISHPES Seminar in Lillehammer on 25–30 January 1993. Published in *Winter Games Warm Traditions*, Goksøyr, von der Lippe, Mo, eds. See above under Goksøyr.

Lindroth, Jan. *Idrott mellan krigen. Organisationer, ledare och idéer i den svenska idrottsrörelsen 1919–1939.* Stockholm: 1987.

Lindroth, Jan. "The Nordic Games, Swedish-Norwegian Relations and Politics, 1905–1913. A Study of Sport and Politics in Conflict." Presented at the ISHPES Seminar in Lillehammer on 25–30 January 1993. Published in *Winter Games Warm Traditions*, Goksøyr, von der Lippe, Mo, eds. See above under Goksøyr.

Lindroth, Jan; Ljunggren, Jens; and Yttergren, Leif. "The Nordic Games." In: *1994 Swedish Media Guide for the Lillehammer Olympics.* Based on paper presented on the Nordic Games at the ISHPES Seminar in Lillehammer on 25–30 January 1993.

Ljunggren, Jens. "The Nordic Games, Nationalism, Sports, and Cultural Conflict." Presented at the ISHPES Seminar in Lillehammer on 25–30 January 1993. Published in *Winter Games Warm Traditions*, Goksøyr, von der Lippe, Mo, eds. See above under Goksøyr.

Mallon, Bill. "The Nordic Games and the Origins of the Olympic Winter Games." In: *Citius, Altius, Fortius*, 3(2): 29–37, May 1994. (Written under pseudonym of Ron Edgeworth.)

Mitch, Dale. "The Nordic Games." In: *Skating*, magazine of the United States Figure Skating Association (USFSA), nd.

Mo, Kristen. "Norwegian Resistance Against the Winter Olympics of the 1920s." In: *The Olympic Games Through the Ages: Greek Antiquity and its Impact on Modern Sport*, eds. R. Renson, M. Lämmer, J. Riordan, D. Chassiotis. Athens: Hellenic Sports Research Institute, 1991.

Newcombe, Jack. *The Best of the Athletic Boys: The White Man's Impact on Jim Thorpe.* Garden City, NY: Doubleday, 1975.

Nordiskt Idrottsliv, Festnumber II 1909. Referenced in Yttergren, "The Nordic Games: Visions of Olympic Winter Games of a Festival?"

Ny Tidning för Idrott, 1901/7, 8. Referenced in Yttergren, "The Nordic Games: Visions of Olympic Winter Games of a Festival?"

Patton, George Smith, 2nd Lieutenant, 15th Cavalry, Fort Myer, Va. *Report on Modern Pentathlon.* To the Adjutant General, U.S. Army, Washington, D.C. 19 September 1912.

Reising, Robert. *Jim Thorpe: The Story of an American Indian.* Minneapolis: Dillon Press, 1974.

Schoor, Gene. *The Jim Thorpe Story: America's Greatest Athlete.* New York: Julian Messner, 1951.

Sparks, Bob. *International Metric Conversion Tables.* 2nd ed. London: Arena Publications Limited, 1979.

Wheeler, Robert W. *Jim Thorpe: World's Greatest Athlete.* Norman, OK: Univ. of Oklahoma Press, 1975.

Wheeler, Robert W. Clipping file of research into Jim Thorpe case.

Wilson, Harold E., Jr. "A Legend in His Own Mind: The Olympic Experience of General George S. Patton, Jr.," *Olympika*, 6: 99–114, 1997.

Yttergren, Leif. "The Nordic Games: Visions of Olympic Winter Games of a Festival?" Presented at the ISHPES Seminar in Lillehammer on 25–30 January 1993.

Zarnowski, Frank. *The Decathlon: A Colorful History of Track and Field's Most Challenging Event.* Champaign, Illinois: Leisure Press, 1989.
Zarnowski, Frank. *Olympic Glory Denied: And a Final Opportunity for Glory Restored.* Glendale, CA: Griffin Publishing, 1996.

1912 Olympic Games — Background and Analysis

History of Sweden

With roots that can be traced back to the 5th century, Sweden is one of the oldest countries in Europe. The Roman historian Tacitius first described it in his work "Germania" in 98 C.E., writing, "Out in the [Baltic] sea are the lands of the Sviones." The oldest known king of the Svear (as they called themselves) is Aun the Old from the late 5th century, who is buried in a huge burial mound, 10 meters high and with a diameter of 60 meters, at Upsala, 70 km. north of Stockholm. His son Egil and great-grandson Adils are buried in adjacent burial mounds of similar size. His grandson Ottar is buried at Vendel, some 30 km. north of Upsala, in a burial mound of about the same size.

Aun and several of his descendants were local kings, but by virtue of the temple at Upsala, which was the most famous in the Scandinavian countries, they were held in higher esteem than the other local kings. Odin, Thor and Frej were the gods worshipped in the Upsala temple. Odin was the foremost God, the God of war and the wisest of all, and known as the All-Father. He had only one eye because he had sacrificed the other to drink from the Well of Wisdom. He rode an eight-legged horse and had two ravens (Hugin and Munin) that flew around the world during the day, and then at night whispered hoarsely into his ear, reporting to him everything they had observed. Thor was the son of Odin, and was known as the God of Lightning and Thunder, and Frej was Odin's wife, the Fertility Goddess. From Odin, Thor, and Frej come our modern words Wednesday, Thursday, and Friday that were named after their names in Anglo-Saxon Norse (*wodnesdæg, thorsdæg,* and *frigedæg*).

The many local communities with their own kings congregated into larger communities, termed "landskap." Around 650 King Ingjald of Upsala, by warfare and trickery, killed the kings of the other landskap of the Svear. All Svear were now united under one king, forming the Kingdom of Svithjod (now Sweden). The English word Sweden comes from the Latin name of the country, Suodia. We will call it Svithjod for as long as it was so called.

In Scandinavia there were four main tribes, the Danes, the Goths, the Norse, and the Svear. They were basically one and the same people, who spoke the same language, worshipped the same Gods, believed in the same conception of justice, and had the same cultures and customs.

1

They had the same written language and all used a runic alphabet. They had no paper so the runes were carved on birch-bark, wood and stones. Written historical sources are scarce, because of the lack of paper, but there is an abundance of rune stones, especially in the districts around Upsala. The Goths were squeezed in between the Danes and the Svear, who both sought to gain control of the Goths. Around 750 the decisive battle for Götaland, the land of the Goths, was fought between the Danes and the Svear at Bråvalla Hed (Moor). The Svear were victorious and the kings of Upsala had expanded their kingdom to all Svithjod and all Götaland.

The kingdom was in reality a federation of landskap but each landskap retained its own laws. The constitution said that the king "was to be elected," not to inherit his crown. It was the prerogative of the Svear to "elect and evict the king," but all Svear did not take part in the election, only those who lived in Tiundaland, the landskap where Upsala was situated, and neighboring Attundaland. Before the newly elected king could take over the kingdom he had to make a tour of the country. In each landskap he had to swear allegiance to the laws of the landskap, stating that he would uphold them. Having done so he was proclaimed king of the landskap in question.

By the late 8th century the Danish tribes had united into Denmark, while the Svear and the Goths were united under the king of Svithjod, and the Norse tribes united into Norway around 870. There was no further opposition by local kings and chieftains, and the countries were overpopulated in some areas. The warriors could no longer seek glory within their own country and there was a need for people in the overpopulated areas to find new land to settle. Thus was born the Viking Age.

The Viking Age

In the 780s some Vikings began to settle in Ireland. But the Viking Age is usually considered to have begun in 793, when a ship landed at Landisfarne, Holy Island, in northern Northumberland, looking for food and water. The inhabitants of the island, monks in a monastery, were apparently reluctant to share or trade with the Vikings. The Vikings then slaughtered the cattle, killed some of the monks, took the treasures of the monastery, and left as quickly as they had arrived.

For about 275 years Vikings from Denmark, Svithjod and Norway explored the world, traded, settled, and fought, from the Caspian Sea in the east, to the African coast in the South and to the shores of North America in the west. They made settlements in numerous sites, including Iceland, Greenland, Newfoundland, the Færoe, Shetland, and Orkney Islands, the Hebrides, Scotland, Ireland, Isle of Man, England, France, Italy, Sicily, Russia, and the eastern and southern shores of the Baltic Sea. They sailed up the rivers of Dvina and Neva-Volkhov-Lovat, and then dragged their ships across land to the Dnieper and Volga Rivers to proceed south to the Black Sea and Caspian Sea. The expeditions were mostly private enterprises but were sometimes led under royal command. The Vikings were assimilated into the local population in densely populated areas, such as England, Ireland, Scotland, France, Italy, Sicily, and Russia. In sparsely populated areas, such as Iceland and the Færoe Islands, they have survived until today. The settlement in Newfoundland, at l'Anse aux Meadows, had to be abandoned after a few years, because it was too lightly populated to maintain and the communication lines were too long. The settlement in Greenland perished in the 15th or 16th century due to malnutrition. A change of climate made it impossible to continue raising cattle, which was their main means of livelihood.

The Svear had begun to settle on the eastern shores of the Baltic Sea, especially Finland, even before the advent of the Viking age. The Slavic inhabitants in and around Novgorod (current-day Russia) asked Rurik, a chieftain from Roden, the coastal area north of Stockholm, to be their king. The people of Roden were called Ros or Rus, and the country was called Rossija (Russia) after them.

One of the few noticeable setbacks occurred when the Vikings attempted to capture Constantinople. They were met with a new kind of resistance, flame-throwers throwing burning oil at them. After this setback, the Vikings developed peaceful relations with the emperor and were allowed to trade in Constantinople. The emperor took them on and formed an elite security guard of Vikings. It was considered a great honor to be in the private security force of the emperor, and these were highly sought-after positions.

As warriors the Vikings were fearless, and they considered dying in battle to be the greatest honor. One then joined the Gods and was allowed to sit at the dinner table of the war-god Odin in his residence, Valhalla. The worst fate of all was to die the "sootdeath," or to die at home in your own bed.

It is remarkable that the Vikings from sparsely populated Scandinavian countries could dominate the history of Europe for around 250 years. The Viking ships were open and shallow draught, but the construction was ingenious, and the ships could best be described as ocean-going landing crafts. But life on board was harsh — there were no cabins, no indoor plumbing, one slept directly on the wooden planking and with only canvas for blankets.

It is difficult to imagine how the Vikings could stand the harsh life on board their open shallow-draught boats, and still navigate to small islands in the Atlantic Ocean with uncanny precision, using just the sun and the stars. The biggest ships were 50 meters long, but these were exceptions. The standard ships had lengths of about 30 meters, widths of 5 meters, and masts of 10–12 meters. Such ships could hold a crew of 70 and carry a cargo of about 20 tons.

Viking Sports

In their spare time the Vikings practiced sport, not just as part of military training, but for fun and recreation. Among the many athletic events were running, high jump, long jump, backwards jump (useful in battle to stay clear of enemy attacks), javelin throwing at a target, stone throwing, three different wrestling styles (of which one has survived to the present day — Glíma), endurance swimming, weightlifting (of stones and barrels filled with sand or gravel), individual tug-of-war, skating with bone-bladed skates (there were also iron skates, but these were not considered to be as fast as bone blades), cross-country skiing, and a ballgame called knattleikr, which was played with bats and a wooden ball. The rules have not survived to knattleikr, but it seems to have been a very violent game because injuries were frequent. Legend also says that the Vikings invented football when they kicked around the skull of a beheaded enemy, but that story is apocryphal.

In tug-of-war the goal line was often set aflame and the loser would be burned. Competitive swim racing was unknown. In the endurance swim, the competitors swam out into the sea and the one who turned back first lost. This was usually done without any accompanying boat. There are many accounts of how the winner had to help the loser ashore.

Fencing was an important part of military training but it was not practiced as a competitive sport, probably because there were no shields that could prevent the heavy swords from causing serious injuries. Fencing competitions were for real, a kind of duel called "holmgång," whose rules have survived. Each man was allowed three shields and the one that was challenged had the first blow. It could either be for "first blood to the ground," or until one of them was unable to defend himself. A common tactic was to direct the sword blows at the lower parts of the other man's leg so as to cut it off.

How good were the Vikings as compared to the present-day athletes? Some performances have survived but as there were local variations, we are faced with the problem of converting their units of measurements to modern ones. As far as is known, the best jumps recorded were: long jump — 7.20 meters and high jump — 1.85 meters. The latter is likely credible, as there are several accounts of men jumping their own height. There is also an account of a man who could jump "as well forwards as backwards" (probably standing jumps).

The Brännö Games

Every third year the kings of Denmark, Svithjod and Norway met on Brännö, an island just outside present-day Göteborg, to discuss the political agenda of the day and to settle disputes peacefully. A natural outgrowth of these meetings was sporting contests between the followers of the three kings. These contests attracted Vikings not just from the mother countries, but from the settlements as well. Events at these games were: Wrestling; Glíma wrestling; Wrestling in the sea; Weightlifting, deadlift; Running, approximately 2 km.; Long jump; Backwards jump; High jump; Javelin throw for accuracy; Stone throw for accuracy; Stone throw for distance; Archery; Tug-of-war; Knattleikr.

Unfortunately, no results have survived. These games seem to have been conducted peacefully, because had any serious incidents occurred we would surely have learned about them.

Conversion to Christianity

The Viking invasions met little resistance from the Western European nations. Their shallow-draught ships could land almost anywhere and be dragged ashore. They could sail and row far upriver. If they met with rapids, or if cataracts prevented the river from being navigated, they simply dragged the ships across land beyond the obstacles. The Western European countries had no naval power equal to the Vikings, and could not prevent their landing. The solution was to pacify the Vikings by converting them to Christianity.

Attacks on land against Denmark were possible, but the Danes built a defensive wall, Danavirke, across the southernmost part of Jutland between the Baltic Sea and the North Sea. The oldest parts date to 737. In the early 9th century the original wall was apparently in disrepair because King Godfred built a new wall in 808, when the Danes were at war with the empire of Charles the Great. The wall served its purpose and in the peace treaty of 811 the border between Denmark and the empire was settled. It was penetrated in 934 when the German king, Henric, managed to capture Hedeby, just north of the border, and forced the king, Gnupa of Svithjod, to be baptized. A couple of years later the Danes reconquered Hedeby, after which they reinforced and extended Danevirke further. Harald Bluetooth, king from the 940s to 986, allowed Christian missionaries into Denmark and was himself baptized in 960.

The first missionary to Svithjod arrived in 830. The first Svear king to be baptized was Olof Skötkonung, around 1000. After him there were alternating Christian and non–Christian kings. The problem was that the king was not just the earthly king but also the high priest of the Temple of Upsala, and had to perform the religious rites, ceremonies and sacrifices. These religious festivals culminated every ninth year when nine of a number of species were sacrificed — including nine human beings. Christian kings who took a pragmatic view performed their duties as high priest, but some refused to do so. The people then used their constitutional right to remove them and elected kings who would perform the duties.

In 1080 Inge was elected king. In 1084, the ninth year of the religious festival, Inge refused to perform his duties as high priest and was duly removed as King. He had to take refuge in Westgothia where the population was predominantly Christian. There he assembled an army of Christian followers and in 1087, marched against Upsala. He killed the king himself, burned down the temple, and built a church on the site. The last bastion of the old religion was crushed.

From the 12th century crusades were carried out to Finland, to convert the country to Christianity, and to consolidate and expand the supremacy of the Svear. The expansion gradually continued eastwards to also include all the Finnish-speaking population. On one of these crusades the sun was seen radiating its beams like a cross against the blue sky. The crusaders saw this as an omen and adopted as their flag a yellow cross against a blue background. This flag did not become the official flag of Sweden until the 16th century, but by then it had been in traditional use for centuries.

Stockholm

Upsala was the political and religious center of Svithjod, while the land that would eventually become Stockholm was a tiny island, strategically situated in a strait separating the Mälar Bay from the inner waters of the Baltic Sea. To enter Mälar Bay and the heartland of Svithjod by sea, at a time when sea routes were more important than land routes, one had to pass that island, which prevented enemies from entering Mälar Bay. Around 1010 stockades were built in the strait separating the island from the mainland, and it is believed that the name Stockholm came from those stocks. The purpose was not to prevent ships from entering or leaving the Mälar Bay, but to control the ships by making them zigzag through the strait. In the 1180s King Canute built a defense tower. The effigy of his father, King Eric, after his death called Saint Eric, became the coat of arms of Stockholm, but the reason why Saint Eric became the Patron Saint of Stockholm is not known.

There was no further mention of Stockholm until 1252 when Birger Jarl (Earl Birger), the highest state official, equivalent to a prime minister, is credited with founding it, for building defenses, and for establishing it as a commercial city. A castle for defense was built and German merchants were invited to promote trade. The elevation of the land had by then progressed to the point that ships could no longer pass Stockholm, and Mälar Bay had become Lake Mälar. Products to and from the Mälar districts had to be reloaded in Stockholm.

In 1364 King Albrecht of Mecklenburg (1363–1389) adopted three golden crowns as his seal, and these were placed on top of the tower of the Stockholm Castle that was called "Tre Kronor" (Three Crowns). The three crowns were taken on as the national coat of arms.

Stockholm quickly developed into the most important trading center in Sweden and the king began to use the Stockholm Castle, Tre Kronor, as a residence. The king, however, had no permanent residence, but took temporary residence in many castles throughout the country. It was not until the 1520s, when King Gustaf took up permanent residence in Tre Kronor, that Stockholm could be called the capital.

Sweden

From the 12th century the kingdom was made up of three countries, Svealand, Götaland and Österlanden (Eastlands). The name of Österlanden was gradually replaced by Finland, the most important of the landskap of Österlanden (just as the Netherlands are often called Holland after its most important province). With the shift of the name Österlanden to Finland the landskap Finland was renamed Real Finland.

King Charles Sverkersson (1160–1167) adopted the title "Svear's and Götar's [Goths'] King." The name Svithjod fell out of use and was replaced by "Svea och Göta Rige" (Svea and Göta State). Subsequently "Göta" was dropped and the name shortened to "Sverige," the current Swedish name for the country known as Sweden in English.

The mode of electing the king of Sverige was also changed. As we have mentioned, it was previously the prerogative of the Svear to elect the king. But in the 12th or early 13th century, each landskap, including Finland, sent a delegation of 12 electors to Mora äng (Mora Meadow), 15 km. southeast of Upsala, the traditional place where kings were elected. The last king to be elected that way was King Christiern in 1457.

In 1350 a royal commission worked out a new set of laws that would apply to the whole of Sweden. But the new laws had to be adopted by every landskap and that was a slow process as many landskap were reluctant to give up their old statutes. It took 50 years before all the landskap adopted the new laws.

We have described the gradual unification, the first step from local communities to landskap, the second step from landskap to Svithjod, Denmark, and Norway. What about the third step, the unification of these three countries into one? Why did this not occur? Actually it happened several times, by various methods — warfare, negotiations, marriages, and elections.

In the early 10th century Denmark was ruled for about two decades by the kings of Svithjod, until their rule ended in 934 (see above). Canute the Great, King of Denmark, England and Norway 1018–36, was also King of Svithjod for a brief time. However, he was defeated by the Svear in a battle at Helgeå, which was likely situated near Upsala.

The most promising union of the three nations was established in 1389, when Queen Margareta, reigning Queen of Denmark and Norway, was also elected reigning Queen of Sweden. In 1397 Eric of Pomerania, a nephew of Queen Margareta, was crowned King of the three countries in Kalmar, a city on the east coast of southern Sweden. In connection with the coronation a treaty was signed, called the Kalmar Treaty. It stated that from that day forward the three countries would have the same king. This union lasted, on and off, until 1521 when Sweden broke away for good. Denmark and Norway had the same kings, with a few brief interruptions, until 1814, but it never led to an integration of the two.

In 1435 a new institution met for the first time, the Parliament, which had four houses — the Nobility, the Clergy, the Burghers and the Peasants. What was most important for the future development of Sweden was that the Peasants were a major political force to be reckoned with. The peasants in Sweden never lost their freedom as they did in so many other European countries, even Denmark. The king was no threat to their freedom but the Nobility was. The Peasants and the king usually fought the power ambitions of the Nobility successfully.

In 1544 the Parliament decided to make Sweden a hereditary kingdom. However, only eight of the 16 kings and reigning queens inherited the throne from then until 1818, the advent of the House of Bernadotte, which is still the reigning royal House. The other eight were elected by the Parliament.

In 1630 Sweden intervened in the Thirty Years' War, and after the Westphalian Peace in 1648, emerged as one of the Great Powers of Europe. It retained its position for 70 years until the death of Charles XII in 1718. At that time Sweden dominated the Baltic Sea, which was virtually a Swedish lake. Its territory included not only mainland Sweden and Finland, but also present-day Estonia and Latvia, Ingermanland (the coastal areas south of the Gulf of Finland and Lake Ladoga, where present-day St. Petersburg [former Leningrad/Petrograd] is situated) and in Germany, Pomerania, and Wismar at the Baltic Sea and Bremen and Verden at the North Sea. At times it also included a coastal area of Poland (in East Prussia), and Trøndelagen, and the island of Bornholm in middle Norway. When Sweden was at its largest in the 17th century, it had an area of around 990,000 km^2 (382,405 sq. mi.), or more than twice its present area of 450,000 km^2 (173,820 sq. mi.).

Sweden's fall from power began in 1700 when it was simultaneously attacked by Denmark, Poland, and Russia. Denmark and Poland were defeated but the war against Russia persisted. After initial Swedish successes, Russia gained the upper hand and in the peace treaty of 1721 Sweden had to cede Ingermanland, Estonia, and Latvia to Russia.

In the 18th century, after the death of Charles XII, Sweden had Parliamentary rule. The king had no real say, but only rubber-stamped Parliamentary decisions. If he refused to do so, the documents were signed using a signature stamp.

In 1766 Sweden was the first country in the world to adopt a law guaranteeing freedom of the press and forbidding censorship. It was considered so important that it was passed as a constitutional law.

In the 18th century Sweden's possessions in Germany were gradually reduced and the last ones were lost in the Napoleonic Wars. In the ensuing peace treaty the Danish king renounced the throne of Norway, handing it to the king of Sweden. Thus, Sweden and Norway were united under the same king, but Norway retained full autonomy, including its own flag. The only thing that the two nations had in common was foreign policy, and it was because of differences of opinion as to foreign representation that the union dissolved in 1905.

Pehr Henrik Ling

In a war against Russia in 1808–1809, Sweden suffered a humiliating defeat and lost that part of its country now called Finland. The situation was similar to that of France after its loss in the 1870–1871 Franco-Prussian War, and it led to a national reawakening.

The prime proponent of strengthening the Swedish people was Pehr Henrik Ling (1776–1839), called "The Father of Swedish Gymnastics." He was a fencing master at the University of Lund in southern Sweden (1805–1813), and he developed a gymnastic system, eponymically called the Ling system. With the assistance of influential friends he received permission to establish the "Gymnastika Centralinstitutet" (GCI [Central Institute of Gymnastics]) in Stockholm in 1813. In his system there were four types of gymnastics taught: military gymnastics, pedagogical gymnastics to be taught in schools, aesthetic gymnastics, mainly for women, and medical gymnastics, better known as physiotherapy. His goal was to strengthen the will, energy, health, and vitality of the Swedish people by gymnastics. Teachers educated at GCI began to teach gymnastics in the Swedish schools.

In 1825 Ling was given the title of professor, and in 1831 he was elected to the Svenska Läkarsällskapet (Swedish Medical Society). He was also a poet and author and in 1835 was elected to the Svenska Akademien (Swedish Academy), the institution that chooses the Nobel Prize winners in literature.

Olympic Games in Helsingborg in the 19th Century

The successor of Pehr Henrik Ling as a fencing master at the University of Lund was Gustaf Johan Schartau (1794–1852). In 1833 he founded Den Olympiska Föreningen (The Olympic Society), which on Thursday, 17 July 1834, organized Olympiska Täflingar (Olympic Contests) at the racetrack in Helsingborg, 50 km. north of Lund. There were four events: gymnastics, running, wrestling, and climbing a 17 ells (10 meter) high soaped mast.

There were seven participants in gymnastics, with Ernst Krumlinde, a student at the University of Lund, winning the first prize, a gold ring. Thus he could be considered the first Swedish Olympic champion. There were 20 participants in running, who ran 400 ells (238 meters) in the five heats. The five heat winners ran a final of 850 ells (505 meters). The winner was Olof Jönsson, a blacksmith's apprentice, with a time of 1:54, who also received a gold ring. Second behind Jönsson was Olof Olsson, a fiddler. There were no weight classes in wrestling. Nils Lamberg, a hussar, won a silver cup by defeating seven competitors. In climbing the soaped mast there were nine entrants, with the first prize, a silver coin, placed at the top of the mast. The first to reach the top was declared the winner. The fourth contestant, Håkan Isaksson, a stableman, was the first to reach the top.

These contests were much more successful than Schartau and Den Olympiska Föreningen had expected. They were not prepared for the great number of spectators, and order was not maintained. Many spectators broke through the roped-off areas, and many did not see any of the events. The criticism of the lack of order was harsh.

The next Olympiska Täflingar were held on Thursday, 4 August 1836, at the same site, with the same events with one addition, a literary contest on the subject: "The ancient Olympic Games as compared to the medieval tournaments and the benefits of the revival of fighting games in present times." The competition was again considered successful, except for problems managing the many spectators. The papers, however, only wrote about the lack of order, and the difficulties the spectators had trying to watch the events, and no mention was made of the competitions. So we know nothing about the number of competitors or the names of the winners. Den Olympiska Föreningen could not cope with the great number of spectators, and there were no further Olympiska Täflingar in Helsingborg.

Olympic Games in Stockholm in the 19th Century

In the 1840s Gustaf Johan Schartau lived in Stockholm, where he allied himself with Knut Eric Venne Höökenberg (1808–1869), a well-known organizer of festivities. They announced "Popular Entertainment and Olympic Games" to be held on Sunday, 13 August 1843, at Ladugårdsgärde, at that time a training ground for the military. The program was as follows:

Music
Wrestling and boxing
Climbing a soaped mast
Racing
Running
Various "amusement" events, among which was a sack race.

Once again the interest was overwhelming, and newspaper accounts estimated the number of spectators from 8,000 to 25,000. The organizers could not possibly handle such a large number of spectators. Barriers were broken down, the ropes marking the running lanes were torn down, and the spectators swarmed all over. Neither the racing nor the running events could be carried out and it is doubtful whether the wrestling and boxing events took place. The orchestra tried in vain to make itself heard, but it also had to give up.

The only events that were contested were climbing the soaped mast and two amusements: the sack race, and catching a shaved and oiled sow turned loose. As in Helsingborg the first prize, a silver cup, was placed on top of the mast and the winner was the first to reach the top. A 14-year-old boy was the first to do so but as soon as he returned to the ground again an enterprising thief snatched the silver cup from him and set off. Now an extra event started — "To Catch a Thief." It succeeded and the silver cup was returned to the boy.

One paper wrote, "I cannot tell much about the 'Olympic Games' as I only saw the Olympic mast-climbing and the Olympic sow. After having seen these I must say that the most Olympic of all were the roars of laughter coming from the bottom of the hearts of the spectators when a climber who failed crestfallen began to slip down."

These Olympic Games were a complete failure. The resources were inadequate and the organizers lacked the ability to conduct competitions that attracted so many spectators.

The Swedish Sports Movement

The oldest Swedish sports club, Upsala Simsällskap (Upsala Swimming Society), was founded in 1796. It is one of the oldest sports clubs in the world today. Upsala is thus not only the cradle of Sweden, it is also the cradle of Swedish sports. Other swimming clubs were founded beginning in the 1820s — 1823 in Lund, 1824 in Linköping, 1827 in Stockholm, 1829 in Jönköping, and so on. The aims of these swimming societies were not race swimming, but to promote the art of swimming. They performed tests, and those who passed the tests were conferred academic titles — B.A., M.A. and Doctor of Swimming.

In the 19th century other sports began to catch on and clubs began to be founded for those sports as well. In 1830 the Svenska Segel Sällskapet (Swedish Sailing Society) was formed, which in 1878 was allowed to add Kungliga (Royal) to its name. The first society for target shooting was founded in 1831 in Kristianstad, the first rowing club in 1851 in Göteborg, the first skating club in 1863 in Göteborg, the first gymnastics club in 1865 in Stockholm, and the first ball club in 1866 in Göteborg. It was not until the 1880s, with the arrival of Viktor Balck, that track and field athletics began to catch on.

Viktor Gustaf Balck and the Orgnization of Swedish Sports

Viktor Gustaf Balck (1844–1928) is called "The Father of Swedish Sports," and rightly so. He was born in Karlskrona, a naval base in southern Sweden, and set his sights on a career as a naval officer. In 1861 he entered Karlberg, the Swedish Military Academy in Stockholm, where the courses in the first year were the same for future army and navy officers. On the first day at Karlberg he entered the gymnastic hall, although he had not previously practiced sports or gymnastics, and this day was decisive for his future life and career. "I was overwhelmed by enthusiasm for gymnastics and fencing and I promised that from that day forward I would dedicate my life to physical exercises."

This love for physical exercises made Balck change his career to become an army officer. In 1866 he received his commission as a second lieutenant and joined the Nerike Regiment. He also entered Gymnastika Centralinstitutet (GCI), from which he earned his degree in 1868. He served as an extra teacher at GCI in 1868–1870 and 1872–1885, and from 1870–1872 he was a gymnastics and fencing teacher at the Military Equestrian School at Strömsholm. He taught at the military section of GCI (1885–1887), while from 1887–1909 he was the head teacher in military gymnastics at GCI, and served as Principal of GCI from 1907–1909.

In 1875 Balck founded the Stockholms Gymnatiskförening (Stockholm Gymnastics Club), in 1880 he helped form the Stockholms Roddförening (Stockholm Rowing Club), and in 1883 he was instrumental in starting the Stockholms Allmänna Skridskoklubb (Stockholm Public Skating Club).

Through the Stockholms Gymnastikförening, Balck began organizing exhibition trips, to Bruxelles in 1877 and to England, Belgium, and Denmark in 1880. During the visit in England he encountered athletic sports for the first time, and what was meant to be a propaganda tour for Swedish gymnastics also became, upon Balck's return, a propaganda trip for track and field athletics among the Swedes. In the summer of 1881 he went to England on a private trip, where he learned more about English sports and became determined to introduce some of them into Sweden.

The first track and field athletics meet organized by Balck and the Stockholm Garrison, took place in May 1882 at Ladugårdsgärde (in Stockholm). At the training fields of Nerike Regiment in Örebro, Balck also organized an athletics meet in midsummer 1882. These were the first two track and field athletics meets in Sweden.

In 1874 Balck cofounded *Tidskrift för Gymnastik* (*Journal for Gymnastics*), while in 1881 he founded *Tidning för Idrott* (*Newspaper for Sports*), the first general sports paper in Sweden. Balck managed the paper until 1897, when Clarence von Rosen (IOC Member 1901–1948) took over as publisher, and renamed it *Ny Tidning för Idrott*, but Balck remained as the editor. From 1884 to 1886 Balck published a three-volume book, *Illustrerad Idrottsbok* (*Illlustrated Book of Sports*), a manual of different sports and games.

At the Congress on Physical Education at the World Exhibition in Paris in 1889 Sweden was represented by a gymnastics troupe with Balck as team manager. In Paris he met Pierre de Coubertin for the first time. They hit it off immediately, having a similar view of sport, believing in its educational value in shaping the character of youth, and in its ability to strengthen the rising generation and, in that way, the whole nation.

In 1891 Balck took the initiative to found the Svenska Gymnastikförbundet (Swedish Gymnastics Association) and he was elected president. In 1896 it changed its name to Svenska Gymnastik- och Idrottsförbundet (Swedish Gymnastics and Sports Association) when track and field athletics began to form a major portion of its activities.

The International Skating Union (ISU) was founded in 1892. At the time there was no national skating association in Sweden, so the Stockholms Allmänna Skridskoklubb (founded by Balck in 1883) became a founding member of the union for Sweden. The club still retains its membership in the ISU despite the fact that both the Swedish (Speed) Skating Association and the Swedish Figure Skating Association are members. Balck was elected President of the ISU in 1895 and remained in that position until 1925.

When Pierre de Coubertin began organizing the 1894 Sorbonne Congress for the re-establishment of the Olympic Games he invited Balck to be one of eight vice-presidents, and Balck accepted. When the invitations to the Congress were sent out, the one to Sweden was addressed to the Svenska Gymnastikförbundet. Balck responded very favorably and offered Stockholm as a site for the Olympic Games, but not necessarily the first games. This shows that Balck already had plans to hold Olympic Games in Stockholm by 1894.

Balck did not take part in the Sorbonne Congress but Sweden was represented by Fredrik Bergh and Sten Drakenberg, both graduates of GCI and friends of Balck. Both of them took part in the formation of the International Olympic Committee. Pierre de Coubertin handpicked the members of the International Olympic Committee, so it was quite natural that Balck became one of the original 13 members.[1]*

The Svenska Idrottsförbundet (Swedish Sports Association) was founded in 1895 in Göteborg. It was a multisports organization similar to the AAU (Amateur Athletic Union) in the United States. At the time, Sweden had two rival groups organizing Swedish Championships. In 1901 Johannes Sigfrid Edström (1870–1964) was elected President of Svenska Idrottsförbundet, and he realized that two rival sports organizations could not benefit Swedish sports. He took

*See Notes on pages 27–28.

the initiative to merge the two bodies and in 1903 they united under the name of Svenska Gymnastik- och Idrottsföreningarnas Riksförbund (National Union of Swedish Gymnastics and Sports Clubs), usually just called Riksförbundet, or RF, for short. Crown Prince Gustaf became the patron, while his son, Prince Gustaf Adolf, King Gustaf VI Adolf from 1950, became the President. Balck was elected President of the Board and Edström President of the Executive Committee. In 1921 J. Sigfrid Edstöm succeeded Viktor Balck as an IOC member in Sweden and in 1946 he was elected IOC President.

In 1897, on the initiative of Viktor Balck and in the presence of the Crown Prince, (future King Gustaf V), Clarence von Rosen, and Sven Hermelin, an organization called Sveriges Allmänna Idrottsförbund (Swedish Public Sports Association) was founded in the Royal Palace with King Oscar II as patron and the Crown Prince as president. Two years later it changed its name to Sveriges Centralförening för Idrottens Främjande — SCIF (Swedish Central Association for Promotion of Sport). In 1899 Viktor Balck assumed the position as President of the Executive Committee of SCIF and became its driving force. One of its tasks, according to the statutes, was to regularly conduct sports events with the character of national festivals. In 1901 the SCIF held the first Nordiska Spelen, or the Nordic Games. In 1907 the IOC awarded the Olympic Cup to the SCIF for its activities, primarily the organization of the Nordic Games.

Nordiska Spelen — The Nordic Games

What were the Nordic Games? In 1899 Professor E. Johan Widmark made the suggestion to begin a series of Nordic Games in Stockholm.[2] In 1900 he discussed the idea with Balck and other leading representatives of the winter sports. It was decided to hold the first Nordic Games in Stockholm in 1901. The original idea was to hold them every second year, alternately in Stockholm and then in another Nordic capital. But the Norwegians did not want a close cooperation with Sweden at a time when they had their minds set on dissolving the union with Sweden. Denmark did not have much winter sport and Finland thought the idea would not work as long as the Norwegians did not accept it. So the Nordic Games were held every fourth year in Sweden — 1901, 1905, 1909, 1913, 1917, 1922 (postponed from 1921 to better fit in with the Olympic Games) and 1926.

Balck spoke of the reason for establishing the Nordic Games. "Above all we placed the national goal of rendering a service to the fatherland and bringing honour to our country. The Nordic Games have now become a national concern for our entire people." In 1901, the Swedish sporting paper *Ny Tidning för Idrott*, wrote, "It is in the winter season that Scandanavians are able to achieve a sport week as no other people in Europe, and we should hold our banner high where we are able; we should make the Swedish name known and respected. That has thus been a fundamental idea with the arrangement of the Nordic Games."

Some people think that the purpose of the Nordic Games was to establish an early Olympic Winter festival. Swedish sports history Professor Jan Lindroth has written: "The goal was to thus create something for winter sports to correspond with the Olympic Games for summer sports." Others differ, pointing to the more nationalistic aspects of the Nordic Games. According to *Ny Tidning för Idrott*, "The most fundamental implications of the Nordic Games have been, in addition to the fostering of a hardy species, the rallying of the Swedes around something really national. It had long been a weakness among us that we have not had something acceptably national, which could assemble the entire people."

The Nordic Games included the usual popular winter sports, notably ski jumping, cross-country skiing, Nordic combined, ski-orienteering, skeleton races, ice yachting, skate sailing, speed skating, figure skating, curling, bandy, sled-dog racing and, in the 1920s, ice hockey. But non-winter sports were also contested, such as fencing, swimming and long-distance equestrian races on winter roads. In addition, some sports we would now consider unusual were also contested, such as ski-joring behind horses, kicksled-joring behind horses, ski-joring behind reindeers, kick-sledding, and pulka racing.

Whatever the original motive, the Nordic Games developed into the winter equivalent to the Olympic Games. When the Olympic Winter Games were instituted in 1924 the Nordic countries opposed them, as they did not see any need for separate Olympic Winter Games since the Nordic Games filled that function. Nonetheless, the Nordic Games died out with the advent of the Olympic Winter Games, and with the death of Viktor Balck in 1928.

Swedish Participation at the Early Olympic Games

Balck was unable to raise a Swedish team for the first Olympic Games in Athens in 1896, but he went to Athens as an IOC member together with the only participating Swede, Henrik Sjöberg. Sjöberg took part in five events: 100 meters, long jump, high jump, discus and gymnastics long horse vault. His best performance was fourth place behind three Americans in the high jump, clearing 1.60 meters, far from his personal best of 1.78. Sjöberg was also entered in the 110 meter hurdles but did not compete. There were two other Swedes entered at Athens: Harald Andersson (later Arbin) in the 100 meters, 110 meter hurdles, long jump and long horse vault; and Johan Bergman, a swimmer from Upsala SS, who was temporarily residing in Greece while doing archaeological research. Neither competed at Athens.

For the 1900 Olympic Games in Paris a committee was formed to raise money and to organize a Swedish team. Ten Swedes took part in Paris: eight athletes, one fencer and one swimmer. Sweden had its first Olympic champions when a combined Swedish-Danish team won the tug-of-war. The first individual Olympic success was also recorded when Ernst Fast finished third in the marathon footrace.

In 1900, Sweden was also represented in the jury of the yachting events by Herman af Peterséns, Vice President of Kungliga Svenska Segel Sällskapet (KSSS). It is not known why he was invited to be a jury member and it is rather unusual since Sweden did not take part in yachting. In 1901 Clarence von Rosen was co-opted as an IOC member. Balck also tried to get a third Swedish member but Coubertin resisted his efforts.

Sweden did not take part in the 1904 Olympic Games, as Balck did not think it was worthwhile to send a team to St Louis, deeming it more important to concentrate on the Nordic Games of 1905. Sweden sent a large team to the 1906 Greek Olympic Games in Athens with Viktor Balck at the helm and Sigfrid Edström as manager of the track and field athletics team. These Games were also a breakthrough for Swedish sports, both nationally and internationally. With three gold, three silver and six bronze medals, Sweden was the second best nation in track and field behind the United States. After this success, Swedish newspapers took a greater interest in sports and began devoting more space to sports.

Sweden sent an even larger team to London in 1908 — 165 men and three women in 14 sports. Viktor Balck again headed the delegation, now with Sigfrid Edstöm as second in command. With eight gold, six silver and 11 bronze medals Sweden was the third-best nation after Great Britain and the United States. Whereas the 1906 team had its main emphasis on track and field athletics, the 1908 team was more diverse. Sweden won medals in eight sports in 1908: track and field athletics, gymnastics, shooting, swimming, lawn tennis, wrestling, yachting and figure skating. The only sports in which Sweden participated and failed to win medals were cycling and fencing. It was in London in 1908 that Viktor Balck put forward the candidacy of Stockholm for the 1912 Olympic Games.

Choice of the Host City for the 1912 Olympic Games

By the late 19th and early 20th centuries, Stockholm was a rapidly expanding city. It had a population of 170,000 in 1880, 300,000 in 1900, and 350,000 in 1912. From an administrative and trade center it had also developed into a major industrial town, one large enough to consider organizing the Olympic Games.

Originally, there were two candidates for the 1912 Olympic Games: Stockholm and Berlin. After pressure from Pierre de Coubertin in 1904, Berlin had withdrawn its candidacy for the 1908 Games in favor of Rome, which was later replaced by London. In London the two Swedish IOC members announced to the session that Stockholm was interested in being the host city. But the IOC noted that Berlin had already been promised the 1912 Olympic Games after its previously generous offer to withdraw its 1908 bid. However, Pierre de Coubertin later noted, "Actually, the choice of the Swedish capital had been practically decided in London."[3]

The decision to award the 1912 games was to be made at the 1909 IOC session in Berlin opening 27 May. In a tactical move the Germans had persuaded the IOC to hold the session in their capital. They were counting on the IOC members being impressed with what they saw in Berlin, the excellent facilities and good conditions for holding the games, and the benevolent and positive attitude towards the games by the citizens of Berlin, of Germany, and the emperor himself.

However, the Germans had problems, primarily with the question of building the Olympic stadium. General Count Egbert van der Asseburg, then the President of "Deutscher Reichsausschuß für die Olympische Spiele" (DRAfOS [German Committee for the Olympic Games]), died on 31 March 1909, and DRAfOS was then at a standstill. At their annual meeting on 17 May 1909 they planned to decide definitively whether or not to bid to host the 1912 Olympic Games. When the meeting reached that point on the agenda contemporary reports state that "there reigned an icy silence." Without any discussion the DRAfOS decided to refrain from seeking the 1912 Olympic Games.

So when the IOC met in Berlin in 1909, Stockholm was the only candidate. But Stockholm was still not an automatic choice. Pierre de Coubertin was in favor of Stockholm, and spoke on their behalf. "The present moment is a most favourable one for Sweden if she wishes to celebrate the Olympic Games. To delay doing so will confer no advantage but rather the opposite."[4] But many IOC Members wanted assurances that Stockholm had the organizational and financial resources to hold the Olympics, as both the 1904 and the 1908 games had been transferred to other cities.

The Swedish application for the Olympic Games was well prepared. The leading sports organizations stood behind it and the government promised to assist in financing the games via the state lottery. The Swedish IOC members, Balck and von Rosen, were able to convince the IOC of Stockholm's ability to hold the games, and on 28 May 1909, the IOC unanimously chose Stockholm. The IOC immediately cabled the Swedish Prince Royal and his reply came within five hours. "Sincere thanks for Your kind cable I am very glad and pleased that Sweden has been honoured to organise the next Games We shall do our best to make them a success Gustaf Adolf."[5]

During the same IOC session, Viktor Balck was awarded the Olympic Diploma. There is little doubt that without Viktor Balck, Stockholm would not have been awarded the 1912 games. Without his enthusiasm, driving force and organizational ability, Swedish sport would not have developed the way it did. His national and international contacts were invaluable. Balck belonged to the inner circle of Pierre de Coubertin's close friends, and he had good contacts with the royal family and several government ministers. No one else in Sweden had the position or the contacts to dare suggest that Stockholm should organize the Olympic Games.

The Olympic Program

Which sports and events should figure on the 1912 Olympic Program? The opinion of Pierre de Coubertin was crystal clear, "It was too much in London, it must not be that extensive. It must above all be less expensive."[6] The same problems existed then as they do now, and probably will forever. The Olympic Games were too large and too expensive. No decisions were taken at the 1909 session concerning the program but it was discussed. The Swedes were instructed to work out a proposal to present to the next IOC session, taking into account the points of view put forward during the discussions.

The Swedes wanted to limit the program to four sports: athletics, gymnastics, swimming, and wrestling. But the discussions in Berlin clearly indicated that cycling, fencing, rowing, and yachting should be included on the Olympic program.

The proposal presented at the IOC session in Luxembourg in 1910 included athletics, cycling (road), equestrian sports, gymnastics, lawn tennis, shooting, swimming (including water polo), wrestling, and yachting. The IOC expressed its view that football (soccer), rowing, modern pentathlon and, after pressure from the Fédération Internationale de Natation Amateur (FINA), ladies' swimming, should be included. Other voices were heard advocating boxing, track cycling, weightlifting, and art competitions. The IOC also asked Sweden to include winter sports and Balck promised to discuss this at the next IOC session. As Pierre de Coubertin was a big proponent of modern pentathlon and art competitions, it was difficult to turn these events down.

At the IOC session in Budapest in 1911, Sweden had to make further concessions. Rowing, modern pentathlon, women's swimming, and art competitions were added to the 1912 Olympic program. Swedish organizers would not allow boxing because there was no national association in Sweden to organize the sport. In his arguments against boxing, Balck said that it was forbidden in Sweden. That was not quite true but one needed special permission by the local police and that was sometimes difficult to obtain. Balck also wanted to delete road cycling, as he maintained that the roads were so bad that it was not feasible to organize road events, which was a gross exaggeration. Balck just did not want cycling on the program, but he failed in his efforts, as road cycling remained.

The IOC reminded Balck of his promise to include winter sports on the program, but he stated that winter sports could not be organized because of the 1913 Nordic Games. Italy's Eugenio Brunetta d'Usseaux then suggested that the Nordic Games should be part of the 1912 Olympic Games, and this was put to a vote. It was finally decided that the Nordic Games should not be part of the 1912 Olympic Games and that there would not be any winter sports on the 1912 Olympic program. (For a more complete explanation of the origin of Winter Olympic sports, see the section on "Winter Olympic Sports" in the chapter "Other Sports and Events," and also the earlier discussion of the Nordic Games in this section.)

Eventually, Sweden had to accede to IOC demands and add more and more sports to the Olympic Program. From an original four sports, the 1912 Olympic program eventually included 13 and the art competitions. The Swedish Organizing Committee successfully opposed the inclusion only of boxing, track cycling and winter sports.

At that time Olympic organizing committees tried to include typical national sports and events on the Olympic program, and Sweden did likewise. There were five events that were practiced almost exclusively in Sweden and Scandinavia — both-hands javelin throwing, both-hands discus throwing, both-hands shot put, inrigger coxed fours, and a shooting event, individual military rifle at 300 meters.

The harmonious development of the body was a cornerstone in Swedish sports and Swedish, or Ling, gymnastics. The system espoused the concept that one should not develop one arm or one side of the body at the expense of the other, as in best-hand throws. Both hands javelin throwing was already practiced during the Viking age, in which both javelins, one in each hand, were thrown simultaneously.

Swedish championships in discus, javelin and shot put were both hands only. Not until 1924 were championships in best-hand throws introduced. It is indeed odd that the both-hands throws figured on the program because at the session in Budapest in 1911, the IOC had voted against the both-hands throws, 11–8. That the Stockholm Organizing Committee could override this, and include them nevertheless, shows how deep-rooted the feelings for the both-hands throws were in Sweden.

Military rifle was not a typical Swedish event per se, but the format at the 1912 games was the same as the event on the national Swedish shooting program — ten shots at a target of five conventional scoring rings, and ten shots at a half-figure from a distance of 300 meters.

What is most important is that the IOC gained the upper hand in this process. Previously the local organizing committees had decided the Olympic program and the IOC had little say in the matter. From 1912 onwards, it was the IOC that decided what events to include and the local organizing committee had to comply.

The 1912 Olympic Organizing Committee

The 1912 Olympic Organizing Committee was founded in the fall of 1909 with three members and one deputy each from Sveriges Centralförening för Idrottens Främjande and Svenska Gymnastik- och Idrottsföreningarnas Riksförbund. The Organizing Committee met for the first time on 7 October 1909. Viktor Balck was the natural choice as president, and Sigfrid Edström became vice-president. The latter attended the IOC sessions in 1910 and 1911, as a representative of the organizing committee.

Crown Prince Gustaf Adolf was asked to become the Honorary President of the Organizing Committee. An executive committee was appointed with Balck as president and Edström as vice-president. Balck turned 65 in 1909 and retired as the principal of GCI, so he could then devote all his time to the Olympic Organizing Committee.

Kristian Hellström was appointed as secretary-general. He was a former middle distance runner, having taken part in the Olympic Games of 1906 in Athens and in 1908 in London. In 1906 he was a bronze medallist in the 1,500 meters and finished fifth in the 800 meters. In 1908 he competed in the 800 meters but was eliminated in the heats. His assistant secretary was John Widenfelt, who was known for his linguistic proficiency, being fluent in several languages, and his encyclopaedic knowledge.

The main question facing the organizing committee was the Olympic stadium. The original plans of the committee were to rebuild an existing sports ground, Idrottsparken. A concrete grandstand was to be erected, but on the three other sides there were to be temporary wooden stands that would be dismantled after the games. The estimated costs were 400,000 Swedish kronor.[7] However, the architect, Torben Grut,[8] also sketched plans for a permanent stadium. When they were negotiating with the government agency, the temporary solution was rejected, as the government wanted a permanent stadium. Since it was providing the finance, the stadium would be the responsibility and property of the state.

The first estimate of the cost for a permanent stadium was 820,000 Swedish kronor,[9] but it was not possible to keep the costs within the original budget, and the final cost amounted to 1,187,880 Swedish kronor,[10] which was paid for by the state lottery. The stadium remained state property until 1964, when it was taken over by the City of Stockholm for a symbolic amount. The ground, however, is still owned by the state.

The stadium was built in classical Gothic style with handmade red brick from Helsingborg. It had horseshoe-shaped stands and two 33 meter high towers at either end of the short end stand. It had a capacity of around 19,000 spectators, but a provisional stand was erected above the short end stand during the games, which increased the capacity to around 22,000.

Charles Perry, groundskeeper at Stamford Bridge, home ground of Chelsea Football Club in London, was employed to build the track. He had previously laid the track for the Olympic Stadium in Athens in 1896 (also used in 1906), and in London in 1908, and would again be responsible for the track at the Antwerp Olympic Stadium in 1920.

The size of the track was 383 meters, with an inner lane radius of 28 meters. The infield for the football matches measured 105 × 65 meters. It was not until the European Athletics Championships in 1958 that the track was enlarged to 400 meters. The size of the football (soccer) field caused some concern, since in the invitations to the football tournament, the size of the pitches was described as 105 × 68½ meters. The participating teams had to sign a document that they would not lodge any protests against the size of the Olympic Stadium football field as long as it was at least 105 × 65 meters.

Construction work on the Olympic Stadium started on 23 November 1910, and it was opened for training on Tuesday, 23 April 1912. The first competition was held there on Sunday, 28 April 1912, and the King, Gustaf V, officially inaugurated it on Saturday, 1 June 1912 at the Swedish Olympic trials.

Financing the stadium via the state lottery was a clever move, as the government could dispose of the lottery money without asking the Parliament, which would probably have been futile. The largest parties in the Parliament were the Agrarians and the Social Democrats, and although on opposite ends of the political spectrum, they had one thing in common — they did not like sports. The Agrarians were of the opinion that if a person wanted to exercise they could work in the fields, fell timber in the forests, or chop wood, while the Social Democrats thought that sports took valuable time from the necessary political and union work, and they deemed it more important to fight for the right to vote and to improve the living conditions of the workers. At a time when the right to vote depended on a person's income — and the bigger the income, the more votes one was allowed — they probably had a point.

Innovations at the 1912 Olympic Games

There were several innovations at the 1912 Olympic Games. There was a semiautomatic electrical timing device. The stopwatches were automatically started by the trigger of the gun and stopped manually by the timekeepers. There was a photo-finish camera that took a series of photos as the runners passed the finishing line. As far as is known it was only necessary to consult the finishing photos once, for second place in the final of the 1,500 meters.

The decathlon was a new event on the Olympic program. A scoring table based on a mathematical formula was worked out, with the formula for the points being based on the Olympic records. A result equal to the previous Olympic record was worth 1,000 points.

Modern pentathlon was another new event, included on the initiative of Pierre de Coubertin. He wanted a multisports event according to modern conceptions and suggested shooting, swimming, fencing, riding, and running. It was left to the Swedish Organizing Committee to propose an event in each sport and to work out the rules and regulations. It was not obvious which events to choose. The organizing committee assessed it as follows:

> The five events ought to be such as would test the endurance, resolution, presence of mind, intrepidity, agility and strength of those taking part in the competi-

tion, while, in drawing up the detailed programme, it was necessary to have all the events of equivalent value, in order to make the Modern Pentathlon a competition of really all-around importance.[11]

Based upon these prerequisites the following events were chosen:

Shooting: Dueling pistol from 25 meters
Swimming: 300 meters freestyle
Fencing: Épée, three hits/match
Riding: 5,000 meter steeplechase cross-country
Running: 4,000 meter cross-country

The greatest problem was whether the modern pentathlon participants could bring their own horses or whether the organizing committee should provide them. Many feared that the latter alternative would be unfair, as at a drawing of lots some riders would get better horses than others. Arguments for the latter alternative were that one of the basic ideas was that the participants should show that, at any time, they could ride an unknown horse over unknown terrain.

It resulted in a compromise. Those who wanted could bring their own horse, but for those who did not, the organizing committee would provide mounts by a drawing of lots. It turned out that those who brought their own horses did not fare better in general than those who received theirs by draw.

The 1912 Olympic Schedule

The London Olympic Games in 1908 began on 27 April and the closing ceremony took place over six months later, on 31 October. This was similar to the situation at the 1900 Olympics in Paris and the 1904 Olympics in St. Louis. In Athens in 1906 all the events were carried out in 11 days, from 22 April to 2 May.

The Swedish Organizing Committee considered three different time frames:

6 July–15 July   The Olympic week beginning with the opening ceremony
29 June–22 July   The Olympic Games
5 May–27 July   First event to closing ceremony

All events, save the lawn tennis covered court events, which took place 5–12 May, were held within the framework of the Olympic Games. Before the Olympic week, 28 June–5 July, lawn tennis hard court events, football (soccer), and shooting took place. The Olympic week included track and field athletics, cycling, gymnastics, swimming, wrestling, modern pentathlon, and water polo, except for the water polo third-place game that was played on 16 July. Equestrian sport and fencing started during the Olympic week but finished on 17 July and 18 July, respectively. Rowing, held 17–19 July, and yachting, contested 20–22 July, were the last events of the 1912 Olympic Games.

The closing ceremony took place at the Restaurant Hasselbacken in Stockholm on 27 July, during the closing banquet and awards ceremony for the yachting events. It was not possible to hold it earlier because, after the Olympic Regatta at Nynäshamn, there were post-Olympic races at Sandhamn, a yachting centre 45 km. east of Stockholm.

Accommodations

The concept of an Olympic village had not yet been conceived, as the first true Olympic village would be built only in 1924 at Paris. At Stockholm in 1912, the foreign teams lived in hotels, boarding homes, schools and one military barracks in Stockholm, with the exception of the Americans, the Russians and the Swedes. The Americans lived onboard the ship that took them to Stockholm, the S.S. *Finland*; the Russians did likewise, staying on the S.S. *Birma*.

The Swedish athletes were quartered in a new building called Allmänna BB, adjacent to the Olympic Stadium. It was completed in time for the Olympic Games and was called Idrottshemmet (The Sports Home) while the Swedish athletes stayed there. After the Games Allmänna BB became the major maternity hospital in Stockholm and numerous children were born there (including the Swedish coauthor of this book and his children).

Big teams could not be accommodated in one place, but were spread out in several hotels and boarding houses. The British team was scattered the most, as it stayed in no fewer than nine different locations: Hotel Excelsior (footballers and male swimmers), Hotel Clara Larsson (cyclists, male swimmers, and modern pentathletes), Hotel Germania (male swimmers), Carlesons Boarding House (rowers, track and field athletes, and male swimmers), Birger Jarl Boarding House (cyclists), Hotel Sylvia (female swimmers), Cosmopolite Boarding House (rowers), Hotel Continental (fencers), and Zander Boarding House (wrestlers and gymnasts).

Prizes[12]

Prizes and medals were beginning to assume more importance by the time of the 1912 Olympics. At Stockholm, the prizes in the individual events were as follows:

1st place	Olympic gold medal
2nd place	Olympic silver medal
3rd place	Olympic bronze medal

It should also be noted that the 1912 gold medals were pure gold, which was the case only in 1904, 1908, and 1912. At all other Olympics, gold medals have actually been gilded silver. As they weighed 24 grams (0.846 oz.), these medals were thus quite valuable, not just for their rarity and as status symbols, but for their precious metal content.

In the team events the prizes were given as follows:

1st place	Olympic silver-gilt medal to each member of the team
2nd place	Olympic silver medal to each member of the team
3rd place	Olympic bronze medal to each member of the team

But there were the following exceptions for team events:

Lawn tennis	In the doubles, an Olympic gold medal was awarded to both players
Equestrian events	Olympic gold medal awarded to each member of the team
Yachting	Olympic gold medal to the helmsmen and also to the mate in the 12 meter class

Bronze medals were not awarded in rowing, as there were only two boats in the finals, and the losing semifinalists were not given bronze medals. There were also no bronze medals awarded in the tug-of-war or the 4 × 100 meter relay (track and field athletics). In tug-of-war there were only two participating teams and in the 4 × 100 relay final there were three teams, of which one was disqualified. There was no gold medal awarded in middleweight B (light-heavyweight) wrestling, as there was no winner in the final, which was declared a double loss.

The obverse, permanent, side of the prize medal was the same as in London in 1908 — an athlete being crowned — which had been designed for 1908 by Bertram Mackennal. The reverse side was designed by the medal engraver Erik Lindberg. It depicted a young herald and a bust of Pehr Henrik Ling and had the text OLYMPISKA SPELEN I STOCKHOLM 1912 (OLYMPIC GAMES IN STOCKHOLM 1912). All medalists also received a diploma.

The obverse, permanent, side of the commemorative medal, also designed by Lindberg, was the same as in London in 1908 — an antique Greek four-horse chariot with a charioteer and a judge. It depicted Zeus sitting on the top of a Ionian pillar with the Goddess of Victory in his hand. In the background there was a view of Stockholm, the Old Town, the Royal Palace and the Parliament Building.

The commemorative medal was struck in four different metals: gold, silver, bronze, and pewter. The King and the Crown Prince received the only two gold medals. The members of the International Olympic Committee and the organizing committee received the silver medals, while the presidents of the international juries and the presidents of the special committees were given bronze medals. The medals in pewter were given to ordinary committee members, athletes, officials, staff members of the organizing committee and other people who had contributed to the organization of the games.

A special Diploma of Merit was awarded to athletes who, without having won a medal, had achieved remarkably good results. It was primarily awarded to nonmedal finalists, but it was also given to all cyclists that finished the road race within 25 percent of the winning time, and also to all the marathon runners who finished within 20 percent of the winning time.

Olympic challenge trophies were first conceived as special awards given by wealthy donors, to be held by the winning athletes or teams, in addition to their medals. The challenge trophy was to be kept until the next Olympics and then returned to the IOC to be awarded to the next winner of the event. One was awarded in 1906 at Athens, for the ancient pentathlon. In London in 1908 there were 12 challenge trophies, but this number increased to 20 in Stockholm in 1912, as follows:

Sport	Event	Year	Donor
Athletics	Ancient Pentathlon	1906	The Crown Prince of Greece
	Marathon	1908	The King of Greece
	Discus throw	1908	Mrs. G. de Montgomery
	Pentathlon	1912	The King of Sweden
	Decathlon	1912	The Czar of Russia
Cycling	100 kilometers	1908	The Prince of Wales
Equestrian	Dressage individual	1912	The Emperor of Austria
	Jumping individual	1912	Count Géza Andrassy
	Jumping team	1912	The King of Italy
	3-day event team	1912	The Emperor of Germany
	Polo	1908	Hurlingham Club
	Best nation	1912	The Swedish Cavalry
Fencing	Épée team	1908	The English Fencers
	Sabre team	1912	The City of Budapest
Football		1908	The Football Association

Sport	Event	Year	Donor
Gymnastics	All-around individual	1908	The City of Prague
Modern Pentathlon		1912	Baron Pierre de Coubertin
Rowing	Coxed eights	1908	Count Eugenio Brunetta d'Usseaux[13]
Shooting	Clay pigeon trap	1908	Lord Westbury
Swimming	1,500 meter freestyle	1908	Count Eugenio Brunetta d'Usseaux
	Plain high diving women	1912	Countess de Casa Miranda (Christina Nilsson)
Wrestling	Greco-Roman Heavyweight	1908	The Gold and Silversmiths
Yachting	6-meter class	1908	The Government of France

The challenge trophies in 100 kilometer track cycling, polo, and the ancient pentathlon could not be distributed as those events were not on the 1912 program. The challenge trophies were designated as the property of the IOC, and the recipients and official representatives of their national Olympic committee, had to sign a form saying that they should return the prize to the organizing committee of the next games no later than 1 January 1916 and that they should pay for any damages incurred in transit. The winners and NOC representatives were required to sign a similar form in 1908. This required signature eventually helped the IOC in 1982, during the resolution of the Thorpe Amateur Status problem (see Appendix II). Thorpe's relatives demanded the return of the challenge trophies for the decathlon and pentathlon, in addition to his gold medals, but the signed form was located in the Swedish National Archives, the Riksarkivet, and legally the IOC did not need to return them.

After 1912 challenge trophies were no longer awarded to the winners. They were considered too valuable and too fragile to be shipped worldwide. In 1920 the winners' names were inscribed on the challenge trophies, but they remained in the custody of the IOC. In 1923 the IOC decided to abolish awarding the challenge trophies altogether.

Political Problems

Before the commencement of the games there was some political trouble and diplomatic posturing caused by the presence of Finland and Bohemia. Finland was a grand duchy with the Russian Czar as Grand Duke. Finland had full inner autonomy, with its own laws and legislation, its own government, and its own parliament. In fact, Finland was the first country in Europe where women were granted the right to vote. Finland was under Russian policy control only in financial matters and in foreign affairs. As an example, Finnish ships carried the Russian flag.

Bohemia did not have the same kind of autonomy as Finland, but one of the many titles of the Austrian emperor was king of Bohemia. The Czechs had entered as Bohemia in the covered court tennis events in May and that went unnoticed. They also entered and played as Bohemia in the hard court events the week prior to the opening ceremony. The Austrian sports paper *Allgemeine Sport-Zeitung* remarked that it was expected that something would be done about that, and as the day of the opening ceremony approached the diplomatic activities of Austria and Russia increased.

Russia and Austria did not want Finland and Bohemia to take part independently, but a compromise was worked out as follows: 1) Finland and Bohemia took part under the Russian and Austrian flags, respectively; 2) at the opening ceremony they marched directly after Russia and Austria, respectively; and 3) Bohemia did not take part under the name of Bohemia but under the name of Austria-Czechs.[14]

The Opening Ceremony

The opening ceremony took place on Saturday, 6 July, in the Olympic Stadium. At 1040 the royal family left the Royal Palace for the stadium. They arrived shortly before 1100 and were greeted by the members of the IOC and the organizing committee. At 1100 the march of the athletes began in alphabetical order according to the Swedish names of the countries: Belgium, Chile, Denmark, France, United States, Greece, the Netherlands, Italy, Japan, Luxembourg, Norway, Portugal, Russia (followed by Finland), Switzerland, Serbia, Great Britain (followed by the British Empire nations of Canada, Australasia, and South Africa), Germany, Austria (followed by Austria-Czechs and Hungary), and Sweden.[15] It should be noted that Greece was not the first nation to enter the stadium, as is now the current practice.

When the Finnish team entered the Stadium behind Russia it momentarily stopped to increase their distance behind the Russian team. The team leaders, Ivar Wilskman and Gustaf "Gösta" Wasenius, ordered the group to take short steps, which led to Finland passing the royal box almost 75 meters behind the Russians.[16] The band began to play a famous Finnish march, "Björneborgarnas marsch" ("March of the Björneborgers")[17] symbolizing the people of Finland, and enormous cheers from the Swedish spectators, who sympathized with their former countrymen, greeted the Finns. At the front of the Finnish team, walking beside Eino Saastamoinen, the male gymnast who served as the standardbearer, was a female gymnast, Siri Börjeson,[18] carrying the flag of Gymnastikföreningen för Fruntimmer i Helsingfors (The Ladies' Gymnastic Club of Helsinki) that had the inscription "*Mens sana in corpore sano.*"[19] But the flag was removed swiftly and discreetly,[20] and few even noticed what had happened.

After the teams, the IOC members, and the members of the organizing committee took their positions on the field, a hymn was sung. The King's chaplain, Clemens Åhfeldt, then delivered a prayer in Swedish, and IOC member, Reverend Robert Stuart de Courcy Laffan, gave one in English. Then the honorary president of the organizing committee, Crown Prince Gustaf Adolf, began to speak. He finished his speech by inviting King Gustaf V to declare the Olympic Games open. The King gave a short speech, which he concluded with:

> Med dessa ord förklarar jag härmed de Olympiska Spelen i Stockholm öppnade.
> [With these words I herewith declare the Olympic Games in Stockholm opened.]

Trumpeters blew from the towers, and a choir sang "Stå stark du ljusets riddarvakt" ("Stand Strong You Knighted Guardian of Light"). The athletes then began to march out of the stadium to the tunes of "The Festival March of the Olympic Games." The athletes did not pass the royal box as they marched in, but did so as they exited the Olympic stadium. It was reported that every national team gave a special salute when passing the royal box.

At 1200, shortly after the athletes had left the stadium, there were exhibitions by male and female Swedish gymnastics troupes. At 1330 the Olympic Games began with the javelin throw and the first round heats of the 100 meters.

The Games of the Vth Olympiad

The games were favored by exceptionally fine and sunny weather, and in Sweden they would later be called the "Solskensolympiaden" (the Sunshine Olympiad). This was good for the spectators and most of the participants, but some athletes suffered from the heat, especially the marathon runners and some of the wrestlers. Only 50 percent of the marathon runners finished the race — the rest victims of the excessive heat — and the paramedics and the ambulances had a tough job in assisting all the runners who retired. The Portuguese runner Francisco Lázaro collapsed during the race and was quickly taken to hospital. The physicians did all they could to revive him but in vain. Without having regained consciousness he passed away the following morning (15 July) at 0620. He was the first athlete, and still one of only two, to die during Olympic competition.[21]

Another incident during the marathon race was "The Japanese Runner Who Disappeared." Japan took part in the Olympic Games for the first time, represented by two athletes, one of them a marathon runner, Shizo Kanaguri. He also suffered from the heat, and at around 20 km., he stopped at a garden alongside the route, exhausted. He was offered lemonade, but sat down and decided to retire from the race. Without notifying any official he returned to Stockholm by train. Years later, in 1967, he was invited to return to Stockholm where, by then 75 years old, he symbolically finished the race.[22]

Wrestling took place on mats in the Olympic Stadium. The sun was shining all day long and the mats became scorching hot. The matches had rounds of 30 minutes. If no decision was scored after 30 minutes, the judges could order another round of 30 minutes, ad infinitum, and thus, matches could theoretically go on for hours. The longest match, between Max Klein (RUS) and Alfred Asikainen (FIN), in Middleweight A (<75 kg.), lasted for 11 hours, before Klein was declared the winner. The next day Klein was scheduled to meet Claes Johansson (SWE), who had already defeated Asikainen, for the gold medal. However, Klein was too exhausted to wrestle so Johansson won the gold medal by default.

In Middleweight B (<82.5 kg., called Light-Heavyweight in many sources) Anders Ahlgren (SWE) and Ivar Böhling (FIN) met in the final. This bout lasted for nine hours but, as no one had gained any advantage or seemed to be really trying, the judges made use of Special Rule 8, which read as follows: "If neither of the competitors has made any real attack during the first 30 minutes, or in the following bouts, the judges can declare both to be defeated; this decision of the judges must be unanimous."[23] Today we would call it double disqualification due to passivity. So there was no winner in this weight class and no gold medal was awarded. Ahlgren and Böhling both received silver medals.

Two athletes towered above the rest in the 1912 Olympic Games — the American Indian Jim Thorpe (né Wa-tho-huck [Bright Path]) and Hannes Kolehmainen of Finland. Thorpe outclassed the other participants in both the pentathlon and decathlon. In the pentathlon he won four of the five events — long jump, 200 meters, discus throw, and 1,500 meters and he was third in the javelin throw. His point score was seven compared to 21 for Ferdinand Bie (NOR), who finished second. In the decathlon Thorpe won three of ten events — shot put, high jump, and the 110 meter hurdles — and he finished almost 700 points ahead of Sweden's Hugo Wieslander in second place and almost 1,000 points ahead of Charles Lomberg (SWE), who placed third. At the awards ceremony, King Gustaf V is reputed to have said to Thorpe, "Sir, you are the greatest athlete in the world." Reportedly, Thorpe answered simply, "Thanks, King."

The story is well known that Thorpe lost his gold medals when it was revealed in January 1913 that he had played minor league pro baseball (See Appendix II). Hugo Wieslander was presented the decathlon gold medal at a ceremony in the Olympic Stadium in 1913. He made plans to return the medal to Jim Thorpe, but it could not be arranged, and in 1951 Wieslander donated the medal to the Swedish Sports Museum in GCI. But the Thorpe/Wieslander medal was stolen from the Swedish Sports Museum in 1954 and has not been seen since.

Jim Thorpe's family pursued a prolonged campaign to get their father's honors restored posthumously and have his medals returned. They were aided by the efforts of American researchers Bob Wheeler and his wife, Florence Ridlon. These efforts met with success on 12 October 1982 when the IOC Executive Committee decided to lift the disqualification, although in an unusual decision, they declared Thorpe and Wieslander equal winners of the decathlon, and Thorpe and Bie equal first in the pentathlon. On 18 January 1983, IOC President Juan Antonio Samaranch handed over copies of the two medals to Thorpe's eldest daughter, Gail, and his son, Bill. On 12 May 1986 a plaque was unveiled in the wall of the Olympic Stadium in Stockholm commemorating Jim Thorpe's Olympic victories.

Hannes Kolehmainen, the Smiling Finn, won three gold medals in Stockholm — 5,000 meters, 10,000 meters, and the 8,000 meter cross-country race — one silver medal in the cross-country team race, and set a new world record for 3,000 meters in the team race. The 5,000 meters and 10,000 meters were new events on the program, replacing the 5 miles (8,046 meters) from London in 1908, and their schedule was difficult, with four races on four consecutive days. It began on Sunday with the 10,000 meter heats, followed on Monday by the 10,000 final, the 5,000 meter heats on Tuesday, and on Wednesday, the 5,000 final. Jean Bouin of France, who held the unofficial world record in the 10,000 (30:58.8), elected to skip that race, because of the schedule, and to concentrate instead on the 5,000 meters. Kolehmainen easily won the 10,000 in 31:20.8, 20 seconds ahead of Lewis Tewanima of the United States.

Kolehminen and Bouin had already met once earlier in 1912, on 28 April in Berlin, over a distance of one German mile, or 7,500 meters, and Kolehmainen had won easily, in a time of 23:05.0, with Bouin 36 seconds back. En route, Kolehmainen had passed 5,000 meters in 15:13. But Bouin was in better condition at the time of the Olympics and was considered a slight favorite, by virtue of having abstained from the 10,000 meters.

The duel between Hannes Kolehmainen and Jean Bouin in the 5,000 is one of the classic races in track and field history. They pulled away from the rest of the field early on. In the early laps the lead changed hand several times, but after half the race Bouin took the lead until near the finish. On the eighth lap Bouin increased his speed in an attempt to drop the Finn, but Kolehmainen hung on. At the bell of the last lap Bouin began his sprint but Kolehmainen responded. On the backstretch Kolehmainen tried to pass Bouin but could not. At the beginning of the final straightaway Kolehmainen attacked again but Bouin was again his equal. The face of the Finn was no longer smiling, but instead wore a look of grim determination. They ran along the finishing straight with the Frenchman half a step ahead when, 20 meters from home, Kolehmainen managed to edge forward inch by inch and win by a narrow margin. Their times were 14:36.6 and 14:36.7, surpassing the unofficial world record of 15:01.2 by almost 25 seconds, and shattering the 15-minute barrier by almost 24 seconds — at the time, a fabulous breakthrough.

With nine gold, eight silver and nine bronze medals, Finland was the fourth-best nation after Sweden, the United States, and Great Britain, but ahead of countries such as Germany, France, Austria, Italy, not to mention Russia, which with two silver and two bronze medals finished well down the list (actually, 15th). Russia may have won the diplomatic battle behind the curtains, but with their Olympic successes, it was the Finns who made their country known worldwide and won the sympathy of world opinion.

When planning the final banquet for participants and officials, there was a problem because there was no hall available with a capacity for 3,000 to 4,000 people. What to do? One member of the committee for the banquet got a bright idea — to lay tables in the stadium. When asked "What if it rains?" he replied, "It won't rain!" It did not rain, and the banquet was a huge success. The public was admitted to the stands where they could watch the banquet on the field and have a banquet of their own. Around 10,000 people paid the admission fee, which helped considerably to finance the banquet.

The Art Competitions

Art competitions figured on the program for the first time, but the organizing committee faced problems with this. The Swedish Royal Academy of Arts and the Swedish art societies did not like the idea of art contests. In fact, they deemed them unsuitable and would have nothing to do with them. As it was not possible to involve Swedish arts circles the organizing committee originally decided to drop the arts contests, which made Pierre de Coubertin furious. He thought that the Swedish artists meddled in something that did not concern them when they questioned the justification of arts contests.

As the Swedish Organizing Committee was unable to organize the arts events, the IOC, or basically Pierre de Coubertin himself, took over. All the Swedish Organizing Committee did was to give 5,000 French francs to the IOC for carrying out the contests. The works were sent to 20, rue Oudinot in Paris, the address of Pierre de Coubertin. It is not known how he selected the juries or who the jury members were, or if perhaps, as seems most likely, he was the sole judge and jury. It is also not known how many works were entered or which artists entered. However, after the decision, all the prize-winning works were brought to Stockholm, where they were exhibited in a hall at Karlaplan,[24] nine blocks away from the Olympic Stadium.

The gold medal in literature went to Georges Hohrod and M. Eschbach for "Ode to Sports," which was submitted in three languages: French, English and German. Georges Hohrod was Pierre de Coubertin himself. In 1899, he had already published an autobiographic novel, "Le Roman d'un rallié," under the pseodonym. It is believed that M. Eschbach was his wife Marie (née Rothan), who grew up partly in Germany, and that she helped him translate the work into German (see the Arts Competitions in the events results sections for more information).

The Awards Ceremony

The awards ceremony for shooting and the sports during the Olympic week, except for cycling, took place on Monday, 15 July at 1700, after the day's events. The last event to be contested was the 1,500 meters of the decathlon.

The prize winners marched into the stadium in three columns, the gold medalists in the middle column, the silver medalists in the left column, and the bronze medalists in the right column. King Gustaf V was standing on a platform in the middle in front of the royal box, with Crown Prince Gustaf Adolf standing on a platform to his right, and Prince Carl, the Duke of Västergötland (Westgothia) and the King's brother, on a platform to his left. The King presented the gold medals and, for the relevant events, the challenge prizes to the winners, and he also placed a laurel wreath of oak leaves on their heads. The Crown Prince distributed the silver medals and Prince Carl the bronze medals.

The medalists were announced by event, beginning with the 100 meters. They approached their respective platforms simultaneously and received their respective medals concurrently. When all the medals were distributed, Viktor Gustaf Balck thanked the royal members for distributing the prizes, and called for four cheers for the King. The ceremony was concluded with the Crown Prince calling for four cheers for the medalists.

The awards ceremony for cycling took place on Monday, 9 July at the Restaurant Hasselbacken. The medals were distributed by the president of the cycling committee, Gösta Drake af Hagelsrum. Several cities along the route had donated special prizes that were also distributed. The Memorial Cup of Eskilstuna went to the winner of the race, Rudolph Lewis of South Africa. The Memorial Cup of Västerås went to the best Swede, Erik Friborg, who finished in seventh place. The Memorial Cup of Enköping went to the best rider between Enköping and the Olympic Stadium, Leonard Meredith of Great Britain. The Memorial Cup of Mariefred was to be awarded to a cyclist not among the prize winners who had nonetheless ridden well, and the cycling committee awarded this cup to Frank Brown of Canada, who finished fifth. The Silver Cup of Sundsvalls Velocipedklubb went to the winner of the team event, Sweden. The Memorial Cup of Köping was presented to the team with the most participants finishing the race, which was Germany.

The awards ceremonies in the sports that finished before or after the Olympic Week — lawn tennis (covered court and hard court), football, equestrian sport and rowing — took place on their respective grounds immediately after the conclusion of the competitions (save for the shooting events). The awards ceremony in yachting took place on 27 July at the Restaurant Hasselbacken. (See the following section on the closing ceremony.)

The Closing Ceremony

The closing ceremony took place in connection with the banquet for the yachtsmen and the yachting officials at Restaurant Hasselbacken on Saturday, 27 July, at 1800. The banquet was presided over by Prince Wilhelm, Duke of Södermanland, second son of the King. The medals and challenge trophy in the 6 meter class were distributed. Each medal-winning yacht received a memorial plate of the Kungliga Svenska Segel Sällskapet (KSSS) to be fastened on the yacht — silver-gilt plates for the gold medal-winning yachts, silver plates for the silver medal-winning yachts, and bronze plates for the bronze medal-winning yachts.

Oscar Holtermann, president of the yachting organizing committee and of KSSS, gave the concluding speech for the hosts. IOC President Pierre de Coubertin gave the final speech, closing the Games of the Vth Olympiad by saying:

> Et maintenant, Messieurs, voici qu'un grand peuple a, par notre entremise, recu de vos mains le flambeau des Olympiades et s'est engagé par là à en préserver et, si possible, à en aviver la flamme précieuse.
>
> Une coutume s'est établie que la dernière parole dite au soir des Jeux Olympiques fut pour saluer l'aurore des Jeux suivants. C'est pourquoi je vais vous proposer au nom du Comité International Olympique, gardien suprême et stable de l'institution renovée, de lever nos verres en l'honneur de la VIe Olympiade.
>
> Puisse-t-elle contribuer comme ses illustres devancières au bien général, au perfectionnement de l'humanité! Puisse-t-elle se préparer dans le labeur fécond des périodes pacifiques! Puisse-t-elle, le jour venu, être célébrée par tous les peuples de l'univers dans l'allégresse et la Concorde!

> (And now, Gentlemen, see how a great people has, by our arrangement, received from your hands the Olympic flame and has undertaken to protect it and, if possible, enhance the radiance of the precious flame.
>
> A custom has been established that the last word spoken in the evening of the Olympic Games is to greet the dawn of the next Games. That is why I will propose to you in the name of the International Olympic Committee, the supreme and solid renovated institution, to raise our glasses in the honour of the VIth Olympiad.
>
> May they, as their brilliant predecessors, contribute to the general good, to the perfection of mankind! May they be prepared in the fruitful labor of peaceful times. May they, when the day has come, be celebrated by all the people of the universe in cheerfulness and Concord!)

Summary

And so the Games of the Vth Olympiad came to an end. They were the most modern Olympic Games yet celebrated, and were certainly the most successful Olympics of the modern era, to that date. The 1896 and 1906 Olympics had small fields, with only a few nations represented. The 1900 and 1904 Olympic Games were sideshows to world fairs and were debacles from which the Olympic Movement was fortunate to recover. The London Olympic Games of 1908 were better, more modern, but the many controversies and the continual bickering between the Americans and the British left a bitter taste long after the successes were remembered. But 1912 showed the world what the Olympic Games could be.

That the 1912 Olympic Games were an organizational success was mainly due to the influence of Viktor Gustaf Balck. Coubertin wrote of him, "Balck dominated the scene with his popular silhouette. No detail was too petty for him to ignore. This Olympiad was his triumph, the culmination of all his past efforts to persuade his country to go in for sport of all kinds without in any way rejecting traditional gymnastics."[25]

Sigfrid Edström was another Swedish sports leader who made his name known for the first time. Before the Olympics Leopold Englund of Sweden launched the idea of an international federation for athletics, and called a meeting for that purpose, to be held in the Swedish Parliament on 17 July 1912. Representatives of 17 countries attended, whose aim was to found the federation then and there, but the United States' James Sullivan opposed the idea. He said that the AAU delegates had no authority to take part in the founding of an international federation, and he wanted the decision to be deferred until the next year. So it was decided to call a meeting in Berlin for 1913, at which the International Amateur Athletic Federation (IAAF) was founded. Edström was elected president and he retained the post until 1946, when he was elected IOC President. (For more on the formation of international federations, see the chapter on "Other Sports and Events.")

What impact did the Olympic Games have on Swedish society and the Swedish sports movement? Many people who were previously uninterested in sports, or had been sceptical of their importance, were carried away by the enthusiasm with which the Swedish successes were met. The public then had a better understanding of sports and what it meant to the country and its people. It had not previously been recognized that sporting success brought good public relations for the country, and was a sign of national strength. This was manifested by the fact that in 1913 the Parliament allocated an unconditional grant to the Swedish sports movement for the first time ever.

The Swedish sports movement, as measured by the number of clubs and the number of club members, had been continually increasing since the 1890s. Did this increase get a boost after the 1912 Olympics? Surprisingly not. The increase continued in 1913 at about the same rate and after 1914 the outbreak of World War I made any comparisons difficult.

One thing that did occur as a result of the 1912 Olympics was the formation of a national Olympic committee in Sweden. In 1900, 1906, 1908 and 1912 there had been temporary committees in Sweden to organize participation at the Olympics, but after the Stockholm Olympic Games it was realized that a permanent committee was needed. So in 1913 Sveriges Olympiska Kommitté, the Swedish Olympic Committee, was founded as a permanent institution.

Pierre de Coubertin was overjoyed, happy that his baby had now grown into at least a successful child, presaging the prominence that the Olympic Games would eventually enjoy in the sporting world. The Vth Olympic Games were the climax of Coubertin's career as a sports leader. Summarizing the 1912 Olympic Games, he wrote as follows in his *Mémoires Olympiques*:

Never had a Swedish summer been more glorious. For five whole weeks, nature was resplendent, the sun perpetually shining, with the light sea breezes, radiant nights, the joyful atmosphere of gaily decked streets, flowers everywhere, and illuminations dimmed only by the brilliance of a light that never paled. In the wonderful setting of the city, the general gaiety of the young knew no bounds. There was little time for sleep, but nobody wanted to sleep anyway. Festivities succeeded festivities without visible adverse effect on muscular feats. The Gothic Stadium, with its pointed arches and towers, its technical perfection, its well-planned and methodical regulations, seemed a model of its kind. Depending on the need, it acted as a banqueting hall, a concert hall, a ballroom and was always ready again the next morning for another series of athletic events. In one evening we saw it covered with squares of grass laid side by side, strewn with obstacles and decorated with banks of flowers for the equestrian games. Everything was done silently, quickly, without error. Whereas in London the life of the huge metropolis had not been influenced by the invasion of Olympism, the whole of Stockholm was impregnated with it. The whole city took part in the effort in honor of the foreigners and we caught a glimpse of what the atmosphere of Olympia must have been like in ancient times — although on a larger scale, embellished and enhanced by the presence of all the modern facilities and amenities, without any of the ugliness they so often bring in their wake, so that Hellenism and progress seemed to have joined forces to act as hosts together.[26]

And so it was.

NOTES

1. Balck has a further, more distant, Olympic connection. His granddaughter, Christine St. Vincent Broke Saumarez married Harry Llewellyn, Welsh equestrian Olympian, and an Olympic gold medalist in team show jumping in 1952.

2. Lindroth, Jan; Ljunggren, Jens; and Yttergren, Leif. "The Nordic Games," in: *1994 Swedish Media Guide for the Lillehammer Olympics*. Based on paper present on the Nordic Games at the ISH-PES Seminar in Lillehammer on 25–30 January 1993.

3. Coubertin, Pierre de. *Olympic Memoirs*, p. 60 (IOC edition).

4. Lyberg, pp. 44.

5. *Ibid.*

6. *Nordiskt Idrottslif,* 36: 336, 24 July 1909.

7. 400,000 Swedish kronor in 1912 was equivalent to $107,527 in 1912 U.S. dollars. The 2000 equivalents are 19,101,419 Swedish kronor and $2,047,312.

8. Torben Grut's son was William Grut, who won the gold medal in the 1948 Olympic modern pentathlon event.

9. 820,000 Swedish kronor in 1912 was equivalent to $220,430 in 1912 U.S. dollars. The 2000 equivalents are 39,157,909 Swedish kronor and $4,196,990.

10. 1,187,880 Swedish kronor in 1912 was equivalent to $319,323 in 1912 U.S. dollars. The 2000 equivalents are 56,725,484 Swedish kronor and $6,079,902.

11. 12OR, p. 640.

12. Most of the material concerning medals awarded at the 1912 Olympics comes from the book *Olympic Medals: A Reference Guide*, by Jim Greensfelder, Oleg Vorontsov, and Jim Lally (Cincinnati: GVL Enterprises, 1999).

13. The Brunetta d'Usseaux Challenge Prize was originally designated to be given to the best nation at the Olympic Games, but as no consensus could be reached as to how to decide this, the prize was transferred to the coxed eights rowing event.

14. Although Bohemia was designated officially as Austria-Czechs (Österrike-Tschecher) (see Uggla), the 1912 Official Report does list the athletes representing it as from "Bohemia" (English text) or "Böhmen" (Swedish text).

15. The nations entered in the following alphabetical order, with the names in Swedish: Belgien, Chile, Danmark, Frankrike, Förenta staterna, Grekland, Holland (Nederländerna), Italien, Japan, Luxemburg, Norge, Portugal, Ryssland (followed by Finland), Schweiz, Serbien, Storbritannien (followed by the British Empire nations of Canada, Australasien, and Sydafrika), Tyskland, Österrike (followed by Österrike-Tschecker and Ungern), and Sverige. The standards, however, were not in Swedish, but were in the language of each nation. From photos of the opening ceremony, the following nameboards have been identified: Belgique, Chilenos, Danmark, France, United States, Hellas, Nederland, Nippon, Luxembourg, Norge, Portugal, Rossia (Finland), Great Britain (Canada, Australasia, South Africa), Deutschland, Österreich (Magyarország), and Sverige. Standards of the following nations have not been seen (possible text on standard): Italy (Italia), Switzerland (Schweiz), Serbia (Srbija) and Austria-Czechs (Österreich-Tschechen).

16. Lyberg W. *Fabulous 100 Years of the IOC. Facts-figures-and much, much more.* Lausanne: IOC, 1996, pp. 190–191.

17. Exactly which famous Finnish march is controversial. Ingmar Björkman, in conversations with Ture Widlund, provided the information about the exact march based on conversations with Valdemar Wickholm, who marched with the Finnish team during the opening ceremony (and competed in the 110 meter hurdles and decathlon). Some sources say it was "30-vuotisen Sodan marssi" ("March of the 30-years War"), also known as "Finska rytteriets marsch" ("March of the Finnish Cavalry"). It is possible that this march was also played during the opening ceremony, but when the Finnish team passed the royal box, the march played was the "Björneborgarnas marsch" ("March of the Björneborgers"). (Björneborg is a city in Finland.)

18. Björkman, Ingmar. *Med idrotten i blodet*, p. 8.

19. Lyberg. *Ibid.*

20. Lyberg notes that this was done "by Swedish police" but Finnish sources (per Markku Siukonen) note that it was done by "a Russian officer." It was most likely the Swedish police, with the Russian officer theory being promulgated by anti–Russian circles within Finland.

21. The second Olympian to die during competition was the Danish cyclist, Knud Enemark Jensen, who collapsed during the 1960 Olympic cycling road race, and later died. Jensen was found to be doped with Ronicol, an amphetamine, which likely hastened his demise. The day was also very hot, and several other cyclists were taken to hospital after the race. This incident was one of several that made the IOC, and other sports authorities, begin drug testing in the late 1960s.

22. Karaki, Kunihiko. "The First Japanese Olympic Delegation in 1912," pp. 261–268, in: *The Olympic Games Through the Ages: Greek Antiquity and its Impact on Modern Sport (Proceedings of the 13th International HISPA Congress, Olympa/Greece, May 22–28, 1989)*, Roland Renson, Manfred Lämmer, James Riordan, Dimitrios Chassiotis, eds. (Athens: Hellenic Sports Research Institute, 1991).

23. 12OR, p. 1095.

24. The 12OR lists the site as Karlavägen 10, but in the Official Program, it is Karlaplan 10. Karlavägen runs through the middle of the Karlaplan section.

25. Coubertin, Pierre de. *op. cit.*, p. 78.

26. *Ibid.*, p. 77–78.

Summary and Statistics

Dates:	5 May–22 July 1912[1]*
Site:	Stockholm, Sweden
Candidate City:	Berlin, Germany
Official Opening By:	King Gustaf V
Number of Countries Competing:	27[2] [27 Men —10 Women]
Number of Athletes Competing:	2,380 [2,327 Men — 53 Women]
Number of Sports:	15 [15 Men — 3 Women —1 Mixed][3]
Number of Events:	102 [95 Men — 5 Women — 2 Mixed]; 5 Art Competitions

Members of the International Olympic Committee in 1912 [45] (years on IOC in brackets)

Australia	Richard Coombes [1905–1932]
Austria	Count Rudolf de Colloredo-Mansfeld [1911–1919]
	Prince Otto zu Windisch-Grätz [1911–1919]
Belgium	Count Henri de Baillet-Latour [1903–1942]
Bohemia	Dr. Jiří Stanislav Guth-Jarkovský [1894–1943]
Canada	Sir John Hanbury-Williams [1911–1921]
Chile	Professor Oscar N. Garcia [1911–1914]
Denmark	Torben Grut [1906–1912][4]
Egypt	Angelos Khristos Bolanaki [1910–1963]
Finland	Baron Reinhold Felix von Willebrand [1908–1919]
France	Abel Ballif [1911–1914]
	Count Albert de Bertier de Sauvigny [1904–1920]
	Ernst Callot [1894–1913]
	Pierre Frédy, Baron Pierre de Coubertin [1894–1925]

Germany	Count Julius Caesar Karl Oskar Erdmann von Wartensleben [1903–1914]
	Count Adalbert von Francken-Sierstorpff [1910–1919]
	Baron Karl von Venningen-Ullner von Diepburg [1909–1914]
Great Britain	Reverend Robert Stuart de Courcy Laffan [1897–1927]
	William Henry Grenfell, Lord Desborough of Taplow [1906–1913]
	Theodore Andrea Cook [1909–1915]
Greece	Count Alexandros Merkati [1897–1925]
Hungary	Count Géza Andrassy [1907–1938]
	Gyula de Muzsa [1909–1946]
Italy	Count Eugenio Brunetta d'Usseaux [1897–1919]
	Attilio Brunialti [1909–1914]
Japan	Professor Jigaro Kano [1909–1938]
Luxembourg	Jean-Maurice Pescatore [1910–1929]
Mexico	Miguel de Beistegui [1901–1931]
Monaco	Count Albert Gautier Vignal [1908–1939]
The Netherlands	Baron Frederik Willem Christiaan Hendrik van Tuyll van Serooskerken [1898–1924]
Norway	Captain Johan Tidemann Sverre [1908–1927]
Peru	Carlos F. de Candamo [1903–1922]
Portugal	Duke Antonio de Lancastre [1906–1912][5]
	Count José Capelo de Penha Garcia (né Franco Frazão) [1912–1940][6]
Romania	Gheorghe A. Plagino [1908–1949]
Russia	Count Nikolao Ribeaupierre [1900–1913]
	Prince Lev Urusov [1910–1933]
Spain	Count Antonio Gonzalo Mejorada del Campo, Marquis de Villamejor [1902–1921]
Sweden	Colonel Viktor Gustaf Balck [1894–1921]
	Count Carl Clarence von Rosen [1900–1948]
Switzerland	Baron Godefroy de Blonay [1899–1937]
Turkey	Selim Sirri Bey Tarcan [1908–1920]
United States	Professor William Milligan Sloane [1894–1924]
	Allison Vincent Armour [1908–1920]
	Evert Jansen Wendell [1911–1917]

Co-opted in 1912 After the Olympic Games Ended

Denmark	Fritz Hansen [1912–1921][7]
Serbia	Svetomir Dukic [1912–1948][8]

The Swedish Olympic Committee for the Olympic Games of Stockholm, 1912

Patron:	King Gustaf V
Honorary President:	Crown Prince Gustaf Adolf
President:	Colonel Viktor Gustaf Balck
Vice-President:	Johannes Sigfrid Edström, Esquire
Secretary-General:	Kristian Hellström, Esquire[9]

Members:	Captain Erik Frestadius; Dr. Astley Levin; Nore Thisell, Esquire; Frits af Sandeberg, Esquire[10]
Deputy Members:	Count Clarence von Rosen, Master of the Horse; Lieutenant Gustaf G:son Uggla
Adjoint Members:	Charles Dickson, Esquire; Colonel, Baron Sven D. A. Hermelin; Captain Oscar Holtermann, Gentleman of the Bedchamber; Sigurd N. Linnér, Esquire, Under-Secretary of State; Fredrik Löwenadler, Esquire, Gentleman-in-Waiting; Walter Murray, Esquire, Under-Secretary of State; Harald Sohlman, Esquire
Exec. Committee:	Colonel Viktor Gustaf Balck; Johannes Sigfrid Edström, Esquire; Kristian Hellström, Esquire; Nore Thisell, Esquire (Deputy Member); Lieutenant Gustaf G:son Uggla (Deputy Member)
Finance Section:	Charles Dickson, Esquire (Bank Director); Dr. Astley Levin; Sigurd N. Linnér, Esquire; Walter Murray, Esquire; Frits af Sandeberg, Esquire; Baron Fredrik Ramel (Adjoint Member pro tem); E. E. Lomm, Esquire (Secretary)
Medals and Badges:	Dr. Astley Levin
Technical Section:	Johannes Sigfrid Edström, Esquire; Lieutenant Gustaf G:son Uggla
Program Section:	Nore Thisell, Esquire; Lieutenant Gustaf G:son Uggla

Committees of the 1912 Olympic Games Organizing Committee

Athletics:	Colonel Viktor Gustaf Balck (President); Leopold Englund, Esquire (Secretary); Kristian Hellström, Esquire (2nd Secretary)
Cycling:	Captain Carl Gustaf "Gösta" Drake af Hagelsrum (President); C. A. Ullén, Esquire (Secretary)
Fencing:	Captain Emil Fick (President); Lieutenant Birger Cnattingius (Secretary)
Football (Soccer):	Christian Ludvig Kornerup, Esquire (President); Anton Johanson, Esquire (Secretary)
Game Shooting:	Count Claes Lewenhaupt, Lord of the Bedchamber (President)
Gymnastics:	Captain Einar Nerman (President); Lieutenant Wilhelm Carlberg (Secretary)
Horse Riding:	HRH Prince Karl (Honorary President); Colonel, Count Erik Carl Gabriel Oxenstierna (President); Count Clarence von Rosen, Master of the Horse (Secretary-General); Lieutenant Carl Emil Otto Trägårdh (Secretary)
Lawn Tennis:	HRH Prince Wilhelm (Honorary President); Captain Axel Fingal Wallenberg (President); Kurt Zetterberg, Esquire (Secretary)
Modern Pentathlon:	Colonel Viktor Gustaf Balck (President); Kristian Hellström, Esquire (Secretary)
Mountain Climbing:	Dr. Erik Ullén (President)
Rowing:	Fredrik Löwenadler, Esquire, Gentleman-in-Waiting (Honorary President); Nils Ljunggren, Esquire (President); Ulrich Salchow, Esquire (Secretary)
Shooting:	Colonel, Count Carl E. Taube (President); Gustaf C. Boivie, Esquire (Secretary); Captain Fredrik Björkenstam, Esquire, Master of the

Hounds (President of Clay Bird Shooting Committee); Ernest Mellin, Esquire (Secretary of Clay Bird Shooting Committee)

Swimming: Erik Bergvall, Esquire (President); Kristian Hellström, Esquire, (Secretary)

Tug-of-War: Captain Carl Gustaf "Gösta" Drake af Hagelsrum (President); Kristian Hellström, Esquire (Secretary)

Wrestling: Carl Helgesson, Esquire (President); Stellan Warelius, Esquire (Secretary)

Yacht Racing: Captain Oscar Holtermann, Gentleman of the Bedchamber (President); Knut Boivin, Esquire, Bank Director (Secretary); Hugo Andersson, Esquire, C. E. (Assistant Secretary)

Accommodations: Captain Otto Bergström (President); C. Fries, Esquire (Secretary); W. Ekström; Kristian Hellström, Esquire; Colonel, Baron Sven D. A. Hermelin; Nore Thisell, Esquire; O. W. Wahlquist

Advertisements: Christian Ludvig Kornerup, Esquire (President); Kristian Hellström, Esquire (Secretary); Gustaf Åsbrink, B.A.; Edvin Molin; Carl Hellberg

Buildings: Colonel Viktor Gustaf Balck (President); Alexandre Lindmann, Esquire (Secretary)

Entertainments: Alex Lilja, Esquire, Court Intendant (President); D. Blomberg, Esquire (Secretary)

Press: Colonel, Baron Sven D. A. Hermelin (President); Erik Pallin, Esquire (Secretary)

Receptions: Captain Erik Frestadius (President); Nils Lundgren, Esquire (Secretary); B. Fale Burman; Gunnar Frestadius; Colonel, Baron Sven D. A. Hermelin; Captain Carl Silfverstolpe

International Juries by Sport

Athletics (T & F): Johannes Sigfrid Edström, Esquire (President/SWE); Captain Carl Silfverstolpe (SWE); John G. Merrick (CAN); Lauri Wilskman (FIN); René Enerlin (FRA); W. A. Brommage (GBR); Carl Diem (GER); Anastasios Metaxas (GRE); Szilárd Stankovits (HUN); James Edward Sullivan (USA)

Fencing: Carl Gustaf Platen (President/SWE); Sten Drakenberg (SWE); Heinrich Tenner (AUT); Albert Feyerick (BEL); Captain H. Jürst (GER); William Henry Grenfell, Lord Desborough of Taplow (GBR); Adrianus Egbertus Willem de Jong (NED); Carlo Compans de Brichanteaux (ITA)

Football (Soccer): Christian Ludvig Kornerup, Esquire (President/SWE); Baron Édouard-Émile de Laveleye (BEL); Daniel Burley Woolfall (GBR); Cornelis August Wilhelm Hirschmann (NED)

Gymnastics: Viktor Gustaf Balck (President/SWE); Captain Einar Nerman (SWE); Holger Christian Valdemar Møller (DEN); Dr. — Lachaud (FRA); Karl von Iszer (HUN); Carl Ferdinand Berthelsen (NOR)

Equestrian Events: Colonel Gustaf Adolf Nyblæus (SWE); Lieutenant-Colonel, Count Reinhol (SWE); Major — Joostens (BEL); Otto August Heinrich Moltke

(DEN); Commander –– Destremau (FRA); Major –– von Giese (GER); Lieutenant-Colonel Johan Henrik Egeberg-Ottesen (NOR); Lieutenant-Colonel Frederick S. Foltz (USA)

Modern Pentathlon: Colonel, Count Carl E. Taube (President/SWE); Captain Carl Silfverstolpe (SWE); Otto Herschmann (AUT); Jiří Rössler-Orovský (BOH); Captain Hans Henrik Bondo (DEN); Lieutenant-Colonel J. F. Noël-Birch (GBR; Désiré Lauber (HUN); Captain Oscar Trygvessøn Klingenberg (NOR); Georges Duperron (RUS); Gustavus Town Kirby (USA)

Rowing: Fredrik Löwenadler, Esquire; Gentleman-in-Waiting (President/SWE); Ulrich Salchow (SWE); Q. L. Deloitte (AUS); L. Annoot (BEL); Joseph Wright (CAN); Henrik Schack Køster (DEN); E. Albert Glandaz (FRA); Dr. Oskar Ruperti (GER); Theodore Andrea Cook (GBR); Consul Einar Wettre (NOR)

Shooting: Colonel, Count Carl E. Taube (President/SWE); Captain Fredrik Björkenstam, Esquire (SWE); Maurice Fauré (FRA); Ioannis Chryssafis (GRE); Anton Frisch (NOR); Colonel Platon Moskov (RUS); Sir Lionel Phillips, Bart (RSA); William Libbey (USA)

Swimming: Major Nils David Edlund (President/SWE); Erik Bergvall (SWE); Ernest Samuel Marks (AUS); Felix Graf (AUT); François Van der Heyden (BEL); Uno Westerholm (FIN); F. Baxter (GBR); A. Witt (GER); Arpád von Füzesséry (HUN); Bartow Summer Weeks (USA)

Tug-of-War: Johannes Sigfrid Edström, Esquire (President/SWE); Captain Carl Silfverstolpe (SWE); John G. Merrick (CAN); Lauri Wilskman (FIN); René Enerlin (FRA); W. A. Brommage (GBR); Carl Diem (GER); Anastasios Metaxas (GRE); Szilárd Stankovits (HUN); James Edward Sullivan (USA)

Wrestling: Carl Helgesson, Esquire (President/SWE); Arthur Walter Björkgren (SWE); Otto Herschmann (AUT); Václav Rudl (BOH); Captain Hans Henrik Bondo (DEN); Eugen Kissling (GER); Moritz Csanádi (HUN); Ludwig Tschaplinsky (RUS)

Flag Bearers at the Opening Ceremony
(27 of 28 nations; 18 bearers known)

Australasia	Malcolm Champion [New Zealand] [Athletics]
Austria	not known[11]
Belgium	not known[12]
Bohemia	Jiří Kodl [Tennis]
Canada	Duncan Gillis [Athletics][13]
Chile	Leopoldo Palma [Athletics]
Denmark	Arne Halfdan Sigurd Højme [Official]
Egypt[14]	Ahmed Mohamed Hassanein [Fencing]
Finland	Eino Saastamoinen [Gymnastics][15]
France	not known[16]
Germany	Karl von Halt [Track & Field Athletics]
Great Britain	Charles Smith [Water Polo]

Greece	Konstantinos Tsiklitiras [Athletics]
Hungary	Jenő Rittich [Gymnastics]
Italy	Alberto Braglia [Gymnastics]
Japan	not known[17]
Luxembourg	Jean-Pierre Thommes [Gymnastics]
The Netherlands	W. Ploeger [Sport Official]
Norway	not known[18]
Portugal	Francisco Lázaro [Track & Field Athletics]
Russia	M. E. Rayevsky [Gymnastics]
Serbia	not known
South Africa	not known[19]
Switzerland	not known[20]
Turkey	no flag bearer[21]
United States	George Bonhag [Athletics]
Sweden	Robert Olsson [Athletics]
Iceland	did not march at the opening ceremony[22]

Credit/Debit Accounting of the 1912 Olympic Games (Swedish kronor — 1912 values)

Income

Olympic Games Fund		13,000.00
Grant from City of Stockholm		50,000.00
Swedish Cent. Assoc. for Sports Promotion (SCFIF)		1,276,019.97
Granberg's Art Industry, Co., Ltd.		12,910.60
Hasselblad & Scholander's, Ltd., Photographers		13,275.02
Östberg & Lenhardtson & Co.		2,299.75
Sale of Cinema Rights		20,446.90
Restaurant in Tennis Pavilion		2,000.00
Series Ticket Sales		429,560.00
Day Ticket Sales		250,762.50
Day Programs and Advertisements		18,848.54
Section for Athletics		
Undergraduates' Amateur Theatricals	411.37	
Choral Society's Matinée	647.14	
Tryouts	509.99	
		1,568.50
Section for Cycling		
Program Sales	2,913.14	
Sundries	67.90	
		2,981.04
Section for Fencing		
Tryouts	76.00	
Ticket Sales	1,636.00	
Inventory Sales	664.50	
		2,376.50

Section for Football (Soccer)
Grant from Football Association	1,000.00	
Tryouts	552.54	
Ticket Sales	62,503.50	
Inventory Sales	350.00	
		64,406.04

Section for Gymnastics
Apparatus and Inventories Sold	1,025.00

Section for Horse Riding (Equestrian Events)   123,539.69

Section for Lawn Tennis
Ticket Sales	21,708.00	
Program Sales	260.93	
Inventory Sales	946.00	
		22,914.93

Section for Rowing
Gift — Fredrik Löwenadler, Esq.	5,000.00	
Ticket Sales	11,664.00	
Program Sales	567.90	
Inventory Sales	567.48	
		17,799.38

Section for Army Rifle Shooting
Sundry Receipts	528.00

Section for Clay Bird Shooting
Gift — Skånska Powder Mfg. Co.	360.56	
Inventory Sales	4,000.00	
		4,360.56

Section for Small-Bore Rifle Shooting
Sundry Receipts	85.30	
Inventory Sales	299.82	
		385.12

Section for Swimming
Tryouts	2,122.74	
Ticket Sales	69,287.50	
Program Sales	1,005.70	
Children's Day Festival	2,040.92	
Timber Sales	5,972.70	
Inventory Sales	370.00	
		80,799.56

Section for Wrestling
Tryouts	1,433.64

Accommodation Committee
Accommodation Fees	8,870.05	
Inventory Sales	568.00	
		9,438.05

Entertainment Committee

Olympia Gardens	28,814.94	
Military Bands' Concerts	7,164.03	
Boy Scouts' Display	685.36	
		36,664.33

Miscellaneous

The Choral Association	13,943.70	
Inventory Sales	1,678.75	
Tryouts	3,105.82	
Racing Club Sundries	625.59	
Stockholm Trotting Club Sundries	103.10	
Commision to hire various sundries	615.95	
		20,072.91

Total Income   **2,479,416.53**

Expenses

General Expenses

Inventories	13,695.57
Interest on Bank Accounts	2,252.26
Posters and Other Advertisements	106,638.47
Ticket Office Expenses	31,995.54
General Secretariat's Office Expenses	16,264.45
Salaries for the General Secretariat	67,768.98
Office Supplies for the General Secretariat	50,421.99
Postage, Telegram, Telephone — General Secretariat	63,137.32
Medals and Diplomas	25,770.40
Program Printing and Distribution	70,878.31
Representation Account	43,474.09
Olympic Games Fund[23]	400.00
Press Committee	3,131.70
Reception Committee	10,423.75
Information Bureau	1,175.22
Entertainments Committee	974.22
Grant to *Idrottstidning (The Olympic News)*	3,000.00
Finance Office	3,444.81
Repairs to Tennis Pavilion	3,050.00
Foreign Committees	2,594.55
Official Report of the Olympic Games	8,455.47
Råsunda Athletic Grounds	25,550.43
Traneberg Athletic Grounds	9,800.00
Miscellaneous	18,423.09

The Stadium — Building Expenses

Preparation and Demolition Work	11,919.51
Foundations	627,319.68
Provisional Stands	43,169.70
Provisional Stand (now removed)	41,918.80

Arena and Running Track	122,609.21	
Railings and Turnstiles	38,545.03	
Entries and Lavatories	43,159.35	
Gardens and Roads	44,743.49	
Gas, water, and heating pipes	100,755.06	
Electric Lighting	15,745.82	
Tower Clock	2,292.59	
Inventories and Furniture	33,118.12	
Architects and Consultants Fees	37,212.50	
Office and Administration Expenses	17,219.84	
Miscellaneous	8,151.27	
		1,187,879.97

The Stadium — Daily Expenses

Office Expenses	2,448.72	
Attendants Uniforms and Salaries	20,770.95	
Competition Expenses	21,986.46	
Decorations	15,427.83	
Inventories	1,825.18	
Miscellaneous Daily Expenses	5,187.74	
		67,646.88

Östermalm Athletic Grounds

Tennis Pavilion	115,000.00	
Arena and Running Track	10,359.10	
Attendants and sundries	3,377.74	
Miscellaneous	7,272.45	
		136,009.29

Accommodation Committee

Administration Expenses	8,469.40	
Office Rent	2,302.32	
Security Salaries	1,298.00	
Inventories	2,092.25	
		14,161.97

Section for Athletics (Track & Field)

Office and Administration Expenses	3,951.52	
Trainer's Salaries	35,666.65	
Training Expenses of Swedish Competitors	32,894.13	
Athletic Materials and Sundries	11,109.10	
Marathon Race Expenses	2,508.70	
Miscellaneous	4,097.10	
		90,227.20

Section for Cycling

Office and Administration Expenses	2,466.78	
Trainer's Salaries	440.00	
Training Expenses of Swedish Competitors	5,696.35	
Athletic Materials and Sundries	624.05	
Miscellaneous	3,528.76	
		12,755.94

Section for Fencing
Office and Administration Expenses	1,149.73	
Trainer's Salaries	750.00	
Training Expenses of Swedish Competitors	304.52	
Athletic Materials and Sundries	2,237.35	
Miscellaneous	3,022.19	
		7,463.79

Section for Football (Soccer)
Office and Administration Expenses	3,284.12	
Trainer's Salaries	2,838.65	
Training Expenses of Swedish Competitors	10,006.15	
Athletic Materials and Sundries	2,132.32	
Miscellaneous	5,792.46	
		24,053.70

Section for Gymnastics
Office and Administration Expenses	1,068.33	
Training Expenses of Swedish Competitors	5,149.87	
Women Gymnasts' Do.	1,200.00	
Athletic Materials and Sundries	8,424.13	
Miscellaneous	5,310.30	
		21,152.63

Section for Horse Riding Competitions (Equestrian Events)
Office and Administration Expenses	40,687.89	
Trainer's Salaries	24,301.78	
Attendants, Decorations, and Music	5,427.47	
Accommodation Charges	15,484.81	
Miscellaneous	18,090.06	
		103,992.01

Section for Lawn Tennis
Office and Administration Expenses	2,028.42	
Trainer's Salaries	1,950.00	
Training Expenses of Swedish Competitors	519.00	
Athletic Materials and Sundries	6,268.98	
Stands, Courts, etc.	17,706.42	
Miscellaneous	2,647.58	
		31,120.40

Section for Modern Pentathlon
Office and Administration Expenses	654.47	
Trainer's Salaries	825.00	
Training Expenses of Swedish Competitors	1,393.95	
Athletic Materials and Sundries	155.92	
Miscellaneous	2,174.64	
		5,203.98

Section for Rowing
Office and Administration Expenses	4,122.14
Trainer's Salaries	3,716.72

Training Expenses of Swedish Competitors	12,790.38	
Athletic Materials and Sundries	7,633.31	
Grandstand	10,376.17	
Miscellaneous	12,458.86	
		51,097.58

Section for Army Rifle Shooting

Office and Administration Expenses	729.49	
Training Expenses	630.35	
Athletic Materials and Sundries	185.24	
Miscellaneous	7,406.96	
		8,952.04

Section for Clay Bird Shooting

Office and Administration Expenses	396.73	
Training Expenses	1,140.62	
Materials (clay birds and cartridges)	2,835.84	
Ranges	7,525.00	
Miscellaneous	2,266.94	
		14,165.13

Section for Small-Bore Rifle Shooting

Training Expenses	318.90	
Athletic Materials and Sundries	18.45	
Miscellaneous	2,279.81	
		2,617.16

Section for Swimming

Office and Administration Expenses	9,370.18	
Trainer's Salaries	5,577.09	
Training Expenses of Swedish Competitors	5,478.21	
Athletic Materials and Sundries	3,984.63	
Stands and Buildings	39,157.39	
Expenses of Competition	5,323.99	
To Swedish Swimming Association, per agreement	4,170.74	
Miscellaneous	11,606.44	
		84,668.67

Section for Tug-of-War

Office and Administration Expenses	668.35	
Training Expenses of Swedish Competitors	1,396.63	
Miscellaneous	344.72	
		2,409.70

Section for Wrestling

Office and Administration Expenses	826.45	
Trainer's Salaries	10,040.20	
Training Expenses of Swedish Competitors	5,933.56	
Athletic Materials and Sundries	3,219.00	
Miscellaneous	3,369.81	
		23,389.02

Section for Baseball
Athletic Materials and Sundries	385.11
Miscellaneous	306.80
	691.91

Section for Art Competitions (Concours d'Art)
Miscellaneous	2,390.43

Miscellaneous
Checking Account — Cervin & Co., Bankers	1,302.06
General Secretariat Balance	344.45
On Deposit	3,000.00
Total Expenses	**2,479,416.53**

Summary

Income
Funds and Grants	1,339,019.97
Ticket and Program Sales at Stadium	699,171.04
Ticket and Program Sales for other Sections	324,117.96
For rights sold and sundry receipts	117,107.56
Total	**2,479,416.53**

Expenses
Organization and Administration	629,179.04
Training expenses	486,351.29
Råsunda Athletics Grounds	25,550.43
Traneberg Athletic Grounds	9,800.00
Östermalm Athletic Grounds	136,009.29
Building of the Stadium	1,187,879.97
Total	**2,474,770.02**
Final Cash on Hand	**4,646.51**

Summary	1912 Sw Kronor	2000 Sw Kronor	1912 US $	2000 US $
Income	2,479,416.53	116,473,190.92	666,509.82	12,483,728.93
Expenses	2,474,770.02	116,254,916.50	665,260.76	12,460,334.03
Profit	4,646.51	218,274.42	1,249.06	23,394.90

Competition Sites

Athletics	Olympic Stadium; marathon race from Stadium to Sollentuna and back to the Olympic Stadium
Cycling	Road race around Lake Mälar
Diving	Swimming Stadium at Djurgårdsbrunnsviken
Equestrian Events	Field Riding Club Stadium (three-day event, long-distance ride)
	Lindarängen (three-day event, steeplechase section)
	Olympic Stadium (three-day event, jumping and dressage sections; individual and team jumping; dressage event)

Fencing	Tennis Pavilion at the Östermalm Athletic Grounds
Football (Soccer)	Olympic Stadium
	Råsunda Idrottsplats
	Traneberg Idrottplats
Gymnastics	Olympic Stadium
Modern Pentathlon	Kaknäs (pistol shooting)
	Swimming Stadium at Djurgårdsbrunnsviken (swimming)
	Tennis Pavilion at the Östermalm Athletic Grounds (fencing)
	Barkaby (steeplechase ride)
	Olympic Stadium (cross-country run start and finish)
Rowing & Sculling	Start at Lido in Djurgårdsbrunnsviken and finish opposite Torstensonsgåtan in Nybroviken
Shooting	Kaknäs (pistol, small-bore rifle, long-range rifle)
	Råsunda (running deer, clay trap)
Swimming	Swimming Stadium at Djurgårdsbrunnsviken
Tennis	Royal Tennis Pavilion (covered courts)
	Tennis Pavilion at the Östermalm Athletic Grounds (lawn tennis)
Tug-of-War	Olympic Stadium
Water Polo	Swimming Stadium at Djurgårdsbrunnsviken
Wrestling	Olympic Stadium
Yachting	Nynäshamn

Paid Attendance and Weather at the Olympic Stadium[24]

	AM	PM	
6 July (Saturday)		13,653	Glorious weather
7 July (Sunday)	6,480	12,666	Glorious day
8 July (Monday)	7,323	10,441	Warm, with brilliant sunshine
9 July (Tuesday)	6,254	10,130	Warm, slightly overcast
10 July (Wednesday)	6,913	14,277	Warm, but not as hot as previous days
11 July (Thursday)	6,758	12,175	A perfect day
12 July (Friday)	8,072	13,300	
13 July (Saturday)	7,417	17,256	Hot and sunny
14 July (Sunday)	8,796	18,713	Hot, near 32° C. (89° F.), slight breeze
15 July (Monday)	12,469	12,469	Warm and sunny
Total Attendance	**70,482**	**135,080**	**205,562**

Paid Attendance at Football (Soccer) Matches

	Olympic Stadium	Råsunda	Traneberg	Total
29 June (Saturday)	5,357	560	231	6,148
30 June (Sunday)	3,397	1,445	239	5,081
1 July (Monday)	0	1,405	134	1,539
2 July (Tuesday)	4,374	–	–	4,374
3 July (Wednesday)	1,340	441	–	1,781

	Olympic Stadium	*Råsunda*	*Traneberg*	*Total*
4 July (Thursday)	13,865	448	–	14,313
5 July (Friday)	–	628	–	628
Totals	**28,333**	**4,927**	**604**	**33,864**

Paid Attendance at Other Olympic Sites

Fencing
Total	1,010

Horse Riding Competitions (Equestrian Events)
16 July (Tuesday)	17,250
17 July (Wednesday)	9,881
Total	**27,131**

Tennis
Indoor (5–12 May)	*c.* 3,000
Outdoor (28 June–5 July)	*c.* 10,000
Total	***c.* 13,000**

Rowing
17 July (Wednesday)	1,679
18 July (Thursday)	1,722
19 July (Friday)	817
Total	**4,218**

Swimming
Afternoon Competitions	14,040
Evening Competitions	34,520
Total	**48,560**

Summary of Paid Attendance
Athletics (Track & Field)	199,505
Equestrian Events	27,131
Fencing	1,010
Football (Soccer)	33,864
Lawn Tennis	13,000
Rowing	4,218
Swimming	48,560
Total	**327,288**

SUMMARY STATISTICS

1912 Olympic Games — Medals Won by Countries

	Gold	*Silver*	*Bronze*	*Medals*
Sweden	23	24	17	64
United States	25	18	20	63

	Gold	*Silver*	*Bronze*	*Medals*
Great Britain	10	15	16	41
Finland	9	8	9	26
Germany	5	13	6	24
France	7	4	3	14
Denmark	1	6	4	11
Hungary	3	2	3	8
Norway	3	2	3	8
Australasia (AUS/NZL)	2	2	3	7 [10]
South Africa	4	2	–	6
Canada	3	2	1	6
Italy	3	1	2	6
Belgium	2	1	3	6
Russia (RUS/EST)	–	2	2	4
Austria	–	2	2	4
The Netherlands	–	–	3	3
Greece	1	–	1	2 [18]
Totals (102 events)*	101	104	98	303
Australia	1	2	2	5
Australasia (AUS/NZL)†	1	–	–	1
New Zealand	–	–	1	1
Russia	–	1	2	3
Estonia	–	1	–	1

*Two seconds and three thirds in pole vault (athletics — men); no third in 400 meter relay (athletics — men); no firsts and two seconds in Greco-Roman wrestling light-heavyweight class; no third in tug-of-war; and no bronze medals awarded to the losing semifinalists in the four rowing events.

†The 1912 800 meter freestyle relay swimming team represented Australasia and was composed of three Australians and one New Zealander.

Note: Decathlon/pentathlon results in 1912 are recorded as they actually occurred; i.e., Decathlon— 1) Thorpe (USA), 2) Wieslander (SWE), 3) Lomberg (SWE); and Pentathlon—1) Thorpe (USA), 2) Bie (NOR), 3) Donahue (USA).

Medals Won by Countries, Men

	Gold	*Silver*	*Bronze*	*Medals*
United States	25	18	20	63
Sweden	22	22	16	60
Great Britain	7	14	13	34
Finland	9	8	9	26
Germany	4	11	6	21
France	6	4	2	12
Denmark	1	5	4	10
Hungary	3	2	3	8
Norway	3	2	2	7
South Africa	4	2	–	6 [10]
Canada	3	2	1	6

	Gold	Silver	Bronze	Medals
Italy	3	1	2	6
Belgium	2	1	3	6
Australasia (AUS/NZL)	1	1	3	5
Russia (RUS/EST)	–	2	2	4
Austria	–	2	1	3
The Netherlands	–	–	3	3
Greece	1	–	1	2 [18]
Totals (95 events)*	94	97	91	282

Medals Won by Countries, Women

	Gold	Silver	Bronze	Medals
Great Britain	2	–	3	5
Australia	1	1	–	2
Sweden	1	1	–	2
Germany	–	2	–	2
France	1	–	–	1
Denmark	–	1	–	1
Austria	–	–	1	1
Norway	–	–	1	1
Totals (5 events)*	5	5	5	15

Medals Won by Countries, Mixed Events

	Gold	Silver	Bronze	Medals
Great Britain	1	1	–	2
Sweden	–	1	1	2
Germany	1	–	–	1
France	–	–	1	1
Totals (2 events)*	2	2	2	6

Art Medals Won by Countries

	Gold	Silver	Bronze	Medals
Italy	2	–	–	2
France	1	1	–	2
Switzerland	1	–	–	1
United States	1	–	–	1
Totals (5 events)*	5	1	–	6

No second or third in designs for town planning; no third in sculptures; no second or third in paintings; no second or third in literature; and no second or third in music.

Most Medals (2 or more) [91: 87 Men, 4 Women]

Men	Gold	Silver	Bronze	Medals
Wilhelm Carlberg (SWE-SHO)	3	2	–	5 [1]
Hannes Kolehmainen (FIN-ATH)	3	1	–	4 [2]
Eric Carlberg (SWE-SHO)	2	2	–	4 [3]
Johan Hübner von Holst (SWE-SHO)	2	1	1	4 [4]
Carl Osburn (USA-SHO)	1	2	1	4 [5]
Alfred Lane (USA-SHO)	3	–	–	3 [6]
Åke Lundeberg (SWE-SHO)	2	1	–	3 [7]
Jean Cariou (FRA-EQU)	1	1	1	3
Charles Dixon (GBR-TEN)	1	1	1	3 [9]
Harold Hardwick (AUS-SWI)	1	–	2	3 [10]
Frederick Hird (USA-SHO)	1	–	2	3
Warren Sprout (USA-SHO)	1	–	2	3 [12]
John Hatfield (GBR-SWI)	–	2	1	3
Gunnar Setterwall (SWE-TEN)	–	2	1	3 [14]
William Leuschner (USA-SHO)	–	1	2	3 [15]
Charles Stewart (GBR-SHO)	–	–	3	3 [16]
Erik Adlerz (SWE-DIV)	2	–	–	2
Paul Anspach (BEL-FEN)	2	–	–	2
Walter Bathe (GER-SWI)	2	–	–	2
Alberto Braglia (ITA-GYM)	2	–	–	2 [20]
Paul Colas (FRA-SHO)	2	–	–	2
Ralph Craig (USA-ATH)	2	–	–	2
Jenő Fuchs (HUN-FEN)	2	–	–	2
André Gobert (FRA-TEN)	2	–	–	2
James Graham (USA-SHO)	2	–	–	2
George Hodgson (CAN-SWI)	2	–	–	2
Ted Meredith (USA-ATH)	2	–	–	2
Axel Nordlander (SWE-EQU)	2	–	–	2
Charles Reidpath (USA-ATH)	2	–	–	2
Alfred Swahn (SWE-SHO)	2	–	–	2 [30]
Armas Taipale (FIN-ATH)	2	–	–	2
Jim Thorpe (USA-ATH)	2	–	–	2
Charles Winslow (RSA-TEN)	2	–	–	2 [33]
Platt Adams (USA-ATH)	1	1	–	2
Hjalmar Andersson (SWE-ATH)	1	1	–	2
Peter Dolfen (USA-SHO)	1	1	–	2
Cecil Healy (AUS-SWI)	1	1	–	2
Harry Hebner (USA-SWI)	1	1	–	2
Duke Kahanamoku (USA-SWI)	1	1	–	2
Harold Kitson (RSA-TEN)	1	1	–	2 [40]
Patrick McDonald (USA-ATH)	1	1	–	2
Paul Palén (SWE-SHO)	1	1	–	2
Joseph Pepe (GBR-SHO)	1	1	–	2
William Pimm (GBR-SHO)	1	1	–	2
Ralph Rose (USA-ATH)	1	1	–	2

Men	Gold	Silver	Bronze	Medals
Julius "Juho" Saaristo (FIN-ATH)	1	1	–	2
Melvin Sheppard (USA-ATH)	1	1	–	2
Walter Winans (USA-SHO/ART)	1	1	–	2 [48]
William Applegarth (GBR-ATH)	1	–	1	2
Carl Björkman (SWE-SHO)	1	–	1	2 [50]
John Eke (SWE-ATH)	1	–	1	2
Mauritz Eriksson (SWE-SHO)	1	–	1	2
John Jackson (USA-SHO)	1	–	1	2
C. Hugo Johansson (SWE-SHO)	1	–	1	2
Bernhard Larsson (SWE-SHO)	1	–	1	2
Edward Lindberg (USA-ATH)	1	–	1	2
Serafino Mazzarocchi (ITA-GYM)	1	–	1	2
Ervin Mészáros (HUN-FEN)	1	–	1	2
Oscar Swahn (SWE-SHO)	1	–	1	2
Norman Taber (USA-ATH)	1	–	1	2 [60]
Konstantinos Tsiklitiras (GRE-ATH)	1	–	1	2 [61]
Frederick Grubb (GBR-CYC)	–	2	–	2
William Milne (GBR-SHO)	–	2	–	2
Friedrich von Rochow (GER-EQU)	–	2	–	2 [64]
Georg Åberg (SWE-ATH)	–	1	1	2
Benjamin Adams (USA-ATH)	–	1	1	2
Alfred Goeldel-Bronikoven (GER-SHO)	–	1	1	2
Kenneth Huszagh (USA-SWI)	–	1	1	2
Georg de Laval (SWE-MOP/SHO)	–	1	1	2
Donald Lippincott (USA-ATH)	–	1	1	2 [70]
Lars Jørgen Madsen (DEN-SHO)	–	1	1	2
W. Neil McDonnell (USA-SHO)	–	1	1	2
Elmer Niklander (FIN-ATH)	–	1	1	2
Albin Stenroos (FIN-ATH)	–	1	1	2
Richard Verderber (AUT-FEN)	–	1	1	2 [75]
Albert Canet (FRA-TEN)	–	–	2	2
Jetze Doorman (NED-FEN)	–	–	2	2
Hugh Durant (GBR-SHO)	–	–	2	2
Willem van Blijenburgh (NED-FEN)	–	–	2	2
George Hutson (GBR-ATH)	–	–	2	2 [80]
Adrianus de Jong (NED-FEN)	–	–	2	2
Albert Kempster (GBR-SHO)	–	–	2	2
Niels Larsen (DEN-SHO)	–	–	2	2
Horatio Poulter (GBR-SHO)	–	–	2	2
George van Rossem (NED-FEN)	–	–	2	2
Carl Schutte (USA-CYC)	–	–	2	2
Nestor Toivonen (FIN-SHO)	–	–	2	2 [87]

Women	Gold	Silver	Bronze	Medals
Edith Hannam (GBR-TEN)	2	–	–	2 [1]
Dorothea "Dora" Köring (GER-TEN)	1	1	–	2 [2]

Women	Gold	Silver	Bronze	Medals
Jennie Fletcher (GBR-SWI)	1	–	1	2 [3]
Sigrid Fick (SWE-TEN)	-	1	1	2 [4]

Most Gold Medals (2 or more) [24: 23 Men, 1 Women]

Men	Gold	Silver	Bronze	Medals
Wilhelm Carlberg (SWE-SHO)	3	2	–	5 [1]
Hannes Kolehmainen (FIN-ATH)	3	1	–	4
Alfred Lane (USA-SHO)	3	–	–	3 [3]
Eric Carlberg (SWE-SHO)	2	2	–	4 [4]
Johan Hübner von Holst (SWE-SHO)	2	1	1	4 [5]
Åke Lundeberg (SWE-SHO)	2	1	–	3 [6]
Eric Adlerz (SWE-DIV)	2	–	–	2
Paul Anspach (BEL-FEN)	2	–	–	2
Walter Bathe (GER-SWI)	2	–	–	2
Alberto Braglia (ITA-GYM)	2	–	–	2 [10]
Paul Colas (FRA-SHO)	2	–	–	2
Ralph Craig (USA-ATH)	2	–	–	2
Jenő Fuchs (HUN-FEN)	2	–	–	2
André Gobert (FRA-TEN)	2	–	–	2
James Graham (USA-SHO)	2	–	–	2
George Hodgson (CAN-SWI)	2	–	–	2
Ted Meredith (USA-ATH)	2	–	–	2
Axel Nordlander (SWE-EQU)	2	–	–	2
Charles Reidpath (USA-ATH)	2	–	–	2
Alfred Swahn (SWE-SHO)	2	–	–	2 [20]
Armas Taipale (FIN-ATH)	2	–	–	2
Jim Thorpe (USA-ATH)	2	–	–	2
Charles Winslow (RSA-TEN)	2	–	–	2 [23]

Woman	G	S	B	Total
Edith Hannam (GBR-TEN)	2	–	–	2 [1]

Youngest Competitors, Men (10 performers)

Yrs-days
16-074 Åke Bergman (SWE/SWI, 100 meter Backstroke)
16-128 Gösta Sjöberg (SWE/DIV, Plain and Fancy High Diving)
16-278 Douglas Melin (SWE/ATH, Standing Long Jump)
16-299 Fredrik Löwenadler (SWE/SWI, 200 meter Breaststroke)
16-320 François Elichagaray (FRA/ROW, Coxed Eights/Fours)
16-354 Frank Meissner (USA/CYC, Road Race, Individual/Team)

17-001   Carlo Speroni (ITA/ATH, Marathon)
17-004   Fredrik Lindgrén (FIN/SWI, 200 meter breaststroke)
17-063   Johan "Juho Aarne" Pekkalainen (FIN/YAC, 10-Meter Class)
17-125   Bohumil Rameš (BOH/CYC, Road Race, Individual/Team)

Youngest Medalists, Men
(10 performers/12 performances)

Yrs-days
17-063   Johan "Juho Aarne" Pekkalainen (FIN-YAC, 10-meter class)
17-302   Thor Henning (SWE-SWI, 400 breaststroke)
18-029   Nedo Nadi (ITA-FEN, Foil)
18-067   Johannes Boutmij (NED-FTB)
18-176   Jacob Opdahl (NOR-GYM, All-Around, Team, Free System)
18-178   Jan van Breda Kolff (NED-FTB)
18-215   Fernando Altimani (ITA-ATH, 10 kilometer walk)
18-233   Donald Lippincott (USA-ATH, 100 meters)
18-237   Lippincott (USA-ATH, 200 meters)
18-267   Hans Luber (GER-DIV, Springboard)
18-271   George Hodgson (CAN-SWI, 1,500 meters)
18-275   Hodgson (CAN-SWI, 400 freestyle)

Youngest Medalists, Men, Individual
(10 performers/13 performances)

Yrs-days
17-302   Thor Henning (SWE-SWI, 400 breaststroke)
18-029   Nedo Nadi (ITA-FEN, Foil)
18-215   Fernando Altimani (ITA-ATH, 10 kilometer walk)
18-233   Donald Lippincott (USA-ATH, 100 meters)
18-237   Lippincott (USA-ATH, 200 meters)
18-267   Hans Luber (GER-DIV, Springboard)
18-271   George Hodgson (CAN-SWI, 1,500 meters)
18-275   Hodgson (CAN-SWI, 400 freestyle)
18-329   John Hatfield (GBR-SWI, 1,500 meters)
18-333   Hatfield (GBR-SWI, 400 freestyle)
19-173   Georg Aberg (SWE-ATH, Long Jump)
19-174   Urho Peltonen (FIN-ATH, Javelin Throw, Both Hands)
19-175   Georg Aberg (SWE-ATH, Triple Jump)

Youngest Gold Medalists, Men
(10 performers/12 performances)

Yrs-days
18-029   Nedo Nadi (ITA-FEN, Foil)

18-176   Jacob Opdahl (NOR-GYM, All-Around, Team, Freestyle)
18-271   George Hodgson (CAN-SWI, 1,500 meters)
18-275   Hodgson (CAN-SWI, 400 freestyle)
18-317   Giovanni Mangiante (ITA-GYM, All-Around, Team)
19-053   Ragnar Malm (SWE-CYC, Road Race, Team)
19-163   Erik Friborg (SWE-CYC, Road Race, Team)
19-174   Alfred Engelsen (NOR-GYM, All-Around, Team, Freestyle)
19-215   Per Daniel Bertilsson (SWE-GYM, All-Around, Team, Swedish System)
19-220   Walther Bathe (GER-SWI, 200 breaststroke)
19-222   Bathe (GER-SWI, 400 breaststroke)
19-272   Luigi Maiocco (ITA-GYM, All-Around, Team)

Youngest Gold Medalists, Men, Individual
(10 performers/14 performances)

Yrs-days
18-029   Nedo Nadi (ITA-FEN, Foil)
18-271   George Hodgson (CAN-SWI, 1,500 meters)
18-275   Hodgson (CAN-SWI, 400 freestyle)
19-220   Walter Bathe (GER-SWI, 200 breaststroke)
19-222   Bathe (GER-SWI, 400 breaststroke)
19-352   Eric Adlerz (SWE-DIV, Plain High Diving)
19-356   Adlerz (SWE-DIV, Platform)
20-224   Gustaf Lindblom (SWE-ATH, Triple Jump)
20-236   Ted Meredith (USA-ATH, 800 meters)
20-282   Alfred Lane (USA-SHO, Rapid-Fire Pistol)
20-285   Lane (USA-SHO, Free Pistol)
20-303   Frederick Kelly (USA-ATH, 110 meter hurdles)
20-353   Juho Saaristo (FIN-ATH, Javelin Throw, Both Hands)
21-029   Harry Hebner (USA-SWI, 100 backstroke)

Oldest Competitors, Men
(10 performers)

Yrs-days
64-257   Oscar Swahn (SWE-SHO, Running Deer, Single, Team)
63-324   Karl Münich (AUT/FEN, Sabre, Individual)
60-103   William Milne (GBR-SHO, Small-bore Rifle, Team, 25 m.)
60-089   Walter Winans (USA-SHO, Running Deer, Single, Team)
60-053   Athanase Sartori (FRA/SHO, Free Rifle, 300 m., 3-pos.)
60-002   Daniel Mérillon (FRA/SHO, Military Rifle, 300 m., 3-pos.)
59-244   John Butt (GBR-SHO, Trap Shooting, Team)
57-355   Henri, Baron de Castex (FRA/SHO, Clay Trap, Individual)
57-265   Johann Olof Ekman (SWE/SHO, Running Deer, Double, Individual)
57-099   William Libbey (USA-SHO, Running Deer, Single, Team)

Oldest Medalists, Men
(10 performers/12 performances)

Yrs-days
64-257 Oscar Swahn (SWE-SHO, Running Deer, Single Shot, Team)
64-256   Swahn (SWE-SHO, Running Deer, Double Shot)
60-103 William Milne (GBR-SHO, Small-bore Rifle, Team, 25 meters)
60-102   Milne (GBR-SHO, Small-bore Rifle, Any Position)
60-089 Walter Winans (USA-SHO, Running Deer, Single Shot, Team)
59-244 John Butt (GBR-SHO, Trap Shooting, Team)
57-099 William Libbey (USA-SHO, Running Deer, Single Shot, Team)
57-005 Bror Brenner (FIN-YAX, 10-meter class)
52-333 Axel Londen (FIN-SHO, Running Deer, Single Shot, Team)
51-147 Alexander Maunder (GBR-SHO, Trap Shooting, Team)
51-104 Gustaf Adolf Boltenstern, Sr. (SWE-EQU, Dressage)
50-175 Henry Sears (USA-SHO, Military Pistol, Team, 50 meters)

Oldest Medalists, Men, Individual
(10 performers/ performances)

Yrs-days
64-256 Oscar Swahn (SWE-SHO, Running Deer Shooting, Single Shot)
60-102 William Milne (GBR-SHO, Small-bore Rifle, Any Position)
51-104 Gustaf Adolf Boltenstern, Sr. (SWE-EQU, Dressage)
47-097 Nestor Toivonen (FIN-SHO, Running Deer Shooting, Single Shot)
41-125 Gideon Ericsson (SWE-SHO, Small-bore Rifle, 25 m., Disappearing Target)
40-348 Lars Jørgen Madsen (DEN-SHO, Free Rifle)
40-077 Carl Gustaf Bonde (SWE-EQU, Dressage)
39-139 James Graham (USA-SHO, Trap Shooting)
39-093 Charles Dixon (GBR-TEN, Indoor Singles)
38-172 Carl Johansson (SWE-DIV, Plain High Diving)

Oldest Gold Medalists, Men
(10 performers/performances)

Yrs-days
64-257 Oscar Swahn (SWE-SHO, Running Deer, Single Shot, Team)
50-175 Henry Sears (USA-SHO, Military Pistol, Team, 50 meters)
48-239 Alfred Larsen (NOR-YAC, 12-meter class)
47-223 Carl Hellstrom (SWE-YAC, 10-meter class)
47-219 Gustaf Boivie (SWE-SHO, Small-bore Rifle, Team, 25 meters)
47-204 William Pimm (GBR-SHO, Small-bore Rifle, Team, 50 meters)
47-197 Per-Olof Arvidsson (SWE-SHO, Running Deer, Single Shot, Team)
46-358 Frank Hall (USA-SHO, Trap Shooting, Team)
46-009 Nils Adlercreutz (SWE-EQU, Three-Day Event, Team)
45-217 Charles Billings (USA-SHO, Trap Shooting, Team)

Oldest Gold Medalists, Men, Individual
(10 performers/performances)

Yrs-days
40-077   Carl Gustaf Bonde (SWE-EQU, Dressage)
39-139   James Graham (USA-SHO, Trap Shooting)
33-346   Patrick McDonald (USA-ATH, Shot Put)
33-208   Matthew McGrath (USA-ATH, Hammer Throw)
32-315   Alfred Swahn (SWE-SHO, Running Deer Shooting, Single Shot)
32-299   Axel Nordlander (SWE-EQU, Three-Day Event)
32-210   Frederick Hird (USA-SHO, Small-bore Rifle, Any Position)
32-154   Kennedy McArthur (RSA-ATH, Marathon)
32-134   Eric Lemming (SWE-ATH, Javelin Throw)
32-090   Wilhelm Carlberg (SWE-SHO, Small-bore Rifle, Disappearing Target)

Youngest Competitors, Women
(10 performers/11 performances)

Yrs-days
15-001   Greta Carlsson (SWE/SWI, 100 freestyle)
15-097   Märta Adlerz (SWE/DIV, Platform)
15-276   Margarete "Grete" Rosenberg (GER/SWI, 100 freestyle)
15-313   Louise Otto (GER/SWI, 100 freestyle)
16-147   Margarete "Grete" Adler (AUT/SWI, 100 freestyle)
16-188   Berta Zahourek (AUT/SWI, 100 freestyle)
16-336   Sonja Jonsson (SWE/SWI, 100 freestyle)
17-177   Elsa Björklund (SWE/SWI, 100 freestyle)
17-182   Johansson (SWE/SWI, 100 freestyle)
17-184   Margareta "Greta" Johansson (SWE/DIV, Platform)
17-187   Karin Lundgren (SWE/SWI, 100 freestyle)

Youngest Medalists, Women
(10 performers/performances)

Yrs-days
15-280   Grete Rosenberg (GER-SWI, 4 × 100 relay)
15-318   Louise Otto (GER-SWI, 4 × 100 relay)
16-152   Margarete Adler (AUT-SWI, 4 × 100 relay)
16-193   Berta Zahourek (AUT-SWI, 4 × 100 relay)
17-185   Margareta "Greta" Johansson (SWE-DIV, Platform)
17-265   Isabella "Belle" Moore (GBR-SWI, 4 × 100 relay)
17-315   Isabelle White (GBR-DIV, Platform)
18-008   Josefine Sticker (AUT-SWI, 4 × 100 relay)
19-041   Wally Dressel (GER-SWI, 4 × 100 relay)

Youngest Medalists, Women, Individual
(6 performers/performances)

Yrs-days
17-185   Margareta "Greta" Johansson (SWE-DIV, Platform)
17-315   Isabelle White (GBR-DIV, Platform)
19-077   Marguerite-Marie Broquedis (FRA-TEN, Singles)
20-182   Wilhelmina "Mina" Wylie (AUS-SWI, 100 freestyle)
22-105   Jennie Fletcher (GBR-SWI, 100 freestyle)
22-248   Sarah "Fanny" Durack (AUS-SWI, 100 freestyle)

Youngest Gold Medalists, Women
(4 performers/performances)

Yrs-days
17-185   Margareta "Greta" Johansson (SWE-DIV, Platform)
17-265   Isabella "Belle" Moore (GBR-SWI, 4 × 100 relay)
19-077   Marguerite-Marie Broquedis (FRA-TEN, Singles)
22-118   Jennie Fletcher (GBR-SWI, 4 × 100 relay)

Youngest Gold Medalists, Women, Individual
(2 performers/performances)

Yrs-days
17-185   Margareta "Greta" Johansson (SWE-DIV, Platform)
19-077   Marguerite-Marie Broquedis (FRA-TEN, Singles)

Oldest Competitors, Women
(10 performers)

Yrs-days
45-148   Ebba Hay (SWE/TEN, Indoor Mixed)
33-242   Ellen Brusewitz (SWE/TEN, Singles)
33-170   Edith Hannam (GBR/TEN, Indoor Singles/Mixed)
33-150   Margareta Cederschiöld (SWE/TEN, Singles)
32-131   Annie Holmström (SWE/TEN, Singles/Mixed)
31-356   Dorothea "Dora" Köring (GER/TEN, Singles/Mixed)
30-290   Mabel Parton (GBR/TEN, Indoor Singles/Mixed)
30-128   Francis Aitchison (GBR/TEN, Indoor Singles/Mixed)
30-099   Sofie Castenschiold (DEN/TEN, Indoor Singles/Mixed)
28-076   Edith Arnheim Lasch (SWE/TEN, Singles/Mixed)

Oldest Medalists, Women
(10 performers/performances)

Yrs-days
33-170   Edith Hannam (GBR-TEN, Indoor Singles)
31-357   Dorothea Koring (GER-TEN, Singles)
30-293   Mabel Parton (GBR-TEN, Indoor Singles)
30-099   Sofie Castenschiold (DEN-TEN, Indoor Singles)
28-119   Molla Bjurstedt (NOR-TEN, Singles)
25-160   Lisa Regnell (SWE-DIV, Platform)
24-193   Hermine Stindt (GER-SWI, 4 × 100 relay)
23-000   Annie Speirs (GBR-SWI, 4 × 100 relay)
22-339   Irene Steer (GBR-SWI, 4 × 100 relay)
22-248   Sarah "Fanny" Durack (AUS-SWI, 100 freestyle)

Oldest Medalists, Women, Individual
(6 performers/performances)

Yrs-days
33-170   Edith Hannam (GBR-TEN, Indoor Singles)
31-357   Dorothea Koring (GER-TEN, Singles)
30-293   Mabel Parton (GBR-TEN, Indoor Singles)
30-099   Sofie Castenschiold (DEN-TEN, Indoor Singles)
28-119   Molla Bjurstedt (NOR-TEN, Singles)
25-160   Lisa Regnell (SWE-DIV, Platform)

Oldest Gold Medalists, Women
(4 performers/performances)

Yrs-days
33-170   Edith Hannam (GBR-TEN, Indoor Singles)
23-000   Annie Speirs (GBR-SWI, 4 × 100 relay)
22-339   Irene Steer (GBR-SWI, 4 × 100 relay)
22-248   Sarah "Fanny" Durack (AUS-SWI, 100 freestyle)

Oldest Gold Medalists, Women, Individual
(2 performers/performances)

Yrs-days
33-170   Edith Hannam (GBR-TEN, Indoor Singles)
22-248   Sarah "Fanny" Durack (AUS-SWI, 100 freestyle)

Total Known Competitors (Men and Women)

	Ath	Cyc	Div	Equ	Fen	Ftb	Gym	Mop	Row	Sho	Swi	Ten	Tow	Wap	Wre	Yac	Subtotals	Multis	Totals
Australasia	5	–	–	–	–	–	–	–	10	–	9	1	–	–	–	–	25	–	25
Austria	12	6	1	–	12	15	–	1	6	7	8	3	–	7	8	–	86	1	85
Belgium	2	1	–	4	11	–	–	–	6	–	5	–	–	9	1	–	39	4	35
Bohemia	11	5	–	–	13	–	1	–	1	–	–	8	–	–	4	–	43	1	42
Canada	18	2	2	–	–	–	–	–	10	3	1	–	–	–	–	–	36	–	36
Chile	6	4	–	2	–	–	–	–	–	2	–	–	–	–	–	–	14	–	14
Denmark	14	8	–	4	6	15	49	4	15	14	1	10	–	–	9	3	152	–	152
Finland	23	5	6	–	–	13	24	–	6	19	6	–	–	–	37	27	166	2	164
France	25	12	–	4	–	–	6	2	17	19	3	6	–	8	6	3	111	2	109
Germany	24	11	4	13	16	22	18	1	25	11	17	7	–	–	14	–	183	–	183
Great Britain	61	26	3	4	22	14	23	3	24	38	18	11	8	7	12	–	274	3	271
Greece	5	–	–	–	6	–	–	–	–	9	1	–	–	–	1	–	22	1	21
Hungary	27	5	–	–	13	14	17	–	11	10	8	6	–	7	10	–	128	5	123
Iceland	1	–	–	–	–	–	–	–	–	–	–	–	–	–	1	–	2	–	2
Italy	12	–	1	–	9	14	18	–	–	–	2	–	–	–	6	–	62	–	62
Japan	2	–	–	–	–	–	–	–	–	–	–	–	–	–	–	–	2	–	2
Luxembourg	2	–	–	–	–	–	19	–	–	–	–	–	–	–	–	–	21	–	21
The Netherlands	1	–	–	–	12	15	–	1	–	1	–	1	–	–	3	–	34	1	33
Norway	21	6	3	3	7	12	46	2	24	28	5	7	–	–	9	18	191	1	190
Portugal	3	–	–	–	1	–	–	–	–	–	–	–	–	–	2	–	6	–	6
Russia	33	10	1	7	24	15	4	5	1	26	4	2	–	–	11	17	160	1	159
Serbia	2	–	–	–	–	–	–	–	–	–	–	–	–	–	–	–	2	–	2
South Africa	7	1	–	–	1	–	–	–	–	8	1	3	–	–	–	–	21	–	21
Sweden	108	12	34	17	18	14	24	12	28	62	24	16	8	7	34	41	459	14	445
Switzerland	1	–	–	–	–	–	–	–	–	–	–	–	–	–	–	–	1	–	1
Turkey	2	–	–	–	–	–	–	–	–	–	–	–	–	–	–	–	2	–	2
United States	109	9	2	4	13	–	–	1	–	26	7	1	–	–	2	–	174	–	174
Totals	537	123	57	62	184	163	249	32	184	283	120	82	16	45	170	109	2,416	36	2,380
Nations	27	18	10	10	16	11	12	10	14	16	17	14	2	6	18	6	27	–	27

Men

	Ath	Cyc	Div	Equ	Fen	Ftb	Gym	Mop	Row	Sho	Swi	Ten	Tow	Wap	Wre	Yac	Subtotals	Multis	Totals
Australasia	5	–	–	–	–	–	–	–	10	–	7	1	–	–	–	–	23	–	23
Austria	12	6	–	–	12	15	–	1	6	7	3	3	–	7	8	–	80	1	79
Belgium	2	1	–	4	11	–	–	–	6	–	4	–	–	9	1	–	38	4	34
Bohemia	11	5	–	–	13	–	1	–	1	–	–	8	–	–	4	–	43	1	42
Canada	18	2	2	–	–	–	–	–	10	3	1	–	–	–	–	–	36	–	36
Chile	6	4	–	2	–	–	–	–	–	2	–	–	–	–	–	–	14	–	14
Denmark	14	8	–	4	6	15	49	4	15	14	1	9	–	–	9	3	151	–	151
Finland	23	5	6	–	–	13	24	–	6	19	4	–	–	–	37	27	164	2	162
France	25	12	–	4	–	–	6	2	17	19	3	5	–	8	6	3	110	2	108
Germany	24	11	4	13	16	22	18	1	25	11	13	6	–	–	14	–	178	–	178
Great Britain	61	26	2	4	22	14	23	3	24	38	12	8	8	7	12	–	264	3	261
Greece	5	–	–	–	6	–	–	–	–	9	1	–	–	–	1	–	22	1	21
Hungary	27	5	–	–	13	14	17	–	11	10	8	6	–	7	10	–	128	5	123
Iceland	1	–	–	–	–	–	–	–	–	–	–	–	–	–	1	–	2	–	2
Italy	12	–	1	–	9	14	18	–	–	–	2	–	–	–	6	–	62	–	62
Japan	2	–	–	–	–	–	–	–	–	–	–	–	–	–	–	–	2	–	2
Luxembourg	2	–	–	–	–	–	19	–	–	–	–	–	–	–	–	–	21	–	21
The Netherlands	1	–	–	–	12	15	–	1	–	1	–	1	–	–	3	–	34	1	33
Norway	21	6	3	3	7	12	46	2	24	28	4	6	–	–	9	18	189	1	188
Portugal	3	–	–	–	1	–	–	–	–	–	–	–	–	–	2	–	6	–	6
Russia	33	10	1	7	24	15	4	5	1	26	4	2	–	–	11	17	160	1	159
Serbia	2	–	–	–	–	–	–	–	–	–	–	–	–	–	–	–	2	–	2
South Africa	7	1	–	–	1	–	–	–	–	8	1	3	–	–	–	–	21	–	21
Sweden	108	12	22	17	18	14	24	12	28	62	18	10	8	7	34	41	435	13	422
Switzerland	1	–	–	–	–	–	–	–	–	–	–	–	–	–	–	–	1	–	1
Turkey	2	–	–	–	–	–	–	–	–	–	–	–	–	–	–	–	2	–	2
United States	109	9	2	4	13	–	–	1	–	26	7	1	–	–	2	–	174	–	174
Totals	*537*	*123*	*43*	*62*	*184*	*163*	*249*	*32*	*184*	*283*	*93*	*69*	*16*	*45*	*170*	*109*	*2,362*	*35*	*2,327*
Nations	27	18	9	10	16	11	12	10	14	16	17	14	2	6	18	6	27	–	27

Women

	Div	Swi	Ten	Subtotal	Multi	Totals
Australasia	–	2	–	2	–	2
Austria	1	5	–	6	–	6
Belgium	–	1	–	1	–	1
Denmark	–	–	1	1	–	1
Finland	–	2	–	2	–	2
France	–	–	1	1	–	1
Germany	–	4	1	5	–	5
Great Britain	1	6	3	10	–	10
Norway	–	1	1	2	–	2
Sweden	12	6	6	24	1	23
Totals	*14*	*27*	*13*	*54*	*1*	*53*
Nations	3	8	6	10	1	10

Known Competitors by Nation

	Sub-Total Men	Sub-Total Women	Sub-Total	Men 2-sport	Men 3-sport	Women 2-sport	Men Total	Women Total	Total
Australasia	23	2	25	–	–	–	23	2	25
Austria	80	6	86	1	–	–	79	6	85
Belgium	38	1	39	4	–	–	34	1	35
Bohemia	43	–	43	1	–	–	42	–	42
Canada	36	–	36	–	–	–	36	–	36
Chile	14	–	14	–	–	–	14	–	14
Denmark	151	1	152	–	–	–	151	1	152
Finland	164	2	166	2	–	–	162	2	164
France	110	1	111	2	–	–	108	1	109
Germany	178	5	183	–	–	–	178	5	183
Great Britain	264	10	274	3	–	–	261	10	271
Greece	22	–	22	1	–	–	21	–	21
Hungary	128	–	128	5	–	–	123	–	123
Iceland	2	–	2	–	–	–	2	–	2
Italy	62	–	62	–	–	–	62	–	62
Japan	2	–	2	–	–	–	2	–	2
Luxembourg	21	–	21	–	–	–	21	–	21
The Netherlands	34	–	34	1	–	–	33	–	33
Norway	189	2	191	1	–	–	188	2	190
Portugal	6	–	6	–	–	–	6	–	6
Russia	160	–	160	1	–	–	159	–	159
Serbia	2	–	2	–	–	–	2	–	2
South Africa	21	–	21	–	–	–	21	–	21
Sweden	435	24	459	9	2	1	422	23	445
Switzerland	1	–	1	–	–	–	1	–	1

	Sub-Total Men	Sub-Total Women	Sub-Total	Men 2-sport	Men 3-sport	Women 2-sport	Men Total	Women Total	Total
Turkey	2	–	2	–	–	–	2	–	2
United States	174	–	174	–	–	–	174	–	174
Totals	*2,362*	*54*	*2,416*	*31*	*2*	*1*	*2,327*	*53*	*2,380*
Nations	27	10	27	12	1	1	27	10	27

Known Competitors, Nations, and Events by Sports

	Total Comp.	Total Nations	Total Events	Men Comp.	Men Nations	Men Events	Women Comp.	Women Nations	Women Events	Mixed Events
Athletics (T&F)	537	27	30	537	27	30	–	–	–	–
Cycling	123	18	2	123	18	2	–	–	–	–
Diving	57	10	4	43	9	3	14	3	1	–
Equestrian Events	62	10	5	62	10	5	–	–	–	–
Fencing	184	16	5	184	16	5	–	–	–	–
Football (Soccer)	163	11	1	163	11	1	–	–	–	–
Gymnastics	249	12	4	249	12	4	–	–	–	–
Modern Pentathlon	32	10	1	32	10	1	–	–	–	–
Rowing & Sculling	184	14	4	184	14	4	–	–	–	–
Shooting	283	16	18	283	16	18	–	–	–	–
Swimming	120	17	9	93	17	7	27	8	2	–
Tennis	82	14	8	69	14	4	13	6	2	2
Tug-of-War	16	2	1	16	2	1	–	–	–	–
Water Polo	45	6	1	45	6	1	–	–	–	–
Wrestling	170	18	5	170	18	5	–	–	–	–
Yachting	109	6	4	109	6	4	–	–	–	–
Subtotals	2,416	27	102	2,362	27	95	54	10	5	2
Multi-Sport Athletes	36	–	–	35	–	–	1	–	–	–
Totals	2,380	27	102	2,327	27	95	53	10	5	2

Athletes Competing in Two or More Sports in 1912 (34: 33 Men, 1 Woman)

Three Sports (2: 2 Men, 0 Women)

Andersson, Robert Theodor "Robban." (SWE-DIV/SWI/WAP)[25]
Carlberg, Gustaf Eric. (SWE-FEN/MOP/SHO)

Two Sports (32: 31 Men, 1 Woman)[26]

Women
Johansson, Ann Theresia Margareta "Greta." (SWE-DIV/SWI)

Men

Andersson, Wilhelm. (SWE-SWI/WAP)
Baronyi, András. (HUN-ATH/SWI)
Beleznai, László. (HUN-SWI/WAP)
Bergqvist, Erik Gustaf. (SWE-SWI/WAP)
Bernhardt, Ing. Edmond. (AUT-MOP/SHO)
Boin, Victor. (BEL-FEN/WAP)
Courbet, Félicien. (BEL-SWI/WAP)
Doorman, Jetze. (NED-FEN/MOP)
Durant, Hugh. (GBR-MOP/SHO)
Engelsen, Alfred. (NOR-DIV/GYM)
Fóti, Samu. (HUN-ATH/GYM)
Godfree, Douglas William. (GBR-FEN/MOP)
Grégoire, Oscar. (BEL-SWI/WAP)
Grönfors, Thorsten G. M. H. (SWE-TEN/YAC)
Grönhagen, Åke Edvard. (SWE-FEN/MOP)
Hanson, Pontus. (SWE-SWI/WAP)
Honzátko, Bohumil. (BOH-ATH/GYM)
Ilmoniemi, Tauno. (FIN-DIV/GYM)
Julin, Harald Alexander Sigfrid. (SWE-SWI/WAP)
de Laval, Claude Patrik Gustaf. (SWE-MOP/SHO)
de Laval, Georg Patrik Fabian. (SWE-MOP/SHO)
Lewenhaupt, Carl Gustaf Sixtenson. (SWE-EQU/MOP)
Meyboom, Herman. (BEL-SWI/WAP)
Nepokupnoy, Boris. (RUS-FEN/MOP)
Paoli, Raoul Lucien. (FRA-ATH/WRE)
Petropoulos, Georgios. (GRE-FEN/SHO)
Radmilovic, Paul. (GBR-SWI/WAP)
Rigal, Georges. (FRA-SWI/WAP)
Tanner, Lauri Arvo. (FIN-FTB/GYM)
Wenk, János. (HUN-SWI/WAP)
Zachár, Imre. (HUN-SWI/WAP)

NOTES

1. These dates are not inclusive. Specifically, competitions took place only 5–12 May and then from 28 June through 22 July.

2. Egypt is usually listed as competing. They had one athlete entered, Ahmed Mohammed Hassanein in fencing. Hassanein carried the Egyptian flag at the Opening Ceremony, but he never actually competed in any fencing event.

3. Theoretically, yachting was a mixed sport, as women could be members of the crews, as a few were in 1908. But no women competed, so we have listed the sport as for "Men."

4. Resigned during the IOC session in Stockholm on 4 July 1912.

5. Resigned during the IOC session in Stockholm on 4 July 1912.

6. Co-opted during the IOC session in Stockholm on 4 July 1912.

7. Co-opted by postal vote on 31 October 1912.

8. Co-opted by postal vote on 1 November 1912.

9. The original secretary was Nore Thisell, Esquire, who served as secretary until 1 May 1910.

10. One of the original members was Bernhard F. Burman, Esquire, representing the Central

Association for the Promotion of Athletics in Sweden. He died in May 1912, and Dr. Astley Levin, who was originally a deputy member, was promoted to full membership.

11. According to the Austrian Olympic Committee.

12. According to the Belgian Olympic Committee and Belgian Olympic historians Roland Renson and Jos Luypaers.

13. Gillis carried the British Union Jack which contained the Canadian coat of arms in the middle of the field.

14. Hassanein carried the Egyptian flag at the Opening Ceremony. He was the only Egyptian athlete entered in 1912. He is usually listed as competing in fencing, but there is no evidence that he actually competed, which means that Egypt had no competitors at the 1912 Olympic Games.

15. Saastamoinen carried a name plate but not the Finnish flag. In 1912, Finland was still not independent of Russia. Although the Finnish athletes were allowed to compete independently they were forced to do so under the Russian flag.

16. According to French Olympic historian Daniel Schamps.

17. According to Bob Miyakawa, Japanese Olympic historian.

18. According to Norwegian Olympic historian Arild Gjerde.

19. Harry Kitson was the captain of the team, but it is not known with certainty who carried the flag for South Africa. This has been checked with South African Olympic historians (Lappe Laubscher, Floris Van Der Merwe) and the South African Olympic Committee. South Africa marched behind the British Union Jack which contained the South African coat of arms in the middle.

20. According to the Swiss Olympic Committee.

21. According to the National Olympic Committee of Turkey. They note that their flag was displayed at the stadium, however.

22. According to the Olympic Committee of Iceland. In 1912 the Icelandic athletes were considered a part of the Danish team, as Iceland was still not independent of Denmark. Iceland was, however, at that time fighting for its independence, and there was a dispute between the Danish chef de mission and the Icelandic athletes concerning how Icelandic athletes should enter the stadium. When the Icelandic team was ordered to march with the Danish team, they protested by not marching at the opening ceremony.

23. From the tug-of-war team's participation in the 1908 Olympic Games in London.

24. Weather notes are from *Olympiska Spelens Tidning/The Olympic News*, the daily newspaper of the 1912 Olympic Games.

25. Andersson also competed in the same three sports at London in 1908.

26. American sources often mention that George Patton competed at the 1912 Olympics in both fencing and modern pentathlon. He competed in modern pentathlon. He was entered in fencing, but there is no evidence that he actually competed.

Athletics (Track & Field)

Track & field athletics was the showcase of the 1912 Olympic Games, as it often is. The biggest stars of the competition were Hannes Kolehmainen, the Finnish distance runner who won the 5,000 and 10,000 meter runs, and the cross-country, and Jim Thorpe, the American Indian multiperformer, who won the decathlon and pentathlon. Further details on their lives can be found in Appendix II (Thorpe) and Appendix III (Kolehmainen).

Track & field athletics was conducted within the Olympic Stadium that had been especially constructed for the 1912 Olympic Games. The track was the unusual distance of just over 383 meters in length. It was constructed by Charles Perry, the British trainer, who had also helped build the tracks that were used at the 1896, 1906, and 1908 Olympic Games.

Site:	Olympic Stadium
Dates:	6–15 July
Events:	30 [30 Men — 0 Women]
Competitors:	537 [537 Men — 0 Women]
Nations:	27 [27 Men — 0 Women]

	Competitors	*Gold*	*Silver*	*Bronze*	*Totals*
Australia	5	–	–	–	–
Austria	12	–	–	–	–
Belgium	2	–	–	–	–
Bohemia	11	–	–	–	–
Canada	18	1	2	1	4
Chile	6	–	–	–	–
Denmark	14	–	–	–	–
Finland	23	6	4	3	13
France	25	–	2	–	2
Germany	24	–	2	–	2
Great Britain	61	2	1	5	8
Greece	5	1	–	1	2
Hungary	27	–	–	1	1
Iceland	1	–	–	–	–
Italy	12	–	–	1	1

Japan	2	–	–	–	–
Luxembourg	2	–	–	–	–
The Netherlands	1	–	–	–	–
Norway	21	–	1	–	1
Portugal	3	–	–	–	–
Russia	33	–	–	–	–
Serbia	2	–	–	–	–
South Africa	7	1	1	–	2
Sweden	108	3	5	6	14
Switzerland	1	–	–	–	–
Turkey	2	–	–	–	–
United States	109	16	13	13	42
Totals	537	30	31	31	92
Nations	27	7	9	8	12

Committee for Athletics (Track & Field)

President: Colonel Viktor Gustaf Balck
Vice-President: Lieutenant Gustaf G:son Uggla
Secretary: Leopold Englund, Esquire
Asst. Secretary: Kristian Hellström, Esquire
Members: Captain Otto Ahnström; Sven Carlson, Esquire; Captain Per Henrik Hedenblad; Elis Juhlin, Jr., Esquire; Hugo Levin, Esquire; Sven Låftman, Esquire; Oscar Löwenadler, Esquire; Edvin Sandborg, Esquire; Sune Smedmark, Esquire; Bruno Söderström, Esquire; Nore Thisell, Esquire
Adjoint Members: Fredrik Bille, Esquire; Colonel, Baron Sven Hermelin
Exec. Comm. Chairman: Lieutenant Gustaf G:son Uggla
Exec. Comm. Secretary: Kristian Hellström, Esquire
Executive Committee: Fredrik Bille, Esquire; Leopold Englund, Esquire; Colonel, Baron Sven Hermelin; Elis Juhlin, Jr., Esquire; Sven Låftman, Esquire; Edvin Sandborg, Esquire; Sune Smedmark, Esquire; Bruno Söderström, Esquire; Nore Thisell, Esquire
International Jury: Johannes Sigfrid Edström (President/SWE); Captain Carl Silfverstolpe (SWE); John G. Merrick (CAN); Lauri Wilskman (FIN); René Enerlin (FRA); W. A. Brommage (GBR); Carl Diem (GER); Anastasios Metaxas (GRE); Szilárd Stankovits (HUN); James Edward Sullivan (USA)

MEN

100 Meters

A: 70[1]*; C: 22[2]; D: 6–7 July.

The event was considered wide open at the beginning of the year, as no sprinter had been dominant since the 1908 Olympics. From 1909 to 1911 three different American sprinters had

*See Notes on pages 123–138.

won the AAU Championship (William Martin [1909], James Rosenberger [1910], Gwinn Henry [1911]), but none of them competed at Stockholm. South Africa's George Patching had won the AAA title in 1910–11 and was present. At the three United States Olympic Trials, Ira Courtney won the western trial, Clement Wilson the central, and Howard Drew the eastern. In the eastern meet, Ralph Craig finished second to Drew. The world record for 100 meters was 10.5, shared by three Germans, Richard Rau, Erwin Kern, and Emil Ketterer. All three competed at Stockholm, but Ketterer did not finish in round one, and Rau and Kern were eliminated in the semifinals.

In the first round, America's Donald Lippincott broke the Olympic record in heat 16 with a 10.6 clocking. The six semifinals advanced only the winner of each heat to the final. Five of the finalists were from the United States — Ralph Craig, Howard Drew, Alvah Meyer, Frank Belote, and Lippincott. The fastest times in the semis were 10.7, posted by both Craig and Meyer.

The final began without Drew, who had strained a muscle at the finish of his semifinal heat and could not start. The final was marked by multiple false starts — listed as six, seven, or eight in various sources. After one of the false starts, Craig and Lippincott ran the entire 100 meters. Craig noted many years later, "There were seven false starts, and I made one of them. Another American who had competed in the Paris Games — those 1900 Games were kind of horrendous, you know — he told me if you ever get to the Olympics, if anyone moves a muscle, you go too. Don Lippincott and I ran the whole hundred meters on one false start. The foreign officials were totally incompetent, and I was afraid not to keep running even though they fired the recall gun. I was told, don't take a chance — *go!* — so I did. They did fire the recall gun, but I didn't believe it."[3]

After the false starts, Patching took the early lead but he was eventually defeated by three Americans, with Craig winning narrowly. Craig would later make the 1948 Olympic team as a yachtsman, and he carried the U.S. flag at the 1948 opening ceremony. He was only an alternate, however, and did not actually compete at the 1948 London Olympics.

Final A: 5; C: 2; D: 7 July; T: 1445.

1. Ralph Craig	USA		10.8
2. Alvah Meyer	USA		10.9est[4]
3. Donald Lippincott	USA		10.9est[5]
4. George Patching	RSA		11.0est
5. Frank Belote	USA		11.0est

[6]

Diplomas of Merit

Howard Drew (USA), Frank Belote (USA), George Patching (RSA)

Semifinals A: 33; C: 12; D: 6 July; T: 1545; F: Winner in each heat advanced to the final.

Heat One A: 6; C: 4.

1. Howard Drew	USA	safe winner	11.0	Q
2. Ira Courtney	USA			[7]
3. Peter Gerhardt	USA			
4. Erwin Kern	GER			
5. Charles Luther	SWE			
6. Vilmos Rácz	HUN			

Heat Two A: 5; C: 5.

1. George Patching	RSA		10.9	Q
2. Knut "Knatten" Lindberg	SWE		11.1est[8]	
3. Richard Rice	GBR			
AC. Franco Giongo	ITA		[9]	
Joseph Aelter(-Freddy)	BEL			

Heat Three A: 5; C: 5.

1. Alvah Meyer	USA		10.7	Q
2. David Jacobs	GBR			
3. Frank Lukeman	CAN			
4. Pál Szalay	HUN			
AC. Rudolf Smedmark	SWE		DNF[10]	

Heat Four A: 6; C: 5.

1. Ralph Craig	USA		10.7	Q
2. Richard Rau	GER		10.9 est[11]	
3. William Stewart	AUS		[12]	
AC. István Jankovich	HUN			
René Mourlon	FRA			
Ferenc Szobota	HUN			

Heat Five A: 6; C: 4.

1. Donald Lippincott	USA		10.7	Q
2. William Applegarth	GBR			
3. Bedřich Vygoda	BOH		[13]	
AC. Clement Wilson	USA			
Victor d'Arcy	GBR			
John Howard	CAN			

Heat Six A: 5; C: 4.

1. Frank Belote	USA		11.1	Q
2. Reuben Povey	RSA			
3. Rupert Thomas	USA			
4. Ivan Möller	SWE			
5. Arthur Anderson	GBR			

Round One A: 70; C: 22; D: 6 July; T: 1330–1415; F: Top two finishers in each heat advanced to the semifinals.

Heat One A: 1; C: 1.

1. Karl August "Charles" Luther	SWE		12.8 [wo]	Q

[14]

Heat Two A: 3; C: 3.

1. Ivan Möller	SWE		11.5	Q
2. Pál Szalay	HUN	at ½ meter		Q
3. Rudolf Rauch	AUT			

[15]

Heat Three A: 6; C: 6.

1. J. Ira Courtney	USA	easy win	11.2		Q
2. István Jankovich	HUN				Q
3. Pierre Failliot	FRA				
4. Henry Blakeney	GBR				
AC. Ladislav Jiránek-Strana	BOH				
Pablo Eitel	CHI				

Heat Four A: 2; C: 2.

1. Richard Rice	GBR	easy win	11.4		Q
2. Rudolf Smedmark	SWE				Q

16

Heat Five A: 3; C: 3.

1. Victor d'Arcy	GBR	at 1 meter	11.2		Q
2. Reuben Povey	RSA				Q
3. António Stromp	POR				

17

Heat Six A: 6; C: 6.

1. Richard Rau	GER	easy win	11.5		Q
2. Vilmos Rácz	HUN				Q
3. Ture Person	SWE				
AC. Robert Schurrer	FRA			18	
Dimitrios Triantafyllakos	GRE				
Leopolds Levensteins	RUS				

Heat Seven A: 5; C: 5.

1. William Stewart	AUS	at 1 meter	11.0		Q
2. Joseph Aelter(-Freddy)	BEL				Q
AC. Charles Lelong	FRA				
Jan Grijseels	NED				
Richard Schwarz	RUS				

19

Heat Eight A: 4; C: 4.

1. Knut "Knatten" Lindberg	SWE	at 2 meters	11.6		Q
2. Bedřich Vygoda	BOH				Q
AC. Dušan Milošević	SRB				
Jón Halldórsson	ISL				

20

Heat Nine A: 4; C: 4.

1. Alvah Meyer	USA	easy win	11.3		Q
2. Franco Giongo	ITA				Q
AC. Robert Duncan	GBR				
Georges Rolot	FRA				

21

Heat Ten A: 5; C: 5.

1. David Jacobs	GBR		10.8	Q =OR
2. Clement Wilson	USA	at a hand		Q
AC. Marius Delaby	FRA		22	
Herman Sotaaen	NOR			
Václav Labík-Gregan	BOH			
23				

Heat Eleven A: 4; C: 4.

1. Frank Belote	USA	safe win	11.0	Q
2. René Mourlon	FRA			Q
3. Henry Macintosh	GBR			
4. Harry Beasley	CAN			
24				

Heat Twelve A: 4; C: 4.

1. Peter Gerhardt	USA	11.1	Q
2. Frank Lukeman	CAN		Q
3. Fritz Weinzinger	AUT		
4. Alex Pedersen	NOR		
AC. Duncan Macmillan[25]	GBR		

Heat Thirteen A: 5; C: 5.

1. John Howard	CAN		11.0	Q
2. George Patching	RSA	bit behind		Q
3. Harold Heiland	USA			
4. Pavel Shtiglits	RUS			
AC. Emil Ketterer	GER		DNF	
26				

Heat Fourteen A: 4; C: 4.

1. Arthur Anderson	GBR	11.0	Q
2. Rupert Thomas	USA		Q
3. Frank McConnell	CAN		
4. Skotte Jacobsson	SWE		
27			

Heat Fifteen A: 4; C: 4.

1. Howard Drew	USA		11.0	Q
2. Erwin Kern	GER	well behind		Q
3. Julien Boullery	FRA			
AC. James Barker	GBR		DNF	
28, 29				

Heat Sixteen A: 5; C: 5.

1. Donald Lippincott	USA		10.6	Q =OR
2. William Applegarth	GBR	at 2 meters		Q
3. Max Herrmann	GER	at 3½ meters		

AC. Ervin Szerelemhegyi	HUN	[30]
Yahiko Mishima JPN		
[31]		

Heat Seventeen A: 4; C: 4.

1. Ralph Craig	USA	11.2	Q
2. Ferenc Szobota	HUN		Q
3. Ragnar Ekberg	SWE		
4. Fritz Fleischer	AUT		
[32]			

200 Meters

A: 61[33]; C: 19; D: 10–11 July.

As in the 100 meters, there was no clear favorite. Again, four different Americans had won the AAU championship since the 1908 Olympics — none of them were in Stockholm. The pre–Olympic favorite was likely Britain's Willie Applegarth, who had won the AAA earlier in 1912. But the world record for 220 yards on a straight had been set at 21⅕ by Ralph Craig at the 1910 IC4A Championships, and he won the eastern U.S. Olympic Trials. After winning the 100 meters three days earlier at Stockholm, Craig was favored.

The six semifinals advanced the winner of each heat to the final, with Applegarth and Germany's Richard Rau joining four Americans, including Craig, to compete for the gold medal. In the final, Applegarth led coming off the turn but was soon passed by Craig and Donald Lippincott. The finish was close but Craig held off a fast-finishing Lippincott to win the sprint double. Lippincott added the 200 silver medal to the bronze medal he had won in the 100.

Final A: 6; C: 3; D: 11 July; T: 1500.

1. Ralph Craig	USA	21.7
2. Donald Lippincott	USA	21.8
3. William Applegarth	GBR	21.9[34]
4. Richard Rau	GER	22.2est
5. Charles Reidpath	USA	22.3est
6. Donnell Young	USA	22.3est

Diplomas of Merit

Richard Rau (GER), Charles Reidpath (USA), Donnell Young (USA)

Semifinals A: 36; C: 11; D: 10 July; T: 1600; F: Winner of each heat advanced to the final.

Heat One A: 6; C: 4.

1. Ralph Craig	USA	21.9	Q
2. David Jacobs	GBR		
3. Ira Courtney	USA		
4. Frigyes Mezei Wiesner	HUN		
5. Ture Person	SWE		
AC. Arthur Anderson	GBR	DNF	

Heat Two A: 6; C: 4.

1.	William Applegarth	GBR		21.9	Q
2.	Clement Wilson	USA			
3.	Harold Heiland	USA			
4.	Cyril Seedhouse	GBR			
5.	Skotte Jacobsson	SWE			
AC.	William Stewart	AUS		DNF	

Heat Three A: 6; C: 5.

1.	Donnell Young	USA	safe winner	21.9	Q
2.	Carl Cooke	USA			
3.[35]	Georges Rolot	FRA			
4.	Max Herrmann	GER			
AC.	George Patching	RSA		DNF[36]	
	Henry Macintosh	GBR		DNF	

Heat Four A: 6; C: 5.

1.	Donald Lippincott	USA	21.8	Q
2.	Alvah Meyer	USA		
3.	John Howard	CAN		
4.	Ivan Möller	SWE	22.4[37]	
5.	Duncan Macmillan	GBR		
6.	Jan Grijseels	NED		

Heat Five A: 6; C: 6.

1.	Richard Rau	GER	22.1	Q
2.	Peter Gerhardt	USA		
3.	Charles Luther	SWE	22.3[38]	
4.	Franco Giongo	ITA		
5.	Reuben Povey	RSA		
AC.	Richard Rice	GBR	DNF	

Heat Six A: 6; C: 5; D: 10 July; T: .

1.	Charles Reidpath	USA	22.1	Q
2.	Victor d'Arcy	GBR	[39]	
3.	Knut Lindberg	SWE	22.5	
4.	István Déván	HUN		
5.	Robert Schurrer	FRA		
AC.	Robert Duncan	GBR	DNF	

Round One A: 61; C: 19; D: 10 July; T: 1030; F: Top two finishers in each heat advanced to the semifinals.

Heat One A: 4; C: 4.

1.	Charles Reidpath	USA	22.6	Q
2.	Georges Rolot	FRA	22.7	Q
3.	Knut Stenborg	SWE		
4.	Václav Labík-Gregan	BOH		

[40]

Heat Two A: 4; C: 4.

1.	Ralph Craig	USA	22.8	Q
2.	Richard Rice	GBR	23.0	Q
3.	Charles Poulenard	FRA		
4.	Karl Lindblom	SWE		

41

Heat Three A: 5; C: 4.

1.	Ira Courtney	USA	22.7	Q
2.	Duncan Macmillan	GBR		Q
3.	Joseph Aelter(-Freddy)	BEL		
4.	Haralds Hahne	RUS		
AC.	Herberts Baumanis	RUS	DNF[42]	

43

Heat Four A: 2; C: 2.

1.	Charles Luther	SWE	23.6	Q
2.	Jan Grijseels	NED		Q

44

Heat Five A: 2; C: 2.

1.	William Applegarth	GBR	24.7	Q
2.	Harold Heiland	USA	24.7 est[45]	Q

46

Heat Six A: 3; C: 3.

1.	Richard Rau	GER	easy win	22.5	Q
2.	Arthur Anderson	GBR			Q
3.	Rudolf Rauch	AUT			

47

Heat Seven A: 5; C: 5.

1.	Carl Cooke	USA	22.2	Q
2.	Reuben Povey	RSA		Q
3.	Algernon Wells	GBR	48	
AC.	Harry Beasley	CAN	49	
	Georges Malfait	FRA		

50

Heat Eight A: 2; C: 2.

1.	John Howard	CAN	25.0	Q
2.	Franco Giongo	ITA	25.0 est[51]	Q

52

Heat Nine A: 3; C: 3.

1.	Knut Lindberg	SWE	23.1	Q
2.	Frigyes Mezei Wiesner	HUN	at 1½ meters[53]	Q
3.	Charles Lelong	FRA		

54

Heat Ten A: 3; C: 3.

1. Peter Gerhardt	USA	22.9	Q
2. Victor d'Arcy	GBR	22.9	Q
3. Gustav "Gösta" Möller	SWE		

55

Heat Eleven A: 5; C: 5.

1. Donald Lippincott	USA	22.8	Q
2. Ivan Möller	SWE	at 1 meter[56]	Q
3. Pierre Failliot	FRA		
4. Ernest Haley	GBR		
5. Pablo Eitel	CHI		

Heat Twelve A: 2; C: 2.

1. Alvah Meyer	USA	24.1	Q
2. Robert Duncan	GBR		Q

57

Heat Thirteen A: 5; C: 5.

1. Donnell Young	USA	22.8	Q
2. Cyril Seedhouse	GBR		Q
AC. Fritz Fleischer	AUT	[58]	
Yahiko Mishima	JPN		
Heinrich Wenseler	GER		

Heat Fourteen A: 5; C: 5.

1. George Patching	RSA	22.3	Q
2. Clement Wilson	USA		Q
3. Frank McConnell	CAN		
4. Ervin Szerelemhegyi	HUN	[59]	
AC. Emil Grandell	SWE	DNF[60]	

Heat Fifteen A: 4; C: 4.

1. Max Herrmann	GER	22.9	Q
2. István Déván	HUN		Q
3. Herman Sotaaen	NOR		
4. Wladyslaw Ponurski	AUT	[61]	

62

Heat Sixteen A: 2; C: 2.

1. William Stewart	AUS	26.0	Q
2. Henry Macintosh	GBR		Q

63

Heat Seventeen A: 2; C: 2.

1. David Jacobs	GBR	23.2	Q
2. Skotte Jacobsson	SWE	23.2 est[64]	Q

65

Heat Eighteen A: 3; C: 3.

1. Ture Person	SWE		23.2	Q
2. Robert Schurrer	FRA	at a hand		Q
3. António Stromp	POR			

66

400 Meters

A: 49; C: 16; D: 12–13 July.

Three Americans were highly considered for this event. Edward Lindberg had won the AAU Championship in 1909 and 1911 and won the Central U.S. Olympic Trial. Donnell Young won the 1911 IC4A title and the eastern U.S. Olympic Trial. The 1912 IC4A 440 yard champion had been Syracuse's Charles Reidpath.

In the fifth semifinal, Young was involved in a controversial incident with Germany's Hanns Braun. On the first curve, Braun tried to cut in front of Young, who reacted by pushing Braun violently to the outside of the track. Young finished first but was disqualified and Braun was advanced to the final, where he would compete against four Americans — Reidpath, Lindberg, Ted Meredith, and Carroll Haff.

The first round and semifinals had been run without lanes. But the Braun-Young incident changed that and strings were put up for the final, and the runners ran in lanes. Braun took the lead until he was passed on the last curve by Reidpath. Reidpath held on to narrowly defeat Braun, with Lindberg taking the bronze medal.

Final A: 5; C: 2; D: 13 July; T: 1500.

1. Charles Reidpath	USA	48.2	OR
2. Hanns Braun	GER	48.3	
3. Edward Lindberg	USA	48.4	
4. James "Ted" Meredith	USA	49.2	
5. Carroll Haff	USA	49.5	

Diplomas of Merit

James "Ted" Meredith (USA), Carroll Haff (USA)

Semifinals A: 27; C: 9; D: 12 July; T: 1615; F: Winner of each heat advanced to the final.

Heat One A: 5; C: 4.

1. Charles Reidpath	USA	48.7	Q
2. Clarence Edmundson	USA		
3. George Nicol	GBR		
4. Frigyes Mezei Wiesner	HUN		
5. Charles Poulenard	FRA		

67

Heat Two A: 6; C: 5.

1. Edward Lindberg	USA	48.9	Q
2. Eric Lindholm	SWE	50.2	

3. Charles Lelong	FRA			
AC. Cyril Seedhouse	GBR		DNF	
Julius Person	GER		DNF	68
Algernon Wells	GBR		DNF	

Heat Three A: 6; C: 5.

1. James "Ted" Meredith	USA	48.8	Q
2. Melvin Sheppard	USA	48.9 est	
3. George Patching	RSA	50.5 est	
4. Knut Stenborg	SWE	50.5[69]	
5. Ole Jacob Pedersen	NOR		
AC. Ernest Henley	GBR	DNF	

Heat Four A: 5; C: 4.

1. Carroll Haff	USA		49.7	Q
2. Emilio Lunghi	ITA			
3. Ervin Szerelemhegyi	HUN			
AC. Ernest Haley	GBR	DNF		
James Rosenberger	USA	DNF		
70				

Heat Five A: 5; C: 4.

1. Hanns Braun	GER		49.2	Q
AC. Ira Davenport	USA			
James Soutter	GBR			
Paul Zerling	SWE			
Donnell Young	USA		DQ[71]	

Round One A: 49; C: 16; D: 12 July; T: 1100; F: Top two finishers in each heat advanced to the semifinals.

Heat One A: 4; C: 4.

1. James Rosenberger	USA	50.6	Q
2. Charles Poulenard	FRA	50.7	Q
3. Wladyslaw Ponurski	AUT		
AC. Claude Ross	AUS	DNF	
72			

Heat Two A: 2; C: 2.

1. Ernest Haley	GBR	1:06.6	Q
2. Melvin Sheppard	USA	1:06.6	Q
73			

Heat Three A: 3; C: 3.

1. Hanns Braun	GER	50.6	Q
2. James "Ted" Meredith	USA		Q
3. Armando Luzarte-Cortesão	POR		
74			

Heat Four A: 2; C: 2.

1. Paul Zerling	SWE	55.4	Q
2. Yahiko Mishima	JPN	55.5	Q
75				

Heat Five A: 4; C: 4.

1. Charles Lelong	FRA	50.2	Q
2. Donnell Young	USA	50.4	Q
3. István Déván	HUN		
4. Gustav "Gösta" Möller	SWE		
76				

Heat Six A: 1; C: 1.

1. Knut Stenborg	SWE	1:01.6	Q
77			

Heat Seven A: 3; C: 3.

1. Carroll Haff	USA	50.4	Q
2. Emilio Lunghi	ITA	50.5	Q
3. Max Herrmann	GER		
78			

Heat Eight A: 3; C: 3.

1. Frigyes Mezei Wiesner	HUN	50.8	Q
2. John Dahlin	SWE	51.0	Q
3. Georges Malfait	FRA		
79			

Heat Nine A: 4; C: 4.

1. Eric Lindholm	SWE	51.4	Q
2. Ole Jacob Pedersen	NOR	51.6	Q
3. Hermann Burkowitz	GER	51.7 est	
4. Václav Labík-Gregan	BOH		
80			

Heat Ten A: 3; C: 3.

1. Edward Lindberg	USA	50.6	Q
2. James Soutter	GBR		Q
3. Franco Giongo	ITA		
81			

Heat Eleven A: 4; C: 4.

1. Clarence Edmundson	USA	50.2	Q
2. Ernest Henley	GBR		Q
3. Melville Brock	CAN		
4. Pyotr Gayevsky	RUS		
82			

Heat Twelve A: 6; C: 6.

1. George Nicol	GBR	50.0		Q
2. Ira Davenport	USA			Q
3. Thomas Gallon	CAN			
4. Erich Lehmann	GER			
5. Georges Rolot	FRA			
6. Ödön Bodor	HUN			

Heat Thirteen A: 2; C: 2.

1. Julius Person	GER	55.4	Q
2. Algernon Wells	GBR	1:01.2[83]	Q
84, 85			

Heat Fourteen A: 3; C: 3.

1. Cyril Seedhouse	GBR	51.5	Q
2. Ervin Szerelemhegyi	HUN		Q
AC. Alex Pedersen	NOR	DQ [51.9]	
86			

Heat Fifteen A: 5; C: 5.

1. George Patching	RSA	51.1	Q
2. Charles Reidpath	USA	51.2	Q
3. Heinrich Wenseler	GER	87	
4. Alan Patterson	GBR		
5. Robert Schurrer	FRA		
88			

800 Meters

A: 48; C: 15; D: 6–8 July.

The defending Olympic champion was America's Mel Sheppard, who had won the AAU title over 880 yards in 1911 and won the eastern U.S. Olympic trial in 1912. But two other Americans began to challenge him in the interim between Olympics. John Paul Jones, a college runner at Cornell, won the IC4A title in both 1911 and 1912. But a Philadelphia high school student, James Edwin "Ted" Meredith, of Mercersburg Academy, came to prominence at both 440 and 880 yards early in 1912, setting interscholastic records at both distances only a few weeks before the Olympic trials. At the Eastern Olympic Trials, Meredith ran third behind Sheppard.

The best of the Europeans were Germany's Hanns Braun, who had won the AAA title in 1911 and 1912, and Italy's Emilio Lunghi, who equalled Sheppard's world record of 1:52.8 (set at the London Olympics) in winning the 1909 Canadian Championship. At La Spezia, on 23 June, Lunghi confirmed his fitness with a 400/800 double of 49.0 and 1:55.0.

The five favorites all survived the first round, but John Paul Jones did not compete in the semifinals. The American trainer, Michael Murphy, thought he had a better chance at 1,500 meters, so he withdrew Jones to save him for the longer race. In the second semi, Lunghi faltered in the stretch and finished fifth, one place from qualifying for the final.

In the final, Mel Sheppard led out at a very fast pace, reaching 400 meters in 52.4. But entering the homestretch, Sheppard could not hold off Ted Meredith, who won by inches in a world record time of 1:51.9. Ira Davenport (USA) came up fast in the last 200 meters to take the bronze medal. Meredith continued to a second tape set at 880 yards, passing that mark in 1:52.5, also a world record.

The official results for the nonmedalists, from the *Official Report*, were 4) Braun 1:52.2; 5) Caldwell 1:52.3; and 6) Brock — no time.[89] Concerning places 4–6, *Olympic Track & Field* states that, "However, these places and times do not stand up under close scrutiny of available photographs and reports from various sources. We here list 'revised' results." The revised results that they listed were 4) Brock 1:52.7e; 5) Caldwell 1:52.8e; and 6) Braun 1:53.1e.[90]

Quercetani and Kök describe this problem as follows: "Even the expert Swedish judges made mistakes in determining the other places, notably in giving a fourth place to Braun in 1:52.2, a time which the German federation recognized in … 1924. In reality, the most dependable witnesses say that the exhausted Braun finished in slow motion, beaten by Caldwell and possibly even by Brock. Without guaranteeing absolute exactness (photographs, taken mostly before the finish and at different angles, don't help much) the order of finish from fourth onwards can be tentatively reconstructed as follows (times are estimated): 4. Caldwell 1:52.8; 5. Brock 1:53; 6. Braun 1:53; 7. Edmundsen; 8. Putnam."[91]

Final A: 8; C: 3; D: 8 July; T: 1700.

1.	James "Ted" Meredith	USA	1:51.9	WR
2.	Melvin Sheppard	USA	1:52.0	
3.	Ira Davenport	USA	1:52.0	
4.[92]	David Caldwell	USA	1:52.8 est	
5.	Melville Brock	CAN	1:53.0 est	
6.	Hanns Braun	GER	1:53.0 est	
7.	Clarence Edmundson	USA		
8.	Herbert Putnam	USA		

Diplomas of Merit

Hanns Braun (GER), Melville Brock (CAN), David Caldwell (USA)

Semifinals A: 17; C: 7; D: 7 July; F: Top four finishers in each heat advanced to the final.

Heat One A: 8; C: 4; D: 7 July; T: 1515.

1.	James "Ted" Meredith	USA	1:54.4	Q
2.	Hanns Braun	GER	1:54.6	Q
3.	Melvin Sheppard	USA	1:54.8	Q
4.	Herbert Putnam	USA	1:55.0	Q
5.[93]	Lindsay Tait	CAN		
6.	Percy Mann	GBR		
AC.	Frederick Hulford	GBR	DNF	[94]
	James Soutter	GBR	DNF	[95]
	[96]			

Heat Two A: 9; C: 6; D: 7 July; T: 1530.

1.	G. Melville Brock	CAN	1:55.7	Q
2.	Clarence Edmundson	USA	1:55.8	Q
3.	David Caldwell	USA	1:55.9	Q

4.	Ira Davenport	USA		1:55.9	Q
5.[97]	Emilio Lunghi	ITA			
AC.	Harlan Holden	USA			
	Ernest Henley[98]	GBR			
	Evert Björn	SWE			
	Armando Luzarte-Cortesão	POR			
99					

Round One A: 48; C: 15; D: 6 July; T: 1445; F: Top two finishers in each heat advanced to the semifinals.

Heat One A: 6; C: 5.

1.	David Caldwell	USA		1:58.6[100]	Q
2.	Emilio Lunghi	ITA	at 7 meters		Q
3.	Walter McClure	USA			
4.	Eric Lindholm	SWE		2:01.5[101]	
5.	Joseph Caulle	FRA			
102					

Heat Two A: 4; C: 4.

1.	Percy Mann	GBR		1:56.0	Q
2.	Herbert Putnam	USA	at 5 meters		Q
3.	Ole Jacob Pedersen	NOR			
	Leopoldo Palma	CHI		DNF	
103					

Heat Three A: 4; C: 4.

1.	John Paul Jones	USA		2:01.8	Q
2.	Armando Luzarte-Cortesão	POR			Q
3.	Oscar Larsen	NOR			
AC.	Guido Calvi	ITA			
104					

Heat Four A: 5; C: 5.

1.	Clarence Edmundson	USA		1:56.5	Q
2.	Lindsay Tait	CAN			Q
3.	Charles Poulenard	FRA			
4.	Richard "Willi" Jahn	GER		2:02.0	
AC.	Robert Burton	GBR		DNF	
105					

Heat Five A: 7; C: 6.

1.	Ira Davenport	USA		1:59.0	Q
2.	Frederick Hulford	GBR			Q
3.	Ödön Bodor	HUN			
4.	Julius Person	GER			
5.	Dmitry Nazarov	RUS			
AC.	Zdeněk Městecký	BOH		DNF	
	Philip Baker	GBR		DNF	
106					

Heat Six A: 8[107]; C: 7.

1. Harlan Holden	USA	1:58.1		Q
2. Evert Björn	SWE			Q
3. Richard Yorke	GBR			
4. Karl Haglund	SWE	2:01.2[108]		
AC. Ferenc Forgács-Faczinek	HUN			
Federico Mueller	CHI			
Aleksandr Yelizarov	RUS			
Vahran Papazyan	TUR			

109, 110

Heat Seven A: 5; C: 5.

1. James Soutter	GBR	2:00.4[111]		Q
2. Melvin Sheppard	USA			Q
3. Erich Lehmann	GER			
AC. Janos Antal	HUN	DNF		
Leopolds Villemson	RUS	DNF		

112

Heat Eight A: 4; C: 4.

1. Melville Brock	CAN	1:57.0		Q
2. James "Ted" Meredith	USA			Q
3. John Victor	RSA			
AC. Alan Patterson	GBR	DNF		

113

Heat Nine A: 6; C: 6.

1. Ernest Henley	GBR	1:57.6		Q
2. Hanns Braun	GER			Q
=3. Erik Frisell	SWE	1:59.2		
AC. Károly Radóczy	HUN	DNF		
Thomas Halpin	USA	1:59.2		
Lauri Pihkala	FIN	DNF		

114

1,500 Meters

A: 45[115]; C: 14; D: 9–10 July.

As late as 1985, Cordner Nelson and Roberto Quercetani, two distinguished track & field historians, labeled this "the greatest race ever run," noting, "The 1912 Olympic Games at Stockholm produced the greatest mile or 1500 meter race ever run from the standpoint of exciting competition between fast runners."[116] Much of what follows is based on their excellent summary.

There were five highly considered runners who started this event at Stockholm. One was the defending Olympic champion, Mel Sheppard. He was primarily a half-miler, and only the day before this event started, he lost narrowly in the 800 meters semifinal.

There were three other top Americans. John Paul Jones had won the 1911 and 1912 IC4A title at 880 yards and one mile. On 27 May 1911, Jones set a world amateur record in the mile with 4:15.4 in winning the IC4A at Cambridge. After the 1912 IC4A meet, he stopped training, not planning on competing at the Olympics, but he was convinced to resume training and travel to Stockholm.

Norman Taber of Brown University had done little prior to 1912. But on 1 June he finished in a dead heat with Jones in the IC4A mile. At the Eastern Olympic Trial, one week later, he ran 1,500 meters in 3:56.4, bettering the world record, but he finished only second in the race.

Taber finished second in the Eastern Olympic Trial because of a highly talented, diminutive runner named Abel Kiviat. Kiviat had first achieved prominence in 1909, winning the Canadian mile championship. In 1911 he won the AAU mile championship. On 26 May 1912, Kiviat ran in the New York Post Office Clerk's Association Games at Celtic Park on Long Island, winning the mile narrowly over Mel Sheppard, but setting a new mile world record of 3:59.2 in doing so. In a handicap race at the same track on 2 June, he bettered that mark off scratch, recording 3:56.8. The record would be short-lived, as on 8 June, at the Eastern Olympic Trial, he defeated Taber with another world record of 3:55.8. His hot running and three world records in only a few weeks made him the Olympic favorite.

Despite the four great American runners, Britain had a top talent in Arnold Nugent Strode Jackson, but one who had little background as a miler. A well-rounded athlete who attended Brasenose College, Oxford, in 1912 he won the Oxford University Athletic Club mile and won the mile against Cambridge in a good time of 4:21.6. Based on those performances, he was named to the British Olympic team for Stockholm.

There were seven heats in round one, with the top two finishers in each heat advancing to the final. The five favorites qualified easily, although Jackson and Jones had been drawn in the same heat. The final comprised 14 runners — seven Americans, three Swedes, two Brits, and a lone Frenchman and German. The four top Americans would be well protected by their group of seven teammates.

The "greatest race ever run" began at 3:30 P.M. (1530) on Wednesday, 10 July 1912. The pace was set by the Frenchman, Henri Arnaud, who passed 400 meters in 1:05 and 800 in 2:08. Taber led at 1,000 meters in 2:39, but at 1,200, Kiviat took the lead in 3:09, closely followed by his teammates, Taber and Jones. Jackson had been running last most of the race, but passed Sheppard on the backstretch and began moving up the field. On the final curve, Kiviat continued to lead, followed by Taber, Jackson, Jones, and Sheppard. Taber pulled even with Kiviat at the start of the straightaway. With 50 meters remaining, Jackson pulled even with Kiviat and Taber, with Jones close behind and Sweden's Ernst Wide closing fast as well. It was only 10 meters from the tape that Jackson edged ahead to win by one tenth of a second from Kiviat (silver medal) and Taber (bronze medal). Kiviat and Taber were so close that the finish camera was needed to determine the final medal placements, the only time this was used to determine a placement at the 1912 Olympics. Jones finished fourth with Wide in fifth.

Jackson described the race in his own words. "Perhaps it is impossible in an Olympic mile to notice who got the lead, when and where, and Kiviat seemed to me to have the lead inside most of the way and Mr P. J. Baker and I had to get along the best way we could and not very near the front either. There we rubbed along until the bell went for the last lap. We then moved up and dropped Sheppard and several others who no doubt were rather tired after the general bustle and their previous efforts. With three hundred and fifty yards to go Paul Jones and Kiviat were well placed but coming round the last bend I got in behind them and running wide caught them with about a hundred yards to go. Running neck and neck for fifty yards I passed them and got home by about two yards, as far as I am told. A perfect day and capital fellow competitors helped the Olympic record to go and I am very grateful and proud to have run with

Mr Kiviat, Taber, and Jones and all the others. I believe that the result of the second and third places was not given out until the photograph had been developed and Mr Kiviat just beat Mr Taber on the post with Mr Jones right on to them. 'U.S.A. right there all the time!'"[117]

Arnold Nugent Strode Jackson (who later changed his name spelling to Arnold Nugent Strode Strode-Jackson) ran only a few more races in a very short, yet meteoric career. He won the Oxbridge mile race again in 1913 and 1914, and his career totaled no more than six top quality races. He joined the British army in World War I, serving with distinction, and becoming its youngest brigadier-general. He won the DSO and three bars, decorations matched by only six other British officers. He was later a British delegate to the Paris Peace Conference in 1921, and was awarded the CBE for his works. He settled in the United States, eventually becoming an American citizen.[118]

Final A: 14; C: 5; D: 10 July; T: 1530.

1.	Arnold Jackson	GBR	3:56.8	OR
2.	Abel Kiviat	USA	3:56.9	
3.	Norman Taber	USA	3:56.9	
4.	John Paul Jones	USA	3:57.2	
5.	Ernst Wide	SWE	3:57.6[119]	
6.	Philip Baker[120]	GBR	4:01.0 est[121]	
7.	John Zander	SWE	4:02.0 est	
8.	Walter McClure	USA	[122]	
AC.	Melvin Sheppard[123]	USA	[124]	
	Henri Arnaud	FRA	[125]	
	Frederick Hedlund	USA		
	Erwin von Sigel	GER	[126]	
	Louis Madeira	USA		
	Evert Björn	SWE		

Diplomas of Merit

John Paul Jones (USA), Ernst Wide (SWE)

Round One A: 45; C: 14; D: 9 July; T: 1430; F: Top two finishers in each heat advanced to the final.

Heat One A: 3; C: 2.

1.	Melvin Sheppard	USA	4:27.6	Q
2.	Louis Madeira	USA	4:27.9	Q
3.	Albert Hare	GBR	4:39.4	
	[127]			

Heat Two A: 6; C: 5.

1.	Norman Taber	USA	4:25.5	Q
2.	Philip Baker	GBR	4:26.0	Q
3.	Georg Amberger	GER	4:27.0	
AC.	Teofil Savniki-Marschalko	HUN		
	Rudolfs Vitols	RUS		
	Dmitry Nazarov	RUS	DNF	
	[128]			

Heat Three A: 8; C: 7.

1. Abel Kiviat	USA	4:04.4	Q
2. Henri Arnaud	FRA	4:05.4	Q
3. Norman Patterson	USA	4:05.5	
4. Lindsay Tait	CAN		
5. Ferenc Forgács-Faczinek	HUN		
AC. François Delloye	BEL		
Ole Jacob Pedersen	NOR		
Edward Owen	GBR	DNF	
129			

Heat Four A: 7; C: 5.

1. Arnold Jackson	GBR	4:10.8	Q
2. John Paul Jones	USA	4:12.4	Q
3. John Victor	RSA	4:12.7	
4. Lewis Anderson	USA		
5. Oscar Larsen	NOR		
6. Arnolds Indriksons	RUS		
7. Alfreds Ruks	RUS		
130			

Heat Five A: 8; C: 5.

1. John Zander	SWE	4:05.5	Q
2. Evert Björn	SWE	4:07.2	Q
3. Herbert Putnam	USA	4:07.6	
4. Richard Yorke	GBR		
5. Georg Mickler	GER		
Aleksandr Yelizarov	RUS		
Nikolay Kharkov	RUS		
Charles Ruffell	GBR	DNF	
131			

Heat Six A: 7; C: 6.

1. Erwin von Sigel	GER	4:09.3	Q
2. Frederick Hedlund	USA	4:10.8	Q
3. William Moore	GBR	4:11.2	
4. Nils Frykberg	SWE	4:11.2 est	
AC. Andrejs Kruklins	RUS		
Frederick Hulford	GBR		
Guido Calvi	ITA	DNF	
132			

Heat Seven A: 6; C: 6.

1. Ernst Wide	SWE	4:06.0	Q
2. Walter McClure	USA	4:07.3	Q
3. William Cottrill	GBR		
4. Efraim Harju	FIN		

5. Yevgeny Petrov	RUS		
Vahran Papazyan	TUR		DNF
133			

5,000 Meters

A: 31; C: 11; D: 9–10 July.

The 5,000 meters individual race was held at the Olympics for the first time in 1912. A team event over this distance had been contested in 1900. The distance was rarely run internationally, and neither America nor Britain had contested a 5,000 meters or three-mile championship as of 1912.

Finland's Hannes Kolehmainen had won the 10,000 meters the day before the first round of this event but he was not pressed in winning heat four to advance to the final. In the final, Kolehmainen and France's Jean Bouin quickly pulled away from the field. For the remainder of the race, until the final straight, Bouin led with Kolehmainen on his heels. Finally, after repeated attempts to pass Bouin, Kolehmainen pulled ahead only 20 meters from the finish. The two leaders shattered the previous world record, as nobody had previously broken 15 minutes for the distance.

In September 1914, both Bouin and the bronze medalist, Britain's George Hutson, were killed in World War I.

Final A: 11; C: 6; D: 10 July; T: 1400.

1. Hannes Kolehmainen	FIN	14:36.6[134]	WR
2. Jean Bouin	FRA	14:36.7	
3. George Hutson	GBR	15:07.6	
4. George Bonhag	USA	15:09.8 est	
5. Tell Berna	USA	15:10.0 est	
6. Alex Decoteau	CAN	[135]	
7. Mauritz "Sörle" Carlsson	SWE	15:18.6	
AC. Louis Scott	USA		
Joseph Keeper	CAN		
Frederick Hibbins	GBR	[136]	
Cyril Porter	GBR		
137, 138			

Diplomas of Merit

George Bonhag (USA), Tell Berna (USA), Alex Decoteau (CAN), Mauritz "Sörle" Carlsson (SWE)

Round One A: 31; C: 11; D: 9 July; F: Top three finishers in each heat advanced to the final.

Heat One A: 5; C: 5; T: 0930.

1. George Bonhag	USA	15:22.6	Q
2. Alex Decoteau	CAN	15:24.2	Q
3. Frederick Hibbins	GBR	15:27.6	Q

4.	George Hill	AUS/NZL	15:56.8	
AC.	Klas Lundström [140]	SWE	DNF[139]	

Heat Two A: 7; C: 4; T: c. 1000.

1.	Louis Scott	USA	15:23.5	Q
2.	Joseph Keeper	CAN	15:28.9	Q
3.	George Hutson	GBR	15:29.0	Q
4.	Bror Modigh	SWE	16:07.1	
AC.	Martin Persson	SWE	DNF[141]	
	Charles Ruffell	GBR	DNF[142]	
	Edward Fitzgerald [144]	USA	DNF[143]	

Heat Three A: 6; C: 5; T: c. 1030.

1.	Mauritz "Sörle" Carlsson	SWE	15:34.6	Q
2.	Ernest Glover	GBR	16:09.1	Q
3.	Cyril Porter	GBR	16:23.4	Q
4.	Mikhail Nikolsky	RUS	17:21.7	
AC.	Garnett Wikoff	USA	DNF[145]	
	K. Aarne Lindholm (Linnolahti) [147]	FIN	DNF[146]	

Heat Four A: 5; C: 5; T: 1615.

1.	Hannes Kolehmainen	FIN	15:38.9	Q
2.	Henrik Nordström	SWE	15:49.1	Q
3.	Tell Berna	USA	15:53.3	Q
4.[148]	George Lee	GBR		
AC.	Gregor Vietz [149]	GER	DNF	

Heat Five A: 8; C: 7; T: c. 1645.

1.	Jean Bouin	FRA	15:05.0	Q	OR
2.	Thorild Olsson	SWE	15:25.2	Q	
3.	Franz "Viljam" Johansson	FIN	15:31.4	Q	
AC.	Alfonso Orlando	ITA	DNF		
	Alfonso Sanchez Rodriguez	CHI	DNF		
	Arnold Treble	GBR	DNF		
	Gaston Heuet	FRA	DNF		
	Wallace McCurdy [151]	USA	DNF[150]		

10,000 Meters

A: 30; C: 13; D: 7–8 July.

Two of the three heats were won by Finland's Kolehmainen brothers—Hannes and Tatu. The final was held on a very hot day and four of the 15 qualifiers did not start. Hannes

Kolehmainen took the lead on the second lap and eventually dropped the field by the sixth lap. He eventually ran uncontested to win by over 45 seconds. The silver medal went to Lewis Tewanima, a Hopi Indian and Jim Thorpe's teammate at the Carlisle Indian School.

Hannes Kolehmainen's winning time was "somewhat" of a world record. At the beginning of 1912 there was no official world record, as the IAAF did not start recognizing marks until 1913. Until 1911, the best mark on record by an amateur was 31:40.0 by Walter George (GBR), set in London on 28 July 1884 during a 12-mile handicap race. The professional best had been set by Alfred Shrubb (GBR) in Glasgow on 5 November 1904 during a one-hour race. But on 16 November 1911, Jean Bouin ran 30:58.8 at Colombes, France. Bouin did not run the 10K at Stockholm but finished a very close second to Hannes Kolehmainen in the 5K.

When the IAAF began to recognize world records, they thought that Bouin had run his mark in 1913. They recognized only Kolehmainen's winning Stockholm time as the initial IAAF-approved world record. Bouin's mark did not receive official recognition until 1926.

Final A: 11; C: 7; D: 8 July; T: 1615.

1.	Hannes Kolehmainen	FIN	31:20.8	WR
2.	Lewis Tewanima	USA	32:06.6	
3.	Albin Stenroos	FIN	32:21.8	
4.	Joseph Keeper	CAN	32:36.2	
5.	Alfonso Orlando	ITA	33:31.2	
AC.	Mauritz "Sörle" Carlsson	SWE	DNF[152]	
	Taavetti "Tatu" Kolehmainen	FIN	DNF[153]	
	Louis Scott[154]	USA	DNF	
	William Scott[155]	GBR	DNF[156]	
	Hugh Maguire	USA	DNF	
	Leonard Richardson	RSA	DNF[157]	

158

Diploma of Merit

Joseph Keeper (CAN)

Round One A: 30; C: 13; D: 7 July; F: Top five finishers in each heat advanced to the final.

Heat One A: 12; C: 8; D: 7 July; T: 0900.

1.	Hannes Kolehmainen	FIN	33:49.0[159]	Q	OR
2.	Joseph Keeper	CAN	33:58.8	Q	
3.	Gaston Heuet	FRA	34:50.0	Q	
4.	John Eke	SWE	34:55.8	Q	
5.	Ernest Glover	GBR	35:12.2	Q	
6.	Albert Öberg	SWE	35:45.0		
AC.[160]	George Lee	GBR	DNF		
	Charles Ruffell	GBR	DNF		
	Vladimír Penc	BOH	DNF		
	William Kramer	USA	DNF		
	Mikhail Nikolsky	RUS	DNF		
	Harry Hellawell	USA	DNF		

161

Heat Two A: 11; C: 8; D: 7 July; T: 0945.

1.	Leonard Richardson	RSA	32:30.3	Q=OR
2.	Lewis Tewanima	USA	32:31.4	Q
3.	Mauritz "Sörle" Carlsson	SWE	33:06.2	Q
4.	Albin Stenroos	FIN	33:28.4	Q
5.	Alfonso Orlando	ITA	33:44.6	Q
6.	Alfonso Sanchez Rodriguez	CHI		
7.	Brynolf Larsson	SWE		
AC.[162]	Bror Fock	SWE	DNF	
	Thomas Humphreys	GBR	DNF	
	Frederick Hibbins	GBR	DNF	
	Gregor Vietz	GER	DNF	
[163]				

Heat Three A: 7; C: 5; D: 7 July; T: 1330.

1.	Taavetti "Tatu" Kolehmainen	FIN	32:47.8	Q
2.	William Scott	GBR	32:55.2	Q
3.	Louis Scott	USA	34:14.2	Q
4.	Martin Persson	SWE	34:18.6	Q
5.	Hugh Maguire	USA	34:32.0	Q
AC.[164]	George Wallach	GBR	DNF[165]	
	George Hill	AUS/NZL	DNF[166]	
[167]				

Marathon

A: 68; E: 98; C: 19; D: 14 July; T: 1348[168]; F: 40,200 meters.

The marathon at Stockholm was the first time the Olympic marathon was conducted as an out-and-back race. The runners started at the Olympic Stadium, ran north to the small town of Sollentuna, where they turned just beyond the main village church and returned to the Olympic Stadium. Unfortunately the day of the race dawned very hot for Stockholm, a common occurrence in Olympic marathon racing. Gynn and Martin have noted "Unconfirmed reports have suggested a temperature of 32° C. (89.6° F.) in the shade."[169]

Most of the world's top long-distance runners were present. The Americans entered 12 runners, the maximum, including the Boston Marathon champions of 1911 (Clarence DeMar) and 1912 (Mike Ryan), two Indian runners (Lewis Tewanima, a Hopi; and Andrew Sockalexis, a Penobscot), and Joseph Forshaw, who had run the Olympic marathon in 1906 and 1908, winning the bronze medal at London. The British entered eight runners, including Fred Barrett, who won the 1909 Polytechnic race, and the third- to eighth-place finishers at the 1912 Polytechnic race.

The top two finishers from the 1912 Polytechnic Marathon were not British but both were present at Stockholm. Canada's James Corkery had won the race, followed by South Africa's Chris Gitsham. South Africa also entered Ken McArthur, who was little known outside his native country. But between 1909 and 1911 he had won three marathon distance races in South Africa, and had never been defeated at marathon distances.

The race was led through the early stages by Taavetti "Tatu" Kolehmainen, Hannes's brother.

At the turnaround at Sollentuna, Chris Gitsham was the leader in 1-12:40, followed by Kolehmainen and McArthur, with a group of five (Fred Lord [GBR], Carlo Speroni [ITA], Alexis Ahlgren [SWE], Sigge Jacobsson [SWE], and Corkery) within a minute of the leader.

By 25 km. Kolehmainen had caught Gitsham and the two ran together for several miles. But Kolehmainen dropped out by 35 km. and McArthur caught his teammate at that point (reached in 2-14:20) and they led by over one minute from Jacobsson and America's virtual unknown, Gaston Strobino.

At the base of a hill, a few kilometers outside the stadium, Gitsham stopped to drink, and McArthur pulled away to take the lead for good. He entered the stadium comfortably ahead, and the two South Africans finished one, two. Strobino finished third. Almost a phantom among American track & field medalists, he had qualified for the Olympic team when he had finished second in a half-marathon in New York earlier in 1912. After the Olympics, Strobino retired and never raced again.

The 1912 Olympic marathon also saw the games' first tragedy. Portuguese marathoner Francisco Lázaro was never near the leaders but at around 30 km. (19 miles) he collapsed from the effects of the race and the hot weather. Taken to Seraphim Hospital, he was never revived and died on the morning after the race at 0620, the first fatality during an Olympic event.

Kennedy McArthur may be the least known Olympic marathon gold medalist. South African historians know little of his life. But Roger Gynn and Dave Martin, in their book on Olympic marathons, note that he is known to have run six marathons in his running career, and never lost.[170]

In addition to the gold medal, Kennedy McArthur was awarded the challenge trophy for the marathon race, that had been donated in 1908 by the King of Greece. The runners who finished in places four to 28 in the marathon were also awarded diplomas of merit. This was all runners finishing within 20 percent of the winning time.

1.	Kennedy McArthur	RSA	2-36:54.8
2.	Christopher Gitsham	RSA	2-37:52.0
3.	Gaston Strobino	USA	2-38:42.4
4.	Andrew Sockalexis	USA	2-42:07.9
5.	James Duffy	CAN	2-42:18.8
6.	Sigfrid "Sigge" Jacobsson	SWE	2-43:24.9
7.	John Gallagher	USA	2-44:19.4
8.	Joseph Erxleben	USA	2-45:47.2[171]
9.	Richard Piggott	USA	2-46:40.7
10.	Joseph Forshaw	USA	2-49:49.4
11.	Edouard Fabre	CAN	2-50:36.2
12.	Clarence DeMar	USA	2-50:46.6
13.	Jean Boissière	FRA	2-51:06.6
14.	Henry Green	GBR	2-52:11.4
15.[172]	William Forsyth	CAN	2-52:23.0
16.	Lewis Tewanima	USA	2-52:41.4
17.	Harry Smith	USA	2-52:53.8
18.	Thomas Lilley	USA	2-59:35.4
19.	Arthur Townsend	GBR	3-00:05.0
20.	Felix Lixl-Kwieton	AUT	3-00:48.0
21.	Fred Lord	GBR	3-01:39.2
22.	Jacob Westberg	SWE	3-02:05.2
23.	Axel Simonsen	NOR	3-04:59.4

24.	Carl Andersson	SWE	3-06:13.0
25.	Edgar Lloyd	GBR	3-09:25.0
26.	Iraklis Sakellaropoulos	GRE	3-11:37.0
27.	Hjalmar Dahlberg	SWE	3-13:32.2
28.	Ivar Gustaf Lundberg	SWE	3-16:35.2
29.	Johannes Christensen	DEN	3-21:57.4
30.	Olaf Lodal	DEN	3-21:57.6
31.	Ödön Kárpáti Kraml	HUN	3-25:21.6
32.	Calle Nilsson	SWE	3-26:56.4
33.	Emmerich Rath	AUT	3-27:03.8
34.	Otto Osen	NOR	3-36:35.2
AC.	Stuart Poulter	AUS	DNF
	Karl Hack	AUT	DNF
	Bohumil Honzatko	BOH	DNF
	Vladimír Penc	BOH	DNF
	František Slavík	BOH	DNF
	James Corkery	CAN	DNF
	Aarne Kallberg	FIN	DNF
	Taavetti "Tatu" Kolehmainen	FIN	DNF
	Louis Pauteux	FRA	DNF
	Harry Barrett	GBR	DNF
	James Beale	GBR	DNF
	Septimus Francom	GBR	DNF
	Henry "Tim" Kellaway	GBR	DNF
	Henrik Ripszám, Jr.	HUN	DNF
	Francesco Ruggero	ITA	DNF
	Carlo Speroni	ITA	DNF
	Shizo Kanaguri[173]	JPN	DNF
	Oscar Fonbæk	NOR	DNF
	Francisco Lázaro[174]	POR	DNF
	Arthur St. Norman	RSA	DNF
	Andrejs Kapmals	RUS	DNF
	Andrejs Kruklins	RUS	DNF
	Nikolajs Rasso	RUS	DNF
	Elmar Reimann	RUS	DNF
	Aleksandrs Upmals	RUS	DNF
	Dragutin Tomašević	SRB	DNF
	Alexis Ahlgren	SWE	DNF
	Thure Bergvall	SWE	DNF
	Wilhelm "William" Grüner	SWE	DNF
	David Guttman	SWE	DNF
	Ivan Lönnberg	SWE	DNF
	Gustaf Törnros	SWE	DNF
	John Reynolds	USA	DNF
	Michael Ryan	USA	DNF
	Lindsay Tait[175]	CAN	DNF

176, 177

Diplomas of Merit

Andrew Sockalexis (USA), Arthur Townsend (GBR), Axel Simonsen (NOR), Carl Andersson (SWE), Clarence DeMar (USA), Edgar Lloyd (GBR), Edouard Fabre (CAN), Felix Lixl-Kwieton (AUT), Fred Lord (GBR), Harry Smith (USA), Henry Green (GBR), Hjalmar Dahlberg (SWE), Iraklis Sakellaropoulos (GRE), Ivar Gustaf Lundberg (SWE), Jacob Westberg (SWE), James Duffy (CAN), Jean Boissière (FRA), John Gallagher (USA), Joseph Erxleben (USA), Joseph Forshaw (USA), Lewis Tewanima (USA), Richard Piggott (USA), Sigfrid "Sigge" Jacobsson (SWE), Thomas Lilley (USA), and William Forsyth (CAN).

Cross-Country Race, Individual

A: 45[178]; C: 10; D: 15 July; T: 1415; F: c. 12,000 meters.[179] Two laps with a start and finish in the Olympic Stadium. The runners ran one-quarter lap in the stadium, returned to the stadium later and ran another one-half lap, and eventually finished with three-quarters lap inside the stadium.

This was the first time that a cross-country event was held on the Olympic program, although it would also be conducted in 1920 and 1924. The course was not revealed to the participants prior to the start, but was marked just before the race began with red ribbons. It was very hilly, through the forest with steep inclines and descents, and many natural obstacles. The British and Continental runners were not used to this kind of terrain and the race was dominated by the Swedes and Finns.

The international cross-country championship had been won in 1911 by Jean Bouin, who would also win in 1912–1913. But Hannes Kolehmainen had already won the 5,000 and 10,000 meters at Stockholm, and when he elected to run the cross-country, he had to be favored. Kolehmainen won easily by over 30 seconds. Two Swedes, Hjalmar Andersson and John Eke, won the silver and bronze medals, respectively. Bouin ran in this race, but did not finish.

1.	Hannes Kolehmainen	FIN	45:11.6
2.	Hjalmar Andersson	SWE	45:44.8
3.	John Eke	SWE	46:37.6
4.	Jalmari "Lauri" Eskola	FIN	46:54.8
5.	Josef Ternström	SWE	47:07.7[180]
6.	Albin Stenroos	FIN	47:23.4
7.	Ville Kyrönen	FIN	47:32.0
8.	Leonard Richardson	RSA	47:33.5
9.	Brynolf Larsson	SWE	47:37.4
10.	Johan Sundkvist	SWE	47:40.0
11.	Franz "Viljam" Johansson	FIN	48:03.0
12.	Harry Hellawell	USA	48:12.0
13.	Klas Lundström	SWE	48:45.4
14.	Lauritz Christiansen	DEN	49:06.4
15.	Frederick Hibbins	GBR	49:18.2
16.	Ernest Glover	GBR	49:53.7
17.	Bror Fock	SWE	50:15.8
18.	Thomas Humphreys	GBR	50:28.0
19.	Olaf Hovdenak	NOR	50:40.8

20.	Parelius Finnerud	NOR	51:16.2
21.	Gustav "Gusten" Carlén	SWE	51:26.8
22.	Johannes Andersen	NOR	51:47.4
23.	Viggo Pedersen	DEN	53:00.8
24.	Louis Scott	USA	53:51.4
25.	Väinö Heikkilä	FIN	54:08.0
26.	Gerhard Topp[181]	DEN	54:24.9
27.	Gregor Vietz	GER	54:40.6
28.	Steen Rasmussen	DEN	55:27.0
AC.	Emmerich Rath	AUT	DNF
	Holger Baden	DEN	DNF
	Fritz Danild	DEN	DNF
	Karl Jensen	DEN	DNF
	Efraim Harju	FIN	DNF
	K. Aarne Lindholm (Linnolahti)	FIN	DNF
	Jean Bouin	FRA	DNF
	William Cottrill	GBR	DNF[182]
	William Scott	GBR	DNF
	Nils Dahl	NOR	DNF
	Edvin Hellgren	SWE	DNF
	John Klintberg	SWE	DNF
	Axel Lindahl	SWE	DNF
	Henrik Nordström	SWE	DNF
	George Bonhag	USA	DNF[183]
	Tell Berna	USA	DNF
	William Kramer	USA	DNF
184			

Diplomas of Merit[185]

Wilhelm "Ville" Kyrönen (FIN), Leonard Richardson (RSA), Brynolf Larsson (SWE), Johan Sundkvist (SWE), Franz "Viljam" Johansson (FIN), and Harry Hellawell (USA)

Cross-Country Race, Team

A: 41[186]; C: 6; D: 15 July; T: 1415; F: c. 12,000 meters. Point-for-place scoring from the individual event, with the top three finishers for each team counting in the team scoring (ns = nonscoring team member).

The team cross-country title was determined by using the scores of the top three finishers from each team competing in the individual cross-country event. At the international cross-country meet, England would win the championship from 1903 to 1914, but this event was basically contested by the British Isles nations and France.

Although Hannes Kolehmainen won the race, Sweden's finishes of second, third, and fifth narrowly brought Sweden the gold medal over Finland. Great Britain was a distant third.

1. Sweden   10
(Hjalmar Andersson [2], John Eke [3], Josef Ternström [5], Axel Lindahl [ns], Bror Fock [ns], Brynolf Larsson [ns], Edvin Hellgren [ns], Gustav "Gusten" Carlén [ns], Henrik Nordström [ns], Johan Sundkvist [ns], John Klintberg [ns], Klas Lundström [ns])

2. Finland   11
(Hannes Kolehmainen [1], Jalmari "Lauri" Eskola [4], Albin Stenroos [6], K. Aarne Lindholm (Linnolahti) [ns], Efraim Harju [ns], Franz "Viljam" Johansson [ns], Väinö Heikkilä
[ns], Wilhelm "Ville" Kyrönen [ns])

3. Great Britain   49
(Frederick Hibbins [15], Ernest Glover [16], Thomas Humphreys [18], William Cottrill
[ns/dnf], William Scott [ns/dnf][187])

4. Norway   61
(Olaf Hovdenak [19], Parelius Finnerud [20], Johannes Andersen [22], Nils Dahl [ns])

5. Denmark   63
(Lauritz Christiansen [14], Viggo Pedersen [23], Gerhard Topp [26], Karl Jensen [ns], Fritz
Danild [ns], Holger Baden [ns], Steen Rasmussen [ns])

AC. United States   DNF
(Harry Hellawell [12], Louis Scott [24], George Bonhag [ns], Tell Berna [ns][188], William
Kramer [ns])

110 Meter Hurdles

A: 22[189]; C: 10; D: 11–12 July.

America's hurdlers had been pre-eminent at all the early Olympics, and in 1912 it was
difficult to pick a favorite among the nine American hurdlers entered. The three U.S. Olympic
Trials had been won by Fred Kelly (west), John Case (central), and Vaughn Blanchard (east).
Case had also been AAU champion in 1910.

All nine Americans advanced to the six semifinals, where only the winner of each heat
advanced to the final. There, in the final, Britain's Kenneth Powell met five Americans. Kelly,
John Nicholson, and James Wendell held the lead at the halfway mark, but Nicholson fell at
the eighth hurdle. Kelly held on to win by a narrow margin over Wendell.

Final A: 6; C: 2; D: 12 July; T: 1500.

1. Frederick Kelly	USA	15.1	
2. James Wendell	USA	15.2	
3. Martin Hawkins	USA	15.3	
4. John Case	USA	15.3 est	
5. Kenneth Powell	GBR	15.5 est	
AC. John Nicholson	USA	DNF[190]	

Diplomas of Merit

John Case (USA), Kenneth Powell (GBR), John Nicholson (USA)

Semifinals A: 20; C: 9; D: 11 July; T: 1615; F: Winner of each heat
advanced to the final.

Heat One A: 4; C: 4.

1. Kenneth Powell	GBR	15.6	Q
2. John Eller, Jr.	USA	15.7 est	

3. Ferdinand Bie	NOR	15.8 est	
4. Pablo Eitel	CHI		

Heat Two A: 4; C: 4.

1. Martin Hawkins	USA	15.7	Q
2. Daciano Colbacchini	ITA	16.0 est	
3. Marius Delaby	FRA	16.2 est	
Károly Solymár Stollmár	HUN	DNF	

Heat Three A: 3; C: 2.

1. John Nicholson	USA	15.4	Q
2. Hermann von Bönninghausen	GER	15.9 est	
3. Vaughn Blanchard	USA	16.0 est	

Heat Four A: 3; C: 2.

1. James Wendell	USA	15.5	Q
2. George Chisholm	USA	15.7 est	
AC. Gerard Anderson	GBR	DNF[191]	

Heat Five A: 3; C: 3.

1. Frederick Kelly	USA	15.6	Q
2. Valdemar Wickholm	FIN	16.6 est	
3. Henry Blakeney	GBR	[192]	

Heat Six A: 3; C: 3.

1. John Case	USA	15.6	Q
2. Edwin Pritchard	USA	15.6 est	
3. Georges André	FRA		

Round One A: 22; C: 10; D: 11 July; T: 0930; F: Top two finishers in each heat advanced to the semifinals.

Heat One A: 2; C: 2.

1. George Chisholm	USA	15.3	Q
2. Károly Solymár Stollmár[194]	HUN	15.8[193]	Q

Heat Two A: 2; C: 2.

1. John Eller, Jr.	USA	16.0[195]	Q
2. Gerard Anderson[197]	GBR	18.6[196]	Q

Heat Three A: 2; C: 2.

1. Martin Hawkins	USA	16.1	Q
2. Georges André[198]	FRA	16.8	Q

Heat Four A: 2; C: 2.

1. Ferdinand Bie	NOR	16.2	Q
2. Valdemar Wickholm	FIN	16.6	Q

199

Heat Five A: 1; C: 1.

1. Pablo Eitel	CHI	17.2[200]	Q (walkover)

201

Heat Six A: 3; C: 3.

1. Marius Delaby	FRA	16.0[202]	Q
2. Vaughn Blanchard	USA	16.0[203]	Q
3. Alfredo Pagani	ITA		

204

Heat Seven A: 2; C: 2.

1. Edwin Pritchard	USA	16.4[205]	Q
2. Henry Blakeney	GBR	17.4[206]	Q

207

Heat Eight A: 2; C: 2.

1. John Nicholson	USA	15.5	Q
2. Daciano Colbacchini	ITA	16.1	Q

Heat Nine A: 1; C: 1.

1. Frederick Kelly	USA	16.4[208]	Q (walkover)

Heat Ten A: 2; C: 2.

1. John Case	USA	16.3	Q
2. Hermann von Bönninghausen	GER	17.0[209]	Q

Heat Eleven A: 3; C: 3.

1. Kenneth Powell	GBR	15.6[210]	Q
2. James Wendell	USA	15.7	Q
3. Frank Lukeman	CAN		

Heat Twelve not held[211]

10 Kilometer Walk

A: 22; C: 11; D: 8, 11 July.

The ten-kilometer walk appeared on the Olympic program for the first time in 1912, although it would be an Olympic event in 1912–1924, and 1948–52. The pre–Olympic favorites were both British — George Larner who had won both walks at the 1908 Olympics, and had won the AAA seven-mile walk in 1911, and Ernest Webb who had won the AAA seven-mile walk 1908–1910, and was the silver medalist in both walks at the 1908 Olympics. The world best in 1912 was 45:43.5 set by Paul Gunia (GER) in Berlin on 24 October 1908. For unknown reasons, neither Larner nor Gunia competed and in their absence, Webb was expected to win easily.

However, Webb could not match Canada's George Goulding, who had also competed at the 1908 Olympics. At London, Goulding had placed fourth in the 3,500 meter walk, did not finish in his heat of the ten-mile walk, and also ran the marathon, finishing 22nd. However, since 1908, Goulding had greatly improved and had beaten Webb at match races in Toronto in the summer of 1910. After winning the gold medal, Goulding's first act was to send a telegram to his wife. It read only, "Won — George."

Goulding spoke more of the final, as given in Henry Roxborough's *Canada at the Olympics*. "In the final, I took the lead right from the start. When I was about 40 yards ahead of Webb, I thought the judges were after me. One of them said something in Swedish which I didn't understand; but when I turned toward him I saw a broad grin on his face and concluded he must have said something nice. Still, it was a ticklish moment, for the judges had the right to pull anyone off the track without previous warnings. With other judges, I could have improved my time; but during the last mile, when I had a lead of about 75 yards, I slowed considerably and took no chance of being disqualified. Besides, in the first heat, I had rubbed the skin off my toes, while wearing almost new shoes; and in the final my feet were really torturing. However, in winning, I soon forgot the pain and remembered only the pleasure."[212]

Final A: 10; C: 6; D: 11 July; T: 1115.

1.	George Goulding	CAN	46:28.4	OR
2.	Ernest Webb	GBR	46:50.4	
3.	Fernando Altimani	ITA	47:37.6	
4.	Aage Rasmussen	DEN	48:00.0	
AC.	Vilhelm Gylche	DEN	DNF[213]	
	William Palmer	GBR	DNF[214]	
	Frederick Kaiser	USA	DNF[215]	
	Arthur St. Norman	RSA	DQ[216]	
	Thomas Dumbill	GBR	DQ[217]	
	William Yates	GBR	DQ[218]	

Diploma of Merit

Aage Rasmussen (DEN)

Round One A: 22; C: 11; D: 8 July; T: 0930; F: Top five finishers in each heat advanced to the final.

Heat One A: 9; C: 7; D: 8 July.

1.	George Goulding	CAN	47:14.5	Q	OR
2.	Ernest Webb	GBR	47:25.4	Q	
3.	Aage Rasmussen	DEN	48:15.8	Q	
4.	Fernando Altimani	ITA	48:54.2	Q	
5.	William Palmer	GBR	51:21.0	Q	
6.	Samuel Schwartz	USA	53:30.8		
7.	Edward Renz	USA	53:30.8		
AC.	Rudolf Richter	BOH	DNF		
	Kaarel Lukk	RUS	DNF		

219

Heat Two A: 13; C: 8; D: 8 July.

1.	William Yates	GBR	49:43.6	Q

2.	Arthur St. Norman	RSA	50:17.9	Q
3.	Thomas Dumbill	GBR	50:57.6	Q
4.	Vilhelm Gylche	DEN	51:13.8	Q
5.	Frederick Kaiser	USA	51:31.8	Q
6.	Alfred Voellmeke	USA	52:29.2	
7.	Rolando Salinas	CHI	55:02.0	
8.	Henrik Ripszám, Jr.	HUN[220]	55:20.6	
9.	Aleksis Ayde	RUS	59:24.2	
AC.	Niels Pedersen	DEN	DQ[221]	
	Robert Bridge	GBR	DQ[222]	
	William Murray	AUS	DQ	
	István Drubina	HUN	DNF/DQ[223]	

[224]

4 × 100 Meter Relay

A: 33; C: 8; D: 8–9 July.

With five of the six finalists in the 100 meters, the United States was a heavy favorite. But after walking over in round one, the U.S. was disqualified in the first heat of the semis for a baton exchange outside the zone.

The finalists were Great Britain, Sweden, and Germany. In the semifinals, each of the winners broke the previous world record of 43.5, which had been set by a German team on 19 May 1912. Germany recorded 42.3 in winning heat three and was favored in the final, in the United States' absence. But Germany also fell prey to a faulty baton pass in the final, and was disqualified.

However, the later penalty notwithstanding, Germany did not win the race. Great Britain held them off, with Willie Applegarth refusing to allow Richard Rau to pass him in the final straight. Both were timed at 42.4, but Britain won by a few centimeters. After the German disqualification, Sweden was awarded the silver medal.

Final A: 12; C: 3; D: 9 July; T: 1600.

1. Great Britain   42.4
   (David Jacobs, Henry Macintosh, Victor d'Arcy, William Applegarth)

2. Sweden   42.6
   (Ivan Möller, Karl August "Charles" Luther, Ture Person, Knut "Knatten" Lindberg)

AC. Germany   DQ [42.4][225]
   (Otto Röhr, Max Herrmann, Erwin Kern, Richard Rau[226])

Semifinals A: 24; C: 6; D: 8 July; T: 1530; F: Winner of each heat advanced to the final.

Heat One A: 8; C: 2.

1. Great Britain   43.0   Q   WR
   (David Jacobs, Henry Macintosh, Victor d'Arcy, William Applegarth)

AC. United States   DQ [42.2][227]
   (J. Ira Courtney, Frank Belote, Clement Wilson, Carl Cooke)

Heat Two A: 8; C: 2.

1. Sweden   42.5   Q   WR
(Ivan Möller, Karl August "Charles" Luther, Ture Person, Knut "Knatten" Lindberg)

2. Hungary   42.9
(Ferenc Szobota, Vilmos Rácz, Pál Szalay, István Jankovich)

Heat Three A: 8; C: 2.

1. Germany   42.3   Q   WR
(Otto Röhr, Max Herrmann, Erwin Kern, Richard Rau)

2. Canada   43.5
(Frank McConnell, Frank Lukeman, Harry Beasley, John Howard)

    Round One A: 32; C: 8; D: 8 July; T: 1200; F: Winner of each heat
    advanced to the semifinals.

Heat One A: 4; C: 1.

1. Canada   46.2[228]   Q   OR
(Frank McConnell, Frank Lukeman, Harry Beasley, John Howard)
[229]

Heat Two A: 4; C: 1.

1. United States   43.7[230]   Q   OR
(Ira Courtney, Frank Belote, Clement Wilson, Carl Cooke)
[231]

Heat Three A: 4; C: 1.

1. Great Britain   45.0   Q   (walkover)
(David Jacobs, Henry Macintosh, Victor d'Arcy, William Applegarth)
[232]

Heat Four A: 4; C: 1.

1. Sweden   43.6[233]   Q   OR
(Ivan Möller, Karl August "Charles" Luther, Ture Person, Knut "Knatten" Lindberg)
[234]

Heat Five A: 8; C: 2.

1. Germany   43.6   Q   =OR
(Karl von Halt, Max Herrmann, Erwin Kern, Richard Rau)

2. Austria   44.8
(Gustav Krojer, Rudolf Rauch, Fritz Weinzinger, Fritz Fleischer)

Heat Six A: 8; C: 2.[235]

1. Hungary   43.7   Q
(Ferenc Szobota, Vilmos Rácz, Pál Szalay, István Jankovich)

2. France   43.8
(Pierre Failliot, Georges Rolot, Charles Lelong, René Mourlon)
[236]

4 × 400 Meter Relay

A: 28; C: 7; D: 14–15 July.

This was the first time this event was on the Olympic program. In 1908, a 1,600 meter medley relay (200, 200, 400, 800) had been contested at the London Olympics. The world record for the 4 × 400 relay was 3:18.2 which had been set on 4 September 1911 by the Irish-American Athletic Club of New York.

With four of the five 400 meter finalists, the United States was heavily favored. There were three heats, and the U.S., Great Britain, and France advanced to the final, with Britain posting the fastest qualifying time — 3:19.0.

The final was no contest as the favored Americans shattered the world record, running 3:16.6. Britain was hampered when their lead-off runner, George Nicol, pulled up and limped most of his lap, allowing France to garner the silver medal.

Britain's third runner was James Soutter. Shortly after the Olympics, in 1913, he forsook track athletics in favor of the gospel ministry and was ordained the minister of the Scots Kirk in Nairobi, the first Scottish minister in Kenya. He returned to Scotland in 1917 and became minister of the parish of Whitekirk and Tynninghame, East Lothian where he served until he retired in 1949. In early August 1966, he oddly disappeared one day, and was never found, being presumed dead on 8 August 1966.

Final A: 12; C: 3; D: 15 July; T: 1430.

1. United States					3:16.6					WR
(Melvin Sheppard, Edward Lindberg, James "Ted" Meredith, Charles Reidpath)

2. France						3:20.7
(Charles Lelong, Robert Schurrer, Pierre Failliot, Charles Poulenard)

3. Great Britain					3:23.2
(George Nicol, Ernest Henley, James Soutter, Cyril Seedhouse)

Round One A: 28; C: 7; D: 14 July; T: 1445; F: Winner of each heat advanced to the final.

Heat One A: 8; C: 2.[237]

1. Great Britain					3:19.0			Q			OR
(George Nicol, Ernest Henley, James Soutter, Cyril Seedhouse)

2. Canada						3:22.2
(G. Melville Brock, John Howard, Thomas Gallon, J. Lindsay Tait)
[238]

Heat Two A: 8; C: 2.[239]

1. United States					3:23.3			Q
(Melvin Sheppard,[240] Edward Lindberg, James "Ted" Meredith, Charles Reidpath)

2. Germany						3:28.2
(Hanns Braun, Max Herrmann, Hermann Burkowitz, Erich Lehmann)
[241]

Heat Three A: 12; C: 3.[242]

1. France						3:22.5			Q
(Charles Lelong, Robert Schurrer, Pierre Failliot, Charles Poulenard)

2. Sweden   3:25.0
(Paul Zerling, John Dahlin, Eric Lindholm, Knut Stenborg)

3. Hungary   3:29.4
(Ervin Szerelemhegyi, Ödön Bodor, István Déván, Frigyes Mezei Wiesner)
[243]

3,000 Meter Team Race

A: 24; C: 5; D: 12–13 July.

A team race had been contested at the 1900 Olympics over 5,000 meters. A 3,000 meter team race was held at the Olympics in 1912, 1920, and 1924. In 1912, the event was decided by teams of five runners each, with the places of the best three runners constituting the team score.

In a major upset in heat one of the first round, the United States defeated Finland, which was led by the redoubtable Hannes Kolehmainen. In the final, the United States won the gold medal, with Sweden second and Britain third. Great Britain's bronze medal was earned despite the fact that they did not defeat a single team in the event—in round one, they received a walkover, and in the final, they finished last.

Final A: 15; C: 3; D: 13 July; T: 1530.

1. United States   9
(Tell Berna [1/8:44.6], Norman Taber [3/8:45.2], George Bonhag [5/8:46.6], Abel Kiviat [ns{dnf}/—, Louis Scott [ns{dnf}/—)

2. Sweden   13
(Thorild Olsson [2/8:44.6], Ernst Wide [4/8:46.2], Bror Fock [7/8:47.1], John Zander [ns{10}/8:48.9], Nils Frykberg [ns{11}/8:49.0])

3. Great Britain   23
(William Cottrill [6/8:46.8], George Hutson [8/8:47.2], Cyril Porter [9/8:48.0], Edward Owen [ns{12}/—[244]], William Moore [ns{dnf}/—)

> *Round One* A: 24; C: 5; D: 12 July; T: 1500; F: Winning team in each heat advanced to the final. Only the top three scorers for each team counted towards the final team score.

Heat One A: 10; C: 2[245]; D: 12 July.

1. United States   9   Q
(Abel Kiviat [2/8:46.3], Tell Berna [3/8:50.1], Norman Taber [4/8:51.1], George Bonhag [ns{5}/8:52.2], H. Louis Scott [ns{6}/8:53.4])

2. Finland   12
(Hannes Kolehmainen [1/8:36.9 (WR)], Albin Stenroos [5{7}/8:54.1], Franz "Viljam" Johansson [6{8}/8:57.2], Aarne Lindholm [ns{9}/9:46.4], Efraim Harju [ns{10}/10:10.6])
[246]

Heat Two A: 9; C: 2; D: 12 July.

1. Sweden   9[247]   Q
(Bror Fock [=2/9:14.7], Nils Frykberg [=2/9:14.7], Ernst Wide [=2/9:14.7], Thorild Olsson [=2/9:14.7], John Zander [=2/9:14.7])

2. Germany   12
(Erwin von Sigel [1/9:06.8], Georg Amberger [5{7}/9:32.5], Gregor Vietz [6{8}/9:34.2],
   Georg Mickler [ns{dnf}/—])
[248]

Heat Three A: 5; C: 1[249]; D: 12 July.

1. Great Britain   walkover   Q
(William Cottrill [10:21.6], George Hutson [10:21.6], Cyril Porter [10:21.6], Edward Owen
   [10:21.6], William Moore [10:21.6])[250]
[251]

High Jump

A: 37[252]; C: 10; D: 7–8 July.

Based on recent results, the favorite was definitely George Horine of the United States, although there were several top American jumpers. Horine had set a world record on 29 March 1912, clearing 1.985 (6-6⅛) at Stanford to break Mike Sweeney's record of 1.97 (6-5⅝) which had stood since 1895. And at the western Olympic trial, held on 18 May, he set another world record, clearing 6-7, the first person to jump two meters (6-7 = 2.007). Horine was a pioneer of a new high jumping style, which later became termed the Western Roll, somewhat similar to the straddle roll, the standard jumping style until Dick Fosbury pioneered the Fosbury Flop. The other top Americans were Egon Erickson, who had won the AAU title in 1909 and the Eastern Olympic Trial in 1912, and Alma Richards, who had recently won the Central Olympic Trial.

The competition initially went about as expected, with Horine, Richards and Erickson lasting until the final five jumpers, joined by Germany's Hans Liesche, and Jim Thorpe. Erickson and Thorpe went out first, failing to clear 1.89 meters. At 1.91, Liesche cleared on his second attempt, Richards on his last attempt, and Horine failed, leaving him with the bronze medal. When the bar was raised to 1.93 (6-4), Richards cleared easily on his first attempt. David Wallechinsky has described the problems that then ensued for Liesche, "Liesche was completely unnerved. He failed twice. Then, just as he had composed himself for his final attempt, a gun went off to signal the start of a race. Liesche waited for the race to end and then composed himself once more. This time the band began to play. After nine minutes, a Swedish official approached him and asked him to hurry up. This was the final blow. Liesche ran at the bar, but missed completely."[253]

Final A: 11; C: 5; D: 8 July; T: 1500.

					160	170	175	180	183	185	187	189	191	193
1.	Alma Richards	USA	1.93	OR	o	o	o	xo	xxo	o	xxo	xxo	xxo[254]	o[255]
2.	Hans Liesche	GER	1.91		o	o	o	o	o	o	o	xo	xo[256]	xxx
3.	George Horine	USA	1.89		o	o	o	o	xo	o	o	xo	xxx	
=4.	Egon Erickson	USA	1.87		o	o	o	o	o	xo	xo	xxx		
	Jim Thorpe[257]	USA	1.87		xo	o	o	o	o	o	o	xxx		
=6.[258]	Harry Grumpelt	USA	1.85		o	o	o	xo	o	xxo	xxx			
	John Johnstone	USA	1.85		o	o	o	o	xxo	xo	xxx			
8.	Karl-Axel Kullerstrand	SWE	1.83		o	o	o	xo	o	xxx				
=9.	Iván, Baron Wardener	HUN	1.80		o	o	o	xo	xxx					
	Timothy Carroll	GBR	1.80		o	o	o	xo	xxx					
11.	Benjamin Baker	GBR	1.75		o	o	o	xxx						

Diplomas of Merit

Egon Erickson (USA), Jim Thorpe (USA), Harry Grumpelt (USA), John Johnstone (USA), Karl-Axel Kullerstrand (SWE)

> *Qualifying Round* A: 37; C: 10; D: 7 July; T: 0900; F: Qualifiers were separated into three groups. All those clearing 1.83 meters qualified for the final.

Group One A: 19; C: 8.

				160	*170*	*175*	*180*	*183*
=1. Timothy Carroll	GBR	1.83	Q	xo	o	xxo	o	xo
Benjamin Baker	GBR	1.83	Q	xo	o	o	o	o
John Johnstone	USA	1.83	Q		o	o	xo	xo
=4. Gösta Hallberg	SWE	1.75		x	o	xo	xxx	
Otto Monsen	NOR	1.75			xo	xo	xxx	
Gerhard Meling (Olsen)	NOR	1.75			xo	xxxo	xxx	
=7. Ragnar Mattson	SWE	1.70		x	xo	xxx		
Paulus af Uhr	SWE	1.70		x	xo	xxx		
Thomas O'Donoghue	GBR	1.70			o			
Platt Adams	USA	1.70		o	o			
=11. Lajos Ludinszky	HUN	1.60		o	x—			
Gustaf "Gösta" Holmér	SWE	1.60		o	x—			
Rodolfo Hammersley	CHI	1.60		o	x—			
Michel Henri Meerz	FRA	1.60		o	x—			
Thage Brauer	SWE	1.60		o	x—			
AC. Marius Delaby	FRA	NH			x—			
Angelo Tonini	ITA	NH		x	xxx			
John Nicholson	USA	NH			xxx			
Armand Estang	FRA	NH			x—			

259

Group Two A: 10; C: 5.

				160	*170*	*175*	*180*	*183*
=1. Hans Liesche	GER	1.83	Q	o	o	o	o	o
Iván, Baron Wardener	HUN	1.83	Q	o	o	o	o	o
Egon Erickson	USA	1.83	Q	o	o	o	xo	o
Harry Grumpelt	USA	1.83	Q	o	o	xo	o	o
George Horine	USA	1.83	Q	o	o	o	o	xo
6. Jervis Burdick	USA	1.80		o	o	o	xo	xxx
=7. Harold Enright	USA	1.75		o	o	xo	xxx	
Richard Sjöberg	SWE	1.75		o	o	o	xxx	
Otto Röhr	GER	1.75		o	xo	xxo	xxx	
Arvo Laine	FIN	1.75		o	xo	o	xxx	

260

Group Three A: 8; C: 5.

				160	*170*	*175*	*180*	*183*
=1. Karl-Axel Kullerstrand	SWE	1.83	Q	o	o	o	o	o

				160	170	175	180	183
Alma Richards	USA	1.83	Q	o	o	o	xo	o
Jim Thorpe	USA	1.83	Q	o	o	xo	o	xxo
=4. André Labat[261]	FRA	1.75		o	xo	xxo	xxx	
Wesley Oler	USA	1.75		o	o	o	xxx	
Ole Aarnæs	NOR	1.75		o	xo	xxo	xxx	
7. Georges André	FRA	1.70		xo	xo	xxx		
8. Alfredo Pagani	ITA	1.60		o	xxx			

[262]

Standing High Jump

A: 18[263]; C: 9[264]; D: 13 July.

Ray Ewry had won the standing high jump every time it had been contested at the Olympics, from 1900 to 1908, with four consecutive victories. But he retired in early 1911 and was not present in Stockholm. In 1909 and 1910, Platt Adams had won the AAU indoor title in this event, although Ewry did not compete in either year. After Ewry's retirement, Adams seemed poised to take over as the top standing jumper. For the second time in Olympic history, brothers won the gold and silver medals, with Platt defeating his brother, Ben. This feat had been accomplished at Athens in 1896, in the 25-meter military pistol event, in which John Paine won the gold medal and his brother, Sumner, the silver. The standing high jump was never again contested at the Olympics.

Final A: 6; C: 3; D: 13 July; T: 1600.

			130	140	145	150	155	160	163	166
1. Platt Adams	USA	1.63	o	o	o	o	o	xo	o	xxx
2. Ben Adams	USA	1.60	o	o	o	o	o	o	xxx	
3. Konstantinos Tsiklitiras	GRE	1.55	o	o	o	xo	xo	xxx		
=4. Leslie Byrd	USA	1.50	o	o	o	xo	xxx			
Leo Goehring	USA	1.50	o	xo	o	o	xxx			
Edvin Möller	SWE	1.50	o	o	o	o	xxx			

Diplomas of Merit

Leslie Byrd (USA), Leo Goehring (USA), Edvin Möller (SWE)

Qualifying Round A: 18; C: 9; D: 13 July; T: 0930; F: Qualifiers were separated into three groups. All those clearing 1.50 meters advanced to the final.

Group One A: 5; C: 5.

			130	135	140	145	148	150
1. Platt Adams	USA	1.50	Q o	o	o	o	o	o
2. Karl Bergh	SWE	1.45	o	o	o	xo	xxx	
=3. Rodolfo Hammersley	CHI	1.40	o	o	o	xxx		
Birger Brodtkorb	NOR	1.40	xo	xo	xo	xxx		
5. Benjamin Baker	GBR	1.35	xo	o	xxx			

[265]

Group Two A: 8; C: 4.

				130	*135*	*140*	*145*	*150*
=1. Ben Adams	USA	1.50	Q	o	o	o	o	o
Konstantinos Tsiklitiras	GRE	1.50	Q	o	o	o	o	o
Leslie Byrd	USA	1.50	Q	o	o	o	o	xxo
Leo Goehring	USA	1.50	Q	o	o	o	xxo	xo
=5. Forest Fletcher	USA	1.45		o	o	o	o	xxx
Rudolf Smedmark	SWE	1.45		o	o	o	o	xxx
Frank Belote	USA	1.45		o	o	xxo	o	xxx
8. Alfred Schwarz	RUS	1.40		o	o	o	xxx	

266

Group Three A: 5; C: 3.

				130	*135*	*140*	*145*	*150*
1. Edvin Möller	SWE	1.50	Q	o	o	o	o	o
=2. Leif Ekman	SWE	1.45		o	o	o	xxo	xxx
Georges André	FRA	1.45		p	o	xo	xo	xxx
4. Helmer Måhl[267]	SWE	1.30		o	p			
AC. Andor Horvag[268]	HUN	NH		p	xxx			

269

Pole Vault

A: 25[270]; C: 11; D: 10–11 July.

In this era, the United States absolutely dominated pole vaulting. In fact, the final came down to 11 vaulters, eight of them American, with lone athletes from Canada, Germany, and Sweden. There was no clear American favorite.

A review of recent performances shows how open the competition would be among the United States' vaulters. The most recent AAU titles had been won as follows: 1909 — Roy Paulding; 1910 — Harold Babcock; and 1911 — a three-way tie between Edwin Cook, Frank Coyle, and Sam Bellah. Cook was the defending Olympic champion, having shared the 1908 gold medal with A. C. Gilbert. The three U.S. Olympic trials went as follows: Western — Bellah won; Central — Frank Murphy won, with Coyle second; and Eastern — Marc Wright won, with Frank Nelson second.

The world record had also taken a recent beating by the American vault crew. At the beginning of 1912, the mark stood at 3.93, set in Boulder, Colorado on 27 May 1910 by Leland Scott. But at the IC4A title in Philadelphia on 1 June 1912, Yale's Robert Gardner won, clearing 3.985 (13-1), the first 13-foot vault. The mark lasted only a week, as Marc Wright won the eastern Olympic trial with the first four-meter vault, clearing 13-2¼ (4.02).

Of the abovementioned American vaulters, all but Cook, Gilbert, Paulding, and Gardner competed at Stockholm, giving the United States six top vaulters from which to choose. Among other nations, the Swedes championed Bertil Uggla, while Canada sent William Happenny, who had been United States AAU champion in 1908 and would win the Canadian championship 1911–1913.

The final six vaulters came down to Uggla, Happenny, and four Americans — Babcock, Nelson, Wright and Murphy. At 3.85 meters, Happenny had to withdraw, having broken two ribs in clearing 3.80. He was joined by Uggla and Murphy who failed to clear 3.85. At 3.85, Harold Babcock cleared on his first attempt, while Nelson and Wright needed two efforts. But when the bar was raised to 3.95, only Babcock was successful, again on one attempt. He took three shots at a new world record of 4.06 (13-3¾) but failed.

Final A: 11; C: 4; D: 11 July; T: 1515.

				340	350	360	365	375[271]	380[272]	385[273]	395[274]	406
1.	Harold Babcock	USA	3.95 OR	o	o	o	p	o	o	o	o	xxx
=2.	Frank Nelson	USA	3.85	o	o	o	xo	o	o	xo	xxx	
	Marc Wright	USA	3.85	o	o	o	o	xo	xo	xo	xxx	
=3.	Bertil Uggla	SWE	3.80	o	o	o	o	o	xo	xxx		
	William Happenny	CAN	3.80	o	xo	o	o	xo	xo	p[275]		
	Frank Murphy	USA	3.80	o	o	xo	xo	o	o	xxx		
7.	Samuel Bellah	USA	3.75	o	o	xo	o	xo	xxx			
=8.	Frank Coyle	USA	3.65	o	o	xo	xo	xxx				
	Gordon Dukes	USA	3.65	o	o	o	xxo	xxx				
	Bill Fritz	USA	3.65	o	xo	xo	xxo	xxx				
11.	Robert Pasemann	GER	3.40	xo	xxx							

Diploma of Merit

Samuel Bellah (USA)

> *Qualifying Round* A: 25; C: 11; D: 10 July; T: 1415; F: Qualifiers were separated into two groups. All those clearing 3.65 meters advanced to the final.

Group One A: 11; C: 7.

					300	320	340	350	360	365
=1.	Frank Nelson	USA	3.65	Q	o		o	o	o	xo
	Robert Pasemann	GER	3.65	Q	o	o	o	o	xxo	o
	Bertil Uggla	SWE	3.65	Q	o	o	o	o	o	xo
	Harold Babcock	USA	3.65	Q		o	o	o	o	o
	William Happenny	CAN	3.65	Q			o	o	o	o
	Gordon Dukes	USA	3.65	Q		xxo	o	xxo	o	o
7.	Carl Hårleman	SWE	3.60			xo	o	xo	o	xxx
8.	Fernand Gonder	FRA	3.50		xo	xo	o	o	xxx	
=9.	Georgios Banikas	GRE	3.20		xo	xo	xxx			
	Magnus "Manne" Nilsson	SWE	3.20			o	xxx			
AC.	Johannes Martin	RUS	NH		xxx					

276

Group Two A: 14; C: 7.

					300	320	340	350	360	365
=1.	Marc Wright	USA	3.65	Q			o	o	o	xo
	Frank Murphy	USA	3.65	Q		o	o	o	xxo	o
	Samuel Bellah	USA	3.65	Q			xo	xxo	xo	o
	Frank Coyle	USA	3.65	Q			o	o	o	xxo
	Bill Fritz	USA	3.65	Q		o	o	o	o	o

			300	320	340	350	360	365
=6. Richard Sjöberg	SWE	3.60	o	o	o	o	xxo	xxx
Clas Gille	SWE	3.60		o	o	xxo	xxx	
=8. Fritz Bøchen Vikke	DEN	3.40	o	o	o	xxx		
Ulrich Baasch	RUS	3.40	o	o	o	xxx		
=10. Hugo Svensson	SWE	3.20	o	o	xxx			
Carl Sander Santesson	SWE	3.20	xo	o	xxx			
Viktor Franzl	AUT	3.20	xxo	o	xxx			
=13. Jindřich Jirsák	BOH	3.00	o	xxx				
Manlio Legat	ITA	3.00	o	xxx				

[277]

Broad (Long) Jump

A: 30[278]; C: 13[279]; D: 12 July.

Frank Irons (USA) was the defending champion and Olympic record holder and in 1912 he won the central U.S. Olympic trial. He was present at Stockholm and was a slight favorite, having won the AAU Championship in 1909 and 1910. But he did not jump well, placing fifth in group one of the qualifying, failing to advance to the final, and finishing ninth overall.

In his first jump in qualifying, America's Albert Gutterson set a new Olympic record with 7.60, which easily qualified him for the final and led the qualifiers. He was joined there by Canada's Calvin Bricker and Sweden's Georg Åberg. In the final, neither Bricker nor Åberg threatened Gutterson, who won the gold medal although he did not approach his qualifying mark with his final jumps. Bricker did not improve his qualifying mark of 7.21 and placed second. Åberg did improve to 7.18 in the final, but still finished third.

Final A: 3; C: 2; D: 12 July; T: 1400.

1.	Albert Gutterson	USA	7.60	OR	(718 709 709)
2.	Calvin Bricker	CAN	7.21		(704 685 -)
3.	Georg Åberg	SWE	7.18		(698 718 663)

Diplomas of Merit

Harry Worthington (USA), Eugene Mercer (USA), Fred Allen (USA)

Final Standings

1.	Albert Gutterson	USA	7.60
2.	Calvin Bricker	CAN	7.21
3.	Georg Åberg	SWE	7.18
4.	Harry Worthington	USA	7.03
5.	Eugene Mercer	USA	6.97
6.	Fred Allen	USA	6.94
7.	Jim Thorpe[280]	USA	6.89
8.[281]	Robert Pasemann	GER	6.82
9.	Francis Irons	USA	6.80
10.	Henry Ashington	GBR	6.78
11.	Ferdinand Bie	NOR	6.75

12.	Sidney Abrahams	GBR	6.72	
13.	Nils Fixdal	NOR	6.71	[6.65]
14.	Edward Farrell	USA	6.71	[6.46]
15.	Philip Kingsford	GBR	6.65	
16.	Andre Campana	FRA	6.64	
17.	Charles Lomberg	SWE	6.62	
18.	Viktor Franzl	AUT	6.57	
19.	Angelo Tonini	ITA	6.44	
20.	Patrik Ohlsson	SWE	6.28	
21.	Gustav Betzén	SWE	6.24	
22.	Aleksandr Schultz	RUS	6.15	
23.	Philipp Ehrenreich	AUT	6.14	
24.	Emil Kukko (Skarra)	FIN	6.11	
25.	Pál Szalay	HUN	5.98	
26.	Nándor Kovács	HUN	5.96	
27.	Alfredo Pagani	ITA	5.95	
28.	Arthur Maranda	CAN	5.87	
29.	Manlio Legat	ITA	5.50	
AC.	Paul Fournelle	LUX	NM	

Qualifying Round A: 30; C: 13; D: 12 July; T: 1400; F: Qualifiers were separated into four groups (combined into three).[282] Top three jumpers qualified for the final.

Group One A: 10; C: 8.

1.	Albert Gutterson	USA	7.60	Q OR	(760or 748 725)
2.	Georg Åberg	SWE	7.04	Q	(704 670 699)
3.	Fred Allen	USA	6.94		(- 694 691)
4.	Robert Pasemann	GER	6.82		(682 680 654)
5.	Francis Irons	USA	6.80		(- 680 672)
6.	Andre Campana	FRA	6.64		(621 664 655)
7.	Angelo Tonini	ITA	6.44		(625 644 -)
8.	Aleksandr Schultz	RUS	6.15		(580 597 615)
9.	Emil Kukko (Skarra)	FIN	6.11		(611 592 598)
10.	Pál Szalay	HUN	5.98		(598 - -)

283

Groups Two and Three[284] A: 12; C: 8.

1.	Calvin Bricker [G3]	CAN	7.21	Q	(692 707 721)
2.	Eugene Mercer [G2]	USA	6.97		(697 684 684)
3.	Henry Ashington [G3]	GBR	6.78		(661 678 -)
4.	Ferdinand Bie [G2]	NOR	6.75		(675 670 636)
5.	Sidney Abrahams [G2]	GBR	6.72		(672 654 652)
6.	Nils Fixdal [G3]	NOR	6.71		(671 - 665)
7.	Charles Lomberg [G3]	SWE	6.62		(644 652 662)
8.	Viktor Franzl [G3]	AUT	6.57		(657 653 650)
9.	Philipp Ehrenreich [G2]	AUT	6.14		(595 610 614)
10.	Nándor Kováts [G3]	HUN	5.96		(- - 596)

| 11. | Arthur Maranda [G3] | CAN | 5.87 | (587 572 586) |
| AC. | Paul Fournelle [G2] | LUX | NM | (- - -) |

285

Group Four A: 8; C: 4.

1.	Harry Worthington	USA	7.03	(703 696 665)
2.	Jim Thorpe	USA	6.89	(667 689 662)
3.	Edward Farrell	USA	6.71	(671 636 646)
4.	Philip Kingsford	GBR	6.65	(652 665 633)
5.	Patrik Ohlsson	SWE	6.28	(606 628 -)
6.	Gustav Betzén	SWE	6.24	(624 - -)
7.	Alfredo Pagani	ITA	5.95	(589 595 -)
8.	Manlio Legat	ITA	5.50	(- 550 -)

286

Standing Long Jump

A: 19; C: 8; D: 8 July.

The defending champion was America's Ray Ewry, who had won the Olympic title in this event in 1900, 1904, 1906, and 1908. In 1904 at St. Louis he had set the then still-standing world and Olympic record of 3.47 (11-4⅞). But Ewry had retired in 1911 and in his absence, Greece's Konstantinos Tsiklitiras won the gold medal, ahead of America's Adams brothers, Platt and Ben. The standing long jump was never again contested at the Olympics.

Final A: 3; C: 2; D: 8 July; T: c. 1200, directly after the qualifying round.

1.	Konstantinos Tsiklitiras	GRE	3.37	(330 324 334)
2.	Platt Adams	USA	3.36	(336 334 324)
3.	Ben Adams	USA	3.28	(318 323 328)

Diplomas of Merit

Gustaf Malmsten (SWE), Leo Goehring (USA), Edvard Möller (SWE)

Final Standings

1.	Konstantinos Tsiklitiras	GRE	3.37
2.	Platt Adams	USA	3.36
3.	Ben Adams	USA	3.28
4.	Gustaf Malmsten	SWE	3.20
=5.[287]	Leo Goehring	USA	3.14
	Edvin Möller	SWE	3.14
7.	András Baronyi	HUN	3.13
8.	R. Leslie Byrd	USA	3.12
9.	Forest Fletcher	USA	3.11
10.	Alfred Motte	FRA	3.10
11.	Gustav Ljunggren	SWE	3.09
12.	Birger Brodtkorb	NOR	3.05
13.	O. Ragnar Ekberg	SWE	3.03

14.	Douglas Melin	SWE	3.02
15.	Henry Ashington	GBR	3.02
16.	Georges André	FRA	3.02
17.	Arthur Maranda	CAN	2.98
18.	Karl Bergh	SWE	2.95
19.	Philip Kingsford	GBR	2.75

Qualifying Round A: 19; C: 8; D: 8 July; T: 1030; F: Qualifiers were separated into four groups. Top three jumpers qualified for the final.

Group One A: 5; C: 4.

1.	Platt Adams	USA	3.32	Q	(323 318 332)
2.	Alfred Motte	FRA	3.10		(310 310 307)
3.	Birger Brodtkorb	NOR	3.05		(300 305 303)
4.	Douglas Melin	SWE	3.02		(302 301 299)
5.	Karl Bergh	SWE	2.95		(286 295 291)

288

Group Two A: 4; C: 3.

1.	Ben Adams	USA	3.28	Q	(328 321 324)
2.	Forest Fletcher	USA	3.11		(305 311 309)
3.	Gustav Ljunggren	SWE	3.09		(301 304 309)
4.	Arthur Maranda	CAN	2.98		(280 283 298)

289

Group Three A: 4; C: 3.

1.	Konstantinos Tsiklitiras	GRE	3.37	Q	(314 326 337)
2.	Leo Goehring	USA	3.14		(- 314 313)
3.	R. Leslie Byrd	USA	3.12		(312 311 305)
4.	Henry Ashington	GBR	3.02		(295 279 302)

290

Group Four A: 6; C: 4.

1.	Gustaf Malmsten	SWE	3.20		(311 320 312)
2.	Edvin Möller	SWE	3.14		(313 314 309)
3.	András Baronyi	HUN	3.13		(312 313 302)
4.	O. Ragnar Ekberg	SWE	3.03		(300 302 303)
5.	Georges André	FRA	3.02		(302 296 -)
6.	Philip Kingsford	GBR	2.75		(260 275 272)

291

Hop, Step, and Jump (Triple Jump)

A: 20[292]; C: 8[293]; D: 15 July.

The Ahearn(e) brothers were the top triple jumpers in the world in 1912. Tim Ahearne (GBR/IRL) was the defending champion and Olympic record holder. His brother, Daniel Ahearn (USA), who had emigrated to the United States and changed the spelling of his last name, was the world record holder and had won the AAU Championship in 1910 and 1911. But neither was present in Stockholm.

In their absence the Swedes dominated the hop, step, and jump. They swept the first three places and garnered six of the top 12 places. Gustaf "Topsy" Lindblom, in his only Olympic appearance ever, had the two longest jumps with his first efforts in the qualifying, and won the gold medal easily over teammate, Georg Åberg, who had won the bronze medal in the long jump.

Final A: 3; C: 1; D: 15 July; T: c. 1600, directly after the qualifying round.

1.	Gustaf "Topsy" Lindblom	SWE	14.76	(- 1435 1432)
2.	Georg Åberg	SWE	14.51	(- 1403 -)
3.	Erik Almlöf	SWE	14.17	(- 1385 1410)

Diplomas of Merit

Erling Vinne (NOR), Platt Adams (USA), Edvard Larsen (NOR), Hjalmar Ohlsson (SWE)

Final Standings

1.	Gustaf "Topsy" Lindblom	SWE	14.76
2.	Georg Åberg	SWE	14.51
3.	Erik Almlöf	SWE	14.17
4.	Erling Vinne	NOR	14.14
5.	Platt Adams	USA	14.09
6.	Edvard Larsen	NOR	14.06
7.	Hjalmar Ohlsson	SWE	14.01
8.	Nils Fixdal	NOR	13.96
9.	Charles Brickley	USA	13.88
10.	Gustaf Nordén	SWE	13.81
11.	Juho Halme	FIN	13.79
12.	Inge Lindholm	SWE	13.74
13.	Edward Farrell	USA	13.57
14.	Otto Bäurle	GER	13.52
15.	Patrik Ohlsson	SWE	13.45
16.	Gustav Krojer	AUT	13.45
17.	Skotte Jacobsson	SWE	13.33
18.	Calvin Bricker	CAN	13.25
19.	Timothy Carroll	GBR	12.56
20.	Arthur Maranda	CAN	12.53

Qualifying Round A: 20; C: 8; D: 15 July; T: 1400; F: Qualifiers were separated into four groups, which were combined into three groups.[294] Top three jumpers qualified for the final.

Group One A: 5; C: 4.

1.	Georg Åberg	SWE	14.51	Q	(1358 1390 1451)
2.	Platt Adams	USA	14.09		(1372 1409 f)
3.	Hjalmar Ohlsson[295]	SWE	14.01		(1401 1387 1391)
4.	Juho Halme	FIN	13.79		(1379 1343 1351)
5.	Timothy Carroll	GBR	12.56		(f 1254 1256)

[296]

Group Two A: 9; C: 4;.

1.	Gustaf "Topsy" Lindblom[297]	SWE	14.76	Q	(1474 1476 1420)
2.	Erik Almlöf[298]	SWE	14.17	Q	(f 1346 1417)
3.	Edvard Larsen	NOR	14.06		(1327 1390 1406)
4.	Nils Fixdal	NOR	13.96		(1396 1358 1366)
5.	Gustaf Nordén	SWE	13.81		(1381 1276 -)
6.	Gustav Krojer	AUT	13.45		(1290 1345 1295)
7.	Skotte Jacobsson	SWE	13.33		(1333 - 1271)
8.	Calvin Bricker[299]	CAN	13.25		(1325 p p)
9.	Arthur Maranda	CAN	12.53		(1253 1207 1225)

[300]

Group Three A: 6; C: 4.

1.	Erling Vinne[301]	NOR	14.14		(1363 1414 1334)
2.	Charles Brickley[302]	USA	13.88		(1388 1384 1377)
3.	Inge Lindholm	SWE	13.74		(1314 1357 1374)
4.	Edward Farrell	USA	13.57		(- 1342 1357)
5.	Otto Bäurle[303]	GER	13.52		(1312 - 1352)
6.	Patrik Ohlsson[304]	SWE	13.45		(1298 1337 1345)

[305]

Shot Put

A: 22; C: 14; D: 10 July.

Since 1904, the world's top shot putter had been Ralph Rose. He had won the Olympic gold medal in both 1904 and 1908 and had set eight world records between 1904 and 1908. His last, and final world record, was 15.54 (51-0), set at a meeting of the Olympic Club in San Francisco on 21 August 1909. He was still dominant, winning the AAU title in 1909 and 1910, but that was his last major title. In 1911 Pat McDonald (né McDonnell) won the AAU Championship after having finished second to Rose in 1910. McDonald would win the AAU title again in 1912 and 1914. At the 1912 U.S. Olympic Trials, Rose won the Western Trial while McDonald won the eastern trial. The battle for world shot put supremacy would certainly come down to these two at Stockholm.

In the qualifying, Rose seemed ready to resume his dominance, setting an Olympic record of 14.98 on his first effort, and raising that to 15.25 with his third put to easily lead the qualifying. Pat McDonald was far behind at that point. He led group three of the qualifying, but posted a mark of almost half a meter behind Rose — 14.78. In the final, McDonald took the lead with his first put, setting a new Olympic record of 15.34. Rose could not improve his qualifying mark and had to settle for the silver medal.

Final A: 3; C: 1; D: 10 July; T: c. 1100, directly after qualifying round.

1.	Patrick McDonald	USA	15.34	OR	(1534or - -)
2.	Ralph Rose	USA	15.25		(1496 - -)
3.	Lawrence Whitney	USA	13.93		(- - -)

Diplomas of Merit

Elmer Niklander (FIN), George Philbrook (USA), Imre Mudin (HUN), Einar Nilsson (SWE)

Final Standings

1.	Patrick McDonald	USA	15.34
2.	Ralph Rose	USA	15.25
3.	Lawrence Whitney	USA	13.93
4.	Elmer Niklander	FIN	13.65
5.	George Philbrook	USA	13.13
6.	Imre Mudin	HUN	12.81
7.	Einar Nilsson	SWE	12.62
8.	Patrick Quinn	GBR	12.53
9.	André Tison	FRA	12.41
10.	Paavo Aho	FIN	12.40
11.	Mikhail Dorizas	GRE	12.05
12.	Aurelio Lenzi	ITA	11.57
13.	Josef Schäffer	AUT	11.44
14.	Karl von Halt	GER	11.16
15.	František Janda-Suk	BOH	11.15
16.	Raoul Paoli	FRA	11.11
17.	Marcel Pelletier	LUX	11.04
18.	Paul Willführ	GER	10.90
19.	Mıgır Mıgıryan	TUR	10.63
20.	Eriks Vanags	RUS	10.44
21.	Arvids Ozols-Berne	RUS	10.33
22.	Charles Lagarde	FRA	9.41

Qualifying Round A: 22; C: 14; D: 10 July; T: 0930; F: Qualifiers were separated into four groups, but groups one and two were combined into one group. Top three throwers qualified for the final.

Groups One and Two[306] A: 8; C: 8.

1.	Lawrence Whitney	USA	13.93	Q	(- - 1393)
2.	Imre Mudin	HUN	12.81		
3.	Einar Nilsson	SWE	12.62		(1218 - 1262)
4.	Patrick Quinn	GBR	12.53		
5.	Paavo Aho	FIN	12.40		
6.	Mikhail Dorizas	GRE	12.05		
7.	Karl von Halt [G2]	GER	11.16		
8.	Frantisek Janda-Suk	BOH	11.15		

[307]

Group Three A: 8; C: 8.

1.	Ralph Rose	USA	15.25	Q OR	(1498or 1468 1525or)
2.	Elmer Niklander	FIN	13.65		(1352 f 1365)
3.	Josef Schäffer	AUT	11.44		(1144 - -)
4.	Raoul Paoli	FRA	11.11		(981 1061 1111)
5.	Marcel Pelletier	LUX	11.04		(1068 1104 -)
6.	Paul Willführ	GER	10.90		(- - 1090)
7.	Mıgır Mıgıryan	TUR	10.63		(1033 - 1063)
8.	Arvids Ozols-Berne	RUS	10.33		(- 1033 -)

[308]

Group Four A: 6; C: 4.

1.	Patrick McDonald	USA	14.78	Q	(1454 1427 1478)
2.	George Philbrook	USA	13.13		(1284 1313 -)
3.	André Tison	FRA	12.41		(- 1174 1241)
4.	Aurelio Lenzi	ITA	11.57		(1052 1125 1157)
5.	Eriks Vanags	RUS	10.44		(- - 1044)
6.	Charles Lagarde	FRA	9.41		(941 - -)

[309]

Shot Put, Both Hands

A: 7; C: 4; D: 11 July.

This was the only time this event was held at the Olympic Games. It was rarely contested at major meets, but the world record was 28.00 meters, set by America's Ralph Rose at Oakland just a month before the Olympics (2 June). Rose barely qualified for the final, placing third behind his teammate, Pat McDonald, who led the qualifying, and Finland's Elmer Niklander. In the final, McDonald improved with both hands and led until Rose's very last throw with his left hand. Until then, Rose was in third place, still trailing the other two finalists. But his last left-handed mark was an improvement of almost one meter, and vaulted him to the gold medal.

Final A: 3; C: 2; D: 11 July; T: c. 1530, directly after the qualifying round; F: Each athlete in the final had three further throws with each hand, with the best mark with each hand, qualifying or final, being totalled to arrive at the total mark.

		Total	(Right/Left)	Right Hand	Left Hand
1. Ralph Rose	USA	27.70	(15.23/12.47)	(1478 — 1510)	(1134 1165 1247)
2. Patrick McDonald	USA	27.53	(15.08/12.45)	(1508 —-)	(1179 1229 1245)
3. Elmer Niklander	FIN	27.14	(14.71/12.43)	(1355 — 1471)	(1242 —-)

Diplomas of Merit

Lawrence Whitney (USA), Einar Nilson (SWE), Paavo Aho (FIN)

Final Standings

		Total	Right	Left
1. Ralph Rose	USA	27.70	15.23	12.47
2. Patrick McDonald	USA	27.53	15.08	12.45
3. Elmer Niklander	FIN	27.14	14.71	12.43
4. Lawrence Whitney	USA	24.09	13.48	10.61
5. Einar Nilsson	SWE	23.37	12.52	10.85
6. Paavo Aho	FIN	23.30	12.72	10.58
7. Mıgır Mıgıryan	TUR	19.78[310]	10.85	8.93

Qualifying Round A: 7; C: 4; D: 11 July; T: 1400; F: Qualifiers were separated into two groups. Three puts with each hand, the best put with each hand to be totaled for the final result. Top three throwers advanced to the final.

Group One A: 3; C: 3.

			Total	(Right/Left)	Right Hand	Left Hand
1.	Lawrence Whitney	USA	24.09	(13.48/10.61)	(1348 - -)	(1061 - -)
2.	Einar Nilsson	SWE	23.37	(12.52/10.85)	(1252 - -)	(1005 1085 -)
3.	Paavo Aho	FIN	23.30	(12.72/10.58)	(1254 1272 -)	(1025 1029 1058)

311

Group Two A: 4; C: 3.

			Total	(Right/Left)	Right Hand	Left Hand
1.	Patrick McDonald	USA	26.77	(14.92/11.85)	(1395 1492 -)	(1137 1174 1185)
2.	Elmer Niklander	FIN	26.67	(14.24/12.43)	(1424 - -)	(1184 - 1243)
3.	Ralph Rose	USA	26.50	(15.23/11.27)	(1511 - 1523)	(1104 1119 1127)
4.	Mıgır Mıgıryan	TUR	19.78	(10.85/8.93)	(- 1085 -)	(893 - -)

312

Discus Throw

A: 41[313]; C: 15; D: 12 July.

Since 1902, the discus throw had been the private property of Martin Sheridan of the United States. He had won the Olympic gold medal in 1904, 1906, and 1908; he had won the AAU Championship in 1904, 1906–07, and 1911; and he had also set approximately 16 world records. However, after winning the AAU title in 1911, he retired, leaving the 1912 Olympic discus throw wide open.

There were several challengers for Sheridan's crown. On 5 August 1911, Finland's Elmer Niklander broke Sheridan's world record with a throw of 44.01. But shortly before the Olympics, America's James Duncan shattered that mark by throwing 47.58 on 27 May 1912 in a both hands handicap competition at the New York Post Office Clerk's Association Games. Duncan also won the Eastern Olympic Trial.

However, neither Niklander nor Duncan could match Finland's Armas Taipale. Taipale led the qualifying easily with a throw of 43.91, which set an Olympic record. Duncan qualified for the final with 42.28, but Niklander did not qualify, finishing fourth. In the final, Taipale improved even more, setting two more Olympic records with his first and third throws in the final. Duncan did not improve in the final and finished third.

The day after his discus gold medal, Taipale doubled with another gold medal in the both-hands discus competition. In 1920, he added a silver medal in the discus to his overall record. In 1913, he set his only world record, breaking Duncan's mark with 47.85 at Magdeburg on 20 July. In addition to his gold medal, Taipale won the challenge trophy for the discus throw, which had been donated in 1908 by Mrs. G. de Montgomery.

Final A: 3; C: 2; D: 12 July; T: c. 1200, directly after the qualifying round.

1.	Armas Taipale	FIN	45.21	OR	[4434or - 4521or]
2.	Leslie Byrd	USA	42.32	[4109 - -]	
3.	James Duncan	USA	42.28	[4133 - -]	

Diplomas of Merit

Elmer Niklander (FIN), Hans Tronner (AUT), Arlie Mucks (USA), George Philbrook (USA)

Final Standings

1.	Armas Taipale	FIN	45.21
2.	R. Leslie Byrd	USA	42.32
3.	James Duncan	USA	42.28
4.	Elmer Niklander	FIN	42.09
5.	Hans Tronner	AUT	41.24
6.	Arlie Mucks	USA	40.93
7.	George Philbrook	USA	40.92
8.	Emil Magnusson	SWE	39.91
9.	Resző Ujlaki	HUN	39.82
10.	Einar Nilsson	SWE	39.69
11.	Ralph Rose	USA	39.65
12.	Emil Muller	USA	39.35
13.	Mikhail Dorizas	GRE	39.28
14.	Duncan Gillis	CAN	39.01
15.	Venne "Verner" Järvinen	FIN	38.60
16.	Josef Waitzer	GER	38.44
17.	František Janda-Suk	BOH	38.31
18.	Aurelio Lenzi	ITA	38.19
19.	Károly Kobulszky	HUN	38.15
20.	Lawrence Whitney	USA	37.91
21.	György "Juraj" Luntzer	HUN	37.88
22.	Avery Brundage	USA	37.85
23.	E. Gunnar Nilsson	SWE	37.44
24.	Emil Welz	GER	37.24
25.	Samu Fóti	HUN	36.37
26.	Gunnar Bolander	SWE	36.22
27.	Carl Johan "Masse" Lind	SWE	36.07
28.	Folke Fleetwood	SWE	35.06
29.	Josef Schäffer	AUT	34.87
30.	André Tison	FRA	34.73
31.	Marcel Pelletier	LUX	33.73
32.	Walter Henderson	GBR	33.61
33.	Móric Kóczán-Kovács	HUN	33.30
34.	Mıgır Mıgıryan	TUR	32.98
35.	Nikolay Neklepayev	RUS	32.59
36.	Charles Lagarde	FRA	32.35
37.	Henning Möller	SWE	32.23
38.	Miroslav Šustera	BOH	31.83
39.	Eriks Vanags	RUS	31.34
40.	Otto Nilsson	SWE	31.07
AC.	Paul Willführ	GER	NM

Qualifying Round A: 41; C: 15; D: 12 July; T: 0930; F: Qualifiers were separated into five groups. Top three throwers qualified for the final.

Group One A: 9; C: 7.

1.	Armas Taipale	FIN	43.91	Q OR	(3684 4391or -)
2.	Hans Tronner	AUT	41.24		(3997 - 4124)

3.	Emil Magnusson	SWE	39.91		(3991 - -)
4.	Einar Nilsson	SWE	39.69		(3726 3877 3969)
5.	Mikhail Dorizas	GRE	39.28		(- 3928 -)
6.	Josef Waitzer	GER	38.44		(3844 - -)
7.	Károly Kobulszky	HUN	38.15		(3781 3815 -)
8.	Avery Brundage	USA	37.85		(3748 3785 -)
9.	Otto Nilsson	SWE	31.07		(3107 - -)

314

Group Two A: 7; C: 5.

1.	Arlie Mucks	USA	40.93		(4054 4093 -)
2.	Emil Muller	USA	39.35		(3791 3869 3935)
3.	Venne "Verner" Järvinen	FIN	38.60		(3415 3860 -)
4.	Lawrence Whitney	USA	37.91		(3487 3791 -)
5.	Samu Fóti	HUN	36.37		(3551 - 3637)
6.	Carl Johan "Masse" Lind	SWE	36.07		(- 3504 3607)
7.	Nikolay Neklepayev	RUS	32.59		(3259 - -)

315

Group Three A: 9; C: 8.

1.	Elmer Niklander	FIN	42.09		(4209 - -)
2.	Ralph Rose	USA	39.65		(3734 3882 3965)
3.	Duncan Gillis	CAN	39.01		(3901 - -)
4.	František Janda-Suk	BOH	38.31		(3241 3683831)
5.	Gunnar Nilsson	SWE	37.44		(- 3744 -)
6.	Móric Kóczán-Kovács	HUN	33.30		(3330 - -)
7.	Mıgır Mıgıryan	TUR	32.98		(- - 3298)
8.	Miroslav Šustera	BOH	31.83		(3183 - -)
AC.	Paul Willführ	GER	NM		(- - -)

316

Group Four A: 6; C: 5.

1.	Leslie Byrd	USA	42.32	Q	(3748 4232 -)
2.	James Duncan	USA	42.28	Q	(4161 4228 -)
3.	Resző Ujlaki	HUN	39.82		(3982 - -)
4.	Emil Welz	GER	37.24		(3616 3724 -)
5.	Josef Schäffer	AUT	34.87		(- 3487 -)
6.	Marcel Pelletier	LUX	33.73		(3373 - -)

317

Group Five A: 10; C: 7.

1.	George Philbrook	USA	40.92		(3814 3855 4092)
2.	Aurelio Lenzi	ITA	38.19		(3558 3819 -)
3.	György "Juraj" Luntzer	HUN	37.88		(3788 - -)
4.	Gunnar Bolander	SWE	36.22		(- 3622 -)
5.	Folke Fleetwood	SWE	35.06		(3202 3289 3506)
6.	André Tison	FRA	34.73		(3473 - -)
7.	Walter Henderson	GBR	33.61		(- 3361 -)
8.	Charles Lagarde	FRA	32.35		(3076 - 3235)

9.	Henning Möller	SWE	32.23	(– 3223 –)
10.	Eriks Vanags	RUS	31.34	(– 3134 –)

318

Discus Throw, Both Hands

A: 20; C: 6; D: 13 July.

The both-hands discus throw was conducted at the Olympics only in 1912. No world record for the event is known for 1912, but the Swedish record at the time was held by Eric Lemming, who had thrown 71.29 in 1910. The day before this event, Finland's Armas Taipale had won the conventional discus throw event. In the both-hands event, he was unchallenged. He led the qualifying and the final, posting the best throw with each hand in all portions of the event to win by almost five meters. He returned to the Olympics in both 1920 and 1924, winning a silver medal in the 1920 discus throw. At that event he was defeated by his teammate, Elmer Niklander, who finished second in this event.

Final A: 3; C: 2; D: 13 July; T: c. 1600, directly after the qualifying round; F: Each athlete in the final had three further throws with each hand, with the best mark with each hand, qualifying or final, being totaled to arrive at the total mark.

			Total	*(Right/Left)*	*Right Hand*	*Left Hand*
1.	Armas Taipale	FIN	82.86	(44.68/38.18)	(4278 – 4468)	(3818 – –)
2.	Elmer Niklander	FIN	77.96	(40.28/37.68)	(3704 3794 –)	(3310 3768 –)
3.	Emil Magnusson	SWE	77.37	(40.58/36.79)	(3703 3890 4058)	(3605 3613 3679)

Diplomas of Merit

Einar Nilsson (SWE), James Duncan (USA), Emil Muller (USA), Folke Fleetwood (SWE), Carl Johan "Masse" Lind (SWE)

Final Standings

			Total	*Right*	*Left*
1.	Armas Taipale	FIN	82.86	44.68	38.18
2.	Elmer Niklander	FIN	77.96	40.28	37.68
3.	Emil Magnusson	SWE	77.37	40.58	36.79
4.	Einar Nilsson	SWE	71.40	40.99	30.41
5.	James Duncan	USA	71.13	39.78	31.35
6.	Emil Muller	USA	69.56	39.83	29.73
7.	Folke Fleetwood	SWE	68.22	36.95	31.27
8.	Carl "Masse" Lind	SWE	68.02	34.20	33.82
9.	Nils Linde	SWE	67.10	34.98	32.12
10.	E. Gunnar Nilsson	SWE	67.09	36.86	30.23
11.	Eric Lemming	SWE	67.08	37.86	29.22
12.	"Verner" Järvinen	FIN	66.69	37.84	28.85
13.	Hans Tronner	AUT	66.66	39.95	26.71
14.	Resző Ujlaki	HUN	66.18	40.32	25.86
15.	Arlie Mucks	USA	63.83	42.63	21.20

			Total	Right	Left
16.	Josef Schäffer	AUT	63.50	36.59	26.91
17.	Leslie Byrd	USA	62.32	40.10	22.22
18.	Károly Kobulszky	HUN	59.48	37.01	22.47
19.	Vasily Molokanov	RUS	47.37	24.79	22.58
AC.	György "Juraj" Luntzer	HUN	NM	37.68	—

Qualifying Round A: 20; C: 6; D: 13 July; T: 1400; F: Qualifiers were separated into three groups. Each athlete took three throws with each hand, with the three athletes having the top totals with both hands advancing to the final.

Group One A: 9; C: 6.

			Total	(Right/Left)	Right Hand	Left Hand
1.	Armas Taipale	FIN	80.03	(44.68/35.35)	(4268 4370 4468)	(3415 3535 -)
2.	Emil Magnusson	SWE	75.35	(40.28/35.07)	(4028 - -)	(3507 - -)
3.	Einar Nilsson	SWE	71.40	(40.99/30.41)	(3960 3099 -)	(- 2578 3041)
4.	Emil Muller	USA	69.56	(39.83/29.73)	(3983 - -)	(2973 - -)
5.	Carl "Masse" Lind	SWE	68.02	(34.20/33.82)	(- 3358 3420)	(3382 - -)
6.	Eric Lemming	SWE	67.08	(37.86/29.22)	(3627 - 3786)	(2881 - 2922)
7.	Hans Tronner	AUT	66.66	(39.95/26.71)	(3445 3854 3995)	(2073 2235 2671)
8.	Károly Kobulszky	HUN	59.48	(37.01/22.47)	(3462 3522 3701)	(- 2247 -)
9.	Vasily Molokanov	RUS	47.37	(24.79/22.58)	(2479 - -)	(2219 2258 -)

319

Group Two A: 5; C: 3.

			Total	(Right/Left)	Right Hand	Left Hand
1.	Elmer Niklander	FIN	72.05	(40.28/31.77)	(- 4028 -)	(3177 - ?)
2.	Nils Linde	SWE	67.10	(34.98/32.12)	(- 3431 3498)	(3212 - -)
3.	Gunnar Nilsson	SWE	67.09	(36.86/30.23)	(3589 3650 3686)	(2693 3023 -)
4.	"Verner" Järvinen	FIN	66.69	(37.84/28.85)	(3784 - -)	(2788 2885 -)
5.	Arlie Mucks	USA	63.83	(42.63/21.20)	(4263 - -)	(2120 - -)

320

Group Three A: 6; C: 4.

			Total	(Right/Left)	Right Hand	Left Hand
1.	James Duncan	USA	71.13	(39.78/31.35)	(3978 - -)	(3135 - -)
2.	Folke Fleetwood	SWE	68.22	(36.95/31.27)	(3505 3695 -)	(3096 3127 -)
3.	Resző Ujlaki	HUN	66.18	(40.32/25.86)	(3593 - 4032)	(2528 - 2586)
4.	Josef Schäffer	AUT	63.50	(36.59/26.91)	(3659 - -)	(2677 2691 -)
5.	R. Leslie Byrd	USA	62.32	(40.10/22.22)	(- 4010 -)	(- 2222 ?)
AC.	György Luntzer[321]	HUN	NM	(37.68/-)	(3267 3697 3768)	(f f f)

322

Hammer Throw

A: 14; C: 4; D: 14 July.

Since the late 1890s, the hammer throw had been dominated by the Irish-born American John Flanagan. He had won three Olympic gold medals (1900, 1904, 1908), won seven AAU Championships (1897–99, 1901–02, 1906–07), and set 15 world records. But since 1907 he had had competition from American Matt McGrath, who had finished second to Flanagan at the 1908 Olympics.

McGrath had one of the longest careers of any track & field athlete ever. He finished second in the 1907 AAU meet, and he last competed in that meet in 1928, finishing fifth at 48 years old. He competed in the Olympic hammer throw four times — 1908 (second), 1912 (first), 1920 (fifth), and 1924 (second). He set two world records, one in 1907 and one in 1911. At Stockholm, McGrath was absolutely dominant. He won the event with 54.74, a margin of 6.35 meters over Canada's Duncan Gillis. McGrath had four measured throws, the shortest of which was 4.44 meters longer than Gillis's best mark.

Final A: 3; C: 2; D: 14 July; T: c. 1530, directly after the qualifying round.

1.	Matthew McGrath	USA	54.74	OR	(5283 5390 5474or)
2.	Duncan Gillis	CAN	48.39	(- 4724 -)	
3.	Clarence Childs	USA	48.17	(- - -)	

Diplomas of Merit

Robert Olsson (SWE), Carl Johan "Masse" Lind (SWE), Denis Carey (GBR), Nils Linde (SWE), Carl Jahnzon (SWE)[323]

Final Standings

1.	Matthew McGrath	USA	54.74
2.	Duncan Gillis	CAN	48.39
3.	Clarence Childs	USA	48.17
4.	Robert Olsson	SWE	46.50
5.	Carl Johan "Masse" Lind	SWE	45.61
6.	Denis Carey	GBR	43.78
7.	Nils Linde	SWE	43.32
=8.[324]	Ralph Rose	USA	42.58
	Carl Jahnzon	SWE	42.58
10.	Arvid Åberg	SWE	41.11
11.	Gunnar Johnson	SWE	39.92
12.	Benjamin Sherman	USA	38.77
13.	Wiktor Hackberg	SWE	38.44
AC.	Simon Gillis	USA	NM

[325]

Qualifying Round A: 14; C: 4; D: 14 July; T: 1330; F: Qualifiers were separated into two groups. Top three throwers qualified for the final.

Group One A: 8; C: 3.

1.	Clarence Childs	USA	48.17	Q	(4817 - -)
2.	Robert Olsson	SWE	46.50		(3956 4650 -)

3.	Carl Johan "Masse" Lind	SWE	45.61			(4506 - 4561)
4.	Denis Carey	GBR	43.78			(3899 4378 -)
5.	Carl Jahnzon	SWE	42.58			(3918 4258 -)
6.	Arvid Åberg	SWE	41.11			(- - 4111)
7.	Gunnar Johnson	SWE	39.92			(3866 3992 -)
8.	Benjamin Sherman[326]	USA	38.77			(3871 - 3877)

Group Two A: 6; C: 3.

1.	Matthew McGrath	USA	54.13	Q	OR	(5413or - -)
2.	Duncan Gillis	CAN	48.39	Q		(4617 - 4839)
3.	Nils Linde	SWE	43.32			(4232 - -)
4.	Ralph Rose	USA	42.58			(- 4080 4258)
5.	Wiktor Hackberg	SWE	38.44			(- - 3844)
AC.	Simon Gillis[327]	USA	NM			(f wd)

[328]

Javelin Throw

A: 25; C: 7; D: 6 July.

Javelin throwing in 1912 was immensely popular in Scandinavia, and there was little doubt that an athlete from that region would win. Of the 24 competitors in this event, 17 were from Scandinavia (plus three Germans, two Russians, one Austrian, one Hungarian), and 14 of the top 15 places went to Scandinavian athletes. The world record at the time of the Olympics was 61.45, set on 25 May 1912 by Finland's Julius Saaristo. Saaristo was likely the cofavorite with the defending champion, Sweden's Eric Lemming.

However, Lemming dominated the event. He defeated Saaristo in both the qualifying and the final, winning by two meters. It was his fourth, and final, javelin gold medal at the Olympics. In 1906 he had won the event at Athens, while at London in 1908, had he won both the conventional and freestyle javelin events.

Final A: 3; C: 3; D: 6 July; T: c. 1500, directly after the qualifying round.

1.	Eric Lemming	SWE	60.64	OR	(6064or - c. 5900)
2.	Juho Saaristo	FIN	58.66		(5621 - 5866)
3.	Móric Kóczán-Kovács	HUN	55.50		(- - 5550)

Diplomas of Merit

Juho Halme (FIN), Väinö Siikaniemi (FIN), Richard Åbrink (SWE)

Final Standings

1.	Eric Lemming	SWE	60.64
2.	Juho Saaristo	FIN	58.66
3.	Móric Kóczán-Kovács	HUN	55.50
4.	Juho Halme	FIN	54.65
5.	Väinö Siikaniemi	FIN	52.43
6.	Richard Åbrink	SWE	52.20

7.	Arne Halse	NOR	51.98	
8.	Jonnas "Jonni" Myyrä	FIN	51.33	
9.	Urho Peltonen	FIN	49.20	
10.	Otto Nilsson	SWE	49.18	
11.	Karl Hilding Sonne	SWE	47.85	
12.	Daniel Johansen	NOR	47.61	
13.	Bror Olsson	SWE	46.94	
14.	Anders Krigsman	SWE	46.71	
15.	Janne Dahl	SWE	45.67	
16.	Arvid Ohrling	SWE	45.32	
17.	Nikolay Neklepayev	RUS	44.98	
18.	Emil Kukko (Skarra)	FIN	44.66	
19.	Josef Waitzer	GER	43.71	
20.	Nikolajs Svedrevits	RUS	43.21	
21.	Algot Larsson	SWE	43.18	
22.	Karl von Halt	GER	41.99	
23.	Paul Willführ	GER	41.05	
AC.	Gustav Krojer	AUT	NM	
	Eskil Falk	SWE	NM	

Qualifying Round A: 25; C: 7; D: 6 July; T: c. 1300; F: Qualifiers were separated into four groups. Top three throwers qualified for the final.

Group One A: 9; C: 3.

1.	Eric Lemming	SWE	57.42	Q OR	(5302 5478 5742or)
2.	Juho Saaristo	FIN	55.37	Q	(5475 5537or f)
3.	Juho Halme	FIN	54.65		(5381 5465 foul)
4.	Urho Peltonen	FIN	49.20		(4920 - -)
5.	Otto Nilsson	SWE	49.18		(4759 4801 4918)
6.	Karl Hilding Sonne	SWE	47.85		(- 4785 -)
7.	Bror Olsson	SWE	46.94		(4694 - -)
8.	Arvid Ohrling	SWE	45.32		(4500 4532 -)
9.	Josef Waitzer	GER	43.71		(4199 4320 4371)

329

Group Two A: 6; C: 3.

1.	Joonas "Jonni" Myyrä	FIN	51.33		(4877 5133 -)
2.	Nikolay Neklepayev	RUS	44.98		(- 4478 4498)
3.	Emil Kukko (Skarra)	FIN	44.66		(4450 - 4466)
4.	Nikolajs Svedrevits	RUS	43.21		(- 4321 -)
5.	Karl von Halt	GER	41.99		(- 4199 -)
6.	Paul Willführ	GER	41.05		(4105 - -)

330

Group Three A: 6; C: 4.

1.	Móric Kóczán-Kovács	HUN	54.99	Q	(5406 - 5499)
2.	Richard Åbrink	SWE	52.20		(4656 4825 5220)
3.	Arne Halse	NOR	51.98		(5198 - -)
4.	Anders Krigsman	SWE	46.71		(4514 4548 4671)

5.	Algot Larsson	SWE	43.18	(4318 – -)
AC.	Gustav Krojer	AUT	NM	(- – -)

331

Group Four A: 4; C: 3.

1.	Väinö Siikaniemi	FIN	52.43	(5219 – 5243)
2.	Daniel Johansen	NOR	47.61	(4618 4687 4761)
3.	Janne Dahl	SWE	45.67	(- 4409 4567)
AC.	Eskil Falk	SWE	NM	(- – -)

332

Javelin Throw, Both Hands

A: 14; C: 4; D: 9 July; T: 1400.

This was the only time this event was held at the Olympics. There is no known world record for the event at the time of the 1912 Olympics. In the scheduled final, the three qualifiers were to have had three further throws with each hand, with the best of each hand being totaled. When all three finalists were from Finland, they elected not to contest a final. The officials agreed with this decision and allowed the results of the qualifying round to count as the final results. Julius Saaristo's winning right-handed throw of 61.00 broke the Olympic record set by Lemming (60.64) in winning the single-arm javelin throw three days earlier. Eric Lemming, who had won the one-handed competition and the Olympic gold medal in 1906 and 1908, finished only fourth in this event. He was second to Saaristo with the right hand, but threw very poorly with his left hand, placing only ninth of the 14 competitors.

Diplomas of Merit

Eric Lemming (SWE), Arne Halse (NOR), Richard Åbrink (SWE), Daniel Johansen (NOR), Otto Nilsson (SWE)

Final Standings

			Total	*Right*	*Left*
1.	Juho Saaristo	FIN	109.42	61.00or	48.42
2.	Väinö Siikaniemi	FIN	101.13	54.09	47.04
3.	Urho Peltonen	FIN	100.24	53.58	46.66
4.	Eric Lemming	SWE	98.59	58.33	40.26
5.	Arne Halse	NOR	96.92	55.05	41.87
6.	Richard Åbrink	SWE	93.12	50.04	43.08
7.	Daniel Johansen	NOR	92.82	48.78	44.04
8.	Otto Nilsson	SWE	88.90	50.21	38.69
9.	Juho Halme	FIN	88.54	54.90	33.64
10.	Arvid Ohrling	SWE	87.17	46.51	40.66
11.	Sten Hagander	SWE	86.80	46.39	40.41
12.	Móric Kóczán-Kovács	HUN	86.39	55.74	30.65
13.	Anders Krigsman	SWE	85.80	46.85	38.95
14.	Karl Hilding Sonne	SWE	84.96	48.48	36.48

Qualifying Round A: 14; C: 4; D: 9 July; T: 1400; F: Qualifiers were separated into three groups. Each athlete took three throws with each hand, with the three athletes having the top totals with both hands advancing to the final.

Group One A: 6; C: 2.

			Total	(Right/Left)	Right Hand	Left Hand
1.	Julius Saaristo	FIN	109.42	(61.00/48.42)	(5764 5988 6100)	(- - 4842)
2.	Eric Lemming	SWE	98.59	(58.33/40.26)	(5223 5833 -)	(3578 4026 -)
3.	Otto Nilsson	SWE	88.90	(50.21/38.69)	(4824 5021 -)	(3869 - -)
4.	Juho Halme	FIN	88.54	(54.90/33.64)	(- 5276 5490)	(3364 - -)
5.	Arvid Ohrling	SWE	87.17	(46.51/40.66)	(4651 - -)	(4066 - -)
6.	Karl Sonne	SWE	84.96	(48.48/36.48)	(- 4948 -)	(3352 3600 3648)

333

Group Two A: 4; C: 3.

			Total	(Right/Left)	Right Hand	Left Hand
1.	Urho Peltonen	FIN	100.24	(53.58/46.66)	(- 5322 5358)	(4630 4663 4666)
2.	Richard Åbrink	SWE	93.12	(50.04/43.08)	(4878 5004 -)	(4171 4308 -)
3.	Sten Hagander	SWE	86.80	(46.39/40.41)	(4258 4639 -)	(3768 4041 -)
4.	Móric Kóczán-Kovács	HUN	86.39	(55.74/30.65)	(5574 - -)	(2923 3065 -)

334

Group Three A: 4; C: 3.

			Total	(Right/Left)	Right Hand	Left Hand
1.	Väinö Siikaniemi	FIN	101.13	(54.09/47.04)	(5409 - -)	(4376 4509 4704)
2.	Arne Halse	NOR	96.92	(55.05/41.87)	(5205 5505 -)	(4148 - 4187)
3.	Daniel Johansen	NOR	92.82	(48.78/44.04)	(4838 - 4878)	(4099 4319 4404)
4.	Anders Krigsman	SWE	85.80	(46.85/38.95)	(4378 4685 -)	(4609 3895 -)

335

Decathlon

A: 29; C: 12; D: 13–15 July; F: The order of events was as follows: Day 1 (13 July)—100 meters, long jump, shot put; Day 2 (14 July)—high jump, 400 meters, discus throw, 110 meter hurdles; Day 3 (15 July)—pole vault, javelin throw, 1,500 meters; T: 1000 (all days).

Prior to 1911, the multievent for track & field athletes was the all-around championship, a ten-event competition emphasizing strength events. But in preparation for the 1912 Olympics, the Swedes devised another ten-event multievent with more emphasis placed on speed and jumping ability. The first known competitions in the decathlon were both conducted on 15 October 1911, in Münster, Germany (won by Karl von Halt) and Göteberg, Sweden (won by Hugo Wieslander). In June 1912, Wieslander won two further Swedish decathlons in preparation for the Olympic Games. He was the Swedish favorite.

The American favorite was a remarkable Native American named Jim Thorpe. A descendant of the Sauk and Fox tribe with an Irish father, Thorpe had starred in both football and baseball, as well as track, at the Carlisle Indian School in Carlisle, Pennsylvania. He had never competed in a decathlon prior to Stockholm, but at the Eastern Olympic Trial in the pentathlon, he was so dominant that he was named to represent the United States in both the decathlon and the pentathlon. The Stockholm decathlon was expected to be a closely fought contest between Wieslander and Thorpe.

It was not. One week after winning the pentathlon, Jim Thorpe won the decathlon by an almost laughable margin, establishing a new world record, and defeating Wieslander by almost 700 points. He won three events, had one second place, four thirds, and two fourths in the ten events. Using point-for-place scoring, he scored 25 points to Wieslander's 67 and Charles Lomberg's 75.

At the closing ceremonies, Thorpe was presented his trophies by Sweden's King Gustaf V. The legend is that the King told him, "Sir, you are the greatest athlete in the world," and that Thorpe replied, "Thanks, King." Whether the legend is true or not, the King was correct. But from 1913 until 1982 the Olympic record books invariably listed Hugo Wieslander as the 1912 Olympic decathlon champion.

In January 1913, newspaper stories broke noting that Jim Thorpe had played minor-league baseball in North Carolina in 1909 and 1910. The United States AAU reacted quickly and declared Thorpe a professional. The IOC followed suit. Thorpe's Olympic victories were taken from him and he was ordered to return his medals and trophies.

However, the story never died. For years, many efforts were made to right what many perceived as a wrong and have the medals, the trophies, and the recognition returned to Jim Thorpe or his family. The trophies included the challenge trophy for the decathlon, which had been donated by the Czar of Russia. In 1982, the International Olympic Committee made partial restitution when they restored Thorpe's amateur status, and declared him, in an unusual ruling, cochampion with Hugo Wieslander.

The story of Thorpe's disqualification, the many attempts to restore his name, and their final success, is a long and complicated one. For a full retelling of the Jim Thorpe saga, see Appendix II.

			1912A	*1985*	
1. Jim Thorpe[336]	USA		8,412.955	6,564	WR
(11.2 679 1289 187 52.2 3698 15.6 325 4570 4:40.1)					
2. Hugo Wieslander	SWE		7,724.495	5,965	
(11.8 642 1214 175 53.6 3629 17.2 310 5040 4:45.0)					
3. Charles Lomberg	SWE		7,413.510	5,721	
(11.8 687 1167 180 55.0 3535 17.6 325 4183 5:12.2)					
4. Gustaf "Gösta" Holmér	SWE		7,347.855	5,768[337]	
(11.4 598 1098 170 53.2 3178 17.0 320 4628 4:41.9)					
5. James Donahue	USA		7,083.450	5,701	
(11.8 648 967 165 51.6 2995 16.2 340 3709 4:44.0)					
6. Eugene Mercer	USA		7,074.995	5,825	
(11.0 684 976 165 49.9 2195 16.4 360 3232 4:46.3)					
7. J. Valdemar Wickholm	FIN		7,058.795	5,676	
(11.5 595 1109 160 52.3 2978 17.0 325 4258 4:33.9)					
8. Erik Kugelberg	SWE		6,758.780	5,346	
(12.3 620 999 165 55.7 3148 17.2 300 4567 4:43.5)					

		1912A	1985
9. Karl von Halt (12.1 608 1112 170 54.2 3546 17.7 270 3982 5:02.8)	GER	6,682.445	5,286
10. Josef Schäffer (12.3 604 1150 155 58.2 3714 18.9 325 4106 5:05.3)	AUT	6,568.585	5,049
11. Aleksandr Schultz (12.3 575 1008 155 54.5 3134 17.8 270 3899 4:46.4)	RUS	6,134.470	4,976
12. Alfreds Alslebens (12.2 627 848 170 59.0 2921 19.5 nh 3734 5:08.6)	RUS	5,294.615	4,329[338]
AC. George Philbrook (12.4 634 1279 180 56.7 4156 16.8 250 4167)	USA	DNF	
Ferdinand Bie (11.7 669 1020 165 53.2 3165 16.4 290 4852)	NOR	DNF	
Frank Lukeman (11.2 614 929 175 52.1 3052 16.3 270)	CAN	DNF	
Avery Brundage (12.2 640 1112 170 55.2 3407 17.1 290)	USA	DNF	
Georges André (11.6 560 990 175 54.4 2537 16.4)	FRA	DNF	
Alfredo Pagani (12.4 583 967 165 56.1 3020 17.2)	ITA	DNF	
Einar Nilsson (11.5 572 1283 170)	SWE	DNF	
Otto Röhr (11.3 643 981 170)	GER	DNF	
Skotte Jacobsson (11.0 646 935 155)	SWE	DNF	
Gunnar Rönström (12.3 599 1069 160)	SWE	DNF	
Alexander Abraham (12.0 552 1129 150)	GER	DNF	
Pierre Failliot (11.3 605 1054)	FRA	DNF	
Harold Babcock (11.6 629 1016)	USA	DNF	
Svend Langkjær (12.0 589 986)	DEN	DNF	
Wiktor Hackberg (12.5 564 1030)	SWE	DNF	
Manlio Legat (12.1 556 823)	ITA	DNF	
Mıgır Mıgıryan (13.3 543 1105)	TUR	DNF	

339

Diplomas of Merit

Gustaf "Gösta" Holmér (SWE), James Donahue (USA), Eugene Mercer (USA), J. Valde-mar Wickholm (FIN), Erik Kugelberg (SWE), Karl von Halt (GER)

Pentathlon

A: 26; C: 11; D: 7 July; F: Scored by points for place in each event. Twelve top finishers after three events advanced to the fourth event (discus throw). Six top finishers (and ties) advanced to the fifth event (1,500 meters). After three events, the totals were rescored counting the marks among only the 12 qualifiers for the final two events. Ties were broken using the decathlon scoring tables. The order of events was as follows: long jump, javelin throw, 200 meters, discus throw, and 1,500 meters; T: 1330.[340]

At the Eastern Olympic Trials on 18 May 1912, held in New York, Jim Thorpe won easily, setting what is considered the first world record in the pentathlon with 3,656.980 points (3,372 on the 1985 tables). He was considered the American favorite in the Olympic pentathlon, but it was difficult to handicap the field as the event had never been contested internationally.

Thorpe solved the problem rather simply by winning four of the five events contested. Only in the javelin throw was he beaten by any athlete, as both Sweden's Hugo Wieslander and Oscar Lemming posted longer javelin throws. Thorpe's dominance was almost complete. Using 1912 scoring tables, his margin of victory was over 400 points.

However, as in the decathlon, Jim Thorpe only kept his pentathlon gold medal until early 1913 when he was disqualified for professionalism. The gold medal reverted to Norway's Ferdinand Bie. For a complete description of the Thorpe controversy, see Appendix II. Thorpe was also awarded the challenge trophy for the pentathlon, which had been donated by the King of Sweden.

		Points	*1912A*	*1985*
1. Jim Thorpe[341]	USA	7	4,041.530	3,660
(707[342] [1/1] 4671 [3/3] 22.9[343] [1/1] 3557 [1] 4:44.8 [1])				
2. Ferdinand Bie	NOR	21[344]	3,623.840	3,336
(685 [2/2] 4645 [4/4] 23.5 [7/5] 3179 [4] 5:07.8 [6])				
3. James Donahue	USA	29[345]	3,475.865	3,316
(683 [3/3] 3828 [16/10] 23.0 [2/2] 2964 [11] 4:51.0 [3])				
4. Frank Lukeman	CAN	29	3,396.975	3,204
(645 [8/6] 3602 [19/11] 23.2 [5/4] 3376 [3] 5:00.2 [5])				
5. J. Austin Menaul	USA	30	3,378.210	3,225
(640 [11/8] 3585[346] [20/12] 23.0 [2/2] 3138 [6] 4:49.6 [2])				
6. Avery Brundage	USA	31	3,451.930	3,184
(658 [4/4] 4285 [9/7] 24.2[347] [15/11] 3472 [2] DNF[348] [7])				
7. Hugo Wieslander	SWE	32	3,540.560	3,255
(627 [14/10] 4956 [1/1] 24.1 [14/10] 3074 [7] 4:53.1[349] [4])				
8. Gustaf "Gösta" Holmér	SWE	30	2,716.785	4 events
(602 [20/12] 4546 [5/5] 24.0 [11/8] 3178 [5])				

9. Inge Lindholm   SWE   30   2,706.205   4 events
(632 [12/9] 4194 [12/8] 23.5 [7/5] 3047 [8])

10. Oscar Lemming   SWE   31   4 events
(655 [5/5] 4951 [2/2] 24.6 [18/12] 2764 [12])

11. Nils Fjästad   SWE   32   4 events
(643 [10/7] 4015 [14/9] 23.6 [9/7] 3043 [9])

12. Emil Kukko (Skarra)   FIN   35   4 events
(619 [17/11] 4443 [6/6] 24.0 [11/8] 2997 [10])

13. Otto Bäurle   GER   38   3 events
(652 [7] 3429 [22] 23.6 [9])

14. Einar Nilsson   SWE   39   3 events
(623 [15] 4367 [8] 24.3 [16])

15. Erik Kugelberg   SWE   40   1,982.875   3 events
(645 [8] 4202 [11] 24.9 [21])

16. Charles Lomberg   SWE   40   1,931.050   3 events
(653 [6] 3715 [17] 24.4 [17])

17. Pierre Failliot   FRA   42   3 events
(629 [13] 3346 [24] 23.2 [5])

18. Hugo Ericson   SWE   44   3 events
(558 [26] 4374 [7] 24.0 [11])

19. John Eller, Jr.   USA   47   3 events
(617 [18] 3336 [25] 23.1 [4])

20. Julius Wagner   SUI   52   3 events
(622 [16] 4131[350] [13] 25.3 [23])

21. Gustav Krojer   AUT   54   3 events
(610 [19] 3989[351] [15] 24.7 [20])

22. Georges André   FRA   60   3 events
(598 [21] 3483 [21] 24.6 [18])

23. Mıgır Mıgıryan   TUR   67   3 events
(559 [25] 3687 [18] 26.4 [24])

24. Alfredo Pagani   ITA   68   3 events
(586 [23] 3423 [23] 25.2 [22])

AC. Karl von Halt   GER   DNF   2 events
(- - - [22/24??][352] 4275 [10])

   Josef Waitzer[353]   GER   DNF   2 events
(- - - [22/24??] DNS [26])
[354]

Diplomas of Merit

Frank Lukeman (CAN), Austin Menaul (USA), Avery Brundage (USA), Hugo Wieslander (SWE)

NOTES

1. FW has 71. DW, EK, and OSVK have 68.
2. FW has 21.
3. Johnson WO. *All That Glitters is Not Gold*, p. 138.
4. At 0.6 meters per 12OR.
5. At 0.15 meters per 12OR.
6. Howard Drew (USA) qualified for the final but did not start because of a pulled muscle.
7. 12OR does not give any positions except noting that Drew won, with "Courtney being his most dangerous competitor." German sources (per Ralf Ragnitter) list the results as given above: 2) Courtney, 3) Gerhardt, 4) Kern, 5) Luther, and 6) Rácz. 12ORes has Kern in second.
8. Uggla has the margin as 0.5 meters.
9. EzM has Giongo 4th and Aelter 5th, but no sources are given and we cannot find this in a 1912 source.
10. Smedmark stopped running because he thought there had been a false start, but the race was not called back.
11. 12OR has the margin as "more than a meter."
12. EzM and OSVK have very different results from ours, listing 3) Jankovich, 4) Stewart, 5) Szobota, and 6) Mourlon. But no sources are given and we cannot find this in a 1912 source.
13. EzM and OSVK have very different results from ours, listing 3) Wilson, 4) d'Arcy, 5) Howard, and 6) Vygoda. But no sources are given and we cannot find this in a 1912 source. In particular, Uggla has Vygoda third.
14. Also entered in this heat, but not competing, were Leopoldo Palma (CHI), Maurice Colman (BEL), Ernest Samazeuil (FRA), Angelo Rossi (ITA), and Tadeusz Garczynski (AUT).
15. Also entered in this heat, but not competing, were Henri Puncet (FRA), Jean Schols (BEL), and Francesco Bicchi (ITA).
16. Also entered in this heat, but not competing, were Émile Paul Lesieur (FRA), Zdislav Prágr (BOH), Tivadar Csató (HUN), and Charles Rice (USA).
17. Also entered in this heat, but not competing, were André Paul Louis Rémy Gauthier (FRA), R. L. Lange (USA), and István Ondrus (HUN).
18. EzM and OSVK have the following results: 4) Triantafyllakos, 5) Schurrer, 6) Levensteins. Ralf Regnitter notes that German sources give the results as: 4) Schurrer, 5) Triantafyllakos, 6) Levensteins. 12OR, 12ORes, Uggla, Spalding, and Diem do not give results past third place.
19. Eric Lindholm (SWE) was also entered in this heat, but did not compete.
20. Fernand Rapin (FRA) may have competed in this heat. He is listed as such in 12ORes. But he is not listed in 12OR, ONews, or Uggla, which are basically all the 1912 sources. Further, he is not listed in the French Olympic index given in *La Galaxie Olympique*. He is not listed in EzM, or in OSVK, although these are contemporary accounts. He is also not listed in master Olympic indices compiled by Wolf Lyberg (*The Athletes of the Summer Olympic Games 1896–1996*) and Gennadi Marichev (*Who is Who at the Summer Olympics 1896–1992*).
21. Vilmos Rádi (HUN) was also entered in this heat, but did not compete.
22. EzM and OSVK have the following results: 3) Delaby, 4) Sotaaen, 5) Labík-Gregan. But no source is given and we cannot find this in any 1912 source.
23. S. Levin (SWE) may have competed in this heat, although it is unlikely. He is listed as such in 12ORes. But he is not listed in 12OR, ONews, or Uggla, which are basically all the 1912 sources. Further, he is not listed in the Swedish Olympic index given in *Sverige och OS*. He is not listed in EzM, or in OSVK, although these are contemporary accounts. He is also not listed in master Olympic indices compiled by Wolf Lyberg (*The Athletes of the Summer Olympic Games 1896–1996*) and Gennadi Marichev (*Who is Who at the Summer Olympics 1896–1992*).
24. Ivan Zakharov (RUS) and Emil Grandell (SWE) may have competed in this heat, although it is unlikely. They are listed as such in 12ORes. But they are not listed in 12OR, ONews, or Uggla, which are basically all the 1912 sources. Further, Grandell is not listed as competing in the 100 in the Swedish Olympic index given in *Sverige och OS*. They are not listed in EzM, or in OSVK, although

these are contemporary acconts. They are also not listed as competing in the 100 in the master Olympic index compiled by Gennadi Marichev (*Who is Who at the Summer Olympics 1896–1992*) (Zakharov is not listed as competing at all). Zakharov is not listed in the master index compiled by Wolf Lyberg (*The Athletes of the Summer Olympic Games 1896–1996*) although Grandell is. But Lyberg's index does not list events, and it is known that Grandell competed in other events in 1912, so this does not in any way show that he competed in the 100.

25. Not listed in most sources, including ones EzM and OSVK, but Macmillan is listed as competing in this heat in Uggla and 12ORes.

26. Knut Stenborg (SWE) may have competed in this heat, although it is unlikely. He is listed as such in 12ORes. But he is not listed in 12OR, ONews, or Uggla, which are basically all the 1912 sources. Further, he is not listed as competing in the 100 in the Swedish Olympic index given in *Sverige och OS*. He is not listed in EzM, or in OSVK, although these are contemporary accounts. He is also not listed as competing in the 100 in the master Olympic index compiled by Gennadi Marichev (*Who is Who at the Summer Olympics 1896–1992*). Stenborg is listed by Wolf Lyberg in his master Olympian index (*The Athletes of the Summer Olympic Games 1896–1996*), but that index does not give information on events, so it does not show that he competed in the 100. He did compete in other events in 1912 though.

27. Gaston Wems (BEL) may have competed in this heat, although it is unlikely. He is listed as such in 12ORes. But he is not listed in 12OR, ONews, or Uggla, which are basically all the 1912 sources. He is not listed in EzM, or in OSVK, although these are contemporary accounts. He is also not listed in master Olympic indices compiled by Wolf Lyberg (*The Athletes of the Summer Olympic Games 1896–1996*) and Gennadi Marichev (*Who is Who at the Summer Olympics 1896–1992*).

28. Robert Kerr (CAN) may have competed in this heat, although it is highly unlikely. He is listed as such in 12ORes. But he is not listed in 12OR, ONews, or Uggla, which are basically all the 1912 sources. He is not listed in the Canadian Olympic Association database of competitors as competing in 1912. He is not listed in the chapter on 1912 in Henry Roxborough's book, *Canada at the Olympics*. Further, in *Olympic Gold*, by Glynn Leyshon and Frank Cosentino, they note, "In 1912, Kerr had an opportunity to represent his city and country once more in the Olympic Games. Even after having earned his position, he deferred and stepped aside to offer his place to a younger athlete who would benefit from the experience." He is not listed in EzM, or in OSVK, although these are contemporary accounts. He is also not listed in master Olympic indices compiled by Wolf Lyberg (*The Athletes of the Summer Olympic Games 1896–1996*) and Gennadi Marichev (*Who is Who at the Summer Olympics 1896–1992*).

29. Gustav "Gösta" Möller (SWE) was also entered in this heat, but did not compete.

30. EzM and OSVK have the following results: 4) Szerelemhegyi, 5) Mishima. But no source is given and we cannot find this in any 1912 source.

31. Rodolfo Hammersley (CHI) may have competed in this heat, although it is unlikely. He is listed as such in 12ORes. But he is not listed in 12OR, ONews, or Uggla, which are basically all the 1912 sources. He is not listed in EzM, or in OSVK, although these are contemporary accounts. He is also not listed in master Olympic indices compiled by Wolf Lyberg (*The Athletes of the Summer Olympic Games 1896–1996*) and Gennadi Marichev (*Who is Who at the Summer Olympics 1896–1992*).

32. Nils Fixdal (NOR) may have competed in this heat, although it is highly unlikely. He is listed as such in 12ORes. But he is not listed in 12OR, ONews, or Uggla, which are basically all the 1912 sources. Further, a Norwegian Olympic historian notes, "I consider Nils Fixdal as competitor only in LJ and TJ, not in 100m. No Norwegian sources gives him as competitor in 100m." He is not listed in EzM, or in OSVK, although these are contemporary accounts. He is also not listed as competing in the 100 in master Olympic indices compiled by Wolf Lyberg (*The Athletes of the Summer Olympic Games 1896–1996*) and Gennadi Marichev (*Who is Who at the Summer Olympics 1896–1992*).

33. DW, EK, FW, and OSVK have 60.

34. No time given in 12OR, but Uggla has the time of 21.9.

35. 12OR has Rolot third, the only source giving this finish. Patching and Macintosh did not finish, so Herrmann must have placed fourth, assuming he finished. No source mentions that he did not.

36. Patching and Henry Macintosh (GBR) are not listed per the OR, but are listed in Uggla, 12ORes, ONews, and EzM and OSVK. ONews also lists Patching and Macintosh as "also starting" but does not mention their finish, and it implies that they DNF. Per Uggla, Patching and Macintosh stopped when they had no chance.

37. Time according to Uggla.

38. Time according to Uggla.

39. EzM gives the following times: 2) d'Arcy 22.3, 3) Lindberg 22.4, 4) Déván 22.5. No source is given and we cannot confirm these times. They are likely estimates, but the only margin we have seen is 12OR noting that "there was very little to choose between d'Arcy and Lindberg at the end of the race."

40. Also entered in this heat, but not competing, were Dimitrios Triantafyllakos (GRE), and Alexandre Correa Leal (POR).

41. Also entered in this heat, but not competing, were Claude Ross (AUS), and István Ondrus (HUN).

42. Ugglad notes that Baumanis did not finish. EzM and OSVK have Baumanis 4th and Hahne 5th.

43. Károly Radóczy (HUN) was also entered in this heat, but did not compete.

44. Also entered in this heat, but not competing, were Dušan Milošević (SRB), Victor Jacquemin (BEL), Émile Paul Lesieur (FRA), and Ulrich Baasch (RUS).

45. According to Uggla, Applegarth and Heiland crossed the line "simultaneously."

46. Also entered in this heat, but not competing, were Pál Szalay (HUN), Maurice Gallisa (FRA), Jack Sweet (AUS), and Angelo Rossi (ITA).

47. Also entered in this heat, but not competing were Bedřich Vygoda (BOH), and Francesco Bicchi (ITA).

48. Placement given in ONews.

49. EzM and OSVK have the following results: 3) Malfait, 4) Beasley, 5) Wells. No source is given and we cannot find this in 1912 sources.

50. Rudolf Smedmark (SWE) may have competed in this heat, although it is unlikely. He is listed as such in 12ORes. But he is not listed in 12OR, ONews, or Uggla, which are basically all the 1912 sources. Further, he is not listed as competing in the 200 in the Swedish Olympic index given in *Sverige och OS*. He is not listed in EzM, or in OSVK, although these are contemporary accounts. He is also not listed as competing in the 200 in the master Olympic index compiled by Gennadi Marichev (*Who is Who at the Summer Olympics 1896–1992*). Stenborg is listed by Wolf Lyberg in his master Olympian index (*The Athletes of the Summer Olympic Games 1896–1996*), but that index does not give information on events, so it does not show that he competed in the 200. He did compete in other events in 1912.

51. According to Uggla, Howard and Giongo crossed the line "simultaneously."

52. Also entered in this heat, but not competing, were Raymond Ali Jules Saladin (FRA), Howard Drew (USA), Fritz Weinzinger (AUT), and Ragnar Ekberg (SWE).

53. Margin according to Uggla.

54. Also entered in this heat, but not competing, were Jean Schols (BEL), Vilmos Rácz (HUN), and Alexander Pedersen (NOR).

55. Also entered in this heat, but not competing, were André Paul Louis Rémy Gauthier (FRA), Rodolfo Hammersley (CHI), and Erwin Kern (GER).

56. Margin according to Uggla.

57. Also entered in this heat, but not competing, were Stanislaus Rudsit (RUS), Maurice Colman (BEL), Robert Kerr (CAN), and Vilmos Rádi (HUN).

58. 12ORes has Fleischer, Wenseler, and Frank Lukeman (CAN) in Heat 13. None are noted as DNS. But both 12OR, Uggla, and ONews have only four participants, thus Lukeman probably DNS. ONews has Wenseler 3rd. 12ORes has Fleischer 3rd. EzM and OSVK have the following: 3) Fleischer, 4) Wenseler, 5) Mishima. No source is given and no result in that order is found in any 1912 source. We think the result is too much in question to assign positions to any finishers other than Young and Seedhouse. Fleischer's participation is highly questionable.

59. 12OR also lists Frederick Thomas Browne (GBR) as competing, and EzM and OSVK have the following results: 3) McConnell, 4) Browne, 5) Grandell, and do not list Szerelemhegyi. According to Arild Gjerde (NOR), Szerelemhegyi competed and Browne did not. However, Gjerde notes that this is an "unknown source," but sources exist to confirm this. Uggla has Szerelemhegyi and not Browne. Also, Browne was a member of the Blackheath Harriers and in their journal, *Gazette & Club Record* for August 1912, they noted, "First Browne hurt his leg, then Soutter, and then Seedhouse… We feel very sorry for them but especially Browne as he lost his place in the Olympic team thereby."

60. Grandell retired at 20 meters with a pulled leg muscle.

61. ONews has Ponurski as 4th. Ponurski is not even listed in 12OR, but he is listed by Uggla and 12ORes.

62. Leopoldo Palma (CHI) is listed in 12OR and 12ORes, but not in Uggla and ONews. He is also not listed in modern sources EzM and OSVK. Eric Lindholm (SWE) may have competed in this heat, but it is more likely that he did not compete.

63. Also entered in this heat, but not competing, were Philipp Ehrenreich (AUT), Jacob Pedersen (NOR), Ernest Samazeuil (RUS), and Bernhard Vogel (RUS).

64. According to Uggla they finished almost together.

65. Also entered in this heat, but not competing, were István Jankovich (HUN), Eugene Mercer (USA), Emil Ketterer (GER), and Fernand Rapin (FRA).

66. Also entered in this heat, but not competing, were Mıgır Mıgıryan (TUR), Gaston Wems (BEL), and Jón Halldórsson (ISL).

67. John Dahlin (SWE) qualified for this heat, but did not compete.

68. Neither Wells nor Person is listed as having competed in this heat in the OR.

69. Time given in Uggla.

70. Yahiko Mishima (JPN) qualified for this heat, but did not compete.

71. Young finished first but was disqualified for obstructing Braun. See the description at the beginning of the event.

72. Also entered in this heat, but not competing, were Jan Grijseels (NED), and Gerard Anderson (GBR).

73. Also entered in this heat, but not competing, were Robert Kerr (CAN), James Hill (GBR), and Bernhard Vogel (RUS).

74. Also entered in this heat, but not competing, were Federico Mueller (CHI), Raymond Ali Jules Saladin (FRA), and Ture Person (SWE).

75. Also entered in this heat, but not competing, were Aleksandr Schultz (RUS), André Fouache (FRA), and Ralph Craig (USA).

76. Alexandre Correa Leal (POR) was also entered in this heat, but did not compete.

77. Also entered in this heat, but not competing, were Victor Jacquemin (BEL), Naum Filimonov (RUS), Herman Sotaaen (NOR), Clément Célestin Mentrel (FRA), and Zdeněk Městecký (BOH).

78. Also entered in this heat, but not competing, were Joseph Caulle (FRA), Karl Haglund (SWE), and Duncan Macmillan (GBR).

79. Also entered in this heat, but not competing, were Leopoldo Palma (CHI), Herberts Baumanis (RUS), and Robert Burton (GBR).

80. Tivadar Kiss (HUN) was also entered in this heat, but did not compete.

81. Also entered in this heat, but not competing, were Lauri Pihkala (FIN), John Howard (CAN), and Erik Frisell (SWE).

82. Jack Sweet (AUS) was also entered in this heat, but did not compete.

83. Wells' time given only in 12ORes.

84. Uggla has Pierre Failliot (FRA) as 3rd place, but 12ORes, 12OR, and ONews do not list him as starting.

85. Also entered in this heat, but not competing, were Carl Cooke (USA), Pierre Failliot (FRA), Robert Alexander Lindsay (GBR), and T. Österlund (SWE).

86. Also entered in this heat, but not competing, were Károly Radóczy (HUN), Harold Heiland (USA), and Karl August "Charles" Luther (SWE).

87. Wenseler is not mentioned in Uggla which specifically states "4 men at the starting line." 12ORes has no did-not-start listed. These results are given in ONews and 12OR lists these five as starters.

88. Maurice Colman (BEL) was also entered in this heat, but did not compete.

89. These are listed as such in ORes, 12OR, and Uggla.

90. OTAF, p. 32.

91. QK, p. 26.

92. Places 4–8 are from QK — see the description above in the race summary.

93. Places for Tait and Mann given only in ONews.

94. Hulford is not listed as running in Uggla, but he is in 12OR and ONews, both of which stated he did not finish. TF noted, "F. H. Hulford did not finish."

95. Soutter (GBR) is not listed in 12OR as having competed, but he is listed in ONews, and Uggla. TF did not mention Soutter at all in the semifinals, which is a bit unusual, considering that he won a heat in round one. It is likely he did not actually compete in the semifinals.

96. John Paul Jones (USA) was scheduled for this heat but did not start.

97. Place for Lunghi given in ONews. However, TF states, "E. J. Henley, Great Britain, finished fifth; he lay last till 500 yards, then sprinted strongly and got up with his men, but fell away in the last 200 yards."

98. See previous footnote — listed as fifth by TF.

99. John Paul Jones (USA) had qualified for this heat, but did not compete.

100. Caldwell's time was 1:58.4 in 12OR, but 1:58.6 in 12ORes, ONews, and Uggla.

101. Time per 12ORes.

102. Also entered in this heat, but not competing, were Eugène Geriot (FRA), Erling Sjøland (NOR), Václav Labík-Gregan (BOH), and Pyotr Gayevsky (RUS).

103. Also entered in this heat, but not competing, were Naum Filimonov (RUS), Ernst Wide (SWE), Zdenek Latavice (AUT), and L. Andrén (SWE).

104. Also entered in this heat, but not competing, were Teofil Savniki-Marschalko (HUN), Nils Frykberg (SWE), James Hill (GBR), Gerard Anderson (GBR), and Marius Etcheparré (FRA), according to the 12ORes. ONews and 12OR do list Savniki-Marschalko as competing.

105. Also entered in this heat, but not competing, were Henri Arnaud (FRA), Thorild Olsson (SWE), and Otto Palotai (HUN).

106. Robert Hales (GBR) was also entered in this heat, but did not compete.

107. See next footnote.

108. Time per 12ORes.

109. Vahran Papazyan is not listed in 12OR or ONews, but he is listed in 12ORes and Uggla. On page 417 in Uggla, a photo shows only seven competitors. All of the runners can be identified except Mueller, and Yelizarov. Mueller and Yelizarov are listed in every source as competing. One runner has a crest on his jersey, which is likely Papazyan. There may have been only seven runners, not eight as we have listed, and if that is the case, then either Mueller or Yelizarov likely did not start.

110. Josef Lindbom (SWE) was also entered in this heat, but did not compete.

111. Time was 2:00.8 per Uggla, but 2:00.4 per 12OR and ONews.

112. The late Zoltan Subert (HUN), a usually reliable ATFS member, claims that Antal was entered but did not start. Alex Dubourg (FRA) and Harry Edward Gissing (USA) are listed as did-not-starts in 12ORes, but there is no such notation for Antal. Uggla has Dubourg as starting, while 12OR and ONews do not. 12OR lists Antal and Villemson as did-not-finishes.

113. Also entered in this heat, but not competing, were John Dahlin (SWE), Georges Alexandre Berretrot (FRA), Lester Bermond (USA), and Konstant Gern (RUS).

114. Also entered in this heat, but not competing, were August Meos (RUS) and Imre László (HUN).

115. FW has 45.

116. NQ, p. 21.

117. ONews, 12 July 1912, p. 7.

118. Buchanan, *British Olympians,* pp. 94–95.

119. The 12ORes has three times given for Wide — 3:57.5, 3:57.6, and 3:57.8, with "3:57.6" underlined. These are probably the three stopwatch times and the middle one was chosen as the official mark.

120. FW has Sheppard incorrectly in sixth.

121. Listed as 3:59.6 in OSVK.

122. Uggla lists only eight names among the finishers. The order in Uggla is the same as ours for 1–7, with no definite places mentioned for sixth to eighth. The eighth name listed in Uggla is McClure, implying that he finished eighth. ONews also lists McClure as eighth.

123. FW has Sheppard incorrectly in sixth.

124. EzM has 8) Arnaud, 9) Sheppard, 10) Hedlund, 11) von Sigel, 12) McClure, 13) Madeira, 14) Björn. As for the only 1912 sources, they list results no deeper than eighth, stopping at McClure.

125. Listed as eighth place in DW.

126. AG/MT lists von Sigel as ninth with 4:05.3. The places and times are from H/A.

127. Also entered in this heat, but not competing, were Pyotr Timofeyev (RUS), József Nady (HUN), Iosif Zaytsev (RUS), Janos Antal (HUN), Georges Dumonteuil (FRA), Emilio Lunghi (ITA), Ödön Bodor (HUN), George Hill (AUS/NZL), and Anton Nilsson (SWE).

128. Also entered in this heat, but not competing, were Klas Lundström (SWE), Robert Hales (GBR), Charles Denis (FRA), Thorild Olsson (SWE), Imre László (HUN), Otto Palotai (HUN), and Wallace McCurdy (USA).

129. Also entered in this heat, but not competing, were Mihály Váradi (HUN), Gyula Belu (HUN), Marcel Quilbeuf (FRA), and August Elmik (RUS).

130. Also entered in this heat, but not competing, were Georges Renaux (FRA), Zdenek Latavice (AUT), L. Andrén (SWE), and Frederick McNair (USA).

131. Also entered in this heat, but not competing, were Federico Mueller (CHI), Georges Renaux (FRA), Fréderic Belarge (BEL). Strangely, Renaux was entered in both heats four and five, but started in neither.

132. Also entered in this heat, but not competing, were Erling Sjøland (NOR), William Crabbie (GBR), Josef Lindbom (SWE), Paul Charles Fonseca (FRA), and Frederick McNair (USA).

133. Also entered in this heat, but not competing, were Pyotr Gayevsky (RUS), Bror Modigh (SWE), René Giraud (FRA), Gyula Kiss (HUN), Eugène Bats (FRA), and Douglas Frank McNicol (GBR).

134. Kolehmainen/Bouin's three-mile time was an estimated 14:07.4.

135. Listed as 8th place in DW and OSVK with Karlsson in 6th and Henry [Louis] Scott in 7th.

136. According to 12ORes, Hibbins DNS, but he is listed as "also started" in 12OR, Uggla, and ONews.

137. Ernest Glover (GBR), Henrik Nordström (SWE), Thorild Olsson (SWE), and Franz "Viljam" Johansson (FIN) qualified for the final but did not start.

138. EzM, FW, OSVK, and H/A have the finish as follows: 6) Carlsson, 7) Scott, 8) Decouteau, 9) Keeper, 10) Hibbins, 11) Porter. However, no sources are given and 1912 sources give no place beyond seventh. The deepest sources are Uggla and ONews, which have Decoteau sixth and Carlsson seventh. In 12OR, Carlsson was sixth.

139. Retired on the last lap according to Uggla.

140. Also entered in this heat, but not competing, were Mihály Váradi (HUN), Harry Smith (USA), Marcel Radique (FRA), John Victor (RSA), Felix Lixl-Kwieton (AUT), Albert Öberg (SWE), Armand Fayollat (FRA), Guglielmo Becattini (ITA), Louis Cephas Madeira (USA), and William Scott (GBR).

141. Retired after four laps according to Uggla.

142. Retired after 1½ laps according to Uggla.

143. Retired after 1½ laps according to Uggla.

144. Also entered in this heat, but not competing, were Pyotr Timofeyev (RUS), Henri Arnaud (FRA), Carlo Speroni (ITA), Ödön Kárpáti Kraml (HUN), Edward Owen (GBR), Lucien Armand Fremont (FRA), Norman Taber (USA), and Jean-Marie Roche (FRA).

145. Retired three laps from the finish according to Uggla.

146. Retired immediately after Wikoff, about three laps from the finish, according to Uggla.

147. Also entered in this heat, but not competing, were Bror Fock (SWE), Pierre Lalaimode (FRA), Iosif Zaytsev (RUS), Karl Hack (AUT), Georges Dudant (FRA), Vahran Papazyan (TUR), Iraklis Sakellaropoulos (GRE), Paul Lixandier (FRA), Gregor Vietz (GER), and Frederick McNair (USA). Vietz competed in Heat Five, for unknown reasons.

148. Lee's fourth-place finish is according to Uggla. 12OR lists him as did-not-finish.

149. Also entered in this heat, but not competing, were Leonard Richardson (RSA), Efraim Harju (FIN), George Wallach (GBR), Gustave Henri Lauvaux (FRA), Lewis Anderson (USA), Francis Joseph O'Neill (GBR), Filip Löwendahl (SWE), John Lindsay Tait (CAN), Grigory Voronkov (RUS), Sándor Kertész (HUN), William Kramer (USA), and Antal Lovass (HUN).

150. According to Uggla, McCurdy fell about 50 meters from the finish and retired.

151. Also entered in this heat, but not competing, were Nils Frykberg (SWE), Nikolay Kharkov (RUS), Ferenc Forgács-Faczinek (HUN), Christopher Gitsham (RSA), Georges Dumonteuil (FRA), John Eke (SWE), William Cottrill (GBR), and Anton Nilsson (SWE).

152. Retired after 16 laps according to 12ORes.

153. Retired after 17 laps according to 12ORes.

154. EL lists Louis Scott as from the USA in the heats and from GBR in the final. He was an American runner and the GBR is incorrect.

155. EL lists this athlete as Walter Scott. William Scott is the listing in Buchanan's *British Olympians.*

156. Retired at about 4:25.

157. Retired at about 7,000 meters.

158. Gaston Heuet (FRA), Ernest Glover (GBR), John Eke (SWE), and Martin Persson (SWE) had qualified for the final but did not start.

159. According to ONews, it appears that the runners in this heat ran one lap too many.

160. EL has the following places — 7) Lee, 8) Ruffell, 9) Penc, 10) Kramer, 11) Nikolsky, and 12) Hellawell. AG/MT state that those six runners did not finish. This is confirmed by Uggla, who notes that Penc and Hellawell retired at four laps, and Kramer retired with nine laps to go.

161. Also entered in this heat, but not competing, were Klas Lundström (SWE), William Murray (AUS), Karl Hack (AUT), Ödön Kárpáti Kraml (HUN), Marcel Radique (FRA), Bror Modigh (SWE), Filip Löwendahl (SWE), Garnett Wikoff (USA), and Carl Holmberg (DEN).

162. EL has the places as follows: 6) Fock, 7) Larsson, 8) Sanchez, 9) Humphreys, 10) Hibbins, and 11) Vietz. AG/MT state that these six runners actually did not finish. Confirming this, ORes notes that Fock retired after 14 laps, and according to 12OR and Uggla, Hibbins and Humphreys retired shortly after Fock. Uggla listed Sanchez Rodriguez as sixth, and Larsson seventh, but ONews had Larsson sixth, and did not list seventh place.

163. Also entered in this heat, but not competing, were Henri Teyssedou (FRA), Gustave Henri Lauvaux (FRA), Nikolay Kharkov (RUS), François Delloye (BEL), John Gallagher (USA), Edouard Fabre (CAN), Francis Joseph O'Neill (GBR), Joseph Erxleben (USA), Henrik Nordström (SWE), Holger Baden (DEN), Iraklis Sakellaropoulos (GRE), Grigory Voronkov (RUS), Sándor Kertész (HUN), Felix Lixl-Kwieton (AUT), Lucien Armand Fremont (FRA), and Michael Ryan (USA).

164. EL has 6) Wallach and 7) Hill. AG/MT state that they did not finish. Confirming this, Uggla notes that Wallach retired after 10 laps and Hill retired at 5,000 meters.

165. Retired after 10 laps according to Uggla.

166. Retired after 5,000 meters according to Uggla.

167. Also entered in this heat, but not competing, were Pyotr Timofeyev (RUS), František Slavík (BOH), George Bonhag (USA), Clovis Pierre Cambon (FRA), Mihály Váradi (HUN), Iosif Zaytsev (RUS), Hjalmar Andersson (SWE), Harry Smith (USA), Carlo Speroni (ITA), Thomas Jack (GBR), Dragutin Tomašević (SRB), Alex Decoteau (CAN), Jan Mrzygtodzki (AUT), Christopher Gitsham (RSA), Viggo Pedersen (DEN), Jean Bouin (FRA), John Klintberg (SWE), Georges Dumonteuil (FRA), Louis Pauteux (FRA), and Antal Lovass (HUN).

168. The scheduled start was 1345 (1:45 P.M.), but the time is given in G/M as 1348 and this is confirmed in the 12OR.

169. G/M, p. 85.

170. G/M, p.94.

171. DW ha 2-45:47.4.

172. 12ORes has 15) Smith, 16) Forsyth, and 17) Tewanima, but has the same times as given here, which are from 12OR. The times seems reliable, which places Forsyth 15th, Tewanima 16th, and Smith 17th.

173. Kanaguri gave up shortly after the 20 kilometer mark with a foot injury, and was not seen again during the Olympics. In fact, his whereabouts for the rest of the Stockholm Olympics and what happened to him during this race remained a mystery until 1962, when Swedish journalist Oscar Söderlund located him in Japan and invited him to Stockholm where he symbolically finished the marathon he had started 50 years earlier. Kaniguri told how he had abandoned the race shortly after 20 kilometers, and had been invited in by a family to drink some fruit juice in their garden. He was ashamed of failing to finish, so he a took a tram to Stockholm, and without contacting the organizing committee, or his Japanese team, returned home on his own. Kanaguri did compete in the Olympic marathon again, however, in both 1920 (16th) and 1924 (did not finish).

174. Lázaro collapsed during the race from the effects of sunstroke. He died the next day, one of only two Olympic athletes to have died during an Olympic competition — the other being the Danish cyclist, Knut Enemark Jensen, who died during the 1960 cycling road race.

175. According to 12OR, he did not start, but he is not listed as a "DNS" in the 12ORes.

176. Also entered in this event, but not starting, were Alex Decoteau (CAN), George Goulding (CAN), Joseph Keeper (CAN), Alfonso Sanchez Rodriguez (CHI), Bel Ali Allel (FRA), Jean Capelle (FRA), Paul Coulond (FRA), Gaston Heuet (FRA), Jean Lespielle (FRA), Henry Lorgnat (FRA), Edmond Neyrinck (FRA), Ahmed Djebella (FRA), Charles Davenport (GBR), George Joseph Day (GBR), Henry Arthur Lewis (GBR), Samuel Raynes (GBR), Nino Cazzaniga (ITA), Orlando Cesaroni (ITA), Alfred August Nilsen (NOR), Ole Olsen (NOR), J:s Chr. Pedersen (NOR), Mathias de Carvalho (POR), Nikolay Kharkov (RUS), Aleksandr Krachenin (RUS), Mikhail Nikolsky (RUS), Iosif Zaytsev (RUS), René Wilde (RUS), Leonard Richardson (RSA), and Zivko Vastitsch (SRB).

177. According to Yves Pinaud's book, *L'Athletisme Africain*, Ahmed Djebella (FRA) started but did not finish. Pinaud notes that Djebella, an Algerian born in Tunis, is the first African outside South Africa to have competed in Olympic track & field. Swedish track & field historian, Rooney Magnusson, says it is most likely that Djebella was a nonstarter, and he is not listed in 12ORes.

178. DW, EK, FW, and OSVK have 46.

179. The race was supposed to be of 8,000 meters, but the times make it certain that it was nearer 12,000 meters.

180. Time according to 12ORes. 12OR has 47:07.1. DW and OSVK use 47:07.1.

181. Listed as Carl Holmberg (DEN) in 12OR, but according to *De Olympiske*, Topp replaced Holmberg and Holmberg did not start in this event.

182. Buchanan did not list Cottrill as competing in this event in *British Olympians*. *The Field* lists Cottrill as finishing 16th instead of Glover.

183. The athletes who did not finish are hard to clarify. Some sources (Gjerde) list Gerhard Topp (DEN) and Efraim Harju (FIN). EzM has Tell Berna on the USA team instead of George Bonhag. Q4G does not list Bonhag or Kramer. The *New York Times* lists the American team members as Hellawell, Bonhag, Berna, Kramer, and Scott, which seems most reliable for the American team members. The OR lists Hellawell, Scott, Bonhag, Kramer, and John Paul Jones.

184. Also entered in this event, but not competing, were Henri Arnaud (FRA), Charles Ruffell (GBR), George Wallach (GBR), Henri Teyssedou (FRA), Pyotr Timofeyev (RUS), František Slavík (BOH), Hans Andersen (NOR), George Lee (GBR), Mihály Váradi (HUN), Rudolf Richter (BOH), Vladimír Penc (BOH), Iosif Zaytsev (RUS), William Murray (AUS), and Nikolay Kharkov (RUS).

185. The fourth to sixth place finishers (Jalmari Eskola [FIN], Josef Ternström [SWE], and Albin Stenroos [FIN]) do not appear to have been awarded diplomas of merit. It is not certain why they did not receive the diplomas, while the seventh to 12th place finishers did, but this is based on 12OR.

186. EK and OSVK have 42.
187. According to 12ORes, Scott started and Charles Ruffell and George Wallach did not start.
188. According to 12ORes, Berna started, and John Paul Jones, who is listed in some American sources, did not start.
189. DW, EK, FW, and OSVK have 21.
190. Fell at the eighth hurdle.
191. Fell at the eighth hurdle.
192. 12ORes has Wickholm second in 16.6 est, but ONews has Blakeney second.
193. According to 12ORes.
194. Also entered in this heat, but not competing, were Gustaf "Gösta" Holmér (SWE), Albert Martin (FRA), and Richard Rice (GBR).
195. Eller knocked down two hurdles.
196. According to 12ORes.
197. Also entered in this heat, but not competing, were Béla Mészáros (HUN), Gaston Sabarthez (FRA), and Thorwald Norling (SWE).
198. Also entered in this heat, but not competing, were Andor Horvag (HUN), Skotte Jacobsson (SWE), and Edward Ives Beeson (USA).
199. Also entered in this heat, but not competing, were Louis Saint-Aubert (FRA), Einar Nilsson (SWE), and James Donahue (USA).
200. Eitel knocked down two hurdles.
201. Also entered in this heat, but not competing, were Hugo Wieslander (SWE), Camille Leunckens (BEL), Raymond de Guanderax (FRA), and Paul Zerling (SWE).
202. Delaby knocked down one hurdle.
203. Blanchard knocked down one hurdle.
204. Also entered in this heat, but not competing, were Bertil Uggla (SWE), and Richard Rau (GER).
205. Pritchard knocked down three hurdles.
206. Blakeney knocked down one hurdle.
207. Also entered in this heat, but not competing, were
208. Kelly knocked down two hurdles.
209. Von Bönninghausen knocked down 2 hurdles.
210. Powell won despite knocking down three hurdles.
211. There was also a heat twelve scheduled but it was canceled, because none of the five competitors (including Jim Thorpe [USA]) showed up to race.
212. Roxborough, Henry. *Canada at the Olympics.* Toronto: Ryerson Press, 1963, pp. 50–51.
213. Glyche was the first to abandon the race.
214. Stopped at about 5,000 meters.
215. Stopped slightly before 5,000 meters.
216. Disqualified at about 5,000 meters.
217. Disqualified shortly after St. Norman.
218. Disqualified shortly after Dumbill.
219. Also entered in this heat, but not competing, were Eduard Hermann (RUS), Walery Jaworski (AUT), Peter Szbalyár (HUN), Henrik Ripszám, Jr. (HUN), John Karlsen (USA), George Morton (USA), Peter Paxián (HUN), and Thomas Edgar Hammond (GBR). For reasons not known, Ripszám was allowed to take part in heat two.
220. Ripszám was actually entered in heat one, but did not take part in that heat. For unknown reasons, he started in heat two.
221. Disqualified shortly after 5,000 meters.
222. Disqualified in the 11th lap.
223. It is not certain if Drubina was disqualified for abandoning, but he did not finish.
224. Also entered in this heat, but not competing, were Miklóz Fekete (HUN), Henry Scott (USA), Mario Vitali (ITA), and János Patak (HUN).
225. Exchanged outside the passing zone.

226. Uggla has Kern, Halt, Herrmann, Rau; while the above roster is from 12OR, ORes, and Diem.

227. The United States finished first in 42.2 but was disqualified. The second baton pass between Belote and Wilson occurred outside of the exchange zone.

228. Walkover.

229. Also entered, but not starting, was Chile (Leopoldo Palma, Pablo Eitel, Rodolfo Hammersley, Federico Mueller).

230. Walkover.

231. Also entered, but not starting, was Italy (Franco Giongo, Francesco Bicchi, Angelo Rossi, Emilio Lunghi).

232. Also entered, but not starting, was Russia (Richard Schwarz, Ivan Zakharov, Pavel Shtiglits, Leopolds Levensteins).

233. Walkover.

234. Also entered, but not starting, was Norway (Herman Sotaaen, Edvard Larsen, Ferdinand Bie, Alexander Pedersen).

235. Bohemia did not start.

236. Also entered, but not starting, was Bohemia (Bedřich Vygoda, Ladislav Jiránek-Strana, Václav Labík-Gregan, Jindřich Jirsák).

237. Italy did not start.

238. Also entered in this heat, but not competing, was a team from Italy (Franco Giongo, Angelo Rossi, Emilio Lunghi, Guido Calvi).

239. Bohemia did not start.

240. In 12ORes, Sheppard is listed as did-not-start, implying that only three ran for the USA.

241. Also entered in this heat, but not competing, was a team from Bohemia (Václav Labík-Gregan, Jindřich Jirsák, Zdislav Prágr, Zdeněk Městecký).

242. Russia did not start.

243. Also entered in this heat, but not competing, was a team from Russia (Naum Filimonov, Aleksandr Schultz, Herberts Baumanis, Pyotr Gayevsky).

244. Owen finished 12th according to ORes but with no time given.

245. South Africa was also entered but did not start.

246. Also entered in this heat, but not competing, was a team from South Africa (Leonard Richardson, Arthur St. Norman, John Victor, Christopher Gitsham, Kennedy McArthur).

247. The five Swedish runners crossed the line simultaneously, effectively being all equal second although no places were actually given. They finished between von Sigel, who was first in 9:06.8, and Amberger, seventh in 9:32.5. The team score of 9 reflects that the "first" three Swedish runners essentially placed second, third, and fourth, for nine points.

248. Also entered in this heat, but not competing, was a team from Russia (Nikolay Kharkov, Aleksandr Yelizarov, Grigory Voronkov, Mikhail Nikolsky, Dmitry Nazarov).

249. Also entered in this heat, but not competing, were teams from France (Henri Arnaud, Georges Dudant, Paul Lixandier, Jean Bouin, Georges Dumonteuil) and Italy (Carlo Speroni, Alfonso Orlando, Guglielmo Becattini, Emilio Lunghi, Guido Calvi).

250. All the British runners crossed the line simultaneously.

251. Also entered in this heat, but not competing, were teams from France and Italy.

252. DW, EK, FW, and OSVK have 26.

253. DW, p. 115.

254. Equalled the Olympic record, set by Liesche, who cleared this height on his second attempt.

255. New Olympic record.

256 New Olympic record.

257. Thorpe was actually disqualified in early 1913. Most sources omit him from the results, save DW and OSVK. For more information, see the more detailed footnote concerning him in the decathlon section and Appendix II.

258. FW has Grumpelt and Johnstone in equal fifth, but he omitted Thorpe. OSVK lists Grumpelt and Johnstone as equal fifth, perhaps rationalizing that Thorpe's placement does not actually count.

259. Also entered in this group, but not competing, was Einar Nilsson (SWE).

260. Also entered in this group, but not competing, were Jean René Labat (FRA), Daniel Campbell (GBR), András Somodi (HUN), István Somodi (HUN), Miklós Nagy (HUN), Géza Vadon (HUN), Charles Lomberg (SWE), Konstantinos Tsiklitiras (GRE), Félix Mathey (FRA), and C. Hellstedt (SWE).

261. Sometimes listed as his brother, Jean René Labat, who was originally entered in Group Two, but withdrew and was replaced by André.

262. Also entered in this group, but not competing, were Carlo Butti (ITA), Fritz Weinzinger (AUT), Manlio Legat (ITA), Georg Holmqvist (SWE), Maurice Menier (FRA), Giulio Alvisi (ITA), Béla Szabó (HUN), Clive Taylor (GBR), Victor Dore (FRA), Edward Ives Beeson (USA), and Furio Bini (ITA).

263. DW and EK have 16. OSVK has 17.

264. DW and EK have 8.

265. Also entered in this group, but not competing, were Francis Irons (USA), Timothy Carroll (GBR), Svend Langkjær (DEN), Georg Åberg (SWE), Douglas Melin (SWE), Alfred Motte (FRA), Francis Louis Delaby (FRA), Angelo Tonini (ITA), John Johansson (SWE), Armand Estang (FRA), Carl-Einar Frick (SWE), Robert Isaac Khan (FRA), Ladislav Jiránek-Strana (BOH), and Henri Alphonse Jardin (FRA).

266. Also entered in this group, but not competing, were Endré Száll (HUN), Thomas O'Donahue (GBR), Gustav Nilsson (SWE), Andor Szende (HUN), Daniel Campbell (GBR), Iván, Baron Wardener (HUN), Maurice Garon (FRA), Géza Vadon (HUN), Carl Russell Palmer (USA), Leone Linardi (ITA), and Russell Lawrence Beatty (USA).

267. Listed in ONews and also in SOOS, but not in 12OR.

268. Jatekok lists Ernö Holecsek as equal 13th in qualifying with 1.40 while ATFS member Zoltán Subert (HUN) lists him as competing, but with no height. Holecsek is not listed in 12OR. ORes lists Andor Horvag but not Holecsek.

269. Also entered in this group, but not competing, were Paul Smutný (BOH), Manlio Legat (ITA), Martin Jacobsen (NOR), John Biller (USA), Georg Holmqvist (SWE), Giulio Alvisi (ITA), Walter Henderson (GBR), André Peux (FRA), Clive Taylor (GBR), Rafael Peltonen (FIN), Colombo Zevola (ITA), André Pettre (ITA), Francesco d'Ercole (ITA), and Hans Langkjær (DEN).

270. DW, EK, FW, and OSVK have 24.

271. All seven athletes who cleared 3.75 broke the existing Olympic record of 3.71.

272. All six athletes who cleared 3.80 broke the existing Olympic record of 3.75 which had been set by seven vaulters at the previous height.

273. All three athletes who cleared 3.85 broke the existing Olympic record of 3.80 which had been set by six vaulters at the previous height.

274. Babcock's mark of 3.95 broke the Olympic record of 3.85 which had been set by three vaulters at the previous height.

275. Happenny broke two ribs in clearing 3.80 and thus withdrew from further jumps.

276. Also entered in this group, but not competing, were Hugo Wieslander (SWE), János Szemere (HUN), Gustaf "Gösta" Holmér (SWE), Erik Simonsson (SWE), Eugene Mercer (USA), André Franquenelle (FRA), Skotte Jacobsson (SWE), Barton Haggard (USA), Maurice Garon (FRA), and Charles Lomberg (SWE).

277. Also entered in this group, but not competing, were Kálmán Szathmáry (HUN), Leone Linardi (ITA), Charles Lagarde (FRA), Stanley Wagoner (USA), Alfredo Pagani (ITA), and Furio Bini (ITA).

278. FW and OSVK have 29. DW and EK have 32.

279. DW and EK have 12.

280. Thorpe was actually disqualified in early 1913. See the more detailed footnote concerning him in the decathlon section, and Appendix II.

281. OSVK has Pasemann in seventh, and all subsequent placements one lower than ours — we have 12th, OSVK 11th, and so on. He apparently is not actually counting Thorpe as finishing higher than the athletes he defeated.

282. Groups two and three were combined into one group.

283. Also entered in this group, but not competing, were Carl Otto Silfverstrand (SWE), Paul Lagarde (FRA), Louis Saint-Aubert (FRA), Platt Adams (USA), Rodolfo Hammersley (CHI), Bedřich Vygoda (BOH), Ferenc Szobota (HUN), James Donahue (USA), Henri Puncet (FRA), and John Patrick Nicholson (USA).

284. Groups two and three were merged into one group. We have indicated the original draw showing in which group the athlete was to have competed.

285. Also entered in these groups, but not competing, were: group two — Raymond de Guanderax (FRA), József Kosa (HUN), Pierre Charles Glanzman (FRA), Eornel Kell (HUN), Gaston Martens (BEL), Hjalmar Ohlsson (SWE), William Happenny (CAN), Edvard Larsen (NOR), Hermann von Bönninghausen (GER), Skotte Jacobsson (SWE), Iván, Baron Wardener (HUN), Robert Bergeyer (FRA), Václav Labík-Gregan (BOH), Miklós Nagy (HUN), and Gustaf Nordén (SWE); group three — Géza Vadon (HUN), László Tihanyi (HUN), Gustaf "Topsy" Lindblom (SWE), Erik Almlöf (SWE), Kálmán Szathmáry (HUN), Charles Hervoche (FRA), Robert de la Brosse (FRA), Frank Lukeman (CAN), Leone Linardi (ITA), Emmanuel Tsaloumas (GRE), Zdislav Prágr (BOH), and Carlo Butti (ITA).

286. Also entered in this group, but not competing, were Jean René Labat (FRA), William Hunter (GBR), Paul Zerling (SWE), Louis Picolet (FRA), William Leach (GBR), Erling Vinne (NOR), Georg Holmqvist (SWE), D. V. Johansson (NOR), Giulio Alvisi (ITA), Samuel Bellah (USA), and Béla Szabó (HUN).

287. DW has Goehring fifth and Möller sixth, but no known method was used in 1912 to break a tie for an equal best mark.

288. Also entered in this group, but not competing, were Francis Irons (USA), Olaf Ingebretsen (NOR), Louis Saint-Aubert (FRA), Angelo Pedrelli (ITA), Einar Nilsson (SWE), Albert Gutterson (USA), Rodolfo Hammersley (CHI), Angelo Tonini (ITA), John Johansson (SWE), and Carl-Einar Frick (SWE).

289. Also entered in this group, but not competing, were Isaac Robert Kahn (FRA), Henri Alphonse Jardin (FRA), Ladislav Jiránek-Strana (BOH), Endré Száll (HUN), Claudio Carpi (ITA), Sidney Abrahams (GBR), Fernand Gillard (FRA), Frank Belote (USA), András Somodi (HUN), Laurent Casson (FRA), and Géza Vadon (HUN).

290. Also entered in this group, but not competing, were László Tihanyi (HUN), Carl Russell Palmer (USA), Erik Almlöf (SWE), Robert de la Brosse (FRA), Leone Linardi (ITA), Russell Lawrence Beatty (USA), Emmanuel Tsaloumas (GRE), Zdislav Prágr (BOH), Ignácz Akos (HUN), William Hunter (GBR), and Martin Jacobsen (NOR).

291. Also entered in this group, but not competing, were John Biller (USA), William Leach (GBR), Rafael Peltonen (FIN), Sverre Grøner (NOR), Helmer Måhl (SWE), Maurice Laraigne (FRA), Francesco d'Ercole (ITA), Alfredo Pagani (ITA), Gyula Pivnik (HUN), and Hans Langkjær (DEN).

292. DW and EK have 22.

293. DW and EK have 9.

294. This was done because of no shows. Four from group two were transferred to group one, five from group three were transferred to group four, and the remainder in groups two and three formed the new group two.

295. Originally drawn for group two, but reassigned to group one. The other four competitors were all originally in group one.

296. Also entered in this group (with original group in parentheses), but not competing, were Francis Irons (1) (USA), Pablo Eitel (1) (CHI), Albert Gutterson (1) (USA), Dimitrios Triantafyllakos (1) (GRE), Rodolfo Hammersley (1) (CHI), Sten Hagander (1) (SWE), Pál Szalay (1) (HUN), Harry Babcock (1) (USA), Paul Fournelle (1) (LUX), Benjamin Adams (2) (USA), Sidney Abrahams (2) (GBR), and William Happenny (2) (CAN).

297. Originally assigned to group three.

298. Originally assigned to group three.

299. Originally assigned to group three.

300. Also entered in this group (with original group in parentheses), but not competing, were

Thomas O'Donahue (2) (GBR), Daniel Campbell (2) (GBR), Géza Vadon (2) (HUN), László Tihanyi (2) (HUN), Henry Ashington (3) (GBR), Carl Sander Santesson (3) (SWE), James Wilkinson (3) (USA), and Leone Linardi (3) (ITA).

301. Originally drawn in group four, but reassigned to group three.

302. Originally drawn in group four, but reassigned to group three.

303. Originally drawn in group four, but reassigned to group three.

304. Originally drawn in group four, but reassigned to group three.

305. Also entered in this group (with original group in parentheses), but not competing, were Viktor Franzl (3) (AUT), Leo Goehring (3) (USA), Nándor Kováts (3) (HUN), Manlio Legat (4) (ITA), Jim Thorpe (4) (USA), Giulio Alvisi (4) (ITA), Colombo Zevola (4) (ITA), Alfredo Pagani (4) (ITA), Furio Bini (4) (ITA), James Wasson (4) (USA), and Gustav Betzén (4) (SWE).

306. The exact make-up of groups one and two is not available. All that is known is that Karl von Halt competed in group two.

307. Also entered in this group (with original group in parentheses), but not competing, were Emil Magnusson (1) (SWE), Hugo Wieslander (1) (SWE), Erik Svensson (1) (SWE), André Pierre Desfarges (1) (FRA), Umberto Avattaneo (1) (ITA), Eric Lemming (1) (SWE), Otto Nilsson (1) (SWE), Angelo Pedrelli (1) (ITA), Josef Waitzer (1) (GER), Jannes Andersson (1) (SWE), Carl Johan "Masse" Lind (1) (SWE), Alfred Reich (1) (USA), Pietro Erculei (1) (ITA), Giuseppe Tugnoli (2) (ITA), Thomas Rae Nicolson (2) (GBR), Robert Olsson (2) (SWE), Géza Pogány (2) (HUN), Arlie Mucks (2) (USA), Vencheslav Ostrukhov (2) (RUS), W. A. Ziegler (2) (USA), Pierre Failliot (2) (FRA), and Gunnar Nilsson (2) (SWE).

308. Also entered in this group, but not competing, were Arthur Bartlett (USA), Henry Klages (USA), Edward Barrett (GBR), Nikolaos Georgantas (GRE), Resző Ujlaki (HUN), Alexander Abraham (GER), and Russell Lawrence Beatty (USA).

309. Also entered in this group, but not competing, were August Kihlart (RUS), Carlo Butti (ITA), Herbert Thatcher (USA), Kálmán Kirchhoffer (HUN), Karl Michl (AUT), Henri Alex Lemasson (FRA), Gustave Jules Amoly (FRA), Arthur Kohler (USA), Henning Möller (SWE), and Szilárd Joanovits (HUN).

310. OSVK has 19.51, using Mıgıryan's 10.58 as mark for the right hand. This is a typo, as the mark is given as 10.85 in the 12OR and the total is also given as 19.78.

311. Also entered in this group, but not competing, were Emil Magnusson (SWE), Hugo Wieslander (SWE), Erik Svensson (SWE), Eric Lemming (SWE), Otto Nilsson (SWE), Jannes Andersson (SWE), Carl Johan "Masse" Lind (SWE), Alfred Reich (USA), Robert Olsson (SWE), Géza Pogány (HUN), and Imre Mudin (HUN).

312. Also entered in this group, but not competing, were Gunnar Nilsson (SWE), Henry Klages (USA), Nikolaos Georgantas (GRE), Resző Ujlaki (HUN), Russell Lawrence Beatty (USA), Herbert Thatcher (USA), Kálmán Kirchhoffer (HUN), Jim Thorpe (USA), George Philbrook (USA), Henning Möller (SWE), and Szilárd Joanovits (HUN).

313. DW, EK, FW, and OSVK have 40.

314. Also entered in this group, but not competing, were Hugo Wieslander (SWE), André Pierre Desfarges (FRA), Umberto Avattaneo (ITA), Eric Lemming (SWE), Andrew Joseph Sheridan (USA), and Cesare Rosini (ITA).

315. Also entered in this group, but not competing, were Pietro Erculei (ITA), Giuseppe Tugnoli (ITA), Paavo Aho (FIN), Patrick Quinn (GBR), K. Thelning (SWE), Imre Mudin (HUN), Károly Nyilassy (HUN), and Henri Pelissier (FRA).

316. Also entered in this group, but not competing, were John Hooker (USA), Pál Antal (HUN), Arvids Ozols-Berne (RUS), André Pierre Desfarges (FRA), Raoul Paoli (FRA), and Vilmos Zöldi (HUN).

317. Also entered in this group, but not competing, were Nils Linde (SWE), Edward Barrett (GBR), Nikolaos Georgantas (GRE), Peter Fúle (HUN), István Mudin (HUN), Russell Lawrence Beatty (USA), Patrick McDonald (USA), August Kihlart (RUS), and Carlo Butti (ITA).

318. Also entered in this group, but not competing, were Karl Michl (AUT), Henri Alex Lemasson (FRA), Gustave Jules Amoly (FRA), and John Falchenberg (NOR).

319. Also entered in this group, but not competing, were Hugo Wieslander (SWE), Avery Brundage (USA), Otto Nilsson (SWE), Platt Adams (USA), and Andrew Joseph Sheridan (USA).

320. Also entered in this group, but not competing, were Samu Fóti (HUN), K. Thelning (SWE), Imre Mudin (HUN), Károly Nyilassy (HUN), Lawrence Whitney (USA), Ralph Rose (USA), Pál Antal (HUN), Vilmos Zöldi (HUN), and Miklós Kovács (HUN).

321. Luntzer is not listed in 12OR, presumably because he failed to make a mark. However, he "almost" made a mark. In the third round he threw 37.68 with his best hand, but failed to record a mark with the other hand, giving him no total mark.

322. Also entered in this group, but not competing, were Nikolaos Georgantas (GRE), Peter Fúle (HUN), Matthew McGrath (USA), István Mudin (HUN), Patrick McDonald (USA), Gunnar Bolander (SWE), George Philbrook (USA), John Falchenberg (NOR), and Henning Möller (SWE).

323. This is how the diplomas of merit are listed in the 12OR. It is not known why Jahnzon was awarded a diploma and Ralph Rose, who had the same length mark, was not.

324. OSVK has Jahnzon eighth and Rose ninth, but there was no tie-breaking method available in 1912 for lower places. If the modern method was used, that is, the next best mark, Rose would be eighth (40.80) and Jahnzon ninth (39.18).

325. OSVK has B[ror] Ohlsson [*sic*— Olsson] (SWE) in 14th place with 37.56, and does not list Gillis as competing. But Bror Ohlsson was not entered, and is not mentioned in 12OR, ONews, 12ORes, or in Uggla.

326. Also entered in this group, but not competing, were Hans Tronner (AUT), Erik Larsson (SWE), Thomas Rae Nicolson (GBR), and W. A. Ziegler (USA).

327. Gillis is not listed in the OR, presumably because he did not make a fair mark. He is listed in ONews, and Spalding mentions him as competing in Stockholm. In addition, NYT notes that he attempted to compete but had to withdraw with an injury after his first throw. He is listed in 12ORes with (- - -).

328. Also entered in this group, but not competing, were Miroslav Šustera (BOH), John Hooker (USA), Harold Edwin Marden (USA), István Mudin (HUN), Marcel Pelletier (LUX), and Alfred Tilley (USA).

329. Also entered in this group, but not competing, were Harry Lott (USA), Hugo Wieslander (SWE), André Pierre Desfarges (FRA), Olaf Ingebretsen (NOR), and Platt Adams (USA).

330. Also entered in this group, but not competing, were Hugo Ahrén (SWE), Lawrence Whitney (USA), Jørgen Kornerup Bang (DEN), Cesare Frassine (ITA), Bruno Brodd (USA), Pierre Failliot (FRA), Thomas Lund (USA), Mikhail Nomikos (GRE), and Ferdinand Bie (NOR).

331. Also entered in this group, but not competing, were Mıgır Mıgıryan (TUR), Raoul Paoli (FRA), Máté Szákall (HUN), Konstantinos Tsiklitiras (GRE), Urho Aaltonen (FIN), Leslie Byrd (USA), Resző Ujlaki (HUN), István Mudin (HUN), and Marcel Pelletier (LUX).

332. Also entered in this group, but not competing, were Manlio Legat (ITA), André Tison (FRA), Henri Alex Lemasson (FRA), Giulio Alvisi (ITA), Charles Lagarde (FRA), Samuel Bellah (USA), Colombo Zevola (ITA), James Mitchel (USA), Furio Bini (ITA), Julius Wagner (SUI), and Ubaldo Bianchi (ITA).

333. Also entered in this heat, but not competing, were Harry Lott (USA), Hugo Wieslander (SWE), Bror Olsson (SWE), Platt Adams (USA), and David Nygren (SWE).

334. Also entered in this heat, but not competing, were Vasily Molokanov (RUS), Lawrence Whitney (USA), J. Austin Menaul (USA), Mikhail Nomikos (GRE), Algot Larsson (SWE), Henry Klages (USA), and Máté Szákall (HUN).

335. Also entered in this heat, but not competing, were Konstantinos Tsiklitiras (GRE), Urho Aaltonen (FIN), Resző Ujlaki (HUN), István Mudin (HUN), Janne Dahl (SWE), George Philbrook (USA), and James Mitchel (USA).

336. In 1913, Jim Thorpe was disqualified for professionalism and his gold medals were removed. His crime was playing minor-league baseball. In 1982, his name was restored to the record books by the IOC, although he was to be listed as co-champion in the decathlon with Wieslander and in the pentathlon with Bie. We have simply listed the results as they actually occurred. See Appendix II for further description of the Thorpe situation.

337. Zarnowski (*The Decathlon*) incorrectly gives Holmér's 1985 converted score as 5,748.

338. Zarnowski (*The Decathlon*) incorrectly gives Alslebens' 1985 converted score as 4,823.

339. Also entered in this event, but not competing, were Eugene Schobinger (USA), John Eller, Jr. (USA), Josef Waitzer (GER), André Fouache (FRA), Bertil Uggla (SWE), Paul Fournelle (LUX), Jean-Pierre Thommes (LUX), Jørgen Kornerup Bang (DEN), J. Austin Menaul (USA), Bohumil Honzatko (BOH), Nicola Kanive (LUX), Raoul Paoli (FRA), Konstantinos Tsiklitiras (GRE), Richard Leslie Byrd (USA), Clément Célestin Mentrel (FRA), Jindřich Jirsák (BOH), Emmanuel Tsaloumas (GRE), Giulio Alvisi (ITA), Ulrich Baasch (RUS), Furio Bini (ITA), and Julius Wagner (SUI).

340. Listed below after each event result (for the first three events and top 12 finishers) are two numbers, such as "[19/11]". The first number (19 in this case) is the overall finish among the 26 competitors. The second number (11 in this case) is the finish among the 12 top qualifiers after three events. The second numbers are those which were used for the final scores.

341. In 1913, Jim Thorpe was disqualified for professionalism and his gold medals were removed. His crime was playing minor-league baseball. In 1982, his name was restored to the record books by the IOC, although he was to be listed as co-champion in the decathlon with Wieslander and in the pentathlon with Bie. We have simply listed the results as they actually occurred. See Appendix II for further description of the Thorpe situation.

342. Thorpe's series in the long jump was 707, 704, and 681, although the order of his three jumps is not given.

343. Thorpe started in the last heat, heat nine, of the 200 meters. His only competitor in this heat was Charles Lomberg (SWE) who ran 24.4 to Thorpe's 22.9.

344. Bie's score is given in the 12OR as 16 points. They adjusted the score after Thorpe's disqualification. Interestingly, in one section of the 12OR (p. 412), they left all the other athletes with their original scores, but on p. 413, they rescored the top six competitors (after Thorpe), giving the scores as follows: Bie—16; Donahue—24; Lukeman—24; Menaul—25; Brundage—26; and Wieslander—28. Note that Thorpe defeated Bie in every event and, in fact, of the next six finishers, only Wieslander defeated Thorpe in any event (javelin).

345. Tie for third broken by using the decathlon scoring tables. Listed above are the 1985 point scores for the first seven finishers. Using the 1912A decathlon scoring tables in effect at the time of the 1912 Olympics, Donahue scored 3,475.865 points, and Lukeman scored 3,396.975 points. In 12OR, Lukeman's points per event are given and total, correctly, to 3,396.975 points. Donahue's points are also given, but total, incorrectly, to 3,525.865 points. In 12OR (p. 413), Donahue is incorrectly credited with 875.0 points for the 200 meter run, while his time of 23.0 should have been worth only 825.0 points. Using 825.0 points gives Donahue his correct total of 3,475.865 points.

346. Zarnowski (*The Decathlon*) has 35.83. 12OR and 12ORes have 35.85. Spalding has 117-7½ (35.85).

347. Time given as 24.2 in 12OR and 12ORes but as 24⅖ (24.4) in Spalding, and also as 24.4 in Guttmann (p. 26).

348. 12OR gives Brundage "---" for the 1,500, implying he did not finish. In addition, 12ORes lists only a dash, implying he did not finish. Spalding lists his time as 5:12.9, and this time has since been copied in multiple sources. Interestingly, no time is given for Brundage in Uggla, either, and he is not even mentioned as competing in the 1,500 in Uggla. But 12OR mentioned him specifically as starting. No mark is given for him in ONews, which listed the first six finishers, stopping at Bie with 5:07.8.

349. The mark is listed as 4:53.1 in Zarnowski (*The Decathlon*), Uggla, and Spalding. In 12OR, the mark is given as 4:51.1 in the table on p. 413, but in the description of the 1,500, it is given as 4:53.1. The time in 12ORes is 4:53.1. The 4:51.1 in 12OR must be a typo.

350. Zarnowski in *The Olympic Decathlon* has a typo here, giving 4231. The mark is 4131 in 12ORes.

351. Zarnowski in *The Olympic Decathlon* has a typo here, giving 3889. The mark is 3989 in 12ORes.

352. Neither 12OR, 12ORes, ONews, Diem, Spalding, nor Uggla gives complete results for the pentathlon. It is unknown what marks von Halt and Waitzer made in their two events. German sources also have no knowledge of their marks.

353. EzM and Arild Gjerde list this athlete as Waitzer. Zarnowski (*The Decathlon*) is less certain, stating that it is either Josef Waitzer or Alexander Abraham (GER). German sources list Abraham as competing only in the decathlon.

354. Also entered in this event, but not competing, were Angelo Pedrelli (ITA), Platt Adams (USA), Svend Langkjær (DEN), Rodolfo Hammersley (CHI), Ernö Holecsek (HUN), André Fouache (FRA), Bertil Uggla (SWE), Harry Babcock (USA), Eugene Mercer (USA), Mikhail Nomikos (GRE), Aarne Salovaara (FIN), Raoul Paoli (FRA), Harry Fryckberg (USA), Konstantinos Tsiklitiras (GRE), László Lichtenekkert (HUN), Richard Leslie Byrd (USA), Clément Célestin Mentrel (FRA), Leone Linardi (ITA), Alexander Abraham (GER), Jindřich Jirsák (BOH), Knut "Knatten" Lindberg (SWE), Frigyes Mezei Wiesner (HUN), Carlo Butti (ITA), György "Juraj" Luntzer (HUN), Manlio Legat (ITA), Paul Zerling (SWE), Kay Schwensen (DEN), Giulio Alvisi (ITA), George Philbrook (USA), and Ulrich Baasch (RUS).

Cycling

Only one cycling race was held at the 1912 Olympics. The Swedish Olympic Committee actually attempted to eliminate cycling altogether. No track races were planned, although at the 11th IOC Session in Luxembourg (11–13 June 1910), the British protested this decision but no change was made. The track races were eliminated because the only velodrome in Stockholm was being destroyed to make room for the new Olympic Stadium, and there were no plans to build a new one, even with the advent of the Olympic Games.[1]*

At the 12th session (Budapest, 23–27 May 1911), the Swedes noted that they wanted to eliminate the road race as well. Britain's Robert de Courcy Laffan insisted that a competition of at least 100 km. should be held. Sweden's Viktor Gustaf Balck noted that, "our roads are so bad that it is impossible to organise such a race."[2] Eventually, though, the Swedish Olympic Committee capitulated, and elected to hold it on the course for the Mälaren Rundt (Tour of Lake Mälaren), the most popular road race in Sweden. The Mälaren Rundt was first held in 1892 and 1893, and then again yearly after 1901.

The race was a very long (315.385 km.[3] [196.0 miles]) time trial on the roads around Lake Mälaren. Lake Mälaren is a huge lake formed by a former inlet of the Baltic Sea. Stockholm was originally built on several islands in the outlet of Lake Mälaren into the Baltic, in order to guard the lake from foreign naval invasion. An individual and team competition was decided based on this single race. The event also holds the distinction of starting at the earliest time of any Olympic event ever — 2 A.M. (0200).

The cycling road race was noteworthy because England, Scotland, and Ireland were allowed to enter teams of riders as individual nations, rather than as one combined team representing Great Britain. It is uncertain why this decision was made. However, on the day before the event, 6 July, France protested this ruling. The ruling was discussed all day, and that evening, the committee for cycling announced that the three nations would be allowed to compete separately. The cycling committee noted that they "… regretted that this concession had been made, but declared at the same time that, as the teams from the countries in question had come to Sweden to take part in the event, the Swedish Cycling Committee did not wish to prevent them from doing so, and that the Swedish Cycling Association intended to take the responsibility for their so doing on its own shoulders, should any steps be taken in the matter by the Union Cycliste Internationale."[4]

*See Notes on pages 151–152.

In addition to the Olympic medals, several cities along the route of the road course donated special prizes. The cycling awards ceremony was separate from the events in the stadium and took place on Monday, 9 July, at Restaurant Hasselbacken, where the awards were distributed by the president of the cycling committee, Gösta Drake af Hagelsrum. The special awards given were as follows: Memorial Cup of Eskilstuna — winner of the race — Rudolph Lewis (RSA); Memorial Cup of Västerås — top Swedish cyclist — Erik Friborg; Memorial Cup of Enköping — best rider between Enköping and the Olympic Stadium — Leonard Meredith (GBR); Memorial Cup of Mariefred — given to the cyclist who rode well but did not win a medal — Frank Brown (CAN); Silver Cup of Sundsvalls Velocipedklubb — winner of the team race — Sweden; and Memorial Cup of Köping — team with most participants finishing — Germany.

Site:	Start at the schoolhouse 1,000 meters south of Liljeholmsbron, on the southwest outskirts of Stockholm. The race looped clockwise around Lake Mälaren, to the west of Stockholm, and finished at the main Olympic Stadium.	
Date:	7 July	
Events:	2 [2 Men — 0 Women]	
Competitors:	123 [123 Men — 0 Women]	
Nations:	18 [18 Men — 0 Women]	

	Competitors	Gold	Silver	Bronze	Medals
Austria	6	–	–	–	–
Belgium	1	–	–	–	–
Bohemia	5	–	–	–	–
Canada	2	–	–	–	–
Chile	4	–	–	–	–
Denmark	8	–	–	–	–
England	12	–	2	–	2
Finland	5	–	–	–	–
France	12	–	–	–	–
Germany	11	–	–	–	–
Hungary	5	–	–	–	–
Ireland	6	–	–	–	–
Norway	6	–	–	–	–
Russia	10	–	–	–	–
Scotland	8	–	–	–	–
South Africa	1	1	–	–	1
Sweden	12	1	–	–	1
United States	9	–	–	2	2
Totals	123	2	2	2	6
Nations	18	2	1	1	4
Great Britain	26	–	2	–	2

Committee for Cycling

President: Captain Carl Gustaf "Gösta" Drake af Hagelsrum
Vice-President: Axel Storm
Treasurer: Oscar Kræpelin
Secretary: C. A. Ullén, Esquire
Members: Erik Pallin, Esquire; Frans Pettersson; Severin Åkerstedt; Carl S. Hellberg; C. Fr. Platin; Emil Salmson

Road Race, Individual

A: 123; E: 151; C: 18[5]; D: 7 July; T: 0200; F: 315.385[6] km. (196.0 miles) individual time trial.

The riders were sent off at two minute intervals, with the last scheduled rider starting at 7 A.M. (0700). Of the 151 entrants only 123 riders eventually started. The individual event was won by Rudolph "Okey" Lewis of South Africa. He started quickly and led by 11½ minutes at 120 km. Increasing the lead to 17 minutes at 200 km., he slowed slightly coming in, but still won by almost nine minutes over Fred Grubb of Great Britain. As the second starter, going off at 2:02 A.M., he was the first overall finisher as well. Little is known about Lewis's cycling career, even by South African experts. It was noted that the weather at the start time of 2 A.M. was cool, with no wind, which favored the very early starters. By 7 A.M. a strong westerly wind was blowing directly into the faces of the later starting riders. Lewis was the second starter and definitely benefited from his start position.[7]

The previous record for the Mälaren Rundt was 11-22:07.0, set in 1909 by Henrik Morén of Sweden, a ten-time winner of the race, including nine consecutive wins from 1902 to 1910. Lewis lowered the record by almost 41 minutes. No fewer than 16 riders, including Morén himself, in 15th place, bettered the previous record.

In addition to the Olympic medals, a diploma of merit was given to cyclists who finished within 25 percent of the winner's time. As Lewis finished in 10-42:39, all riders under 13-23:18.8 qualified, and thus 81 of the 94 riders who finished received this special diploma.[8]

1.	Rudolph Lewis	RSA	10-42:39.0
2.	Frederick Grubb	ENG	10-51:24.2
3.	Carl Schutte	USA	10-52:38.8
4.	Leon Meredith	ENG	11-00:02.6
5.	Frank Brown	CAN	11-01:00.0
6.	Antti Raita	FIN	11-02:20.3
7.	Erik Friborg	SWE	11-04:17.0
8.	Ragnar Malm	SWE	11-08:14.5
9.	Axel Wilhelm Persson	SWE	11-10:59.6
10.	Algot Lönn	SWE	11-12:02.5
11.	Alvin Loftes	USA	11-13:51.3
12.	Alexis Ekström	SWE	11-14:50.7
13.	Albert Kruschel	USA	11-17:30.2
14.	Birger Andreassen	NOR	11-20:14.6
15.	Henrik Morén	SWE	11-21:31.9

16.	John Wilson	SCO	11-21:43.0
17.	Walter Martin	USA	11-23:55.2
18.	Charles Moss	ENG	11-23:55.8
19.	Werner Karlsson	SWE	11-24:18.0
20.	Joseph Kopsky	USA	11-27:06.0
21.	Vilho Oskari Tilkanen	FIN	11-28:38.5
22.	William Hammond	ENG	11-29:16.8
23.	Robert Rammer	AUT	11-30:40.8
24.	Robert Thompson	SCO	11-31:16.0
25.	Olaf Meyland-Smith	DEN	11-32:24.2
26.	Franz Lemnitz	GER	11-34:32.2
27.	Rudolf Baier	GER	11-35:01.5
28.	John Becht	USA	11-35:04.8
29.	Stanley Jones	ENG	11-37:40.6
30.	Herbert Gayler	ENG	11-39:01.8
31.	Adolf Kofler	AUT	11-39:32.6[9]
32.	Charles Hansen	DEN	11-40:04.0[10]
33.	Oswald Rathmann	GER	11-40:18.4[11]
34.	Johan Kankkonen	FIN	11-41:35.5
35.	John Miller	SCO	11-44:01.6
36.	Georg Warsow	GER	11-45:24.0
37.	Francis Higgins	ENG	11-45:44.5
38.	Arthur Gibbon	ENG	11-46:00.2
39.	Charles Davey	ENG	11-47:26.3
40.	Joseph Racine	FRA	11-50:32.7[12]
41.	David Stevenson	SCO	11-52:55.0
42.	Alberto Downey	CHI	11-53:02.5
43.	Rudolf Kramer	AUT	11-53:12.8
44.	Otto Männel	GER	11-53:27.4
45.	Josef Hellensteiner	AUT	11-54:00.2
46.	Josef Zilker	AUT	11-54:38.7
47.	Paul Henrichsen	NOR	11-55:23.2
48.	Johannes Reinwaldt	DEN	11-57:20.0
49.	Charles Hill	SCO	11-57:56.5
50.	André Capelle	FRA	11-59:48.4
51.	Gunnar Björk	SWE	12-00:49.4
52.	Alois Wacha	AUT	12-01:12.4
53.	Godtfred Olsen	DEN	12-06:18.8
54.	James "Jesse" Pike	USA	12-06:21.6
55.	Wilhelm Rabe	GER	12-06:55.8
56.	Jerome Steinert	USA	12-08:32.3
57.	Josef Rieder	GER	12-12:32.4
58.	Cárlos Koller	CHI	12-13:49.2
59.	Ernest Merlin	ENG	12-16:08.6
60.	Andrejs Apsits	RUS	12-18:20.6
61.	Martin Koch	GER	12-18:22.5
62.	Robert Birker	GER	12-19:27.6
63.	Bohumil Rameš	BOH	12-20:12.2
64.	René Gagnet	FRA	12-20:32.6[13]

65.	Anton Hansen	NOR	12-21:23.7[14]
66.	Hjalmar Väre	FIN	12-21:29.2
67.	Michael Walker	IRL	12-27:49.9[15]
68.	James Stevenson	SCO	12-27:50.8[16]
69.	Arturo Friedemann	CHI	12-28:20.8
70.	Frank Meissner	USA	12-29:09.0
71.	Francis Guy	IRL	12-32:19.4
72.	Valdemar Nielsen	DEN	12-33:09.2
73.	István Müller	HUN	12-39:28.0
74.	José Torres	CHI	12-39:39.5
75.	János Henzsely	HUN	12-42:16.3
76.	Hermann Smiel	GER	12-49:01.6
77.	Gyula Mazur	HUN	12-50:55.8
78.	George Watson	CAN	12-52:22.2
79.	Carl Lüthje	GER	13-00:31.8
80.	Ralph Mecredy	IRL	13-03:39.0
81.	John Walker	IRL	13-15:50.2[17]
82.	Matthew Walsh	IRL	13-31:17.0
83.	Georges Valentin	FRA	13-33:59.5
84.	Ignác Teiszenberger	HUN	13-38:35.8
85.	Bernhard Doyle	IRL	13-42:11.8
86.	George Corsar	SCO	13-51:22.8
87.	Václav Tintěra	BOH	14-10:34.6
88.[18]	Bohumil Kubrycht	BOH	14-11:21.0
89.	Étienne Cheret	FRA	14-15:18.1
90.	Arthur Griffiths	SCO	14-15:24.0[19]
91.	Gaston Alancourt	FRA	14-23:59.3
92.	Pierre Peinaud	FRA	14-49:59.4
93.	André Lepère	FRA	15-03:18.1
94.	Alexis Michiels	FRA	15-15:59.2

AC.	Fyodor Borisov	RUS	DNF	between Bålsta & Järva
	Károly Teppert	HUN	DNF	between Bålsta & Järva
	Hans Olsen	DEN	DNF	between Enköping & Bålsta
	Carl Olsen	NOR	DNF	in Enköping
	Augusts Köpke	RUS	DNF	in Kungsör
	Janis Pratneek	RUS	DNF	between Eskilstuna & Kungsör
	Valdemar Christoffer Nielsen	DEN	DNF	between Eskilstuna & Kungsör
	Jan Vokoun	BOH	DNF	between Eskilstuna & Kungsör
	Edgars Richters	RUS	DNF	in Eskilstuna
	Carl Lundquist	SWE	DNF	between Strängnäs & Eskilstuna
	Arvid Pettersson	SWE	DNF	between Strängnäs & Eskilstuna
	Friedrich Bosch	RUS	DNF	between Strängnäs & Eskilstuna
	John Kirk	ENG	DNF	in Strängnäs
	Carl Guldbrandsen	NOR	DNF	in Strängnäs
	Jakob Bukse	RUS	DNF	between Strängnäs & Läggesta
	Martin Sæterhaug	NOR	DNF	in Läggestatrakterna
	Hjalmar Levin	SWE	DNF	between Södertälje & Läggesta
	Otto Jensen	DEN	DNF	between Södertälje & Läggesta
	Jean Patou	BEL	DNF	between Södertälje & Läggesta

Sergey Pesteryev	RUS	DNF	between Södertälje & Läggesta
Jacques Marcault	FRA	DNF	outside Södertälje
Janis Lieven	RUS	DNF	outside Södertälje
Louis Bes	FRA	DNF	outside Södertälje
René Rillon	FRA	DNF	2 km. beyond Södertälje
Arthur Stokes	ENG	DNF	in Södertälje
Karlis Köpke	RUS	DNF	in Södertälje
František Kundert	BOH	DNF	before Södertälje
Juho Jaakonaho	FIN	DNF	before Södertälje
Karl Landsberg[20]	SWE	DNF	by Midsommarkransen

21

Diplomas of Merit

Leon Meredith (ENG), Frank Brown (CAN), Antti Raita (FIN), Erik Friborg (SWE), Ragnar Malm (SWE), Axel Wilhelm Persson (SWE), Algot Lönn (SWE), Alvin Loftes (USA), Alexis Ekström (SWE), Albert Kruschel (USA), Birger Andreassen (NOR), Henrik Morén (SWE), John Wilson (SCO), Walter Martin (USA), Charles Moss (ENG), Werner Karlsson (SWE), Joseph Kopsky (USA), Vilho Oskari Tilkanen (FIN), William Hammond (ENG), Robert Rammer (AUT), Robert Thompson (SCO), Olaf Meyland-Smith (DEN), Franz Lemnitz (GER), Rudolf Baier (GER), John Becht (USA), Stanley Jones (ENG), Herbert Gayler (ENG), Adolf Kofler (AUT), Charles Hansen (DEN), Oswald Rathmann (GER), Johan Kankkonen (FIN), John Miller (SCO), Georg Warsow (GER), Francis Higgins (ENG), Arthur Gibbon (ENG), Charles Davey (ENG), Joseph Racine (FRA), David Stevenson (SCO), Alberto Downey (CHI), Rudolf Kramer (AUT), Otto Männel (GER), Josef Hellensteiner (AUT), Josef Zilker (AUT), Paul Henrichsen (NOR), Johannes Reinwaldt (DEN), Charles Hill (SCO), André Capelle (FRA), Gunnar Björk (SWE), Alois Wacha (AUT), Godtfred Olsen (DEN), James "Jesse" Pike (USA), Wilhelm Rabe (GER), Jerome Steinert (USA), Josef Rieder (GER), Cárlos Koller (CHI), Ernest Merlin (ENG), Andrejs Apsits (RUS), Martin Koch (GER), Robert Birker (GER), Bohumil Rameš (BOH), René Gagnet (FRA), Anton Hansen (NOR), Hjalmar Väre (FIN), Michael Walker (IRL), James Stevenson (SCO), Arturo Friedemann (CHI), Frank Meissner (USA), Francis Guy (IRL), Valdemar Nielsen (DEN), István Müller (HUN), José Torres (CHI), János Henzsel (HUN), Hermann Smiel (GER), Gyula Mazur (HUN), George Watson (CAN), Carl Lüthje (GER), Ralph Mecredy (IRL), John Walker (IRL)

Start Order and Time of Starting

#. Name	Nation	Scheduled Start Time	
1. René Rillon	FRA	0200 [2:00 A.M.]	
2. Rudolph Lewis	RSA	0202 [2:02 A.M.]	
3. Axel Wilhelm Persson	SWE	0204 [2:04 A.M.]	
4. José Torres	CHI	0206 [2:06 A.M.]	
5. Adolf Kofler	AUT	0208 [2:08 A.M.]	
6. Gyula Tóth	HUN	0210 [2:10 A.M.]	DNS
7. Walter Pofhal	USA	0212 [2:12 A.M.]	DNS
8. George Herd	SCO	0214 [2:14 A.M.]	DNS
9. John Kirk	ENG	0216 [2:16 A.M.]	
10. Carl Guldbrandsen	NOR	0218 [2:18 A.M.]	
11. Georg Warsow	GER	0220 [2:20 A.M.]	
12. Karlis Köpke	RUS	0222 [2:22 A.M.]	

#. Name	Nation	Scheduled Start Time	
13. Thomas Bulger	CAN	0224 [2:24 A.M.]	DNS
14. René Gagnet	FRA	0226 [2:26 A.M.]	
15. Julien Médecin	MON	0228 [2:28 A.M.]	DNS
16. Erik Friborg	SWE	0230 [2:30 A.M.]	
17. Arturo Friedemann	CHI	0232 [2:32 A.M.]	
18. Robert Rammer	AUT	0234 [2:34 A.M.]	
19. Lajos Merényi	HUN	0236 [2:36 A.M.]	DNS
20. Joseph Kopsky	USA	0238 [2:38 A.M.]	
21. Charles Hill	SCO	0240 [2:40 A.M.]	
22. Stanley Jones	ENG	0242 [2:42 A.M.]	
23. Birger Andreassen	NOR	0244 [2:44 A.M.]	
24. Wilhelm Rabe	GER	0246 [2:46 A.M.]	
25. Ans Pohle	RUS	0248 [2:48 A.M.]	DNS
26. William Spencer	CAN	0250 [2:50 A.M.]	DNS
27. Joseph Racine	FRA	0252 [2:52 A.M.]	
28. Henri Bernardi	MON	0254 [2:54 A.M.]	DNS
29. Ragnar Malm	SWE	0256 [2:56 A.M.]	
30. Alberto Downey	CHI	0258 [2:58 A.M.]	
31. Rudolf Kramer	AUT	0300 [3:00 A.M.]	
32. János Henzsely	HUN	0302 [3:02 A.M.]	
33. Ernest Kockler	USA	0304 [3:04 A.M.]	DNS
34. James Stevenson	SCO	0306 [3:06 A.M.]	
35. Arthur Stokes	ENG	0308 [3:08 A.M.]	
36. Anton Hansen	NOR	0310 [3:10 A.M.]	
37. Oswald Rathmann	GER	0312 [3:12 A.M.]	
38. Edgars Richters	RUS	0314 [3:14 A.M.]	
39. Walter Andrews	CAN	0316 [3:16 A.M.]	DNS
40. André Capelle	FRA	0318 [3:18 A.M.]	
41. Ralph Mecredy	IRL	0320 [3:20 A.M.]	
42. Algot Lönn	SWE	0322 [3:22 A.M.]	
43. Cárlos Koller	CHI	0324 [3:24 A.M.]	
44. Alois Wacha	AUT	0326 [3:26 A.M.]	
45. Ferenc Retzischar	HUN	0328 [3:28 A.M.]	DNS
46. Albert Kruschel	USA	0330 [3:30 A.M.]	
47. John Wilson	SCO	0332 [3:32 A.M.]	
48. Leon Meredith	ENG	0334 [3:34 A.M.]	
49. Paul Henrichsen	NOR	0336 [3:36 A.M.]	
50. Robert Birker	GER	0338 [3:38 A.M.]	
51. Augusts Köpke	RUS	0340 [3:40 A.M.]	
52. George Watson	CAN	0342 [3:42 A.M.]	
53. Alexis Michiels	FRA	0344 [3:44 A.M.]	
54. Charles Anderson	IRL	0346 [3:46 A.M.]	DNS
55. Werner Karlsson	SWE	0348 [3:48 A.M.]	
56. Charles Hansen	DEN	0350 [3:50 A.M.]	
57. Josef Hellensteiner	AUT	0352 [3:52 A.M.]	
58. Gyula Mazur	HUN	0354 [3:54 A.M.]	
59. John Becht	USA	0356 [3:56 A.M.]	

#. Name	Nation	Scheduled Start Time	
60. Robert Thompson	SCO	0358 [3:58 A.M.]	
61. William Hammond	ENG	0400 [4:00 A.M.]	
62. Martin Sæterhaug	NOR	0402 [4:02 A.M.]	
63. Otto Männel	GER	0404 [4:04 A.M.]	
64. Andrejs Apsits	RUS	0406 [4:06 A.M.]	
65. Frank Brown	CAN	0408 [4:08 A.M.]	
66. Pierre Peinaud	FRA	0410 [4:10 A.M.]	
67. Thomas Donaldson	IRL	0412 [4:12 A.M.]	DNS
68. Arvid Pettersson	SWE	0414 [4:14 A.M.]	
69. Valdemar Nielsen	DEN	0416 [4:16 A.M.]	
70. Josef Zilker	AUT	0418 [4:18 A.M.]	
71. Károly Gröger	HUN	0420 [4:20 A.M.]	DNS
72. Alvin Loftes	USA	0422 [4:22 A.M.]	
73. Daniel Quinn	SCO	0424 [4:24 A.M.]	DNS
74. Charles Moss	ENG	0426 [4:26 A.M.]	
75. Josef Bye	NOR	0428 [4:28 A.M.]	DNS
76. Hermann Smiel	GER	0430 [4:30 A.M.]	
77. Friedrich Bosch	RUS	0432 [4:32 A.M.]	
78. Bohumil Rameš	BOH	0434 [4:34 A.M.]	
79. Gaston Alancourt	FRA	0436 [4:36 A.M.]	
80. Bernhard Doyle	IRL	0438 [4:38 A.M.]	
81. Henrik Morén	SWE	0440 [4:40 A.M.]	
82. Valdemar Christoffer Nielsen	DEN	0442 [4:42 A.M.]	
83. Vilho Oskari Tilkanen	FIN	0444 [4:44 A.M.]	
84. István Paraker	HUN	0446 [4:46 A.M.]	DNS
85. Carl Schutte	USA	0448 [4:48 A.M.]	
86. David Stevenson	SCO	0450 [4:50 A.M.]	
87. Arthur Gibbon	ENG	0452 [4:52 A.M.]	
88. Carl Olsen	NOR	0454 [4:54 A.M.]	
89. Josef Rieder	GER	0456 [4:56 A.M.]	
90. Jeannot Eulenberg	RUS	0458 [4:58 A.M.]	DNS
91. Bohumil Kubrycht	BOH	0500 [5:00 A.M.]	
92. André Lepère	FRA	0502 [5:02 A.M.]	
93. David Livingston	IRL	0504 [5:04 A.M.]	DNS
94. Karl Landsberg	SWE	0506 [5:06 A.M.]	
95. Hans Olsen	DEN	0508 [5:08 A.M.]	
96. Johan Kankkonen	FIN	0510 [5:10 A.M.]	
97. Lájos Schwarcz	HUN	0512 [5:12 A.M.]	DNS
98. Walter Martin	USA	0514 [5:14 A.M.]	
99. William Petrie	SCO	0516 [5:16 A.M.]	DNS
100. Charles Davey	ENG	0518 [5:18 A.M.]	
101. Johann Penz	GER	0520 [5:20 A.M.]	DNS
102. Fyodor Borisov	RUS	0522 [5:22 A.M.]	
103. Václav Tintěra	BOH	0524 [5:24 A.M.]	
104. Georges Valentin	FRA	0526 [5:26 A.M.]	
105. Francis Guy	IRL	0528 [5:28 A.M.]	
106. Alex Ekström	SWE	0530 [5:30 A.M.]	

#. Name	Nation	Scheduled Start Time	
107. Otto Jensen	DEN	0532 [5:32 A.M.]	
108. Antti Raita	FIN	0534 [5:34 A.M.]	
109. István Müller	HUN	0536 [5:36 A.M.]	
110. Jerome Steinert	USA	0538 [5:38 A.M.]	
111. Arthur Griffiths	SCO	0540 [5:40 A.M.]	
112. Herbert Gayler	ENG	0542 [5:42 A.M.]	
113. Rudolf Baier	GER	0544 [5:44 A.M.]	
114. Janis Pratneek	RUS	0546 [5:46 A.M.]	
115. František Kundert	BOH	0548 [5:48 A.M.]	
116. Étienne Cheret	FRA	0550 [5:50 A.M.]	
117. John Walker	IRL	0552 [5:52 A.M.]	
118. Hjalmar Levin	SWE	0554 [5:54 A.M.]	
119. Olaf Meyland-Smith	DEN	0556 [5:56 A.M.]	
120. Juho Jaakonaho	FIN	0558 [5:58 A.M.]	
121. Ignác Teiszenberger	HUN	0600 [6:00 A.M.]	
122. Frank Meissner	USA	0602 [6:02 A.M.]	
123. George Corsar	SCO	0604 [6:04 A.M.]	
124. Francis Higgins	ENG	0606 [6:06 A.M.]	
125. Franz Lemnitz	GER	0608 [6:08 A.M.]	
126. Janis Lieven	RUS	0610 [6:10 A.M.]	
127. Jan Vokoun	BOH	0612 [6:12 A.M.]	
128. Louis Bes	FRA	0614 [6:14 A.M.]	
129. Matthew Walsh	IRL	0616 [6:16 A.M.]	
130. Gunnar Björk	SWE	0618 [6:18 A.M.]	
131. Godtfred Olsen	DEN	0620 [6:20 A.M.]	
132. Hjalmar Väre	FIN	0622 [6:22 A.M.]	
133. Gyula Huszár	HUN	0624 [6:24 A.M.]	DNS
134. George Norgauer	USA	0626 [6:26 A.M.]	DNS
135. John Farquhar	SCO	0628 [6:28 A.M.]	DNS
136. Frederick Grubb	ENG	0630 [6:30 A.M.]	
137. Carl Lüthje	GER	0632 [6:32 A.M.]	
138. Jakob Bukse	RUS	0634 [6:34 A.M.]	
139. Omer Bodson	BEL	0636 [6:36 A.M.]	DNS
140. Jacques Marcault	FRA	0638 [6:38 A.M.]	
141. Michael Walker	IRL	0640 [6:40 A.M.]	
142. Carl Lundquist	SWE	0642 [6:42 A.M.]	
143. Johannes Reinwaldt	DEN	0644 [6:44 A.M.]	
144. Carl Lindberg	FIN	0646 [6:46 A.M.]	DNS
145. Károly Teppert	HUN	0648 [6:48 A.M.]	
146. James "Jesse" Pike	USA	0650 [6:50 A.M.]	
147. John Miller	SCO	0652 [6:52 A.M.]	
148. Ernest Merlin	ENG	0654 [6:54 A.M.]	
149. Martin Koch	GER	0656 [6:56 A.M.]	
150. Sergey Pesteryev	RUS	0658 [6:58 A.M.]	
151. Jean Patou	BEL	0700 [7:00 A.M.]	

Road Race, Team

A: 60/69/119[22]; C: 15; D: 7 July; T: 0200; F: 315.385 km. (196.0 miles) individual time trial. Maximum 12 riders per team, with the top four finishers from each team counted towards the team's time.

The team event was based on the total time of the best four riders for each team, with each nation being allowed to start up to 12 cyclists. Sweden won this event by a relatively close margin of nine minutes over England. Interestingly, Sweden's four top riders finished consecutively in places seven to ten.

1. Sweden	44-35:33.6
Erik Friborg	11-04:17.0
Ragnar Malm	11-08:14.5
Axel Wilhelm Persson	11-10:59.6
Algot Lönn	11-12:02.5
Non-scoring Team Members	
Alexis Ekström	11-14:50.7
Henrik Morén	11-21:31.9
Werner Karlsson	11-24:18.0
Gunnar Björk	12-00:49.4
Arvid Pettersson	DNF
Carl Lundquist	DNF
Hjalmar Levin	DNF
Karl Landsberg	DNF
2. England	44-44:39.4[23]
Frederick Grubb	10-51:24.2
Leon Meredith	11-00:02.6
Charles Moss	11-23:55.8
William Hammond	11-29:16.8
Non-scoring Team Members	
Stanley Jones	11-37:40.6
Herbert Gayler	11-39:01.8
Francis Higgins	11-45:44.5
Arthur Gibbon	11-46:00.2
Charles Davey	11-47:26.3
Ernest Merlin	12-16:08.6
John Kirk	DNF
Arthur Stokes	DNF
3. United States	44-47:55.5[24]
Carl Schutte	10-52:38.8
Alvin Loftes	11-13:51.3[25]
Albert Kruschel	11-17:30.2
Walter Martin	11-23:55.2
Non-scoring Team Members	
Joseph Kopsky	11-27:06.0
John Becht	11-35:04.8
James "Jesse" Pike	12-06:21.6

Jerome Steinert	12-08:32.3
Frank Meissner	12-29:09.0

4. Scotland — 46-29:55.6[26]
- John Wilson — 11-21:43.0
- Robert Thompson — 11-31:16.0
- John Miller — 11-44:01.6
- David Stevenson — 11-52:55.0
  - Non-scoring Team Members
  - Charles Hill — 11-57:56.5
  - James Stevenson — 12-27:50.8
  - George Corsar — 13-51:22.8
  - Arthur Griffiths — 14-15:24.0

5. Finland — 46-34:03.5
- Antti Raita — 11-02:20.3
- Vilho Oskari Tilkanen — 11-28:38.5
- Johan Kankkonen — 11-41:35.5
- Hjalmar Väre — 12-21:29.2
  - Non-scoring Team Member
  - Juho Jaakonaho — DNF

6. Germany — 46-35:16.1
- Franz Lemnitz — 11-34:32.2
- P. Rudolf Baier — 11-35:01.5
- Oswald Rathmann — 11-40:18.4
- Georg Warsow — 11-45:24.0
  - Non-scoring Team Members
  - Otto Männel — 11-53:27.4
  - Wilhelm Rabe — 12-06:55.8
  - Josef Rieder — 12-12:32.4
  - Martin Koch — 12-18:22.5
  - Robert Birker — 12-19:27.6
  - Hermann Smiel — 12-49:01.6
  - Carl Lüthje — 13-00:31.8

7. Austria — 46-57:26.4
- Robert Rammer — 11-30:40.8
- Adolf Kofler — 11-39:32.6
- Rudolf Kramer — 11-53:12.8
- Josef Hellensteiner — 11-54:00.2
  - Non-scoring Team Members
  - Josef Zilker — 11-54:38.7
  - Alois Wacha — 12-01:12.4

8. Denmark — 47-16:07.0
- Olaf Meyland-Smith — 11-32:24.2
- Charles Hansen — 11-40:04.0
- Johannes Reinwaldt — 11-57:20.0
- Godtfred Olsen — 12-06:18.8
  - Non-scoring Team Members
  - Valdemar Nielsen — 12-33:09.2

Hans Olsen	DNF
Valdemar Christoffer Nielsen	DNF
Otto Jensen	DNF
9. Chile	49-14:52.0
Alberto Downey	11-53:02.5
Cárlos Koller	12-13:49.2
Arturo Friedemann	12-28:20.8
José Torres	12-39:39.5
10. France	49-44:53.2
Joseph Racine	11-50:32.7
André Capelle	11-59:48.4
René Gagnet	12-20:32.6
Georges Valentin	13-33:59.5
Non-scoring Team Members	
Étienne Cheret	14-15:18.1
Gaston Alancourt	14-23:59.3
Pierre Peinaud	14-49:59.4
André Lepère	15-03:18.1
Alexis Michiels	15-15:59.2
Jacques Marcault	DNF
Louis Bes	DNF
René Rillon	DNF
11. Ireland	51-19:38.5[27]
Francis Guy	12-32:19.4
Michael Walker	12-27:49.9
Ralph Mecredy	13-03:39.0
John Walker	13-15:50.2
Non-scoring Team Members	
Matthew Walsh	13-31:17.0
Bernhard Doyle	13-42:11.8
12. Hungary	51-51:15.9
István Müller	12-39:28.0
János Henzsely	12-42:16.3
Gyula Mazur	12-50:55.8
Ignác Teiszenberger	13-38:35.8
Non-scoring Team Member	
Károly Teppert	DNF
AC. Bohemia	DNF
Bohumil Rameš	12-20:12.2
Václav Tintěra	14-10:34.6
Bohumil Kubrycht	14-11:21.0
František Kundert	DNF
Jan Vokoun	DNF
Norway	DNF
Birger Andreassen	11-20:14.6
Paul Henrichsen	11-55:23.2

Anton Hansen	12-20:23.7
Carl Gulbrandsen	DNF
Carl Olsen	DNF
Martin Sæterhaug	DNF
Russia	DNF
Andrejs Apsits	12-18:20.6
Augusts Köpke	DNF
Edgars Richters	DNF
Friedrich Bosch	DNF
Fyodor Borisov	DNF
Janis Pratneek	DNF
Jakob Bukse	DNF
Janis Lieven	DNF
Karlis Köpke	DNF
Sergey Pesteryev	DNF

NOTES

1. 12OR, p. 427.
2. Lyberg, pp. 51–52.
3. It is usually listed as 320 km. (198.7 miles), but this appears to be an estimate. BWMR calls the distance "197 miles." The best measurement appears to be in *The Field*, which gave 315.385 km. (196.0 miles).
4. 12OR, p. 437.
5. DW, EK, and OSVK have 16. But this likely counts Great Britain as only one nation. For cycling, England, Ireland, and Scotland were definitely allowed to enter separate teams of riders.
6. Often listed as 320 km., the exact distance comes from OlyCyc.
7. BWMR, August 1912.
8. BWMR, August 1912.
9. ONews had Hansen 31st with 11-40:04, Rathmann 32nd with 11-40:18.4, and Kofler 33rd with 11-41:32.6. These results are from 12OR. ONews failed to deduct two minutes from Kofler's time: he was stopped at a street crossing. OlyCyc confirms Kofler's time of 11-39:32.6, and the two-minute deduction.
10. See previous footnote.
11. See previous footnotes.
12. Both ONews and BWMR list Racine's time as 11-54:32.7. They failed to deduct four minutes allowed for being stopped at road crossings. OlyCyc confirms the time of 11-50:32.7 and the four-minute deduction.
13. Gagnet is listed as 65th in 12OR and Uggla. See the next footnote.
14. Hansen's time is given in 12OR as 12-20:23.7. But all other 1912 sources (ONews, Uggla, OlyCyc, BWMR) note that he started at 3:10 A.M. (0310) and finished at 3-31:23.7 P.M. (1521:23.7), which gives a time of 12-21:23.7. There is a misprint somewhere, either in the finishing time or the race time, or a deduction of one minute is not accounted for in the sources. The preponderance of the evidence supports the starting time of 0310, the finishing time of 1531:23.7, and the race time of 12-21:23.7. If Hansen's time was 12-20:23.7, he would be placed 64th ahead of René Gagnet (FRA).
15. If the times in 12OR are given correctly, then 12OR has the order of finish for 67–69 incorrect. They give these times for Walker, J. Stevenson, and Friedemann, but list Friedemann as 67th, Walker as 68th, and Stevenson as 69th. Of note, in the team results, Walker's time is given as 12-17:49.9, ten minutes faster. But that time would have placed him 60th, and he is definitely listed as 68th. His start time was 0640 and his finish time was 1907:49.9, for a race time of 12-27:49.9.

16. Three different times are listed in 1912 for Stevenson: 12-27:50.8 (12OR-Uggla-OlyCyc and correct), 12-29:50.8 (BWMR), and 12-39:50.8 (ONews). BWMR and ONews appear to have the time as 12-29:50.8, with the ONews time of 12-39:50.8 being an obvious typo. Both failed to deduct two minutes which he was allowed for being stopped at road crossings. As noted above, J. Stevenson is listed as 69th by 12OR, which might make the time of 12-29:50.8 the correct one, but we think not.

17. The first 81 riders, or those finishing within 25 percent of the winner's time, were awarded a special diploma of merit.

18. Czech sources have Kubrycht listed as 91st in this event.

19. Griffiths is listed with a time of 14-15:24.0 and 90th place in 12OR, OlyCyc, and Uggla. However, he is strangely listed as "did not finish" in ONews and BWMR. We have used the 12OR time as taking precedence.

20. Retired after only 200 meters, after being hit by a car.

21. Also entered, but not competing, were: Charles Wm. Anderson [54] (IRL), Walter Andrews [39] (CAN), Henri J. Bernardi [28] (MON), Omer Bodson [139] (BEL), Thomas Bulger [13] (CAN), Josef Schweiggard Bye [75] (NOR), Thomas Donaldson [67] (IRL), Jeannot Eulenberg [90] (RUS), John Farquhar [135] (SCO), Károly Gröger [71] (HUN), George R. Herd [8] (SCO), Gyula Huszár [133] (HUN), Ernest Kockler [33] (USA), Carl Lindberg [144] (FIN), David Livingston [93] (IRL), Julien Médecin [15] (MON), Lajos Merényi [19] (HUN), George Fr. Norgauer [134] (USA), István Paraker [84] (HUN), Johann Penz [101] (GER), William Petrie [99] (SCO), Walter L. Pofhal [7] (USA), Ans Pohle [25] (RUS), Daniel Quinn [73] (SCO), Ferenc Retzischar [45] (HUN), Lajos Schwarcz [97] (HUN), William Spencer [26] (CAN), and Gyula Tóth [6] (HUN). Scheduled start numbers are in brackets. It should be noted that Johann Penz (GER) is listed as having started but not finished in Diem, and by German Olympic historian Rupert Kaiser, but 12OR, BWMR, Uggla, and ONews specifically do not list him as starting.

22. The 15 teams that competed had 119 riders. The 12 teams that finished could only count four riders for the team score. Thus most sources state that there were 60 riders from 15 teams. But the three teams that did not finish did not really have four riders to count, so including all 21 riders for those teams gives 69 riders in the team event. Counting all riders for the 15 teams gives 119 cyclists.

23. The time may have been 44-44:39.2. The discrepancy is based on the time for William Hammond. In both 12OR and OlyCyc, his time is given as 11-29:16.8 in the individual results but as 11-29:16.6 in the team results. We have used the time for the individual result, although it is impossible to tell which is correct.

24. See next footnote.

25. This is the time given for Loftes in the individual results in the 12OR. The team results give his time as 11-13:51.2. However, the team score adds up correctly when using the time from the individual results.

26. The time given in the 12OR is 46-29:55.1. But the individual results and the team results for each team member agree and add up to 46-29:55.6, which is also the time given in OlyCyc.

27. The time given in 12OR is 51-39:38.5, which is almost certainly a typo, and is definitely wrong. They used 12-17:49.9 for Michael Walker's time, but he is listed as finishing in 12-27:49.9 in the individual results. Further (see above), the time of 12-17:49.9 would have placed him much higher than his individual result. OlyCyc has the time correct at 51-19:38.5.

Diving

There were four diving events, one for women and three for men, held at Stockholm. The dives were scored by five judges, who gave point scores, but also ranked the divers based on ordinals, similar to figure skating. In the preliminary rounds, the divers were ranked within their heats by ordinals, but advancement to the final was based on points scored independent of the heat. In the finals, placements were decided on total ordinal ranking with total points used to break ties.

Site:	Swimming Stadium at Djurgårdsbrunnsviken
Dates:	6–15 July
Events:	4 [3 Men —1 Women]
Competitors:	57 [43 Men —14 Women]
Nations:	10 [9 Men — 3 Women]

Overall	*Competitors*	*Gold*	*Silver*	*Bronze*	*Medals*
Austria	1	–	–	–	–
Canada	2	–	–	–	–
Finland	6	–	–	–	–
Germany	4	1	2	1	4
Great Britain	3	–	–	1	1
Italy	1	–	–	–	–
Norway	3	–	–	–	–
Russia	1	–	–	–	–
Sweden	34	3	2	2	7
United States	2	–	–	–	–
Totals	57	4	4	4	12
Nations	10	2	2	2	3

Men	*Competitors*	*Gold*	*Silver*	*Bronze*	*Medals*
Canada	2	–	–	–	–
Finland	6	–	–	–	–

153

Men	Competitors	Gold	Silver	Bronze	Medals
Germany	4	1	2	1	4
Great Britain	2	–	–	–	–
Italy	1	–	–	–	–
Norway	3	–	–	–	–
Russia	1	–	–	–	–
Sweden	22	2	1	2	5
United States	2	–	–	–	–
Totals	43	3	3	3	9
Nations	9	2	2	1	2

Women	Competitors	Gold	Silver	Bronze	Medals
Austria	1	–	–	–	–
Great Britain	1	–	–	1	1
Sweden	12	1	1	–	2
Totals	14	1	1	1	3
Nations	3	1	1	1	2

Committee for Swimming, Diving, and Water Polo

President: Erik Bergvall, Esquire
Vice-President: Major Nils David Edlund
Secretary: Kristian Hellström, Esquire
Treasurer: John G. Andersson, Esquire
Members: Carl Blidberg, Esquire; Per Fjästad, Esquire; Thor Friman, Esquire; Anton Johanson, Esquire; Torsten Kumfeldt, Esquire; Sigfrid D. Larsson, Esquire; Konrad Littorin, Esquire; Emil Lundberg, Esquire; J. A. Lönnegren; Mayor Arvid Ulrich, Esquire; Gustaf Wretman, Esquire
Building Committee: Erik Bergvall, Esquire (President); Sigfrid D. Larsson, Esquire; Torsten Kumfeldt, Esquire
Training Committee: Erik Bergvall, Esquire (President); John G. Andersson, Esquire; Torsten Kumfeldt, Esquire

MEN

Springboard Diving

A: 18; C: 7; D: 8–9 July; F: Two springboards of heights of one and three meters.

This competition consisted of two compulsory dives from one meter and two compulsory dives from three meters, followed by three optionals from three meters, which could be selected from a table of 18 allowable dives. Germany swept the first four places. After the compulsory dives, Zürner and Günther led, with Jansson close behind them. Günther dove brilliantly during the optional dives and was placed first by four of the five judges. The competition for the bronze medal was very close, with total ordinal scores of 22-23-24 given to Jansson, Zürner, and Hans Luber. The fourth-place finisher, Albert Zürner, was the defending Olympic champion from this event in London.

Final A: 8; C: 5; D: 9 July; T: 1940.

			Points	Ordinals
1.	Paul Günther	GER	79.23	6
2.	Hans Luber	GER	76.78	9
3.	Kurt Behrens	GER	73.73	22
4.	Albert Zürner	GER	73.33	23
5.	Robert Zimmerman	CAN	72.54	24
6.	Herbert Pott	GBR	71.45	28
7.	Johan "John" Jansson	SWE	69.64	32
8.	George Gaidzik	USA	68.01	36

Diplomas of Merit

Albert Zürner (GER), Robert Zimmerman (CAN), Herbert Pott (GBR), Johan "John" Jansson (SWE), George Gaidzik (USA)

Qualifying A: 18; C: 7; D: 8 July; T: 1900; F: Winner of each heat and the next five leading point scorers advanced to the final.

Heat One A: 7; C: 4.

			Points	Ordinals	
1.	Kurt Behrens	GER	80.14	6	Q
2.	Paul Günther	GER	78.14	9	q
3.	Arthur McAleenan	USA	68.02	15	
4.	Ernst Brandsten	SWE	65.01	20	
5.	Sven Nylund	SWE	62.60	28	
6.	Eskil Brodd	SWE	62.62	29	
7.	Oskar Wetzell	FIN	58.70	33	

1*

Heat Two A: 4; C: 3.

			Points	Ordinals	
1.	Johan "John" Jansson	SWE	77.77	5	Q
2.	Albert Zürner	GER	76.64	10	q
3.	Ernst Eklund	SWE	53.02	16	
4.	Carlo Bonfanti	ITA	46.81	19	

2

Heat Three A: 7; C: 5.

			Points	Ordinals	
1.	Hans Luber	GER	77.50	6	Q
2.	Robert Zimmerman	CAN	76.60	11	q

See Notes on pages 160–161.

		Points	Ordinals	
3. George Gaidzik	USA	74.03	16	q
4. Herbert Pott	GBR	73.94	17	q
5. Ernfred Appelqvist	SWE	62.61	25	
6. Axel Runström	SWE	58.42	30	
7. Erik Tjäder	SWE	53.56	35	

3

Plain and Fancy High Diving

A: 23[4] C: 7[5]; D: 12, 15 July; F: Platform at heights of five and ten meters.

In this event, the divers executed one plain running dive and one backwards somersault dive from five meters, one plain running dive and one plain standing dive from ten meters, and three optional dives from ten meters. The optional dives were to be selected from a table of 13 allowable dives. Erik Adlerz had already won the plain high diving competition. Adlerz was leading on all judges' totals going into his last dive, a flying somersault, but failed badly on it, and was then ranked second by two of the judges, trailing Albert Zürner. However, he was ranked first by three judges, and his total ordinal score of seven enabled him to win the championship.

Final A: 8; C: 4; D: 15 July; T: 1215.

		Points	Ordinals
1. Eric Adlerz	SWE	73.94	7
2. Albert Zürner	GER	72.60	10
3. Gustaf Blomgren	SWE	69.56	16
4. Hjalmar Johansson	SWE	67.80	22
5. George Yvon	GBR	67.66	22
6. Harald Arbin	SWE	62.62	31
7. Alvin Carlsson	SWE	63.16	32
8. Toivo Aro	FIN	57.05	40

Diplomas of Merit

Hjalmar Johansson (SWE), George Yvon (GBR), Harald Arbin (SWE), Alvin Carlsson (SWE)

Qualifying A: 23; C: 7; D: 12 July; T: 1240; F: Winner of each heat and the next five leading point scorers advanced to the final.

Heat One A: 9; C: 4.

		Points	Ordinals	
1. Hjalmar Johansson	SWE	68.06	9	Q
2. Albert Zürner	GER	65.04	14	q
3. Hans Luber	GER	61.66	23	
4. Gösta Sjöberg	SWE	62.08	24	
5. Ernst Brandsten	SWE	61.42	24	
6. George Gaidzik	USA	62.56	25	

		Points	Ordinals	
7. Johan "John" Jansson	SWE	59.75	27	
8. Kurt Behrens	GER	58.35	33	
9. Leo Suni	FIN	48.93	45	

6

Heat Two A: 8; C: 4.

		Points	Ordinals	
1. Eric Adlerz	SWE	74.76	6	Q
2. Gustaf Blomgren	SWE	68.50	9	q
3. Harald Arbin	SWE	62.75	15	q
4. Ernst Eklund	SWE	59.94	20	
5. Sigvard Andersen	NOR	56.40	25	
6. Oskar Wetzell	FIN	50.46	32	
7. Kalle Kainuvaara	FIN	48.10	33	
AC. Arthur McAleenan	USA	DNF		

7

Heat Three A: 6; C: 4.

		Points	Ordinals	
1. Alvin Carlsson	SWE	66.98	7	Q
2. George Yvon	GBR	65.70	9	q
3. Toivo Aro	FIN	62.75	16	q
4. Robert Andersson	SWE	60.59	18	
5. Jens Harald Stefenson	SWE	41.54	25	
AC. John Lyons	CAN	DNF		

8, 9

Plain High Diving

A: 31[10]; C: 9[11]; D: 6–7, 11 July; F: Platforms at heights of five and ten meters.

The plain high diving event consisted of one running dive and one standing dive from five meters and one standing dive and two running dives from ten meters. All the dives were selected from a table of 13 allowable dives. Erik Adlerz won the event relatively easily, placing first on four of the five judges' cards, the fifth judge placing him third. Adlerz won the plain and fancy high diving four days later to win two diving gold medals in Stockholm. The silver medal went to Hjalmar Johansson, who was the defending Olympic champion, in a very close battle with his teammate, Johan "John" Jansson. They tied on total ordinals, but Johansson defeated Jansson by two tenths of a point. The Swedes swept the first four places.

Final A: 8; C: 3; D: 11 July; T: 1930.

		Points	Ordinals
1. Eric Adlerz	SWE	40.0	7
2. Hjalmar Johansson	SWE	39.3	12
3. Johan "John" Jansson	SWE	39.1	12

		Points	Ordinals
4. Victor Gustaf Crondahl	SWE	37.1	22
5. Toivo Aro	FIN	36.5	26
6. Axel Runström	SWE	36.0	26
7. Ernst Brandsten	SWE	36.2	28
AC. Paul Günther	GER	DNF[12]	

Diplomas of Merit

Victor Gustaf Crondahl (SWE), Toivo Aro (FIN), Axel Runström (SWE), Ernst Brandsten (SWE)

Qualifying A: 31; C: 9; D: 6–7 July; F: Winner of each heat and the next four leading point scorers advanced to the final.

Heat One A: 8; C: 5; D: 6 July; T: 1930.

		Points	Ordinals	
1. Paul Günther	GER	36.1	8	Q
2. Torsten Eriksson	SWE	35.8	11	
3. Tauno Ilmoniemi	FIN	35.0	13	
4. Alfred Johansson	SWE	34.7	14	
5. Nils Tvedt	NOR	31.7	25	
6. Sven Elis Holmér	SWE	30.2	31	
7. Sigvard Andersen	NOR	28.6	32	
AC. Viktor Baranov[13]	RUS	DNF		

14

Heat Two A: 7; C: 5; D: 6 July; T: c. 2100.

		Points	Ordinals	
1. Johan "John" Jansson	SWE	38.3	5	Q
2. George Gaidzik	USA	36.2	13	
3. George Yvon	GBR	35.2	17	
4. Gunnar Ekstrand	SWE	35.3	18	
5. Arthur McAleenan	USA	34.9	20	
6. Carlo Bonfanti	ITA	28.5	32	
7. Alfred Engelsen	NOR	28.3	33	

15

Heat Three A: 9; C: 4; D: 7 July; T: 1330.

		Points	Ordinals	
1. Hjalmar Johansson	SWE	40.1	7	Q
2. Toivo Aro	FIN	39.4	10	q
3. Axel Runström	SWE	38.3	15	q
4. Ernst Brandsten	SWE	37.7	19	q
5. Victor Gustaf Crondahl	SWE	37.0	22	q
6. Hans Luber	GER	36.2	27	
7. Kurt Behrens	GER	35.1	31	

		Points	*Ordinals*	
8. John Lyons	CAN	32.5	40	
9. Jens Harald Stefenson	SWE	31.2	44	

16

Heat Four A: 7; C: 3; D: 7 July; T: c. 1500.

		Points	*Ordinals*	
1. Eric Adlerz	SWE	39.9	5	Q
2. Oskar Wetzell	FIN	33.8	13	
3. Kalle Kainuvaara	FIN	33.2	14	
4. Albert Nyman	FIN	32.0	21	
5. Leo Suni	FIN	32.1	22	
6. Albert Zürner	GER	31.7	26	
7. Sven Magnus Montan	SWE	30.2	31	

17

WOMEN

Plain High Diving

A: 14; C: 3; D: 10, 13 July; F: Platforms at heights of five and ten meters.

This was the first Olympic diving competition for women and it consisted of two compulsory dives from five meters and three compulsory dives from ten meters. Twelve of the 14 competitors were Swedish and seven of the eight finalists were Swedes. Margareta "Greta" Johansson won easily, being placed first by all five judges. She was awarded a gold medal and the challenge trophy for the women's plain high diving, which was donated in 1912 by Christina Nilsson, the Countess de Casa Miranda.

Johansson emigrated to the United States in 1913, where she married Ernst Brandsten, seventh in 1912 men's plain high diving. They settled in California and Ernst was coach at Stanford for many U.S. Olympic divers. He was also coach of the U.S. Olympic diving team for the 1936 games in Berlin.

Finals A: 8; C: 2; D: 13 July; T: 1915.

		Points	*Ordinals*
1. Margareta "Greta" Johansson	SWE	39.9	5
2. Lisa Regnell	SWE	36.0	11
3. Isabelle "Belle" White	GBR	34.0	17
4. Elsa Regnell	SWE	33.2	20
5. Ella Eklund	SWE	31.9	22
6. Elsa Andersson	SWE	31.3	25
7. Selma Andersson	SWE	28.3[18]	36
8. A. Viktoria "Tora" Larsson	SWE	26.8	39

Diplomas of Merit

Elsa Regnell (SWE), Ella Eklund (SWE), Elsa Andersson (SWE), Selma Andersson (SWE), A. Viktoria "Tora" Larsson (SWE)

Qualifying A: 14; C: 3; D: 10 July; T: 1900; F: Winner of each heat and the next six leading point scorers advanced to the final.

Heat One A: 8; C: 2.

			Points	Ordinals	
1.	Margareta "Greta" Johansson	SWE	36.2	5	Q
2.	Lisa Regnell	SWE	34.1	13	q
3.	Isabelle "Belle" White	GBR	33.9	14	q
4.	A. Viktoria "Tora" Larsson	SWE	31.0	21	q
5.	Selma Andersson	SWE	30.6	23	q
6.	Elsa Andersson	SWE	29.7	25	q
7.	Wilhelmina "Willy" Thulin	SWE	25.0	35	
8.	Märta Adlerz	SWE	21.9	39	

19

Heat Two A: 6; C: 2.

			Points	Ordinals	
1.	Ella Eklund	SWE	34.4	7	Q
2.	Elsa Regnell	SWE	34.9	8	q
3.	Gerda Johansson	SWE	28.7	16	
4.	Dagmar Nilsson	SWE	27.3	19	
5.	Ester Edström	SWE	26.3	23	
AC.	Hanny Kellner	AUT	DNF		

20, 21

NOTES

1. Also entered in this heat, but not competing, were Albert Mikael Nyman (FIN) and Julius Stern (GER).

2. Also entered in this heat, but not competing, were Ludwig Valentich (AUT), August Müller (GER), George Godfrey (RSA), and Harry Edwin Burton (USA).

3. Also entered in this heat, but not competing, was Frank Bornamann (USA).

4. DW, EK, FW, and OSVK have 21.

5. DW, EK, and OSVK have 6.

6. Also entered in this heat, but not competing, were Frank Bornamann (USA) and Alfred Engelsen (NOR).

7. Also entered in this heat, but not competing, were George Godfrey (RSA), and Harry Edwin Burton (USA).

8. There were originally four scheduled heats.

9. Also entered in this heat, but not competing, were Ludwig Valentich (AUT), Paul Günther (GER), Nils Tvedt (NOR), Torsten Eriksson (SWE), and Edwin George Schaal (USA).

10. DW, EK, and OSVK have 30.

11. DW and EK have 8.

12. Günther struck his arm against his head on a dive in the final, spraining his wrist, and had to withdraw. His injury dive is listed as the fourth in Uggla and ONews, but as the first in 12OR.

13. Not listed in OSVK.

14. Also entered in this heat, but not competing, were Ludwig Valentich (AUT) and Frank Bornamann (USA).

15. Also entered in this heat, but not competing, were Leslie Boardman (AUS), Walter Weber (GER), and Andreas Asimakopoulos (GRE).

16. Also entered in this heat, but not competing, was Robert Zimmerman (CAN).

17. Also entered in this heat, but not competing, were Elias Arnesen (NOR) and George Godfrey (RSA).

18. DW has 27.3, but all 1912 sources list the mark as 28.3.

19. Also entered in this heat, but not competing, were Sarah "Fanny" Durack (AUS) and Famia Elda (ITA).

20. There were originally at least four scheduled heats.

21. Also entered in this heat, but not competing, were Jessie Kerr (AUS), Wilhelmina Wylie (AUS), Hermine Thum (AUT), and Astrid Garpestad (NOR).

Equestrian Events

In the resolution adopted at the Sorbonne Congress in Paris in 1894, equestrian sports and polo were among the sports mentioned to be included on the Olympic Program. However, there were no equestrian sports conducted at the 1896 Olympic Games, which greatly disappointed Baron Pierre de Coubertin.

At the Paris Olympics of 1900, there were five competitions which can be considered Olympic equestrian events.[1]* But the equestrian events of the 1912 Olympics were really the first time that this sport was held in an organized manner at the Olympics. The idea of Olympic equestrian competition was first formally broached at the seventh IOC session (1906 in Athens), and equestrian events were scheduled to be conducted at the 1908 Olympic Games in London.[2] In one British book discussing the 1908 Olympics, Webster listed the 14th event from the preliminary program as "Military riding (referred to a committee, which requested Count von Rosen [SWE] to look into the matter and report to the British Olympic Council)."[3] Other than polo, though, no equestrian competition took place at the 1908 Olympic Games, for reasons which are not exactly clear.

In 1909 at the tenth IOC session (Berlin), the Swedish committee made a proposal concerning equestrian events at Stockholm, which was adopted in principle by the IOC. A Swedish committee was formed, under the patronage of HRH Prince Karl, for what was termed the "Horse Riding Competitions."[4] At the 12th IOC Session (1911 in Budapest) a committee of IOC members was organized to assist with the preparations for equestrian sports at the 1912 Olympic Games. This committee comprised of the following IOC members, all nobility: Prince Otto zu Windisch-Grätz (AUT), Baron Karl von Venningen-Ullner von Diepburg (GER), Count Géza Andrassy (HUN), Count Eugenio Brunetta d'Usseaux (HUN), and Count Clarence von Rosen (SWE).

Cash prizes were normally given at equestrian events of the kind included in the Olympic Games. However, there were no cash prizes at the Olympics, only medals to be won. The organizing committee feared that the absence of cash prizes would severely limit the number of entrants. In order to counter that, and to spur the interest of the better riders, they persuaded kings and emperors to set up prestigious challenge prizes.

Several challenge prizes were awarded for the winners of the equestrian events in Stockholm, as follows: three-day event — the German Emperor's Challenge Prize, a silver shield with the portrait of the Emperor engraved upon it; dressage — the Emperor of Austria's Prize, an equestrian stauette in silver; show jumping, team — the King of Italy's Prize, a silver-gilt "Vic-

*See Notes on pages 170–171.

tory" on a marble base; and show jumping, individual — Count Géza Andrassy (HUN) Prize, a gold statuette of a Greek goddess; and to the best overall nation in equestrian sport — the Swedish Cavalry's Prize, a statuette of a Swedish 18th century mounted rider. Andrassy's Challenge Cup was announced for the 1908 Olympics in London but not awarded, as no equestrian competition was conducted that year. With four first places, one second, and one third place, Sweden won the challenge prize of the Swedish Cavalry.

Only "gentlemen" riders, as determined by the equestrian federations in their respective nations, were allowed to compete in the 1912 Olympic equestrian events. Thus, women and non-commissioned officers were excluded.

Site:	Stockholm Fältridklubb's — Stockholm Field Riding Club — Stadium (three-day event, start and finish of long-distance ride); Lindarängen (three-day event, steeplechase course); Olympic Stadium (individual and team jumping; dressage event; jumping and dressage, three-day event).
Dates:	13–17 July
Events:	5 [5 Men — 0 Women]
Competitors:	62 [62 Men — 0 Women]
Nations:	10 [10 Men — 0 Women]

	Competitors	Gold	Silver	Bronze	Medals
Belgium	4	–	–	1	1
Chile	2	–	–	–	–
Denmark	4	–	–	–	–
France	4	1	1	1	3
Germany	13	–	3	1	4
Great Britain	4	–	–	–	–
Norway	3	–	–	–	–
Russia	7	–	–	–	–
Sweden	17	4	1	1	6
United States	4	–	–	1	1
Totals	62	5	5	5	15
Nations	10	2	3	5	5

Committee for Horse Riding Competitions

Honorary President: HRH Prince Karl
President: Colonel, Count Erik Carl Gabriel Oxenstierna
Treasurer: Captain, Count Fabian F:son Wrede
Secretary: Colonel, Count Clarence von Rosen, Master of the Horse
Members: Colonel Gabriel Torén; Major, Baron Claes Arvid Bror Cederström; Count Carl Bonde, Master of the Horse; Colonel Bror Olivier Claes Munck; Jacob Philipson, Esquire; Captain, Baron Nils Palmstierna; Lieutenant, Count Carl Gustaf Lewenhaupt; Lieutenant Carl Emil Otto Trägårdh

Secretariat
  Secretary-General: Colonel, Count Clarence von Rosen, Master of the Horse
  Secretary: Lieutenant Carl Emil Otto Trägårdh
  Treasurer: Captain, Count Fabian F:son Wrede

Executive Committee
  President: Major, Baron Claes Arvid Bror Cederström
  Secretary-General: Colonel, Count Clarence von Rosen, Master of the Horse
  Secretary: Lieutenant Carl Emil Otto Trägårdh
  Treasurer: Captain, Count Fabian F:son Wrede
  Members: Captain, Baron Nils Palmstierna; J. Philipson, Esquire

Reception Committee
  President: Colonel Gabriel Torén
  Secretary: Lieutenant, Count Carl Gustaf Lewenhaupt

Accommodation Bureau
  Director: Captain, Count Gustaf Ludvig Hamilton
  Secretary: Lieutenant Carl Henning von Horn
  Guides: Captain Lars Birger G:son Holm (BEL); Lieutenant Frank Hugo Martin (DEN);
Captain Robert Theofron Cederschiöld (FRA); Lieutenant Wilhelm Gudmund Löwenhjelm
(GER); Lieutenant Carl Björnstierna (GBR/CAN); Lieutenant Carl William Kleen (NOR);
Lieutenant Carl Henning von Horn (RUS/USA)

Stabling Bureau
  Director: Lieutenant Carl Gustaf Julius Hernlund
  Assistant: Lieutenant Roy Johan Henrik Malmstén; Lieutenant, Baron Samuel Lars Åkerhielm

Traveling Bureau
  Director: Lieutenant Ivar Osterman
  Representatives: Lieutenant Lars Martin Knut Henrik von Sydow; Lieutenant, Baron Fredrik
Herman Bennet; Lieutenant, Baron Melcher Falkenberg

Entertainments Committee
  President: Colonel, Baron Carl Rosenblad
  Vice-President: Lieutenant-Colonel, Count Reinhold von Rosen
  Secretary: Lieutenant Erik Alb:son Uggla
  Members: Major Carl Gustaf Oscar Ankarcrona, Major Gustaf Björnström; Captain, Baron
Carl Reinhold von Essen; Lieutenant Hugo Nicolaus Otto Theodor Ankarcron; Lieutenant,
Baron Samuel Lars Åkerhielm

Jury
  President: Colonel Bror Olivier Claes Munck
  Secretary: Captain John Maule
  Field President: Colonel, Count Carl Thorsten Gotthard Rudenschöld
  Field Adjutant: Captain Carl Erik Knös
  Prize President: Lieutenant-Colonel, Baron Carl Gustaf Bror Cederström
  Prize Adjutant: Lieutenant, Baron Fredrik Herman Bennet
  Prize Members: Major Ulrick Edmund Wilhelm Croneborg, Major Per Vilhelm Karsten
  Jumping President: Lieutenant-Colonel Baron Adolf Adelswärd

Jumping Adjutant: Lieutenant Frans Bror Daniel Salmson
Adjoint Member: Captain Axel Ahnström; Lieutenant-Colonel Gustaf Richard Joachim

International Jury
    President: Colonel Gustaf Adolf Nyblæus (SWE)
    Members: Lieutenant-Colonel, Count Reinhold von Rosen (SWE); Major — Joostens (BEL); Otto August Heinrich Moltke (DEN); Commander — Destremau (FRA); Major — von Giese (GER); Lieutenant Colonel Johan Henrik Egeberg-Ottesen (NOR); Lieutenant Colonel Frederick S. Foltz (USA)

Advertisement Committee
    Secretary-General: Colonel, Count Clarence von Rosen, Master of the Horse
    Member: Lieutenant, Count Carl Gustaf Lewenhaupt

Press Bureau
    Member: Lieutenant Sture Hemming Gadd

Military Riding (Three-Day) Event, Individual

A: 27; C: 7; D: 13, 15–17 July; T: 0800–1030 (13/7); 1100–1500 (15/7); 0900–1130 (16/7); 0700–1200 (17/7); F: 13/7 — long-distance ride of 55 km., 50 km. road (1), and 5 km. cross-country, scored separately (2); 15/7 — 3,500 meter steeplechase (3); 16/7 — jumping competition (4); 17/7 — dressage (5).

The event was only for commissioned officers on active duty. Each nation was allowed a maximum of four competitors. Not strictly a true three-day event as we now know it, the event was termed the "Military Riding Competition" in 1912. In addition, it took place over four days, not three. Section scores were calculated by using the percentage of possible scores in each section multipled by ten. The maximum by sections were the following: section one — long-distance ride of 55 km., maximum ten points; section two — 5 km. cross-country ride with natural obstacles of fences, ditches, and streams, held as a portion of the long-distance ride, maximum 130 points, scaled down to ten points; section three — 3,500 meter steeplechase, maximum 100 points, scaled down to ten points; section four — jumping competition, maximum 150 points, scaled down to ten points; and section five — dressage, maximum 770 points, scaled down to ten points. As an example, in dressage (section five), Nordlander scored 590 in the dressage or .766 of maximum, which gave him a score of 7.66 for the dressage.

The event opened with the 55 km. ride on a day that was described as oppressively hot.[5] Still, 26 of the 27 riders finished the course, with only one (Albert Seigner [FRA]) outside the time limit of four hours. In the cross-country portion of the ride, held concurrently, three riders rode the wrong way and were disqualified, but 13 posted perfect scores of 130. Thus after two sections, 13 riders were tied for first place. Two days later, 22 riders started the steeplechase section, but it did little to separate the logjam at the top. Seventeen of the 22 posted perfect scores of 100 in this section, and nine riders remained tied for first with total scores of 30 after this section.

The jumping (section four) was won by Ernst Casparsson (SWE) who scored 145 of 150 points. Bernard Meyer (FRA) and Friedrich von Rochow (GER) each scored 143 to move into a tie for first place with totals of 39.53, with only the dressage remaining. Only 15 riders started the dressage, which was won by Jean Cariou (FRA), who scored 594.2 points (of 770 possible) to move into third place overall. The second best dressage score was posted by Axel Nordlander of Sweden, who had been in seventh place going into the last section. Nordlander scored 590 points in the dressage, and his adjusted score of 7.66 enabled him to move into first place overall. Nordlander won, in addition to his gold medal, the German Emperor's Challenge Prize.

Rider	Horse		1	2	3	4	5	Total
1. Axel Nordlander	Lady Artist	SWE	10.0	10.00	10.0	8.93	7.66	46.59
2. Friedrich von Rochow	Idealist	GER	10.0	10.00	10.0	9.53	6.89[6]	46.42
3. Jean Cariou	Cocotte	FRA	10.0	10.00	10.0	8.60	7.72	46.32
4. Nils Adlercreutz	Atout	SWE	10.0	9.85	10.0	9.00	7.46	46.31
=5. Ernst Casparsson	Irmelin	SWE	10.0	9.62	10.0	9.67	6.87	46.16
Rudolf, Count von Schaesberg–Tannheim	Grundsee	GER	10.0	10.00	10.0	9.40	6.76	46.16
7. Benjamin Lear	Poppy	USA	10.0	10.00	10.0	9.07	6.84	45.91
8. Eduard von Lütcken	Blue Boy	GER	10.0	10.00	10.0	9.27	6.63	45.90
9. John Montgomery	Deceive	USA	10.0	10.00	10.0	9.40	6.48	45.88
10. Henric Horn af Åminne	Omen	SWE	10.0	10.00	10.0	8.27	7.58	45.85
11. Guy Henry	Chiswell	USA	10.0	9.46	10.0	9.13	6.95	45.54
=12. Ephraim Graham	Connie	USA	10.0	9.62	10.0	9.40	6.28	45.30
Bernard Meyer	Allons-y	FRA	10.0	10.00	10.0	9.53	5.77	45.30
14. Albert Seigner	Dignité	FRA	9.0	9.23	10.0	9.33	7.59	45.15
15. Carl von Moers	May-Queen	GER	10.0	10.00	8.2	8.67	7.56	44.43
AC. Paul Covert	La Sioute	BEL	10.0	9.85	10.0	8.33	DNS	DNF
Gaston de Trannoy	Capricieux	BEL	10.0	9.69	10.0	8.53	DNS	DNF
Paul Kenna	Harmony	GBR	10.0	10.00	9.4	8.80	DNS	DNF
Edward Radcliffe-Nash	The Flea	GBR	10.0	9.69	8.4	8.20	DNS	DNF
Frode Kirkebjerg	Dibbe–Libbe	DEN	10.0	5.69	10.0	DNS	DNF	DNF
Bryan Lawrence	Patrick	GBR	10.0	9.85	DNF	DNS	DNF	DNF
Herbert Scott	Whisper II	GBR	10.0	10.00	DQ[7]	DNS	DNF	DNF
Carl Adolph Kraft	Gorm	DEN	10.0	10.00	DNS	DNF		DNF
Michel Dufort d'Astafort	Castibalza	FRA	10.0	DQ[8]	DNS	DNF		
Emanuel de Blommaert de Soye	Clonmore	BEL	10.0	DQ[9]	DNS	DNF		
Guy Reyntiens	Beau Soleil	BEL	10.0	DQ[10]	DNS	DNF		
Carl Høst Saunte	Streg	DEN	DNF	DNF	DNS	DNF		

Military Riding (Three-Day) Event, Team

A: 27; C: 7; D: 13, 15–17 July; T: 0800–1030 (13/7); 1100–1500 (15/7); 0900–1130 (16/7); 0700–1200 (17/7); F: Four-man teams, best three scores from the individual competition to count for the team total.

After the first day of competition, Germany led with a perfect score of 60, followed by Sweden and Great Britain, who both scored 59.85. Germany continued to lead after the third and fourth sections, scoring a perfect 90 through section three, and with 118.20 points going into the dressage. Entering the last event, the United States was in second with 117.49 points, and Sweden third with 117.07. But Sweden fared the best in the dressage to win the gold medal, with Germany second and the United States third. Only four of the original seven teams had three riders finish all five phases of the competition.

1. Sweden   139.06
   (Axel Nordlander <Lady Artist> [46.59], Nils Adlercreutz <Atout> [46.31], Ernst Casparsson <Irmelin> [46.16], Henric Horn af Åminne <Omen> [45.85])

2. Germany   138.48
   (Friedrich von Rochow <Idealist> [46.42], Rudolf, Count von Schaesberg-Tannheim <Grundsee> [46.16], Eduard von Lütcken <Blue Boy> [45.90], Carl von Moers <May-Queen> [44.43])

3. United States   137.33
   (Benjamin Lear <Poppy> [45.91], John Montgomery <Deceive> [45.88], Guy Henry <Chiswell> [45.54], Ephraim Graham <Connie> [45.30])

4. France   136.77
   (Jean Cariou <Cocotte> [46.32], Bernard Meyer <Allons-y> [45.30], Albert Seigner <Dignité> [45.15], Michel Dufort d'Astafort <Castibalza> [DQ])

AC. Great Britain   DNF
   (Paul Kenna <Harmony> [DNF], Bryan Lawrence <Patrick> [DNF], Edward Radcliffe-Nash <The Flea> [DQ], Herbert Scott <Whisper II> [DQ])

   Denmark   DNF
   (Carl Adolph Kraft <Gorm> [DNF], Carl Høst Saunte <Streg> [DNF], Frode Kirkebjerg <Dibbe-Libbe> [DNF])

   Belgium   DNF
   (Emanuel de Blommaert de Soye <Clonmore> [DQ], Paul Covert <La Sioute> [DNF], Guy Reyntiens <Beau Soleil> [DQ], Gaston de Trannoy <Capricieux> [DNF])

Dressage, Individual

A: 21; C: 8; D: 15 July; T: 0800–1100, 1200–1500.

This event was called the Prize Riding Event in the *Official Report*, and was similar to, but not precisely the same as, what we now know as dressage. In addition to the dressage tests, there were a number of obstacles to negotiate. Four of these had a height between 0.8 and 1.1 m. one had a length of 3.0 m. and one was a rolling barrel 0.8 m. in diameter. The Swedes dominated the competition, their six riders finishing in the top eight places, and sweeping the medals. The gold medalist, Carl Bonde, did not compete at the 1920 or 1924 Olympics, but in 1928 at Amsterdam, he was on the Swedish dressage team which won the silver medal. In the 1928 individual dressage he placed 19th. Bonde was awarded the the Emperor of Austria's Challenge Prize, in addition to his gold medal.

	Rider	Horse	Nation		Judges' Scores						Total
1.	Carl Bonde	Emperor	SWE	1	1	1	1	3	3	5	15
2.	Gustaf Adolf Boltenstern, Sr.	Neptun	SWE	1	2	2	2	3	5	6	21
3.	Hans von Blixen-Finecke, Sr.	Maggie	SWE	2	3	4	5	5	5	8	32
4.	Friedrich von Osterley	Condor	GER	2	2	3	4	6	9	10	36
5.	Carl Rosenblad	Miss Hastings	SWE	3	4	4	5	7	9	11	43
6.	Oscar af Ström	Irish Lass	SWE	4	6	6	6	8	8	9	47
7.	Felix Bürkner	King	GER	1	2	6	7	8	13	14	51[12]
8.	Carl Kruckenberg	Kartusch	SWE	4	6	7	8	8	8	10	51
9.	Mikhail Yekimov	Tritonich	RUS	3	7	7	10	10	12	13	62
10.	Albert Seigner	Dignité	FRA	1	4	12	13	13	13	17	73
11.	Andreas von Flotow	Senta	GER	7	9	9	9	12	13	18	77
12.	Carl von Moers	New Bank	GER	10	10	11	11	11	15	15	83
13.	Guy Henry	Chiswell	USA	9	12	12	13	14	15	18	93
14.	Jean Cariou	Mignon	FRA	5	7	11	15	17	19	20	94
15.	Jens Baltazar Falkenberg	Hjørdis	NOR	12	14	14	14	16	16	17	103
16.	Rudolf Jakob Poul Keyper	Kinley Princess	DEN	12	14	15	15	17	18	20	111
17.	Gaston de Trannoy	Capricieux	BEL	10	14	17	18	19	19	20	117
18.	Carl Høst Saunte	Streg	DEN	11	15	16	16	20	21	21	120
19.	Michel Dufort d'Astafort	Castibalza	FRA	11	17	18	18	19	19	21	123
20.	John Montgomery	Deceive	USA	16	17	18	19	19	20	21	130
21.	Emanuel de Blommaert de Soye	Clonmore	BEL	16	16	20	20	21	21	21	135

Judges

Bror Cederström, President; Wilhelm Croneborg; Per Karstén; Captain Chodron de Courcel (FRA); Major –– Wiel-Gjedde (NOR); Captain Gavril Bertrain (RUS); Lieutenant-Colonel –– Seiffert (GER)
[13]

Show Jumping, Individual

A: 31; C: 8; D: 16 July; T: 1400–1800; F: One round. Maximum points 190.

There were 15 obstacles, with four of them jumped twice, or a total of 19 obstacles. Ten points were given for each obstacle cleared. The maximum height of the jumps was 1.4 m. The water jump was 4.0 m. in length. Deductions were as follows: first refusal — two points; second refusal — four points; third refusal — six points; fall from horse — six points; hitting fence with horse's foreleg — one point; hitting fence with horse's hindleg — one point; knocking down a fence with the horse's foreleg — four points; knocking down a fence with the horse's hindleg — two points; hitting the water with the horse's hindleg — two points; hitting the water with the horse's foreleg — four points; and exceeding the time limit — two points for each five-second interval beyond the time limit. The course was 1,533 meters in length, and the time limit was 3:50.0, for a calculated speed of 400 meters/minute.

Jean Cariou (FRA) tied for first place with Rabod Wilhelm von Kröcher (GER) with four faults, or a score of 186. In the jump-off, shortened to six obstacles (maximum score of 60), Cariou had five faults to seven for von Kröcher. (Of interest, Cariou had competed in the three-day event, finishing third in the individual. He had the highest total score in sections one to three, and five, but was brought down by his performance in the jumping section, where he finished 15th of 19 competitors.) Cariou won the Count Géza Andrassy (HUN) Challenge Prize, in addition to his gold medal.

	Rider	Horse	Nat	Score	Time	JO/Score/Time
1.	Jean Cariou	Mignon	FRA	186	3:46.0	55 1:16.0
2.	Rabod Wilhelm von Kröcher	Dohna	GER	186	3:37.2	53 1:10.0
3.	Emanuel de Blommaert de Soye	Clonmore	BEL	185	3:18.0	
4.	Herbert Scott	Shamrock	GBR	184	3:26.4	
5.	Sigismund Freyer	Ultimus	GER	183	3:24.0	
=6.	Wilhelm, Count von Hohenau	Pretty Girl	GER	181	3:19.0	
	Ernst Casparsson[14]	Kiriki	SWE	181	3:29.4	
	Nils Adlercreutz	Ilex	SWE	181	3:30.0	
=9.	Dmitry Pavlovich Romanov	Unité	RUS	180	3:23.6	
	Charles Lewenhaupt	Arno	SWE	180	3:33.0	
	Carl Gustaf Lewenhaupt	Medusa	SWE	180	3:35.0	
	Ernst Hubertus Deloch	Hubertus	GER	180	3:39.0	
=13.	Michel Dufort d'Astafort	Amazone	FRA	179	3:38.6	
	Carl-Axel Torén	Falken	SWE	179	3:41.2	
15.	Karol Rómmel	Siablik	RUS	178	3:49.0	
=16.	Enrique Deichler	Chile	CHI	176	3:40.0	
	Aleksandr Rodzhianko	Eros	RUS	176	3:21.0	
=18.	Sergey Zagorsky	Bandoura	RUS	174	3:18.0	
	Friedrich Karl, Prince von Preußen	Gibson Boy	GER	174	3:25.0	
	Friedrich Ernst, Count von Grote	Polyphem	GER	174	3:39.8	
21.	Mikhail Plechkov	Eveta	RUS	173	3:46.8	
=22.	Åke Hök	Mona	SWE	170	3:38.8	
	Aleksey Selikhov	Tugela	RUS	170	3:42.4	
24.	Karl Kildal	Garcia	NOR	168	3:34.2	
25.	Elias Yanes	Patria	CHI	166	3:35.0	
26.	Jørgen Jensen	Jossy	NOR	165	3:38.6	
27.	Paul Kenna	Harmony	GBR	162	4:12.0	
28.	Jens Falkenberg	Florida	NOR	161	4:31.6[15]	
29.	Edward Radcliffe-Nash	The Flea	GBR	153	4:30.2	
30.	Guy Reyntiens	Beau Soleil	BEL	147	4:23.0	
AC.	Bernard Meyer	Ursule	FRA	DNF[16]		

[17]

Show Jumping, Team

A: 22; C: 6; D: 17 July; T: 1300–1600; F: Four-man teams, best three scores to count for the team total. Competition held separately from the individual event. The point scoring system was the same as for the individual event. Maximum individual possible 190; maximum team possible 570.

The team jumping event was conducted separately from the individual competition, and on the following day. Sweden won the gold medal, led by Count Carl Gustaf Lewenhaupt whose score of 188 was the best individual performance, although equaled by Belgium's Emanuel de Blommaert de Soye. For their victory, the Swedish team was awarded the King of Italy's Challenge Prize.

		Time	Time Faults	Other Faults	Total Points
1. Sweden			2	23	545
Carl Gustaf Lewenhaupt	Medusa	3:36.0	0	2	188
Gustaf Kilman	Gåtan	3:45.0	0	10	180
Hans von Rosen	Lord Iron	3:51.0	2	11	177
Fredrik Rosencrantz	Drabant	4:03.0	6	13	171
2. France			2	30	538
Michel Dufort d'Astafort	Amazone	3:37.0	0	5	185
Jean Cariou	Mignon	3:38.0	0	8	182
Bernard Meyer	Allons-y	3:51.0	2	17	171
Albert Seigner	Cocotte	3:26.0	0	20	170
3. Germany			0	40	530
Sigismund Freyer	Ultimus	3:22.0	0	9	181
Wilhelm, Count von Hohenau	Pretty Girl	3:14.0	0	13	177
Ernst Hubertus Deloch	Hubertus	3:42.0	0	18	172
Friedrich Karl, Prince von Preußen	Gibson Boy	3:23.0	0	24	166
4. United States			0	43	527
John Montgomery	Deceive	3:31.0	0	10	180
Guy Henry	Chiswell	3:42.0	0	16	174
Benjamin Lear	Poppy	3:36.0	0	17	173
5. Russia			2	48	520
Aleksandr Rodzhianko	Eros	3:31.0	0	14	176
Mikhail Plechkov	Yvette	3:39.6	0	18	172
Aleksey Selikhov	Tugela	3:53.0	2	16	172
Dmitry Pavlovich Romanov	Unité	3:06.8	0	21	169
6. Belgium			2	58	510
Emanuel de Blommaert de Soye	Clonmore	3:30.0	0	2	188
Gaston de Trannoy	Capricieux	3:44.0	0	28	162
Paul Covert	La Sioute	3:50.4	2	28	160

NOTES

1. Mallon, Bill. *The 1900 Olympic Games*. Jefferson, NC: McFarland, 1998., p. 101.
2. 12OR, p. 564.
3. Webster, p. 206.
4. 12OR, p. 565.
5. 12OR, p. 583.
6. Given in both 12OR and Rau as 6.39. However, this score would give a final total of only 45.92, which would have placed von Rochow in seventh place, not second. The error can be seen when looking at his gross score for the dressage, which was 530.7. As 770 was the dressage maxi-

mum, this represented .689 of maximum, for a correct dressage score of 6.89 and a correct final score of 46.42.

7. Rode the wrong way.

8. Rode the wrong way.

9. Rode the wrong way.

10. Rode the wrong way.

11. Denmark entered four riders and two reserves in this event. R. Oluf Pontoppidan [Cai] and Captain H. C. A. Jessen [Geisha], who were both entered, did not take part. Frode Kirkebjerg was originally a reserve, but did compete.

12. Ties in place scores were decided by point scores. However, the point scores have not been found, and were probably not preserved.

13. Also entered in this event, but not competing, were Paul Covert [La Sioute] (BEL), Guy Reyntiens [Beau Soleil] (BEL), Carl Adolph Kraft [Gorm] (DEN), R. Oluf Pontoppidan [Cai] (DEN), J. C. A. Dornonville de la Cour [Selma] (DEN), Bernard Meyer [Allons-y/Ursule] (FRA), Lieutenant –– de Meslon [Amazone] (FRA), Herbert Scott [Whisper II] (GBR), Edward Radcliffe-Nash (Betty/The Flea) [GBR], Bryan Lawrence [Patrick] (GBR), Paul Kenna [Harmony] (GBR), Lieutenant-Colonel –– Jobst [Regina] (GER), Friedrich von Rochow [Else] (GER), Jørgen Jensen [Biro] (NOR), Karl Kildal [Nelly] (NOR), Benjamin Lear [Poppy/Fencing Girl] (USA), and Ephraim Graham [Connie] (USA).

14. FW has only Count von Hohenau in sixth, and did not list Casparsson or Adlercreutz.

15. Falkenberg's time of 4:31.6 should have incurred 18 fault points. But no time faults are noted in 12OR or Rau. An additional 18 faults would have lowered Falkenberg's score to 143 and 30th place. It is likely that 4:31.6 is a misprint for 3:41.6.

16. Meyer retired at the 11th obstacle.

17. Also entered in this event, but not competing, were Paul Covert [La Sioute] (BEL), Gaston de Trannoy [Capricieux] (BEL), Carl Adolph Kraft [Gorm] (DEN), R. Oluf Pontoppidan [Cai] (DEN), Carl Høst Saunte [Streg] (DEN), J. C. A. Dornonville de la Cour [Selma] (DEN), Captain H. C. A. Jessen [Geisha] (DEN), Frode Kirkebjerg [Dibbe-Libbe] (DEN), Albert Seigner [Allons-y/Dignité] (FRA), Lieutenant –– de Meslon [Amazone] (FRA), Bryan Lawrence [One-Two-Three] (GBR), Captain C. F. Michelet [Helmsman] (NOR), Benjamin Lear [Poppy/Fencing Girl] (USA), Guy Henry [Chiswell/Connie] (USA), Ephraim Graham [Fencing Girl/Bazan] (USA), John Montgomery [Deceive/Bazan] (USA), and George Patton [Deceive/Connie] (USA).

Fencing

Fencing is one of the few sports that has been conducted on the program of every Olympic Games of the modern era, and 1912 was no exception. Nevertheless, the sport was controversial in 1912, as the French and Italians, who were the dominant nations in foil and épée fencing, did not agree with the rules for the competitions. The French responded by withdrawing, and sent no competitors to Stockholm. Italy withdrew only from the épée events.

From the point of view of this book, fencing has been the most difficult sport in terms of finding the complete results. The *Official Report* appears to contain almost complete results, but these are but a façade. The *Official Report* seems to have listed all the entrants in the results of the pools of the individual events, whether or not they competed. Programs and entries for the fencing events are available and seem to give the same entry lists as the result summaries of the *Official Report*, supporting the contention that the final results therein are not accurate.

Several sources have been searched to find the full fencing results, but not with complete success. The following results are based mainly on the British sporting newspaper, *The Field*, which gave the most detailed summaries. *The Field* is our only relatively complete source. Where it differs from the *Official Report*, we were able to check the results against a few other sources from 1912, notably Austrian sporting journals (*Allgemeine Sport Zeitung*) and Hungarian newspaper sources, and they invariably supported *The Field*, and not the *Official Report*. But many questions remain, including the exact make-up of the teams in certain pools in the team events. Still, we think these results are the most accurate yet published for the 1912 Olympic fencing competitions. Because they are so different from what we have usually seen, we have not diligently footnoted other sources, as we have done with all other sports. Suffice to say that we have examined the usual sources — Kamper, Kluge, Mező, Wallechinsky, and Wasner — but we have instead relied on primary 1912 sources for our information.

Site:	Tennis Pavilion at the Östermalm Idrottsplats
Dates:	6–18 July
Events:	5 [5 Men — 0 Women]
Competitors:	184 [184 Men — 0 Women]
Nations:	16 [16 Men — 0 Women]

	Competitors	Gold	Silver	Bronze	Medals
Austria	12	–	1	1	2
Belgium	11	2	–	1	3
Bohemia	13	–	–	–	–
Denmark	6	–	1	–	1
Germany	16	–	–	–	–
Great Britain	22	–	1	–	1
Greece	6	–	–	–	–
Hungary	13	2	1	1	4
Italy	9	1	1	–	2
The Netherlands	12	–	–	2	2
Norway	7	–	–	–	–
Portugal	1	–	–	–	–
Russia	24	–	–	–	–
South Africa	1	–	–	–	–
Sweden	18	–	–	–	–
United States	13	–	–	–	–
Totals	184	5	5	5	15
Nations	16	3	5	4	7

Committee for Fencing

President: Captain Emil Fick
Secretary: Lieutenant Birger Cnattingius
Members: Captain, Baron Hans Henrik von Essen; Lieutenant Carl Hjalmar Reinhold Hjorth; I. Tagtström, Esquire; Lieutenant Nils Brambeck
International Jury: Carl Gustaf Platen (President/SWE); Sten Drakenberg (SWE); Heinrich Tenner (AUT); Albert Feyerick (BEL); H. Jürst (GER); William Henry Grenfell, Lord Desborough of Taplow (GBR); Adrianus Egbertus Willem de Jong (NED); Carlo Compans de Brichanteaux (ITA)

Foil, Individual

A: 94[1]*; C: 15; D: 6–8 July; F: Each match was the first to record five hits.

In international fencing shortly after 1900, the top swordsmen were divided between two styles — the French school and the Italian school. But the French boycotted the Olympic fencing competition, upset with the rules. They proposed that the touch surfaces should include the upper arm but this was rejected. With the best French fencers absent, the foil event was left to the Italians.

The foil gold medal went to Italy's Nedo Nadi, who advanced through four rounds with the loss of only one match. In 1920 at Antwerp, Nadi defended his foil gold medal, and won five gold medals in fencing at the 1920 Olympics.

*See Notes on pages 202–209.

Final Pool A: 8; C: 4; D: 8 July; T: 1300–1600.

			nn	ps	rv	lb	ea	es	bb	rm	W	L	TF	TR
1.	Nedo Nadi	ITA	–	o	o	o	o	o	o	o	7	0	35	8
2.	Pietro Speciale	ITA	x	–	o	o	x	o	o	o	5	2	29	24
3.[2]	Richard Verderber	AUT	x	x	–	x	o	o	o	o	4	3	27	25
4.	László Berti	HUN	x	x	o	–	o	x	o	o	4	3	23	25
5.	Edoardo Alaimo	ITA	x	o	x	x	–	o	o	o	4	3	27	26
6.	Edgar Seligman	GBR	x	x	x	o	x	–	o	o	3	4	23	29
7.	Béla Békessy	HUN	x	x	x	x	x	x	–	o	1	6	20	34
8.	Robert Montgomerie	GBR	x	x	x	x	x	x	x	–	0	7	22	35

Diplomas of Merit

László Berti (HUN), Edoardo Alaimo (ITA), Edgar Seligman (GBR), Béla Békessy (HUN), Robert Montgomerie (GBR)

Semifinal Pools A: 24; C: 9; D: 8 July; T: 0900–1200; F: First two in each pool advance to the final.

Pool One[3] A: 6; C: 5.

			L	
=1.	Edoardo Alaimo	ITA	1	Q
	Edgar Seligman	GBR	1	Q[4]
=3.	Pál Pajzs	HUN	2	
	Zoltán Schenker	HUN	2	
5.	Robert Hennet	BEL	3	
6.	Vilém Tvrzsky	BOH	4	

Pool Two A: 6; C: 6.

			L	
1.	Nedo Nadi	ITA	0	Q
2.	Béla Békessy	HUN	1	Q
=3.	Emil Schön	GER	2	
	Paul Anspach	BEL	2	
5.	Ivan Osiier	DEN	3	
AC.	Edgar Amphlett	GBR	DNF[5]	

Pool Three[6] A: 6; C: 5.

			L	
1.	Pietro Speciale	ITA	0	Q
2.	Robert Montgomerie	GBR	2	Q
3.	Péter Tóth	HUN	2	
=4.	Béla Zulavszky	HUN	3	
	Henri Anspach	BEL	3	
	Julius Lichtenfels	GER	3	

Pool Four[7] A: 6; C: 5.

			L	
=1.	László Berti	HUN	0	Q
	Richard Verderber	AUT	0	Q

3.	Sherman Hall	USA	2	8
4.	Victor Willems	BEL	3	
AC.	Dezső Földes	HUN	DNF[9]	
	Fernando Cavallini	ITA	DNF	

Quarterfinal Pools A: 47; C: 12; D: 7 July; F: First three in each pool advance to the semifinals.

Pool One[10] A: 6; C: 6; T: 1300–1600.

			L	
1.	Zoltán Schenker	HUN	0	Q
2.	Nedo Nadi	ITA	1	Q
3.	Julius Lichtenfels	GER	1	Q
4.	Gordon Alexander	GBR	3	11
=5.	Léon Tom	BEL	4	
	Marc Larimer	USA	4	

Pool Two[12] A: 5; C: 5; T: 1300–1600.

			L	
1.	Béla Zulavszky	HUN	0	Q
2.	Vilém Tvrzsky	BOH	1	Q
3.	Edgar Amphlett	GBR	2	Q[13]
4.	Jens Ole Berthelsen	DEN	3	
5.	Francesco Pietrasanta	ITA	4	

14

Pool Three[15] A: 6; C: 6; T: 1300–1600.

			L	
1.	Pietro Speciale	ITA	0	Q
=2.	Edgar Seligman	GBR	1	Q[16]
	Dezső Földes	HUN	1	Q
=4.	Marcel Berré	BEL	3	
	Scott Breckinridge	USA	3	
6.	Josef Pfeiffer	BOH	5	

Pool Four[17] A: 6; C: 6; T: 1300–1600.

			L	
=1.	Edoardo Alaimo	ITA	0	Q
	Béla Békessy	HUN	0	Q
3.	Sherman Hall	USA	1	Q
=4.	Adolf Davids	GER	3	
	Axel Jöhncke	SWE	3	
	Fernand de Montigny	BEL	3	

Pool Five[18] A: 6; C: 6; T: 1600–1900.

			L	
=1.	Ivan Osiier	DEN	1	Q
	Péter Tóth	HUN	1	Q
	Victor Willems	BEL	1	Q
=4.	Sotirios Notaris	GRE	3	

			L	
	Wilhelm Löffler	GER	3	
6.	Harold Rayner	USA	4	

Pool Six[19] A: 6; C: 6; T: 1600–1900.

			L	
=1.	Henri Anspach	BEL	1	Q
	Fernando Cavallini	ITA	1	Q
3.	Pál Pajzs	HUN	2	Q
4.	Carl Hjorth	SWE	3	
=5.	Arthur Fagan	GBR	4	[20]
	Friedrich Golling	AUT	4	

Pool Seven[21] A: 6; C: 6; T: 1600–1900.

			L	
1.	Robert Hennet	BEL	1	Q
2.	Robert Montgomerie	GBR	2	Q[22]
3.	Richard Verderber	AUT	2	Q
=4.	Lauritz Christian Østrup	DEN	3	
	Vilém Goppold z Lobsdorfu, Jr.	BOH	3	
6.	Hermann Plaskuda	GER	4	

Pool Eight A: 6; C: 6; T: 1600–1900.

			L	
1.	László Berti	HUN	1	Q
2.	Paul Anspach	BEL	2	Q
3.	Emil Schön	GER	3	Q
=4.	Bjarne Eriksen	NOR	3	
	Ejnar Levison	DEN	3	
	Jacques Ochs	BEL	3	

Round One Pools A: 94; C: 15; D: 6–7 July; F: First three in each pool advanced to the quarterfinals.

Pool One A: 5; C: 5; D: 6 July; T: 0800–1030.

			L	
1.	Léon Tom	BEL	0	Q
2.	Vilém Tvrzský	BOH	1	Q
3.	Dezső Földes	HUN	2	Q
=4.	Dmitry Knyazhevich	RUS	3	
	Andreas Suttner	AUT	3	
	[23]			

Pool Two A: 5; C: 5; D: 6 July; T: 0800–1030.

			L	
1.	Marcel Berré	BEL	0	Q
=2.	Marc Larimer	USA	2	Q[24]
	Edgar Amphlett	GBR	2	Q[25]
=4.	Johannes Adam	GER	3	
	Feliks Leparsky	RUS	3	
	[26]			

Pool Three A: 5; C: 5; D: 6 July; T: 0800–1030.

			L	
=1.	Gordon Alexander	GBR	1	Q[27]
	Albertson Van Zo Post	USA	1	Q[28]
3.[29]	Josef Pfeiffer	BOH	2	Q
4.	Bertalan Dunay	HUN	2	
5.	Pavel Guvorsky [30]	RUS	4	

Pool Four A: 7; C: 7; D: 6 July; T: 0800–1030.

			L	
1.	Nedo Nadi	ITA	0	Q
2.	Zoltán Schenker	HUN	1	Q
3.	Scott Breckinridge	USA	3	Q
4.	Miroslav Klika	BOH	3	
=5.	Walter Gates	RSA	4	
	Percival Davson	GBR	4	
7.	Julius Thomson [31]	GER	6	

Pool Five A: 7; C: 7; D: 6 July; T: 1300–1600.

			L	
1.	Julius Lichtenfels	GER	1	Q
2.	Arthur Fagan	GBR	2	Q[32]
3.	Jens Ole Berthelsen	DEN	3	Q
=4.	Gaston Salmon	BEL	3	
	Graeme Hammond	USA	3	
6.	Gustaf Armgarth	SWE	4	
7.	Vladimir Keyser	RUS	5	

Pool Six A: 7; C: 7; D: 6 July; T: 1300–1600.

			L	
1.	Francesco Pietrasanta	ITA	0	Q
2.	Fernand de Montigny	BEL	1	Q
3.	Sotirios Notaris	GRE	2	Q
=4.	Stenson Cooke	GBR	4	
	Lars Thorlaksøn Aas	NOR	4	
	John MacLaughlin	USA	4	
7.	Nikolay Gorodetsky	RUS	6	

Pool Seven A: 7; C: 7; D: 6 July; T: 1300–1600.

			L	
=1.	Sherman Hall	USA	1	Q
	Victor Willems	BEL	1	Q
3.	Pietro Speciale	ITA	2	Q
=4.	Sydney Martineau	GBR	3	[33]
	Aleksandr Mordovin	RUS	3	
=6.	Birger Personne	SWE	4	
	Hans Olsen	DEN	4	

Pool Eight A: 5; C: 5; D: 6 July; T: 1300–1600.

			L	
1.	Harold Rayner	USA	0	Q
2.	Béla Zulavszky	HUN	1	Q
3.	Adolf Davids	GER	2	Q
4.	Nils Grönwall	SWE	3	
5.	Vladimir Samoylov	RUS	4	

34

Pool Nine A: 6; C: 6; D: 6 July; T: 1600–1900.

			L	
=1.	Edgar Seligman	GBR	1	Q
	Béla Békessy	HUN	1	Q
3.	Wilhelm Löffler	GER	2	Q
4.	Josef Javůrek	BOH	3	
5.	Franz Dereani	AUT	4	
6.	Ernest Gignoux	USA	5	

35

Pool Ten A: 6; C: 6; D: 6 July; T: 1600–1900.

			L	
1.	Ejnar Levison	DEN	0	Q
2.	Pál Pajzs	HUN	1	Q
3.	Hermann Plaskuda	GER	2	Q
=4.	Josef Puhm	AUT	3	
	William Bowman	USA	3	
6.	Zdeněk Vávra	BOH	5	

36

Pool Eleven A: 4; C: 4; D: 6 July; T: 1600–1900.

			L	
1.	Ivan Osiier	DEN	0	Q
=2.	Axel Jöhncke	SWE	2	Q
	Friedrich Golling	AUT	2	Q
4.	Gavril Bertrain	RUS	2	

37

Pool Twelve A: 6; C: 6; D: 6 July; T: 1600–1900.

			L	
1.	Edoardo Alaimo	ITA	0	Q
2.	Péter Tóth	HUN	1	Q
3.	Vilém Goppold z Lobsdorfu, Jr.	BOH	2	Q
4.	Alfred Sauer	USA	3	
=5.	Vladimir Sarnavsky	RUS	4	
	Albert Naumann	GER	4	

38

Pool Thirteen A: 7; C: 7; D: 7 July; T: 0800–1100.

			L	
1.	Paul Anspach	BEL	0	Q

=2.	Carl Hjorth	SWE	1	Q
	Robert Montgomerie	GBR	1	Q[39]
=4.	Leonid Martuchev	RUS	3	
	Oluf Berntsen	DEN	3	
=6.	Georges von Tangen	NOR	5	
	Reinhold Trampler	AUT	5	

[40]

Pool Fourteen A: 5; C: 5; D: 7 July; T: 0800–1100.

			L	
=1.	Henri Anspach	BEL	1	Q
	Richard Verderber	AUT	1	Q
	Bjarne Eriksen	NOR	1	Q
4.	Adrianus de Jong	NED	3	
5.	Anatoly Zhakovlev	RUS	4	

[41]

Pool Fifteen A: 6; C: 6; D: 7 July; T: 0800–1100.

			L	
=1.	Jacques Ochs	BEL	1	Q
	László Berti	HUN	1	Q
3.	Lauritz Christian Østrup	DEN	2	Q
4.	Heinrich Ziegler	GER	2	
5.	Rudolf Cvetko[42]	AUT	3	
6.	František Kříž	BOH	5	

[43]

Pool Sixteen A: 6; C: 6; D: 7 July; T: 0800–1100.

			L	
=1.	Fernando Cavallini	ITA	1	Q
	Robert Hennet	BEL	1	Q
	Emil Schön	GER	1	Q
4.	George Breed	USA	3	
5.	Leonid Grinev	RUS	4	
6.	Gunnar Böös	SWE	5	

[44]

Épée, Individual

A: 93; C: 15; D: 11–13 July.

The épée events were somewhat "empty" competitions, as the best épée fencers in the world were the French and the Italians. As noted above, the French boycotted the entire Olympic fencing competition, and the Italians refused to compete in the épée, upset with the rules. The Italian Fencing Federation had proposed that the blade of the épée be lengthened to 94 cm., and when this proposal was rejected, they refused to participate.

With the French and Italians absent, the Belgians did well, advancing four fencers to the final. Paul Anspach of Belgium won the gold medal. Anspach competed as a fencer at the

Olympics of 1908, 1912, 1920, and 1924, winning five Olympic medals as follows: 1908 épée team bronze; 1912 épée individual gold; 1912 épée team gold; 1920 épée team silver; and 1924 épée team silver.

Final Pool A: 8; C: 4; D: 13 July; T: 1400–1700.

		pa	io	lhdb	vb	esö	ese	lt	mh	W	L	T
1. Paul Anspach	BEL	–	o	o	o	o	x	o	o	6	1	0
2. Ivan Osiier	DEN	x	–	o	x	o	o	o	o	5	2	0
3. Philippe Le Hardy de Beaulieu	BEL	x	x	–	o	o	o	o	=	4	2	1
4. Victor Boin	BEL	x	o	x	–	o	o	o	=	4	2	1
5. Einar Sörensen	SWE	x	x	x	x	–	o	o	o	3	4	0
6. Edgar Seligman	GBR	o	x	x	x	x	–	o	=	2	4	1
7. Léon Tom	BEL	x	x	x	x	x	x	–	o	1	6	0
8. Martin Holt	GBR	x	x	=	=	x	=	x	–	0	4	3

Diplomas of Merit

Victor Boin (BEL), Einar Sörensen (SWE), Edgar Seligman (GBR), Léon Tom (BEL), Martin Holt (GBR)

Semifinal Pools A: 24; C: 9; D: 13 July; F: First two in each pool advanced to the final.

Pool One A: 6; C: 6; T: 0900–1200.

		L	
=1. Einar Sörensen	SWE	1	Q
Léon Tom	BEL	1	Q
=3. Petros Manos	GRE	3	
William Bowman	USA	3	
=5. Edgar Amphlett	GBR	4	[45]
Zdeněk Vávra	BOH	4	

Pool Two A: 6; C: 5; T: 0900–1200.

		L	
=1. Edgar Seligman	GBR	0	Q[46]
Paul Anspach	BEL	0	Q
3. Adrianus de Jong	NED	2	
=4. Gerald Ames	GBR	3	
Pál Rosty	HUN	3	
6. Miroslav Klika	BOH	5	

Pool Three A: 6; C: 5; T: 0900–1200.

		L	
=1.[47] Victor Boin	BEL	2	Q
Ivan Osiier	DEN	2	Q
3. Henri Anspach	BEL	2	
=4. Gustaf Lindblom	SWE	3	
Robert Montgomerie	GBR	3	[48]
6. Frantisek Kšíž	BOH	5	

Pool Four A: 6; C: 6; T: 0900–1200.

			L	
=1.	Martin Holt	GBR	2	Q[49]
	Philippe Le Hardy de Beaulieu	BEL	2	Q
3.	Georgios Petropoulos	GRE	2	
=4.	Ejnar Levison	DEN	4	
	Georg Branting	SWE	4	
6.[50]	Vilém Goppold z Lobsdorfu, Jr.	BOH	4	

Quarter-Final Pools A: 48; C: 13; D: 12 July; F: First three in each pool advanced to the semifinals.

Pool One A: 6; C: 6; T: 1200–1500.

			L	
=1.	Zdeněk Vávra	BOH	1	Q
	Ivan Osiier	DEN	1	Q
3.	Edgar Seligman	GBR	2	Q[51]
=4.	Fernand de Montigny	BEL	3	
	Fredric Schenck	USA	3	
6.	Hendrik de Iongh	NED	4	

Pool Two A: 6; C: 6; T: 1200–1500.

			L	
1.	Philippe Le Hardy de Beaulieu	BEL	0	Q
=2.	William Bowman	USA	2	Q
	Miroslav Klika	BOH	2	Q
4.	Sotirios Notaris	GRE	2	
=5.	Arthur Everitt	GBR	4	[52]
	Gavril Bertrain	RUS	4	

Pool Three A: 6; C: 6; T: 1200–1500.

			L	
1.	František Kříž	BOH	1	Q
=2.	Edgar Amphlett	GBR	2	Q[53]
	Ejnar Levison	DEN	2	Q
=4.	Hans Thomson	GER	4	
	Jacques Ochs	BEL	4	
6.	Lars Thorlaksøn Aas	NOR	5	

Pool Four A: 6; C: 6; T: 1200–1500.

			L	
1.	Paul Anspach	BEL	2	Q
2.	Robert Montgomerie	GBR	2	Q[54]
3.	Georgios Petropoulos	GRE	2	Q
=4.	Arthur Griez von Ronse	AUT	3	
	Jan de Beaufort	NED	3	
6.	Severin Finne	NOR	4	

Pool Five A: 6; C: 6; T: 1500–1800.

			L	
1.	Einar Sörensen	SWE	1	Q
=2.	Petros Manos	GRE	2	Q
	Gerald Ames	GBR	2	Q[55]
=4.	George Breed	USA	3	
	Sigurd Mathiesen	NOR	3	
6.	Emil Schön	GER	4	

Pool Six A: 6; C: 6; T: 1500–1800.

			L	
1.	Vilém Goppold z Lobsdorfu, Jr.	BOH	1	Q
=2.	Gustaf Lindblom	SWE	2	Q
	Victor Boin	BEL	2	Q
4.	Trifon Triantafyllakos	GRE	3	
5.	Charles Vander Byl	GBR	4	
6.	Jens Ole Berthelsen	DEN	5	

Pool Seven A: 6; C: 6; T: 1500–1800.

			L	
1.	Henri Anspach	BEL	0	Q
=2.	Adrianus de Jong	NED	2	Q
	Pál Rosty	HUN	2	Q
4.	Konstantinos Kotzias	GRE	3	
=5.	Karel Goppold z Lobsdorfu	BOH	4	
	Louis Sparre[56]	SWE	4	

Pool Eight A: 6; C: 6; T: 1500–1800.

			L	
=1.	Léon Tom	BEL	1	Q
	Georg Branting	SWE	1	Q
3.	Martin Holt	GBR	2	Q[57]
4.	Georgios Versis	GRE	3	
=5.	Albertson Van Zo Post	USA	4	
	Zdeněk Bárta	BOH	4	

Round One Pools A: 87; C: 15; D: 11–12 July; F: First three in each pool advanced to the quarterfinals.

Pool One A: 8; C: 8; D: 11 July; T: 0900–1200.

			L	
=1.	Ejnar Levison	DEN	1	Q
	Hendrik de Iongh	NED	1	Q
3.	Sotirios Notaris	GRE	2	Q
4.	Victor Willems	BEL	3	
5.	Julius Lichtenfels	GER	4	
6.	Åke Grönhagen	SWE	5	
=7.	Pavel Guvorsky	RUS	6	
	Gordon Alexander	GBR	6	[58]

Pool Two A: 6; C: 6; D: 11 July; T: 0900–1200.

			L	
=1.	Paul Anspach	BEL	1	Q
	Petros Manos[59]	GRE	1	Q
3.	Jens Ole Berthelsen	DEN	3	Q
4.	Friedrich Schwarz	GER	3	
=5.	Aleksandr Soldatenkov	RUS	4	
	Knut Enell	SWE	4	

60

Pool Three A: 7; C: 7; D: 11 July; T: 0900–1200.

			L	
1.	Konstantinos Kotzias	GRE	1	Q
2.	Léon Tom	BEL	2	Q
3.	Arthur Griez von Ronse	AUT	4	Q
=4.	Hans Bergsland	NOR	4	
	Vladimir Keyser	RUS	4	
AC.	Fernando Correia	POR	DQ	
	Vilém Tvrzský	BOH	DQ	

61

Pool Four A: 6; C: 6; D: 11 July; T: 0900–1200.

			L	
=1.	Einar Sörensen	SWE	1	Q
	Vilém Goppold z Lobsdorfu, Jr.	BOH	1	Q
3.	Severin Finne	NOR	2	Q
=4.	Sherman Hall	USA	4	
	Vladimir Sarnavsky	RUS	4	
	George van Rossem	NED	4	

62

Pool Five A: 4; C: 4; D: 11 July; T: 1200–1500.

			L	
1.	Zdeněk Vávra	BOH	1	Q
2.	Gavril Bertrain	RUS	1	Q
3.	George Breed	USA	1	Q
4.	Georges von Tangen	NOR	3	

63

Pool Six A: 5; C: 5; D: 11 July; T: 1200–1500.

			L	
=1.	Edgar Seligman	GBR	1	Q[64]
	Jacques Ochs	BEL	1	Q
3.	Miroslav Klika	BOH	3	Q
4.	Bjarne Eriksen	NOR	3	
5.	Leonid Martuchev	RUS	4	

65

Pool Seven A: 7; C: 7; D: 11 July; T: 1200–1500.

			L	
1.	Lars Thorlaksøn Aas	NOR	2	Q
=2.	Philippe Le Hardy de Beaulieu	BEL	3	Q
	Martin Holt	GBR	3	Q[66]
4.	Alfred Sauer	USA	3	
=5.	Albertus Perk	NED	4	
	Josef Javůrek	BOH	4	
7.	Walter Gates	RSA	5	

Pool Eight A: 6; C: 6; D: 11 July; T: 1200–1500.

			L	
1.	Robert Montgomerie	GBR	1	Q
=2.	Fernand de Montigny	BEL	2	Q
	František Kříž	BOH	2	Q
=4.	Marc Larimer	USA	3	
	Harald Platou	NOR	3	
6.	Heinrich Schrader	GER	5	

67

Pool Nine[68] A: 5; C: 5; D: 11 July; T: 1500–1800.

			L	
1.	Victor Boin	BEL	0	Q
2.	Arthur Everitt	GBR	1	Q[69]
3.	Sigurd Mathiesen	NOR	2	Q
4.	Graeme Hammond	USA	3	
5.	Jacob van Geuns	NED	4	

70

Pool Ten[71] A: 7; C: 7; D: 11 July; T: 1500–1800.

			L	
1.	Hans Thomson	GER	2	Q
2.	Jan de Beaufort	NED	2	Q
3.	Louis Sparre	SWE	2	Q
4.	Gaston Salmon	BEL	3	
=5.	Percival Davson	GBR	4	72
	Josef Pfeiffer	BOH	4	
7.	John MacLaughlin	USA	5	

73

Pool Eleven[74, 75] A:—; C:—; D: 11 July; T: 1500–1800.

			L	
=1.	Fredric Schenck	USA	bye	Q
	Edgar Amphlett	GBR	bye	Q
	Henri Anspach	BEL	bye	Q

76

Pool Twelve[77] A: 4; C: 4; D: 11 July; T: 1500–1800.

			L	
1.	Ivan Osiier	DEN	0	Q

2.	Zdeněk Bárta	BOH	1	Q
3.	William Bowman	USA	2	Q
4.	Stenson Cooke	GBR	3	[78]

[79]

Pool Thirteen[80] A: 8; C: 8; D: 12 July; T: 0900–1200.

			L	
1.	Gustaf Lindblom	SWE	3	Q
2.	Adrianus de Jong	NED	3	Q
3.	Georgios Versis[81]	GRE	3	Q
=4.	Hermann Plaskuda	GER	3	
	Sydney Martineau	GBR	3	
6.	Marcel Berré	BEL	4	
7.	J. Ernest Gignoux	USA	5	
8.	Hans Olsen	DEN	6	

Pool Fourteen[82, 83] A:—; C:—; D: 12 July; T: 0900–1200.

			L	
=1.	Charles Vander Byl	GBR	bye	Q
	Pál Rosty	HUN	bye	Q
	Albertson Van Zo Post	USA	bye	Q

[84]

Pool Fifteen[85] A: 8; C: 8; D: 12 July; T: 0900–1200.

			L	
1.	Georg Branting	SWE	1	Q
=2.	Emil Schön	GER	2	Q
	Trifonos Triantafillakos	GRE	2	Q
4.	Willem Hubert van Blijenburgh	NED	3	
=5.	John Blake	GBR	4	[86]
	Oluf Berntsen	DEN	4	
=7.	James Moore	USA	5	
	Béla Békessy	HUN	5	

Pool Sixteen[87] A: 6; C: 6; D: 12 July; T: 0900–1200.

			L	
1.	Georgios Petropoulos	GRE	1	Q[88]
=2.	Gerald Ames	GBR	2	Q[89]
	Karel Goppold z Lobsdorfu	BOH	2	Q[90]
4.	Lauritz Østrup	DEN	3	
5.	Walther Meienreis	GER	4	
6.	Willem Molijn	NED	5	

[91]

Épée, Team

A: 58[92]; C: 11; D: 9–10 July; F: Teams of eight fencers, with four fencers to take part in a single match. Each fencer met all four fencers of the other team, thus 16 bouts per match. Each bout was the first to three touches. The match could be discontinued once one team won nine matches. The captain of the losing team could decide whether or not to continue to 16 matches. In case of a tie in matches, the team with the least number of touches received won the match. If the touches received were equal, a barrage took place to decide the match.

The Belgians greatly benefited from the absence of the French and Italians from the épée competitions, as described above. Belgium had advanced four fencers to the final of the individual épée event, and provided the individual champion in Paul Anspach. Led by Anspach, the Belgians won this event, although they did lose a match to the Swedes in the semifinal pools. The Belgian team won possession of the challenge trophy for the team épée, which had been donated in 1908 by the English Fencers.

Final Standings

1. Belgium
(Gaston Salmon, Henri Anspach, Jacques Ochs, Paul Anspach, Robert Hennet, Victor Willems)[93]

2. Great Britain
(Arthur Everitt, Edgar Seligman, Martin Holt, Percival Davson, Robert Montgomerie, Sydney Martineau)[94]

3. The Netherlands
(Adrianus de Jong, Jetze Doorman, Leonardus Nardus, Willem Hubert van Blijenburgh)[95]

4. Sweden
(Einar Sörensen, Eric Carlberg, Georg Branting, Gustaf Lindblom, Louis Sparre, Pontus von Rosen)[96]

=5. Denmark
(Ejnar Levison, Hans Olsen, Ivan Osiier, Lauritz Christian Østrup)[97]

Greece
(Georgios Petropoulos, Georgios Versis, Konstantinos Kotzias, Petros Manos, Trifonos Triantafillakos)[98]

=7. Bohemia
(Vilém Goppold z Lobsdorfu, Jr., Vilém Goppold z Lobsdorfu, Sr., Josef Pfeiffer, František Kříž)[99]

Germany
(Emil Schön, Friedrich Schwarz, Heinrich Ziegler, Hermann Plaskuda)[100]

=9. Russia
(Gavril Bertrain, Dmitry Knyazhevich, Vladimir Sarnavsky, Pavel Guvorsky, Vladimir Keyser, Aleksandr Soldatenkov, Leonid Martuchev)[101]

Norway
(Hans Bergsland, Severin Finne, Lars Thorlaksøn Aas, Georges von Tangen)[102]

United States
(Albertson Van Zo Post, George Breed, John MacLaughlin, Scott Breckinridge, Sherman Hall, William Bowman)[103]

Diplomas of Merit

Sweden (Einar Sörensen, Eric Carlberg, Georg Branting, Gustaf Lindblom, Louis Sparre, Pontus von Rosen)

Final Pool A: 19; C: 4; D: 10 July; T: 0900–1500.

	W	L	MW[104]	ML
1. Belgium	3	0	32 (27)	21 (16)

(Henri Anspach, Robert Hennet, Jacques Ochs, Gaston Salmon, Paul Anspach)

2. Great Britain	1	2	26 (20)	28 (22)

(Percival Davson, Arthur Everitt, Martin Holt, Edgar Seligman, Robert Montgomerie)

3. The Netherlands	1	2	28 (18)	30 (20)

(Adrianus de Jong, Willem Hubert van Blijenburgh, Jetze Doorman, Leonardus Nardus)

4. Sweden	1	2	25 (16)	32 (23)

(Einar Sörensen, Gustaf Lindblom, Pontus von Rosen, Louis Sparre, Georg Branting)

Pool Summary

Belgium 10 (9) Great Britain 7 (6)
(BEL — P Anspach 4, Ochs 3, H Anspach 3 (2), Hennet 0) (GBR — Holt 3 (2), Davson 2, Montgomerie 1, Seligman 1)

Belgium 10 (8) The Netherlands 8 (6)
(BEL — H Anspach 3, Ochs 2,[105] P Anspach 2, Salmon 3 (1)) (NED — van Blijenburgh 2, de Jong 2, Nardus 1, Doorman 1)

Belgium 12 (10) Sweden 6 (4)
(BEL — Hennet 4, Ochs 4, P Anspach 2, H Anspach 2[106]) (SWE — Sörensen 3, Lindblom 1, von Rosen 1, Sparre 1)

The Netherlands 10 (7) Great Britain 9 (6)
(NED — Doorman 4, van Blijenburgh 3, Nardus 1, de Jong 1) (GBR — Seligman 2, Montgomerie 2, Holt 1, Davson 1)

Sweden 11 (6) The Netherlands 10 (5)
(SWE — Sörensen 2, Lindblom 2, Branting 2, von Rosen 0) (NED — van Blijenburgh 3, Nardus 1, de Jong 1, Doorman 0)

Great Britain 10 (8) Sweden 8 (6)
(GBR — Montgomerie 3, Holt 3, Davson 2, Everitt 0[107]) (SWE — Sörensen 2, von Rosen 2, Lindblom 1, Branting 1)

Match Summaries (matches won–lost)

Belgium vs. Great Britain (10–7 [9–6])

	Seligman	Montgomerie	Holt	Davson	Wins	Wins+Draws
Ochs	1–0	1–0	0–1	1–0	3	3
H Anspach	1–0	1–0	1–1	0–1	2	3
P Anspach	1–0	1–0	1–0	1–0	4	4
Hennet	0–1	0–1	0–1	0–1	0	0
Wins (GBR)	*1*	*1*	*2*	*2*	*9*	*10*
Wins+Draw (GBR)	*1*	*1*	*3*	*2*	*7*	

Semifinal Pools A: 40–48??; C: 8; D: 9 July; T: 1400–1830; F: First two
teams in each pool advanced to the final.

Pool One A: 19–27??; C: 4.

	W	L	MW	ML	
1. The Netherlands	3	0	28 (25)	25 (22)	Q

(Adrianus de Jong, Willem Hubert van Blijenburgh, Leonardus Nardus, Jetze Doorman)

2. Great Britain	2	1	30 (23)	27 (20)	Q

(Arthur Everitt, Robert Montgomerie, Martin Holt, Percival Davson, Edgar Seligman, Sydney Martineau[108])

3. Denmark	1	2	25 (21)	27 (23)

(rosters not known for any matches in this pool — minimum four/maximum eight fencers)

4. Bohemia	0	3	24 (20)	28 (24)

(rosters not known for any matches in this pool — minimum four/maximum eight fencers)

Pool Summary

The Netherlands	10 (8)	Great Britain	10 (8)	
The Netherlands	10 (8)	Great Britain	8 (6)	(barrage)

(NED — roster not known; GBR — Everitt, Montgomerie, Holt, Davson)

The Netherlands	8	Bohemia	8[109]	
The Netherlands	9	Bohemia	5	(barrage)

(NED — van Blijenburgh, de Jong, Nardus, Doorman; BOH — roster not known)

The Netherlands	10 (9)	Denmark	7 (6)[110]

(NED — de Jong 3, van Blijenburgh 2, Nardus 2, Doorman 3 (2); DEN — roster not known)

Great Britain	10 (8)	Denmark	8 (6)

(GBR — Everitt, Montgomerie, Holt, Martineau/Seligman[111]; DEN — roster not known)

Great Britain	10 (7)	Bohemia	9 (6)

(GBR — Everitt, Montgomerie, Holt, Martineau/Seligman[112]; BOH — roster not known)

Denmark	10 (9)	Bohemia	7 (6)

(rosters not known)

Pool Two A: 21; C: 4.

	W	L	MW	ML	
1. Sweden	3	0	33 (28)	20 (15)	Q

(Einar Sörensen, Gustaf Lindblom, Pontus von Rosen, Eric Carlberg)

2. Belgium	2	1	32 (28)	20 (16)	Q

(Henri Anspach, Robert Hennet, Jacques Ochs, Paul Anspach, Victor Willems, Gaston
Salmon)

3. Greece	1	2	25 (19)	29 (23)

(Petros Cambas, Konstantinos Kotzias, Petros Manos, Sotirios Notaris, Georgios Petropoulos, Georgios Versis, Trifonos Triantafillakos)[113]

4. Germany	0	3	16 (11)	37 (32)

(Hermann Plaskuda, Emil Schön, Friedrich Schwarz, Heinrich Ziegler)[114]

Pool Summary

Sweden	11 (9)	Belgium	7 (5)

(SWE — Sörensen, Lindblom, von Rosen, Carlberg; BEL — H Anspach 2, Hennet 2, Ochs 2 (1), P Anspach 1 (0))

Sweden	12 (11)	Germany	5 (4)

(SWE — Sörensen, Lindblom, von Rosen, Carlberg; GER — roster not known)

Sweden	10 (8)	Greece	8 (6)

(SWE — Sörensen, Lindblom, von Rosen, Carlberg; GRE — roster not known)

Belgium	15 (14)	Germany	2 (1)

(BEL — P Anspach 4 (3), H Anspach 4, Willems 4, Hennet 3; GER — Plaskuda, Schwarz, Schön, Ziegler)

Belgium	10 (9)	Greece	7 (6)[115]

(BEL — Hennet 4, Willems 3, Ochs 3 (2), Salmon 0; GRE — roster not known)

Greece	10 (7)	Germany	9 (6)

(rosters not known)

Round One A: 42; C: 9; D: 9 July; T: 0900–1330; F: First two teams in each pool advance to the semifinals.

Pool One A:—; C:—.[116]

=1. The Netherlands   Q
(Entered — Adrianus de Jong, Willem Hubert van Blijenburgh, Jetze Doorman, Leonardus Nardus, George van Rossem, Jan de Beaufort, Adriaan Bos, Albertus Perk)

=1. Germany   Q
(Entered — Jakob Erckrath de Bary, Friedrich "Fritz" Jack, Julius Lichtenfels, Walther Meienreis, Hermann Plaskuda, Emil Schön, Friedrich Schwarz, Heinrich Ziegler)

Pool Two A: 15; C: 3.

	W	L	MW	ML	
=1. Great Britain	1	0	12 (11)	5 (4)	Q
Belgium	1	0	9 (8)	2 (1)	Q
3. Russia	0	2	7 (5)	21 (19)	

(Robert Montgomerie, Percival Davson, Arthur Everitt, Martin Holt) [Great Britain]

(Paul Anspach, Henri Anspach, Jacques Ochs, Gaston Salmon) [Belgium]

(Gavril Bertrain, Dmitry Knyazhevich, Vladimir Sarnavsky, Pavel Guvorsky, Vladimir Keyser, Aleksandr Soldatenkov, Leonid Martuchev) [Russia]

Pool Summary

Great Britain	12 (11)	Russia	5 (4)

(GBR — Everitt 3, Holt 3, Davson 3, Montgomerie 2; RUS — Keyser, Soldatenkov, Martuchev, Bertrain)

Belgium	9 (8)	Russia	2 (1)[117]

(BEL — P Anspach 2, Salmon 2, H Anspach 3, Ochs 2; RUS — Bertrain, Sarnavsky, Guvorsky, Knyazhevich)

Pool Three A: 12; C: 3.

	W	L	MW	ML	
=1. Bohemia	1	0	10 (7)	9 (6)	Q

(Vilém Goppold z Lobsdorfu, Jr., Vilém Goppold z Lobsdorfu, Sr., Josef Pfeiffer, František Kříž)

	W	L	MW	ML	
Sweden	1	0	9 (7)	9 (7)	Q

(Einar Sörensen, Gustaf Lindblom, Pontus von Rosen, Eric Carlberg)

	W	L	MW	ML	
3. Norway	0	2	18 (13)	19 (14)	

(Hans Bergsland, Severin Finne, Lars Aas, Georges von Tangen)

Pool Summary[118]

Bohemia   10 (7)   Norway   9 (6)
(BOH — Goppold z Lobsdorfu, Jr., Goppold z Lobsdorfu, Sr., Pfeiffer, Kříž; NOR — Bergsland, Finne, Thorlaksøn Aas, von Tangen)

Sweden   9 (7)   Norway   9 (7)
(SWE — Sörensen, Lindblom, von Rosen, Carlberg; NOR — Finne 4, Thorlaksøn Aas 3, Bergsland 2, von Tangen 0)

Sweden[119]   9   Norway   3
(SWE — Sörensen, Lindblom, von Rosen, Carlberg; NOR — Finne, Thorlaksøn Aas, Bergsland, von Tangen)

Pool Four A: 15; C: 3.

	W	L	MW	ML	
1. Denmark	2	0	19 (18)	13 (12)	Q

(Ejnar Levison, Hans Olsen, Ivan Osiier, Lauritz Christian Østrup[120])

	W	L	MW	ML	
2. Greece	1	1	17 (15)	17 (15)	Q

(Konstantinos Kotzias, Petros Manos, Georgios Petropoulos, Georgios Versis, Trifon Triantafyllakos)

	W	L	MW	ML	
3. United States	0	2	13 (12)	19 (18)	

(William Bowman, Scott Breckinridge, George Breed, Sherman Hall, John MacLaughlin, Albertson Van Zo Post)[121]

Pool Summary

Denmark   10 (9)   Greece   7 (6)
(DEN — Levison, Olsen, Osiier, Østrup; GRE — Kotzias, Petropoulos, Versis, Triantafyllakos)

Denmark   9   United States   6
(DEN — roster not known; USA — Bowman 2, Breckinridge 2, MacLaughlin 2, Breed 0)

Greece   10 (9)   United States   7 (6)
(GRE — Manos, Petropoulos, Versis, Triantafyllakos; USA — Breckinridge 2, MacLaughlin 2, Van Zo Post 2 (1), Hall 1)

Sabre, Individual

A: 64[122]; C: 12; D: 16–18 July.

In 1908 at London, Hungary began its dominance of Olympic sabre fencing. They won the team event, and Jenő Fuchs won the individual sabre gold medal. Fuchs was back in Stockholm, the leader of a powerful Hungarian sabre team. Seven of the eight finalists were Hungarian, and Fuchs defended his Olympic gold medal.

From 1908 through 1964, a Hungarian fencer always won the sabre gold medal at the Olympics, with the exception of 1920, when Hungary was not invited as it was considered an aggressor nation in World War I. Hungarians also won all the world championships in individual sabre from 1923 through 1937 and, after World War II, 1951–55.

Final Pool[123] A: 8; C: 2; D: 18 July; T: 1400–1700.

		jf	bb	em	zs	nn	pt	lw	df	W	L	TF	TR
1. Jenő Fuchs	HUN	–	3	3	0	3	3	3	3	6	1	18	10
2. Béla Békessy	HUN	0	–	2	3	3	3	3	3	5	2	17	11
3. Ervin Mészáros	HUN	2	3	–	3	3	0	3	3	5	2	17	12
4. Zoltán Schenker	HUN	3	2	1	–	2	3	3	3	4	3	17	13
5. Nedo Nadi	ITA	2	0	2	3	–	3	3	3	4	3	16	17
6. Péter Tóth	HUN	1	0	3	1	2	–	3	2	2	5	12	17
7. Lajos Werkner	HUN	2	2	1	1	2	2	–	3	1	6	13	19
8. Dezső Földes	HUN	0	1	0	2	2	3	1	–	1	6	9	20

Diplomas of Merit

Zoltán Schenker (HUN), Nedo Nadi (ITA), Péter Tóth (HUN), Lajos Werkner (HUN), Dezső Földes (HUN)

Semifinal Pools A: 20; C: 7; D: 18 July; T; 0900–1200; F: First two in each pool advanced to the final.[124]

Pool One[125] A: 5; C: 3.

			W	L	
1.	Béla Békessy	HUN	5	0	Q
2.	Nedo Nadi	ITA	4	1	Q
3.	Béla Zulavszky	HUN	3	2	
4.	Bertalan Dunay	HUN	2	3	
5.	Friedrich Schwarz	GER	1	4	
	[126]				

Pool Two[127] A: 3; C: 2.

			W	L	
1.	Péter Tóth	HUN	2	0	Q
2.	Jenő Fuchs	HUN	1	1	Q
3.	Alfred Syson	GBR	0	2	
	[128]				

Pool Three[129] A: 6; C: 4.

			W	L	
1.	Ervin Mészáros	HUN	5	0	Q
2.	Dezső Földes	HUN	4	1	Q
3.	Pál Pajzs	HUN	3	2	
4.	Charles Vander Byl	GBR	2	3	
5.	Boris Arsenyev	RUS	1	4	
6.	Birger Personne	SWE	0	5	

Pool Four[130] A: 6; C: 4.

			W	L	
1.	Lajos Werkner	HUN	5	0	Q
2.	Zoltán Schenker	HUN	4	1	Q
3.	László Berti	HUN	3	2	
4.	Apollon Guiber von Greifenfels	RUS	2	3	
5.	William Marsh	GBR	1	4	
6.	Oluf Berntsen	DEN	0	5	

Quarterfinal Pools A: 39; C: 9; D: 17 July; T: 1200–1800; F: First three in each pool advanced to the semifinals.

Pool One A: 6; C: 5; T: 1200–1500.

			W	L	
1.	László Berti	HUN		0	Q
2.	Bertalan Dunay	HUN		1	Q
3.	Vladimir Andreyev	RUS		2	Q
4.	Giovanni Benfratello	ITA		3	
=5.	Ejnar Levison	DEN		4	
	Georg Stöhr	GER		4	

Pool Two A: 5; C: 4; T: 1200–1500.

			W	L	
1.	Lajos Werkner	HUN		0	Q
2.	Oszkár Gerde	HUN		1	Q
3.	Anatoly Timofeyev	RUS		2	Q
=4.	Alfred Sauer	USA		3	
	Harry Butterworth[131]	GBR		3	

Pool Three A: 4; C: 4; T: 1200–1500.

			W	L	
1.	Ervin Mészáros	HUN		0	Q
2.	Friedrich Schwarz	GER		1	Q
3.	William Marsh	GBR		2	Q
4.	Prince Ernest zu Hohenlohe[132]	AUT		3	

Pool Four A: 5; C: 4; T: 1200–1500.

			W	L
=1.	Béla Békessy	HUN	1	Q
	Dezső Földes	HUN	1	Q
3.	Oluf Berntsen	DEN	2	Q
=4.	Aristide Pontenani	ITA	3	
	Nikolay Kuznyetsov	RUS	3	

133

Pool Five A: 5; C: 4; T: 1500–1800.

			W	L
1.	Zoltán Schenker	HUN	1	Q
=2.[134]	Charles Vander Byl	GBR	2	Q
	Apollon Guiber von Greifenfels	RUS	2	Q
4.	Hans Thomson	GER	2	
5.	Edward Brookfield	GBR	3	

135

Pool Six A: 4; C: 4; T: 1500–1800.

			W	L
=1.	Alfred Syson	GBR	0	Q
	Jenő Fuchs	HUN	0	Q
3.	Boris Arsenyev	RUS	2	Q
4.	Jens Ole Berthelsen	DEN	3	

136

Pool Seven A: 5; C: 4; T: 1500–1800.

			W	L
=1.[137]	Nedo Nadi	ITA	1	Q
	Pál Pajzs	HUN	1	Q
3.[138]	Béla Zulavszky	HUN	2	Q
4.	Alfred Keene	GBR	2	
5.	Martin Nordenström	SWE	4	

139

Pool Eight A: 5; C: 5; T: 1500–1800.

			W	L
1.	Péter Tóth	HUN	0	Q
=2.[140]	Julius Lichtenfels	GER	1	Q
	Birger Personne	SWE	1	Q
4.	Francesco Pietrasanta	ITA	1	
5.	A. Ridley Martin	GBR	4	

141

Round One Pools A: 52[142]; C: 12; D: 16–17 July; T: 0900–1800 (16/7), 0900–1200 (17/7); F: First three in each pool advanced to the quarterfinals. 63 per FW and that appears to be correct based on TF

Pool One A: 4; C: 4; D: 16 July; T: 0900–1200.

			W	L	
1.	Giovanni Benfratello	ITA	3	0	Q
2.	Lajos Werkner	HUN	2	1	Q
3.	Vladimir Danich	RUS	1	2	Q
4.	Gustaf Armgarth	SWE	0	3	

143

Pool Two A: 5; C: 5; D: 16 July; T: 0900–1200.

			W	L	
=1.	Béla Zulavszky	HUN	3	1	Q
	Julius Lichtenfels	GER	3	1	Q
3.[144]	Vladimir Andreyev	RUS	2	2	Q
4.	Friedrich Golling	AUT	2	2	
5.	Helge Werner	SWE	0	4	

145

Pool Three A: 4; C: 4; D: 16 July; T: 0900–1200.

			W	L	
1.	Karl Münich	AUT	3	0	Q
2.	Hans Thomson	GER	2	1	Q
3.	Jens Ole Berthelsen	DEN	1	2	Q
4.	Boris Nepokupnoy	RUS	0	3	

146

Pool Four A: 5; C: 5; D: 16 July; T: 0900–1200.

			W	L	
1.	Edoardo Alaimo	ITA	4	0	Q
=2.	Albert Bogen	AUT	2	2	Q
	Oluf Berntsen	DEN	2	2	Q
=4.	Aleksandr Shkylev	RUS	1	3	
	Zdeněk Bárta	BOH	1	3	

147

Pool Five A: 5; C: 5; D: 16 July; T: 1200–1500.

			W	L	
1.[148]	Charles Vander Byl	GBR	3	1	Q
2.	Josef Javůrek	BOH	3	1	Q
3.	Josef Puhm	AUT	2	2	Q
=4.	Carl-Gustaf Klerck	SWE	1	3	
	Georgy Zakyrich	RUS	1	3	

149

Pool Six A: 4; C: 4; D: 16 July; T: 1200–1500.

			W	L	
1.	Ejnar Levison	DEN	3	0	Q
2.	A. Ridley Martin	GBR	2	1	Q

3.	Anatoly Timofeyev	RUS	1	2	Q
4.	Johannes Kolling	NED	0	3	

150

Pool Seven A: 4; C: 4; D: 16 July; T: 1200–1500.

			W	L	
1.	Béla Békessy	HUN	3	0	Q
2.[151]	Franz Dereani	AUT	1	2	Q
3.[152]	William Marsh	GBR	1	2	Q
4.	Konstantin Vaterkampf	RUS	1	2	

153

Pool Eight A: 5; C: 5; D: 16 July; T: 1200–1500.

			W	L	
=1.	Hendrik de Iongh	NED	3	1	Q
	Péter Tóth	HUN	3	1	Q
3.	Martin Nordenström	SWE	2	2	Q
=4.	Douglas Godfree	GBR	1	3	
	Aleksandr Mordovin	RUS	1	3	

154

Pool Nine[155] A: —; C: —; D: 16 July; T: 1500–1800.

			W	L	
=1.	Georg Stöhr	GER	bye		Q
	Ervin Mészáros	HUN	bye		Q
	Nikolay Kuznyetsov	RUS	bye		Q

156

Pool Ten[157] A: —; C: —; D: 16 July; T: 1500–1800.

			W	L	
=1.	Apollon Guiber von Greifenfels	RUS	bye		Q
	Jenő Fuchs	HUN	bye		Q
	Birger Personne	SWE	bye		Q

158

Pool Eleven[159] A: —; C: —; D: 16 July; T: 1500–1800.

			W	L	
=1.	Bertalan Dunay	HUN	bye		Q
	Prince Ernest zu Hohenlohe	AUT	bye		Q
	Boris Arsenyev	RUS	bye		Q

160

Pool Twelve A: 4; C: 4; D: 16 July; T: 1500–1800.

			W	L	
1.	Zoltán Schenker	HUN	3	0	Q
2.	Friedrich Schwarz	GER	2	1	Q
3.	Harry Butterworth	GBR	1	2	Q
4.	Pavel Filatov	RUS	0	3	

161

Pool Thirteen A: 4; C: 4; D: 17 July; T: 0900–1200.

			W	L	
1.	Francesco Pietrasanta	ITA	3	0	Q
2.[162]	Pál Pajzs	HUN	1	2	Q
3.[163]	Alfred Syson	GBR	1	2	Q
4.	Walter Gates	RSA	1	2	
	164				

Pool Fourteen A: 4; C: 4; D: 17 July; T: 0900–1200.

			W	L	
1.	Oszkár Gerde	HUN	3	0	Q
2.	Nedo Nadi	ITA	2	1	Q
3.	Albertson Van Zo Post	USA	1	2	Q
4.	Archibald Corble	GBR	0	3	
	165				

Pool Fifteen[166] A:—; C:— D: 17 July; T: 0900–1200.

			W	L	
=1.	Alfred Sauer	USA	bye		Q
	Dezső Földes	HUN	bye		Q
	Alfred Keene	GBR	bye		Q
	167				

Pool Sixteen A: 4; C: 4; D: 17 July; T: 0900–1200.

			W	L	
1.	László Berti	HUN	3	0	Q
2.	Aristide Pontenani	ITA	2	1	Q
3.	Edward Brookfield	GBR	1	2	Q
4.	Gunnar Lindholm	SWE	0	3	
	168				

Sabre, Team

A: 69; C: 11; D: 14–15 July; F: Teams of eight fencers, with four fencers to take part in a single match. Each fencer met all four fencers of the other team, thus 16 bouts per match. Each bout was the first to three touches. The match could be discontinued once one team won nine matches. The captain of the losing team could decide whether or not to continue to 16 matches. In case of a tie in matches, the team with the least number of touches received won the match. If the touches received were equal, a barrage took place to decide the match.

With seven of the eight finalists from the individual sabre event, Hungary had a very easy time of it in the team sabre event, winning all its matches, with the closest match being a 9–5 victory over Italy in the semifinals. The Hungarian team won possession of the challenge trophy for the team épée, which was donated in 1912, appropriately enough, by the City of Budapest.

Hungary won all the gold medals in team sabre at the Olympics from 1908 to 1960, except for 1920 when the nation was not invited because of its role in World War I. Hungary has also been dominant in the team sabre at the world championships. World championships in the team sabre began in 1930, and were held through the 1950s in non–Olympic years. Hungary won the title in 1930–31, 1933–35, 1937, 1951, 1953–55, and 1957–58, failing to win the title only in 1938, 1947, and 1949–50.

Final Standings

1. Hungary
(Jenő Fuchs, Zoltán Schenker, László Berti, Ervin Mészáros, Péter Tóth, Lajos Werkner, Oszkár Gerde, Dezső Földes)

2. Austria
(Richard Verderber, Otto Herschmann, Rudolf Cvetko, Andreas Suttner, Friedrich Golling, Albert Bogen, Reinhold Trampler)[169]

3. The Netherlands
(Jetze Doorman, Dirk Scalongne, Adrianus de Jong, Willem Hubert van Blijenburgh, Hendrik de Iongh, George van Rossem)[170]

4. Bohemia
(Josef Pfeiffer, Vilém Goppold z Lobsdorfu, Sr., Bedřich Schejbal, Josef Čipera, Otakar Švorčík)[171]

=5. Belgium
(Henri Anspach, Léon Tom, Marcel Berré, Philippe Le Hardy de Beaulieu, Robert Hennet)[172]

Italy
(Edoardo Alaimo, Giovanni Benfratello, Fernando Cavallini, Nedo Nadi, Ugo Di Nola, Gino Belloni)[173]

=7. Germany
(Friedrich Schwarz, Friedrich Jack,[174] Johannes Adam, Georg Stöhr, Walther Meienreis, Hermann Plaskuda, Jakob Erckrath de Bary, Emil Schön, Julius Lichtenfels)

Great Britain
(Archibald Corble, Edward Brookfield, A. Ridley Martin, Harry Butterworth, Richard Crawshay, William Marsh)[175]

=9. Russia
(Vladimir Andreyev, Aleksandr Shkylev, Vladimir Danich, Apollon Guiber von Greifenfels, Nikolay Kuznyetsov, Aleksandr Mordovin, Georgy Zakyrich, Anatoly Timofeyev)[176]

Sweden
(Axel Jöhncke, Helge Werner, Birger Personne, Carl-Gustaf Klerck)[177]

Denmark
(Jens Ole Berthelsen, Ejnar Levison, Hans Olsen, Ivan Osiier, Lauritz Christian Østrup)

Final Pool A: 23; C: 4; D: 15 July; T: 0900–1500.

	W	L	MW	ML
1. Hungary	3	0	24	8

(Jenő Fuchs, Zoltán Schenker, László Berti, Ervin Mészáros, Péter Tóth, Lajos Werkner, Oszkár Gerde, Dezső Földes)

2. Austria	2	1	24	20

(Richard Verderber, Otto Herschmann, Rudolf Cvetko,[178] Friedrich Golling, Albert Bogen)

3.   The Netherlands   1   2   14   30
(Jetze Doorman, Dirk Scalongne, Adrianus de Jong, Willem Hubert van Blijenburgh, Hendrik de Iongh, George van Rossem)

4.   Bohemia   0   3   14   18
(Josef Pfeiffer, Vilém Goppold z Lobsdorfu, Sr., Bedřich Schejbal, Josef Čipera)

Pool Summary

Hungary   11   Austria   5
(HUN — Fuchs 4, Schenker 3, Berty 2, Mészáros 2) (AUT — Cvetko 2, Verderber 2, Herschmann 1, Golling 0)

Hungary   13   The Netherlands   3
(HUN — Tóth 4, Werkner 3, Gerde 3, Földes 3) (NED — Doorman 1, Scalongne 1, de Jong 1, van Blijenburgh 0)

Hungary   wo   Bohemia   scratched
(HUN — Fuchs, Mészáros, Berty, Schenker[179])

Austria   10   Bohemia   6
(AUT — Verderber 4, Herschmann 4, Cvetko 2, Bogen 0) (BOH — Pfeiffer 2, Goppold z Lobsdorfu, Sr. 2, Schejbal 1, Čipera 1)

Austria   9   The Netherlands   3
(AUT — Verderber 3, Herschmann 3, Cvetko 2, Golling 1) (NED — Doorman 0, de Iongh 1, Scalongne 1, de Jong 1)

The Netherlands   8 (34)[180]   Bohemia   8 (36)
(NED — de Jong 3, Scalongne 3, Doorman 2, van Rossem 0) (BOH — Goppold z Lobsdorfu, Sr. 3, Pfeiffer 2, Čipera 2, Schejbal 1)

Match Summary

Hungary vs. Austria (11–5)

	Herschmann	Cvetko	Golling	Verderber	Wins (HUN)	Touches
Schenker	3–1	2–3	3–1	3–1	3	11–6
Fuchs	3–1	3–0	3–1	3–1	4	12–3
Berty	3–1	1–3	3–0	2–3	2	9–7
Mészáros	1–3	3–1	3–2	2–3	2	9–9
Wins (AUT)	*1*	*2*	*0*	*2*		*41–25*
Touches	*10–6*	*9–7*	*12–4*	*10–8*	*41–25*	

Semifinal Pools A: 48; C: 8; D: 14 July; T: 1500–1930; F: First two teams in each pool advanced to the final.

Pool One A: 20; C: 4.

	W	L	MW	ML	
1. Bohemia	3	0	23	9	Q

(Vilém Goppold z Lobsdorfu, Sr., Josef Čipera, Bedřich Schejbal, Josef Pfeiffer, Otakar Švorčík)

2. The Netherlands   2   1   26   18   Q
(Adrianus de Jong, George van Rossem, Jetze Doorman, Dirk Scalongne, Willem Hubert van Blijenburgh)

3. Belgium   1   2   13   18
(Léon Tom, Robert Hennet, Marcel Berré, Philippe Le Hardy de Beaulieu, Henri Anspach)

4. Great Britain   0   3   14   31
(Archibald Corble, Harry Butterworth, Edward Brookfield, Richard Crawshay, A. Ridley Martin)

Pool Summary

Bohemia   10   The Netherlands   6
(BOH — Lobsdorfu, Sr. 4, Čipera 3, Švorčík 2, Schejbal 1) (NED — van Rossem 3, de Jong 2, Doorman 1, van Blijenburgh 0)

Bohemia   wo   Belgium   scratch
Bohemia   13   Great Britain   3
(BOH — Lobsdorfu, Sr. 4, Čipera 4, Pfeiffer 3, Schejbal 2) (GBR — Butterworth 1, Corble 1, Martin 1, Crawshay 0)

The Netherlands   11   Belgium   4
(NED — de Jong 4, van Rossem 3, Scalongne 3, Doorman 1) (BEL — Hennet 2, Berré 1, H Anspach 1, Tom 0)

The Netherlands   9   Great Britain   4
(NED — van Rossem 3, Scalongne 3, Doorman 2, de Jong 1) (GBR — Butterworth 1, Corble 1, Crawshay 1, Brookfield 1)

Belgium   9   Great Britain   7
(BEL — Tom 3, Hennet 3, Berré 2, Le Hardy de Beaulieu 1) (GBR — Corble 3, Martin 3, Crawshay 1, Brookfield 0)

Match Summaries

Bohemia vs. Great Britain (13–3)

	Pfeiffer	Schejbal	Čipera	Lobsdorfu, Sr.	Wins (GBR)	Touches
Butterworth	2–3	3–1	1–3	1–3	1	7–10
Corble	1–3	3–1	0–3	1–3	1	5–10
Crawshay	1–3	1–3	1–3	1–3	0	4–12
Martin	3–2	1–3	1–3	0–3	1	5–11
Wins (BOH)	*3*	*2*	*4*	*4*		*21–43*
Touches	*7–11*	*8–8*	*3–12*	*3–12*	*21–43*	

The Netherlands vs. Great Britain (9–4)

	de Jong	van Rossem	Scalongne	Doorman	Wins (GBR)	Touches
Butterworth	3–2	–	2–3	1–3	1	6–8
Corble	3–2	2–3	–	1–3	1	6–8
Crawshay	3–2	0–3	1–3	–	1	4–8
Brookfield	0–3	1–3	1–3	3–1	1	5–10
Wins (NED)	*1*	*3*	*3*	*2*		*34–21*
Touches	*9–9*	*3–9*	*4–9*	*5–7*	*21–34*	

Belgium vs. Great Britain (9–7)

	Tom	Berré	Beaulieu	Hennet	Wins (GBR)	Touches
Corble	0–3	3–2	3–2	3–0	3	9–7
Brookfield	2–3	2–3	1–3	0–3	0	5–12
Crawshay	1–3	2–3	3–1	0–3	1	6–10
Martin	3–1	3–1	3–1	1–3	3	10–6
Wins (BEL)	*3*	*2*	*1*	*3*		*30–35*
Touches	*6–10*	*10–9*	*10–7*	*4–9*	*30–35*	

Pool Two A: 28; C: 4.

	W	L	MW	ML	
1. Hungary	3	0	33	13	Q

(Jenő Fuchs, Ervin Mészáros, László Berty, Lajos Werkner, Péter Tóth, Oszkár Gerde, Dezső Földes)

	W	L	MW	ML	
2. Austria	2	1	27	21	Q

(Richard Verderber, Otto Herschmann, Rudolf Cvetko, Andreas Suttner, Friedrich Golling, Albert Bogen, Reinhold Trampler)

	W	L	MW	ML
3. Italy	1	2	19	24

(Nedo Nadi, Ugo Di Nola, Giovanni Benfratello, Fernando Cavallini, Edoardo Alaimo, Gino Belloni)

	W	L	MW	ML
4. Germany	0	3	12	33

(Friedrich Schwarz, Johannes Adam, Georg Stöhr, Walther Meienreis, Hermann Plaskuda, Jakob Erckrath de Bary, Emil Schön, Julius Lichtenfels)

Pool Summary

Hungary　　　　11　　　　　　Austria　　　　5[181]
 (HUN — Fuchs 4, Mészáros 3, Berty 2, Werkner 2) (AUT — Verderber 3, Herschmann 1[182], Cvetko 1, Suttner 0)

Hungary　　　　9　　　　　　Italy　　　　5[183]
 (HUN — Fuchs 4, Berty 3, Mészáros 2, Tóth 0) (ITA — Nadi 3, Di Nola 1, Benfratello 1, Cavallini 0)

Hungary　　　　13　　　　　　Germany　　　　3
 (HUN — Mészáros 4, Földes 3, Gerde 3, Fuchs 3) (GER — Adam 1, Schwarz 1, Stöhr 1, Meienreis 0)

Austria　　　　11　　　　　　Italy　　　　5
 (AUT — Verderber 4, Trampler 4, Herschmann 3, Cvetko 0) (ITA — Nadi 3, Alaimo 1, Belloni 1, Benfratello 1)

Austria　　　　11　　　　　　Germany　　　　5
 (AUT — Verderber 4, Golling 3, Trampler 2, Bogen 2) (GER — Schwarz 2, Adam 1, Plaskuda 1, Stöhr 1)

Italy　　　　9　　　　　　Germany　　　　4
 (ITA — Di Nola 4, Nadi 2, Alaimo 2, Belloni 1) (GER — Schön 3, Plaskuda 1, Erckrath de Bary 0, Lichtenfels 0)

Round One Pools A: 51; C: 9/11; D: 14 July; T: 0800–1100, 1300–1330;
   F: First two teams in each pool advanced to the semifinals.

Pool One A:—; C:—.[184]

=1.   Bohemia   bye
      Hungary   bye
      [185]

Pool Two A: 18; C: 3.

	W	L	MW	ML	
=1. Belgium	1	0	9	7	Q

(Henri Anspach, Paul Anspach, Philippe Le Hardy de Beaulieu, Jacques Ochs, Gaston Salmon, Léon Tom[186])

=1. Italy	1	0	10	6	Q

(Gino Belloni, Giovanni Benfratello, Nedo Nadi, Ugo Di Nola)

3. Russia	0	2	13	19	

(Vladimir Andreyev, Aleksandr Shkylev, Vladimir Danich, Apollon Guiber von Greifenfels, Nikolay Kuznyetsov, Aleksandr Mordovin, Georgy Zakyrich, Anatoly Timofeyev[187])

Pool Summary

Belgium   9   Russia   7
   (rosters not known)

Italy   10   Russia   6
   (ITA — Belloni, Benfratello, N Nadi, Di Nola) (RUS — roster not known)

Belgium   Italy   [188]

Pool Three A: 13[189]; C: 3.

	W	L	MW	ML	
1. Great Britain	1	0	12	1	Q

(Harry Butterworth, Richard Crawshay, Archibald Corble, William Marsh, A. Ridley Martin[190])

2. Germany	0	0	0	3	Q

(Jakob Erckrath de Bary, Julius Lichtenfels, Hermann Plaskuda, Friedrich "Fritz" Jack[191])

3. Sweden	0	1	1	9	

(Axel Jöhncke, Helge Werner, Birger Personne, Carl-Gustaf Klerck)

Pool Summary

Great Britain   9   Sweden   1
   (GBR — Corble 3, Butterworth 2, Crawshay 2, Marsh 2) (SWE — Personne 1, Klerck 0, Jöhncke 0, Werner 0)

Great Britain   3   Germany   0   [192]
   (GBR — Butterworth 1, Crawshay 1, Corble 1, [Martin]) (GER — Erckrath de Bary 0, Werner 0, Plaskuda 0, [Jack])

Match Summaries (matches won–lost)

Great Britain vs. Sweden (9–1)

	Jöhncke	Werner	Personne	Klerck	Wins (GBR)
Butterworth	1–0	1–0	–	–	2
Crawshay	1–0	1–0	–	–	2
Corble	–	1–0	1–0	1–0	3
Marsh	1–0	–	0–1	1–0	2
Wins (SWE)	*0*	*0*	*1*	*0*	*9–1*

Great Britain vs. Germany (3–0)

	de Bary	Lichtenfels	Pascuda	Jack	Wins (GBR)
Butterworth	1–0	–	–	–	1
Crawshay	–	1–0	–	–	1
Corble	–	–	1–0	–	1
Martin	–	–	–	–	–
Wins (GER)	*0*	*0*	*0*	*–*	*3–0*

Pool Four A: 18; C: 3.

	W	L	MW	ML	
1. Austria	2	0	17	6	Q

(Richard Verderber, Otto Herschmann, Rudolf Cvetko, Friedrich Golling, Andreas Suttner, Albert Bogen, Reinhold Trampler[193])

2. The Netherlands	1	1	14	15	Q

(Adrianus de Jong, Willem Hubert van Blijenburgh, George van Rossem, Jetze Doorman, Dirk Scalongne, Hendrik de Iongh[194])

3. Denmark	0	2	7	17

(Jens Ole Berthelsen, Ejnar Levison, Hans Olsen, Ivan Osiier, Lauritz Christian Østrup[195])

Pool Summary

Austria (rosters not known)	9	The Netherlands	5
Austria (rosters not known)	8	Denmark	1
The Netherlands (rosters not known)	9	Denmark	6

NOTES

1. TF noted "there were 117 competitors, as follows (RUS/SWE/GER 12, ITA/USA 11, BEL 10, BOH 9, GBR/DEN/HUN 8, AUT 7, NED 3, NOR 3, GRE 2, RSA 1)." They were certainly referring to entrants, although 12OR and FenPro both list 129 entrants.

2. Places three to five were decided on hits received during the final pool. The tie between Verderber and Berty on hits received (25) was broken by a one-touch fence-off, won by Verdeber.

3. Called Pool Three in TF.

4. Lost to Alaimo.

5. Amphlett lost to Anspach (5–3) and also to Schön. In his assault again Bekessy, he became upset with the judging and retired.

6. Called Pool Four in TF.

7. Called Pool One in TF.

8. Defeated only Willems.

9. According to TF, Földes and Cavallini retired during this pool, upset with the judging.

10. Called Pool Four in TF.

11. Lost to Schenker, Nadi, and Lichtenfels.

12. Called Pool Three in TF.

13. Lost to Tvrzský and Zulavszky.

14. Albertson Van Zo Post (USA) was also entered in this pool, but scratched, according to TF.

15. Called Pool One in TF.

16. Lost to Földes. Seligman did not fence against Speciale in this pool.

17. Called Pool One in TF.

18. Called Pool One in TF.

19. Called Pool One in TF.

20. Defeated Golling for his only victory.

21. Called Pool One in TF.

22. Lost to Hennet and Verderber.

23. Eric Carlberg (SWE), and Friedrich Jack (GER) were entered in this pool but did not compete.

24. Larimer lost to Berré and Amphlett.

25. Amphlett lost to Berré and to Leparsky (5–4), but defeated Larimer 5–4.

26. Giovanni Benfratello (ITA), and Carl-Gustaf Krokstedt (SWE) were entered in this pool but did not compete.

27. Lost to Pfeiffer.

28. Lost to Alexander.

29. Listed as third in this pool in ONews.

30. Aristide Pontenani (ITA), and Georg Stöhr (GER) were entered in this pool but did not compete.

31. Perikles Georgakopoulos (GRE) was entered in this pool but did not compete.

32. Lost to Licht and Salmon.

33. Lost to Hall, Speciale, Willems.

34. Ugo Di Nola (ITA), and Vincenc Rechner (BOH) were entered in this pool but did not compete.

35. Dino Diana (ITA) was entered in this pool but did not compete.

36. Carlo Castorina (ITA) was entered in this pool but did not compete.

37. Gino Belloni (ITA), Walter Kudloff (GER), and François Rom (BEL) were entered in this pool but did not compete.

38. Henry Peyron (SWE) was entered in this pool but did not compete.

39. Lost to Hjorth. Did not compete against Anspach.

40. Raphaël "Felix" Vigeveno (NED) was entered in this pool but did not compete.

41. Ahmed Mohamed Hassanein (EGY), and Gustaf Lindblom (SWE) were entered in this pool but did not compete.

42. Cvetko was born in Senoze, near Kranj, in present day Slovenia. Though it was not a country at the time, Cvetko can be considered the first Slovenian to have competed in the Olympic Games.

43. Carl Setterberg (SWE) was entered in this pool but did not compete.

44. Jaroslav Tuček (Šourek) (BOH) was entered in this pool but did not compete.

45. Lost to Manos and Bowman. Double-hit matches with Sörensen, Tom.

46. Seligman and Anspach did not compete against each other.

47. The 12OR has H. Anspach and Osiier as equal first, with Boin third; but Osiier and Boin competed in the final and H. Anspach did not. TF has Osiier and Boin as equal first after a tie with H. Anspach, broken on number of points. This must be correct.

48. Defeated Kříž and Boin. Double-hit match with Osiier.

49. Lost to Le Hardy de Beaulieu. Double-hit match with Goppold z Lobsdorfu, Jr.

50. TF has Goppold z Lobsdorfu, Jr. as equal fourth, while Czech/Bohemian sources list him as sixth.

51. Lost to Osiier. Double-hit match with Vávra.

52. Defeated Bertrain.

53. Double-hit matches with Levison and Ochs.

54. Lost to de Beaufort and Petropoulos.

55. Lost to Sörensen and Manos.

56. See the notes concerning Louis Sparre in pool ten of round one.

57. Lost to Branting. Double-hit match with Versis.

58. Defeated Lichtenfels.

59. Listed as Manos in 12OR but as Petros Georgopoulos in FenPro.

60. Ahmed Mohammed Hassanein (EGY) and Jaroslav Tuček (Šourek) (BOH) were entered in this pool but did not compete.

61. Jakob Erckrath de Bary (GER)) was entered in this pool but did not compete.

62. Panagiotis Kabas (GRE) and Reinhold Trampler (AUT) were entered in this pool but did not compete.

63. François Rom (BEL), Rudolf Cvetko (AUT), Erik de Laval (SWE), and Alexandros Kharalambopoulos (GRE) were entered in this pool but did not compete.

64. Lost to Ochs.

65. Patrik de Laval (SWE), Andreas Suttner (AUT), and Scott Breckinridge (USA) were entered in this pool but did not compete.

66. Lost to Le Hardy de Beaulieu. Double-hit match with Sauer and Gates.

67. Leonardus Nardus (NED) was entered in this pool but did not compete.

68. Called Pool 12 in one section of TF, but Pool 9 in another section.

69. Lost to Boin.

70. Heinrich Ziegler (GER) and Vincenc Rechner (BOH) were entered in this pool but did not compete.

71. Called Pool 12 in one section of TF, but Pool 10 in another section.

72. Defeated Sparre. Double-hit match with Thomson.

73. Giorgios Versis (GRE) was also entered in this pool, but did not compete.

74. This pool was not actually contested as only three fencers presented for the matches. All three were advanced to the quarterfinal round.

75. Called Pool 10 in one section of TF, but Pool 11 in another section.

76. Richard Verderber (AUT), Vilém Goppold z Lobsdorfu, Sr. (BOH), Rudolf von Buchholz (NED), Pontus von Rosen (SWE), and Walter Kudloff (GER) were entered in this pool but did not compete.

77. Called Pool 9 in one section of TF, but Pool 12 in another section.

78. Double-hit match with Bowman.

79. Herman Dooijewaard (NED), Henry Peyron (SWE), Friedrich Jack (GER), and Robert Hennet (BEL) were entered in this pool but did not compete.

80. Called Pool 16 in one section of TF, but Pool 13 in another section.

81. Listed as Triantafilos Kordogiannis (GRE) in FenPro, but as C. Versis in 12OR.

82. This pool was not actually contested, but as only three fencers presented for the matches. All three were advanced to the quarterfinal round.

83. Called Pool 15 in TF in one section, but Pool 14 in another section.

84. Herbert Sander (DEN), Ioannis Georgiadis (GRE), Adriaan Bos (NED), Albert Naumann (GER), and Eric Carlberg (SWE) were entered in this pool but did not compete.

85. Called Pool 14 in TF in one section, but Pool 15 in another section.

86. Defeated van Blijenburgh, Berntsen, and Schön.

87. Called Pool 13 in one section of TF, but Pool 16 in another section.

88. Lost to Ames.

89. Defeated Petropoulos. Double-hit matches with Østrup and Goppold z Lobsdorfu.

90. Lost to Petropoulos. Double-hit match with Ames.

91. Carl-Gustaf Krokstedt (SWE), and Dmitry Knyazhevich (RUS) were entered in this pool but did not compete.

92. This number is counting strictly only fencers for whom we can confirm participation in at least one match. There were likely a few more competitors than this, but precise rosters for several of the matches cannot be found.

93. Fernand de Montigny may have competed in the final pool match against The Netherlands. See footnote concerning this in the match summary. According to Uggla, both de Montigny and François Rom were members of the team, but we cannot confirm them competing in any match. According to *L'Étoile Belge* and *L'Expresse Liège*, Philippe Le Hardy de Beaulieu was a member of the team but we cannot confirm him competing in any match. However, those two newspapers do not mention de Montigny as a member of the team.

94. Edgar Amphlett and John Blake were entered as members of the team, but did not take part in any matches.

95. Jan de Beaufort, Adriaan Bos, and Albertus Perk were also entered as members of the team. We cannot confirm them as competing in any match.

96. Carl-Gustaf Krokstedt, Erik de Laval, and Henry Peyron were also entered as members of the Swedish team, but we cannot confirm them as competing in any match.

97. Only the roster against Norway is known. The rosters against the United States, the Netherlands, Bohemia, and Greece are not known. Oluf Berntsen, Paul Georg Cohn, and Jens Peter Berthelsen were entered as members of the team, but it is not known if they competed.

98. Rosters known against Denmark and the United States. No rosters are known for the matches against Belgium, Germany, and Sweden. Four other Greek fencers were entered in this event, but they are not known to have competed: Sotirios Notaris, Georgios Balakakis, Konstantinos Nikolopoulos, and Ioannis Vallas.

99. Only the lineup against Norway is known. The lineups against Great Britain, Denmark, and the Netherlands are not known. Also entered for Bohemia in this event were Josef Javůrek, Miroslav Klika, Vilém Tvrzský, and Zdeněk Vávra.

100. Only the roster against Belgium is known. Also entered for Germany in this event were Friedrich Jack, Jakob Erckrath de Bary, Julius Lichtenfels, and Walther Meienreis.

101. Aleksandr Mordovin was also entered as a member of the Russian team but we cannot confirm him as competing in any match.

102. Bjarne Eriksen, Sigurd Mathiesen, Harald Platou, and Henrik Calmeyer Norby were also entered as members of the Norwegian team, but we cannot confirm them as competing in any match.

103. The United States had also entered John Gignoux, Graeme Hammond, Marc Larimer, James Moore, Harold Rayner, Alfred Sauer, and Fredric Schenck. A team could consist of only eight members, so no more than two of these seven could possibly have taken part. We cannot confirm any of them as competing in any matches.

104. The first number indicates the number of matches won or tied. Matches ending in double hits are counted for both teams. The number in parentheses omits the double hit-ending matches.

105. According to *Tilburgsche Courant* (11 July 1912), a Dutch newspaper, Fernand de Montigny competed in this match, and not Jacques Ochs.

106. Swedish papers have the hits for the Belgian fencers as follows: Hennet 3, Ochs 3, P Anspach 3 (2), H Anspach 3 (2).

107. Swedish papers have the hits for the British fencers in this match as follows: Holt 3, Davson 3, Montgomerie 2, Seligman 2.

108. It can be determined that both Seligman and Martineau must have competed in this pool, and one against Bohemia and Denmark, although it is uncertain who competed in which match. See the footnote after the match summaries below.

109. Also reported as 9–9.

110. Also seen as 9–8 (8–7) in TF.

111. Either Sydney Martineau or Edgar Seligman. It can be determine that Martineau competed against either Denmark or Bohemia, based on the *Times* (16 July 1912) noting that he took part

in only one match. The same article in the *Times* notes that Seligman took part in three matches. Two of these are known; thus he competed against either Denmark or Bohemia.

112. Either Sydney Martineau or Edgar Seligman. It can be determined that Martineau competed against either Denmark or Bohemia, based on the *Times* (16 July 1912) noting that he took part in only one match. The same article in the *Times* notes that Seligman took part in three matches. Two of these are known, thus he competed against either Denmark or Bohemia.

113. None of the rosters for the Greek matches are known. This is the list of entries according to OFen, although Petropoulos is not mentioned in Uggla.

114. The roster is known for only one of Germany's three matches. The other four team members were Jakob Erckrath de Bary, Friedrich Jack, Julius Lichtenfels, and Walther Meienreis.

115. This score is seen variably in several different sources, and it is difficult to be certain of the precise score. It is 11–7 (9–5) in *L'Étoile Belge* (17 July 1912) and *L'Express Liège* (18 July 1912); 9–6 in *Le Petit Bleu* (15 July 1912) (Bruxelles); and 9–7 (with one tie, which implies 17 matches which is impossible) in *Le Journal de Liège* (17 July 1912).

116. No matches were held in this pool as only two teams entered and both were then advanced to the semifinals.

117. Seen as 9–1 in *Journal de Liège* (17/7/1920).

118. The Sweden vs. Bohemia match was not contested as both teams had defeated Norway, and thus were qualified to advance to the semifinal round.

119. The 9–3 victory was a barrage fence-off of the original tie.

120. Oluf Berntsen and Jens Peter Berthelsen may have competed in this pool, but the roster for the match against the United States is not known.

121. The U.S. competitors are from the *Winged Foot*, the journal of the New York Athletic Club (1912).

122. Most recent sources list differing numbers of competitors, to wit: DW — 40; EK — 63; FW- 63; OSVK — 64 (although he lists 125 competitors in the various pools); VK — 63. But note TF: "In one sense it was disappointing. Although there were 126 entries, only sixty-four *sabreurs* remained to compete. Among those who withdrew were all the members of the Austrian, Bohemian, and Dutch teams. Of the British representatives Mr. Crawshay did not stay to compete, and Lieut. Fiellman [*sic*], R.N., and Capt. C. Fitzclarence were also absentees. The sixty-four competitors were: Hungary, 12; Russia, 11; Great Britain, 9; Austria, 6; Germany, 5; Italy, 5; Sweden, 5; Denmark, 3; Holland, 2; United States, 2; Bohemia, 2; Greece, 1; and South Africa, 1. The British representatives were: Mr. A. Ridley, Mr. H. R. Butterworth, Mr. Archie Corble, Mr. W. W. Marsh, Lieut. E. Brookfield, R.N., Capt. D. W. Godfree, Mr. A. V. Keene, Capt. A. Syson, and Capt. C. F. Vander Byl, the English sabre champion." (TF, 120: 436, 24 August 1912).

123. This scoring summary is from Jatekok, the only source we have found which has detailed scores for the final round of the individual sabre. While not a contemporary source (we used the second edition from 1932), it is a Hungarian source, which is important given that seven of the eight finalists were Hungarian.

124. The semifinal pool results are from Hungarian newspaper sources, supplied by Gabriel Szabó. They differ slightly from TF, mainly in the number of victories and losses. Both sources differ slightly from 12OR.

125. Called Pool One in TF.

126. Anatoly Timofeyev (RUS) was also entered in this pool, but did not compete.

127. Called Pool Three in TF.

128. Also entered in this pool, but not competing, were Julius Lichtenfels (GER), Oszkár Gerde (HUN), and Vladimir Andreyev (RUS).

129. Called Pool Two in TF.

130. Called Pool One in TF.

131. Albert Bogen (AUT) was also entered in this pool, but did not compete.

132. Edoardo Alaimo (ITA) and Vladimir Danich (RUS) were also entered in this pool, but did not compete.

133. Karl Münich (AUT) was also entered in this pool, but did not compete.

134. Vander Byl and Guiber von Greifenfels also tied for second based on number of hits.

135. Franz Dereani (AUT) was also entered in this pool, but did not compete.

136. Hendrik de Iongh (NED) and Josef Javůrek (BOH) were also entered in this pool, but did not compete.

137. Nadi and Pajzs also tied for first based on number of hits.

138. Zulavszky was placed third, ahead of Keene, based on number of hits.

139. Josef Puhm (AUT) was also entered in this heat, but did not compete.

140. Based on number of hits, Lichtenfels and Personne were ranked equal second, and were placed ahead of Pietrasanta.

141. Albertson Van Zo Post (USA) was also entered in this pool, but did not compete.

142. There were actually 64 fencers that presented for Round One, but 12 were in pools that were not contested, and they received byes into the quarterfinals.

143. Martin Steffan (GER), Rudolf Cvetko (AUT), Panagiotis Kabas (GRE), and Lauritz Østrup (DEN) were entered in this pool but did not compete.

144. Placed third ahead of Golling based on hits received.

145. Gino Belloni (ITA), Bedřich Schejbal (BOH), and Ivan Osiier (DEN) were entered in this pool but did not compete.

146. Josef Čipera (BOH), Fernando Cavallini (ITA), and Perikles Georgakopoulos (GRE) were entered in this pool but did not compete.

147. Triantafilos Kordogiannis (GRE) and George van Rossem (NED) were entered in this pool but did not compete.

148. Placed first ahead of Javůrek based on hits received.

149. Hans Olsen (DEN), Ugo Di Nola (ITA), and Jetze Doorman (NED) were entered in this pool but did not compete.

150. Reinhold Trampler (AUT), Vilém Tvrzský (BOH), Anders Boo Kullberg (SWE), and Dino Diana (ITA) were entered in this pool but did not compete.

151. Placed second ahead of Marsh based on hits received.

152. Marsh defeated Vaterkampf in a barrage for third place.

153. Victor Boin (BEL), Axel Jöhncke (SWE), Adrianus de Jong (NED), and František Kříž (BOH) were entered in this pool but did not compete.

154. Friedrich Jack (GER), Jacques Ochs (BEL), and Josef Pfeiffer (BOH) were entered in this pool but did not compete.

155. This pool was not actually contested as only three fencers presented for the matches. All three were advanced to the quarterfinal round.

156. Philippe Le Hardy de Beaulieu (BEL), Charles Fitzclarence (GBR), Sidney Stranne (SWE), Karel Goppold z Lobsdorfu (BOH), and Rudolf von Buchholz (NED) were entered in this pool but did not compete.

157. This pool was not actually contested as only three fencers presented for the matches. All three were advanced to the quarterfinal round.

158. Paul Anspach (BEL), Vilém Goppold z Lobsdorfu, Sr. (BOH), Herman Dooijewaard (NED), Ferdinand Fiellman (GBR), and Emil Schön (GER) were entered in this pool but did not compete.

159. This pool was not actually contested as only three fencers presented for the matches. All three were advanced to the quarterfinal round.

160. Willem Hubert van Blijenburgh (NED), Ioannis Georgiadis (GRE), Richard Crawshay (GBR), Jaroslav Tuček (Šourek) (BOH), and Heinrich Ziegler (GER) were entered in this pool but did not compete.

161. Otakar Švorčik (BOH), Khambopoulos Versis (GRE), Dirk Scalongne (NED), and Léon Tom (BEL) were entered in this pool but did not compete.

162. Placed second ahead of Syson and Gates based on hits received.

163. Syson defeated Gates in a barrage for third place.

164. Henri Anspach (BEL), Trifon Triantafyllakos (GRE), Jakob Erckrath de Bary (GER), and Andreas Suttner (AUT) were entered in this pool but did not compete.

165. Gaston Salmon (BEL), Hermann Plaskuda (GER), Georgios Petropoulos (GRE), and Vilém Goppold z Lobsdorfu, Jr. (BOH) were entered in this pool but did not compete.

166. This pool was not actually contested as only three fencers presented for the matches. All three were advanced to the quarterfinal round.

167. Sotirios Notaris (GRE), Pietro Speciale (ITA), Nils Brambeck (SWE), Walther Meienreis (GER), and Otto Herschmann (AUT) were entered in this pool but did not compete.

168. George Patton, Jr. (USA), Johannes Adam (GER), Konstantinos Kotzias (GRE), and Richard Verderber (AUT) were entered in this pool but did not compete.

169. Josef Puhm was also entered as a member of the team but we cannot confirm him as competing in any matches. The late Erich Kamper of Austria, well-known Olympic historian, stated that he did not compete.

170. Rudolf von Buchholz and Herman Dooijewaard were also entered as members of the Dutch team, but we cannot confirm them as competing in any match.

171. Zdeněk Bárta, Josef Javůrek, and František Kříž were also entered as members of the Bohemian team, but we cannot confirm them as competing in any matches.

172. Gaston Salmon, Jacques Ochs, and Paul Anspach were also entered as members of the Belgian team, but we cannot confirm that they competed in any match. Marcel Barré was not entered, according to Uggla, but was according to OFen.

173. Francesco Pietrasanta and Pietro Speciale were also entered as members of the Italian team, but we cannot confirm that they competed in any match.

174. Technically, Jack is not known to have competed in any match, but he was about to compete in round one when the German team defaulted. See the footnote concerning the German team in round one.

175. Ferdinand Fiellman and Douglas Godfree were also entered as members of the British team, but we cannot confirm them as competing in any match. Fiellman definitely did not compete, as this is mentioned in TF.

176. This is the only entry list for the Russian team. We do not know the lineups for Russia in any match in team sabre. It is possible that some of these fencers did not compete in this event.

177. Gustaf Armgarth, Nils Brambeck, Axel Jöhncke, and Martin Nordenström were also entered as members of the Swedish team, but we cannot confirm them as competing in any match.

178. Cvetko was born in Senoze, near Kranj, in present day Slovenia. Though it was not a country at the time, Cvetko can be considered the first Slovenian to have competed in the Olympic Games.

179. Tentative lineup according to *Magyar Nemzet* (17 July 1912), had the match taken place.

180. Match decided by touches received, 34 against the Netherlands, and 36 against Bohemia. It is given as 36–37 in *Het Vaterland*, but 34–36 in *De Courant* (16 July 1912), and 34–36 is supported by ASZ (23 July 1912, dateline 15 July 1912), which noted that Bohemia lost by two touches.

181. The score was 10–6 according to Hungarian and Austrian sources. These marks are from TF, which gave individual victory totals.

182. The Hungarian roster is from TF and confirmed by Jatekok. According to *Magyar Nemzet* (17 July 1912), Reinhold Trampler competed, rather than Herschmann.

183. The score was 11–5 according to Hungarian sources. These marks are from TF, which gave individual victory totals.

184. No matches were conducted in this pool, because Greece did not present. Both teams were advanced to the quarterfinals.

185. Greece was also entered in this pool, but scratched and did not compete. No matches were held in this pool, and Bohemia and Hungary advanced directly to the semifinal pools. The team entered for Greece, according to OFen, comprised Petros Kambas, Konstantinos Kotzias, Petros Manos, Sotirios Notaris, Georgios Petropoulos, Trifon Triantafyllakos, and Georgios Versis.

186. No rosters known for pool four matches, so precise make-up of Belgian team in this pool is conjectural, and based on entrants and who we know competed in later rounds.

187. No rosters known for pool four matches, so precise make-up of Russian team in this pool is conjectural, and based on entrants and who we know competed in later rounds.

188. Match not held as both teams had qualified for the semifinals.

189. Technically, neither Martin (GBR) nor Jack (GER) actually competed in this round. See footnotes 190 and 191.

190. Technically, Martin did not compete in this round, although he was about to do so. He did not compete in the first round against Sweden, but was scheduled to compete against the German team and Jack, when the Swedes withdrew. The Great Britain vs. Germany match was then discontinued and Martin did not have to fence.

191. Technically, Jack did not compete in this round, although he was about to do so. He was scheduled to compete against the British team and Martin, when the Swedes withdrew. The Great Britain vs. Germany match was then discontinued and Jack did not have to fence.

192. The withdrawal of the Swedish team was announced after the first three assaults of the Britain-Germany match. The match was then discontinued with the score 3–0 and both teams advanced.

193. No rosters known for pool four matches, so precise make-up of Austrian team in this pool is conjectural, and based on entrants and who we know competed in later rounds.

194. No rosters known for pool four matches, so precise make-up of Dutch team in this pool is conjectural, and based on entrants and who we know competed in later rounds.

195. No rosters known for pool four matches, so precise make-up of Danish team in this pool is conjectural, and based on entrants. Only five Danish fencers entered in the team sabre event.

Football (Association Football [Soccer[1]*])

The Swedish Olympic football committee made the plans for the 1912 Olympic football (soccer) tournament. The original plans allowed each nation to enter as many as four teams, but at the annual meeting of the Fédération Internationale de Football Association (FIFA) in 1911, the following ruling was made: "Although the rules for the Football Competitions at the Olympic Games of Stockholm in 1912 permit every nation affiliated to Fédération Internationale de Football Association to send four teams to the competition, the Fédération considers it most suitable that each nation should send only one." The original ruling was made to allow Great Britain to enter four teams — one each for England, Ireland, Scotland, and Wales. However, the Scottish Football Association (founded in 1873), the Football Association of Wales (founded in 1876), and the Irish Football Association (founded in 1880), all decided not to enter.[2] It was left to The Football Association, founded in 1863, and governing football in England, to enter a team.

The entries closed on 29 May and 13 teams were entered. France and Belgium[3] entered but withdrew, leaving 11 teams to compete for the championship. Bohemia also tried to enter a team but its entry was refused as it was no longer a member of FIFA.[4]

The event was planned as a single-elimination competition and the draw was held on 18 June 1912 at the office of Svenska Gymnastik — och Idrottsföreningarnas Riksförbund, or the National Football of Swedish Gymnastics and Sports Club. The two losing semifinalists competed for the bronze medals. A consolation tournament was also conducted with all losing teams from the first two rounds allowed to compete. First prize in the consolation tournament was silver medals from the Svenska Fotbollförbundet (Swedish Football Association), while second prize was bronze medals from the same organization.

The games were at three arenas in or near Stockholm: The Olympic Stadium, Råsunda Idrottsplats, and Tranebergs Idrottsplats. Råsunda Idrottsplats was inaugurated in 1910 and was jointly owned by Svenska Fotbollförbundet and several football clubs in Stockholm. It had a stand for 2,000 spectators and a total capacity of around 12,000. In 1937 it was rebuilt with concrete stands for 40,000 spectators, becoming the national arena for Swedish football (the Wembley of Sweden), and renamed Fotbollstadion. It was further enlarged to 50,000 seats for the 1958

See Notes on pages 220–221.

World Cup finals when it was the main stadium. Tranebergs Idrottsplats was the home ground of Djurgårdens IF, one of the leading football clubs in Stockholm. It was inaugurated in 1911, with a stand for 2,000 spectators and a total capacity of around 10,000.

The weather during the 1912 Olympic football tournament was exceptionally warm for Sweden, so much so that buckets of water were placed besides the touch-lines so players could refresh themselves during play.

England won the gold medal fairly easily, winning their first two matches by 7–0 against Hungary and 4–0 against Finland. In the semifinal match against Finland, Harold Walden scored three goals for England, and in the first round against Hungary, he had scored five of Britain's seven goals. In addition to the medals awarded to the British players, Great Britain earned possession of the challenge trophy for football, which had been donated in 1908 by the Football Association of Great Britain.

In the final, Denmark was hampered by the loss of Poul "Tist" Nielsen, who had sprained his knee against the Netherlands in the semifinals. The first goal of the final was scored by England's Walden at ten minutes. At 22 minutes, Gordon Hoare made the score England 2, Denmark 0. Shortly thereafter, Denmark's Anton Olsen scored from 25 meters out to tighten up the match. Unfortunately, just before the interval Charles Buchwald of Denmark, after a heading duel with Viv Woodward, dislocated his shoulder and was sent off. England took advantage of this by scoring two goals within three minutes to lead 4–1 at the half. Although playing a man down in the second half, Denmark managed to reduce the lead to 4–2, which was the final score.

In the first round of the consolation series, Germany defeated Russia 16–0, led by Gottfried Fuchs, who scored ten goals, equaling the Olympic record which had been set by Denmark's Sophus Nielsen in 1908.

Site:	Olympic Stadium; Råsunda Idrottsplats; Tranebergs Idrottsplats
Dates:	29 June–5 July
Event:	1 [1 Men—0 Women]
Competitors:	163 [163 Men—0 Women]
Nations:	11 [11 Men—0 Women]

	Competitors	*Gold*	*Silver*	*Bronze*	*Medals*
Austria	15	–	–	–	–
Denmark	15	–	1	–	1
Finland	13	–	–	–	–
Germany	22	–	–	–	–
Great Britain/England	14	1	–	–	1
Hungary	14	–	–	–	–
Italy	14	–	–	–	–
The Netherlands	15	–	–	1	1
Norway	12	–	–	–	–
Russia	15	–	–	–	–
Sweden	14	–	–	–	–
Totals	163	1	1	1	3
Nations	11	1	1	1	3

Committee for Football (Association Football [Soccer])

President: Christian Ludvig Kornerup, Esquire
Secretary: Anton Johanson, Esquire
Members: Rickard Andersson; Gösta Dalman; Oscar Forshell; Wilhelm Friberg; Erik Grahn; Alexander Hammar; Carl Hellberg; Erland Hjärne; Ivar Holm; Rybin Johansson; John Ohlsson, Esquire; Gotthold Ohrling; Edvin Sandborg, Esquire
Finance Committee: Carl Hellberg; Anton Johanson, Esquire; John Ohlsson, Esquire; Gotthold Ohrling; Edvin Sandborg, Esquire
Reception Committee: Gösta Dalman; Oscar Forshell; Carl Hellberg; Anton Johanson, Esquire; Ernst Killander; Christian Ludvig Kornerup, Esquire; Gustaf C. A. Lindencrona
Technical Committee: Oscar Forshell; Wilhelm Friberg; Erik Grahn; Alexander Hammar; Carl Hellberg; Erland Hjärne; Anton Johanson, Esquire; Rybin Johansson; John Ohlsson, Esquire; Gotthold Ohrling; Edvin Sandborg, Esquire
Referees: Christiaan Jacobus Groothoff (NED); Ede Herczog (HUN); Hugo Meisl (AUT); David Philip (SCO); George Wagstaffe-Simmons (ENG); Herbert James Willing (NED); Ruben Gelbord (SWE); Per Sjöblom (SWE)
International Jury: Christian Ludvig Kornerup, Esquire (President/SWE); Baron Édouard-Émile de Laveleye (BEL); Daniel Burley Woolfall (GBR); Cornelis August Wilhelm Hirschmann (NED)

Final Standings

A: 163[5]; C: 11; D: 29 June–5 July.

1. Great Britain/England
(Ronald Brebner, Thomas Burn, Arthur Knight, Douglas McWhirter, Henry Littlewort, Joseph Dines, Arthur Berry, Vivian Woodward [captain], Harold Walden, Gordon Hoare, Ivor Sharpe, Edward Hanney, Edward Wright, Harold Stamper)

2. Denmark
(Sofus Hansen, Nils Middelboe [captain], Harald Hansen, Charles von Buchwald, Emil Jørgensen, Paul Berth, N. C. Oscar Nielsen,[6] M. Axel Tufvesson, O. Anton Olsen, Sofus Nielsen, Vilhelm Wolfhagen, Hjalmar Christoffersen, Axel Petersen, Ivar-Lykke Seidelin-Nielsen, N. Poul Nielsen)

3. The Netherlands
(Marius Göbel, David Wijnveldt, Pieter Bouman, Gerardus Fortgens, Constant Feith, Nicolaas de Wolf, Dirk Lotsij [co-captain], Johannes Boutmij, Jan van Breda Kolff, Henri de Groot, Caesar ten Cate, Jan van der Sluis, Jan Vos, Nicolaas Bouvy, Johannes de Korver [co-captain])

4. Finland
(August Syrjäläinen, Hjalmar "Jalmari" Holopainen, Gösta Löfgren [co-captain], Knut Lund, Eino Soinio, Viljo Lietola, Lauri Tanner, Bror Wiberg, Algoth Niska, Artur Nyssönen, Jari "Lali" Öhman, Kaarlo Soinio (Salin) [co-captain], August Wickström)

=5. Hungary
(Gáspár Borbás, Imre Schlosser [captain], Mihály Pataky, Sándor Bodnár, Béla Sebestyén, Antal Vágó, Jenő Károly, Gyula Biró, Imre Payer, Gyula Rumbold, László Domonkos, Kálmán Szury, Zoltán Blum, Miklóz Fekete)

Norway

(Erling Maartmann, Rolf Maartmann, Hans Endrerud, Kristian Krefting, Henry Reinholt, Gunnar Andersen, Charles Herlofsen [captain], Harald Johansen, Einar Friis Baastad, Per Skou, Carl Ingolf Pedersen, Sverre Jensen)

Austria

(Alois Müller, Leopold Neubauer, Johann Studnicka [co-captain], Robert Merz, Ludwig Hussak, Robert Cimera, Karl Braunsteiner, Josef Brandstätter, Bernhard Graubart, Ladislavs Kurpiel, Otto Noll, Franz Weber, Gustav Blaha, Josef Kaltenbrunner [co-captain], Leopold "Grundi" Grundwald)

Russia

(Sergey Filipov, Vasily Zhitaryev, Vladimir Butusov [captain], Aleksandr Filipov, Mikhail Smirnov, Nikolas Kynin, Nikita Khromov, Andrey Akimov, Vladimir Markov, Pyotr Sokolov, Leonid Favorsky, Fyodor Rimsha, Grigory Nikitin, Mikhail Yakovlev, Aleksey Uversky)

=9. Germany

(Julius Hirsch, Eugen Kipp, Willi Worpitzky, Adolf Jäger, Karl Wegele, Hermann Bosch, Max Breunig [co-captain], Georg Krogmann, Ernst Hollstein, Helmuth Röpnack, Albert Weber, Adolf Werner, Gottfried Fuchs, Hans Reese, Walter Hempel, Karl Burger, Josef Glaser, Camillo Ugi [co-captain], Karl Uhle, Fritz Förderer, Emil Oberle, Otto Thiel)

Italy

(Edoardo "Dino" Mariani, Enrico Sardi, Felice Berardo, Franco Bontadini, Enea Zuffi, Pietro Leone, Giuseppe Milano [captain], Carlo De Marchi, Renzo De Vecchi, Angelo Binaschi, Piero Campelli, Luigi Barbesino, Modesto Valle, Vittorio Morelli di Popolo)

Sweden

(Karl Ansén, Helge "Ekis" Ekroth, Erik Börjesson, Ivar Svensson, Herman Myhrberg [captain], Karl Gustafsson, Gustaf Sandberg, Ragnar Wicksell, Jacob Lewin, Erik Bergström, Josef Börjesson, Erik Dahlström, Götrik Frykman, Konrad Törnqvist)

7

Tournament Summary

		Olympic Tournament					Consolation Tournament				
		Won	*Lost*	*Tied*	*Goals For*	*Goals Agst*	*Won*	*Lost*	*Tied*	*Goals For*	*Goals Agst*
1.	England	3	0	0	15	2					
2.	Denmark	2	1	0	13	5					
3.	The Netherlands	3	1	0	17	7					
4.	Finland	2	2	0	5	16					
=5.	Hungary	0	1	0	0	7	2	0	0	6	1
	Austria	1	1	0	5	4	2	1	0	6	4
	Norway	0	1	0	0	7	0	1	0	0	1
	Russia	0	1	0	1	2	0	1	0	0	16
=9.	Germany	0	1	0	1	5	1	1	0	17	3
	Italy	0	1	0	2	3	1	1	0	2	5
	Sweden	0	1	0	3	4	0	1	0	0	1
	Totals	*11*	*11*	*0*	*62*	*62*	*6*	*6*	*0*	*31*	*31*

Tournament Draw

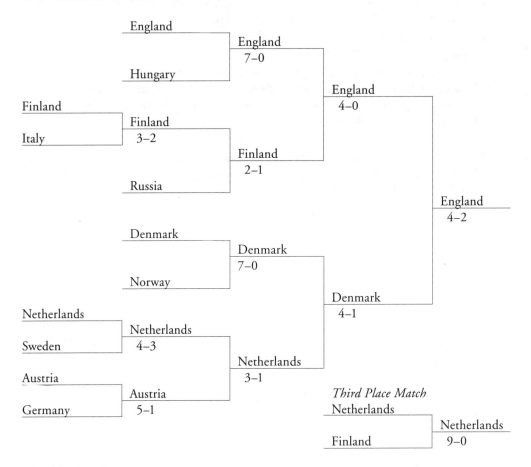

Third Place Match

Consolation Tournament

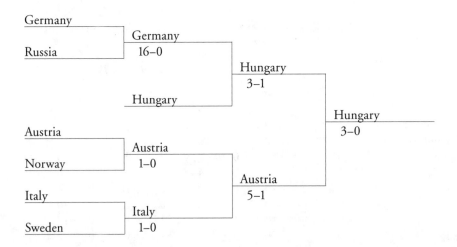

Match Summaries

Round One — 29 June

| Finland | 3 | Italy | 2 (extra time) |

Time: 1100
Site: Tranebergs Idrottsplats
Attendance: 231
Referee: Hugo Meisl (AUT)
Halftime: 2–2
Fulltime: 2–2
Goals: Öhman [2: 1–0], Bontadini [10: 1–1], Sardi [25: 2–1], E Soinio [40: 2–2], Wiberg [105: 3–2].
Rosters: *Finland:* Syrjäläinen [G], Holopainen [FB], Löfgren [FB], E. Soinio [HB], K. Soinio (Salin) [HB], Lund [HB], Wickström [F], Wiberg [F], Nyssönen [F], Öhman [F], Niska [F]; *Italy:* Campelli [G], De Vecchi [FB], Binaschi [FB], Leone [HB], Milano [HB], De Marchi/Morelli di Popolo [HB][8], Mariani [F], Sardi [F], Berardo [F], Bontadini [F], Zuffi [F].

| Austria | 5 | Germany | 1 |

Time: 1500
Site: Råsunda Idrottsplats
Attendance: 560
Referee: Herbert James Willing (NED)
Halftime: 0–1
Goals: Jäger [35: 0–1], Studnicka [58: 1–1], Neubauer [62: 2–1], Merz [75: 3–1], Merz [81: 4–1], Cimera [89: 5–1].
Rosters: *Austria:* Noll [G], Graubart [FB], Kurpiel [FB], Brandstätter [HB], Braunsteiner [HB], Cimera [HB], Hussak [F], Merz [F], Studnicka [F], Neubauer [F], Müller [F]; *Germany:* Weber [G], Röpnack [FB], Hollstein [FB], Krogmann [HB], Breunig [HB], Bosch [HB], Wegele [F], Jäger [F], Worpitzky [F], Kipp [F], Hirsch [F].

| The Netherlands | 4 | Sweden[9] | 3 (extra time) |

Time: 1900
Site: Olympic Stadium
Attendance: 5,357
Referee: George Wagstaffe-Simmons (ENG/GBR)
Halftime: 2–1
Fulltime: 3–3
Goals: Svensson [3: 0–1], Bouvy [28: 1–1], Vos [43: 2–1], Bouvy [52: 3–1], Börjesson [62: 3–2], Svensson [80: 3–3], Vos [91: 4–3].
Rosters: *The Netherlands:* Göbel [G], Wijnveldt [FB], Feith [FB], de Wolf [HB], de Korver [HB], Lotsij [HB], van Breda Kolff [F],[10] de Groot [F], ten Cate [F], Vos [F], Bouvy [F]; *Sweden:* J. Börjesson [G], Lewin [FB], Bergström [FB], Wicksell [HB], Sandberg [HB], Gustafsson [HB], Myhrberg [F], Svensson [F], E. Börjesson [F], Ekroth [F], Ansén [F].

Quarterfinals — 30 June

| Finland | 2 | Russia | 1[11] |

Time: 239
Site: Tranebergs Idrottsplats

Attendance: 200
Referee: Per Sjöblom (SWE)
Halftime: 1–0
Goals: Wiberg [30: 1–0], Butusov [72: 1–1], Öhman [80: 2–1].
Rosters: *Finland:* Syrjäläinen [G], Holopainen [FB], Löfgren [FB], Lund [HB], E. Soinio [HB], Lietola [HB], Wickström [F], Wiberg [F], Nyssönen [F], Öhman [F], Niska [F]; *Russia:* Favorsky [G], Sokolov [FB], Markov [FB], Akimov [HB], Khromov [HB], Kynin [HB], Smirnov [F], A. Filipov [F],[12] Butusov [F], Zhitaryev [F], S. Filipov [F].

England   7   Hungary   0
Time: 1330
Site: Råsunda Idrottsplats
Attendance: 8,000
Referee: Christiaan Jacobus Groothoff (NED)
Halftime: 3–0
Goals: Walden [21: 1–0], Walden [23: 2–0], Woodward [45: 3–0], Walden [49: 4–0], Woodward [53: 5–0], Walden [55: 6–0], Walden [85: 7–0].[13]
Rosters: *England:* Brebner [G], Burn [FB], Knight [FB], Littlewort [HB], Hanney [HB],[14] Dines [HB], Berry [F], Woodward [F], Walden [F], Hoare [F], Sharpe [F]; *Hungary:* Domonkos [G], Rumbold [FB], Payer [FB], Biró [HB], Károly [HB], Vágó [HB], Sebestyén [F], Bodnár [F], Pataky [F], Schlosser [F], Borbás [F].

Denmark   7   Norway   0
Time: 1630
Site: Råsunda Idrottsplats
Attendance: 1,445
Referee: Ruben Gelbord (SWE)
Halftime: 3–0
Goals: Olsen [4: 1–0], Wolfhagen [25: 2–0], Middelboe [37: 3–0], S. Nielsen [60: 4–0], Olsen [70: 5–0], S. Nielsen [85: 6–0], Olsen [88: 7–0].
Rosters: *Denmark:* S. Hansen [G], von Buchwald [FB], H. Hansen [FB], I. L. Seidelin-Nielsen [HB], Middelboe [HB], Berth [HB], Petersen [F], S. Nielsen [F], Olsen [F], Christoffersen [F], Wolfhagen [F]; *Norway:* Pedersen [G], Skou [FB], Baastad [FB], Johansen [HB], Herlofsen [HB], Andersen [HB], Reinholt [F], Krefting [F], Endrerud [F], R. Maartmann [F], E. Maartmann [F].

The Netherlands   3   Austria   1
Time: 1900
Site: Råsunda Idrottsplats
Attendance: 1,445
Referee: James Philip (SCO/GBR)
Halftime: 3–1
Goals: Bouvy [8: 1–0], ten Cate [12: 2–0], Vos [30: 3–0], Müller [41: 3–1].
Rosters: *The Netherlands:* Göbel [G], Wijnveldt [FB], Bouman [FB], Lotsij [HB], Boutmij [HB], Fortgens [HB], van Breda Kolff [F], de Groot [F], ten Cate [F], Vos [F], Bouvy [F]; *Austria:* Noll [G], Graubart [FB], Kurpiel [FB], Brandstätter [HB], Braunsteiner [HB], Cimera [HB], Hussak [F], Merz [F], Studnicka [F], Müller [F], Neubauer [F].

Semifinals — 2 July

England 4 Finland 0

Time: 1500
Site: Olympic Stadium
Attendance: 4,374
Referee: Ruben Gelbord (SWE)
Halftime: 2–0
Goals: Own goal Holopainen [1: 1–0], Walden [7: 2–0], Walden [75: 3–0], Walden [-: 4–0].
Rosters: *England:* Brebner [G], Burn [FB], Knight [FB], Littlewort [HB], Stamper [HB], Dines [HB], Wright [F], Woodward [F], Walden [F], Hoare [F], Sharpe [F]; *Finland:* Syrjäläinen [G], Holopainen [FB], Löfgren [FB], Lund [HB], E. Soinio [HB], Lietola [HB], Wickström [F], Wiberg [F], Öhman [F], Nyssönen [F], Niska [F].

Denmark 4 The Netherlands 1

Time: 1900
Site: Olympic Stadium
Attendance: 4,374
Referee: Ede Herczog (HUN)
Halftime: 3–0
Goals: Jørgensen [7: 1–0], Olsen [14: 2–0], N. P. Nielsen [37: 3–0], Own goal H. Hansen [85: 3–1], Olsen [87: 4–1].
Rosters: *Denmark:* S. Hansen [G], Middelboe [FB], H. Hansen [FB], von Buchwald [HB], Jørgensen [HB], Berth [HB], N. C. O. Nielsen [F], N. P. Nielsen [F], Olsen [F], S. Nielsen [F], Wolfhagen [F]; *The Netherlands:* Göbel [G], Wijnveldt [FB], Bouman [FB], Fortgens [HB], Boutmij [HB], Lotsij [HB], van Breda Kolff [F], de Groot [F], ten Cate [F], Vos [F], Bouvy [F].

Final — 4 July

England 4 Denmark 2

Time: 1900
Site: Olympic Stadium
Attendance: 13,865
Referee: Christiaan Jacobus Groothoff (NED)
Halftime: 4–1
Goals: Walden [10: 1–0], Hoare [22: 2–0], Olsen [27: 2–1], Hoare [41: 3–1], Berry [43: 4–1], Olsen [81: 4–2].
Rosters: *England:* Brebner [G], Burn [FB], Knight [FB], McWhirter [HB], Littlewort [HB], Dines [HB], Berry [F], Woodward [F], Walden [F], Hoare [F], Sharpe [F]; *Denmark:* S. Hansen [G], Middelboe [FB], H. Hansen [FB], von Buchwald [HB], Jørgensen [HB], Berth [HB], N. C. O. Nielsen [F], Tufvesson [F], Olsen [F], S. Nielsen [F], Wolfhagen [F].

Third-Place Match — 4 July

The Netherlands 9 Finland 0

Time: 1500
Site: Råsunda Idrottsplats
Attendance: 448

Referee: Per Sjöblom (SWE)

Halftime: 4–0

Goals: van der Sluis [24: 1–0], de Groot [28: 2–0], Vos [29: 3–0], Vos [43: 4–0], Vos [46: 5–0], van der Sluis [57: 6–0], Vos [74: 7–0], Vos [78: 8–0], de Groot [86: 9–0].

Rosters: *The Netherlands:* Göbel [G], Wijnveldt [FB], Feith [FB], Boutmij [HB], Lotsij [HB], de Wolf [HB], van Breda Kolff [F], de Groot [F], van der Sluis [F], Vos [F], Bouvy [F]; *Finland:* Syrjäläinen [G], Holopainen [FB], Löfgren [FB], Lund [HB], Lietola [HB], E. Soinio [HB], Tanner [F], Wiberg [F], Öhman [F], Nyssönen [F], Niska [F].

Consolation Series — Round One — 1 July

Austria   1   Norway   0

Time: 1100

Site: Tranebergs Idrottsplats

Attendance: 134

Referee: Per Sjöblom (SWE)

Halftime: 1–0

Goals: Neubauer [2: 1–0]

Rosters: *Austria:* Kaltenbrunner [G], Kurpiel [FB], Braunsteiner [FB], Weber [HB], Brandstätter [HB], Cimera [HB], Müller [F], Blaha [F], Merz [F], Grundwald [F], Neubauer [F]; *Norway:* Pedersen [G], Skou [FB], Baastad [FB], Johansen [HB], Herlofsen [HB], Jensen [HB], Reinholt [F], Krefting [F], Endrerud [F], R. Maartmann [F], E. Maartmann [F].

Germany   16   Russia   0

Time: 1700

Site: Råsunda Idrottsplats

Attendance: 1,405

Referee: Christiaan Jacobus Groothoff (NED)

Halftime: 8–0

Goals: Fuchs [2: 1–0], Förderer [6: 2–0], Fuchs [9: 3–0], Fuchs [21: 4–0], Förderer [27: 5–0], Fuchs [28: 6–0], Burger [30: 7–0], Fuchs [34: 8–0], Fuchs [46: 9–0], Fuchs [51: 10–0], Förderer [53: 11–0], Fuchs [55: 12–0], Oberle [58: 13–0], Fuchs [65: 14–0], Förderer [66: 15–0], Fuchs [69: 16–0].

Rosters: *Germany:* Werner [G], Reese [FB], Hempel [FB], Burger [HB], Glaser [HB], Ugi [HB], Uhle [F], Förderer [F], Fuchs [F], Oberle [F], Thiel [F]; *Russia:* Favorsky [G], Sokolov [FB], Rimsha [FB], Uversky [HB], Khromov [HB], Yakovlev [HB], Smirnov [F], Zhitaryev [F], Butusov [F], Nikitin [F], S. Filipov [F].

Italy   1   Sweden   0

Time: 1900

Site: Råsunda Idrottsplats

Attendance: 1,405

Referee: Herbert James Willing (NED)

Halftime: 1–0

Goals: Sardi [15: 1–0].

Rosters: *Italy:* Campelli [G], De Vecchi [FB], Valle [FB], Binaschi [HB], Milano [HB], Leone [HB], Bontadini [F], Berardo [F], Sardi [F], Barbesino [F], Mariani [F]; *Sweden:* J. Börjesson [G], Bergström [FB], Törnqvist [FB], Wicksell [HB], Frykman [HB], Gustafsson [HB], Myhrberg [F], Svensson [F], E. Börjesson [F], Dahlström [F], Ansén [F].

Consolation Series — Semifinals — 3 July

Hungary   3   Germany   1
   Time: 1500
   Site: Råsunda Idrottsplats
   Attendance: 441
   Referee: Christiaan Jacobus Groothoff (NED)
   Halftime: 2–0
   Goals: Schlosser [5: 1–0], Schlosser [39: 2–0], Förderer [56: 2–1], Schlosser [82: 3–1].
   Rosters: *Hungary:* Domonkos [G], Rumbold [FB], Payer [FB], Vágó [HB], Szury [HB], Blum [HB], Sebestyén [F], Bodnár [F], Fekete [F], Schlosser [F], Borbás [F]; *Germany:* Werner [G], Röpnack [FB], Hollstein [FB], Krogmann [HB], Ugi [HB], Bosch [HB], Wegele [F], Förderer [F], Fuchs [F], Hirsch [F], Oberle [F].

Austria   5   Italy   1
   Time: 1900
   Site: Djurgården Stadium
   Attendance: 1,340
   Referee: Herbert James Willing (NED)
   Halftime: 2–0
   Goals: Müller [30: 1–0], Grundwald [40: 2–0], Hussak [49: 3–0], Studnicka [65: 4–0], Berardo [81: 4–1], Grundwald [89: 5–1].
   Rosters: *Austria:* Kaltenbrunner [G], Braunsteiner [FB], Graubart [FB], Weber [HB], Brandstätter [HB], Cimera [HB], Hussak [F], Müller [F], Studnicka [F], Neubauer [F], Grundwald [F]; *Italy:* Campelli [G], De Vecchi [FB], Valle [FB], Binaschi [HB], Milano [HB], Leone [HB], Zuffi [F], Bontadini [F], Berardo [F], Barbesino [F], Mariani [F].

Consolation Series — Final — 5 July

Hungary   3   Austria   0
   Time: 1900
   Site: Råsunda Idrottsplats
   Attendance: 628
   Referee: Herbert James Willing (NED)
   Halftime: 1–0
   Goals: Schlosser [32: 1–0], Pataky [60: 2–0], Bodnár [76: 3–0].
   Rosters: *Hungary:* Domonkos [G], Rumbold [FB], Payer [FB], Biró [HB], Vágó [HB], Blum [HB], Sebestyén [F], Bodnár [F], Pataky [F], Schlosser [F], Borbás [F]; *Austria:* Kaltenbrunner [G], Graubart [FB], Kurpiel [FB], Brandstätter [HB], Braunsteiner [HB], Cimera [HB], Hussak [F], Müller [F], Merz [F], Neubauer [F], Grundwald [F].

   Goal Scoring Summary

	Olympic Tournament	Consolation Tournament	Total Goals
Harold Walden (GBR)	9	–	9
Jan Vos (NED)	8	–	8
O. Anton Olsen (DEN)	7	–	7
Nicolaas Bouvy (NED)	3	–	3
Robert Merz (AUT)	2	–	2
Sofus Nielsen (DEN)	2	–	2

	Olympic Tournament	Consolation Tournament	Total Goals
Bror Wiberg (FIN)	2	–	2
Jari Öhman (FIN)	2	–	2
Gordon Hoare (GBR)	2	–	2
Vivian Woodward (GBR)	2	–	2
Henri de Groot (NED)	2	–	2
Jan van der Sluis (NED)	2	–	2
Ivar Svensson (SWE)	2	–	2
Alois Müller (AUT)	1	1	2
Leopold Neubauer (AUT)	1	1	2
Johann Studnicka (AUT)	1	1	2
Robert Cimera (AUT)	1	–	1
Emil Jørgensen (DEN)	1	–	1
Nils Middelboe (DEN)	1	–	1
N. Poul Nielsen (DEN)	1	–	1
Vilhelm Wolfhagen (DEN)	1	–	1
Eino Soinio (FIN)	1	–	1
Arthur Berry (GBR)	1	–	1
Adolf Jäger (GER)	1	–	1
Enrico Sardi (ITA)	1	1	2
Franco Bontadini (ITA)	1	–	1
Caesar ten Cate (NED)	1	–	1
Vladimir Butusov (RUS)	1	–	1
Erik Börjesson (SWE)	1	–	1
Gottfried Fuchs (GER)	–	10	10
Fritz Förderer (GER)	–	5	5
Imre Schlosser (HUN)	–	4	4
Leopold "Grundi" Grundwald (AUT)	–	2	2
Ludwig Hussak (AUT)	–	1	1
Karl Burger (GER)	–	1	1
Emil Oberle (GER)	–	1	1
Sándor Bodnár (HUN)	–	1	1
Mihály Pataky (HUN)	–	1	1
Felice Berardo (ITA)	–	1	1

Own Goals

Harald Hansen (DEN)	1	against The Netherlands
Hjalmar "Jalmari" Holopainen (FIN)	1	against England

NOTES

1. The term soccer is derived as a slang term from the English universities Oxford and Cambridge. The word's origins date to the 1870s when the split in the forms of football became final. The students at the Oxbridge schools had a penchant for adding "-er" to names of words, thus breakfast became "breaker," rugby football became "rugger," and association football became "soccer."

2. 12OR, pp. 479–480.

3. Belgium withdrew on the day of the draw for the tournament.

4. Česka Svaž Footballový, the association governing football in Bohemia, was granted provisional membership of FIFA in 1906 and full membership in 1907. Due to objections from Austria, however, its membership was canceled in 1908.

5. EK and OSVK are grossly in error here, giving the number of competitors as 221.

6. Changed his name to Oscar Nielsen-Nørlund in 1914.

7. France and Belgium were also entered in the tournament, but did not start. Bohemia tried to enter but its entry was rejected as it was no longer a member of FIFA. See the introduction above for a discussion of this.

8. It is difficult to understand how this occurred, as substitutes were definitely not allowed in 1912. De Marchi played the first half and di Popolo the second half, as is noted in the official publication of Federazione Giuoco Calcio (Italian Football Association). The only possible explanation is that the illegal substitution was by the Italians at halftime, with the referee and their opponents not noticing the change.

9. With five minutes to play in regular time, Erik Börjesson was upended in the Dutch penalty area. He took the penalty kick himself. Although he had converted a penalty for Sweden in the 62nd minute, his shot was too loose and was saved by the Dutch keeper Marius Göbel.

10. Jan van Breda Kolff later emigrated to the United States. His son, Butch van Breda Kolff later became a well-known basketball coach, first in college at Princeton, and later in the NBA.

11. At the conclusion of this match, the winning flag was raised to the top of the flagpole. Because of the political situation between Russia and Finland, the Russian flag was raised. But the Finnish supporters affixed a small plate below the flag, which read, "Finland Won."

12. ASZ has Grigory Nikitin instead of Aleksandr Filipov.

13. Hungarian penalty shot at 15 minutes taken by Sándor Bodnár, but save by English keeper Ronald Brebner. With the score 6–0 in the second half, an English penalty shot was taken by Gordon Hoare, but was saved by László Domonkos.

14. Hanney was injured in the first moments and was off the field for ten minutes before he returned. But the injury was serious and he was unable to play in the second half; nor could he play the remainder of the Olympic tournament. England thus played the second half a man down.

Gymnastics

At the time of the 1912 Olympics, international gynmastics was split among several schools. There was the Swedish, or Ling school; the Sokol, or Bohemian, school; and the German turnen, or European school. Each method had its supporters and the gymnastics community compromised by providing a team competition in three different systems at Stockholm — the European (German), the Swedish, and a Free System, with free choice of movements and apparatus. This would be repeated in 1920 at Antwerp, when the same three styles were used for three separate team events.

Individual gymnastics also had its exponents and its detractors. In particular, the Swedes did not like the idea of gymnastics as an individual competition, as it was against their basic concept of gymnastics. In 1908 the Swedish press did not publish the results of the individual gymnastics competition at London, as there were no Swedish participants. Still, the Swedish Olympic committee agreed to organize an individual gymnastics event in Stockholm. In fact, at the 11th IOC session (1910 in Luxembourg), the Swedish Olympic committee revealed that it was not planning on conducting any competitive gymnastics but only displays. The committee soon capitulated to the wishes of the IOC and agreed to organize competitive events.

All the Olympic gymnastics events were held outdoors in the Olympic Stadium, a common practice in that era.

Site:	Olympic Stadium	
Dates:	8, 10–12 July	
Events:	4 [4 Men — 0 Women]	
Competitors:	249 [249 Men — 0 Women]	
Nations:	12 [12 Men — 0 Women]	

	Competitors	Gold	Silver	Bronze	Medals
Bohemia	1	–	–	–	–
Denmark	49	–	1	1	2
Finland	24	–	1	–	1
France	6	–	1	–	1
Germany	18	–	–	–	–

*See Notes on page 229.

Great Britain	23	–	–	1	1
Hungary	17	–	1	–	1
Italy	18	2	–	1	3
Luxembourg	19	–	–	–	–
Norway	46	1	–	1	2
Russia	4	–	–	–	–
Sweden	24	1	–	–	1
Totals	249	4	4	4	12
Nations	12	3	4	4	8

Committee for Gymnastics

President: Captain Einar Nerman
Secretary: Lieutenant Wilhelm Carlberg; Lieutenant Torsten Oswald Magnus Holmberg
Members: Captain Ebbe Lieberath; Captain Bernhard Erik Littorin; Georg Löfgren, Esquire; Emil Löfvenius, Esquire
International Jury: Viktor Gustaf Balck (President/SWE); Captain Einar Nerman (SWE); Holger Christian Valdemar Møller (DEN); –– Lachaud (FRA); Karl von Iszer (HUN); Carl Ferdinand Berthelsen (NOR)

Combined All-Around, Individual

A: 44; C: 9; D: 12 July; T: 0930–1230, 1400–1700; F: Performances on horizontal bar, parallel bars, rings, and pommeled horse. Maximum of six gymnasts per nation. Each performance scored 0–12 by three judges. Possible score of 36 on each apparatus and total possible of 144.

In the absence of the German gymnasts, this event was dominated by the French and Italians, as they took the first 11 places. No Swedes or Norwegians competed, even though those nations won two of the three team gymnastics events in 1912. The reason is that the Swedes and Norwegians were opposed to the concept of individual gymnastics competition. They believed that gymnastics was a team sport, which should be practiced in mass displays.

The individual event was won by Italy's Alberto Braglia, who defended the individual all-around gold medal he had won at London in 1908. In addition to his gold medal, he retained possession of the challenge trophy for the individual all-around. This trophy had been donated for the 1908 Olympics by the City of Prague. Braglia had also been runner-up in both individual events at the 1906 Olympics in Athens. After his 1908 Olympic championships, Braglia used his Olympic fame to become a circus performer. Working on a trapeze, he sustained a serious injury from a fall in 1910. But he recovered from that setback to return to the Olympics in 1912 at Stockholm. After the 1912 Olympics, Braglia turned professional, returning to the circus as an acrobat. He later returned to gymnastics to coach the Italian team for the 1932 Olympics.

		HB	*PB*	*Rg*	*PH*	*Total*
1. Alberto Braglia	ITA	32.75	34.75	31.75	35.75	135.00
2. B. Louis Ségura	FRA	30.00	35.75	32.25	34.50	132.50

		HB	PB	Rg	PH	Total
3. Adolfo Tunesi	ITA	30.25	35.00	30.50	35.75	131.50
=4. Giorgio Zampori	ITA	29.00	35.00	30.75	33.25	128.00
Guido Boni	ITA	29.75	35.25	28.25	34.75	128.00
6. Pietro Bianchi	ITA	29.50	33.75	30.75	33.75	127.75
=7. Marcel Lalue	FRA	29.25	35.50	30.50	31.75	127.00
Marco Torrès	FRA	30.25	35.00	31.00	30.75	127.00
9. Guido Romano	ITA	29.25	32.50	30.00	34.50	126.25
10. Antoine Costa	FRA	29.75	34.25	29.75	30.75	124.50
11. Louis-Charles Marty	FRA	26.75	34.75	30.50	30.50	122.50
12. Leonard Hanson	GBR	28.50	31.75	31.50	29.50	121.25
13. Elemér Pászti	HUN	27.75	30.50	27.00	33.75	119.00
14. Auguste Pompogne	FRA	27.00	32.00	28.00	31.00	118.00
=15. József Szalai	HUN	28.00	33.00	29.75	26.50	117.25
Antoine Wehrer	LUX	26.50	33.00	28.75	29.00	117.25
17. Imre Gellért	HUN	24.00	34.00	26.75	32.25	117.00
18. Pierre Hentges	LUX	26.00	29.50	29.25	30.75	115.50
19. János Krizmanich	HUN	26.50	28.75	26.75	33.00	115.00
20. Nicolas Kanive	LUX	22.25	31.25	29.50	28.50	111.50
21. John Whitaker	GBR	26.50	27.75	29.75	27.25	111.25
22. Jean-Pierre Thommes	LUX	22.75	32.00	27.50	28.50	110.75
23. François Hentges	LUX	20.75	32.50	27.00	30.25	110.50
24. Emile Lanners	LUX	25.00	29.00	27.00	28.75	109.75
25. Samuel Hodgetts	GBR	25.25	27.75	28.25	27.25	108.50
26. Arvor Hansen	DEN	27.00	29.50	28.50	22.50	107.50
27. Viljami Nieminen	FIN	26.50	30.00	25.00	24.25	105.75
28. Charles Simmons[1]	GBR	23.50	30.50	28.50	23.00	105.50
29. William Cowhig	GBR	25.75	29.50	26.75	22.50	104.50
30. Charles Jensen	DEN	25.25	27.00	26.25	25.25	103.75
31. Edvard Jansson	FIN	28.25	30.75	24.25	19.75	103.00
32. Reginald Potts	GBR	25.50	23.25	28.25	24.75	101.75
33. Axel Andersen	DEN	22.25	30.00	26.50	20.00	98.75
=34. Niels Petersen	DEN	20.75	28.25	28.25	20.00	97.25
Carl Alfred Pedersen	DEN	25.00	26.25	25.25	20.75	97.25
36. Bohumil Honzátko	BOH	17.00	25.00	25.50	23.75	91.25
37. Antti Tamminen	FIN	23.00	23.25	26.00	18.25	90.50
38. Pavel Kushnikov	RUS	24.75	24.50	21.50	19.25	90.00
39. Aleksandr Akhyun	RUS	20.75	25.25	23.25	18.50	87.75
40. Ejnar Møbius	DEN	13.50	27.00	26.25	20.00	86.75
41. Semyon Kulikov	RUS	16.50	24.00	21.50	17.50	79.50
42. Fyodor Zabelin	RUS	14.75	22.00	22.50	17.00	76.25
AC. Kaarle "Kalle" Ekholm	FIN	25.00	25.50	DNS	DNF	
Yrjö Vuolio	FIN	23.25	29.00	DNS	DNF	

[2]

Judges

Professor Cesare Tifi (ITA); Captain Alfred E. Syson (GBR); Dr. Ivar Wilskman (FIN); Dr. J. F. Allum (NOR); Dr. -- Lachaud (FRA)

Diplomas of Merit

Giorgio Zampori (ITA), Guido Boni (ITA), Pietro Bianchi (ITA), Marcel Lalue (FRA), Marco Torrès (FRA), Guido Romano (ITA)

Combined All-Around, Swedish System, Team

A: 74; C: 3; D: 8 July; T: 1400–1700; F: One team per nation. Teams of 16 to 40 gymnasts performing simultaneously. Time limit: one hour, including march in and march out. The organizing committee provided fixed apparatus necessary for Swedish gymnastics, including four balance beams, eight beam saddles, 20 wall bars, 24 climbing ropes, two wooden horses, and three box horses. The teams could choose any combination of apparatuses. The judges evaluated 11 components: 1) entry exercises [5]; 2) flexion movements [8]; 3) heaving exercises [7]; 4) balance exercises [4]; 5) shoulder-blade exercises [6]; 6) abdominal exercises [6]; 7) marching and running [7]; 8) lateral trunk movements [7]; 9) vaulting exercises [7]; 10) closing exercises [4]; and 11) uniformity and precision [8]. Maximum points for each component 15, with the score multiplied by the tariff (in brackets above). Maximum possible 1,035. Five judges scoring with all five scores to count.

This event figured on the Olympic program for the first time in 1912, and would appear only once more, in 1920 at Antwerp. The Swedes easily won the team event based on their own method of gymnastics. This event had only three entrants from three of the five Scandinavian nations. Four of the five judges placed Sweden first, while the Danish judge narrowly voted for Denmark. Sweden repeated its Olympic victory in their own style at Antwerp in 1920. Only John Sörenson competed for Sweden in both 1912 and 1920.

	1	2	3	4	5	Total	Average
1. Sweden	970.50	953.50	957.80	841.50	964.00	4,687.30	937.46

    (Per Bertilsson, Carl Ehrenfried Carlberg, Nils Daniel Granfelt, Curt Hartzell, Oswald Holmberg, Anders Hylander, Axel Janse, Anders Boo Kullberg, Sven Landberg, Per Nilsson, Benkt Rudolf Norelius, Axel Norling, Daniel Norling, Sven Rosén, Nils Silfverskiöld, Carl Silfverstrand, John Sörenson, Yngve Stiernspetz, Carl-Erik Svensson, Karl-Johan Svensson (Sarland), Knut Torell, Edward Wennerholm, Claës Wersäll, David Wiman) (Team Leader: Ebbe Lieberath; Flag Bearer: Karl Erik Ekblad)

2. Denmark	889.00	932.50	962.50	793.00	917.20	4,494.20	898.84

    (Peter Andersen, Søren Christensen, Ingvald Eriksen, George Falcke, Torkild Garp, Hans Trier Hansen, Johannes Hansen, Rasmus Hansen, Jens Kristian Jensen, Søren Jensen, Valdemar Bøggild, Karl Kirk, Jens Kirkegaard, Olaf Kjems, Carl Larsen, Jens Peter Laursen, Marius Lefevre, Poul Mark, Einar Olsen, Hans Pedersen, Hans Eiler Pedersen, Jens Thorup Pedersen, Peder Larsen Pedersen, Jørgen Christian Ravn, Aksel Sørensen, Søren Thorborg, Kristen Vadgaard, Johannes Vinther) (Team Leader: Niels Bukh[3]; Flag Bearer: Kornerup Bang)

3. Norway	796.50	952.00	875.80	749.75	912.00	4,286.05	857.21

    (Arthur Amundsen, Jørgen Andersen, Trygve Bøyesen, Georg Brustad, Conrad Christensen, Oscar Engelstad, Marius Eriksen, Aksel Henry Hansen, Peter Hol, Eugen Ingebretsen, Olaf Ingebretsen, Olof Jacobsen, Erling Jensen, Thor Jensen, Frithjof Olsen, Oscar Olstad,

Edvin Paulsen, Carl Alfred Pedersen, Paul Pedersen, Rolf Robach, Sigurd Smebye, Torleif Torkildsen) (Team Leader: C. Frøhlich-Hansen)

Judges

1	=	Major O. Lefebure (BEL)
2	=	Major Jean Louis Adolph Bentzen (NOR)
3	=	H. N. Rasmussen, B.A. (DEN)
4	=	Captain Alfred E. Syson (GBR)
5	=	Captain L. Konrad Wallenius (SWE)

Combined All-Around, Team, European System

A: 91[4]; C: 5; D: 11 July; T: 0930–1230, 1400–1600; F: One team per nation. Teams of 16 to 40 gymnasts performing simultaneously. Time limit: one hour, including march in and march out. The organizing committee provided fixed apparatus: four horizontal bars, four parallel bars, four pommeled horses, and four Roman rings. Each team had to provide their own hand apparatus for the free-standing exercises. Exercises on the horizontal bar, parallel bars, and pommeled horse were mandatory. Maximum points on each apparatus 12. Maximum points for free-standing exercises 12 and for free exercises ten. Maximum possible points 58. Scoring by five judges, with all scores to count.

This event figured on the Olympic program for the first time in 1912, and would appear only once more, in 1920 at Antwerp. Deutsche Turnerschaft, the German Gymnastic Association, the world's foremost gymnastic association, declined to send a team. The German team at Stockholm was a mediocre university team from Leipzig. Had the Deutsche Turnerschaft team appeared, it would likely have won easily.

The Italian team had finished sixth in the only team competition at the 1908 Olympics, which was free gymnastics without apparatus. At Stockholm, they dominated this event, winning with almost a 20 percent margin of victory over the runner-up, Hungary. Of the five judges, four placed Italy first, while the Hungarian judge placed Hungary first. The Italians would win this event again at the 1920 Olympics in Antwerp. Sweden had won the team gymnastics event in 1908 but did not enter this event, as German *Turnen* (gymnastics) was not practiced in Sweden. In Sweden, German *Turnen* was considered to be acrobatics and to belong in a circus arena rather than the gymnastics hall.

	1	*2*	*3*	*4*	*5*	*Total*	*Average*
1. Italy	56.00	55.75	48.00	52.50	53.50	265.75	53.15

(Guido Boni, Giuseppe Domenichelli, Luciano Savorini, Guido Romano, Angelo Zorzi, Giorgio Zampori, Giovanni Mangiante, Lorenzo Mangiante, Adolfo Tunesi, Pietro Bianchi, Paolo Salvi, Alberto Braglia, Alfredo Gollini, Serafino Mazzarocchi, Francesco Loy, Carlo Fregosi, Luigi Maiocco, Umberto Zanolini[5]) (Team Leader: Cornelio Cavalli)

	1	*2*	*3*	*4*	*5*	*Total*	*Average*
2. Hungary	37.25	44.00	39.50	52.00	54.50	227.25	45.45

(József Bittenbinder, Imre Erdődy, Samu Fóti, Imre Gellért, Győző Haberfeld, Ottó Hellmich, István Herczeg, József Keresztessy, Lajos Kmetykó, János Krizmanich, Elemér Pászti, Árpád Pédery, Jenő Rittich, Ferenc Szűts, Ödön Téry, Géza Tuli) (Team Leader: Rezső Bábel)

3. Great Britain   47.50   30.75   35.00   43.00   28.25   184.50   36.90
(Albert Betts, Harold Dickason, Samuel Hodgetts, Alfred Messenger, Edward Pepper, Charles Vigurs, Samuel Walker, John Whitaker, Sidney Cross, Bernard Franklin, Edward Potts, Reginald Potts, George Ross, Henry Oberholzer, Charles Simmons,[6] Arthur Southern, Ronald McLean, Charles Luck, Herbert Drury, William MacKune, William Titt, William Cowhig, Leonard Hanson) (Team Leader: Charles Joseph West/R. Oberholzer[7])

4. Luxembourg   50.50   36.75   22.00   38.00   32.50   179.75   35.95
(Nicolas Adam, Charles Behm, André Bordang, François Hentges,[8] Pierre Hentges, Michal Hemmerling, Jean-Baptiste Horn, Nicolas Kanive, Nicolas Kummer, Marcel Langsam, Emile Lanners, Jean-Pierre Thommes, François Wagner, Antoine Wehrer, Ferdinand Wirtz, Joseph Zuang[9]) (Team Leader: Valentin Peffer)

5. Germany   32.75   27.25   30.25   49.00   22.75   162.00   32.40
(Walter Engelmann, Adolf Seebaß, Alfred Staats, Hans Roth, Arno Glockauer, Alexander Sperling, Kurt Reichenbach, Rudolf Körner, J. Erwin Buder, Wilhelm Brülle, Heinrich Pahner, Johannes Reuschle, Walter Jesinghaus, Eberhard Sorge, Karl Richter, M. Erich Worm, Karl Jordan, Hans Werner) (Team Leader: Dr. Herman Kuhr)

Judges

1	=	Dr. Abraham Clod-Hansen (DEN)
2	=	Professor Cesare Tifi (ITA)
3	=	Captain Alfred E. Syson (GBR)
4	=	Dr. Erich Wagner-Hohenlobbese (GER)
5	=	Michel Bély (HUN)

Combined All-Around, Free System, Teams

A: 101[10]; C: 5; D: 10 July; T: 0930–1230, 1400–1600; F: One team per nation. Teams of 16 to 40 gymnasts performing simultaneously. Time limit: one hour, including march in and march out. The organizing committee provided fixed apparatus as for the Swedish and European team events. The judges could assess the execution of the exercises, the composition of the program, and the posture and attention of the team. Each scored the entire program from zero to 25 points. Five judges, with all five scores to count.

This event figured on the Olympic program for the first time in 1912, and would appear only once more, in 1920 at Antwerp. This was the closest of the three team gymnastic competitions at the 1912 Olympics. Three judges placed Norway first, while the Danish judge placed Denmark first, and the Finnish judge placed Finland first. The Swedes and the Italians, who had won the other team events, did not compete in the free system team competition. Eight years later, in 1920, Norway finished second, trailing Denmark, which was the only other team to compete in this style at Antwerp.

	1	*2*	*3*	*4*	*5*	*Total*	*Average*
1. Norway	20.00	24.00	22.00	23.25	25.00	114.25	22.85

(Isak Abrahamsen, Hans Beyer, Hartman Bjørnson, Alfred Engelsen, Sigurd Jørgensen, Bjarne Johnsen, Knud Knudsen, Alf Lie, Rolf Lie, Tor Lund, Petter Martinsen, Per Mathiesen, Jacob Opdahl, Nils Opdahl, Bjarne Pettersen, Frithjof Sælen, Øistein Schirmer, Georg

Selenius, Sigvard Sivertsen, Robert Sjursen Rafto, Einar Strøm, Gabriel Thorstensen, Thomas Thorstensen, Nils Voss [Repål]) (Team Leader: Johannes Dahl)

2. Finland   20.00   20.00   23.00   22.25   24.00   109.25   21.85
(Kaarle "Kalle" Ekholm, Eino Forsström, Eero Hyvärinen, Mikko Hyvärinen, Tauno Ilmoniemi, Ilmari Keinänen, Jalmari Kivenheimo, Karl Lund, Aarne Pelkonen, K. Ilmari Pernaja, Arvid Rydman, K. Eino Saastamoinen, Aarne Salovaara, Heikki Sammallahti, Hannes Sirola, Klaus Uuno Suomela [Lindholm], Lauri Tanner, Väinö Tiiri, Kaarlo Vähämäki, Kalle Vasama) (Team Leader: Arvid Vartia)

3. Denmark   23.00   19.00   21.50   20.75   22.00   106.25   21.25
(Axel Sigurd Andersen, Hjalmar "Hjallis" Nørregaard Andersen, Halvor Birch, Wilhelm Grimmelmann, Arvor Hansen, Christian Hansen, Aage Marius Hansen, Charles Jensen, Hjalmar Johansen, Poul Preben Jørgensen, Carl Immanuel Krebs, Vigo Meulengracht-Madsen, Lukas Nielsen, Rikard Nordstrøm, Steen Lerche Olsen, Oluf Olsson, Carl Julius Pedersen, Kristian Pedersen, Olaf Pedersen, Niels Petersen, Christian Valdemar Svendsen) (Team Leader: H. Mølgaard)

4. Germany   18.00   12.00   14.00   16.25   24.00   84.25   16.85
(Walter Engelmann, Adolf Seebaß, Alfred Staats, Hans Roth, Arno Glockauer, Alexander Sperling, Kurt Reichenbach, Rudolf Körner, J. Erwin Buder, Wilhelm Brülle, Heinrich Pahner, Johannes Reuschle, Walter Jesinghaus, Eberhard Sorge, Karl Richter, M. Erich Worm, Karl Jordan, Hans Werner) (Team Leader: Dr. Herman Kuhr)

5. Luxembourg   19.00   15.50   18.00   17.00   12.00   81.50   16.30
(Nicolas Adam, Charles Behm, André Bordang, François Hentges,[11] Pierre Hentges, Michal Hemmerling, Jean-Baptiste Horn, Jean-Pierre Frantzen, Nicolas Kanive, Émile Knepper, Nicolas Kummer, Marcel Langsam, Maurice Palgen, Emile Lanners, Jean-Pierre Thommes, François Wagner, Antoine Wehrer, Ferdinand Wirtz, Joseph Zuang) (Team Leader: Valentin Peffer)

Judges
1   =   Dr. Abraham Clod-Hansen (DEN)
2   =   Dr. J. F. Allum (NOR)
3   =   Dr. Ivar Wilskman (FIN)
4   =   Captain Alfred E. Syson (GBR)
5   =   Dr. Erich Wagner-Hohenlobbese (GER)

NON-OLYMPIC EVENTS

Gymnastics Exhibitions

A number of gymnastic exhibitions were conducted during the 1912 Olympic Games. They were as follows:

Date	Times	Teams
6 July	1200–1330	Display by 192 Swedish men gymnasts. Leader: Ebbe Lieberath
6 July	1200–1330	Display by 48 Swedish women gymnasts. Leader: Marrit Hallström
8 July	0930–1100	Display by 150 Danish men gymnasts. Leader: Miss –– Bentzen

8 July	0930–1100	Display by 320 Danish women gymnasts. Leader: Wilhelm Kristensen Skaarup
8 July	1100–1145	Display by 22 Norwegian women gymnasts. Leader: Reidar Fabritius
8 July	1145–1230	Display by 24 Finnish women gymnasts. Leader: Elli Björkstén
10 July	1600–1645	Display by 16 Hungarian men gymnasts. Leader: Rezső Bábel
11 July	1600–1645	Display by 18 Russian men gymnasts. Leader: Captain –– Fock

Diplomas of Merit

Russian Men Gymnastics Squad

NOTES

1. Charles Simmons was the father of well-known actress, Jean Simmons.

2. Also entered in this event, but not competing, were Josef Kovařík (BOH), Orvil Elliott (CAN), George Alan Keith (CAN), Conrad Christensen (NOR), Bjarne Pettersen (NOR), Nikolay Freuendorff (RUS), Nikolay Lyshchik (RUS), Petr Pelipeychenko (RUS), and Paul Krimmel (USA).

3. Bukh is listed in the Danish Olympic book, *De Olympiske*, while 12OR lists A. Hansen.

4. EK and OSVK have 92. However, only 91 gymnasts are listed in OSVK. However, his 91 and our 91 are not precisely the same. See following footnotes.

5. Maiocco and Zanolini are not listed in 12OR, or in OSVK. But they are listed in Colasante's book *La nascita del Movimento Olimpico in Italia, 1894–1914*. Rome: CONI, 1996.

6. Charles Simmons was the father of well-known actress, Jean Simmons.

7. West is listed in 12OR, while Oberholzer is listed in Uggla.

8. Not listed in OSVK.

9. Many sources, including DW, EK, and OSVK, also list Jean-Pierre Frantzen, Émile Knepper, and Maurice Palgen, but they are not listed in 12OR and do not appear to have competed.

10. OSVK has 101. However, OSVK lists only 100 gymnasts in his results. See the following footnotes for more information.

11. Not listed in OSVK.

Modern Pentathlon

The modern pentathlon is a sport proposed by the founder of the modern Olympic Games, Baron Pierre de Coubertin. He envisioned a competition which would determine the greatest all-around sportsman, similar to the pentathlon of the ancient Olympic Games, as described by Aristotle. "The most perfect sportsmen, therefore, are the Pentathletes because in their bodies strength and speed are combined in beautiful harmony."[1]*

However, Coubertin's all-around competition differed greatly from the ancient pentathlon, which consisted of the long jump, discus and javelin throwing, a sprint race of about 200 meters, and wrestling. At the 1909 IOC session in Berlin, he first proposed the modern pentathlon, which was then noted to consist of "... equestrian, running, jumping, swimming, and wrestling. Fencing or shooting could replace wrestling."[2]

It was not until the 12th IOC session at Budapest in 1911 that Coubertin's idea was accepted by the IOC membership. He stated, "I had already submitted the idea to the IOC on two previous occasions, and my proposal had always been greeted with a lack of understanding and almost hostility. I had not insisted. This time however the grace of the Holy Sporting Ghost enlightened my colleagues and they accepted an event to which I attached great importance: a veritable consecration of the complete athlete, the modern pentathlon was to comprise a footrace, a horse-race, a swimming race, a fencing match, and finally, a shooting contest, which I would prefer to have had replaced by a rowing race, but this would have added greatly to the difficulties of the organization, which was already quite complicated enough."[3]

At that 1911 IOC session, there was some concern on the part of the Stockholm organizers about providing horses for the competitors. Lyberg wrote, "The matter of the horses to be used started a heated discussion. Balck had reported that the organisers could not provide horses to the competitors, [and] de Coubertin got very upset. This competition was 'his baby' and told [Viktor Gustaf] Balck that he and his friends had badly misunderstood his intentions. As not all competitors could bring their own horses the only solution was that the organisers must supply all with horses and that a draw was to be made for the horses. Balck was not happy but promised to provide the horses!"[4]

The 1912 modern pentathlon consisted of rapid-fire pistol shooting, épée fencing, a 300 meter swimming race, a cross-country steeplechase equestrian event, and a 4,000 meter cross-country run. It is probably better termed the military pentathlon. A press release from the UIPMB

*See Notes on pages 240–241.

(Union Internationale de Pentathlon Moderne et Biathlon) described the choice of the events. "The choice of the five diverse and unrelated sports which make up the Modern Pentathlon arose out of the romantic, rough adventures of a liaison officer whose horse is brought down in enemy territory; having defended himself with his pistol and sword he swims across a raging river and delivers the message on foot."[5]

The 1912 Olympic modern pentathlon was the first ever contested, with the exception of the Olympic trials in Sweden shortly before the Olympics. Because of its military imagery, most of the competitors were military officers. Many of the competitors also came to the modern pentathlon from other sports, using their skills in those sports to aid their training for the combined event. At Stockholm, 12 of the 32 modern pentathletes competed in another sport during the Olympics. The oldest participant in 1912 was Carl Pauen (GER) who was born on 7 April 1859 and was thus 53 years old in 1912. He retired, for reasons not known, after the first event, the shooting.

Sweden trained athletes specifically for the modern pentathlon in 1912, and their athletes dominated, as would be expected from their training. They entered 12 athletes, and Swedes finished in the first four places, six of the top seven, and seven of the top nine. Scoring was by a point-for-placed system for each of the five separate competitions.

The first event was shooting and three Swedes led, with Gösta Åsbrink winning the event with 20 hits, no misses, and 193 points. His teammates, Georg de Laval and Gösta Lilliehöök finished second and third. Swimming was held on the second day, and de Laval and Åsbrink were equal first with five points after the swim competition ended. The best swim time was made by Ralph Clilverd (GBR) who swam the 300 meters in 4:58.4.

The third and fourth days of the competition were devoted to the round-robin épée fencing. The best performance in fencing was by Sweden's Åke Grönhagen, who won 24 of 26 matches. After three events, Georg de Laval led with 15 points, Lilliehöök second with 18 points, Åsbrink third with 20 points, and Clilverd fourth with 22 points.

Georg de Laval maintained his lead after the riding competition. He finished third in the riding, for 18 points after four events and a four-point lead over Lilliehöök going in to the final cross-country run. The riding was also won by Grönhagen, who moved up to third place with 25 points.

After four events, Gösta Åsbrink was in fourth place with 27 points. He won the final event, the 4,000 meter run in 19:00.9, to finish with 28 points, but it was not enough. Gösta Lilliehöök finished fifth in the run to beat Åsbrink by one point, 27–28, and win the first Olympic modern pentathlon. Georg de Laval finished 12th in the run to fall to third place overall. In addition to his gold medal, Lilliehöök was awarded possession of the challenge trophy for the modern pentathlon, which had been donated for the Stockholm Olympics by de Coubertin.

All of the 32 competitors at Stockholm were men, and through 1996, women's modern pentathlon was never contested at the Olympics, although it had been a World Championship event since 1981. Women débuted in Olympic modern pentathlon at Sydney in 2000. However, a British woman did attempt to compete in the 1912 modern pentathlon. The story was first reported in the newspapers on 7 July 1912, oddly in the *Louisville Courier-Journal*. The headline noted, "GIRL TO ENTER OLYMPIC GAMES. Miss Helen Preece, Women's Hope, to Take Part in the Contests to Be Held at Stockholm." Sections of this story are as follows:

> LONDON, July 6.— Englishwomen are expecting Miss Helen Preece, a 15-year-old horsewoman, to accomplish great things at the Olympic games at Stockholm this month.
>
> Miss Preece, who will be the only female representative at the games, has won fame here as an expert horsewoman and athlete generally, and her abilities are not

[un]known in the United States. At New York in November last, at the Madison Square Garden Horse Show, Miss Preece won outright the $1,000 gold cup, open to the world for riding, in addition to many other "blues."

"I have entered for several contests there," she said, "but my particular ambition is to carry off the first prize in the great competition. That is a stiff proposition, I admit, since it includes five different events: A cross-country ride of 4,000 meters (about two and one-half miles); riding over a course of 5,000 meters; swimming 300 meters; fencing and shooting with a revolver at a target twenty-five meters distant.

"A formidable list, you will agree, and all have to be won, but father and friends, under whose guidance I am now undergoing quite an arduous course of training, seem to have every confidence in me, and, of course, I myself am enthusiastic.

"I have obtained special leave of absence from my school in Hertfordshire, and my day's work now commences as early as 5 o'clock every morning, and only ends with bedtime at 8 o'clock.

"A varied program is mapped out for me each day, but it always includes riding, shooting, swimming, running and walking practice, and today I have been put on a special diet, also, so that I should be absolutely fit for the Pentathlon on July 11.

"The one thing that worries me is the fact that I shall be the only woman competitor in this particular contest; it may make me nervous."

Referring to her New York visit, Miss Preece said:

"I had a great time out there. Everybody was so good to me and I made many friends. The American women are fine riders and their sportsmanship is great. They seem to take a far greater active interest in sports generally than do the women in England."[6]

Her dreams never came to pass, however, and Miss Preece did not compete at Stockholm. Robert de Courcy Laffan, honorary secretary of the British Olympic Association, wrote to the Stockholm organizing committee on 2 May 1912, "We have had an application from a lady to be allowed to enter for the Modern Pentathlon in the Olympic Games of Stockholm. I presume from your telegram of March 22nd. stating that the Horse Riding Competitions are only open to gentlemen riders, that the Modern Pentathlon is not open to ladies. I do not however feel authorised to decide this question absolutely, and therefore beg to refer it to you for a definite decision." Laffan's sign-off may reveal something about his own feelings on this matter, "Believe me, Gentlemen, Very sincerely yours ..."[7]

On 8 May 1912, Kristian Hellström, secretary of the Stockholm organizing committee forwarded a copy of the letter to Coubertin. Coubertin wrote of the situation in *Revue Olympique*. "The other day an application came signed by a neo–Amazon who wanted to compete in the Modern Pentathlon and the Swedish Committee, who was left free to decide in the absence of fixed legislation, refused that application."[8] Coubertin answered Hellström, presumably shortly thereafter, although the letter has no date:

As to the Modern Pentathlon I am personnally [sic] opposed *to the admittance of ladies* as competitors in the Olympic Games. But as they are this time admitted as tennis players, swimmers etc. I do not see on what ground we should stand to refuse them in the Pentathlon. However, I repeat that I greatly *regret the fact*. Therefore I leave to you to decide and if you refuse or accept the engagement, I shall agree with you.[9]

Given Coubertin's letter, and the date of the newspaper article (7 July), it is possible that Hellström allowed Miss Preece to enter, but that some other circumstance prevented her from competing. There is no mention of this situation in the *Official Report*. Nothing further is known about Helen Preece.

The first non–Swedish finisher was an American, Lieutenant George Patton, who finished fifth, and later became a very famous American general. Patton attended college at the United States Military Academy at West Point (NY), where he competed in football, track, fencing, and shooting. He graduated in 1909, then excelled as a horseman in the military. His all-around athletic prowess made him a natural to compete in an event such as the modern pentathlon. He never came close to winning, because his worst event was the first one, the shooting, and it put him hopelessly behind. He scored only 150 points, finishing in 21st place. But in the remaining four events, he finished seventh, fourth, sixth, and third, to move up into fifth place overall.

As a military man, Patton wrote a summary of his competition in the modern pentathlon, and this has been well chronicled by Harold "Rusty" Wilson, Ph.D. in "A Legend in His Own Mind: The Olympic Experience of General George S. Patton, Jr."[10] In Wilson's article, Patton's actual performances are compared to those in his report. To be kind, it is obvious that Patton exaggerated.

Lieutenant Patton was eventually promoted to general and served with honor in Northern Africa and Europe during World War II. He led the United States Third Army, fighting against Rommel's Africa Corps, and participated in the United States' invasion of Sicily, and at the Battle of the Bulge. His career has been immortalized in several biographies, and also in a movie of his life entitled simply "Patton," with George C. Scott in the Academy Award–winning title role.

Sites:	Kaknäs (pistol shooting); Swimming Stadium at Djurgårdsbrunnsviken (swimming); Tennis Pavilion at the Östermalm Athletic Grounds (fencing); Barkaby to Rinkeby (steeplechase ride); Olympic Stadium (cross-country run start and finish)
Dates:	7–12 July (7 July — Shooting; 8 July — Swimming; 9–10 July — Fencing; 11 July — Riing; 12 July — Running)
Events:	1 [1 Men — 0 Women]
Competitors:	32 [32 Men — 0 Women]
Nations:	10 [10 Men — 0 Women]

	Competitors	Gold	Silver	Bronze	Medals
Austria	1	–	–	–	–
Denmark	4	–	–	–	–
France	2	–	–	–	–
Germany	1	–	–	–	–
Great Britain	3	–	–	–	–
The Netherlands	1	–	–	–	–
Norway	2	–	–	–	–
Russia	5	–	–	–	–
Sweden	12	1	1	1	3

United States	1	–	–	–	–
Totals	32	1	1	1	3
Nations	10	1	1	1	1

Committee for the Modern Pentathlon

President: Colonel Viktor Gustaf Balck
Secretary-General: Kristian Hellström, Esquire
Members: Colonel, Count Carl E. Taube; Captain Carl Silfverstolpe; Lieutenant F. Samuel Granfelt
Athletics Members: Lieutenant Gustaf G:son Uggla; Sune Smedmark, Esquire
Fencing Members: Captain Emil Fick; Lieutenant Birger Cnattingius
Equestrian Members: Lieutenant, Count Charles Gustaf Lewenhaupt; Lieutenant Claes König
Swimming Members: Erik Bergvall, Esquire; Gustaf Wretman, Esquire
Shooting Members: Colonel, Count Carl E. Taube; Lieutenant Eric Carlberg
International Jury: Colonel, Count Carl E. Taube (President/SWE); Captain Carl Silfverstolpe (SWE); Otto Herschmann (AUT); Jiří Rössler-Orovský (BOH); Captain Hans Henrik Bondo (DEN); Lieutenant Colonel J. F. Noël-Birch (GBR); Désiré Lauber (HUN); Captain Oscar Trygvessøn Klingenberg (NOR); Georges Duperron (RUS); Gustavus Town Kirby (USA)

Individual

A: 32; C: 10; D: 7–12 July; T: 0900 (7/7 — Shooting); 1100 (8/7 — Swimming); 0900–1700 (9–10/7 — Fencing); 1215 (11/7 — Riding); 1100 (12/7 — Running); F: Point-for-place scoring.

	Athlete	Nat	1	2	3	4	5	6	7	8	9	10	Total
1.	Gustaf "Gösta" Lilliehöök	SWE	20/192[11]	3	6:05.8	10	17	5	100	4	20:32.9	5	27
2.	Gösta Åsbrink	SWE	20/193	1	5:46.0	4	12	15	100	7	19:00.9	1	28
3.	Georg de Laval	SWE	20/192[12]	2	5:28.0	3	15	10	100	3	21:56.2	12	30
4.	Åke Grönhagen	SWE	18/158	18	5:49.6	5	24	1	100	1	21:41.6	10	35
5.	George Patton	USA	17/150	21	5:55.6	7	20	4	100	6	20:01.9	3	41
6.	Sidney Stranne	SWE	20/176[13]	11	6:00.8	9	21	3	100	8	21:45.1	11	42
7.	Karl Mannström	SWE	19/171	14	6:28.8	14	12	16	100	2	21:21.9	9	55
8.	Edmond Bernhardt	AUT	16/135	26	5:03.6	2	17	6	100	12	22:34.0	14	60
9.	Gustaf Wersäll	SWE	20/182	9	5:56.2	8	7	21	93	19	20:36.0	6	63[14]
10.	Douglas Godfree	GBR	18/166	16	5:54.0	6	12	17	100	11	22:03.8	13	63
11.	Ralph Clilverd	GBR	20/172	12	4:58.4	1	16	9	19	23	24:06.2	18	63
12.	Nils Hæggström	SWE	19/180	13	6:35.8	15	11	18	93	20	19:04.0	2	68
13.	Carl Paaske	NOR	18/147	19	6:49.2	16	13	14	100	14	21:19.8	8	71
14.	C. Patrik de Laval	SWE	20/188	5	6:54.4	17	13	13	98	17	24:19.6	20	72
15.	Oskar Wilkman	RUS	20/176[15]	10	8:11.6	23	7	20	100	5	2:57.8	15	73[16]
16.	Jean de Mas Latrie	FRA	19/161	15	10:03.0	27	23	2	100	10	24:17.4	19	73
17.	C. Gustaf Lewenhaupt	SWE	16/148	24	6:10.4	12	8	19	98	15	20:16.7	4	74

	Athlete	Nat	1	2	3	4	5	6	7	8	9	10	Total
18.	Hugh Durant	GBR	20/191	4	10:07.0	28	17	7	95	18	24:37.5	21	78
19.	Georges Brulé	FRA	12/100	30[17]	7:04.4	18	16	8	62	22	20:48.4	7	85[18]
20.	Arno Almqvist	RUS	17/143	23	6:06.0	11	3	27	100	13	23:16.1	16	90
21.	Weli Gunnar Hohenthal	RUS	18/159	17	7:38.8	19	5	25	98	16	23:28.6	17	94
22.	Kai Jølver	DEN	7/52	32	9:32.6	26	7	22	86	21	26:08.6	22	123
AC.	Johannes Blom Ussing	DEN	7/57	31	7:40.4	20	6	23	100	9	WD		
	Erik de Laval	SWE	20/185[19]	7	6:20.0	13	15	11	100	DQ			
	Henrik Norby	NOR	13/110	27	7:48.6	21	14	12	100	DQ			
	Vilhelm Laybourn	DEN	16/140	25	12:09.6	29	6	24	69[20]	DQ			
	Theodor Zeilau	DEN	13/93	28	7:59.4	22	4	26	DNF				
	Boris Nepokupnoy	RUS	20/185[21]	6	8:16.6	24	WD						
	Carl "Kalle" Aejemelaeus	RUS	17/151	20	8:59.8	25	WD						
	Eric Carlberg	SWE	20/185[22]	8	WD								
	Jetze Doorman	NED	17/149	22	WD								
	Carl Pauen	GER[23]	12/102	29	WD								

1	=	Shooting score (200 possible; targets hit/total score)
2	=	Point-for-place score for shooting
3	=	300 meter swim time
4	=	Point-for-place score for swimming
5	=	Fencing wins
6	=	Point-for-place score for fencing
7	=	Riding score (points)
8	=	Point-for-place score for riding
9	=	4,000 meter run time
10	=	Point-for-place score for running

Diplomas of Merit

Åke Grönhagen (SWE), George Patton (USA), Sidney Stranne (SWE), Karl Mannström (SWE), Edmond Bernhardt (AUT)

Shooting — Detailed Results

A: 32; C: 10; D: 7 July; T: 0900; F: Dueling (rapid-fire) pistols at 25 meters, with the target visible for each series of five shots for three seconds. Four series of five shots. In the event of ties, shoot-offs of four series of five shots.

			S1-H/P	S2-H/P	S3-H/P	S4-H/P	Totals
1.	Gösta Åsbrink	SWE	5/47	5/49	5/48	5/49	20/193
2.	Georg de Laval	SWE	5/50	5/47	5/47	5/48	20/192
3.	Gustaf "Gösta" Lilliehöök	SWE	5/48	5/47	5/49	5/48	20/192
4.	Hugh Durant	GBR	5/46	5/48	5/49	5/48	20/191
5.	C. Patrik de Laval	SWE	5/47	5/46	5/48	5/47	20/188
6.	Boris Nepokupnoy	RUS	5/47	5/45	5/47	5/46	20/185

		S1-H/P	S2-H/P	S3-H/P	S4-H/P	Totals
7. Erik de Laval	SWE	5/47	5/47	5/45	5/46	20/185
8. Eric Carlberg	SWE	5/44	5/47	5/48	5/46	20/185
9. E. Gustaf Wersäll	SWE	5/49	5/45	5/43	5/45	20/182
10. Oskar Wilkman	RUS	5/43	5/45	5/45	5/43	20/176
11. Sidney Stranne	SWE	5/42	5/46	5/42	5/46	20/176
12. Ralph Clilverd	GBR	5/46	5/41	5/44	5/41	20/172
13. Nils Hæggström	SWE	5/46	4/40	5/47	5/47	19/180
14. Karl Mannström	SWE	5/44	5/49	5/41	4/37	19/171
15. Jean de Mas Latrie	FRA	5/43	5/41	4/32	5/45	19/161
16. Douglas Godfree	GBR	5/49	4/36	5/45	4/36	18/166
17. Weli Gunnar Hohenthal	RUS	5/46	5/47	4/32	4/34	18/159
18. Åke Grönhagen	SWE	5/45	4/34	4/33	5/46	18/158
19. Carl Paaske	NOR	4/31	5/43	4/33	5/40	18/147
20. Carl "Kalle" Aejemelaeus	RUS	5/47	4/33	5/45	3/26	17/151
21. George Patton	USA	5/45	3/30	4/34	5/41	17/150
22. Jetze Doorman	NED	4/34	4/36	5/43	4/36	17/149
23. Arno Almqvist	RUS	3/23	5/41	4/36	5/43	17/143
24. C. Gustaf Lewenhaupt	SWE	3/28	4/35	5/45	4/40	16/148
25. Vilhelm Laybourn	DEN	3/25	4/36	5/44	4/35	16/140
26. I. Edmond Bernhardt	AUT	5/39	5/45	3/27	3/24	16/135
27. Henrik Norby	NOR	4/30	4/38	3/23	2/19	13/110
28. Theodor Zeilau	DEN	5/39	3/21	2/16	3/17	13/93
29. Carl Pauen	GER	4/39	2/15	3/22	3/26	12/102
30. Georges Brulé	FRA	2/16	3/27	3/23	4/34	12/100
31. Johannes Blom Ussing	DEN	0/0	2/17	3/24	2/16	7/57
32. Kai Jølver	DEN	2/17	0/0	3/20	2/15	7/52

Shoot-Offs

		S1-H/P	S2-H/P	S3-H/P	S4-H/P	Totals
2. Georg de Laval	SWE	5/46	5/48	5/47	5/47	20/188
3. Gustaf "Gösta" Lilliehöök	SWE	5/45	5/48	5/45	5/45	20/183
6. Boris Nepokupnoy	RUS	5/46	5/48	5/47	5/50	20/191
7. Erik de Laval	SWE	5/49	5/49	5/46	5/45	20/189
8. Eric Carlberg	SWE	5/46	5/46	5/47	5/46	20/185
10. Oskar Wilkman	RUS	4/37	4/37	5/44	5/47	18/165
11. Sidney Stranne	SWE	4/33	5/45	5/45	3/27	17/150

S1-H/P = Series One — Hits/Points
S2-H/P = Series Two — Hits/Points
S3-H/P = Series Three — Hits/Points
S4-H/P = Series Four — Hits/Points

Swimming — Detailed Results

A: 29; C: 8; D: 8 July; T: 1100; F: 300 meter freestyle. No swim-off for ties, both competitors being given equal points.

Heat One A: 5; C: 4.

			Time	Place
1.	Sidney Stranne	SWE	6:00.8	9th
2.	Gustaf "Gösta" Lilliehöök	SWE	6:05.8	10th
3.	Carl Paaske	NOR	6:49.2	16th
4.	Theodor Zeilau	DEN	7:59.4	22nd
5.	Carl "Kalle" Aejemelaeus	RUS	8:59.8	25th

Heat Two A: 2; C: 2.

			Time	Place
1.	Gösta Åsbrink	SWE	5:46.0	4th
2.	Weli Gunnar Hohenthal	RUS	7:38.8	19th

Heat Three A: 4; C: 4.

			Time	Place
1.	Georg de Laval	SWE	5:28.0	3rd
2.	Henrik Norby	NOR	7:48.6	21st
3.	Jean de Mas Latrie	FRA	10:03.0	27th
4.	Hugh Durant	GBR	10:07.0	28th

Heat Four A: 4; C: 3.

			Time	Place
1.	Ralph Clilverd	GBR	4:58.4	1st
2.	E. Gustaf Wersäll	SWE	5:56.2	8th
3.	Arno Almqvist	RUS	6:06.0	11th
4.	Erik de Laval	SWE	6:20.0	13th

Heat Five A: 5; C: 4.

			Time	Place
1.	Åke Grönhagen	SWE	5:49.6	5th
2.	George Patton	USA	5:55.6	7th
3.	Karl Mannström	SWE	6:28.8	14th
4.	Oskar Wilkman	RUS	8:11.6	23rd
5.	Vilhelm Laybourn	DEN	12:09.4	29th

Heat Six A: 5; C: 4.

			Time	Place
1.	I. Edmond Bernhardt	AUT	5:03.6	2nd
2.	C. Gustaf Lewenhaupt	SWE	6:10.4	12th
3.	C. Patrik de Laval	SWE	6:54.4	17th
4.	Georges Brulé	FRA	7:04.4	18th
5.	Boris Nepokupnoy	RUS	8:16.6	24th

Heat Seven A: 4; C: 3.

			Time	Place
1.	Douglas Godfree	GBR	5:54.0	6th
2.	Nils Hæggström	SWE	6:35.8	15th

		Time	Place
3. Johannes Ussing	DEN	7:40.4	20th
4. Kai Jølver	DEN	9:32.6	26th

24

Fencing — Detailed Results

A: 27; C: 8; D: 9–10 July; T: 0900–1700 (both days); F: Épée, round robin tournament, best of five hits in each match. Ties decided by number of hits received. If still tied, a one-hit rematch was held.

25

		Won	Hits Against
1. Åke Grönhagen	SWE	24	28
2. Jean de Mas Latrie	FRA	23	34
3. Sidney Stranne	SWE	21	36
4. George Patton	USA	20	44
5. Gustaf "Gösta" Lilliehöök	SWE	17	39
6. I. Edmond Bernhardt	AUT	17	45
7. Hugh Durant	GBR	17	46
8. Georges Brulé	FRA	16	43
9. Ralph Clilverd	GBR	16	46
10. Georg de Laval	SWE	15	44
11. Erik de Laval	SWE	15	49
12. Henrik Norby	NOR	14	53
13. C. Patrik de Laval	SWE	13	49
14. Carl Paaske	NOR	13	54
15. Gösta Åsbrink	SWE	12	50
16. Karl Mannström	SWE	12	52
17. Douglas Godfree	GBR	12	57
18. Nils Hæggström	SWE	11	59
19. C. Gustaf Lewenhaupt	SWE	8	57
20. Oskar Wilkman	RUS	7	64
21. E. Gustaf Wersäll	SWE	7	68
22. Kai Jølver	DEN	7	70
23. Johannes Ussing	DEN	6	68
24. Vilhelm Laybourn	DEN	6	70
25. Weli Gunnar Hohenthal	RUS	5	70
26. Theodor Zeilau	DEN	4	73
27. Arno Almqvist	RUS	3	74

26

Equestrian Riding — Detailed Results

A: 26; C: 8; D: 11 July; T: 1215; F: 5,000 meter cross-country course with 12 fixed obstacles. Time limit of 15:00. Two penalty points assessed for each five seconds over the time limit. Penalties given as follows: first refusal or break-out at an obstacle — two points; subsequent refusals or break-outs — five points; fall of horse — five points; fall of rider from horse — ten points. Each rider began with 100 points from which penalty points were deducted. In the event of ties, each athlete was given equal points. The course started at Barkarby and went via Hjulsta, Tenstad, and Spånga Church to finish at Rinkeby.[27]

	Own Horse[28]		Penalty	Time	Time Pen	Pts	Place[29]
1. Åke Grönhagen	X	SWE	0	9:04.4	0	100	1st
2. Karl Mannström	X	SWE	0	9:36.0	0	100	2nd
3. Georg de Laval	X	SWE	0	9:39.4	0	100	3rd
4. Gustaf "Gösta" Lilliehöök	X	SWE	0	9:45.5	0	100	4th
5. Oskar Wilkman	X	RUS	0	10:34.2	0	100	5th
6. George Patton		USA	0	10:42.0	0	100	6th
7. Gösta Åsbrink		SWE	0	11:12.4	0	100	7th
8. Sidney Stranne		SWE	0	11:14.5	0	100	8th
10. Johannes Ussing		DEN	0	11:21.0	0	100	9th
11. Jean de Mas Latrie	X	FRA	0	11:26.0	0	100	10th
12. Douglas Godfree		GBR	0	11:43.9	0	100	11th
13. I. Edmond Bernhardt		AUT	0	12:01.6	0	100	12th
14. Arno Almqvist		RUS	0	12:03.4	0	100	13th
15. Carl Paaske[30]	X	NOR	fault	12:33.0	0	100	14th
16. C. Gustaf Lewenhaupt	X	SWE	2	11:00.0	0	98	15th
17. Weli Gunnar Hohenthal	X	RUS	2	11:11.8	0	98	16th
18. C. Patrik de Laval	X	SWE	2	13:15.0	0	98	17th
18. Hugh Durant	X	GBR	5	10:00.4	0	95	18th
19. E. Gustaf Wersäll	X	SWE	7	9:44.0	0	93	19th
20. Nils Hæggström	X	SWE	7	13:26.0	0	93	20th
21. Kai Jølver		DEN	14	10:49.5	0	86	21st
22. Georges Brulé	X	FRA	38	14:44.6	0	62	22nd
23. Ralph Clilverd		GBR	61	15:46.6	20	19	23rd
AC. Erik de Laval	X	SWE	fault	9:59.4	0	100	DQ
Henrik Norby	X	NOR	fault	13:10.0	0	100	DQ
Vilhelm Laybourn		DEN	fault[31]	12:41.6	0	69[31]	DQ
Theodor Zeilau		DEN					DNF

Cross-Country Running — Final Placements

A: 22; C: 8; D: 12 July; T: 1100; F: 4,000 meter cross-country with the start and finish in the Olympic Stadium. The runners started at one-minute intervals.

1.	Gösta Åsbrink	SWE	19:00.9
2.	Nils Hæggström	SWE	19:04.0
3.	George Patton	USA	20:01.9
4.	C. Gustaf Lewenhaupt	SWE	20:16.7
5.	Gustaf "Gösta" Lilliehöök	SWE	20:32.9
6.	E. Gustaf Wersäll	SWE	20:36.0
7.	Georges Brulé	FRA	20:48.4
8.	Carl Paaske	NOR	21:19.8
9.	Karl Mannström	SWE	21:21.9
10.	Åke Grönhagen	SWE	21:41.6
11.	Sidney Stranne	SWE	21:45.1

12.	Georg de Laval	SWE	21:56.2
13.	Douglas Godfree	GBR	22:03.8
14.	I. Edmond Bernhardt	AUT	22:34.0
15.	Oskar Wilkman	RUS	22:57.8
16.	Arno Almqvist	RUS	23:16.1
17.	Weli Gunnar Hohenthal	RUS	23:28.6
18.	Ralph Clilverd	GBR	24:06.2
19.	Jean de Mas Latrie	FRA	24:17.4
20.	C. Patrik de Laval	SWE	24:19.6
21.	Hugh Durant	GBR	24:37.5
22.	Kai Jølver	DEN	26:08.6

32

NOTES

1. UIPMB Press Release, "Introduction to Modern Pentathlon," p.1.

2. Lyberg, p. 45.

3. Coubertin. *Mémoires Olympiques.* IOC 1979 reprinted edition, pp. 125–126.

4. Lyberg, p. 52.

5. UIPMB Press Release, "Introduction to Modern Pentathlon," p.1.

6. *Louisville Courier-Journal,* 7 July 1912.

7. This letter is contained in the Riksarkivet, the archives of the 1912 Olympics held at the Swedish National Library, the Kungliga Biblioteket.

8. *Revue Olympique,* July 1912.

9. Both Hellström's letter to Coubertin and Coubertin's reply (above) are found at the Riksarkivet. The underlines in Coubertin's letter are his, and are found in the original.

10. *Olympika,* 6: 99–114, 1997.

11. Shoot-off of tie at 192 points between Lilliehöök and G. de Laval: de Laval —188; Lilliehöök —183 (see below).

12. Shoot-off of tie at 192 points between Lilliehöök and G. de Laval: de Laval —188; Lilliehöök —183 (see below).

13. Shoot-off of tie at 176 points between Stranne and Wilkman: Wilkman —165; Stranne —150 (see below).

14. According to the rules as listed in 12OR, ties in total points were to be decided by time in the final event. OSVK lists Wersäll, Godfree, and Clilverd as equal ninth.

15. Shoot-off of tie at 176 points between Stranne and Wilkman: Wilkman —165. Stranne —150 (see below).

16. According to the rules as listed in 12OR, ties in total points were to be decided by time in the final event. OSVK lists both Wilkman and de Mas Latrie as equal 15th.

17. Brulé is listed in 12OR as 28th in shooting, but his scores (as noted below) definitely place him 30th. This changes his overall score from 83 to 85 points, but does not affect his final placement.

18. See previous footnote concerning Brulé's shooting score and placement.

19. Shoot-off of tie at 185 points between E. de Laval, Nepokupnoy, and E. Carlberg: Nepokupnoy —191; de Laval —189, Carlberg —185 (see below).

20. Laybourn is credited with 79 points in 12OR for the riding event. However, details of the event are available in 12OR and show that he had 31 penalty points, giving him correctly a score of 69. This did not change his placement in the riding event, however, and since he withdrew, had no effect on the final outcome.

21. Shoot-off of tie at 185 points between E. de Laval, Nepokupnoy, and E. Carlberg: Nepokupnoy —191; de Laval —189; Carlberg —185 (see below).

22. Shoot-off of tie at 185 points between E. de Laval, Nepokupnoy, and E. Carlberg: Nepokupnoy—191; de Laval—189; Carlberg—185 (see below).

23. A second German considered entering, in fact a prince. Carl Diem wrote, "Our two competitors were not first class, of course…. The German competitors gave in after the first discipline. Also nominated was the Prince Friedrich Karl von Preußen, who competed in equestrian events in Stockholm. He did not get permission to start in the modern pentathlon by the Prussian dynasty who was afraid that the modern pentathlon would be too difficult for the Prince." In Carl Diem, *Die olympischen Spiele 1912*. Berlin: Bürger, 1912. In fact, the prince never actually entered.

24. Carl Pauen (GER), Eric Carlberg (SWE), and Jetze Doorman (NED) did not start in the swimming.

25. Originally, we listed wins and losses, but a problem arose. The number of wins recorded and losses recorded did not match. Now in épée fencing in 1912, a double-hit match, in which both fencers were scored as having lost, was a possibilty. But the modern pentathlon fencing was the first to record three hits. It is still a possibility that some matches were recorded as draws, with a score of 3–3, and that both fencers were accorded a loss for that match. This still does not solve the problem.

The 12OR lists a table on pp. 652–653 for the modern pentathlon fencing results, which is effectively a spreadsheet. By looking carefully at this spreadsheet, we note that the number of wins appears to be correct for all fencers on first inspection, so no change to the fencing results, or the overall results, is necessary. But there are 18 matches that do not make much sense in the scoring. Twelve of these may be explained as "double-hit matches," or a score of 3–3. But the other six still are difficult to explain. Two of these are listed in 12OR (pp. 652–653) as 0–0. Perhaps they did not take place, but that is difficult to fathom, as they are recorded as wins for the fencers. Further, there are still four matches that make no sense at all, in which touches are recorded, but neither fencer appears to have had three hits against.

Unfortunately, there is no checking the match results, as detailed numbers do not exist, and only 12OR gives the results of all the matches. The matches in question are as follows: double-hit matches: Jølver vs. P. de Laval [3–3], Jølver vs. Paaske [3–3], Jølver vs. Durant [3–3], Jølver vs. Åsbrink [3–3], Grönhagen vs. P. de Laval [3–3], Almqvist vs. Paaske [3–3], Almqvist vs. Mannström [3–3], de Mas Latrie vs. Stranne [3–3], G. de Laval vs. Zeilau [3–3], E. de Laval vs. Lilliehöök [3–3], Zeilau vs. Wersäll [3–3], Mannström vs. Wersäll [3–3]. Matches That Possibly Did Not Take Place: Brulé vs. P. de Laval [0–0], Grönhagen vs. Mannström [0–0], Unexplainable Results: Brulé vs. Paaske [1–1], Grönhagen vs. de Mas Latrie [1–1], Grönhagen vs. Durant [1–0], and Grönhagen vs. Åsbrink [1–1].

26. Boris Nepokupnoy (RUS) and Carl "Kalle" Aejemelaeus (RUS) did not start in the fencing.

27. In 1912, this was wilderness territory, but it is now highly populated, and Hjulsta, Tensta, and Rinkeby are stations of the Stockholm underground system.

28. X indicates the rider rode his own horse. The other riders used horses provided by the organizing committee.

29. Place refers to the correct placement in the riding event for all 26 competitors. This takes into account the three riders who finished the course but then withdrew prior to the running event. Their scores and placements were disregarded in figuring the final riding placements.

30. Carl Paaske (NOR), Erik de Laval (SWE), Henrik Norby (NOR) and Vilhelm Laybourn (DEN) were disqualified for riding on the wrong side of a flag (fault). Paaske's disqualification was lifted, for unknown reasons, and he was allowed to continue in the event.

31. Laybourn is credited with 79 points in 12OR for the riding event. However, details of the event are available in 12OR and show that he had 31 penalty points, giving him correctly a score of 69. This did not change his placement in the riding event, however, and since he withdrew, it had no effect on the final outcome.

32. Johannes Ussing (DEN) did not start in this section due to an injury.

Rowing & Sculling

The rowing events at Stockholm were conducted at Djurgårdsbrunnsviken. The course allowed two boats to race concurrently with a straighaway of 1,200 meters and then a very slight starboard turn, followed later by a very slight port turn.

The program was decided in early 1910 and approved by the IOC at its session in Budapest in 1911. After the IOC session, the Swedish rowing committee was approached about including events for coxless fours, double sculls, and coxed pairs. But with the course encompassing two turns, the committee felt that these boats would be too difficult to handle. Each nation could enter two boats per event. The inrigger coxed fours event was contested at Stockholm — for the only time in Olympic history.

There were no bronze medals awarded in rowing at the 1912 Olympic Games. The rowing course allowed only two boats at a time, so the finals consisted of only two crews, who won the gold and silver medals. The losing semifinalists were not awarded bronze medals, but they were awarded Diplomas of Merit. In both the inrigger coxed fours and the coxed eights, there was only one losing semifinalist.

Site:	Start at Lido in Djurgårdsbrunnsviken and finish opposite Torstensonsgåtan in Nybroviken. Provisional stands built at the finish on the embankment of Strandvägen.
Dates:	17–19 July
Events:	4 [4 Men — 0 Women]
Competitors:	184 [184 Men — 0 Women]
Nations:	14 [14 Men — 0 Women]

	Competitors	Gold	Silver	Bronze	Medals	Semis
Australasia	10	–	–	–	–	–
Austria	6	–	–	–	–	–
Belgium	6	–	1	–	1	–
Bohemia	1	–	–	–	–	–
Canada	10	–	–	–	–	1
Denmark	15	1	–	–	1	1

Finland	6	–	–	–	–	–
France	17	–	–	–	–	–
Germany	25	1	–	–	1	1
Great Britain	24	2	2	–	4	–
Hungary	11	–	–	–	–	–
Norway	24	–	–	–	–	2
Russia	1	–	–	–	–	1
Sweden	28	–	1	–	1	–
Totals	184	4	4	–	8	6
Nations	14	3	3	–	5	5

Committee for Rowing

Honorary President: Fredrik Lowenädler
President: Nils Ljunggren, Esquire
Secretary: Ulrich Salchow, Esquire
Treasurer: Per O. S. Fjästad, Esquire
Boat-House Chief: Walfrid Clemens
Members: Otto Andersson; J. Magnusson; Victor Zetterlund; K. K. Stamsö
International Jury: Fredrik Löwenadler (President/SWE); Ulrich Salchow, Esquire (SWE); Q. L. Deloitte (AUS); L. Annoot (BEL); Joseph G. Wright (CAN); Henrik Schack Køster (DEN); E. Albert Glandaz (FRA); Dr. Oskar Ruperti (GER); Theodore Andrea Cook (GBR); Consul Einar Wettre (NOR)

Single Sculls

A: 13; C: 11; D: 17–19 July; F: 2,000 meters.

Other than Cecil McVilly of Australia and Everard Butler of Canada, all the scullers were European. Butler was the top North American sculler, being superior to any of the United States men of the time. He had won the 1911 and 1912 championship of the National Association of Amateur Oarsmen in the single sculls.

The top European sculler was likely William Kinnear, who had won the Diamond Challenge Sculls at Henley in 1910 and 1911. But Kinnear lost at Henley early in 1912 to A. A. Stuart, who had also won the same event in 1909. The European championships were held later in 1912 and would be won by Belgium's Polydore Veirman.

Kinnear, Butler, and Veirman made it through to the semifinals. The biggest early casualty was McVilly, who was disqualified in the first round for colliding with Martin Stahnke's (GER) boat. In the semifinals, Veirman defeated Hugo Maksimilian Kusick of Russia. The other semi was closely fought with Kinnear holding off Butler by one length. This set up a final between Kinnear and Veirman, probably the two favorites. In the final, Veirman led from the start, and was up by half a length at 500 meters. Kinnear pulled even at the halfway mark, though, and inched away to win by one length.

Final A: 2; C: 2; D: 19 July; T: 1700.

1.	William Kinnear	GBR	7:47.3[1]*
2.	Polydore Veirman	BEL	7:56[2]

    Semifinals A: 4; C: 4; D: 19 July.

    Heat One A: 2; C: 2; T: 1230.

1.	Polydore Veirman	BEL	7:41.0	Q
2.	Hugo Maksimilian Kusick	RUS	at 1½ lengths	

    Heat Two A: 2; C: 2; T: 1300.

1.	William Kinnear	GBR	7:37.0[3]	Q
2.	Everard Butler[4]	CAN	7:41.0[5]	

    Diploma of Merit

Everard Butler (CAN)[6]

    Quarterfinals A: 7; C: 7; D: 18 July.

    Heat One A: 2; C: 2; T: 1100.

1.	József Mészáros	HUN	8:23[7]
AC.	Polydore Veirman	BEL	DNF

    Heat One Rerace A: 2; C: 2; T: 1930.

1.	Polydore Veirman	BEL	7:52	Q [8]
2.	József Mészáros	HUN	at 3 lengths[9]	

    Heat Two[10] A: 1; C: 1; T: 1120.

1.	Everard Butler	CAN	7:39.9[11]	Q
[12]				

    Heat Three[13] A: 2; C: 2; T: 1200.

1.	William Kinnear	GBR	7:49.9[14]	Q
2.	Martin Stahnke	GER	7:58.8[15]	

    Heat Four[16] A: 2; C: 2; T: 1210.

1.	Hugo Maksimilian Kusick	RUS	7:45.2[17]	Q
2.	Károly Levitzky[18]	HUN	a 2 lengths[19]	

    Round One A: 13; C: 11; D: 17–18 July.

    Heat One A: 2; C: 2; D: 17 July; T: 1500.

1.	Hugo Maksimilian Kusick	RUS	7:46.0	Q[20]
2.	Alfred Heinrich	AUT	2 lengths[21]	

Heat One A: 2; C: 2; D: 18 July; T: 1140.

1.	Hugo Maksimilian Kusick	RUS	7:45.2[22]	Q[23]
AC.	Alfred Heinrich	AUT	DQ[24]	

Heat Two A: 2; C: 2; D: 17 July; T: 1520.

1.	Martin Stahnke	GER	8:28.8[25]	Q[26]
AC.	Cecil McVilly	AUS	DQ [8:11][27]	

Heat Three[28] A: 2; C: 2; D: 17 July; T: 1540.

1.	Everard Butler	CAN	7:55.6[29]	Q
2.	Axel Matias Haglund	FIN	at 8 lengths[30]	

Heat Four[31] A: 2; C: 2; D: 17 July; T: 1600.

1.	William Kinnear	GBR	7:44	Q
2.	Kurt Hoffmann	GER	at 1½ lengths[32]	

Heat Five[33] A: 1; C: 1; D: 17 July; T: 1620.

1.	József Mészáros [34]	HUN	wo [8:29]	Q

Heat Six[35] A: 2; C: 2; D: 17 July; T: 1640.

1.	Mikael Simonsen	DEN	8:14.0	Q
AC.	Jaroslav Šourek	BOH	DNF[36]	

Heat Seven[37] A: 1; C: 1; D: 17 July; T: 1700.

1.	Károly Levitzky [39]	HUN	8:04[38]	Q

Heat Eight A: 1; C: 1; D: 17 July; T: 1720.

1.	Polydore Veirman [41]	BEL	7:59.2[40]	Q

Coxed Fours, Outriggers

A: 55; C: 9; D: 17–19 July; F: 2,000 meters.

In the Stewards' Challenge Cup at the Henley Regatta, the Thames Rowing Club had won in 1909 and 1911. The European Championships had been won in 1909 and 1910 by crews from Italy, and in 1911 and 1912 by Switzerland. However, neither Italy nor Switzerland entered the Olympic event in 1912.

This left the field to the British crew from the Thames Rowing Club and the somewhat unknown German crew from the Ludwigshafener Ruderverein. The Thames crew barely survived the semifinals. Germany's Ludwigshafener crew was not pressed in getting to the final where they defeated the British by two lengths.

Final A: 10; C: 2; D: 19 July; T: 1730.

1. Germany [Ludwigshafener Ruderverein]   6:59.4[42]
    (Albert Arnheiter [bow], Hermann Wilker [2], Rudolf Fickeisen [3], Otto Fickeisen [stroke], Otto Maier [cox])

2. Great Britain [Thames Rowing Club]   at 2 lengths[43]
    (Julius Beresford [bow], Karl Vernon [2], Charles Rought [3], Bruce Logan [stroke], Geoffrey Carr [cox])

Semifinals A: 20; C: 4; D: 19 July.

Heat One A: 10; C: 2; T: 1330.

1. Germany [Ludwigshafener Ruderverein]   6:59   Q
    (Albert Arnheiter [bow], Hermann Wilker [2], Rudolf Fickeisen [3], Otto Fickeisen [stroke], Otto Maier [cox])

2. Denmark [Polyteknisk Roklub]   at 2½ lengths[44]
    (Erik Bisgaard, Rasmus Frandsen, Mikael Simonsen, Poul Thymann, Ejgil Clemmensen [cox])

Heat Two A: 10; C: 2; T: 1400.

1. Great Britain [Thames Rowing Club]   7:04.4[45]   Q
    (Julius Beresford [bow], Karl Vernon [2], Charles Rought [3], Bruce Logan [stroke], Geoffrey Carr [cox])

2. Norway [Kristiania Roklub][46]   7:04.8[47]
    (Henry Larsen [bow], Mathias Torstensen [2], Theodor "Thea" Klem [3], Haakon Tønsager [stroke], Ejnar Tønsager [cox])

Diplomas of Merit

Denmark [Polyteknisk Roklub] (Erik Bisgaard, Rasmus Frandsen, Mikael Simonsen, Poul Thymann, Ejgil Clemmensen)
Norway [Kristiania Roklub] (Henry Larsen, Mathias Torstensen, Theodor "Thea" Klem, Haakon Tønsager, Ejnar Tønsager)

Quarterfinals A: 35; C: 6; D: 18 July.

Heat One A: 10; C: 2; T: 1220.

1. Denmark [Polyteknisk Roklub]   7:09   Q
    (Erik Bisgaard, Rasmus Frandsen, Mikael Simonsen, Poul Thymann, Ejgil Clemmensen [cox])

2. Finland [Helsingfors R. K.]   7:12.5[48]
    (Johan Valdemar Nyholm [bow], Oskar Edvin Forsman [2], Edvin Lönnberg [3], Emil Nylund [stroke], Valdemar Henriksson [cox])

Heat Two A: 10; C: 2; T: 1240.

1. Great Britain [Thames Rowing Club]   7:145[49]   Q
    (Julius Beresford [bow], Karl Vernon [2], Charles Rought [3], Bruce Logan [stroke], Geoffrey Carr [cox])

2. Norway [Studenternes Roklub]   at 1½ lengths[50]
   (Øivin Davidsen, Leif Rode, Theodor "Tommy" Schjøth, Olaf Dahll [stroke], Einar Eriksen [cox])

   Heat Three A: 10; C: 2; T: 1300.

1. Norway [Kristiania Roklub]   7:05   Q
   (Henry Larsen [bow], Mathias Torstensen [2], Theodor "Thea" Klem [3], Haakon Tønsager [stroke], Ejnar Tønsager [cox])

2. Belgium [Royal Club Nautique de Gand]   at 3 lengths[51]
   (Guillaume Visser [bow], Georges Van den Bossche [2], Edmond Van Waes [3], Georges
   Willems [stroke], Leonard Nuytens [cox])

   Heat Four A: 5; C: 1; T: 1320.

1. Germany [Ludwigshafener Ruderverein]   7:14.4[52]   Q
   (Albert Arnheiter [bow], Hermann Wilker [2], Rudolf Fickeisen [3], Otto Fickeisen
   [stroke], Otto Maier [cox])

   Round One A: 55; C: 9; D: 17 July.

   Heat One A: 5; C: 1; T: 1820.

1. Denmark [Polyteknisk Roklub]   7:20   Q
   (Erik Bisgaard, Rasmus Frandsen, Mikael Simonsen, Poul Thymann, Ejgil Clemmensen
   [cox])

   Heat Two[53] A: 10; C: 2; T: 1840.

1. Finland [Helsingfors R. K.]   7:18.2[54]   Q
   (Johan Valdemar Nyholm [bow], Oskar Edvin Forsman [2], Edvin Lönnberg [3], Emil
   Nylund [4], Valdemar Henriksson [cox])

2. France [Société Nautique de Bayonne]   at 1½ lengths[55]
   (André Mirambeau, Louis Thomaturgé, René Saintongey, Pierre Allibert [stroke],
   François Elichagaray [cox])

   Heat Three[56] A: 10; C: 2; T: 1900.

1. Norway [Kristiania Roklub]   7:15   Q
   (Henry Larsen [bow], Mathias Torstensen [2], Theodor "Thea" Klem [3], Haakon Tønsager [stroke], Ejnar Tønsager [cox])

AC. Austria [Ruderverein Germania, Leitmeritz] DNF[57]
    (Fritz Kromholz [bow], Richard Mayer [2], Hugo Cuzna [3], Georg Kröder [stroke],
    Emil Jand [cox])

   Heat Four A: 5; C: 1; T: 1920.

1. Norway [Studenternes Roklub]   7:27.4[58]   Q
   (Øivin Davidsen, Leif Rode, Theodor "Tommy" Schjøth, Olaf Dahll [stroke], Einar Eriksen [cox])
[59]

Heat Five[60] A: 10; C: 2; T: 1940.

1. Belgium [Royal Club Nautique de Gand]   7:15   Q
   (Guillaume Visser [bow], Georges Van den Bossche [2], Edmond Van Waes [3], Georges
   Willems [stroke], Leonard Nuytens [cox])

2. Denmark [København Roklubb][61]   at 1 length[62]
   (M. Hans Jørgensen, Knud Gøtke, Johan Praem, Theodor Eyrich, Silva Smedberg [cox])

   Heat Six[63] A: 10; C: 2; T: 2000.

1. Germany [Ludwigshafener Ruderverein]   7:06.6[64]   Q
   (Albert Arnheiter [bow], Hermann Wilker [2], Rudolf Fickeisen [3], Otto Fickeisen
   [stroke], Otto Maier [cox])

2. Sweden [Vaxholm Roddklubb]   at 1½ lengths[65]
   (John Lager, Axel Eriksson, Ernst Wetterstrand, Gunnar Lager [stroke], Karl Sundholm
   [cox])

   Heat Seven A: 5; C: 1; T: 2020.

1. Great Britain [Thames Rowing Club]   7:27.0   Q
   (Julius Beresford [bow], Karl Vernon [2], Charles Rought [3], Bruce Logan [stroke],
   Geoffrey Carr [cox])
   [66]

Coxed Fours, Inriggers

A: 30; C: 4; D: 17–18 July; F: 2,000 meters.

The inrigger coxed fours event has only been contested once at the Olympics — in 1912.
Inriggers is a rowing format only popular in the Nordic countries as is evidenced by the entry
list. Two Swedish, two Norwegian, and one Danish crew were joined by a French boat. The
French boat was trounced in round one by one of the Norwegian teams.

   Final A: 10; C: 2; D: 18 July; T: 1910.

1. Denmark [Nykjøbings paa Falster Roklub]   7:44.6[67]
   (Ejler Allert, Jørgen Hansen, Carl Møller, Carl Pedersen, Poul Hartmann [cox])

2. Sweden [Roddklubben af 1912]   7:56.9[68]
   (Ture Rosvall, William Bruhn-Möller, Conrad Brunkman, Herman Dahlbäck [stroke],
   Wilhelm "Willie" Wilkens [cox])

   Semifinals A: 15; C: 3; D: 17 July.
   Heat One A: 10; C: 2; T: 1740.

1. Sweden [Roddklubben af 1912]   7:39.2[69]   Q
   (Ture Rosvall, William Bruhn-Möller, Conrad Brunkman, Herman Dahlbäck [stroke],
   Wilhelm "Willie" Wilkens [cox])

2. Norway [Ormsund Roklub][70]   at ¾ length[71]
   (Claus Høyer, Reidar Holter, Magnus Herseth, Frithjof Olstad [stroke], Olav Bjørnstad
   [cox])

Heat Two A: 5; C: 1; T: 1800.

1. Denmark [Nykjøbings paa Falster Roklub]   7:59.5[72]   Q
    (Ejler Allert, Jørgen Hansen, Carl Møller, Carl Pedersen, Poul Hartmann [cox])

Round One A: 30; C: 4; D: 17 July.

Heat One A: 10; C: 2; T: 1100.

1. Sweden [Roddklubben af 1912]   7:51.5[73]   Q
    (Ture Rosvall, William Bruhn-Möller, Conrad Brunkman, Herman Dahlbäck [stroke],
    Wilhelm "Willie" Wilkens [cox])

2. Norway [Kristiania Roklub]   at 2 lengths[74]
    (Gunnar Grantz [bow], Olaf Solberg [2], Gustav Hæhre [3], O. Hannibal Fegth [stroke],
    John Bjørnstad [cox])

Heat Two A: 10; C: 2; T: 1120.

1. Denmark [Nykjøbings paa Falster Roklub]   7:52.0   Q
    (Ejler Allert, Jørgen Hansen, Carl Møller, Carl Pedersen, Poul Hartmann [cox])

2. Sweden [Göteborgs Roddförening]   at 1½ lengths[75]
    (Tage Johnson, Axel Johansson, Axel Gabrielsson, Charles Gabrielsson [stroke], Wilhelm
    Brandes [cox])

Heat Three A: 10; C: 2; T: 1140.

1. Norway [Ormsund Roklub]   8:03.0   Q
    (Claus Høyer, Reidar Holter, Magnus Herseth, Frithjof Olstad [stroke], Olav Bjørnstad
    [cox])

2. France [Société Nautique de Bayonne]   at 5 lengths[76]
    (Charles Garnier, Alphonse Meignant, Auguste Richard, Gabriel Poix, François Elicha-
    garay [cox])

Coxed Eights

A: 99; C: 8[77]; D: 17–19 July; F: 2,000 meters.

The last four European Championships had been won by France, Belgium, Italy, and
Switzerland. The Grand Challenge Cup at the Henley Regatta had been won in 1910 and 1911
by a Magdalen College (Oxford) crew. In 1909 that title had been won by the Belgian crew from
the Royal Club Nautique de Gand. Unfortunately the Gand crew was not at Stockholm nor
was Magdalen College. The British were represented by the Leander Club and New College
(Oxford). Canada did send a Toronto Argonauts eight, which had won the 1911 championships
of the National Association of Amateur Oarsmen (United States' championship).

In a bad draw, Leander and the Argonauts were drawn against each other in round one,
with Leander narrowly defeating the Toronto crew. Leander also survived close races against
Australasia in the quarters (by less than a boat length) and Germany in the semis. On the other
hand, the New College crew had a relatively easy time of it, winning the first two rounds hand-
ily against Norway and Sweden, and receiving a bye in the semifinals.

The final was closely fought. The two boats were even for 1,000 meters, when Leander pulled ahead before the series of turns. They were never caught, eventually winning by about one length. Leander was awarded possession of the challenge trophy for the coxed eights event, which had been donated in 1908 by the Italian Count and IOC member, Eugenio Brunetta d'Usseaux.

Final A: 18; C: 1; D: 19 July; T: 1800.

1.   Great Britain [Leander Club]   6:15.7[78]
     (Edgar Burgess [bow], Sidney Swann [2], Leslie Wormwald [3], Ewart Horsfall [4], James
        Gillan [5], Arthur Garton [6], Alister Kirby [7], Philip Fleming [stroke], Henry Wells
        [cox])

2.   Great Britain [New College, Oxford]   6:19.2[79]
     (William Fison [bow], William Parker [2], Thomas Gillespie [3], Beaufort Burdekin [4],
        Frederick Pitman [5], Arthur Wiggins [6], Charles Littlejohn [7], Robert Bourne
        [stroke], John Walker [cox])

Semifinals A: 27; C: 2; D: 19 July.

Heat One A: 9; C: 1; T: 1130.

1.   Great Britain [New College, Oxford]   7:22.4[80]   Q
     (William Fison [bow], William Parker [2], Thomas Gillespie [3], Beaufort Burdekin [4],
        Frederick Pitman [5], Arthur Wiggins [6], Charles Littlejohn [7], Robert Bourne
        [stroke], John Walker [cox])

Heat Two A: 18; C: 2; T: 1200.

1.   Great Britain [Leander Club]   6:16.2[81]   Q
     (Edgar Burgess [bow], Sidney Swann [2], Leslie Wormwald [3], Ewart Horsfall [4], James
        Gillan [5], Arthur Garton [6], Alister Kirby [7], Philip Fleming [stroke], Henry Wells
        [cox])

2.   Germany [Berliner Ruderverein von 1876][82]   6:18.6[83]
     (Otto Liebing, Max Bröske, Max Vetter, Willi Bartholomae, Fritz Bartholomae, Werner
        Dehn, Rudolf Reichelt, Hans Matthiae, Kurt Runge [cox])

Quarterfinals A: 54; C: 4; D: 18 July.

Heat One A: 18; C: 2; T: 1540.

1.   Great Britain [New College, Oxford]   6:19.0   Q
     (William Fison [bow], William Parker [2], Thomas Gillespie [3], Beaufort Burdekin [4],
        Frederick Pitman [5], Arthur Wiggins [6], Charles Littlejohn [7], Robert Bourne
        [stroke], John Walker [cox])

2.   Sweden [Roddklubben af 1912]   at 1 length[84]
     (Gustaf Brunkman, Per Mattson, Sebastian Tamm, Schering "Ted" Wachtmeister, Con-
        rad Brunkman, William Bruhn-Möller, Ture Rosvall, Herman Dahlbäck [stroke],
        Wilhelm "Willie" Wilkens [cox])

Heat Two A: 18; C: 1; T: 1600.

1. Germany [Berliner Ruderverein von 1876]   6:22.2[85]   Q
   (Otto Liebing, Max Bröske, Max Vetter, Willi Bartholomae, Fritz Bartholomae, Werner Dehn, Rudolf Reichelt, Hans Matthiae, Kurt Runge [cox])

2. Germany [Sport Borrussia, Berlin]   at 2 lengths[86]
   (Carl Eichhorn, Ludwig Weihnacht, Richard Friesicke, Andreas Wegener, Fritz Eggebrecht, Heinrich Landrock, Egbert Reinsfeld, Gottfried Gelfort, Otto Charlet [cox])

Heat Three A: 18; C: 2; T: 1620.

1. Great Britain [Leander Club]   6:10.2[87]   Q
   (Edgar Burgess [bow], Sidney Swann [2], Leslie Wormwald [3], Ewart Horsfall [4], James Gillan [5], Arthur Garton [6], Alister Kirby [7], Philip Fleming [stroke], Henry Wells [cox])

2. Australasia [Sydney Rowing Club]   at ½ length[88]
   (John Ryrie [bow], Simon Fraser [2], Hugh Ward [3], Thomas Parker [4], Henry Hauenstein [5], Sydney Middleton [6], Harry Ross-Boden [7], Roger Fitzhardinge [stroke], Robert Waley [cox])

Round One A: 99; C: 8; D: 17 July.

Heat One A: 18; C: 2; T: 1200.

1. Germany [Sport Borrussia, Berlin]   6:45   Q
   (Carl Eichhorn, Ludwig Weihnacht, Richard Friesicke, Andreas Wegener, Fritz Eggebrecht, Heinrich Landrock, Egbert Reinsfeld, Gottfried Gelfort [stroke], Otto Charlet [cox])

2. France [Société Nautique de Bayonne]   at 1¼ lengths[89]
   (Jean Arné, Gabriel St. Laurent, Marius Lenjeune, Louis Lafitte, Jean Elichagaray, Joseph Campot, Etienne Lesbats, Pierre Alvarez [stroke], François Elichagaray [cox])

Heat Two A: 18; C: 2; T: 1220.

1. Australasia [Sydney Rowing Club]   6:57.0   Q
   (John Ryrie [bow], Simon Fraser [2], Hugh Ward [3], Thomas Parker [4], Henry Hauenstein [5], Sydney Middleton [6], Harry Ross-Boden [7], Roger Fitzhardinge [stroke], Robert Waley [cox])

2. Sweden [Göteborgs Roddklubb]   at 2 lengths[90]
   (Einar Amundén, Ragnar Bergstedt, Gustaf Broberg, Simon Ericsson, Ivar Rydberg, Anders Almqvist, Arvid Svendel, Leif Sörvik, Gillis Ahlberg [cox])

Heat Three A: 18; C: 2; T: 1240.

1. Germany [Berliner Ruderverein]   6:32[91]   Q
   (Otto Liebing, Max Bröske, Max Vetter, Willi Bartholomae, Fritz Bartholomae, Werner Dehn, Rudolf Reichelt, Hans Matthiae [stroke], Kurt Runge [cox])

2. Hungary [Hungarian Evezős Egylet]   at 2½–3 lengths[92]
   (István Szebeny [bow], Artúr Baján [2], Miltiades Manno [3], István Jenei [4], Lajos Gráf [5], Miklós Szebeny [6], Antal Szebeny [7], Georg Szebeny [stroke], Kálmán Vasko [cox])

Heat Four A: 18; C: 2; T: 1300.

1. Great Britain [New College, Oxford]   6:42.5[93]   Q
    (William Fison [bow], William Parker [2], Thomas Gillespie [3], Beaufort Burdekin [4], Frederick Pitman [5], Arthur Wiggins [6], Charles Littlejohn [7], Robert Bourne [stroke], John Walker [cox])

2. Norway [Kristiania Roklub]   at 1½ lengths[94]
    (Einar Sommerfeldt, Thomas Høie, Harald Herolfson, Olaf Solberg, Gustav Hæhre, O. Hannibal Fegth, Gunnar Grantz, Otto Theodor Krohg [stroke], John Bjørnstad [cox])

Heat Five A: 18; C: 2; T: 1320.

1. Great Britain [Leander Club]   6:22.2[95]   Q
    (Edgar Burgess [bow], Sidney Swann [2], Leslie Wormwald [3], Ewart Horsfall [4], James Gillan [5], Arthur Garton [6], Alister Kirby [7], Philip Fleming [stroke], Henry Wells [cox])

2. Canada [Toronto Argonauts]   at ½ + length[96]
    (Charles Riddy [bow], Phil Boyd [2], Albert Kent [3], William Murphy [4], Alex Sinclair [5], Becher Gale [6], Richard Gregory [7], Geoffrey Taylor [stroke], Winslow McCleary [cox])

Heat Six A: 9; C: 1; T: 1340.

1. Sweden [Roddklubben af 1912]   7:05.2[97]   Q
    (Gustaf Brunkman, Per Mattson, Sebastian Tamm, Schering "Ted" Wachtmeister, Conrad Brunkman, William Bruhn-Möller, Ture Rosvall, Herman Dahlbäck [stroke], Wilhelm "Willie" Wilkens [cox])

Diplomas of Merit[98]

Canada [Toronto Argonauts] (Charles Riddy, Phil Boyd, Albert Kent, William Murphy, Alex Sinclair, Becher Gale, Richard Gregory, Geoffrey Taylor, Winslow McCleary)

Australasia [Sydney Rowing Club] (John Ryrie, Simon Fraser, Hugh Ward, Thomas Parker, Henry Hauenstein, Sydney Middleton, Harry Ross-Boden, Roger Fitzhardinge, Robert Waley)

Germany [Berliner Ruderverein von 1876] (Otto Liebing, Max Bröske, Max Vetter, Willi Bartholomae, Fritz Bartholomae, Werner Dehn, Rudolf Reichelt, Hans Matthiae, Kurt Runge)

NOTES

1. 12OR has 7:37, while Uggla has the time as 7:47. This time is from ONews, and corresponds to the time they give for second place, 7:56.

2. Time from ONews. The margin was as follows in various reports: 12OR—one length; TF—two lengths; and ASZ—six lengths.

3. Time according to 12OR and Uggla; TF has 7:37.4.

4. Listed as 3rd placed in FM, who notes, "Butler is entitled to the place, for his time in the semifinals was better than that of M. Kusik." However, there was no provision for using this rule to award third place and no third places are listed in 12OR.

5. Time according to ONews.

6. It is unknown why Hugo Maksimilian Kusick (RUS) was also not awarded a diploma of merit, but this is based on 12OR.

7. This heat was declared void and a rerace was held later in the day. TF described this heat as follows: "Veirman appeared to be crowding his opponent as the bend was reached, and Mészáros signalled a protest, and appeared to ease. Veirman then fouled the bridge, and Mészáros came up and finished an easy winner. The committee ordered a re-row. Veirman won by three lengths." (*The Field*, 120: p. 146, 20 July 1912.)

8. TF described this heat as follows: "Veirman appeared to be crowding his opponent as the bend was reached, and Mészáros signalled a protest, and appeared to ease. Veirman then fouled the bridge, and Mészáros came up and finished an easy winner. The committee ordered a re-row. Veirman won by three lengths." (*The Field*, 120: p. 146, 20 July 1912.) The time is given as 7:52.0 according to 12OR, but that was the time for the first race. The time for the rerow is given in Uggla as 8:23.0.

9. The margin was as follows in various reports: TF — at three lengths; 12OR —<three lengths; Uggla — several lengths.

10. Listed as Heat Three in TF.

11. The time was 7:39.9 according to ONews and ASZ. It was 7:39 in 12OR.

12. Mikael Simonsen (DEN) had qualified for round two and was to start in heat two but he did not appear.

13. Listed as Heat Two in TF and Heat Four in Uggla.

14. Time per ASZ, ONews, and TF. 12 OR has 7:49.

15. Time according to ONews. The margin was as follows in various reports: 12OR — four lengths; TF — two lengths; ASZ — one and one-half lengths.

16. Listed as Heat Three in Uggla.

17. Time according to TF. 12OR has 7:45, while Uggla has, inexplicably, 7:58.0.

18. Uggla has Kusick racing Alfred Heinrich (AUT) in this heat, although Heinrich lost in heat one of round one. Levitzky won heat seven in round one and advanced to the quarterfinals.

19. Margin according to 12OR and Uggla; TF has it as one length.

20. This race was rerowed after Heinrich protested that Kusick had interfered with him during the first race on 17 July. Kusick won the original race in 7:46.0, leading Heinrich by two lengths in that race.

21. Margin according to ONews, while TF has 2½ lengths.

22. Time according to ONews and ASZ. TF has 7:56 and Uggla has 7:58.

23. This race was rerowed after Heinrich protested that Kusick had interfered with him during the first race on 17 July. Kusick won the original race in 7:46.0, leading Heinrich by two lengths in that race.

24. TF and ASZ list Heinrich as DQ in this rerace, while 12OR lists him as DNF.

25. Time according to TF and ONews. 12OR has 8:05. But TF gives the time for McVilly, who actually finished ahead of Stahnke before being disqualified, and that was 8:11, a time also given in ONews. Thus 8:28.8 appears to be more accurate.

26. McVilly finished several lengths in front of Stahnke but was disqualified for colliding with Stahnke's boat.

27. Timed in 8:11 according to ONews and TF.

28. Listed as Heat Six in TF.

29. Time according to ONews, while 12OR has 7:55.

30. The margin was as follows in various reports: 12OR — at eight lengths; Uggla — at seven lengths; ASZ — at ten lengths.

31. Listed as Heat Seven in TF.

32. The margin was as follows in various reports: ONews — at 1½ lengths; Uggla/ASZ — at one length.

33. Listed as Heat Three in TF and Heat Six in Uggla.

34. Ivan Schweizer (BOH) is listed in 12OR, but Mészáros's victory in this heat is described as "won as he liked." It appears that Schweizer did not actually start. He is listed as "scratched" in

TF, while ASZ lists him specifically as "DNS," and ONews describes Mészáros's victory as a walkover (wo), implying that Schweizer did not start.

35. Listed as Heat Four in TF and Heat Five in Uggla.

36. Retired at Djurgårdsbron, about 300 meters from the finish.

37. Listed as Heat Five in TF.

38. Listed as 8:05 in 12OR, but 8:04 in ONews, which seems to have the more reliable times.

39. Alexander McCulloch (GBR), the 1908 silver medalist, was also entered in this heat, but never left England due to illness.

40. Time from ONews, while 12OR has 7:59.

41. Samuel Finley Gordon (USA) was also entered in this heat, but did not compete.

42. Uggla has the time as 6:59.0. The time is from 12OR and ONews (English version). ONews (Swedish version) has 6:59.2.

43. The margin was given in various reports as follows: 12OR/ONews/Uggla — at two lengths; TF/ASZ — at three lengths.

44. The margin was given in various reports as follows: ONews — at 2½ lengths; TF — at two lengths; 12OR — at 2½ lengths; ASZ/Uggla — at 1½ lengths.

45. Time was 7:04.8 according to 12OR, 7:04.4 according to Uggla, and 7:04.2 TF.

46. Listed as third place in FM, for unknown reasons. 12OR lists no third places.

47. Uggla gave the time of 7:04.8, and 12OR had 7:05.2. We are using Uggla for this heat as it seems the "intermediate" time between 12OR and TF. Margin according to TF, who gave the winning time as 7:04.2, was ¼ length.

48. The margin is given in various reports as follows: TF — at 1+ length; 12OR — at almost three lengths; ASZ — at three lengths. The time is from ONews.

49. Time according to TF and ONews. 12OR and Uggla gave 7:14.

50. The margin is given in various reports as follows: ONews — at 1½ lengths; TF — at two lengths; 12OR — at 2½ lengths; Uggla — at three lengths.

51. The margin is given in various reports as follows: TF — at three lengths; 12OR — at one clear length; Uggla — at one length.

52. Time according to ASZ. 12OR gave the time as 7:14.

53. Listed as Heat One according to TF.

54. Time according to TF and ONews. 12OR and Uggla have 7:18.

55. The margin was given in various reports as follows: ONews/Uggla — at 1½ lengths; TF — at two lengths.

56. Listed as Heat Two according to TF.

57. TF noted "The Austrians retired at the bend." Uggla also noted that they retired at 1,500 meters. ASZ notes that Kröder collapsed at around 1,500 meters and Austria had to retire.

58. Time according to TF. OR and Uggla have 7:27.

59. An Austrian crew from "Donau" was also entered in heat four but scratched. The crew entered was Theodor Jakobi, Georg Hölzl, Karl Korber, Rudolf Kramer, Karl Meystrik, and Josef Petraseck.

60. Listed as Heat Three in TF.

61. According to TF, Denmark protested this result, but the protest was withdrawn.

62. The margin is given in various reports as follows: ONews — at one length; TF — at a "bare" length; 12OR — at two lengths; Uggla — at several lengths.

63. Listed as Heat Four in TF.

64. Time according to TF and ASZ. 12OR and Uggla have 7:06.

65. The margin is given in various reports as follows: ONews — at 1½ lengths; 12OR/TF — at two lengths; Uggla — at barely a length.

66. Germany (Mainzer Ruder-Verein) was also entered in this heat. 12OR lists them as did-not-start. However, ASZ notes, "Die Deutschen verstuerten sich und England zog als sicher Sieger durchs Ziel." ("The Germans mis-steered and England passed the finishing line as a sure winner.") Diem lists the Mainzer team as "nicht angetr," or "did not start." Still, it is difficult to know what to make of the ASZ report. Mainzer entered eight rowers in this event, and we do not know which

of the eight may have competed, although it is unlikely that any did so. The entrants were as follows: Oskar Cordes, Lorenz Eismayer, Josef Falk, Hans Kalkhof, Max Minthe, Rudolf Namen, Richard Piez, and Philipp Schreiner. The German Olympic committee has a detailed list of all their Olympians, and do not list any of the above as having competed in 1912.

67. Time according to ONews and ASZ. Uggla has 7:44.0, while 12OR has 7:47, a likely typo.

68. Time according to ONews. The margin was given in various reports as follows: ONews/TF — at four lengths; ASZ — at five lengths.

69. Time as given in ONews and ASz. 12OR and Uggla have 7:39.

70. Listed as third place in FM, whose rationale is obviously that Norway was the third boat in the semifinals. But the 12OR lists no third places.

71. The margin was given in various reports as follows: ONews/TF/Uggla — at ¾ lengths; ASZ — at 2½ lengths.

72. Time according to ONews, which seems to have the most reliable times. 12OR and Uggla have 7:39 which is likely a repetition of the time for heat one of the semifinals. As a walkover, it is unlikely that the Danish crew rowed as fast as the crews in the competitive heat one.

73. According to TF the time was 7:51.2, but 12OR and Uggla have 7:51.5.

74. The margin was given in various reports as follows: ONews/ASZ/Uggla — at two lengths; TF — at 2½ lengths.

75. The margin was given in various reports as follows: 12OR/ONews/TF — at 1½ lengths; Uggla — at one length.

76. The margin is given in various reports as follows: ONews/TF — at five lengths; ASZ — at seven lengths.

77. DW, EK, and OSVK have 7.

78. Time according to ONews. 12OR has 6:15.

79. Time according to ONews. 12OR has no time, but gives the margin as "at 1 length."

80. Time according to ONews. Uggla and ASZ have the time as 7:22. 12OR has the time as 7:47. It is unclear why this discrepancy exists, but ONews has the most reliable times, and the 12OR time of 7:47 is likely a typo.

81. Time according to ONews and Uggla. 12OR has 6:16.4 and Diem has 6:16.0.

82. Listed as third place in FM, whose rationale is obviously that Germany was the third boat in the semifinals. But the 12OR lists no third places.

83. Time according to ONews. The other sources had only margins, as follows: 12OR — at ½ length; ASZ — at ⅓ length.

84. The margin was given in various reports as follows: 12OR — at one length; TF — at 1¼ lengths; ASZ — at 1½ lengths.

85. Time according to Diem. The time was 6:22 according to 12OR/TF/Uggla.

86. The margin was given in various reports as follows: ONews — at 2 lengths; 12OR — at 2½ lengths; ASZ — at ½ length.

87. The time was 6:10.0 according to 12OR, while TF, Diem, and Uggla have 6:10.2.

88. The margin was given in various reports as follows: ONews (English) — at ½ length; ONews (Swedish)/ASZ — at ¾ lengths; TF — at ¼ length; 12OR — at three meters.

89. The margin was given in various reports as follows: ONews — at 1¼ lengths; 12OR — at four lengths;, TF/Uggla/ASZ — at 1½ lengths.

90. The margin was given in various reports as follows: 12OR — at 3+ lengths; TF — at two lengths; Uggla — at 1½ lengths.

91. The time was given in various reports as follows: ONews/Uggla/TF/Diem — 6:32; 12OR — 6:57. The 6:57 in 12OR must be typo and likely a repeat of the winning time in heat two.

92. "Won easily" according to 12OR. TF has the margin as 2½ lengths, while Uggla has three lengths. ONews has the margin as "more than 2 lengths."

93. The time is 6:42.2 in 12OR, while TF/Diem/Uggla and ONews (Swedish) have 6:42.5. The English version of ONews has 6:43.5 which is likely typo for 6:42.5.

94. The margin was given in various reports as follows: 12OR/ASZ — at one length; TF — at 1¼ lengths; ONews — at 1½ lengths.

95. The time is 6:19.0 in 12OR, while TF has 6:22.2 and 6:22.0 (in two different places), and Diem, ONews, and Uggla have 6:22.2.

96. The margin was given in various reports as follows: 12OR — at ½ + length; ASZ — at ½ length.

97. Time according to Diem. 12OR has 7:05, while TF has 7:52. The 7:52 in TF is likely a typo for 7:5.2 (7:05.2).

98. There is no rationale for how these were chosen, but the information is based on 12OR. Notably, the Canadian team did not win any race, and did not advance beyond the first round.

Shooting

As at London in 1908, the 1912 Olympic shooting program had a large number of events — 18 at Stockholm as compared to 15 at London. And similarly, the events could basically be separated into five categories: 1) long-range rifle shooting, 2) small-bore rifle shooting, 3) pistol shooting, 4) clay bird trap shooting, and 5) running deer shooting. The pistol and rifle events were held at Kaknäs, while the running deer and clay trap events were held at Råsunda.

Sweden and the United States dominated the competitions. Both won seven gold medals, with Sweden winning 17 medals in all to the 14 won by the United States.

Site: Kaknäs (pistol, small-bore rifle, long-range rifle); Råsunda (running deer, clay trap)
Dates: 29–30 June, 1–5 July
Events: 18 [18 Men — 0 Women]
Competitors: 283 [283 Men — 0 Women]
Nations: 16 [16 Men — 0 Women]

	Competitors	*Gold*	*Silver*	*Bronze*	*Medals*
Austria	7	–	–	–	–
Canada	3	–	–	–	–
Chile	2	–	–	–	–
Denmark	14	–	1	2	3
Finland	19	–	–	2	2
France	19	2	–	–	2
Germany	11	–	1	1	2
Great Britain	38	1	4	4	9
Greece	9	–	–	–	–
Hungary	10	1	–	–	1
The Netherlands	1	–	–	–	–
Norway	28	–	1	1	2
Russia	26	–	1	1	2
South Africa	8	–	–	–	–

Sweden	62	7	6	4	17
United States	26	7	4	3	14
Totals	283	18	18	18	54
Nations	16	5	7	8	10

Committee for Shooting

Shooting Committee
  President: Colonel, Count Carl E. Taube
  Vice-President: Captain Fredrik Björkenstam, Esquire; Master of the Hounds to His Majesty
  Secretary: Gustaf C. Boivie, Esquire
  Members: Per-Olof Arvidsson, Esquire; Edward Benedicks, Esquire; Lieutenant Eric Carlberg; Folke Fagrell, Esquire; M. N. Hallman, Esquire; Emil W. Lindewald, Esquire; Ernest Mellin, Esquire; Captain, Baron Stig Rålamb; Major C. P. K. Otto Sjögren; Alfred Swahn, Esquire; Oscar G. Swahn, Esquire
  Deputy Members: Johann E. Ekman, Esquire; Baron Axel Klinckowström
  International Jury: Colonel, Count Carl E. Taube (President/SWE); Captain Fredrik Björkenstam, Esquire, Master of the Hounds to His Majesty (SWE); Maurice Fauré (FRA); Ioannis Chryssafis (GRE); Anton Frisch (NOR); Colonel Platon Moskov (RUS); Sir Lionel Phillips, Bart (RSA); William Libbey (USA)

Rifle Shooting Committee
  President: Colonel, Count Carl E. Taube
  Members: Lieutenant-Colonel Erik Otto; Per-Olof Arvidsson, Esquire; Gustaf C. Boivie, Esquire; Lieutenant Eric Carlberg; Folke Fagrell, Esquire; Major C. P. K. Otto Sjögren

Small-Bore Rifles, Revolvers and Pistol Committee
  President: Captain, Baron Stig Rålamb
  Members: Lieutenant Nils Gustaf Knut Bildt; Lieutenant Carl Hugo Adelborg

Clay Bird and Running Deer Committee
  President: Captain Fredrik Björkenstam, Esquire, Master of the Hounds to His Majesty
  Secretary: Ernest Mellin, Esquire
  Adjoint Member: Oscar G. Swahn, Esquire
  Members: Emil W. Lindewald, Esquire; M. N. Hallman, Esquire; Alfred Swahn, Esquire; Edward Benedicks, Esquire
  Deputy Members: Johan E. Ekman, Esquire; Baron Axel Klinckowström

Long-Range Rifle Shooting

Free Rifle, 300 meters, Three Positions (Event E)

A: 84; C: 9; D: 2 July; T: 1100–1400, 1600–1900; F: 120 shots, 40 each standing, kneeling, and prone. 400 posible in each position, 1,200 possible total. Target 100 cm. in diameter with ten five-centimeter scoring rings. Centre-10 ten centimeters in diameter. Black center 60 centimeters in diameter. Ties decided by 1) number of hits on target, and 2) number of black center hits, number of tens, number of nines, and so on.

Despite a relatively poor score in the standing shooting, placing only 13th in that section, France's Paul Colas won the gold medal in the free rifle event because he had the highest score in both the kneeling and prone positions. Both Colas and the runner-up, Lars Jørgen Madsen (DEN), had competed in this event at London in 1908, with Madsen finishing 14th and Colas 25th. Colas competed in five shooting events in Stockholm, and also won the gold medal in the 600 meter military rifle event. He also competed in Olympic shooting in 1920 and 1924. In addition to his individual gold medals at Stockholm, he won team shooting medals in 1908 (bronze in small-bore rifle team) and 1924 (silver in free rifle team).

		Stdng	Knlg	Prone	Total
1. Paul Colas	FRA	283	342	362	987
2. Lars Jørgen Madsen	DEN	318	333	330	981
3. Niels Larsen	DEN	273	334	355	962
4. C. Hugo Johansson	SWE	292	326	341	959
5. Gudbrand Gudbrandsen Skatteboe	NOR	305	308	343	956
6. Bernhard Larsson	SWE	274	339	341	954
7. Albert Helgerud	NOR	281	317	354	952
8. Tönnes Björkman	SWE	285	322	340	947
9. Ole Sæther	NOR	276	316	349	941
10. Erik Blomqvist	SWE	269	326	337	932
11. Gustaf Adolf Jonsson	SWE	275	316	337	928
12. Ole Olsen	DEN	315	291	320	926
13. Voitto Kolho	FIN	290	313	320	923
14. Mauritz Eriksson	SWE	276	316	330	922
15. Einar Liberg	NOR	275	316	330	921
16. Hans Christian Tauson	DEN	263	324	334	921
17. Carl Osburn	USA	278	300	337	915
18. Olaf Sæter	NOR	304	299	311	914
19. Gustav "Kustaa" Nyman	FIN	302	289	322	913
20. Verner Jernström	SWE	265	315	332	912
21. Cornelius Burdette	USA	263	300	349	912
22. Paul Vighals	NOR	264	318	329	911
23. Østen Østensen	NOR	270	308	333	911
24. Léon Johnson	FRA	270	298	340	908
25. Heikki Huttunen	FIN	290	298	318	906
26. Thomas Refsum	NOR	294	306	305	905
27. Olaf Husby	NOR	263	307	335	905
28. Harry Adams	USA	246	297	360	903
29. Julius Braathe	NOR	289	292	319	900
30. Arne Sunde	NOR	282	304	314	900
31. Embret Skogen	NOR	279	286	334	899
32. Warren Sprout	USA	270	299	327	896
33. Laurits Larsen	DEN	300	277	317	894
34. Carl Björkman	SWE	239	308	341	888
35. Allan Briggs	USA	239	308	341	888

		Stdng	Knlg	Prone	Total
36. Harold Bartlett	USA	238	293	353	884
37. S. Robert Jonsson	SWE	260	290	325	875
38. Frederick Hird	USA	227	326	322	875
39. Huvi Tuiskunen	FIN	264	322	289	875
40. George Harvey	RSA	240	288	346	874
41. Vilho Vauhkonen	FIN	281	285	304	870
42. August Wikström	SWE	266	291	313	870
43. Nils J:son Skog	SWE	225	315	329	869
44. Louis Percy	FRA	245	314	309	868
45. Auguste Marion	FRA	254	303	311	868
46. Frants Nielsen	DEN	268	290	293	851
47. Anders Peter Nielsen	DEN	244	292	313	849
48. Per-Olof Arvidsson	SWE	245	279	315	839
49. Emil Holm	FIN	243	280	312	835
50. Emil, Ritter Bömches von Boor	HUN	220	282	326	828
51. Robert Patterson	RSA	205	277	328	810
52. Hans Schultz	DEN	236	296	276	808
53. Raoul, Count de Boigne	FRA	203	285	318	806
54. Teotan Lebedev	RUS	243	274	289	806
55. Robert Bodley	RSA	150	310	346	806
56. Ernest Keeley	RSA	188	289	323	800
57. Lauri Kolho	FIN	238	265	284	787
58. Dmitry Kuskov	RUS	228	269	283	780
59. Jalo Urho Autonen	FIN	211	279	286	776
60. Povl Gerlow	DEN	233	256	283	772
61. George Whelan	RSA	185	242	335	762
62. Pavel Valdayne	RUS	204	260	294	758
63. Athanase Sartori	FRA	193	258	303	754
64. Arthur Smith	RSA	176	252	324	752
65. Boris Belinsky	RUS	201	261	284	746
66. Aleksandr Tillo	RUS	251	232	261	744
67. Albert Johnstone	RSA	181	228	332	741
68. Konstantin Kalinin	RUS	231	254	251	736
69. Zoltán Jelenffy-Tóth von Csejthe	HUN	187	241	290	718
70. Charles Jeffreys	RSA	166	207	342	715
71. Pavel Leche	RUS	186	254	273	713
72. Rezs Velez	HUN	183	240	289	712
73. Osvald Rechke	RUS	170	252	277	699
74. László Hauler	HUN	162	250	265	677
75. Aladár von Farkas	HUN	154	238	261	653
76. Georgy Davidov	RUS	177	207	251	635
77. Davids Weiss	RUS	181	293	249	623
78. Aleksandr Dobrzhansky	RUS	149	149	165	463
AC. Hans Peter Denver	DEN	277	265	WD	
Nestor Toivonen	FIN	252	207	WD	
István Prihoda	HUN	134	WD		
Pierre Gentil	FRA	231	WD		

		Stdng	*Knlg*	*Prone*	*Total*
Jens Madsen Hajslund	DEN	226	WD		
Géza Mészöly von Sárbogárd	HUN	84	WD		
1*					

Diplomas of Merit

C. Hugo Johansson (SWE), Gudbrand Gudbrandsen Skatteboe (NOR), Bernhard Larsson (SWE), Albert Helgerud (NOR), Tönnes Björkman (SWE)

Military Rifle, 300 meters, Three Positions (Event C)

A: 91; C: 12; D: 1 July; T: 0900–1400; F: Fired in two stages. First stage: four shots kneeling, four shots prone, and two shots standing in a time limit of three minutes fired at a 140 × 170 centimeter five-ring target. Bullseye 30 centimeters across, with center five scoring rings 50 centimeters across, and four 10 centimeter scoring rings. Second stage: five shots prone and five shots kneeling in a time limit of three minutes fired at a half-figure target, width 50 centimeters, height 90 centimeters, with five points for each hit. Possible 50 for each stage, 100 overall. Ties decided by the greatest number of hits on the half-figure.

With one shot to go, Nils Romander, an 18-year-old Swedish schoolboy, was in the lead, having missed only one shot to that point. All he had to do was hit the half-figure with his last shot and the gold medal was his. The Swedish crowd was excited and gathered around him, but he became nervous by all the fuss and excitement, and missed the last shot.

Hungary's Sándor Prokopp was tied for sixth place after the first stage, but in the second stage he recorded one of the seven perfect scores of 50. His combined total of 97 won him the gold medal. Prokopp had competed at London in 1908, but only in the free rifle event, in which he finished 43rd.

Carl Osburn (USA), Embret Skogen (NOR) and Nikolaos Levidis (GRE) tied for second with 95 points. In the shoot-off for the medals, Osburn scored 99, the highest score of the event, winning easily over Skogen (91) and Levidis (70).

1.	Sándor Prokopp	HUN	47	50	97	
2.	Carl Osburn	USA	45	50	95	99
3.	Embret Skogen	NOR	45	50	95	91
4.	Nikolaos Levidis	GRE	45	50	95	70
5.	Nils Romander	SWE	49	45	94	
6.	Arthur Fulton	GBR	42	50	92	
7.	Rezső Velez	HUN	42	50	92	
8.	Carl Flodström	SWE	46	45	91	
9.	Harold Bartlett	USA	45	45	90	
10.	George Harvey	RSA	45	45	90	
11.	Pavel Valdayne	RUS	45	45	90	
12.	Harry Adams	USA	44	45	89	
13.	Ernest Keeley	RSA	44	45	89	
14.	Tönnes Björkman	SWE	43	45	88	
15.	Julius Braathe	NOR	48	40	88	

*See Notes on pages 282–285.

16. Gustaf Adolf Jonsson	SWE	48	40	88
17. Frangiskos Maurommatis	GRE	37	50	87
18. Per-Olof Arvidsson	SWE	42	45	87
19. S. Robert Jonsson	SWE	46	40	86
20. Per August Stridfeldt	SWE	46	40	86
21. Erik Ohlsson	SWE	46	40	86
22. Paul Colas	FRA	46	40	86
23. Louis Percy	FRA	41	45	85
24. Aladár von Farkas	HUN	40	45	85
25. Allan Briggs	USA	45	40	85
26. Georgy Vishnyakov	RUS	39	45	84
27. László Hauler	HUN	39	45	84
28. Frederick Hird	USA	49	35	84
29. Géza Mészöly von Sárbogárd	HUN	43	40	83
30. Pavel Leche	RUS	48	35	83
31. W. Neil McDonnell	USA	42	40	82
32. Johann Dulnig	AUT	42	40	82
33. John Jackson	USA	42	40	82
34. Charles Jeffreys	RSA	47	35	82
35. Mathias Glomnes	NOR	47	35	82
36. Hans Schultz	DEN	47	35	82
37. Warren Sprout	USA	41	40	81
38. John Sedgewick	GBR	41	40	81
39. Robert Davies	GBR	41	40	81
40. Torsten Nyström	SWE	46	35	81
41. Johannes Jordell	NOR	35	45	80
42. Teotan Lebedev	RUS	40	40	80
43. Harald Ekwall	CHI	45	35	80
44. Arne Sunde	NOR	45	35	80
45. Robert Bodley	RSA	38	40	78
46. Boris Belinsky	RUS	38	40	78
47. Osvald Rechke	RUS	43	35	78
48. Felix Alegria	CHI	42	35	77
49. Dmitry Kuskov	RUS	42	35	77
50. Fleetwood Varley	GBR	31	45	76
51. Aleksandr Tillo	RUS	46	30	76
52. Cornelius Burdette	USA	40	35	75
53. Verner Jernström	SWE	40	35	75
54. John Somers	GBR	40	35	75
55. Albert Helgerud	NOR	45	30	75
56. Edward Parnell	GBR	45	30	75
57. Langford Lloyd	GBR	39	35	74
58. Raoul, Count de Boigne	FRA	28	45	73
59. Robert Patterson	RSA	37	35	72
60. Davids Weiss	RUS	42	30	72
61. Pierre Gentil	FRA	36	35	71
62. Herman Skjerven	NOR	41	30	71
63. Niels Larsen	DEN	35	35	70
64. J. Arvid Hoflund	SWE	40	30	70

65. Philip Richardson	GBR	34	35	69
66. Emil, Ritter Bömches von Boor	HUN	39	30	69
67. Alexandros Theofilakis	GRE	39	30	69
68. Georgy Davidov	RUS	38	30	68
69. William McClure	GBR	38	30	68
70. Maxime Landin	FRA	42	25	67
71. Aleksandr Dobrzhansky	RUS	31	35	66
72. Iakovos Theofilas	GRE	41	25	66
73. George Whelan	RSA	34	30	64
74. Povl Gerlow	DEN	44	20	64
75. Ioannis Theofilakis	GRE	33	30	63
76. Ludvig Thielemann	NOR	32	30	62
77. Albert Johnstone	RSA	37	25	62
78. Daniel Mérillon	FRA	37	25	62
79. Konstantin Kalinin	RUS	42	20	62
80. Ole Bjerke	NOR	41	20	61
81. Johannes "Johs" Espelund	NOR	30	30	60
82. Birger Lie	NOR	44	15	59
83. Carl Wallenborg	SWE	36	20	56
84. Arthur Smith	RSA	36	20	56
85. István Prihoda	HUN	29	20	49
86. Philip Plater	GBR	34	15	49
87. Zoltán Jelenffy-Tóth von Csejthe	HUN	33	15	48
88. Spyridon Mostras	GRE	19	25	44
89. Carl Weydahl	NOR	25	15	40
90. Athanase Sartori	FRA	23	15	38
91. Béla von Darányi	HUN	7	5	12

2

Diplomas of Merit

Nikolaos Levidis (GRE), Nils Romander (SWE), Arthur Fulton (GBR), Rezső Velez (HUN), Carl Flodström (SWE), Harold Bartlett (USA), George Harvey (RSA), Pavel Valdayne (RUS)

Military Rifle, 600 meters, Any Position (Event B)

A: 85; C: 12; D: 1 July; T: 1500–1800; F: 20 shots at 600 meters. 100 possible. Target 180 × 170 centimeters, with a five-ring 40 centimeters in diameter, black centre 60 centimeters in diameter, four-ring ten centimeters, three-ring 15 centimeters, two-ring 20 centimeters. Ties decided by shoot-off on the spot.

Carl Osburn had finished second in the 300 meter military rifle event, and Paul Colas would win the free rifle event the next day. In this event, they tied for first with scores of 94. In the shoot-off, Osburn led early but after 19 shots they were tied with 86 points. Colas scored a perfect five on the final shot, to defeat Osburn, who scored only a four, by one point, 91–90. Jackson and Briggs also shot off for the bronze medal, Jackson winning by one point.

1. Paul Colas	FRA	94	91
2. Carl Osburn	USA	94	90

3. John Jackson	USA	93	90
4. Allan Briggs	USA	93	89
5. Philip Plater	GBR	90	
6. Verner Jernström	SWE	88	
7. Harcourt Ommundsen	GBR	88	
8. Cornelius Burdette	USA	87	
9. Arthur Fulton	GBR	87	
10. Henry Burr	GBR	87	
11. Carl Wallenborg	SWE	87	
12. Harry Adams	USA	86	
13. James Reid	GBR	86	
14. Warren Sprout	USA	85	
15. Erik Gustafsson	SWE	85	
16. Edward Skilton	GBR	85	
17. Ole Christian Degnes	NOR	84	
18. Edward Parnell	GBR	84	
19. Harold Bartlett	USA	83	
20. Louis Percy	FRA	83	
21. George Harvey	RSA	83	
22. Frangiskos Maurommatis	GRE	82	
23. Hugo Johansson	SWE	82	
24. Carl-Johan Sund	SWE	82	
25. Tönnes Björkman	SWE	81	
26. Frederick Hird	USA	81	
27. Fleetwood Varley	GBR	81	
28. Erik Ohlsson	SWE	81	
29. Leonard Lagerlöf	SWE	81	
30. Arne Sunde	NOR	80	
31. John Sedgewick	GBR	80	
32. W. Neil McDonnell	USA	80	
33. Philip Richardson	GBR	79	
34. Ioannis Theofilakis	GRE	79	
35. Hans Nordvik	NOR	79	
36. S. Robert Jonsson	SWE	79	
37. Robert Davies	GBR	78	
38. Mauritz Eriksson	SWE	77	
39. Konstantin Kalinin	RUS	77	
40. Gudbrand Gudbrandsen Skatteboe	NOR	77	
41. Thomas Refsum	NOR	76	
42. Charles Jeffreys	RSA	76	
43. Albert Johnstone	RSA	75	
44. Hans Schultz	DEN	75	
45. Pavel Valdayne	RUS	75	
46. John Somers	GBR	74	
47. Albert Helgerud	NOR	74	
48. Rasmus Friis	DEN	74	
49. Ruben Örtegren	SWE	74	
50. Raoul, Count de Boigne	FRA	73	
51. Davids Weiss	RUS	73	

52. Nikolaos Levidis	GRE	73
53. Robert Patterson	RSA	73
54. Robert Bodley	RSA	73
55. Ragnvald Maseng	NOR	73
56. Ole Jensen	NOR	73
57. Paul Vighals	NOR	72
58. Osvald Rechke	RUS	71
59. Dmitry Kuskov	RUS	71
60. Olaf Sæter	NOR	70
61. Georgy Davidov	RUS	70
62. Aleksandr Tillo	RUS	70
63. Auguste Marion	FRA	69
64. Daniel Mérillon	FRA	69
65. Boris Belinsky	RUS	69
66. Torsten Nyström	SWE	69
67. Harald Ekwall	CHI	67
68. Alexandros Theofilakis	GRE	66
69. Pierre Gentil	FRA	65
70. Pavel Leche	RUS	62
71. Aleksandr Dobrzhansky	RUS	61
72. Felix Alegria	CHI	61
73. Rezső Velez	HUN	60
74. Teotan Lebedev	RUS	59
75. Ludvig Thielemann	NOR	57
76. Aladár von Farkas	HUN	56
77. Georgy Vishnyakov	RUS	56
78. Zoltán Jelenffy-Tóth von Csejthe	HUN	54
79. Géza Mészöly von Sárbogárd	HUN	54
80. Emil, Ritter Bömches von Boor	HUN	51
81. Johann Dulnig	AUT	41
82. Søren Christian Bough	NOR	40
83. László Hauler	HUN	35
84. Athanase Sartori	FRA	32
85. Iakovos Theofilas	GRE	13

3

Diplomas of Merit

Allan Briggs (USA), Philip Plater (GBR), Verner Jernström (SWE), Harcourt Ommundsen (GBR), Cornelius Burdette (USA), Arthur Fulton (GBR), Henry Burr (GBR), Carl Wallenborg (SWE)

Free Rifle, 300 meters, Three Positions, Teams (Event D)

A: 42; C: 7; D: 4 July; T: 1100–1400; F: 6-man teams. 120 shots per shooter, 40 each standing, kneeling, and prone. 400 posible in each position, 1,200 possible total per shooter, 7,200 possible per team. Target 100 cm. in diameter with ten five-centimeter scoring rings. Center-10 ten centimeters in diameter. Black center 60 centimeters in diameter. Ties decided by 1) number of hits on target, and 2) number of black center hits, number of tens, number of nines, and so on.

Denmark had the highest score in the standing position, Sweden the highest in the kneeling position, and Norway in the prone position. These three teams shared the medals, with Sweden winning by 50 points overall over Norway.

	Standing	Kneeling	Prone	Total
1. Sweden	1,728	1,913	2,014	5,655

    (Mauritz Eriksson [291/339/346-976], C. Hugo Johansson [294/335/346-975], Erik Blomqvist [274/345/343-962], Carl Björkman [306/308/340-954], Bernhard Larsson [277/298/300-914], Gustaf Adolf Jonsson [286/288/300-874])

2. Norway	1,697	1,885	2,023	5,605

    (Gudbrand Gudbrandsen Skatteboe [283/315/347-945], Ole Sæther [278/325/342-945], Østen Østensen [278/322/340-940], Albert Helgerud [296/312/330-938], Olaf Sæter [291/316/328-935], Einar Liberg [271/295/336-902])

3. Denmark	1,770	1,845	1,914	5,529

    (Ole Olsen [301/329-353-983], Lars Jørgen Madsen [327/335/311-973], Niels Larsen [295/319/317-931], Niels Andersen [281/302/313-896], Laurits Larsen [280/282/328-890], Jens Madsen Hajslund [286/278/292-856])

4. France	1,650	1,839	1,982	5,471

    (Paul Colas [308/331/365-1,004], Louis Percy [267/313/351-931], Léon Johnson [303/305/300-908], Pierre Gentil [278/301/320-899], Raoul, Count de Boigne [239/309/326-874], Auguste Marion [255/280/320-855])

5. Finland	1,651	1,751	1,921	5,323

    (Voitto Kolho [306/308/337-951], Heikki Huttunen [287/321/338-946], Gustav "Kustaa" Nyman [287/306/304-897], Emil Holm [248/270/327-845], Huvi Tuiskunen [273/267/304-844], Vilho Vauhkonen [250/279/311-840])

6. South Africa	1,238	1,679	1,980	4,897

    (George Harvey [229/309/349-887], Robert Bodley [225/290/342-857], Robert Patterson [223/271/345-839], Arthur Smith [219/270/332-821], Ernest Keeley [207/305/300-812], George Whelan [135/234/312-681])

7. Russia	1,505	1,612	1,775	4,892

    (Pavel Valdayne [260/288/312-860], Teotan Lebedev [254/256/317-827], Aleksandr Tillo [261/264/297-822], Konstantin Kalinin [252/265/286-803], Dmitry Kuskov [236/280/295-811], Pavel Leche [242/259/268-769])
4

Diplomas of Merit

France (Paul Colas, Louis Percy, Léon Johnson, Pierre Gentil, Raoul, Count de Boigne, Auguste Marion)

Military Rifle, 200, 400, 500, and 600 Meters, Teams (Event A)

A: 60; C: 10; D: 29 June; T: 1000; F: 6-man teams. 15 shots each at 200, 400, 500, and 600 meters. 75 possible per shooter at each distance, 300 possible per shooter, 1,800 possible per team. Target for 200 meters: 140 × 170 centimeters, with a five-ring 20 centimeters in diameter, black center 30 centimeters across, four-ring five centimeters, three-ring ten centimeters, two-ring 15 centimeters; and one-ring 20 centimeters. Target for 400/500/600 meters: 180 × 170 centimeters, with a five-ring 40 centimeters in diameter, black centre 60 centimeters in diameter, four-ring 10 centimeters, three-ring 15 centimeters, two-ring 20 centimeters. Ties decided by shoot-off on the spot.

This event figured on the Olympic Program in 1912, 1920, and 1924, but with varying distances and formats. In 1912, the United States completely dominated this event. They had the highest score at all four distances. The lowest scoring American, Warren Sprout, had a total of 276, which equaled the highest individual total of any non–American shooter — Harcourt Ommundsen of Great Britain also scored 276.

	200m.	400m.	500m.	600m.	Total
1. United States	438	444	424	381	1,687

(Cornelius Burdette [74/73/71/70-288], Allan Briggs [72/75/70/66-283], Harry Adams [74/74/73/62-283], John Jackson [71/73/69/66-279], Carl Osburn [73/75/72/58-278], Warren Sprout [74/74/69/59-276])

	200m.	400m.	500m.	600m.	Total
2. Great Britain	428	410	391	373	1,602

(Harcourt Ommundsen [74/75/69/58-276], Henry Burr [70/68/68/60-266], Edward Skilton [73/66/66/61-266], James Reid [70/70/63/63-266], Edward Parnell [68/70/62/66-266], Arthur Fulton [73/61/63/65-262])

	200m.	400m.	500m.	600m.	Total
3. Sweden	417	416	384	353	1,570

(Mauritz Eriksson [69/69/71/57-266], Verner Jernström [72/68/58/64-262], Carl Björkman [71/68/64/58-261], Tönnes Björkman [70/71/62/58-261], Bernhard Larsson [68/70/62/61-261], C. Hugo Johansson [67/70/67/55-259])

	200m.	400m.	500m.	600m.	Total
4. South Africa	415	387	393	336	1,531

(George Harvey [67/65/70/56-258], Robert Bodley [74/64/66/52-256], Arthur Smith [67/66/59/64-256], Ernest Keeley [68/69/63/55-255], Charles Jeffreys [71/64/63/56-254], Robert Patterson [68/59/72/53-252])

	200m.	400m.	500m.	600m.	Total
5. France	405	407	377	326	1,515

(Louis Percy [69/69/66/59-263], Paul Colas [67/71/62/62-262], Raoul, Count de Boigne [71/65/66/60-262], Pierre Gentil [69/70/67/51-257], Léon Johnson [68/68/62/42-240], Maxime Landin [61/64/54/62-231])

	200m.	400m.	500m.	600m.	Total
6. Norway	408	378	358	329	1,473

(Ole Christian Degnes [70/69/64/65-268], Arne Sunde [70/65/62/56-253], Ole Jensen [68/61/60/59-248], Hans Nordvik [67/64/63/48-242], Olaf Husby [67/61/61/44-233], Mathias Glomnes [66/58/48/57-229])

	200m.	400m.	500m.	600m.	Total
7. Greece	390	385	356	314	1,445

(Frangiskos Maurommatis [71/67/62/61-261], Alexandros Theofilakis [67/67/60/64-258], Ioannis Theofilakis [67/64/65/53-249], Nikolaos Levidis [66/61/56/48-231], Iakovos Theofilas [67/65/55/42-229], Spyridon Mostras [52/61/58/46-217])

	200m.	400m.	500m.	600m.	Total
8. Denmark	398	380	338	303	1,419

(Niels Andersen [69/70/61/50-250], Lars Jørgen Madsen [70/65/63/49-247], Hans Schultz [62/64/59/59-244], Niels Larsen [69/61/55/52-237], Jens Madsen Hajslund [68/61/48/46-223], Rasmus Friis [60/59/52/47-218])

9. Russia   385   389   345   284   1,403
   (Pavel Valdayne [68/64/56/63-251], Dmitry Kuskov [66/66/67/47-246], Teotan Lebedev
   [60/68/56/53-237], Davids Weiss [64/67/54/41-226], Aleksandr Tillo [65/64/52/45-
   226], Georgy Davidov [62/60/60/35-217])

10. Hungary   379   353   338   263   1,333
    (Emil, Ritter Bömches von Boor [63/59/59/56-237], István Prihoda [70/58/57/42-227],
    Rezső Velez [64/63/60/39-226], László Hauler [67/61/50/41-219], Géza Mészöly von
    Sárbogárd [61/58/57/41-217], Aladár von Farkas [54/54/55/44-207])

   Diplomas of Merit

   South Africa (George Harvey, Robert Bodley, Arthur Smith, Ernest Keeley, Charles Jeffreys,
Robert Patterson)

Small-Bore Rifle Shooting

Small-Bore Rifle, Prone Position (English Match), 50 Meters (Event G)

A: 41; C: 9; D: 4 July; T: 1200–1900; F: 40 shots prone position. Target 40 × 40 centimeters, with a five-ring of four centimeters in diameter, black center six centimeters in diameter, four-ring three centimeters, three-ring three centimeters, two-ring seven centimeters. 200
possible. Ties decided by the greatest number of 1) 5s, 2) black center hits, 3) 4s, 4) 3s, and so
on.

Although America's Frederick Hird won the gold medal with 194 points, the next five positions and six of the top ten were taken by British shooters. Hird won three Olympic shooting
medals in 1912 — the individual gold in this event and bronze medals in the two team small-bore
events. He also competed in Olympic shooting in 1920, but did not fare as well.

1.	Frederick Hird	USA	194
2.	William Milne	GBR	193
3.	Harold Burt	GBR	192
4.	Edward Lessimore	GBR	192
5.	Francis Kemp	GBR	190
6.	Robert Murray	GBR	190
7.	William Leuschner	USA	189
8.	Erik Boström	SWE	189
9.	Johan Hübner von Holst	SWE	189
10.	William Pimm	GBR	189
11.	Axel Wahlstedt	SWE	187
12.	Warren Sprout	USA	187
13.	Carl Osburn	USA	187
14.	Joseph Pepé	GBR	187
15.	J. Fredrik Nyström	SWE	187
16.	Arthur Nordenswan	SWE	186
17.	Eric Carlberg	SWE	186
18.	W. Neil McDonnell	USA	186
19.	Ruben Örtegren	SWE	186

20.	Ernst Johansson	SWE	185
21.	Wilhelm Carlberg	SWE	185
22.	Robert Löfman	SWE	185
23.	Edwin Anderson	USA	185
24.	David Griffiths	GBR	184
25.	Nikolaos Levidis	GRE	181
26.	Frants Nielsen	DEN	180
27.	William Styles	GBR	179
28.	Erik Odelberg	SWE	179
29.	László Hauler	HUN	178
30.	Arne Sunde	NOR	176
31.	Sándor, Count Török von Mura	HUN	174
32.	Ioannis Theofilakis	GRE	173
33.	Aleksandr Dobrzhansky	RUS	172
34.	Frangiskos Maurommatis	GRE	172
35.	Johannes Jordell	NOR	172
36.	Vladimir Potekin	RUS	170
37.	Iakovos Theofilas	GRE	167
38.	Povl Gerlow	DEN	167
39.	Gideon Ericsson	SWE	157
40.	Ragnvald Maseng	NOR	156
41.	André Regaud	FRA	125

5

Diplomas of Merit

Edward Lessimore (GBR), Francis Kemp (GBR), Robert Murray (GBR), William Leuschner (USA), Erik Boström (SWE), Johan Hübner von Holst (SWE), William Pimm (GBR)

Small-Bore Rifle, 25 Meters, Disappearing Target (Event I)

A: 36[6]; C: 8; D: 5 July; T: 1000; F: 5 series of 25 shots. Target was a 12-centimeter high figure, 3.5 centimeters at the widest, which appeared for three seconds, with intervals of five seconds between appearances. After each series of five shots, the figure was changed. Any position allowed. 250 possible. The center 10-mark was an oval 14 mm. high and 10 mm. wide, with subsequent scoring ovals 7 mm. apart. Places determined first by number of hits on target, and ties decided by 1) number of points made, 2) number of 10s, 3) number of 9s, and so on.

Wilhelm Carlberg had competed in the 1908 small-bore rifle disappearing target event, finishing seventh. He had an exceptionally long Olympic career, competing and winning medals in Olympic shooting in 1906, 1908, 1912, and 1924 — he did not compete at Antwerp in 1920. In 1912 he won five Olympic medals — three gold and two silver. Overall, he won eight Olympic medals — three gold, three silver, and two bronze. His twin brother, Eric Carlberg, also competed in shooting for Sweden at the Olympics, and in fact, finished 20th in this event. His Olympic career was shorter, encompassing only the Olympics of 1906, 1908, and 1912, and he won five Olympic medals, two gold and three silver, although he never won an individual shooting medal.

			Hits	Points	10s	9s
1.	Wilhelm Carlberg	SWE	25	242		
2.	Johan Hübner von Holst	SWE	25	233		
3.	Gideon Ericsson	SWE	25	231	12	8
4.	Joseph Pepé	GBR	25	231	9	13
5.	Robert Murray	GBR	25	228		
6.	Axel Gyllenkrok	SWE	25	227[7]		
7.	William Pimm	GBR	25	225		
8.	Frederick Hird	USA	25	221		
9.	Harold Burt	GBR	24	222		
10.	Robert Löfman	SWE	24	221		
11.	Erik Odelberg	SWE	24	219		
12.	Edward Lessimore	GBR	24	218		
13.	William Styles	GBR	24	216		
14.	W. Neil McDonnell	USA	24	212		
15.	Gustaf Boivie	SWE	24	212		
16.	Edwin Anderson	USA	24	208		
17.	Warren Sprout	USA	24	205		
18.	Frangiskos Maurommatis	GRE	24	204		
19.	Léon Johnson	FRA	24	203		
20.	Eric Carlberg	SWE	23	219		
21.	Ioannis Theofilakis	GRE	23	214		
22.	William Milne	GBR	23	212		
23.	Francis Kemp	GBR	23	206		
24.	William Leuschner	USA	23	206		
25.	Axel Wahlstedt	SWE	23	200		
26.	Aleksandr Dobrzhansky	RUS	23	190		
27.	Pierre Gentil	FRA	23	176		
28.	Arthur Nordenswan	SWE	22	200		
29.	David Griffiths	GBR	22	192		
30.	Nikolaos Levidis	GRE	22	192		
31.	Povl Gerlow	DEN	21	174		
32.	Vladimir Potekin[8]	RUS	20	171		
33.	Sándor, Count Török von Mura	HUN	18	146		
34.	Carl Osburn	USA	18	146		
35.	Robert Jonsson	SWE	17	143		
36.	Iakovos Theofilas	GRE	14	116		

[9]

Diplomas of Merit

Joseph Pepé (GBR), Robert Murray (GBR), Axel Gyllenkrok (SWE)

Small-Bore Rifle, 25 Meters, Disappearing Target, Teams (Event H)

A: 16; C: 4; D: 5 July; T: 1500; F: 4-man teams. 5 series of 25 shots. 250 possible per shooter, 1,000 possible per team. Target was a 12-centimeter high figure, 3.5 centimeters at the widest, which appeared for three seconds, with intervals of five seconds between appearances. After each series of five shots, the figure was changed. Any position allowed. The center 10-mark was an oval 14 mm. high and 10 mm. wide, with subsequent scoring ovals 7 mm. apart. Places determined first by number of hits on target, and ties decided by 1) number of points made, 2) number of 10s, 3) number of 9s, and so on.

This team competition was closely fought between Sweden and Great Britain, but Sweden eventually won, led by Johan Hübner von Holst, and the twin Carlberg brothers, Eric and Vilhelm. The Swedish and American shooters used autoloading Winchester M1903 .22 caliber rifles, while the British used single-shot rifles. No Swedish shots missed the target, but one of their competitors failed to discharge his shot in time, and that had to count as a miss.

	Points	*Hits*
1. Sweden	925	99

    (Johan Hübner von Holst [238], Eric Carlberg [238], Wilhelm Carlberg [229], Gustaf Boivie [220])

2. Great Britain	917	99

    (William Pimm [237], Joseph Pepé [235], William Milne [226], William Styles [219])

3. United States	881

    (Frederick Hird [227], Warren Sprout [221], W. Neil McDonnell [217], William Leuschner [216])

4. Greece	716

    (Ioannis Theofilakis [211], Iakovos Theofilas [187], Frangiskos Maurommatis [185], Nikolaos Levidis [133])
10

Small-Bore Rifle, 50 Meters, Prone, Teams (Event F)

A: 24; C: 6; D: 3 July; T: 1200; F: 4-man teams. 40 shots prone position per shooter. Five-ring of four centimeters in diameter. 200 possible per shooter, 800 possible per team. Target 40 × 40 centimeters, with a five-ring of four centimeters in diameter, black center six centimeters in diameter, four-ring three centimeters, three-ring three centimeters, two-ring seven centimeters. Ties decided by the greatest number of 1) 5s, 2) black center hits, 3) 4s, 4) 3s, and so on.

In *Olympic Shooting*, Crossman described the results of this match as follows. "The Americans had not trained especially for the 50-meter prone team match, but they had some hopes of winning with their Stevens M414 single-shot, falling-block rifles. They soon found the sights inadequate. The rules specified the prone position for this match, with no artificial support.[11] The officials ruled that the ground was obviously not artificial and that the shooters therefore could rest their rifles on the ground. Strangely, only the Swedish team seemed to know about this, and they took full advantage of the knowledge, resting both the left hand and forearm and the butt of the rifle on the firing line. The English raised quite a fuss about this, but lost and went on to win by shooting ability, 762 to the Swedes' 748, with the United States four points behind, for a third out of the six teams."[12]

1. Great Britain	762

    (Edward Lessimore [195], William Pimm [193], Joseph Pepé [189], Robert Murray [185])[13]

2. Sweden   748
   (Arthur Nordenswan [190], Eric Carlberg [189], Ruben Örtegren [185], Wilhelm Carlberg [184])

3. United States   744
   (Warren Sprout [193], William Leuschner [188], Frederick Hird [185], Carl Osburn [178])

4. France   714
   (Léon Johnson [189], Pierre Gentil [183], André Regaud [180], Maxime Landin [162])

=5. Denmark   708
   (Povl Gerlow [185], Lars Jørgen Madsen [180], Frants Nielsen [177], Hans Denver [166])

   Greece   708
   (Ioannis Theofilakis [184], Iakovos Theofilas [177], Frangiskos Maurommatis [174], Nikolaos Levidis [173])
   14

Pistol Shooting

Dueling Pistol, 30 Meters (Event M)

A: 42; C: 10; D: 29 June; T: 0900; F: 30 shots in six series of five shots each. Target a figure
1.7 meters high. Figure appeared for each shot for three seconds and then disappeared after ten
seconds. After each series, there was an interval for marking. Scoring by hits on target, with ties
broken by points. 30 hits possible, 300 points possible. Places determined first by number of
hits on target, and ties subsequently broken by number of points made.

Alfred Lane won both of the individual pistol shooting events at the Stockholm Olympics,
although he was only 20 years old in 1912. He won three gold medals in 1912, adding a team
gold in the military pistol event, where he also made the highest score. In the team dueling pistol event, Lane also had the highest individual score, although the United States finished only
fourth. Lane competed again at Antwerp in 1920 and added two more gold medals in team events
and a bronze in the individual free pistol. Johan Hübner von Holst (SWE) and John Dietz
(USA) tied for third place. In the shoot-off for the bronze medal, von Holst scored 284 to
Dietz's 282.

			Hits	Points
1.	Alfred Lane	USA	30	287
2.	Paul Palén	SWE	30	286
3.	Johan Hübner von Holst	SWE	30	283
4.	John Dietz	USA	30	283
5.	C. Ivan Törnmarck	SWE	30	280
6.	Eric Carlberg	SWE	30	278
7.	Georg de Laval	SWE	30	277
8.	Walter Winans	USA	30	276
9.	Sándor, Count Török von Mura	HUN	30	275
10.	Hans Roedder	USA	30	275
11.	Gustaf Boivie	SWE	30	272

			Hits	*Points*
12.	Edmond Sandoz	FRA	30	272
13.	Patrik de Laval	SWE	30	268
14.	Georgy Panteleymonov	RUS	30	265
15.	Wilhelm Carlberg	SWE	29	274
16.	Peter Dolfen	USA	29	274
17.	Erik Boström	SWE	29	274
18.	Frans-Albert Schartau	SWE	29	270
19.	Reginald Sayre	USA	29	268
20.	Adolf Schmal, Jr.	AUT	29	267
21.	Henry Sears	USA	29	266
22.	Nikolay Melnitsky	RUS	29	264
23.	Ioannis Theofilakis	GRE	29	263
24.	Pavel Voyloshnikov	RUS	29	260
25.	Felix Alegria	CHI	29	259
26.	Georges, Marquis de Crequi-Montfort de Courtivron	FRA	28	263
27.	Konstantinos Skarlatos	GRE	28	261
28.	Amosse Kache	RUS	28	260
29.	Frangiskos Maurommatis	GRE	28	256
30.	Axel Gyllenkrok	SWE	28	255
31.	Maurice Fauré	FRA	28	250
32.	Grigory Shesterikov	RUS	28	250
33.	Alexandros Theofilakis	GRE	27	242
34.	Nikolaos Levidis	GRE	27	231
35.	Anastasios Metaxas	GRE	26	232
36.	Charles, Baron de Jaubert	FRA	26	229
37.	Hugo Cederschiöld	SWE	26	225
38.	Harald Ekwall	CHI	25	217
39.	Georg Meyer	GER	25	207
40.	I. Edmond Bernhardt	AUT	25	194
41.	William McClure	GBR	23	180
42.	Henri, Baron de Castex	FRA	17	140

15

Diplomas of Merit

John Dietz (USA), Ivan Törnmarck (SWE), Eric Carlberg (SWE), Georg de Laval (SWE), Walter Winans (USA), Sándor, Count Török von Mura (HUN), Hans Roedder (USA)

Free Pistol, 50 Meters (Event K)

A: 54; C: 12; D: 1 July; T: 1200; F: 60 shots in ten series of six shots each. Target 50 centimeters in diameter. Center ring five centimeters across, with each scoring ring 2.5 centimeters apart, with the black center 20 centimeters in diameter (7–10). 600 possible. Ties settled by countback on 10s, 9s, 8s, and so on.

Alfred Lane added the free pistol gold medal to the one he had earned in the dueling pistol event two days previously. In this event, his 25-point margin of victory was one of the most dominant performances in Olympic shooting history. Charles Stewart (GBR) and Georg de

Laval (SWE) finished equal third with 470, but Stewart won the bronze medal because of having scored more "centers (tens)" than de Laval.[16]

The 8th-place finisher, Nikolay Panin (Kolomenkin) was a well-known figure skater, who had won the special figures gold medal at the 1908 Olympics in London. His real name was Nikolay Kolomenkin, but he competed under the pseudonym of Nikolay Panin, presumably because sports were considered undignified by the elite of Russian society in that era.

1.	Alfred Lane	USA	499
2.	Peter Dolfen	USA	474
3.	Charles Stewart	GBR	470[17]
4.	Georg de Laval	SWE	470
5.	Erik Boström	SWE	468
6.	Horatio Poulter	GBR	461
7.	Henry Sears	USA	459
8.	Nikolay Panin (Kolomenkin)	RUS	457
9.	John Dietz	USA	454
10.	Léon Johnson	FRA	454
11.	C. Ivan Törnmarck	SWE	453
12.	Eric Carlberg	SWE	452
13.	Reginald Sayre	USA	452
14.	Lars Jørgen Madsen	DEN	452
15.	André Regaud	FRA	447
16.	Wilhelm Carlberg	SWE	446
17.	Georgy Panteleymonov	RUS	442
18.	Ioannis Theofilakis	GRE	441
19.	Dmitry Kuskov	RUS	438
20.	Hugh Durant	GBR	433
21.	Laurits Larsen	DEN	432
22.	Hans Roedder	USA	431
23.	Harald Ekwall	CHI	430
24.	Albert Kempster	GBR	426
25.	J. Fredrik Nyström	SWE	426
26.	Frangiskos Maurommatis	GRE	425
27.	Sándor, Count Török von Mura	HUN	424
28.	Heikki Huttunen	FIN	424
29.	Robert Löfman	SWE	423
30.	Konstantinos Skarlatos	GRE	420
31.	Grigory Shesterikov	RUS	420
32.	Peter Jones	GBR	417
33.	Nikolay Melnitsky	RUS	414
34.	Pavel Voyloshnikov	RUS	413
35.	William McClure	GBR	411
36.	Paul Palén	SWE	410
37.	Gideon Ericsson	SWE	408
38.	Felix Alegria	CHI	406
39.	Adolf Schmal, Jr.	AUT	406
40.	Frants Nielsen	DEN	406
41.	Niels Larsen	DEN	405
42.	Gustaf Boivie	SWE	401

43.	Peter Sofus Nielsen	DEN	397
44.	Gerhard Bock	GER	395
45.	Edward Tickell	GBR	387
46.	Amosse Kache	RUS	384
47.	Alexandros Theofilakis	GRE	369
48.	Gustaf Stiernspetz	SWE	357
49.	Walter Winans	USA	356
50.	Anders Peter Nielsen	DEN	355
51.	Hugo Cederschiöld	SWE	352
52.	Zoltán Jelenffy-Tóth von Csejthe	HUN	348
53.	I. Edmond Bernhardt	AUT	245
54.	Heinrich Hoffmann	GER	189

18

Diplomas of Merit

Georg de Laval (SWE), Erik Boström (SWE), Horatio Poulter (GBR)

Dueling Pistol, 30 Meters, Teams (Event L)

A: 28; C: 7; D: 29 June, 3 July[19]; T: 1500 (29/6); F: four-man teams. 30 shots per shooter in six series of five shots each. Target a figure 1.7 meters high. Figure appeared for each shot for three seconds and then disappeared after ten seconds. After each series, there was an interval for marking. Scoring by hits on target, with ties broken by points. 30 hits possible per shooter, 300 points possible per shooter; 120 hits possible per team, 1,200 possible per team. Places determined first by number of hits on target, and ties subsequently broken by number of points made.

Sweden won this event comfortably, with a perfect score of 120 hits on target, led by the Carlberg twins, Wilhelm and Eric. The highest individual score in this event was made by the United States' Alfred Lane, who had won both individual pistol events. The event was decided by the number of hits on target, which enabled Russia to win the silver medal, despite having had only the fourth highest total of points.

	Hits	*Points*
1. Sweden	120	1,145

(Wilhelm Carlberg [290], Eric Carlberg [287], Johan Hübner von Holst [284], Paul Palén [284])

2. Russia	118	1,091

(Amosse Kache [281], Nikolay Melnitsky [273], Pavel Voyloshnikov [270], Georgy Panteleymonov [267])

3. Great Britain	117	1,107[20]

(Hugh Durant [289], Albert Kempster [285], Charles Stewart [284], Horatio Poulter [249])

4. United States	117	1,097

(Alfred Lane [292], Reginald Sayre [273], Walter Winans [271], John Dietz [261])

5. Greece	115	1,057

(Konstantinos Skarlatos [283], Ioannis Theofilakis [275], Frangiskos Maurommatis [273], Georgios Petropoulos [226])

6. France   113   1,041
    (Edmond Sandoz [285], Charles, Baron de Jaubert [275], Georges, Marquis de Crequi-Montfort de Courtivron [259], Maurice Fauré [222])

7. Germany   102   890
    (Bernhard Wandolleck [256], Gerhard Bock [233], Georg Meyer [216], Heinrich Hoffmann [195])

Military Pistol, 50 Meters, Teams (Event J)

A: 20; C: 5; D: 2 July; T: 1200; F: four-man teams. 60 shots per shooter in ten series of six shots each. 600 possible per shooter, 2,400 possible per team. Target 50 centimeters in diameter. Center ring five centimeters across, with each scoring ring 2.5 centimeters apart, with the black center 20 centimeters in diameter (7–10). Ties settled by countback on 10s, 9s, 8s, and so on.

America's Alfred Lane led the team to the gold medal. His score of 509 was 34 points higher than that of the next best individual, Sweden's Georg de Laval (475). This was the final pistol shooting event of the 1912 Olympics.

1. United States   1,916
    (Alfred Lane [509], Henry Sears [474], Peter Dolfen [467], John Dietz [466])

2. Sweden   1,849
    (Georg de Laval [475], Eric Carlberg [472], Wilhelm Carlberg [459], Erik Boström [443])

3. Great Britain   1,804
    (Horatio Poulter [461], Hugh Durant [456], Albert Kempster [452], Charles Stewart [435])

4. Russia   1,801
    (Nikolay Panin (Kolomenkin) [469], Grigory Shesterikov [448], Pavel Voyloshnikov [447], Nikolay Melnitsky [437])

5. Greece   1,731[21]
    (Frangiskos Maurommatis [454], Ioannis Theofilakis [442], Konstantinos Skarlatos [429], Alexandros Theofilakis [406])
    [22]

Diplomas of Merit

Russia (Nikolay Panin (Kolomenkin), Grigory Shesterikov, Pavel Voyloshnikov, Nikolay Melnitsky)

Running Deer Shooting

Running Deer, Single Shot, Individual (Event Q)

A: 34; C: 7; D: 29 June–1 July; T: 1000–1200, 1330–1800; F: Ten shots per man with one shot per run. Deer with scoring rings up to five points per shot. Rifle off shoulder before deer appears. 23-meter wide run at a distance of 100 meters. Target runs for four seconds across the opening. 50 possible, 25 possible in shoot-offs. Ties decided by shoot-offs of five runs.

This event resulted in a three-way tie for first place. In the shoot-off, Finland's Nestori Toivonen took three of the five shots and then withdrew, as he was well behind. Sweden's Alfred Swahn and Åke Lundeberg both took the full five shots. Swahn led by one point after four shots, 15–14, but scored a perfect five on the final shot to win the gold medal. Swedish shooters dominated this event, taking five of the first six and six of the first eight places.

Alfred Swahn won nine Olympic shooting medals between 1908 and 1924, three of each color. His father, Oscar Swahn, was the defending champion from London, but finished tied for fourth in this event at Stockholm.

													Total	SO
1.	Alfred Swahn	SWE	3	5	4	5	4	3	3	5	5	4	41	20
2.	Åke Lundeberg	SWE	4	4	3	4	5	4	4	4	4	5	41	17
3.	Nestor Toivonen	FIN	5	3	4	4	5	4	4	4	5	3	41	11
=4.[23]	Karl Larsson	SWE	4	5	3	4	5	3	4	4	4	3	39	
	Oscar Swahn	SWE	4	4	3	3	5	5	2	5	4	4	39	
	Sven August Lindskog	SWE	4	2	4	5	5	5	5	3	2	4	39	
7.	Heinrich Elbogen	AUT	5	4	3	4	4	5	3	3	3	4	38	
=8.	Adolf Cederström	SWE	5	5	3	3	3	3	3	4	5	3	37	
	William Leuschner	USA	4	4	3	3	5	5	3	3	5	2	37	
10.	Adolf Michel	AUT	3	3	4	4	4	5	4	5	1	3	36	
=11.	Johann Ekman	SWE	4	2	–	3	5	5	4	3	4	4	34	
	Erik Sökjer-Petersén	SWE	3	3	–	3	3	4	3	5	5	5	34	
13.	Erland Koch	GER	3	3	4	2	3	4	3	3	5	3	33	
14.	Ernst Rosenqvist	FIN	4	3	3	2	4	2	3	4	4	3	32	
=15.	Gustaf Lyman	SWE	3	4	3	3	2	4	2	3	3	4	31	
	Vasily Skrotsky	RUS	3	3	1	5	3	4	4	3	5	–	31	
	Peter Paternelli	AUT	5	3	3	3	–	4	3	4	2	4	31	
	Axel Londen	FIN	2	3	3	4	3	4	3	3	3	3	31	
	Nikolaos Levidis	GRE	3	3	3	3	3	3	3	4	3	3	31	
20.	Harry Blau	RUS	2	4	2	3	2	3	2	4	4	3	29	
=21.	Huvi Tuiskunen	FIN	2	3	4	1	5	2	2	3	3	3	28	
	Iivar "Iivo" Väänänen	FIN	3	3	3	–	4	4	2	3	3	3	28	
	Albert Preuß	GER	5	3	2	–	3	4	–	4	3	4	28	
=24.	Horst Goeldel-Bronikoven	GER	3	4	2	4	4	3	3	2	–	2	27	
	Emil Lindewald	SWE	3	3	3	3	–	3	5	–	3	4	27	
=26.	Per-Olof Arvidsson	SWE	5	3	–	2	3	–	5	2	3	3	26	
	Karl Reilin	FIN	–	3	4	2	2	3	3	3	3	3	26	
	Edward Benedicks	SWE	3	2	2	4	4	4	–	3	–	4	26	
=29.	Walter Winans	USA	4	–	4	–	2	2	4	5	–	3	24	
	Ioannis Theofilakis	GRE	4	3	4	–	–	3	3	–	3	4	24	
=31.	Dmitry Barkov	RUS	3	3	2	1	1	1	3	3	3	3	23	
	Eberhard Steinböck	AUT	–	3	3	3	5	–	3	–	3	3	23	
33.	Aleksandr Dobrzhansky	RUS	3	–	3	1	3	3	3	2	1	3	22	
34.	Pavel Lieth	RUS	2	–	–	1	–	3	–	3	–	1	10	

24

Shoot-Off

								Total
1.	Alfred Swahn	SWE	5	5	3	2	5	20
2.	Åke Lundeberg	SWE	3	4	4	3	3	17
3.	Nestor Toivonen	FIN	4	3	4	–	–	11

Diplomas of Merit[25]

Karl Larsson (SWE), Sven Arvid Lindskog (SWE), Heinrich Elbogen (AUT), Adolf Cederström (SWE), William Leuschner (USA), Adolf Michel (AUT), Johann Ekman (SWE)

Running Deer, Double Shot, Individual (Event R)

A: 20; C: 6; D: 3 July; T: 0900–1200, 1330; F: 20 shots per man, with two shots per run. Deer with scoring rings up to five points per shot. Rifle off shoulder before deer appears. 23-meter wide run at a distance of 100 meters. Target runs for four seconds across the opening. 100 possible, 30 possible in shoot-offs. Ties decided by shoot-offs of three runs.

Although there were 45 entries for this event, only 20 shooters started, and 12 of the starters were Swedes. Swedish shooters finished in the first nine places and took 12 of the first 14 places. The winner, Åke Lundeberg, won medals in all three running deer events at Stockholm, but never again competed at the Olympics. He also competed in the two clay trap shooting events at Stockholm, but failed to win a medal in those.

1.	Åke Lundeberg	SWE	3/4	3/5	3/5	4/4	3/4	3/3	3/5	5/5	3/5	4/5	79
2.	Edward Benedicks	SWE	3/4	4/5	3/3	4/4	3/5	3/4	2/3	4/5	3/5	2/5	74
3.	Oscar Swahn	SWE	4/4	3/5	2/2	5/5	3/4	3/5	2/4	3/4	3/4	3/4	72
=4.	Alfred Swahn	SWE	3/5	4/5	5/5	2/5	3/5	–/3	2/3	–/3	2/4	4/5	68
	Per-Olof Arvidsson[26]	SWE	4/5	4/5	–/5	4/5	3/4	4/5	–/3	–/2	3/3	4/5	68
6.	Sven August Lindskog	SWE	3/4	3/4	3/4	3/4	2/4	1/4	4/5	2/3	2/4	3/5	67
7.	Erik Sökjer-Petersén	SWE	2/5	3/4	2/4	3/4	3/4	–/–	5/5	4/4	3/4	2/4	65
8.	Emil Lindewald	SWE	–/3	2/4	4/4	3/4	4/4	–/3	3/4	5/5	3/3	3/3	64
9.	Gustaf Lyman	SWE	2/3	2/4	3/5	3/4	3/3	3/4	–/2	3/4	3/3	3/4	61
10.	Charles, Baron de Jaubert	FRA	–/5	2/3	2/3	4/4	2/4	3/3	2/4	4/3	–/5	3/4	60
11.	Walter Winans	USA	3/4	3/3	2/2	2/4	2/4	–/3	4/4	2/3	3/5	3/3	59
=12.	E. Hjalmar Frisell	SWE	2/4	3/5	4/5	–/3	2/3	–/3	3/5	3/4	4/5	–/–	58
	Johann Ekman	SWE	2/3	–/3	3/5	3/3	3/3	–/4	3/4	–/3	3/4	4/5	58
14.	C. Wilhelm Dybäck	SWE	–/3	2/3	3/–	3/3	–/3	1/3	3/4	4/4	5/5	3/5	57
15.	William Leuschner	USA	2/3	3/3	3/4	3/3	3/3	4/5	3/3	2/2	–/–	–/–	49
16.	Heinrich Elbogen	AUT	3/3	–/5	3/3	–/5	2/3	1/3	2/3	1/3	4/4	–/–	48
=17.	Erland Koch	GER	2/3	–/3	–/3	4/4	–/5	2/3	3/5	–/2	–/3	2/3	47
	Albert Preuß	GER	–/3	3/3	–/3	3/4	–/3	–/3	–/3	3/4	2/3	3/4	47
19.	Dmitry Barkov	RUS	1/2	–/2	–/2	–/3	3/3	4/4	–/–	–/4	1/4	3/3	39
20.	Vasily Skrotsky	RUS	–/3	–/1	–/3	1/1	2/3	1/1	3/3	–/1	2/3	1/3	32

[27]

Diplomas of Merit[28]

Erik Sökjer-Petersén (SWE), Emil Lindewald (SWE)

Running Deer, Single Shot, Teams (Event P)

A: 20; C: 5; D: 4 July; T: 1000–1200, 1330; F: Four-man teams. Ten shots per man with one shot per run. Deer with scoring rings up to five points per shot. Rifle off shoulder before deer appears. 23-meter wide run at a distance of 100 meters. Target runs for four seconds across the opening. 50 possible per shooter, 200 possible per team.

After taking the first nine places in the double-shot running deer event on 3 July, Sweden was heavily favored in the team running deer event, and they won easily. They were led by the individual winners in the two running deer events, Åke Lundeberg and Alfred Swahn. But their leading scorer in the team event was Swahn's father, Oscar Swahn, who was 64 years, 257 days old on 4 July 1912, making him the oldest gold medalist in Olympic history. Oscar Swahn returned to the Olympics in 1920, where he won a silver medal in the team running deer event, aged 72 years, 279 days, making him the oldest medalist in Olympic history. Oscar Swahn was on the Swedish shooting team which was to compete at the 1924 Paris Olympics, but he fell ill shortly before those Games and did not compete. He died on 1 May 1927, a few months shy of his 80th birthday.

1. Sweden   151
   (Oscar Swahn [43], Åke Lundeberg [39], Alfred Swahn [37], Per-Olof Arvidsson [32])
2. United States   132
   (Walter Winans [39], William Leuschner [38], William Libbey [37], Neil McDonnell [18])
3. Finland   123
   (Nestor Toivonen [38], Iivar "Iivo" Väänänen [30], Axel Londen [29], Ernst Rosenqvist [26])
4. Austria   115
   (Peter Paternelli [34], Adolf Michel [33], Heinrich Elbogen [29], Eberhard Steinböck [19])
5. Russia   108
   (Vasily Skrotsky [36], Dmitry Barkov [26], Harry Blau [23], Aleksandr Dobrzhansky [23]) [29]

Clay Trap Shooting

Clay Trap Shooting, Individual (Event O)

A: 61; C: 11; D: 2–4 July; T: 0900 (2/7), 0900 (3/7), 0900 (4/7); F: 100 birds possible per shooter, shot in three stages. Two shots could be fired at each bird. First stage was 20 birds per man in two rounds, with unknown angles and known traps. Second stage was 30 birds per man in two rounds, with unknown angles and known traps. Third stage was 50 birds per man in three stages, with 40 birds from known traps and ten birds from unknown traps. Top 31 shooters and ties advanced to second stage. Top 20 and ties advanced to 3rd stage. [30]

James Graham won this event, posting the highest score in each stage, although his totals were equaled by other shooters at each stage. He was the most consistent shooter by far. After the first round, Graham was tied with Baron von Zedlitz und Leipe (GER), Edward Gleason

(USA), and Horst Göldel-Bronikoven (GER). After two rounds, he remained tied with his teammate, Gleason, but Gleason slumped badly in the last round and finished only 11th. In addition to his gold medal, Graham won Lord Westbury's Challenge Trophy, which in 1908 had been presented to Canada's Walter Ewing.

			Stage 1	*Stage 2*	*Stage 3*	*Total*
1.	James Graham	USA	19	28	49	96
2.	Alfred Goeldel-Bronikoven	GER	18	28	48	94
3.	Harry Blau	RUS	15	27	49	91
=4.	Harold Humby	GBR	18	24	46	88
	Anastasios Metaxas[31]	GRE	18	26	44	88
	Albert Preuß	GER	17	25	46	88
	Gustaf Adolf "Aadolf" Schnitt[32]	FIN	18	26	44	88
	Franz, Baron von Zedlitz und Leipe[33]	GER	19	23	46	88
=9.	Emile Jurgens	NED	17	27	43	87
	Ralph Spotts	USA	16	24	47	87
	Edward Gleason	USA	19	28	40	87
=12.	Erland Koch	GER	18	23	45	86
	Karl Fazer	FIN	16	25	43	86[34]
	Horst Goeldel-Bronikoven	GER	19	23	44	86
	Frank Hall	USA	16	26	44	86
16.	William Grosvenor	GBR	17	24	44	85
=17.	Robert Hutcheson	CAN	15	26	43	84
	Erich, Count von Bernstorff-Gyldensteen	GER	17	24	43	84
	John Butt	GBR	18	24	42	84
	Åke Lundeberg	SWE	17	24	43	84
=21.	Charles Palmer	GBR	15	24	43	82
	Alfred Swahn	SWE	17	25	40	82
=23.	Leonardus Syttin	RUS	15	24	42	81
	Frantz Rosenberg	NOR	15	24	42	81
=25.	Hans Joachim Lüttich	GER	16	23	38	77
	Charles, Baron de Jaubert	FRA	15	25	37	77
=27.	André Fleury	FRA	16	23	35	74
	Carsten Henrik Bruun	NOR	16	24	34	74
=29.	Henri, Baron de Castex	FRA	17	21	—	38
	Robert Huber	FIN	15	23	—	38
	E. Hjalmar Frisell	SWE	15	23	—	38
	Emil Johannes Collan	FIN	15	23	—	38
	George Whitaker	GBR	16	22	—	38
34.	Victor Wallenberg	SWE	17	20	—	37
=35.	Georges de Crequi-Montfort de Courtivron	FRA	15	21	—	36
	Walter Bodneck	RUS	15	21	—	36
	Daniel McMahon	USA	15	21	—	36
38.	Edward Benedicks	SWE	15	19	—	34
39.	George Pinchard	GBR	15	18	—	33
40.	Johann Ekman	SWE	15	16	—	31
=41.	Edouard Creuzé de Lesser	FRA	14	—	—	14
	Charles Billings	USA	14	—	—	14

			Stage 1	Stage 2	Stage 3	Total
	Herman Eriksson	SWE	14	—	—	14
	John Hendrickson	USA	14	—	—	14
=45.	James Kenyon	CAN	13	—	—	13
	William Davies	CAN	13	—	—	13
	C. Edvard Bacher	FIN	13	—	—	13
	René Texier	FRA	13	—	—	13
	Alexander Maunder	GBR	13	—	—	13
	Herman Nyberg	SWE	13	—	—	13
=51.	Henri le Marié	FRA	12	—	—	12
	Pavel Lieth	RUS	12	—	—	12
=53.	Alfred Black	GBR	11	—	—	11
	Emil Ernst Fabritius	FIN	11	—	—	11
	Boris Pertel	RUS	11	—	—	11
=56.[35]	John Goodwin	GBR	10	—	—	10
	Oscar Swahn	SWE	10	—	—	10
	Otto Bökman	SWE	10	—	—	10
	Carl Wollert	SWE	10	—	—	10
60.	Nils Klein	SWE	7	—	—	7
61.	Alfred Stabell	NOR	3	—	—	3

[36]

Diplomas of Merit

Harold Humby (GBR), Anastasios Metaxas (GRE), Albert Preuß (GER), Gustaf Adolf "Aadolf" Schnitt (FIN), Franz, Baron von Zedlitz und Leipe (GER)

Clay Trap Shooting, Teams (Event N)

A: 36; C: 6; D: 29 June, 1 July; T: 0900–1200, 1330 (29/6 — 1st stage); 0900–1200, 1330 (1/7 — 2nd/3rd stages); F: six-man teams. Shot in three stages. First stage was 20 birds per man in two rounds, unknown angles, known traps, continuous fire, with half the teams eliminated after this stage. Second stage was 30 birds per man in two rounds, unknown angles, known traps, continuous fire, with half the remaining teams eliminate after this stage. Third stage was 50 birds per man in three parts; parts one and two were 20 birds each, unknown angles, known traps, continuous fire, while part three was unknown angles and unknown traps. Possibles per team: first stage — 120, second stage — 180, third stage — 300; total — 600.

The United States team had the highest score in all three stages, winning the gold medal quite easily over Great Britain. A seventh team was entered, Russia, but did not compete. Because there were seven entries, only four teams were supposed to advance to the second stage. But Finland and Sweden were tied at 95 after the first stage and both were allowed to continue, eliminating only France after the first day. Both Finland and Sweden were eliminated after the second stage, leaving the final shooting to the United States, Great Britain, and Germany. The real contest was for the silver medal between Great Britain and Germany. After stage one, Germany was in second place, trailing the United States by only one bird, and after two stages, Britain led Germany by only one bird. Both teams scored 247 in the final stage to give Great Britain the silver medal.

1. United States   108   161   263   532
   (James Graham [16/30/48-94], Charles Billings [20/29/44-93], Ralph Spotts [18/28/44-
   90], John Hendrickson [18/26/45-89], Frank Hall [18/25/43-86], Edward Gleason
   [18/23/39-80])

2. Great Britain   104   160   247   511
   (Harold Humby [19/26/46-91], William Grosvenor [17/29/43-89], Alexander Maunder
   [18/27/44-89], George Whitaker [17/27/40-84], John Butt [16/24/39-79], Charles
   Palmer [17/27/35-79])

3. Germany   107   156   247   510
   (Franz, Baron von Zedlitz und Leipe [19/28/44-91], Horst Goeldel-Bronikoven [18/27/43-
   88], Erich, Count von Bernstorff-Gyldensteen [18/24/45-87], Erland Koch [17/26/39-
   82], Albert Preuß [18/25/38-81], Alfred Goeldel-Bronikoven [17/26/38-81])

4. Sweden   95   148   —   243
   (Åke Lundeberg [19/29-48], Alfred Swahn [18/27-45], Johann Ekman [16/25-41], Victor Wallenberg [15/25-40], E. Hjalmar Frisell [13/25-38], Carl Wollert [14/17-31])

5. Finland   95   138   —   233
   (C. Edvard Bacher [17/27-44], Robert Huber [18/25-43], Gustaf Adolf "Aadolf" Schnitt
   [18/23-41], Emil Johannes Collan [16/21-37], Karl Fazer [15/21-36], Axel Londen
   [11/21-32])

6. France   90   —   —   90
   (André Fleury [16], Henri, Baron de Castex [15], Georges, Marquis de Crequi-Montfort
   de Courtivron [15], Charles, Baron de Jaubert [15], René Texier [15], Edouard Creuzé
   de Lesser [14])
   37

NOTES

1. Also entered in this event, but not competing, were Ludwig Ternajgo (AUT), Magnus Vin-
derslev (DEN), Ernst Rosenqvist (FIN), Oscar Rosenqvist (FIN), Iivo Väänänen (FIN), Maurice Fauré
(FRA), Maxime Landin (FRA), Léon Lécuyer (FRA), André Regaud (FRA), Alexandros Theofilakis
(GRE), Ioannis Theofilakis (GRE), Zoltán Zyzda (HUN), Sándor Prokopp (HUN), Béla von Darányi
(HUN), Geza von Hammersberg (HUN), Sándor, Count Török von Mura (HUN), Vasily Skrotsky
(RUS), Edwin L. Anderson (USA), John Jackson (USA), Edward Kingsbury Lang (USA), and W.
Neil McDonnell (USA).

2. Also entered in this event, but not competing, were Ludwig Ternajgo (AUT), Rasmus Friis
(DEN), Laurits Larsen (DEN), Wilhelm Laybourn (DEN), Magnus Vinderslev (DEN), André Regaud
(FRA), Léon Johnson (FRA), Maurice Lecoq (FRA), Auguste Marion (FRA), Philip Plater (GBR),
Spyridon Mostras (GRE), Zoltán Zyzda (HUN), Geza von Hammersberg (HUN), Sándor, Count
Török von Mura (HUN), Edwin L. Anderson (USA), and Edward Kingsbury Lang (USA).

3. Also entered in this event, but not competing, were Ludwig Ternajgo (AUT), E. R. Fox
(AUS), J. J. Wallace (AUS), Niels Hansen Ditlev-Larsen (DEN), Povl Gerlow (DEN), Laurits Larsen
(DEN), Vilhelm Laybourn (DEN), Maurice Fauré (FRA), Maxime Landin (FRA), Maurice Lecoq
(FRA), André Regaud (FRA), Spyridon Mostras (GRE), Deukalion Rediadis (GRE), István Prihoda
(HUN), Zoltán Zyzda (HUN), Sándor Prokopp (HUN), and Béla von Darányi (HUN).

4. Also entered in this event, but not competing, were teams from Hungary and the United
States.

5. Also entered in this event, but not competing, were Ludwig Ternajgo (AUT), Hans Denver (DEN), Niels Hansen Ditlev-Larsen (DEN), Lars Jørgen Madsen (DEN), Ole Olsen (DEN), Hans Schultz (DEN), Paul Colas (FRA), Raoul, Count de Boigne (FRA), Pierre Gentil (FRA), Maxime Landin (FRA), Léon Johnson (FRA), Léon Lécuyer (FRA), Louis Percy (FRA), Jacques Regaud (FRA), Athanase Sartori (FRA), William Grosvenor (GBR), Harry Humby (GBR), Spyridon Mostras (GRE), Deukalion Rediadis (GRE), Alexandros Theofilakis (GRE), Emil, Ritter Bömches von Boor (HUN), Johann Iván (HUN), Alfons Szmazsenka (HUN), Géza von Hammersberg (HUN), Alfred von Tisza-Ujlak (HUN), István Prihoda (HUN), Aladár von Farkas (HUN), Géza Mészöly von Sárbogárd (HUN), Julius Melczer von Kelemesi (HUN), Ole Bjerke (NOR), Johannes Espelund (NOR), Albert Helgerud (NOR), Ole Sæther (NOR), Yevgeny Tevyakhov (RUS), Otto Schmunk (RUS), George Harvey (RSA), Robert Patterson (RSA), George Whelan (RSA), Robert Dennis (USA), John Dooley (USA), Albert Jones (USA), and Harris Laning (USA).

6. There were 66 entries according to the 12OR. There were 36 competitors, thus 30 did not start. However, there are 31 entry forms for shooters who did not start. One competitor, Vladimir Potekin (RUS), has no entry form, and he may have competed without being entered.

7. EK has 228, but 12OR and all 1912 sources have 227.

8. Vladimir Potekin (RUS), has no entry form, and he may have competed without being entered.

9. Also entered in this event, but not competing, were Ludwig Ternajgo (AUT), Hans Denver (DEN), Niels Hansen Ditlev-Larsen (DEN), Lars Jørgen Madsen (DEN), Frants Nielsen (DEN), Ole Olsen (DEN), Hans Schultz (DEN), Paul Colas (FRA), Raoul, Count de Boigne (FRA), Maxime Landin (FRA), Léon Lécuyer (FRA), Louis Percy (FRA), André Regaud (FRA), Jacques Regaud (FRA), Athanase Sartori (FRA), William Grosvenor (GBR), Harry Humby (GBR), Thomas Jenkins (GBR), Anastasios Metaxas (GRE), Spyridon Mostras (GRE), Deukalion Rediadis (GRE), Alexandros Theofilakis (GRE), Aladár von Farkas (HUN), Géza von Hammersberg (HUN), Julius Melczer von Kelemesi (HUN), Zoltán Jelenffy-Tóth von Csejthe (HUN), Johann Iván (HUN), George Harvey (RSA), Robert Patterson (RSA), Hugo Cederschiöld (SWE), and Robert Dennis (USA).

10. Also entered in this event, but not competing, were teams from Denmark, France, and Hungary.

11. The 12OR noted, "Position: Any, without artificial rest," p. 692.

12. Crossman, *Olympic Shooting*, p. 51.

13. 12OR has the individual scores for Great Britain as Pimm—193, Lessimore—192, Pepé—189, and Murray—188. The scores given here are from TF, which noted, "In the official scores, Lessimore's score is given as 192 and Murray's as 188, but this was owing to a mistake in the targets, and the figures given here are correct. Lessimore's score was the highest made at the meeting, and deserves special consideration."

14. Also entered in this event, but not competing, were Hungary and Russia.

15. Also entered in this event, but not competing, were Ludwig Ternajgo (AUT), Lars Jørgen Madsen (DEN), Laurits Larsen (DEN), Vilhelm Laybourn (DEN), Anders Peter Nielsen (DEN), Sofus Peter Nielsen (DEN), Frants Nielsen (DEN), Georges Brulé (FRA), –– de Vanssay (FRA), Gerhard Bock (GER), Bernhard Wandolleck (GER), Heinrich Hoffmann (GER), Hugh Durant (GBR), Guy Edward Granat (GBR), Peter Jones (GBR), Albert Kempster (GBR), Henry Munday (GBR), Horatio Poulter (GBR), Charles Stewart (GBR), Edward James Tickell (GBR), Spyridon Mostras (GRE), Georgios Petropoulos (GRE), Deukalion Rediadis (GRE), Julius Melczer von Kelemesi (HUN), Dmitry Kuskov (RUS), Yevgeny Tevyakhov (RUS), Nikolay Panin (Kolomenkin) (RUS), George Harvey (RSA), Robert Patterson (RSA), Gottfrid Armstrong (USA), James Baker (USA), Irving Calkins (USA), James Edward Gorman (USA), and Thomas le Boutillier (USA).

16. 12OR, p. 700.

17. Noted in TF, "Stewart won the bronze medal after shooting off a tie with Delaval [*sic*], of Sweden," but no scores for the shoot-off were given.

18. Also entered in this event, but not competing, were Heinrich Anton Bartosch (AUT), Ludwig Ternajgo (AUT), Raoul, Count de Boigne (FRA), Maurice Fauré (FRA), Charles, Baron de Jaubert (FRA), Maxime Landin (FRA), Maurice Lecoq (FRA), Léon Lécuyer (FRA), Auguste Mar-

ion (FRA), Louis Percy (FRA), Jacques Regaud (FRA), Athanase Sartori (FRA), Guy Edward Granat (GBR), Henry Munday (GBR), Spyridon Mostras (GRE), Deukalion Rediadis (GRE), Iakovos Theofilas (GRE), Ole Sæther (NOR), Yevgeny Tevyakhov (RUS), Robert Bodley (RSA), George Harvey (RSA), Charles Jeffreys (RSA), Ernest James Keeley (RSA), Robert Patterson (RSA), Arthur Athelstan Smith (RSA), Gottfrid Armstrong (USA), James Baker (USA), Irving Calkins (USA), James Edward Gorman (USA), and Thomas le Boutillier (USA).

19. France, Russia, Sweden, and the United States shot on Saturday, 29 June. Germany, Great Britain, and Greece shot on Wednesday, 3 July.

20. DW has the mark has 1,097.

21. Spalding lists the team score for Greece as 1,761 and the individual score for Ioannis Theofilakis as 472. These scores are from 12OR.

22. Also entered in this event, but not competing, were Denmark, France, Hungary, and South Africa.

23. EK states that there was a shoot-off for fourth to sixth places, but this is not mentioned at all in 12OR, which specifically gives details of the shoot-off for first to third. DW has the results as 4) Larsson, 5) O. Swahn, 6) Lindskog, 7) Elbogen, and 8) Cederström.

24. Also entered in this event, but not competing, were Heinrich Anton Bartosch (AUT), Robert Gollitsch (AUT), Ludwig Ternajgo (AUT), E. R. Fox (AUS), J. J. Wallace (AUS), Vilhelm Laybourn (DEN), Lars Jørgen Madsen (DEN), Paul Colas (FRA), Maurice Fauré (FRA), Georges, Marquis de Crequi-Montfort de Courtivron (FRA), Edouard Creuzé de Lesser (FRA), Charles, Baron de Jaubert (FRA), Georg Meyer (GER), Alexandros Theofilakis (GRE), Alfons Szmazsenka (HUN), Géza von Hammersberg (HUN), Sándor, Count Török von Mura (HUN), Nikolay Melnitsky (RUS), Yevgeny Tevyakhov (RUS), Boris Pertel (RUS), Robert Bodley (RSA), George Harvey (RSA), Charles Jeffreys (RSA), Albert Johnstone (RSA), Ernest James Keeley (RSA), Robert Patterson (RSA), Arthur Athelstan Smith (RSA), Harry Adams (USA), Alfred Lane (USA), William Libbey (USA), and W. Neil McDonnell (USA).

25. It is unknown why Oscar Swahn (SWE), who also finished equal fourth, with Karl Larsson (SWE) and Sven August Lindskog (SWE), was not awarded a diploma of merit. The information is based on 12OR.

26. Listed as fifth in DW and EK, but there is no evidence that there was a tie-breaking decision or shoot-off for fourth and fifth places.

27. Also entered in this event, but not competing, were Robert Gollitsch (AUT), Adolf Michel (AUT), Peter Paternelli (AUT), Ludwig Ternajgo (AUT), E. R. Fox (AUS), J. J. Wallace (AUS), Lars Jørgen Madsen (DEN), Paul Colas (FRA), Georges, Marquis de Crequi-Montfort de Courtivron (FRA), Edouard Creuzé de Lesser (FRA), Maurice Fauré (FRA), Horst Goeldel-Bronikoven (GER), Georg Meyer (GER), Alfons Szmazsenka (HUN), Géza von Hammersberg (HUN), Sándor, Count Török von Mura (HUN), Aleksandr Dobrzhansky (RUS), Nikolay Melnitsky (RUS), Yevgeny Tevyakhov (RUS), George Harvey (RSA), Arthur Athelstan Smith (RSA), Harry Adams (USA), Alfred Lane (USA), William Libbey (USA), and W. Neil McDonnell (USA).

28. Sökjer-Petersén and Lindewald finished seventh and eighth, respectively. It is not known why the equal fourth place finishers (Alfred Swahn [SWE] and Per-Olof Arvidsson [SWE]) were not awarded diplomas of merit. The information is based on 12OR, p. 882.

29. Also entered in this event, but not competing, were teams from France, Germany, and South Africa.

30. More precisely, a maximum of 50 percent of the competitors were to be eliminated after the first stage. With 61 competitors, that meant that the top 31 and ties would advance to the second stage. There were 40 shooters advancing to the second stage, and again, a maximum of 50 percent of the competitors were to be eliminated. As there were 40 shooters in the second stage, 20 were to be advanced to the third stage. The qualifying score for the top 20 was 41 after the second stage; three shooters had 40 and five shooters had 39, and for unknown reasons, these eight shooters were also advanced to the third stage.

31. FW has only Humby in fourth place, and did not list Metaxas, Preuß, or Schnitt.

32. Not listed as equal fourth in EK.

33. Not listed as equal fourth in EK.

34. The scores for Fazer do not total 86, but these are the individual and total marks for each series as given in the OR.

35. Listed as "46" in 12OR, but placed between 55 and 57, an obvious typo.

36. Also entered in this event, but not competing, were Heinrich Anton Bartosch (AUT), Johann Dulnig (AUT), Adolf Michel (AUT), Walter Ewing (CAN), Alexander Bajakin (FIN), Axel Fredrik Londen (FIN), Paul Colas (FRA), André Fleury (FRA), Frangiskos Maurommatis (GRE), Alfons Szmazsenka (HUN), Géza von Hammersberg (HUN), Sándor, Count Török von Mura (HUN), Carl Heyer (HUN), Cristian Moltzer (NED), Hendrik Smith van Gelder (NED), Cornelius Marius Viruly (NED), Dmitry Barkov (RUS), Nikolay Melnitsky (RUS), Dorwin Culver (USA), and Elliott Ranney (USA).

37. Also entered in this event, but not competing, was Russia.

Swimming

Swimming has been contested at every Olympic Games of the modern era and 1912 at Stockholm was no exception. The big swimming news in Stockholm was the inclusion of events for women. While women had competed at the Olympics from 1900 to 1908 in archery, croquet, golf, tennis, and yachting, this was the first time that they were admitted to the Olympic program in one of the "major" sports. It would not be until 1928 that women would be allowed to compete in the Olympic Games in track & field athletics.

This decision was made by the IOC in Luxembourg in 1910 at its 11th session. The IOC membership voted unanimously to accept women in Olympic competition in gymnastics, swimming, and tennis. Originally, the Swedish Olympic committee planned women's competitions in the 100 meter freestyle and in plain high diving (see Diving). Eventually, it was decided to also allow women to compete in a freestyle relay race.

The swimming competitions were held at Djurgårdsbrunnsviken, an inlet not far from the Stockholm city center. A stadium setup was built in the inlet and a swimming course of 100 meters was arranged, bounded on one end by land, on the opposite end by a steamboat pier, and enclosed on each side by pontoons.

Site:	Swimming Stadium at Djurgårdsbrunnsviken
Dates:	6–15 July (6–15 July [Men], 8–9, 11–12, 15 July [Women])
Events:	9 [7 Men — 2 Women]
Competitors:	120 [93 Men — 27 Women]
Nations:	17 [17 Men — 8 Women]

Total	*Competitors*	*Gold*	*Silver*	*Bronze*	*Medals*
Australia	9	2	2	2	6
Austria	8	–	–	1	1
Belgium	5	–	–	–	–
Canada	1	2	–	–	2
Denmark	1	–	–	–	–
Finland	6	–	–	–	–
France	3	–	–	–	–
Germany	17	2	3	2	7

	Competitors	Gold	Silver	Bronze	Medals
Great Britain	18	1	2	3	6
Greece	1	–	–	–	–
Hungary	8	–	–	–	–
Italy	2	–	–	–	–
Norway	5	–	–	–	–
Russia	4	–	–	–	–
South Africa	1	–	–	–	–
Sweden	24	–	1	–	1
United States	7	2	1	1	4
Totals	120	9	9	9	27
Nations	17	6	5	5	7

Men	Competitors	Gold	Silver	Bronze	Medals
Australia	7	1	1	2	4
Austria	3	–	–	–	–
Belgium	4	–	–	–	–
Canada	1	2	–	–	2
Denmark	1	–	–	–	–
Finland	4	–	–	–	–
France	3	–	–	–	–
Germany	13	2	2	2	6
Great Britain	12	–	2	2	4
Greece	1	–	–	–	–
Hungary	8	–	–	–	–
Italy	2	–	–	–	–
Norway	4	–	–	–	–
Russia	4	–	–	–	–
South Africa	1	–	–	–	–
Sweden	18	–	1	–	1
United States	7	2	1	1	4
Totals	93	7	7	7	21
Nations	17	5	5	4	6

Women	Competitors	Gold	Silver	Bronze	Medals
Australia	2	1	1	–	2
Austria	5	–	–	1	1
Belgium	1	–	–	–	–
Finland	2	–	–	–	–
Germany	4	–	1	–	1
Great Britain	6	1	–	1	2
Norway	1	–	–	–	–
Sweden	6	–	–	–	–
Totals	27	2	2	2	6
Nations	8	2	2	2	4

Committee for Swimming, Diving, and Water Polo

President: Erik Bergvall, Esquire
Vice-President: Major Nils David Edlund
Secretary: Kristian Hellström, Esquire
Treasurer: John G. Andersson, Esquire
Members: Carl Blidberg, Esquire; Per Fjästad, Esquire; Thor Friman, Esquire; Anton Johanson, Esquire; Torsten Kumfeldt, Esquire; Sigfrid D. Larsson, Esquire; Konrad Littorin, Esquire; Emil Lundberg, Esquire; J. A. Lönnegren; Mayor Arvid Ulrich, Esquire; Gustaf Wretman, Esquire
Building Committee: Erik Bergvall, Esquire (President); Sigfrid D. Larsson, Esquire; Torsten Kumfeldt, Esquire
Training Committee: Erik Bergvall, Esquire (President); John G. Andersson, Esquire; Torsten Kumfeldt, Esquire
International Jury: Major Nils David Edlund (President/SWE); Erik Bergvall (SWE); Ernest Samuel Marks (AUS); Felix Graf (AUT); François Van der Heyden (BEL); Uno Westerholm (FIN); F. Baxter (GBR); A. Witt (GER); Arpád von Füzesséry (HUN); Bartow Summer Weeks (USA)

MEN

100 Meter Freestyle

A: 34; C: 12; D: 6–7, 9–10 July.

The defending Olympic champion was America's Charles Daniels, who had won the gold medal in this event in both 1906 and 1908. At the beginning of 1912, Daniels also held the world record, having recorded 1:02.8 over 110 yards in New York on 15 April 1910. But Daniels had recently retired and did not compete at Stockholm. The favorite's role in Stockholm probably fell to the German, Kurt Bretting, who on 6 April 1912, had broken Daniels' world record with a mark of 1:02.4.

The Americans were led by the little known Hawaiian, Duke Kahanamoku. Kahanamoku had not competed in the American championships, because he was so far from the mainland in an era when travel was not easy, but supposedly he had set record times in his native Hawaii.

Controversy occurred in the semifinals, which were scheduled for the evening of 7 July, only a few hours after the quarterfinals. For some reason, the American contingent, Kahanamoku, Kenneth Huszagh, and Perry McGillivray, who had all qualified for the semifinals, did not appear, thinking that the afternoon race had qualified them for the final, to be held on 9 July. But this was not the case. The swimming officials made allowances, however, and decided to hold an extra heat among the Americans and Italy's Mario Massa, who had missed the quarterfinals due to a "misunderstanding." They ruled that the winner of the extra semifinal heat could advance to the final, if he posted a time faster than the third-place swimmer in heat one. Kahanamoku proved his ability in this heat, and made certain that he would qualify by giving his best effort, which resulted in his equaling Bretting's world record of 1:02.4. Huszagh was also advanced to the final, as his mark of 1:06.2 was equal to the third-place time from heat one, which had been posted by Australia's William Longworth.

In the final, Kahanamoku took the lead early, and Bretting never challenged. Noting at the halfway mark that he had a comfortable lead, Kahanamoku eased up and still won by almost two meters, although with a slower time than he had posted in the semifinals.

Final A: 5; C: 3; D: 10 July; T: c. 1915.

1. Duke Paoa Kahanamoku	USA	1:03.4
2. Cecil Healy	AUS	1:04.6
3. Kenneth Huszagh	USA	1:05.6
4. Kurt Bretting	GER	1:05.8
5. Walter Ramme	GER	1:06.4

[1]

Diplomas of Merit

Leslie Boardman (AUS), Kurt Bretting (GER), Perry McGillivray (USA), William Longworth (AUS), Walter Ramme (GER)

Semifinals A: 8; C: 4; D: 7, 9 July; F: First two finishers in each heat and the fastest third-place finisher advanced to the final.

Heat One A: 3; C: 2; D: 7 July; T: 2000.

1. Cecil Healy	AUS	1:05.6	Q
2. Walter Ramme	GER	1:05.8	Q
3. William Longworth	AUS	1:06.2	q[2]

Heat Two A: 1; C: 1; D: 7 July; T: 2010.

1. Kurt Bretting	GER	1:04.6[3]	Q

Heat Three A: 4; CF: 1; D: 9 July.[4]

1. Duke Paoa Kahanamoku	USA	1:02.4	Q	WR
2. Kenneth Huszagh	USA	1:06.2	Q	
3. Perry McGillivray	USA	1:06.2		
AC. Mario Massa[5]	ITA	DNF		

Quarterfinals A: 13; C: 5; D: 7 July; T: 1330; F: First two finishers in each heat and the fastest third-place finisher advanced to the semifinals.

Heat One A: 4; C: 3.

1. Kurt Bretting	GER	1:04.2	Q
2. William Longworth	AUS	1:05.2	Q
3. Harold Hardwick	AUS	1:06.0	
4. Robert Andersson	SWE	1:09.5[6]	

Heat Two A: 4; C: 2.

1. Duke Paoa Kahanamoku	USA	1:03.8	Q
2. Walter Ramme	GER	1:07.8	Q

See Notes on pages 304–309.

| =3. | Max Ritter | GER | 1:08.8 | |
| | Nicholas Nerich | USA | 1:08.8 | |

[7]

Heat Three A: 5; C: 3.

1.	Kenneth Huszagh	USA	1:04.2	Q
2.	Perry McGillivray	USA	1:04.4	Q
3.	Cecil Healy	AUS	1:04.8	q
4.	Leslie Boardman	AUS	1:05.4	
5.	Paul Radmilovic	GBR	1:19.0	

[8]

Round One A: 34; C: 12; D: 6 July; T: 1900; F: First two finishers in each heat and the fastest third-place finisher advanced to the semi-finals.

Heat One[9] A: 4; C: 4.

1.	László Beleznai	HUN	1:08.0	Q
2.	Robert Andersson	SWE	1:09.4[10]	Q
3.	Andreas Asimakopoulos	GRE	1:15.4	
4.	Herbert von Kuhlberg	RUS		

[11]

Heat Two[12] A: 4; C: 4.

1.	Kurt Bretting	GER	1:07.0	Q
2.	Paul Radmilovic[13]	GBR	1:10.4	Q
3.	Theodore Tartakover[14]	AUS	1:12.2	
4.	Jules Wuyts[15]	BEL	1:13.6	

[16]

Heat Three[17] A: 6; C: 6.

1.	Leslie Boardman	AUS	1:06.0	Q
2.	Nicholas Nerich[18]	USA	1:07.6	Q
3.	John Henry Derbyshire	GBR	1:09.2	
AC.	Davide Baiardo[19]	ITA		
	Walther Binner[20]	GER		
	Alajos Ferenc Kenyery[21]	HUN		

[22]

Heat Four[23] A: 5; C: 4.

1.	Perry McGillivray	USA	1:04.8	Q
2.	Cecil Healy	AUS	1:05.2	Q
3.	Kenneth Huszagh[24]	USA	1:06.2	Q
4.	Cletus Andersson[25]	SWE		
5.	Georg Kunisch[26]	GER		

[27, 28]

Heat Five[29] A: 4; C: 3.

1. Duke Paoa Kahanamoku	USA	1:02.6	Q	WR
2. William Longworth	AUS	1:05.2	Q	
3. Harry Hebner	USA	1:10.4		
4. Gérard Meister	FRA	1:16.6		

[30]

Heat Six[31] A: 4; C: 4.

1. Harold Hardwick	AUS	1:05.8	Q
2. Max Ritter	GER	1:08.0	Q
3. Herman Meyboom	BEL	1:15.4	
4. James Reilly	USA		

[32]

Heat Seven[33] A: 4; C: 4.

1. Walter Ramme	GER	1:10.2	Q
=2. Mario Massa	ITA	1:11.8	Q
Harald Julin[34]	SWE	1:11.8	Q
4. John Johnsen	NOR	1:19.1	

[35]

Heat Eight[36] A: 3; C: 3.

1. Eric Bergqvist	SWE	1:13.4	Q
2. Georges Rigal	FRA	1:17.8	Q
3. László Szentgróti[37]	HUN		

[38, 39, 40]

400 Meter Freestyle

A: 26[41]; C: 13; D: 11, 13–14 July.

The world record over 440 yards was held by Australia's Frank Beaurepaire, who had won the silver medal in this event at London in 1908. Beaurepaire competed at the 1920 and 1924 Olympic Games as well, but he did not compete in Stockholm as he was declared a professional in 1911 for having lectured on swimming and lifesaving. Australia's best hope in this event was Harold Hardwick, who had won the 1911 Amateur Swimming Association (ASA — Great Britain) title over 440 yards. Hardwick later won the Australian professional heavyweight boxing championship in 1915. The 1912 ASA champion was Britain's John Hatfield, who would also win that event in 1913. Hatfield finished second and Hardwick third in this event.

The victory went to Canada's George Hodgson, who had won the 1,500 meters only four days earlier. Hodgson had come to prominence in 1910 when he won every race he entered at the Canadian Championships. In 1911 he won the mile race at the Festival of the Empire Games in London (GBR), entering McGill University (Montreal) upon his return. In 1912, he again swept his events at the Canadian Championships, while representing the Montreal Amateur Athletic Association (MAAA). With the outbreak of World War I, Hodgson traveled to England where he joined the Royal Air Force (RAF). During his military career, he won the AFC and the London Board of Trade Silver Medal for rescues made at sea. Upon his return to Canada, he resumed his swimming career, and competed at the 1920 Olympics, but in the 400 and 1,500 meter freestyle races at Antwerp, he failed to make the final.

Final A: 5; C: 4; D: 14 July; T: 1900.

1. George Hodgson	CAN	5:24.4	OR
2. John Hatfield	GBR	5:25.8	
3. Harold Hardwick	AUS	5:31.2	
4. Cecil Healy	AUS	5:37.8	
5. Béla von Las-Torres	HUN	5:42.0	

Diplomas of Merit

Cecil Healy (AUS), Béla von Las-Torres (HUN)

Semifinals A: 11; C: 6; D: 13 July; T: 1900; F: First two finishers in each heat and the fastest third-place finisher advanced to the final.

Heat One A: 6; C: 4.

1. George Hodgson	CAN	5:25.4	Q
2. John Hatfield	GBR	5:25.6	Q
3. William Foster	GBR	5:49.0	
4. Nicholas Nerich	USA	5:51.0	
5. Sydney Battersby	GBR	5:51.2	
6. John Haakon Johnsen	NOR		

42

Heat Two A: 5; C: 3.

1. Harold Hardwick	AUS	5:31.0	Q
2. Béla von Las-Torres	HUN	5:34.8	Q
3. Cecil Healy	AUS	5:37.8	q
4. Malcolm Champion	AUS/NZL	5:38.0	
5. Henry Taylor	GBR	5:48.2	

43, 44

Round One[45] A: 26; C: 13; D: 11 July; T: 1210; F: First two finishers in each heat and the fastest third-place finisher advanced to the semifinals.

Heat One A: 6; C: 4.

1. Harold Hardwick	AUS	5:36.0[46]	Q
2. Malcolm Champion	AUS/NZL	5:37.0	Q
3. James Reilly	USA	6:10.2	
4. Nils-Erik Haglund	SWE	6:23.4	
5. Davide Baiardo	ITA		
AC. Mario Massa	ITA	DNF	

47

Heat Two A: 4; C: 4.

1. Sydney Battersby	GBR	6:03.6	Q
2. John Haakon Johnsen	NOR	6:14.4	Q

3. Johan Eskil Wedholm	SWE	6:29.8		
AC. Pavel Avksentyev	RUS	DNF		

48

Heat Three A: 5; C: 5.

1. Max Ritter	GER	5:44.6	Q
2. Alajos Ferenc Kenyery	HUN	5:46.0	Q
3. Nicholas Nerich	USA	5:50.4	q
AC. David Theander	SWE	DNF	
Theodore Tartakover	AUS	DNF	

49

Heat Four A: 3; C: 3.

1. Béla von Las-Torres	HUN	5:36.2	Q
2. Henry Taylor	GBR	5:48.4	Q
AC. Nikolay Voronkov	RUS	DNF	

50

Heat Five A: 3; C: 3.

1. Cecil Healy	AUS	5:34.0	Q	WR
2. John Hatfield	GBR	5:35.6	Q	
3. Franz Schuh	AUT	6:09.4[51]		

52

Heat Six A: 5; C: 5.

1. George Hodgson	CAN	5:50.6	Q
2. William Foster	GBR	5:52.4	Q
3. Oscar Schiele	GER	5:57.0	
4. George Godfrey	RSA	6:30.6	
5. Harry Christian Hedegaard	DEN	7:07.8	

53, 54

1,500 Meter Freestyle

A: 19; C: 11; D: 6–7, 9–10 July.

The defending champion was Britain's Henry Taylor, who also held the world record of 22:48.4, which he had set at London in winning the 1908 Olympic championship. Taylor had won the ASA mile championship in 1911, but in 1912 he was defeated by John Hatfield, who would also win that title in 1913–14.

Hatfield had to know he would have a difficult time when Canada's George Hodgson broke Taylor's world record in the first round, posting a time of 22:23.0. In the final, Hatfield was no match for Hodgson. Hodgson took off at a brisk pace, leading Australia's Harold Hardwick by ten meters at the first turn (100 meters). By 500 meters, he held a 25 meter lead over Hatfield. Hodgson passed 1,000 meters in 14:37.0,[55] a world record for that distance. After winning the race in 22:00.0, Hodgson continued on in an attempt to set a new world record for the mile (1,609 meters), which he did with a time of 23:34.5.[56] Hodgson's world record for 1,500 meters lasted for 11 years, until it was broken by Arne Borg (SWE), with a time of 21:35.3 at Göteborg on 8 July 1923. In addition to his gold medal, Hodgson also won the challenge trophy for the 1,500 meter freestyle event, which had been donated in 1908 by the Italian Count and IOC member, Eugenio Brunetta d'Usseaux.

Final A: 5; C: 4; D: 10 July; T: 1940.

1. George Hodgson	CAN	22:00.0	WR
2. John Hatfield	GBR	22:39.0	
3. Harold Hardwick	AUS	23:15.4	
AC. Béla von Las-Torres	HUN	DNF	
Malcolm Champion	AUS/NZL	DNF	

Diploma of Merit

Wilhelm Andersson (SWE)

Semifinals A: 9; C: 6; D: 9 July; T: 1235; F: First two finishers in each heat and the fastest third-place finisher advanced to the final.

Heat One A: 5; C: 4.

1. George Hodgson	CAN	22:26.0	Q
2. John Hatfield	GBR	22:33.4	Q
3. Harold Hardwick	AUS	23:14.0	q
4. Wilhelm Andersson	SWE	23:14.4	
AC. Henry Taylor	GBR	DNF	

57

Heat Two A: 4; C: 3.

1. Béla von Las-Torres	HUN	23:09.8	Q
2. Malcolm Champion	AUS/NZL	23:24.2	Q
3. William Foster	GBR	23:32.2	
4. Sydney Battersby	GBR		

58

Round One 59 A: 19; C: 11; D: 6–7 July; F: First two finishers in each heat and the fastest third-place finisher advanced to the semifinals.

Heat One A: 4; C: 4; D: 6 July; T: 1945.

1. Wilhelm Andersson	SWE	23:12.2[60]	Q
2. Malcolm Champion	AUS/NZL	23:34.0	Q
3. Henry Taylor	GBR	24:06.4	q
AC. Herbert Mauritz Wetter	NOR	DNF	

61

Heat Two A: 3; C: 3; D: 6 July; T: 2030.

1. Béla von Las-Torres	HUN	22:58.0	Q
2. John Hatfield	GBR	23:16.6	Q
AC. Auguste Caby	FRA	DNF	

62

Heat Three A: 3; C: 3; D: 6 July; T: 2115.

1. George Hodgson	CAN	22:23.0	Q	WR
2. William Longworth	AUS	23:03.6	Q	
3. Harry Hedegaard	DEN	28:32.4		

63

Heat Four A: 4; C: 4; D: 7 July; T: 1415.

1. Sydney Battersby	GBR	23:58.0	Q
2. Franz Schuh	AUT	25:19.8	Q
3. Johan Eskil Wedholm	SWE	27:38.0	
AC. Mario Massa	ITA	DNF	

64

Heat Five A: 5; C: 5; D: 7 July; T: 2020.

1. Harold Hardwick	AUS	23:23.2	Q
2. William Foster	GBR	23:52.2	Q
3. John Haakon Johnsen	NOR	25:45.6	
4. Karl Gustaf Collin	SWE	27:05.2	
AC. Pavel Avksentyev	RUS	DNF	

65, 66

100 Meter Backstroke

A: 18; C: 7; D: 9–10, 13 July.

In an era when the United States did not contest an outdoor backstroke championship, Harry Hebner still dominated American backstroking. Over the indoor distance of 150 yards, he was national champion from 1910 to 1916. He rarely raced over 100 meters or the imperial equivalent of 110 yards, but he held the American records for both 100 and 150 yards. The world record at the beginning of 1912 was held by Hungary's András Baronyi, who had posted 1:18.8 at Budapest on 17 July 1911. But the world record was broken twice before the Stockholm Olympics, first by Germany's Oscar Schiele with 1:18.4 at Brussels on 6 April, and then the mark was destroyed by Germany's Otto Fahr, with 1:15.6 at Magdeburg on 29 April. Schiele was in Stockholm and competed in this event, but he was disqualified in heat one of round one.

Fahr's world record was not threatened in any round. The final came down to him and Hebner. After a false start, Hebner took an early lead and held off Fahr to win by slightly over one second. The *Official Report* noted, "Hebner, who kept his head well out of the water and was able to observe his opponents during the whole of the race, won without any difficulty."

Final A: 5; C: 3; D: 13 July; T: 1940.

1. Harry Hebner	USA	1:21.2
2. Otto Fahr	GER	1:22.4
3. Paul Kellner	GER	1:24.0
4. András Baronyi	HUN	1:25.2
5. Otto Groß	GER	1:25.8

Diplomas of Merit

András Baronyi (HUN), Otto Groß (GER)

Semi-Finals A: 11; C: 5; D: 10 July; F: First two finishers in each heat and the fastest third-place finisher advanced to the final.

Heat One A: 6; C: 4; T: 1900.

1. Harry Hebner	USA	1:20.8	Q
2. Otto Fahr	GER	1:21.8	Q
3. András Baronyi	HUN	1:26.2	q
4. László Szentgróti	HUN	1:26.4	
5. Erich Schultze	GER		
6. George Webster	GBR		

Heat Two A: 5; C: 3; T: 1905.

1. Otto Groß	GER	1:26.0	Q
2. Paul Kellner	GER	1:26.2	Q
3. Herbert Haresnape	GBR	1:26.8	
4. Frank Sandon	GBR	1:32.2	
5. Gunnar Sundman	SWE	1:35.0	

Round One[67] A: 18; C: 7; D: 9–10 July; F: First two finishers in each heat and the fastest third-place finisher advanced to the semifinals.

Heat One A: 4; C: 4; D: 9 July; T: 1215.

1. Harry Hebner	USA	1:21.0	Q
2. Otto Groß	GER	1:24.0	Q
3. Åke Bergman	SWE	1:33.8	
AC. Oscar Schiele	GER	DQ	

[68, 69]

Heat Two A: 4; C: 4; D: 9 July; T: 1225.

1. Otto Fahr	GER	1:22.0	Q
2. George Webster	GBR	1:29.4	Q
3. Hugo Lundevall	SWE	1:46.8	
AC. János Wenk	HUN	DQ [1:28.6][70]	

[71]

Heat Three A: 4; C: 4; D: 9 July; T: 1230.

1. András Baronyi	HUN	1:22.0	Q
2. Paul Kellner	GER	1:26.0	Q
4. Harry Svendsen (Aspestrand)	NOR	1:47.2	
AC. Oscar Grégoire[72]	BEL	DQ [1:29.8]	

[73]

Heat Four A: 4; C: 4; D: 10 July; T: 1300.

1. Herbert Haresnape	GBR	1:27.0	Q
2. Erich Schultze	GER	1:27.2	Q

| 3. Gunnar Sundman | SWE | 1:31.2 | q |
| 4. John Johnsen | NOR | 1:34.2 | |

74

Heat Five A: 2; C: 2; D: 10 July; T: 1305.

| 1. László Szentgróti | HUN | 1:26.6 | Q |
| 2. Frank Sandon | GBR | 1:31.8 | Q |

75, 76, 77

200 Meter Breaststroke

A: 24; C: 11; D: 7, 9–10 July.

International breaststroke competition in this era was dominated by Continental Europeans, notably the Germans. The world record was held by Belgium's Félicien Courbet, with a mark of 3:00.8 set at Schaerback on 2 October 1910. Although Courbet was in Stockholm he did not advance in his semifinal heat. The most recent ASA championships had been won as follows: 1907–09 — Percy Courtman (GBR); 1910 — Harald Julin (SWE); 1911 — Ödön Toldi (HUN); and 1912–13 — Courtman. Thus the event was wide-open.

However, none of the above won a medal, although all but Toldi competed. The event was swept by the Germans, led by Walter Bathe, who challenged, but did not break, Courbet's world record with a mark of 3:01.8.

Final A: 5; C: 3; D: 10 July; T: 1930.

1. Walter Bathe	GER	3:01.8
2. Wilhelm Lützow	GER	3:05.0
3. Paul Malisch	GER	3:08.0
4. Percy Courtman	GBR	3:08.8
AC. Thor Henning	SWE	DNF

Diplomas of Merit

Percy Courtman (GBR), Harald Julin (SWE)

Semifinals A: 12; C: 6; D: 9 July; T: 2015; F: First two finishers in each heat and the fastest third-place finisher advanced to the final.

Heat One A: 6; C: 4.

1. Paul Malisch	GER	3:09.6	Q
2. Thor Henning	SWE	3:10.4	Q
3. Harald Julin	SWE	3:10.6	
4. Karl Gustaf Lindroos	FIN	3:11.6	
5. Carlyle Atkinson	GBR	3:15.2	
6. Arvo Ossian Aaltonen	FIN	3:17.0	

Heat Two A: 6; C: 5.

| 1. Walter Bathe | GER | 3:02.2 | Q |
| 2. Wilhelm Lützow | GER | 3:04.4 | Q |

3. Percy Courtman	GBR	3:09.4	q
4. Oszkár Demján	HUN	3:11.2	
5. Félicien Courbet	BEL	3:11.6	
AC. Pontus Hanson	SWE	DNF	

Round One[78] A: 24; C: 11; D: 7 July; T: 1350 and 1930; F: First two finishers in each heat and the fastest third-place finisher advanced to the semifinals.

Heat One A: 4; C: 4; T: 1350.

1. Wilhelm Lützow	GER	3:07.4	Q
2. Thor Henning	SWE	3:14.0	Q
3. Karl Lindroos	FIN	3:16.6[79]	q
4. Frank Schryver	AUS	3:24.0	
[80]			

Heat Two A: 5; C: 5.

1. Paul Malisch	GER	3:08.8	Q
2. Arvo Ossian Aaltonen	FIN	3:13.0	Q
3. Nils Gustaf Andersson	SWE	3:20.6	
4. Josef Wastl	AUT	3:25.6	
5. Georgy Baymakov	RUS	3:29.0	
[81]			

Heat Four[82] A: 4; C: 4.

1. Walter Bathe	GER	3:03.4	Q
2. Percy Courtman	GBR	3:09.8	Q
3. Fredrik Löwenadler	SWE	3:22.2	
AC. Mike McDermott	USA	DQ [3:18.2]	
[83]			

Heat Five[84] A: 4; C: 4; T: 1930.

1. Félicien Courbet	BEL	3:12.6[85]	Q
2. Pontus Hanson	SWE	3:14.2	Q
AC. George Innocent	GBR	DQ [3:16.0]	
3. Audun Rusten	NOR	DQ [3:39.8]	
[86]			

Heat Six[87] A: 6; C: 3.

1. Oszkár Demján	HUN	3:07.8	Q
2. Harald Julin	SWE	3:12.8	Q
3. Herman Cederberg	FIN	3:18.6	
4. F. Vilhelm Lindgrén	FIN	3:21.2	
5. Sven Hanson	SWE	3:24.4	
6. Oscar Hamrén	SWE		

Extra Heat[88] A: 1; C: 1.

1. Carlyle Atkinson	GBR	3:12.0	Q
[89, 90]			

400 Meter Breaststroke

A: 17; C: 10; D: 8, 11–12 July.

This event appeared on the Olympic program only three times — in 1904 (at 440 yards), 1912, and 1920. Walter Bathe (GER) won his second breaststroke gold medal, adding this to the title he had won at 200 meters two days earlier. Bathe took an early lead, being ahead by four meters at the first turn (100 meters), and led by 10 meters at 250 meters. He won easily.

Final A: 5; C: 3; D: 12 July; T: 1935.

1. Walter Bathe	GER	6:29.6	
2. Thor Henning	SWE	6:35.6	
3. Percy Courtman	GBR	6:36.4	
4. Paul Malisch	GER	6:37.0	
AC. Wilhelm Lützow	GER	DNF	

Diploma of Merit

Paul Malisch (GER)

Semifinals A: 10; C: 6; D: 11 July; T: 1930; F: First two finishers in each heat and the fastest third-place finisher advanced to the final.

Heat One A: 5; C: 5.

1. Walter Bathe	GER	6:32.0	Q
2. Thor Henning	SWE	6:32.0	Q
3. Percy Courtman	GBR	6:36.6	q
4. Félicien Courbet	BEL	6:59.8	
AC. Zeno von Singalewicz	AUT	DNF	

[91]

Heat Two A: 5; C: 3.

1. Wilhelm Lützow	GER	6:44.6	Q
2. Paul Malisch	GER	6:47.6	Q
3. Arvo Ossian Aaltonen	FIN	6:56.8	
4. Karl Gustaf Lindroos	FIN	7:00.4	
AC. George Innocent	GBR	DNF	

Round One[92] A: 17; C: 10; D: 8 July; T: 1200; F: First two finishers in each heat and the fastest third-place finisher advanced to the semifinals.

Heat One A: 4; C: 4.

1. Thor Henning	SWE	6:52.4	Q
2. George Innocent	GBR	7:07.8	Q
AC. Josef Wastl	AUT	DNF	
Oszkár Demján	HUN	DQ [6:35.8][93]	

[94]

Heat Two A: 4; C: 4.

1. Paul Malisch	GER	6:47.0	Q
2. Karl Gustaf Lindroos	FIN	7:00.0	Q
3. Nils Gustaf Andersson	SWE	7:17.0	
AC. Mike McDermott	USA	DQ [7:07.0]	
95			

Heat Three A: 4; C: 4.

1. Wilhelm Lützow	GER	6:49.8	Q
2. Félicien Courbet	BEL	6:52.6	Q
3. Zeno von Singalewicz	AUT	7:04.0	q
4. Frank Schryver	AUS	7:07.8	
96			

Heat Four A: 3; C: 2.

1. Percy Courtman	GBR	6:43.8	Q
2. Arvo Ossian Aaltonen	FIN	6:48.8	Q
3. F. Vilhelm Lindgrén	FIN	7:12.6	
97			

Heat Five A: 2; C: 1.

1. Walter Bathe	GER	6:34.6	Q
2. Georgy Baymakov	RUS	7:28.6	Q
98, 99			

4 × 200 Meter Freestyle Relay

A: 20; C: 5; D: 12, 15 July.

The world record of 10:55.6 in this event had been set in 1908 at the London Olympics by the winning British relay team. That record took a beating in these games as, in the first round, the United States bettered the mark with a time of 10:26.4. The record lasted only a few minutes as it was bettered in the second heat by the Australasian team, which won the heat in 10:14.0.

The final was expected to be a close battle between the United States and Australasia, but Australasia dominated it. The two teams were almost tied at the end of the first leg, but New Zealand's Malcolm Champion pulled away on the second leg and the Australasians were never again challenged. They won by almost nine seconds in a world record of 10:11.6.

Final A: 16; C: 4; D: 15 July; T: 1245.

1.   Australasia   10:11.2[100]   WR
   (Cecil Healy [AUS/1], Malcolm Champion [NZL/2], Leslie Boardman [AUS/3], Harold Hardwick [AUS/4])

2.   United States   10:20.2
   (Kenneth Huszagh [1], Perry McGillivray [2], Harry Hebner [3], Duke Paoa Kahanamoku [4])

3. Great Britain   10:28.6[101]
   (William Foster, Sydney Battersby, John Hatfield, Henry Taylor)

4. Germany   10:37.0
   (Oscar Schiele, Georg Kunisch, Kurt Bretting, Max Ritter)
   [102]

Diplomas of Merit

Germany (Oscar Schiele, Georg Kunisch, Kurt Bretting, Max Ritter)

Round One   A: 20; C: 5; D: 12 July; T: 1900; F: First two finishers in each heat and the fastest third-place finisher advanced to the final.

Heat One   A: 12; C: 3.

1. United States   10:26.4   Q   WR
   (Kenneth Huszagh [1], Duke Paoa Kahanamoku [2], Perry McGillivray [3], Harry Hebner [4])

2. Hungary   10:34.6   Q
   (László Beleznai [1], Imre Zachár [2], Alajos Ferenc Kenyery [3], Béla von Las-Torres [4])

3. Great Britain   10:39.4   q
   (William Foster [1], Sydney Battersby [2], John Hatfield [3], Henry Taylor [4])

Heat Two   A: 8; C: 2.

1. Australasia   10:14.0   Q   WR
   (Harold Hardwick [AUS/1], Malcolm Champion [NZL/2], Leslie Boardman [AUS/3], Cecil Healy [AUS/4])

2. Germany   10:42.2   Q
   (Oscar Schiele [1], Georg Kunisch, Kurt Bretting, Max Ritter)

WOMEN

100 Meter Freestyle

A: 27; C: 8; D: 8–9, 11–12 July.

Women had never competed internationally in swimming prior to the Stockholm Olympics, so it was difficult to choose favorites. The British ASA title had been won in 1909, 1911, and 1912 by Britain's Jennie Fletcher. The world record at the beginning of 1912 was held over 110 yards by Daisy Curwen (GBR) with 1:24.6, set in Liverpool on 29 September 1911. In preparation for the Olympics, Curwen herself broke that mark on 10 June 1912, posting 1:20.6 at Birkenhead.

Australia was to be represented by Sarah "Fanny" Durack and Wilhelmina Wylie, but not without some effort. Originally the Australian sports authorities did not wish to "waste" money on sending women to the Olympics. Finally, the New South Wales Ladies' Amateur Swimming Association voted to allow the two to go to the Olympics, providing they paid their own way. A fund was raised which paid Durack's expenses and Wylie's family and friends provided her support. Durack's sister, Mary, served as their chaperone on the long boat trip.

Wilhelmina Wylie had been the better of the two swimmers up to a year before the 1912 Olympics, and she had never lost to Durack to that time. But Durack changed to the new crawl stroke, from the Trudgeon, and after that, Wylie never defeated Durack. Prior to the 1912 Olympics, Durack posted world records over 50 yards (27.0), 100 yards (66.0), and 220 yards (2:56.0). In her first round heat at Stockholm, she broke Curwen's world record for 100 meters with a time of 1:19.8.

The final came down to Durack, Wylie, and Fletcher. Daisy Curwen competed in Stockholm and qualified for the final, but had to withdraw when she was rushed to hospital for an emergency appendectomy. It is unlikely she would have challenged Durack in the final, who won easily in 1:22.2. A few days later, in an exhibition in the Stockholm Swimming Stadium, Durack broke the world record for 300 meters with a time of 4:43.6. She eventually set 11 world records between 1906 and 1921. Although she planned to compete at the 1920 Olympics in Antwerp, the plan was derailed when, shortly before the games, she suffered the same fate as Daisy Curwen, and missed the Olympics due to an appendectomy.

Final A: 5; C: 3; D: 12 July; T: 1900.

1. Sarah "Fanny" Durack	AUS	1:22.2	
2. Wilhelmina Wylie	AUS	1:25.4	
3. Jennie Fletcher	GBR	1:27.0	
4. Margareta "Grete" Rosenberg	GER	1:27.2[103]	
5. Annie Speirs	GBR	1:27.4	
[104]			

Diplomas of Merit

Margareta "Grete" Rosenberg (GER), Annie Speirs (GBR), Daisy Curwen (GBR)

Semifinals A: 11; C: 3; D: 11 July; T: 1200; F: First two finishers in each
heat and the fastest third-place finisher advanced to the final.

Heat One A: 6; C: 3.

1. Sarah "Fanny" Durack	AUS	1:20.2	Q
2. Daisy Curwen	GBR	1:26.8	Q
3. Annie Speirs	GBR	1:27.0	q
4. Isabella Moore	GBR	1:27.4	
5. Mary Langford	GBR	1:29.2	
6. Louise Otto	GER	1:32.0	

Heat Two A: 5; C: 3.

1. Wilhelmina Wylie	AUS	1:27.0	Q	
2. Jennie Fletcher	GBR	1:27.2	Q	
3. Margareta "Grete" Rosenberg	GER	1:29.2	[q]	[105]
4. Wally Dressel	GER	1:33.4		
AC. Irene Steer	GBR	DQ [1:29.0]		

Round One A: 27; C: 8; D: 8–9 July; F: First two finishers in each heat and the fastest third-place finisher advanced to the semifinals.

Heat One A: 6; C: 6; D: 8 July; T: 1930.

1. Isabella Moore	GBR	1:29.8	Q	
2. Louise Otto	GER	1:34.4	Q	
3. Klara Milch	AUT	1:37.2		
4. Margareta "Greta" Johansson	SWE	1:41.4		
5. Tyyne Maria Järvi	FIN	1:42.4		
AC. Aagot Normann	NOR	DNF		

Heat Two A: 6; C: 4; D: 8 July; T: 1935.

1. Daisy Curwen	GBR	1:23.6	Q	
2. Jennie Fletcher	GBR	1:26.2	Q	
3. Berta Zahourek	AUT	1:38.6		
4. Josefa "Pepi" Kellner	AUT	1:41.2		
5. Karin Lundgren	SWE	1:44.8		
6. Sonja Jonsson	SWE			

Heat Three A: 6; C: 6; D: 9 July; T: 1200.

1. Wilhelmina Wylie	AUS	1:26.8	Q	
2. Mary Langford	GBR	1:28.0	Q	
3. Hermine Stindt	GER	1:29.2		
4. Josefine Sticker	AUT	1:31.8		
5. Claire Guttenstein	BEL			
6. Elsa Björklund	SWE			

Heat Four A: 6; C: 6; D: 9 July; T: 1205.

1. Sarah "Fanny" Durack	AUS	1:19.8	Q	WR
2. Irene Steer	GBR	1:27.2	Q	
3. Wally Dressel	GER	1:28.6	q	
4. Margareta "Grete" Adler	AUT	1:34.4		
5. Greta Carlsson	SWE			
6. Regina Kari	FIN			

Heat Five A: 3; C: 3; D: 9 July; T: 1210.

1. Margareta "Grete" Rosenberg	GER	1:25.0	Q
2. Annie Speirs	GBR	1:25.6	Q
3. Vera Thulin	SWE	1:44.0	

4 × 100 Meter Freestyle Relay

A: 16; C: 4; D: 15 July; F: Final only.

Australia was represented at the 1912 Olympics by two swimmers, Sarah "Fanny" Durack and Wilhelmina "Mina" Wylie, who had finished first and second in the 100 meters. They offered to compete in the relay, and swim two legs each, but this request was turned down.[106] In their absence, Great Britain won the race easily.

Final A: 16; C: 4; D: 15 July; T: 1200.

1. Great Britain   5:52.8
   (Isabella Moore, Jennie Fletcher, Annie Speirs, Irene Steer)

2. Germany   6:04.6
   (Wally Dressel, Louise Otto, Hermine Stindt, Margareta "Grete" Rosenberg)

3. Austria   6:17.0
   (Margareta "Grete" Adler, Klara Milch, Josefine Sticker, Berta Zahourek)

4. Sweden
   (Greta Carlsson, Margareta "Greta" Johansson, Sonja Jonsson, Vera Thulin)

Swimming Exhibitions

Several swimming exhibitions were given during the Olympics. On Sunday, 7 July, at 7:00 P.M. (1900), a display was given by male Swedish swimmers. Another display, this one by female swimmers, was given on Tuesday evening, 9 July. On the next to last night of swimming competition, 14 July (Sunday), the program listed an exhibition as a "Grand General Display of Swimming."

In the evening of 15 July, the last night on which swimming events were held, Fanny Durack (AUS), who had easily won the 100 meter freestyle for women, gave an exhibition swim in which she tried to break the women's world record for 300 meters. She succeeded, setting a new record of 4:43.6, with splits of 1:24.0 at 100 meters, and 3:05.0 at 200 meters. That same night, at the Djurgårdsbrunnsviken Swimming Stadium, at 8:00 P.M. (2000), the program listed the following exhibition, "Aquatic Festival (illuminations, etc.) arranged by the Stockholms Kappsimningsklubb (the Stockholm Swimming Club), the Swedish Amateur Swimming Association and the Committee for the 'Barnens Dag' Fund (Children's Summer Holiday Fund)." The Aquatic Festival was repeated the following evening, 16 July.

NOTES

1. Although qualified, William Longworth did not start in the final, because he was undergoing an operation to drain an infection from his head. He was noted to have had this during the earlier rounds but continued to swim.

2. Longworth was not advanced to the final, although he originally qualified. This was due to confusion concerning the Americans and Mario Massa (ITA) not showing up for scheduled heats, despite having qualified. When a third semifinal was added, it was decided to allow the winner to advance to the final if his time was faster than the third-place finisher in heat one (Longworth). Duke Paoa Kahanamoku won that heat in world-record time. When the second-place finisher behind Kahanamoku (Huszagh) also equaled Longworth's time, he was allowed to advance to the final. Longworth was originally still allowed in the final but he did not compete because of an illness — see note 1 above.

3. Time according to 12OR, 12ORes, and ONews; 1:04.8 according to Uggla.

4. The Americans did not show up for heats one or two by mistake. They thought that all the Americans who had qualified in round two were to advance to the final. Mario Massa of Italy also made the same mistake. A third semifinal heat was scheduled, and it was decided that the winner of the heat could advance to the finals, if he posted a faster time than the third place time in heat one.

5. Massa had qualified for the second round, but did not start in heat three, "due to a misunderstanding," according to 12OR. He did not qualify for the semifinal, but was added to this extra heat in the semifinals — see above footnotes.

6. Also entered in this heat, but not competing, were László Beleznai (HUN), and Georges Rigal (FRA).

7. Also entered in this heat, but not competing, were Harald Julin (SWE), and Eric Bergqvist (SWE).

8. Mario Massa (ITA) did not start in heat three although he had qualified for round two. The OR noted "…but from some misunderstanding, he did not put in an appearance." The Americans who qualified via round two also did not start in the semifinals (see above), and an extra semifinal was added to accommodate them and give them a chance to qualify for the final. Massa was also added to this extra semifinal, but the reasons for this are not known.

9. The heats and heat assignments were changed dramatically at the last minute. This was originally heat two. The scheduled heat one was not held. Paul Radmilovic (GBR), Theodore Tartakover (AUS), and Jules Wuyts (BEL) were entered in the original heat one, but competed in the redrawn heat two.

10. Time according to 12ORes, ONews, and Uggla. It is given as 1:09.2 in 12OR.

11. Also entered in this heat, but not competing, were Jacques Martin (FRA) and George Hodgson (CAN).

12. Originally heat three.

13. Originally assigned to heat one, which was not held.

14. Originally assigned to heat one, which was not held.

15. Originally assigned to heat one, which was not held.

16. Also entered in this heat, but not competing, were George Godfrey (RSA), Attilio Bellezza (ITA), Eben Cross (USA), and Henri Decoin (FRA).

17. Originally heat four.

18. Originally assigned to heat five.

19. Originally assigned to heat five.

20. Originally assigned to heat five.

21. Originally assigned to heat five.

22. Also entered in this heat, but not competing, were Josef Scheibler (AUT), Richard Frizell (USA), Henri Dubois (FRA), Josef Munk (HUN).

23. Originally heat six. The original heat five was not contested. The scheduled entrants in that heat were Nicholas Nerich (USA), Davide Baiardo (ITA), Walther Binner (GER), Alajos Ferenc Kenyery (HUN), and Cletus Andersson (SWE).

24. Originally assigned to heat eight.

25. Originally assigned to heat five.

26. Originally assigned to heat eight.

27. Also entered in this heat, but not competing, were Heinrich Brandstetter (AUT), Jean Roldes (FRA), and Otto Kühne (GER).

28. Harald Julin was entered in this heat, but was reassigned to the redrawn heat seven.

29. Originally heat seven.

30. Also entered in this heat, but not competing, were Eugen von Romanóczy (HUN) and Virgilio Bellazza (ITA).

31. Originally heat nine. The original heat eight was not contested.

32. Also entered in this heat, but not competing, were Otto Scheff (AUT) and Jean Martin (FRA).

33. Originally heat ten.

34. Originally assigned to heat six, which became heat four and was contested. It is not known why Julin was reassigned to this heat.

35. Also entered in this heat, but not competing, were Aldo Cigheri (ITA) and Michael McDermott (USA).

36. Originally heat eleven.

37. According to 12ORes Szentgróti did not start. But he is listed in 12OR and ONews.

38. Also entered in this heat, but not competing, was Aleksey Andreyev (RUS).

39. There were originally 11 scheduled heats. The original heats one, five, and eight were not held. Swimmers in these heats were assigned to other heats or did not start.

40. The following swimmers were entered in this event, but did not compete: original heat one — Max Rosenfeld (AUT), Leo G. "Budd" Goodwin (USA), Emanuel Prüll (AUT); original heat five — Marcel Pernot (FRA); original heat eight — Leslie George Rich (USA), Mario Portolongo (ITA), Bengt Wallin (SWE), Béla von Las-Torres (HUN).

41. EK has obvious typos, reversing the number of competitors (he gives 13) and nations (he gives 26).

42. Max Ritter has qualified for this heat but did not start.

43. Alajos Ferenc Kenyery (HUN) had qualified for this heat, but did not start.

44. Max Ritter (GER) and Alajos Ferenc Kenyery (HUN) did not start in the semifinals, although they had qualified.

45. There were originally 11 scheduled heats. But because there were a large number of entered swimmers who did not appear to compete, the heats were redrawn as follows: the original heats one and two were combined to form heat one; the original heats three and four were combined to form heat two; the original heats five through seven were combined to form heat three; the original heat eight became heat four; the original heat nine became heat five; and the original heats ten and eleven were combined to form heat six.

46. Time according to 12OR, 12ORes, and ONews. It is given as 5:36.2 in Uggla.

47. The original heat assignments were as follows: Champion, Haglund, Baiardo — heat one; Hardwick, Reilly, Massa — heat two.

48. The original heat assignments were as follows: Johnsen — heat three; Battersby, Wedholm, Avksentyev — heat four.

49. The original heat assignments were as follows: Ritter, Theander — heat five; Tartakover — heat six; Kenyery, Nerich — heat seven.

50. Also entered in this heat, but not competing, were Harry Hebner (USA), Otto Fahr (GER), and Otto Scheff (AUT).

51. Time according to Uggla and 12ORes; Schuh gives 6:09.4. It is given as 6:09.2 in ONews and as 6:09.6 in 12OR.

52. Also entered in this heat were Kenneth Huszagh (USA), Emmerich Zachár (HUN), and Andreas Asimakopoulos (GRE).

53. The original heat assignments were as follows: Hodgson, Hedegaard — heat ten; Foster, Schiele, Godfrey — heat eleven.

54. The following swimmers were entered in this event, but did not compete: original heat one — John Knight Shyrock (USA), Jean Rodier (FRA), Isaac Bentham (GBR); original heat two — Georges Hermant (FRA), Wolfgang Siller (AUT), Robert Andersson (SWE); original heat three — Leslie George Rich (USA), Henri Decoin (FRA), Attilio Bellezza (ITA), Josef Scheibler (AUT), Karl Gustaf Collin (SWE); original heat four — J. P. Mantell (USA), René Voisard (FRA), Leslie Boardman (AUS); original heat five — Perry McGillivray (USA), Ilarion Borisovsky (RUS), Georges Rigal (FRA), Virgilio Bellazza (ITA); original heat six — Richard Frizell (USA), Marcel Pernot (FRA), Harry Svendsen (Aspestrand) (NOR), Viktor Baranov (RUS), Wilhelm Andersson (SWE); original heat seven — William Longworth (AUS), S. Matucha (BOH), Émile Bangerter (FRA), Aldo Cigheri (ITA); original heat ten — Leo G. "Budd" Goodwin (USA), Joseph Pletinckx (BEL), Josef Černý (BOH), Gérard Meister (FRA), Mario Portolongo (ITA); original heat eleven — Lincoln Johnson (USA), Henri Dubois (FRA), Herbert Mauritz Wetter (NOR), Aleksey Andreyev (RUS).

55. The three stopwatches on Hodgson's time at 1,000 meters recorded as follows: 14:36.8, 14:37.0, 14:37.2.

56. The three stopwatches on Hodgson's time at one mile recorded as follows: 23:34.5, 23:34.0, 23:34.2.

57. Franz Schuh (AUT) had qualified for this heat but did not start.

58. William Longworth (AUS) had qualified for this heat but did not start.

59. There were originally eight scheduled heats. The heats were redrawn as follows: the origi-

nal heats one and two were combined to form heat one; the original heat three became heat two; the original heat four became heat three; the original heats five and six were combined to form heat four; and the original heats seven and eight were combined to form heat five.

60. Time according to 12OR, 12ORes, and ONews. It is given as 23:12.5 in Uggla.

61. The original heat assignments were as follows: Champion, Taylor — heat one; Andersson, Wetter — heat two.

62. Also entered in this heat, but not competing, were Georges Rigal (FRA), Attilio Bellezza (ITA), and James Reilly (USA).

63. Also entered in this heat, but not competing, were Marcel Pernot (FRA), Leo G. "Budd" Goodwin (USA), and Alois Broft (BOH).

64. The original heat assignments were as follows: Battersby — heat five; Schuh, Wedholm, Massa — heat six.

65. The original heat assignments were as follows: Hardwick, Johnsen, Collin — heat seven; Foster, Avksentyev — heat eight.

66. The following swimmers were entered in this event, but did not compete: original heat one — Georges Drigny (FRA), Jean Thorailler (FRA), J. P. Mantell (USA), Mario Portolongo (ITA); original heat two — André Chenriet (FRA), Georges Hermant (FRA), Davide Baiardo (ITA), Nikolay Voronkov (RUS); original heat five — Henri Dubois (FRA), René Voisard (FRA), Virgilio Bellazza (ITA), Alajos Ferenc Kenyery (HUN), Wolfgang Siller (AUT); original heat six — Louis Bonzom (FRA), Joseph Pletinckx (BEL), Otto Kühne (GER); original heat seven — Alfred Vieilledent (FRA), Emmerich Zachár (HUN), Aldo Cigheri (ITA); original heat eight — Émile Bangerter (FRA), George Godfrey (RSA), Otto Fahr (GER), Joseph Green Morris (USA).

67. There were originally seven scheduled heats. The heats were redrawn as follows: the original heats one and two were combined to form heat one; the original heat three became heat two; the original heat four became heat three; the original heats five and six were combined to form heat four; and the original heat seven became heat five.

68. The original heat assignments were as follows: Groß, Bergman — heat one; Hebner, Schiele — heat two.

69. Oscar Grégoire (BEL) did not start in this heat. He was originally scheduled for heat two, which was combined to form the eventual heat one. Grégoire eventually competed in heat three. See that heat for further footnote information.

70. Listed as second in this heat in Uggla, but he did not compete in the semifinals because he was disqualified.

71. Also entered in this heat, but not competing, were Andreas Asimakopoulos (GRE) and Henri Dubois (FRA).

72. Grégoire was assigned to the original heat two, but did not appear in time for the redrawn heat one start. He appeared for the original heat four (this heat after the redraw), and was for some reason allowed to start in this heat. But the performance was eventually disallowed and his correct place in the results is DNS in heat one (which was original heats one and two). Grégoire's time should have advanced him to the semifinals, as the fastest third-place finisher in round one was supposed to qualify, but it was not allowed.

73. Also entered in this heat, but not competing, were Émile Bangerter (FRA), Davide Baiardo (ITA), and Josef Selmeczi (HUN).

74. The original heat assignments were as follows: Haresnape, Sundman — heat five; Schultze, Johnsen — heat six.

75. Also entered in this heat, but not competing, were Virgilio Bellazza (ITA), Pontus Hanson (SWE), and Maurice Quintard (FRA).

76. The original heat assignments were as follows: Sandon — heat six; Szentgróti — heat seven.

77. The following swimmers were entered in this event, but did not compete: original heat one — Aldo Cigheri (ITA), James Slane (GBR), Ivan Géczy (HUN), Nikolaus Bartkó (HUN); original heat two — Viktor Baranov (RUS), Victor Pierre Eggman (FRA), Mario Massa (ITA); original heat five — George Godfrey (RSA), Stephan Wendelin (HUN), Paudely Psycha (GRE); original heat six — Daniel Pierre Lehn (FRA), Mario Portolongo (ITA), Aleksey Andreyev (RUS).

78. There were originally eight scheduled heats. The heats were redrawn as follows: heats two and three were combined to form a new heat two; heats six to eight were combined to form a new heat six. Heats one, four, and five did not change.

79. Time according to 12ORes, ONews. It is given as 3:16.4 in 12OR, and no time was given in Uggla.

80. Carlyle Atkinson (GBR) was entered in this heat but did not start. See the extra heat listed below.

81. The original heats two and three were combined into this heat. The original heat assignments were as follows: Wastl, Baymakov — heat two; Malisch, Aaltonen, Andersson — heat three.

82. Heat Three according to Uggla.

83. Also entered in this heat, but not competing, were Louis Laufray (FRA), and Heinrich Brandstetter (AUT).

84. Heat Four according to Uggla.

85. Time according to 12ORes, ONews and Uggla. It is given as 3:12.4 in 12OR.

86. Also entered in this heat, but not competing, were Ilarion Borisovsky (RUS) and Virgilio Bellazza (ITA).

87. Heat Five according to Uggla.

88. Heat Six according to Uggla and Heat Three according to 12OR.

89. Atkinson was assigned to heat one but did not appear in time for the heat. When he later appeared he was, for unknown reasons, allowed to swim in an extra heat of his own after the other heats. The 12OR called it heat three probably because, as the original heat three had been combined with the original heat two, there was no true heat three. But 12ORes clearly states "Extra Heat." It is unclear what Atkinson had to do to qualify for the semifinals, but we surmise that he had to better the time of the third-place finishers in the other heats, which he did.

90. The following swimmers were entered in this event, but did not compete: original heat two — Andreas Baronyi (HUN), Davide Baiardo (ITA), John Haakon Johnsen (NOR), and Richard Hallard (FRA); original heat three — Emmerich Elek (HUN), Victor Pierre Eggman (FRA), and Aldo Cigheri (ITA); original heat six — Mario Portolongo (ITA), Walter Krohn (GER), and George Godfrey (RSA); original heat seven — Henri Dubois (FRA), Nikolay Voronkov (RUS), Edmund Toldi (HUN), Mario Massa (ITA), and Rudolf Dlouchy (AUT); original heat eight — Daniel Pierre Lehn (FRA), János Wenk (HUN), Arno Almqvist (RUS), A. Stühmer (GER), Sven Henning (SWE), and Attilio Bellezza (ITA).

91. Georgy Baymakov (RUS) was entered in this heat after qualifying but did not start.

92. There were originally seven scheduled heats. The heats were redrawn as follows: the original heat one remained heat one; the original heats two and three were combined to form heat two; the original heat four became heat three; the original heats five and six were combined to form heat four; and the original heat seven became heat five.

93. Listed as first in this heat in Uggla. He was disqualified because he touched the wall with only one hand at the turn, not with both hands simultaneously, in accordance with the rules in force for breaststroke at the time.

94. Also entered in this heat, but not competing, were Georges Lefevre (FRA), and Audun Rusten (NOR).

95. The original heat assignments were as follows: Malisch, Lindroos — heat two; Andersson, McDermott — heat three.

96. Also entered in this heat, but not competing, were Henri Dubois (FRA) and Pavel Avksentyev (RUS).

97. The original heat assignments were as follows: Courtman, Lindgrén — heat five; Aaltonen — heat six.

98. Also entered in this heat, but not competing, were Rudolf Dlouchy (AUT), Herman Edvard Cederberg (FIN), and Also Cigheri (ITA).

99. The following swimmers were entered in this event, but did not compete: original heat two — Arno Almqvist (RUS), Attilio Bellezza (ITA), Victor Pierre Eggman (FRA), and Pontus Hanson (SWE); original heat three — Paul Harfort (FRA), Virgilio Bellazza (ITA), Samuel Blatherwick

(GBR), and Davide Baiardo (ITA); original heat five — Sven Henning (SWE), Mario Portolongo (ITA), Edmund Toldi (HUN), and Louis André Fanger (FRA); original heat six — Harald Julin (SWE), Nikolay Voronkov (RUS), George Godfrey (RSA), Mario Massa (ITA), and Louis Laufray (FRA).

100. Time 10:11.6 according to 12OR, but 10:11.2 in 12ORes, Uggla, Diem and Spalding. The time in 12OR appears to be a typo. FW used 10:11.6.

101. Time 10:28.2 according to 12OR, likely a typo, but 10:28.6 in 12ORes, Diem, and Spalding.

102. Hungary did not start in the final, despite having qualified to do so.

103. DW has 1:27.4, but the mark is 1:27.4 in all other sources.

104. Daisy Curwen (GBR) also qualified for the final but could not start in it, as she developed appendicitis after the semifinals and underwent surgery for it. She was replaced by Margarete "Grete" Rosenberg (GER), who had the second-fastest third-place time in the semifinals.

105. Rosenberg did not originally qualify for the final, as she did not have the fastest third-place time, but she was advanced to the final when Curwen could not start in it.

106. Gordon, *Australia and the Olympic Games*, p. 85; quoting Mina Wylie interview, Oral History Section, National Library of Australa.

Tennis (Lawn and Covered Courts)

The 1912 Olympic Games began with the covered court tennis events, similar to 1908, when the London Olympics began with racquets, followed by the covered court tennis competition. The covered court tennis at Stockholm began on 5 May at 1:15 P.M. (1315), and ended one week later, on 12 May, with the prizes being given at 5:00 P.M. (1700) later that day.

The covered court events had a reasonable international representation but this was not true of the lawn tennis competitions. The reason for this was that the Olympic lawn tennis schedule was in complete conflict with the 1912 Wimbledon Championships, which ran from 24 June through 8 July. The Olympic lawn tennis championships were held from 28 June through 5 July.

Site:	Royal Tennis Pavilion (covered court events); Tennis Courts at the Östermalm Idrottsplats (lawn tennis events)
Dates:	5–12 May (covered court events); 28 June– 5 July (lawn tennis)
Events:	8 [4 Lawn, 4 Covered Court; 4 Men, 2 Women, 2 Mixed, 2 Men Lawn, 2 Men Covered Court, 1 Women Lawn, 1 Women Covered Court, 1 Mixed Lawn, 1 Mixed Covered Court]
Competitors:	83 [69 Men — 14 Women]
Nations:	14 [14 Men — 6 Women]

Overall	Total	Competitors Lawn	Covered	Both	Gold	Silver	Bronze	Medals
Australasia	1	–	1	–	–	–	1	1
Austria	3	3	–	–	–	1	–	1
Bohemia	8	6	1	1	–	–	–	–
Denmark	10	8	2	–	–	1	–	1
France	6	4	2	–	3	–	2	5
Germany	7	7	–	–	1	1	1	3

310

	Total	Lawn	Covered	Both	Gold	Silver	Bronze	Medals
Great Britain	11	–	11	–	2	2	2	6
Hungary	6	6	–	–	–	–	–	–
The Netherlands	1	1	–	–	–	–	–	–
Norway	7	7	–	–	–	–	1	1
Russia	2	2	–	–	–	–	–	–
South Africa	3	3	–	–	2	1	–	3
Sweden	16	1	3	12	–	2	1	3
United States	1	1	–	–	–	–	–	–
Totals	82	49	20	13	8	8	8	24
Nations	14	12	6	1	4	6	6	9

Men	Total	Competitors Lawn	Covered	Both	Gold	Silver	Bronze	Medals
Australasia	1	–	1	–	–	–	1	1
Austria	3	3	–	–	–	1	–	1
Bohemia	8	6	1	1	–	–	–	–
Denmark	9	8	1	–	–	–	–	–
France	5	3	2	–	2	–	1	3
Germany	6	6	–	–	–	–	1	1
Great Britain	8	–	8	–	–	1	1	2
Hungary	6	6	–	–	–	–	–	–
The Netherlands	1	1	–	–	–	–	–	–
Norway	6	6	–	–	–	–	–	–
Russia	2	2	–	–	–	–	–	–
South Africa	3	3	–	–	2	1	–	3
Sweden	10	–	2	8	–	1	–	1
United States	1	1	–	–	–	–	–	–
Totals	69	45	15	9	4	4	4	12
Nations	14	11	6	2	4	4	7	

Women	Total	Competitors Lawn	Covered	Both	Gold	Silver	Bronze	Medals
Denmark	1	–	1	–	–	1	–	1
France	1	1	–	–	1	–	–	1
Germany	1	1	–	–	–	1	–	1
Great Britain	3	–	3	–	1	–	1	2
Norway	1	1	–	–	–	–	1	1
Sweden	6	1	1	4	–	–	–	–
Totals	13	4	5	4	2	2	2	6
Nations	6	4	3	1	2	2	2	5

Mixed		Gold	Silver	Bronze	Medals
France		–	–	1	1
Germany		1	–	–	1

Great Britain	1	1	–	2
Sweden	–	1	1	2
Totals	2	2	2	6
Nations	2	2	2	4

Committee for Lawn Tennis

Honorary President: HRH Prince Wilhelm
President: Captain Axel Fingal Wallenberg
Secretary: Kurt Zetterberg, Esquire; Assistant Paymaster, R.N.
Members: Mrs. Märtha Adlerstråhle; Miss Ebba Hay; Wollmar Boström, Esquire, First Private Secretary to HM the King; Lieutenant Henrik Fick; Consul, James Keiller, Jr.; Fredrik Bohnstedt, Esquire; B.A.

Diplomas of Merit— Lawn Tennis[1]*

Axel Thayssen (DEN), Charles Wennergren (SWE), L. Eric Tapscott (RSA), Ladislav "Rázný" Žemla (BOH), Ludwig, Count von Salm-Hoogstraeten (AUT), Ludwig Maria Heyden (GER), Vagn Ingerslev (DEN)

Diplomas of Merit— Covered Court Tennis[2]

Carl-Olof Nylén (SWE), Erik Larsen (DEN), F. Gordon Lowe (GBR), Frans Möller (SWE), Hakon Leffler (SWE), Thorsten Grönfors (SWE), Wollmar Boström (SWE)

LAWN TENNIS — MEN

Men's Singles

A: 49; C: 12; D: 28 June–5 July; F: Single-elimination tournaments.

With most of the top British and Commonwealth players absent, playing at Wimbledon, this tournament was not of the top rank. The top player in the world in 1912 was New Zealand's Anthony "Tony" Wilding. Wilding was Wimbledon champion in 1910 and 1911, and won again in 1912, during the Olympic championship, and won his fourth consecutive Wimbledon championship in 1913. The only American who competed at Stockholm, Roosevelt Pell, was not of the top quality, his best finish ever at the United States championships coming in 1915, when he lost in the semifinals.

In Wilding's absence, the Olympic men's singles final came down to two South Africans, Charles Winslow and Harry Kitson. Kitson had the better career record, winning the South African championship in 1905, 1908, 1911, and 1913, while Winslow would win that title only once, in 1914. Nonetheless, at Stockholm, Winslow held on to defeat Kitson and win the Olympic gold medal in four sets.

See Notes on pages 325–326.

1.	Charles Winslow	RSA
2.	Harry Kitson	RSA
3.	Oscar Kreuzer	GER
4.	Ladislav "Rázný" Žemla	BOH
=5.	Ludwig, Count von Salm-Hoogstraeten	AUT
	Otto von Müller	GER
	Ludwig Maria Heyden	GER
	Arthur Zborzil	AUT
=9.	Heinrich Schomburgk	GER
	Charles Wennergren	SWE
	Béla von Kehrling	HUN
	L. Eric Tapscott	RSA
	Vagn Ingerslev	DEN
	T. Roosevelt Pell	USA
	Josef Šebek	BOH
	Mikhail Sumarokov-Elston	RUS
=17.	Frans Möller	SWE
	Robert Spies	GER
	Wollmar Boström	SWE
	L. Leif Rovsing	DEN
	Victor Hansen	DEN
	Jenő von Zsigmondy	HUN
	François Joseph Blanchy	FRA
	Axel Thayssen	DEN
	Thorsten Grönfors	SWE
	Aurél von Kelemen	HUN
	Albert Canet	FRA
	Noble Stibolt	NOR
	Karel "Sláva" Robětín (Fuchs)	BOH
	Gunnar Setterwall	SWE
=31.	Hakon Leffler	SWE
	Jaroslav Just	BOH
	Trygve Smith	NOR
	Richard Petersen	NOR
	Jaromír Zeman	BOH
	Ove Frederiksen	DEN
	Bohuslav "Černý" Hykš	BOH
	F. Felix Piepes	AUT
	Aage Madsen	DEN
	Ernst Frigast	DEN
	Jørgen Arenholt	DEN
	Edouard Marc Mény de Marangue	FRA
	Leó von Baráth	HUN
	Conrad Langaard	NOR
	Curt Benckert	SWE
	Otte Blom	NED
	Herman Bjørklund	NOR
=48.	Jiří Kodl	BOH
	O. Paul Lindpaintner	GER

3

Tournament Draw

Round One D: 28–29 June.

E. Tapscott (RSA)	d. J. Kodl (BOH)	6–4, 6–1, 6–2	28/6
F. Piepes (AUT)	d. O.P. Lindpaintner (GER)	6–2, 6–3, 6–3	28/6
A. Thayssen (DEN)	wo. K. Ardelt (BOH)		29/6 1200

Round Two D: 28–30 June.

H. Kitson (RSA)	d. H. Leffler (SWE)	6–2, 6–1, 6–0	28/6
F. Möller (SWE)	wo. J.P. Samazeuilh (FRA)		
R. Spies (GER)	d. J. Just (BOH)	2–6, 6–3, 3–6, 6–3, 6–1	29/6 0900
H. Schomburgk (GER)	wo. J. Montariol (FRA)		
W. Boström (SWE)	d. T. Smith (NOR)	6–2, 6–4, 6–1	29/6 0900
L. von Salm-Hoogstraeten (AUT)	d. R. Petersen (NOR)	6–1, 7–5, 6–3	29/6 1030
C. Wennergren (SWE)	d. J. Zeman (BOH)	6–1, 6–0, 6–0	28/6
L. Rovsing (DEN)	wo. P. Segner (HUN)		
V. Hansen (DEN)	wo. Ö. Schmid (HUN)		
B. von Kehrling (HUN)	wo. J.C. Kempe (SWE)		
E. von Zsigmondy (HUN)	wo. H. Liebisch (AUT)		
O. von Müller (GER)	d. O. Frederiksen (DEN)	6–2, 6–1, 6–4	30/6 0900
R. Bertrand (AUT)	wo. H. Planner von Plaun (AUT)		
L. Žemla (BOH)	wo. A. Hammacher (GER)		29/6 0900
F.J. Blanchy (FRA)	d. B. Hykš (BOH)	5–7, 6–1, 6–2, 6–1	28/6
E. Tapscott (RSA)	d. F. Piepes (AUT)	3–6, 7–5, 4–6, 7–5, 7–5	30/6 1430
A. Thayssen (DEN)	d. A. Madsen (DEN)	6–1, 6–3, 3–6, 6–3	29/6 1030
C. Winslow (RSA)	d. E. Frigast (DEN)	7–5, 6–2, 6–3	
T. Grönfors (SWE)	wo. E. Tóth (HUN)		
V. Ingerslev (DEN)	d. J. Arenholt (DEN)	6–2, 1–6, 6–0, 6–4	
L.M. Heyden (GER)	d. M. Mény de Marangue (FRA)	7–9, 4–6, 6–2, 7–5, 6–1	29/6 1330
A. von Kelemen (HUN)	d. L. von Baráth (HUN)	6–1, 6–3, 6–4	
A. Canet (FRA)	d. C. Langaard (NOR)	6–3, 6–0, 6–1	29/6 1030
R. Pell (USA)	wo. G. Paller (HUN)		
N. Stibolt (NOR)	wo. D. Lawton (FRA)	29/6 1500	
J. Šebek (BOH)	wo. O. Froitzheim (GER)		
K. Robětín (Fuchs) (BOH)	wo. C. Ritter von Wessely (AUT)		
A. Zborzil (AUT)	d. C. Benckert (SWE)	6–2, 6–4, 1–6, 6–3	29/6 1330
G. Setterwall (SWE)	d. O. Blom (NED)	6–3, 6–3, 8–6	29/6 1330
M. Sumarokov-Elston (RUS)	wo. A. Alenitsyn (RUS)		
B. Angell (NOR)	wo. O. Relly (AUT)		
O. Kreuzer (GER)	d. H. Bjorklund (NOR)	6–0, 6–0, 6–1	29/6 1200

Round Three D: 29 June–1 July.

Kitson	d. Möller	6–2, 6–2, 6–3[4]	30/6 1300
Schomburgk	d. Spies	8–6, 6–1, 4–1, retired	30/6 0900
von Salm-Hoogstraeten	d. Boström	7–5, 6–4, 6–1	30/6 1600
Wennergren	d. Rovsing	4–6, 9–7, 6–8, 6–1, 6–1	29/6 1500
von Kehrling	d. Hansen	6–2, 6–1, 6–8, 6–4	29/6 1630
von Müller	d. von Zsigmondy	6–1, 6–2, 6–0	30/6 1600
Žemla	wo. Rudolf Bertrand (AUT)		

Tapscott	d. Blanchy	1–6, 5–7, 6–3, 6–4, 6–4	1/7	1000[5]
Winslow	d. Thayssen	6–4, 3–6, 6–4, 6–4	30/6	0900
Ingerslev	d. Grönfors	6–1, 6–2, 6–2	30/6	1030
Heyden	d. von Kelemen	6–3, 4–6, 7–5, 7–5	30/6	1030
Pell	d. Canet	6–2, 6–3, 6–4[6]	29/6	
Šebek	d. Stibolt	6–1, 6–3, 6–0		
Zborzil	d. Robětín (Fuchs)	6–4, 6–2, 6–1	30/6	1600
Sumarokov-Elston	d. Setterwall	6–2, 6–3, 11–13, 6–2	30/6	1730
Kreuzer	wo. Bjarne Angell (NOR)	29/6 1630		

Round Four D: 1 July.

Kitson	d. Schomburgk	6–2, 6–2, 6–3	1/7 1230
von Salm-Hoogstraeten	d. Wennergren	6–3, 5–7, 7–5, 6–1	1/7 1530
von Müller	d. von Kehrling	6–2, 6–1, 6–1[7]	1/7 1100
Žemla	d. Tapscott	1–6, 4–6, 6–2, 6–4, 6–2[8]	1/7 1530
Winslow	d. Ingerslev	6–4, 8–6, 6–4[9]	1/7 1100
Heyden	d. Pell	2–6, 7–5, 8–6, 7–5	1/7 1530
Zborzil	d. Šebek	6–1, 6–0, 3–6, 6–2	1/7 1700
Kreuzer	d. Sumarokov-Elston	6–2, 10–12, 6–4, 6–0	1/7 1400

Quarterfinals D: 2–3 July.

Kitson	d. von Salm-Hoogstraeten	6–2, 6–2, 6–4	3/7 1500[10]
Žemla	d. von Müller	6–4, 7–5, 6–4	3/7 0900[11]
Winslow	d. Heyden	6–2, 6–4, 8–10, 4–6, 6–3	2/7
Kreuzer	d. Zborzil	6–4, 6–3, 6–2	2/7 1200

Semifinals D: 3–4 July.

Kitson	d. Žemla	2–6, 6–3, 6–2, 4–6, 6–3	4/7 1200
Winslow	d. Kreuzer	9–7, 7–5, 6–2	3/7 1400

Final D: 5 July; T: 1400.

Winslow	d. Kitson	7–5, 4–6, 10–8, 8–6

Bronze Medal Match D: 4 July.

Kreuzer	d. Žemla	6–2, 3–6, 6–3, 6–1

Men's Doubles

A: 44[12]; C: 10; D: 28 June–5 July; F: Single-elimination tournaments.

The two South African finalists from the singles competition, Charles Winslow and Harry Kitson, teamed to win the doubles event. Since the retirement of Britain's Doherty brothers (Laurie and Reggie), there was no dominant doubles team in international tennis. The other men's doubles champions in 1912 were as follows: Wimbledon—Roper Barrett and Charles Dixon; French—Max Décugis and André Germot; United States—Thomas Bundy and Malcolm McLoughlin; and Australian—James Parke and Charles Dixon (GBR/IRL).

1. Harry Kitson/Charles Winslow   RSA
2. F. Felix Piepes/Arthur Zborzil   AUT
3. Albert Canet/Edouard Marc Mény de Marangue   FRA
4. Ladislav "Rázný" Žemla/Jaroslav Just   BOH
=5. Mikhail Sumarokov-Elston/Aleksandr Alenitsyn   RUS
   Wollmar Boström/Curt Benckert   SWE
   Charles Wennergren/Carl-Olof Nylén   SWE
   Robert Spies/Ludwig Maria Heyden   GER
=9. Heinrich Schomburgk/Otto von Müller   GER
   L. Leif Rovsing/Victor Hansen   DEN
   Axel Thayssen/Aage Madsen   DEN
   Béla von Kehrling/Jenő von Zsigmondy   HUN
   Richard Petersen/Conrad Langaard   NOR
   Ernst Frigast/Ove Frederiksen   DEN
=15. Leó von Baráth/Aurél von Kelemen   HUN
   Trygve Smith/Herman Bjørklund   NOR
   Josef Šebek/Bohuslav "Černý" Hykš   BOH
   Ede Tóth/Paul Segner   HUN
   Jaromír Zeman/Karel "Sláva" Robětín (Fuchs)   BOH
   Vagn Ingerslev/Jørgen Arenholt   DEN
   Bjarne Angell/Noble Stibolt   NOR
   Frans Möller/Thorsten Grönfors   SWE[13]

Tournament Draw

Round One D: 28–30 June.

Frigast/Frederiksen	bye		
Schomburgk/von Müller	d. von Baráth/von Kelemen	6–0, 6–0, 6–2	30/6 1300
Canet/Mény de Marangue	wo. D. Lawton/J.P. Samazeuilh (FRA)		
Sumarokov-Elston/Alenitsyn	wo. F.J. Blanchy/J. Montariol (FRA)		
Rovsing/Hansen	wo. J. Kodl/K. Ardelt (BOH)		
Boström/Benckert	wo. O. Froitzheim/O. Kreuzer (GER)		
Lindpaintner/Hammacher	wo. G. Paller/Ö. Schmid (HUN)		
von Salm-Hoogstraeten/ Planner von Plaun	wo. G. Setterwall/C. Kempe (SWE)		
Piepes/Zborzil	d. Smith/Bjorklund	6–0, 6–2, 6–0	29/6
Thayssen/Madsen	d. Šebek/Hykš	6–3, 6–4, 6–4	28/6
Wennergren/Nylén	d. Tóth/Segner		
von Kehrling/von Zsigmondy	d. Zeman/Robětín (Fuchs)	3–6, 6–1, 6–4	28/6
Kitson/Winslow	d. Ingerslev/Arenholt	6–4, 6–1, 6–4	28/6
Žemla/Just	d. Angell/Stibolt	6–1, 6–2, 6–0	29/6 1200
Petersen/Langaard	wo. R. Bertrand/C. von Wessely (AUT)		
Spies/Heyden	d. Möller/Grönfors	3–6, 6–4, 6–2, 4–6, 6–1	29/6 1630

Round Two D: 29 June–1 July.

Canet/Mény de Marangue	d. Schomburgk/von Müller	6–8, 6–3, 6–2, 6–3	1/7 1830
Sumarokov-Elston/Alenitsyn	d. Rovsing/Hansen	2–6, 6–3, 7–5, 6–3	30/6 1030

Boström/Benckert	wo.	O.P. Lindpaintner/ A. Hammacher (GER)		
Piepes/Zborzil	wo.	L. von Salm-Hoogstraeten/ H. Planner von Plaun (AUT)		
Wennergren/Nylén	d.	Thayssen/Madsen	6–1, 6–2, 6–4	30/6 1300
Kitson/Winslow	d.	von Kehrling/von Zsigmondy	6–3, 6–3, 7–9, 6–2	30/6 1730
Žemla/Just	d.	Petersen/Langaard	6–1, 6–2, 6–4	29/6
Spies/Heyden	d.	Frigast/Frederiksen	6–2, 7–5, 6–3	30/6 1430

Quarterfinals D: 1–2 July.

Canet/Mény de Marangue	d.	Sumarokov-Elston/Alenitsyn	6–3, 6–0, 6–1	2/7 1100
Piepes/Zborzil	d.	Boström/Benckert	6–3, 4–6, 6–1, 6–1	1/7 1700
Kitson/Winslow	d.	Wennergren/Nylén	6–3, 7–5, 6–1	1/7 1700
Žemla/Just	d.	Spies/Heyden	6–0, 8–6, 6–4	2/7 1400[14]

Semifinals D: 3 July.

Piepes/Zborzil	d.	Canet/Mény de Marangue	7–5, 2–6, 3–6, 10–8, 10–8	3/7 1100
Kitson/Winslow	d.	Žemla/Just	4–6, 6–1, 7–5, 6–4	3/7 1730[15]

Final D: 4 July; T: 1500.

Kitson/Winslow	d.	Piepes/Zborzil	4–6, 6–1, 6–2, 6–2

Bronze Medal Match D: 5 July; T: 1500.[16]

Canet/Mény de Marangue	d.	Žemla/Just	13–11, 6–3, 8–6.

LAWN TENNIS — WOMEN

Ladies' Singles

A: 8[17]; C: 4; D: 1–4 July; F: Single-elimination tournaments.

The top players in the world were Britain's Dorothea Lambert Chambers, Wimbledon champion in 1903, 1904, 1906, 1910, 1911, 1913 and 1914, and the United States' Margaret Browne, U.S. Champion from 1912 to 1914. However, neither was present at Stockholm. The title went to France's Marguerite Broquedis, who would win the French championship in 1913 and 1914. She defeated Germany's Dora Köring in the final, who was probably the top player at Stockholm. Köring was German champion in 1912 and 1913.

The bronze medalist, however, Anna "Molla" Bjurstedt, would become the best known player among the women at Stockholm. After emigrating to the United States in 1914, she won the U.S. Championship in 1915, 1918, 1920, 1921, 1922, and 1926. She was the only woman to defeat Suzanne Lenglen in singles after World War I, this occurring at the 1921 U.S. Championships.

1. Marguerite Broquedis   FRA
2. Dorothea "Dora" Köring   GER

3. Anna "Molla" Bjurstedt		NOR		
4. Edith Arnheim Lasch		SWE		
=5. Annie Holmström		SWE		
Margareta Cederschiöld		SWE		
=7. Sigrid Fick		SWE		
Ellen Brusewitz		SWE		

18

Tournament Draw

Round One D: 1 July; T: 0900.

A. Holmström (SWE)	bye			
E. Arnheim Lasch (SWE)	bye			
A.M. Bjurstedt (NOR)	bye			
G. Kaminski (GER)	bye			
D. Köring (GER)	d.	S. Fick (SWE)	7–5, 6–3[19]	1/7 0900
V. Bjurstedt (NOR)	wo.	M. Rieck (GER)		
M. Cederschiöld (SWE)	d.	E. Brusewitz (SWE)	8–6, 8–6	1/7 0900
M. Broquedis (FRA)	wo.	J. de Lobkowicz (BOH)		

Quarterfinals D: 3 July.

Arnheim Lasch	d.	Holmström	4–6, 6–4, 6–1[20]	3/7 0900
Köring	wo.	V. Bjurstedt (NOR)		
Broquedis	d.	Cederschiöld	6–1, 6–4[21]	3/7 1000
Bjurstedt	wo.	G. Kaminski (GER)		

Semifinals D: 3 July

Köring	d.	Arnheim Lasch	6–4, 6–3[22]	3/7 1500
Broquedis	d.	M. Bjurstedt	6–3, 2–6, 6–4	3/7 1400

Final D: 4 July; T: 1515.

Broquedis	d.	Köring	4–6, 6–3, 6–4	4/7 1515

Bronze Medal Match D: 4 July; T: 1100.

M. Bjurstedt	d.	Arnheim Lasch	6–2, 6–2	4/7 1100

LAWN TENNIS — MIXED EVENTS

Mixed Doubles

A: 12; C: 4; D: 1, 3–5 July; F: Single-elimination tournaments.

The field was very weak, due to the absence of the British and American players. The gold medalists, Dorothea "Dora" Köring and Heinrich Schomburgk, also won the German mixed championship in 1912 and 1913.

1. Dorothea "Dora" Köring/Heinrich Schomburgk — GER
2. Sigrid Fick/Gunnar Setterwall — SWE
3. Marguerite Broquedis/Albert Canet — FRA
4. Annie Holmström/Thorsten Grönfors — SWE
=5. Edith Arnheim Lasch/Carl-Olof Nylén — SWE
    Anna "Molla" Bjurstedt/Conrad Langaard — NOR[23]

Tournament Draw

Round One D: 1 July.

Cederschiöld/Kempe	bye			
Kaminski/von Müller	bye			
Rieck/Kreuzer	bye			
Broquedis/Canet	d.	Arnheim Lasch/Nylén	6–2, 6–4	1/7 1400
Lobkowicz/Just	wo.	J. Kubešová/A. Kubeš (BOH)		
Köring/Schomburgk	wo.	V. Bjurstedt/T. Smith (NOR)		
Fick/Setterwall	wo.	A. Šebková/J. Šebek (BOH)		
Holmström/Grönfors	d.	M. Bjurstedt/Langaard (NOR)	6–4, 4–6, 7–5	1/7 1000

Quarterfinals D: 3 July.

Broquedis/Canet	wo.	M. Cederschiöld/J.C. Kempe (SWE)		
Fick/Setterwall	d.	Holmström/Grönfors	8–6, 10–8	3/7 1000[24]
Rieck/Kreuzer	wo.	G. Kaminski/O. von Müller (GER)		
Köring/Schomburgk	wo.	J. de Lobkowicz/J. Just (BOH)		

Semifinals D: 4 July.

Köring/Schomburgk	d.	Broquedis/Canet	6–2, 6–3	4/7 1000
Fick/Setterwall	wo.	M. Rieck/O. Kreuzer (GER)		

Final D: 5 July.

Köring/Schomburgk	d.	Fick/Setterwall	6–4, 6–0	5/7

Bronze Medal Match D: 5 July.

Broquedis/Canet	wo.	M. Rieck/O. Kreuzer (GER)	5/7

COVERED COURTS — MEN

Men's Singles

A: 22; C: 6; D: 5–6, 8–12 May; F: Single-elimination tournaments.

The 1912 Olympic Games began at 1315 on 5 May when Sweden's Carl Kempe hit his first serve in his match with Jaroslav Hainz of Bohemia. The covered court competition had a much stronger field than the lawn tennis event which would occur almost two months later. The covered court event was not hampered by the concurrent competition at Wimbledon, which greatly weakened the lawn tennis events. In fact, the Stockholm covered court singles could claim one of the top international fields to date in men's tennis. Although Tony Wilding was considered the top player in the world (see his record under lawn tennis men's singles), he was defeated in the semifinals by the British player, Charles Dixon. Dixon was favored in the final, but fell in straight sets to André Gobert of France. Gobert was the top French player in 1912, having replaced Max Décugis. Gobert was French singles champion in 1911 and 1920 and won the indoor French title in 1911, 1912 and 1913, and again in 1920.

1.	André Gobert	FRA
2.	Charles Dixon	GBR
3.	Anthony Wilding	AUS/NZL
4.	F. Gordon Lowe	GBR
=5.	George Caridia	GBR
	Gunnar Setterwall	SWE
	Karel "Sláva" Robětín (Fuchs)[25]	BOH
	Arthur Lowe[26]	GBR
=9.	Theodore Mavrogordato	GBR
	Thorsten Grönfors	SWE
	Arthur "Wentworth" Gore	GBR
	Maurice Germot	FRA
	J. Carl Kempe	SWE
	H. Roper Barrett	GBR
	Charles Wennergren	SWE
=16.	Lennart Silverstolpe	SWE
	Frans Möller	SWE
	Hakon Leffler	SWE
	Wollmar Boström	SWE
	Alfred Beamish	GBR
	Erik Larsen	DEN
	Jaroslav Hainz	BOH
	[27]	

Tournament Draw

Round One D: 5–6 May.

J. Just (BOH)	wo.	M. Decugis (FRA)		5/7 1315
T. Grönfors (SWE)	wo.	J. Šebek (BOH)		5/7 1315
A. Wilding (AUS/NZL)	d.	L. Silverstolpe (SWE)	6–0, 6–1, 6–1	5/7 1430
G. Caridia (GBR)	d.	F. Möller (SWE)	6–2, 7–5, 3–6, 6–4	5/7 1430
A. Gore (GBR)	d.	H. Leffler (SWE)	7–5, 6–4, 7–5	5/7 1530
A. Lowe (GBR)	d.	W. Boström (SWE)	5–7, 6–4, 6–4, 6–4	5/7 1530
M. Germot (FRA)	d.	A. Beamish (GBR)	4–6, 6–2, 4–6, 6–2, 6–4	6/7 1600[28]
A. Gobert (FRA)	d.	E. Larsen (DEN)	8–6, 6–1, 5–7, 8–6	5/7 1700
J.C. Kempe (SWE)	d.	J. Hainz (BOH)	6–1, 6–4, 3–6, 6–3	5/7 1315

Round Two D: 5–6, 8 May.

Dixon	d.	Mavrogordato	6–2, 9–7, 4–6, 10–8	6/5 1100

Robětín (Fuchs)	wo.	J. Just (BOH)	
Wilding	d.	Grönfors	6–3, 6–3, 6–3	6/5 1300
Caridia	d.	Gore	6–2, 9–7, 7–5	8/5 1430
Lowe	d.	Germot	6–4, 3–6, 6–1, 6–4	8/5 1200
Gobert	d.	Kempe	6–1, 6–2, 7–5	8/5 1500
Setterwall	d.	Barrett	4–6, 6–1, 6–4, 6–8, 6–4	6/5 1515
Lowe	d.	Wennergren	6–4, 6–1, 6–4	5/5 1315

Quarterfinals D: 8–9 May.

Dixon	d.	Robětín (Fuchs)	6–2, 6–4, 6–1	8/5
Wilding	d.	Caridia	6–1, 6–2, 6–2	9/5 1500
Gobert	d.	Lowe	6–1, 6–1, 6–3	9/5 1200
Lowe	d.	Setterwall	6–4, 1–6, 6–3, 8–6	8/5

Semifinals D: 10 May.

Dixon	d.	Wilding	6–0, 4–6, 6–4, 6–4	10/5 1430
Gobert	d.	Lowe	6–4, 10–8, 2–6, 2–6, 6–2	10/5 1300

Final D: 12 May.

Gobert	d.	Dixon	8–6, 6–4, 6–4	12/5 1315

Bronze Medal Match D: 11 May.

Wilding	d.	Lowe	4–6, 6–2, 7–5, 6–0	11/5 1530

Men's Doubles

A: 16; C: 3; D: 6–11 May; F: Single-elimination tournaments.

The British teams of Dixon and Beamish and Gore and Barrett were favored as all had played on winning teams at Wimbledon. The 1911 Wimbledon champions were André Gobert and Max Décugis, while Decugis and Maurice Germot had won the French title from 1911 to 1914. However, with Decugis not present in Stockholm, the Olympic indoor champion, André Gobert, teamed with Germot to upset the British team of Dixon and Beamish in the semifinal, and to defeat Swedes Setterwall and Kempe in the final. Gobert and Germot teamed again to win the 1913 French indoor title.

1.	André Gobert/Maurice Germot	FRA
2.	Gunnar Setterwall/J. Carl Kempe	SWE
3.	Charles Dixon/Alfred Beamish	GBR
4.	Arthur "Wentworth" Gore/H. Roper Barrett	GBR
=5.	F. Gordon Lowe/Arthur Lowe	GBR
	Wollmar Boström/Curt Benckert	SWE
=7.	Charles Wennergren/Carl-Olof Nylén	SWE
	George Caridia/Theodore Mavrogordato	GBR

Tournament Draw

Round One D: 6–7 May.

Dixon/Beamish	bye		
Möller/Grönfors	bye		
Boström/Benckert	bye		
Gore/Barrett	bye		
Robětin (Fuchs)/Just	bye		
Lowe/Lowe	d. Wennergren/Nylén	9–7, 11–9, 6–2	6/5 1330
Gobert/Germot	wo. J. Šebek/J. Hainz (BOH)		
Setterwall/Kempe	d. Caridia/Mavrogordato	6–4, 4–6, 6–8, 6–2, 6–3	7/5 1500

Quarterfinals D: 7–8 May.

Dixon/Beamish	wo. K. Robětín (Fuchs)/J. Just (BOH)		
Gobert/Germot	d. Lowe/Lowe	3–6, 6–8, 6–4, 6–2, 6–3	7/5 1300
Setterwall/Kempe	wo. F. Möller/T. Grönfors (SWE)		8/5 1615
Gore/Barrett	d. Boström/Benckert	7–5, 6–4, 6–1	7/5 1430

Semifinals D: 9–10 May

Gobert/Germot	d. Dixon/Beamish	6–3, 6–1, 6–2	9/5 1630[29]
Setterwall/Kempe	d. Gore/Barrett	4–6, 3–6, 6–1, 6–4, 6–3	10/5 1600

Final D: 11 May; T: 1400.

Gobert/Germot	d. Setterwall/Kempe	6–4, 12–14, 6–2, 6–4	11/5 1400

Bronze Medal Match D: 11 May; T: 1530.

Dixon/Beamish	d. Gore/Barrett	6–2, 0–6, 10–8, 2–6, 6–3	11/5 1530

COVERED COURTS — WOMEN

Ladies' Singles

A: 8; C: 3; D: 6–7, 9–11 May; F: Single-elimination tournaments.

With only eight players, and none of the top British women, this event was not of the top international caliber. Edith Hannam, who won the event without losing a set, had made it to the All-Comers' final at Wimbledon in 1911. Born Edith Boucher, she married Francis Hannam in 1909 and settled briefly in Canada, after which she stopped competing. However, on returning to Britain she resumed playing, and won five Welsh singles' championships between 1912 and 1923.

1.	Edith Hannam	GBR
2.	Sofie Castenschiold	DEN
3.	Mabel Parton	GBR

4. Sigrid Fick	SWE	
=5. Edith Arnheim Lasch	SWE	
Annie Holmström	SWE	
F. Helen Aitchison	GBR	
8. Margareta Cederschiöld	SWE	
30		

Tournament Draw

Round One D: 6 May; T: 1100.

E. Lasch (SWE)	bye			
M. Decugis (FRA)	bye			
A. Holmström (SWE)	bye			
S. Castenschiold (DEN)	bye			
E. Hannam (GBR)	bye			
F.H. Aitchison (GBR)	bye			
M. Parton (GBR)	d.	M. Cederschiöld (SWE)	6–0, 6–1	6/5 1100
S. Fick (SWE)	wo.	E. Magnusson (SWE)		

Quarterfinals D: 6–7 May.

E. Hannam (GBR)	d.	E. Arnheim Lasch (SWE)	7–5, 6–1	7/5 1600
M. Parton (GBR)	wo.	M. Decugis (FRA)		
S. Fick (SWE)	d.	A. Holmström (SWE)	6–1, 6–1	6/5 1200
S. Castenschiold (DEN)	d.	H. Aitchison (GBR)	2–6, 6–2, 6–1	6/5 1700

Semifinals D: 9–10 May.

E. Hannam	d.	M. Parton	7–5, 6–2	9/5 1630
S. Castenschiold	d.	S. Fick	6–4, 6–4	10/5 1200

Final D: 11 May; T: 1300.

E. Hannam	d.	S. Castenschiold	6–4, 6–3	11/5 1300

Bronze Medal Match D: 11 May; T: 1200.

M. Parton	d.	S. Fick	6–3, 6–3	11/5 1200

COVERED COURTS — MIXED EVENT

Mixed Doubles

A: 16; C: 3; D: 6–9, 11–12 May; F: Single-elimination tournaments.

In the final, Edith Hannam and Charles Dixon needed three sets to defeat another British team, Helen Aitchison and H. Roper Barrett. Hannam also won the covered court ladies' singles at Stockholm, while Dixon won the silver medal in the covered court men's singles, and, with Alfred Beamish, a bronze medal in the men's doubles. Two months later, Dixon skipped the Olympic lawn tennis event to play at Wimbledon where he won the doubles with H. Roper Barrett. Later in the year he and James Parke (GBR/IRL) won the doubles title at the Australian championships, and he finished a memorable year by captaining the winning British Davis Cup squad in 1912.

1.	Edith Hannam/Charles Dixon	GBR
2.	Helen Aitchison/H. Roper Barrett	GBR
3.	Sigrid Fick/Gunnar Setterwall	SWE
4.	Margareta Cederschiöld/J. Carl Kempe	SWE
=5.	Sofie Castenschiold/Erik Larsen	DEN
	Mabel Parton/Theodore Mavrogordato	GBR
=7.	Edith Arnheim Lasch/Carl-Olof Nylén	SWE
	Ebba Hay/Frans Möller	SWE

31

Tournament Draw

Round One D: 6–7 May.

Hannam/Dixon	bye			
Fick/Setterwall	bye			
Cederschiöld/Kempe	bye			
Castenschiold/Larsen	bye			
M. Decugis/M. Decugis (FRA)	bye			
Šebková/Šebek (BOH)	bye			
Aitchison/Barrett	d.	Arnheim Lasch/Nylén	6–2, 6–4	7/5 1200
Parton/Mavrogordato	d.	Hay/Möller	6–3, 6–0	6/5 1430

Quarterfinals D: 8 May.

Fick/Setterwall	wo.	A. Šebková/J. Šebek (BOH)		
Aitchison/Barrett	d.	Castenschiold/Larsen	6–0, 6–3	8/5 1330
Hannam/Dixon	d.	Parton/Mavrogordato	6–3, 6–0	8/5 1330
Cederschiöld/Kempe	wo.	M. Decugis/M. Decugis (FRA)		

Semifinals D: 9 May

Aitchison/Barrett	d.	Fick/Setterwall	3–6, 6–1, 6–2	9/5 1330
Hannam/Dixon	d.	Cederschiöld/Kempe	6–2, 6–2	9/5 1200

Final D: 12 May; T: 1530.

Hannam/Dixon	d.	Aitchison/Barrett	4–6, 6–3, 6–2	12/5 1530

Bronze Medal Match D: 11 May; T: 1700.

Fick/Setterwall	wo.	Cederschiöld/Kempe	retired	11/5 1700

NOTES

1. It is difficult to fathom how these were chosen. They do not appear to be definitely based on the finish in any of the separate events.

2. It is difficult to fathom how these were chosen. They do not appear to be definitely based on the finish in any of the separate events.

3. Also entered in this event, but not competing, were Rudolf Bertrand (AUT), Herman Liebisch (AUT), Herbert Plauner von Plaun (AUT), Otto Relly (AUT), Carl von Wessely (AUT), Karel Ardelt (BOH), Jean-Pierre Samazeuilh (FRA), Jean Montariol (FRA), Daniel Edouard Lawton (FRA), Otto Froitzheim (GER), August Hammacher (GER), Paul Segner (HUN), Ödön Schmid (HUN), Ede Tóth (HUN), Gyüla Paller (HUN), Bjarne Angell (NOR), Aleksandr Alenitsyn (RUS), and Carl Kempe (SWE).

4. This is the score in 12OR, but ONews gives 6–1, 6–4, 6–0.

5. Originally scheduled for 30 June at 1730.

6. This is the score given in 12OR, but ONews gives 6–2, 6–3, 6–3.

7. This is the score in 12OR but ONews gives 6–1, 6–2, 6–0.

8. This is the score in 12OR, but ONews gives 1–6, 5–7, 6–3, 6–4, 6–4.

9. This is the score in 12OR but ONews has 6–4, 8–6, 7–5.

10. Originally scheduled for 2 July at 1330.

11. Originally scheduled for 2 July at 0900.

12. DW, EK, FW, and OSVK have 42.

13. Also entered in this event, but not competing, were the teams of Rudolf Bertrand/Carl Ritter von Wessely (AUT), Ludwig, Count von Salm-Hoogstraeten/Herbert Plauner von Plaun (AUT), Jiří Kodl/Karel Ardelt (BOH), Daniel Edouard Lawton/Jean-Pierre Samazeuilh (FRA), François Joseph Blanchy/Jean Montariol (FRA), O. Paul Lindpaintner/August Hammacher (GER), Otto Froitzheim/Oscar Kreuzer (GER), Ede Tóth/Paul Segner (HUN), Gyüla Paller/Ödön Schmid (HUN), and Gunnar Setterwall/J. Carl Kempe (SWE).

14. Originally scheduled for 1 July at 1830.

15. Originally scheduled for 2 July at 1730.

16. Originally scheduled for 4 July at 1700.

17. It is reasonable to consider that there were nine competitors in this event. Valborg Bjurstedt (NOR), sister of Anna "Molla" Bjurstedt, is listed as winning in the first round, but the match was a walkover over Miken Rieck (NOR). In round two, Bjurstedt did not compete and lost by default to Dora Köring (GER). Thus she never actually competed. Norwegian Olympic historians Magne Teigen and Arild Gjerde have examined this situation and are also not certain what to do. It appears that Valborg Bjurstedt may not actually have been in Stockholm, and the first round walkover was merely a matter of record keeping by the officials. Thus, we have not included her as a competitor.

18. Also entered in this event, but not competing, were Josefina de Lobkowicz (BOH), Miken Rieck (GER), Gertrud Kaminski (GER), and Valborg Bjurstedt (NOR).

19. This is the score given in 12OR, but ONews gives the score as 7–5, 6–0.

20. This is the score given in 12OR, but ONews has the score as 4–6, 6–4, 7–5.

21. This is the score given in 12OR, but ONews gives the score as 6–0, 6–4.

22. This is the score given in 12OR, but ONews gives the score as 6–4, 6–4.

23. Also entered in this event, but not competing, were Jiřína Kubešová/Antonín Kubeš (BOH), Josefina de Lobkowicz/Jaroslav Just (BOH), Anna Šebková/Josef Šebek (BOH), Gertrud Kaminski/Otto von Müller (GER), Valborg Bjurstedt/Trygve Smith (NOR), and Margareta Cederschiöld/J. Carl Kempe (SWE).

24. Originally scheduled for 2 July at 1400.

25. Not listed as equal fifth in DW.

26. Not listed as equal fifth in DW.

27. Also entered in this event, but not competing, were Josef Šebek (BOH), Jaroslav Just (BOH), and Max Decugis (FRA).

28. Originally scheduled for 5 May at 1700.

29. Originally scheduled for 8 May at 1615.

30. Also entered in this event, but not competing, were Marie Decugis (FRA) and Elsa Magnusson (SWE).

31. Also entered in this event, but not competing, were the teams of Anna Šebková/Josef Šebek (BOH) and Marie Decugis/Max Decugis (FRA).

Tug-of-War

There were five teams entered: Austria, Bohemia, Great Britain, Luxembourg, and Sweden. The matches were scheduled to take place as a round-robin tournament from 7–9 July and 11–12 July. But Austria, Bohemia, and Luxembourg did not make an appearance, for reasons not known. Thus the only event was a single match between Great Britain and the host Swedish team, held on Monday, 8 July at 5:15 P.M. (1715).

The match was conducted on a sand track at the north end of the Olympic Stadium. The match was to be a best two-of-three pulls. In the first pull Sweden slowly pulled the British team over. During the second pull, some of the British team members sat down for better leverage, which was against the rules prohibiting contact with ground with any part of the body except the feet. When the British did not heed several warnings from the judges, they stopped the pull and declared Sweden the winners of the second pull. The Swedish team was made up of six members of the Stockholm Police Force, one member of the Göteburg police, and one fisherman from Sandhamn, a well-known yachting centre on an island 45 km. east of Stockholm. The British team was made up of members of the London City Police. Three of the eight British team members had pulled on the gold medal winning London Police team at the 1908 Olympics — Edwin Mills, Frederick Humphreys, James Shepherd. In addition, three further British tuggers in 1912 had also competed for the bronze-medal winning team at the 1908 Olympics, then representing the K Division Metropolitan Police Team — Walter Chaffe, Joseph Dowler, Alexander Munro. Sweden also entered a tug-of-war team at the 1908 Olympics, but did not place, and the 1908 and 1912 teams had no tuggers in common.

Site:	Olympic Stadium	
Dates:	8 July	
Events:	1 [1 Men — 0 Women]	
Competitors:	16 [16 Men — 0 Women]	
Nations:	2 [2 Men — 0 Women]	

	Competitors	Gold	Silver	Bronze	Medals
Great Britain	8	–	1	–	1
Sweden	8	1	–	–	1
Totals	16	1	1	–	2
Nations	2	1	1	–	2

Committee for Tug-of-War

President: Captain Carl Gustaf "Gösta" Drake af Hagelsrum
Vice-President: Lieutenant Ernst Killander
Secretary: Kristian Hellström, Esquire
Members: Sergeant Arno Almqvist; Lieutenant Anders Daevel; Paymaster Nils Djurberg; Police-Inspector Alfred Fäldt; Lieutenant G. Gyllenhammar; Johan af Klercker, Esquire; Police-Sergeant G. H. Lindmark; Sergeant A. Hjalmar Wollgarth; Lieutenant Birger Ekström
International Jury: Johannes Sigfrid Edström (President/SWE); Captain Carl Silfverstolpe (SWE); John G. Merrick (CAN); Lauri Wilskman (FIN); René Enerlin (FRA); W. A. Brommage (GBR); Carl Diem (GER); Anastasios Metaxas (GRE); Szilárd Stankovits (HUN); James Edward Sullivan (USA)[1]

Final Standings

A: 16; C: 2; D: 8 July; T: 1715.

1. Sweden
    (Adolf Bergman, Arvid Andersson, Johan Edman, Erik Fredriksson, Carl Jonsson, Erik Larsson, August Gustafsson, Herbert Lindström)

2. Great Britain
    (Alexander Munro, James Shepherd, John Sewell, Joseph Dowler, Edwin Mills, Frederick Humphreys, Mathias Hynes, Walter Chaffe)

Original Tournament Schedule

Date	Time	Match
7 July	1545	Bohemia vs. Great Britain
	1700	Sweden vs. Austria
8 July	1700	Luxembourg vs. Austria
	1715	Great Britain vs. Sweden
9 July		Luxembourg vs. Great Britain
		Bohemia vs. Sweden
11 July		Luxembourg vs. Sweden
		Bohemia vs. Austria
12 July		Great Britain vs. Austria
		Bohemia vs. Luxembourg

NOTES

1. The same international jury served for both track & field athletics and tug-of-war.

Water Polo

Water polo had been contested at the 1900, 1904, and 1908 Olympics. The 1904 Olympic water polo had been conducted under some unusual rules and only American club teams competed. The 1900 and 1908 Olympic water polo tournaments had both been won by teams from Great Britain. The 1900 British team had all been members of the same club, the Osborne Swimming Club of Manchester, while the 1908 team was more a "national" team, with members from four different clubs.

In 1912, the matches consisted of two periods of seven minutes each, effective playing time. In the event of a tie, two extra periods of three minutes each were played. The tournament was played according to the "Bergvall System," named after Erik Bergvall, President of Svenska Simförbundet (Swedish Swimming Association). In the Bergvall System, second place was not awarded to the losing finalist, but a separate second-place tournament was conducted among all teams losing to the winning team. Similarly, a third-place tournament was then conducted among all teams losing to the second-place team.

Great Britain was the favorite again in 1912 and did not disappoint, winning the gold medal. In their first round match, however, they were severely tested by the Belgian team, only winning in overtime by 7–5. In fact, Belgium led 3–2 at the half, and took a 4–2 lead early in the second half before Paul Radmilovic scored two goals to tie the match at 4–4 in regulation. In the semifinals, Great Britain played Sweden. Britain led 2–1 at the half, but Sweden pulled even, 3–3, shortly after intermission. Britain scored the last three goals to win, 6–3. Having survived those two difficult matches, the final was easy for the British team. They defeated an overmatched Austrian team 8–0, scoring four goals in each half.

Four members of the winning 1908 British team returned to Stockholm in 1912 to defend the gold medal: George Wilkinson, Charles Smith, George Cornet, and Paul Radmilovic. Wilkinson, in fact, had also competed in 1900 for the Osborne Swimming Club team and thus had already won two water polo Olympic championships. Considered by many the first great water poloist, he started his career at the Osborne club before moving to the Hyde Seal Swim Club in 1902. He captained that water polo team for 22 years, and led them to nine Amateur Swimming Association titles, and an international victory over Brussels at the "World Championships" of 1904 in Paris.

Charles Smith represented the Salford Swimming Club, and won Olympic water polo gold medals in 1908, 1912, and 1920. He was goalie for the British national team from 1902 through 1926 and also competed at the Olympics of 1924. When he won his 1920 gold medal, he was

41 years, 214 days old, which makes him the oldest Olympic water polo gold medalist. Less is known about George Cornet, a member of the Inverness Swimming Club, but he did represent Scotland 17 times in water polo between 1897 and 1912.

Paul (Pavao) Radmilovic had one of the longest Olympic careers of any Olympic water poloist. He competed in water polo at the Olympics of 1908, 1912, 1920, 1924, and 1928, one of only three Olympians to have competed in five water polo tournaments. But because of World War I, his span of 20 years competing in Olympic water polo is the longest on record, although equaled by Paul Vasseur of France, who competed in 1900, 1906, 1912, and 1920. Radmilovic also competed as a swimmer at the Olympics of 1906, 1908, and 1920, giving him six consecutive Olympic appearances between 1906 and 1928. He won four Olympic gold medals in all–water polo in 1908, 1912, and 1920 and as a member of the winning 4 × 200 meter freestyle relay in 1908. Welsh-born of a Greek/Macedonian father and an Irish mother, in 1967 he became the first Briton to be inducted into the Swimming Hall of Fame.

Site:	Swimming Stadium at Djurgårdsbrunns-viken
Dates:	7–11, 13–16 July
Events:	1 [1 Men–0 Women]
Competitors:	45 [45 Men–0 Women]
Nations:	6 [6 Men–0 Women]

	Competitors	Gold	Silver	Bronze	Medals
Austria	7	–	–	–	–
Belgium	9	–	–	1	1
France	8	–	–	–	–
Great Britain	7	1	–	–	1
Hungary	7	–	–	–	–
Sweden	7	–	1	–	1
Totals	45	1	1	1	3
Nations	6	1	1	1	3

Committee for Swimming, Diving, and Water Polo

President: Erik Bergvall, Esquire
Vice-President: Major Nils David Edlund
Secretary: Kristian Hellström, Esquire
Treasurer: John G. Andersson, Esquire
Members: Carl Blidberg, Esquire; Per Fjästad, Esquire; Thor Friman, Esquire; Anton Johanson, Esquire; Torsten Kumfeldt, Esquire; Sigfrid D. Larsson, Esquire; Konrad Littorin, Esquire; Emil Lundberg, Esquire; J. A. Lönnegren; Mayor Arvid Ulrich, Esquire; Gustaf Wretman, Esquire
Building Committee: Erik Bergvall, Esquire (President); Sigfrid D. Larsson, Esquire; Torsten Kumfeldt, Esquire
Training Committee: Erik Bergvall, Esquire (President); John G. Andersson, Esquire; Torsten Kumfeldt, Esquire

MEN

Final Standings

A: 45[1]*; C: 6; D: 7–11, 13–16 July.

1. Great Britain
   (Charles Smith, George Cornet, Charles Bugbee, Arthur Hill, George Wilkinson, Paul Radmilovic, Isaac Bentham)

2. Sweden
   (Torsten Kumfeldt, Harald Julin, Pontus Hanson, Robert Andersson, Max Gumpel, Wilhelm Andersson, Erik Bergqvist)

3. Belgium
   (Albert Durant, Victor Boin, Joseph Pletinckx, Oscar Grégoire, Herman Donners, Herman Meyboom, Félicien Courbet, Jean Hoffman, Pierre Nijs)

4. Austria
   (Rudolf Buchfelder, Richard Manuel, Walter Schachlitz, Otto Scheff, Josef Wagner, Ernst Kovács, Hermann Buchfelder)

=5. Hungary
   (Sándor Ádám, László Beleznai, Tibor Fazekas, Jenő Hégner Tóth, Károly Rémi, János Wenk, Imre Zachár)

   France
   (Gustave Prouvost, Gaston Vanlaere, Georges Rigal, Paul Louis Beulque, Jean Rodier, Jean Thorailles, Henri Decoin, Paul Vasseur)

   Diplomas of Merit

Austria (Rudolf Buchfelder, Richard Manuel, Walter Schachlitz, Otto Scheff, Josef Wagner, Ernst Kovács, Hermann Buchfelder)

Tournament Summary

	Won	Lost	Tied	Goals For	Goals Against
1. Great Britain	3	0	0	21	8
2. Sweden	3	1	0	22	11
3. Belgium	3	2	0	22	21
4. Austria	1	3	0	10	25
=5. Hungary	0	2	0	9	11
France	0	2	0	3	11
Totals	*10*	*10*	*0*	*87*	*87*

*See Notes on page 335.

Tournament Draw

Tournament for 2nd and 3rd Place

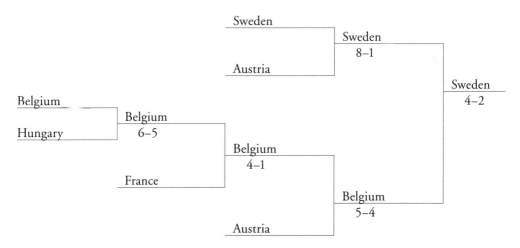

Match Summaries[2]

Round One

7 July[3]

Great Britain	2	2	4	3	7	(overtime)
Belgium	3	1	4	1	5	

    Time: 1515
    Attendance: unknown
    Referee: Gunnar Wennerström (SWE)
    Goals: Hill [2], Wilkinson [2], Radmilovic [2], Bentham; Grégoire [2], Meyboom [2], Nijs
    Rosters: *Great Britain:* Smith [G], Cornet [FB], Bugbee [FB], Hill [HB], Wilkinson [F], Radmilovic [F], Bentham [F]; *Belgium:* Durant [G], Donners [FB], Boin [FB], Pletinckx [HB], Grégoire [F], Meyboom [F], Courbet [F].[4]

8 July

Sweden	4	3	7
France	0	2	2

    Time: 1330
    Attendance: unknown
    Referee: John C. Hurd (GBR)
    Goals: R. Andersson [3], Bergqvist [3]; Prouvost, Decoin
    Rosters: *Sweden:* Kumfeldt [G], Julin [FB], Gumpel [FB], Hanson [HB], R. Andersson [F], W. Andersson [F], Bergqvist [F]; *France:* Thorailles [G], Prouvost [FB], Decoin [FB], Vasseur [HB], Vanlaere [F], Rigal [F], Beulque [F].

    Semifinals

9 July

Austria	1	4	5
Hungary	2	2	4

    Time: 1335
    Attendance: unknown
    Referee: Gunnar Wennerström (SWE)
    Goals: Scheff (final goal for Austria); Fazekas, Hégner Tóth, Rémi
    Rosters: *Austria:* Buchfelder [G], Manuel [FB], Schachlitz [FB], Scheff [HB], Wagner [F], Kovács [F], Buchfelder [F]; *Hungary:* Wenk [G], Ádám [FB], Beleznai [FB], Fazekas [HB], Hégner Tóth [F], Rémi [F], Zachár [F].

11 July

Great Britain	2	4	6
Sweden	1	2	3

    Time: 2000
    Attendance:
    Referee: Gunnar Wennerström (SWE)
    Goals: Wilkinson [3], Radmilovic, Bentham, Hill; R. Andersson [2], W. Andersson
    Rosters: *Great Britain:* Smith [G], Cornet [FB], Bugbee [FB], Hill [HB], Wilkinson [F], Radmilovic [F], Bentham [F]; *Sweden:* Kumfeldt [G], Julin [FB], Gumpel [FB], Hanson [HB], W. Andersson [F], R. Andersson [F], Bergqvist [F].[5]

    Final

13 July

Great Britain	4	4	8
Austria	0	0	0

    Time: 1950
    Attendance: unknown
    Referee: Erik Bergvall (SWE)
    Goals: unknown
    Rosters: *Great Britain:* Smith [G], Cornet [FB], Bugbee [FB], Hill [HB], Wilkinson [F], Radmilovic [F], Bentham [F]; *Austria:* R. Buchfelder [G], Manuel [FB], Schachlitz [FB], Scheff [HB], Wagner [F], Kovács [F], H. Buchfelder [F].[6]

Consolation Round for 2nd–3rd Place

10 July

Belgium	2	4	6
Hungary	3	2	5

  Time: 1430[7]
  Attendance: unknown
  Referee: Gunnar Wennerström (SWE)
  Goals: Fazekas [3], Rémi [2]
  Rosters: *Belgium:* unknown; *Hungary:* Wenk [G], Ádám [FB], Beleznai [FB], Fazekas [HB], Hégner Tóth [F], Rémi [F], Zachár [F].

11 July[8]

Belgium	2	2	4
France	1	0	1

  Time: 1130
  Attendance: unknown
  Referee: Gunnar Wennerström (SWE)
  Goals: unknown
  Rosters: *Belgium:* unknown; *France:* unknown.

14 July

Sweden	5	3	8
Austria	1	0	1

  Time: 2000
  Attendance: unknown
  Referee: George W. Hearn (GBR)
  Goals: R. Andersson [3], Bergqvist [3], W. Andersson [2]; Scheff
  Rosters: *Sweden:* Kumfeldt [G], Julin [FB], Gumpel [FB], Hanson [HB], R. Andersson [F], W. Andersson [F], Bergqvist [F]; *Austria:* R. Buchfelder [G], Manuel [FB], Schachlitz [FB], Scheff [HB], Wagner [F], Kovács [F], H. Buchfelder [F].

15 July

Belgium	2	3	5
Austria	1	3	4

  Time: 1300
  Attendance: unknown
  Referee: Erik Bergvall (SWE)
  Goals: Scheff
  Rosters: *Belgium:* unknown; *Austria:* Buchfelder [G], Manuel [FB], Schachlitz [FB], Scheff [HB], Wagner [F], Kovács [F], Buchfelder [F].

16 July

Sweden	1	3	4
Belgium	1	1	2

  Time: 0900
  Attendance: unknown

Referee: John C. Hurd (GBR)

Goals: Bergqvist [2], R. Andersson, W. Andersson

Rosters: *Sweden:* Kumfeldt [G], Julin [FB], Gumpel [FB], Hanson [HB], R. Andersson [F], W. Andersson [F], Bergqvist [F]; *Belgium:* unknown.

NOTES

1. EK has 46. FW has 65. OSVK has 61.

2. The original schedule was as follows: GBR vs. BEL — 6 July at 2045; SWE vs. FRA — 8 July at 1330; AUT vs. HUN — 9 July at 1335; BEL vs. HUN — 10 July at 1230; GBR vs. SWE — 11 July at 2000; BEL vs. FRA — 12 July at 1240; GBR vs. AUT — 13 July at 1950; SWE vs. AUT — 14 July at 2000; and BEL vs. AUT — 15 July at 1300. SWE vs. BEL was not originally scheduled.

3. Match originally scheduled for 6 July, Saturday evening, but postponed until the next day because of darkness.

4. According to TF, the starters for BEL were Durant, Boin, Nijs, Pletinckx, Courbet, Gregoire, and Meyboom. Thus it was Nijs instead of Donners.

5. According to TF, Sweden also had all three Anderssons compete — R.T., W. and K.E. Sweden had eight players in this match altogether.

6. ASZ in their report says that Heinrich [Harry] Blau and –– Meyer took part for Austria. There were two M[a]yers entered, Victor and Leopold. ASZ does not say which M[a]yer it was. ASZ has no lineup but R. Buchfelder and Scheff were also not mentioned. Thus it is doubtful if Manuel, Schachlitz, Kovacs, and H. Buchfelder all competed.

7. Originally scheduled for 1230.

8. Originally scheduled for 12 July at 1240, but played on 11 July at the request of the French team.

Wrestling (Greco-Roman)

Wrestling was a very popular sport in Sweden in 1912, but only in the Greco-Roman form. In 1908 at London, Olympic competition had been conducted in both Greco-Roman and catch-as-catch-can (freestyle) events, but the Swedes planned Olympic competition only in the Greco-Roman style for the 1912 Olympics. At the 12th IOC session in Budapest in 1911, Luxembourgois IOC member Jean-Maurice Pescatore suggested that freestyle should also be included on the program but he was voted down.[1]*

Wrestling was conducted on three 5×5 meter mats in the Olympic Stadium, exposing the wrestlers to the hot sun throughout the matches. A small nearby enclosure was used as a reserve arena in the event of rain, and a few bouts did take place there. The bouts were in 30-minute rounds, with three judges. After each 30-minute round, the judges could declare a winner or order another round, with no limit to the number of rounds. In the event that neither wrestler was aggressive enough, the judges could declare both wrestlers to have lost (today called disqualification due to passivity).

Sweden's neighbor, Finland, was the dominant nation in wrestling at Stockholm, winning three of the five classes, and seven medals, including at least one medal in every class.

Site:	Olympic Stadium
Dates:	6–15 July
Events:	5 (5 Men — 0 Women)
Competitors:	170 (170 Men — 0 Women)
Nations:	18 (18 Men — 0 Women)

	Competitors	*Gold*	*Silver*	*Bronze*	*Medals*
Austria	8	–	–	–	–
Belgium	1	–	–	–	–
Bohemia	4	–	–	–	–
Denmark	9	–	–	1	1
Finland	37	3	2	2	7
France	6	–	–	–	–

See Notes on pages 353–355.

Germany	14	–	1	–	1
Great Britain	12	–	–	–	–
Greece	1	–	–	–	–
Hungary	10	–	–	1	1
Iceland	1	–	–	–	–
Italy	6	–	–	–	–
The Netherlands	3	–	–	–	–
Norway	9	–	–	–	–
Portugal	2	–	–	–	–
Russia	11	–	1	–	1
Sweden	34	1	2	1	4
United States	2	–	–	–	–
Totals	170	4	6	5	15
Nations	18	2	4	4	6

Committee for Wrestling

President: Carl Helgesson, Esquire

Members: Carl Andersson, Esquire; A. W. Björkgren, Esquire; James Borg, Esquire; Hjalmar Johansson, Esquire; John Olsson, Esquire; Carl Sandberg, Esquire; Stellan Warelius, Esquire

International Jury: Carl Helgesson, Esquire (President/SWE); A. W. Björkgren (SWE); Otto Herschmann (AUT); Václav Rudl (BOH); Captain Hans Henrik Bondo (DEN); Eugen Kissling (GER); Moritz Csanádi (HUN); Ludwig Tschaplinsky (RUS)

Chief Judges: Carl Helgesson (SWE); Arthur Walter Björkgren (SWE); Oscar Nordh (SWE); Ernst Palm (SWE); Carl Sandberg (SWE); John Olsson (SWE)

Judges: Carl Andersson (SWE); Carl Arvidson (SWE); Alfred Bark (SWE); Ivan Holmqvist (SWE); Hjalmar Johansson (SWE); William Malmström (SWE); P. A. Sjöholm (SWE); Arnold Richard Nielsen (DEN); G. A. M. Brands (NED); Johan Karl Lindstedt (FIN); Percy Longhurst Fisher (GBR); Richard Preuß (GER); Franz Xaver Markones (AUT); Rudolf Schindler (BOH); Péter Tatics (HUN)

Notes on Result Abbreviations

bye	=	not scheduled against another opponent in that round
dec.	=	won by decision
dq.	=	won by disqualification
dq2.	=	both wrestlers disqualified for lack of aggression (passivity)
ret.	=	won by retirement of opponent
threw.	=	won by throw (fall)
wo.	=	walkover (other wrestler did not appear or compete)

GRECO-ROMAN

Featherweight (60 kg. [132 lbs.]) Class

A: 38; C: 13; D: 6–9, 11–13, 15 July. Weigh-in and drawing of lots on 6 July.; F: Double-elimination tournament.

In 1910 and 1911, there had been six different competitions considered as world championships, more properly called international meets. They had been won by Karl Wernicke (GER—1910 in Düsseldorf), Antti Hyvönen (FIN—1911 in Helsinki), Hans Lachnit (GER—1911 in Stuttgart), Erich Kockel (GER—1911 in Berlin), R. Walter (GER—1911 in Dresden), and Hans Heinrich Rauss (AUT—1911 in Vienna). Of these, only Rauss competed in this event at Stockholm, but he was eliminated after four rounds. The winner was Kaarlo Koskelo, who never again competed at the Olympics, and never competed in a world or European championship. Finnish wrestlers dominated this class, taking the gold and bronze medal, and six of the top eight places.

1.	Kaarlo Koskelo	FIN	
2.	Georg Gerstacker	GER	
3.	Otto Lasanen	FIN	
AC.	Erik Öberg	SWE	eliminated round 7
	Kalle Leivonen	FIN	eliminated round 7
	Arvo Kangas	FIN	eliminated round 6
	Lauri Haapanen	FIN	eliminated round 6
	H. Vilhelm Lehmusvirta	FIN	eliminated round 6
	Harry Larsson	SWE	eliminated round 5
	Hugo Johansson	SWE	eliminated round 5
	Verner Hetmar	DEN	eliminated round 5
	Carl-Georg Andersson	SWE	eliminated round 4
	Friedrich Schärer	AUT	eliminated round 4
	Hans Heinrich Rauss	AUT	eliminated round 4
	Josef Beránek	BOH	eliminated round 4
	Arvid Beckman	SWE	withdrew round 4
	József Pongrácz	HUN	withdrew round 4
	Pavel Pavlovich	RUS	withdrew round 4
	Aleksandr Ankondinov	RUS	eliminated round 3
	António Pereira	POR	eliminated round 3
	Kristian Arnesen	NOR	eliminated round 3
	Mikael Hestdahl	NOR	eliminated round 3
	Ragnvald Gullaksen	NOR	eliminated round 3
	Bruno Åkesson	SWE	withdrew after round 2
	Aleksanders Meesits	RUS	eliminated round 2
	Alfred Taylor	GBR	eliminated round 2
	András Szoszky	HUN	eliminated round 2
	Carl Hansen	DEN	eliminated round 2
	Conrad Stein	GER	eliminated round 2
	Ewald Persson	SWE	eliminated round 2
	Georg "Jonny" Andersen	GER	eliminated round 2

Mariano Ciai	ITA	eliminated round 2
Percy Cockings	GBR	eliminated round 2
Risto Mustonen	FIN	eliminated round 2
William Lyshon	USA	eliminated round 2
George MacKenzie	GBR	withdrew round 2
George Retzer	USA	withdrew round 2
Karl Karlsson[2]	SWE	withdrew round 2

3

Diplomas of Merit

Erik Öberg (SWE), Kalle Leivonen (FIN), Lauri Haapanen (FIN), H. Vilhelm Lehmusvirta (FIN)

Tournament Summary

Round One			Match Time[4]	Date
H. Vilhelm Lehmusvirta (FIN)	threw.	Percy Cockings (GBR)	2½	6 July
Kalle Leivonen (FIN)	threw.	Mariano Ciai (ITA)	2½[5]	6 July
Mikael Hestdahl (NOR)	dec.	Bruno Åkesson (SWE)	1-00	6 July
Erik Öberg (SWE)	threw.	Alfred Taylor (GBR)	9	6 July
Kristian Arnesen (NOR)	threw.	Josef Beránek (BOH)	10	6 July
Pavel Pavlovich (RUS)	threw.	Karl Karlsson (SWE)	34	6 July
Otto Lasanen (FIN)	dec.	Arvid Beckman (SWE)	30	7 July
Ragnvald Gullaksen (NOR)	dec.	Ewald Persson (SWE)	59[6]	7 July
Arvo Kangas (FIN)	threw.	Aleksandr Ankondinov (RUS)	4	7 July
Harry Larsson (SWE)	dec.	Conrad Stein (GER)	40	7 July
József Pongrácz (HUN)	threw.	William Lyshon (USA)	6	7 July
Hugo Johansson (SWE)	threw.	Georg "Jonny" Andersen (GER)	12	7 July
Georg Gerstacker (GER)	threw.	András Szoszky (HUN)	38	7 July
Verner Hetmar (DEN)	threw.	Risto Mustonen (FIN)	2	
Lauri Haapanen (FIN)	threw.	António Pereira (POR)	2	
George MacKenzie (GBR)	dec.	Aleksanders Meesits (RUS)	30	
Carl-Georg Andersson (SWE)	threw.	Carl Hansen (DEN)	12½	
Kaarlo Koskelo (FIN)	dec.	Hans Heinrich Rauss (AUT)	1-00	9 July
Friedrich Schärer (AUT)	threw.	George Retzer (USA)	15	9 July

Round Two			Match Time	Date
H. Vilhelm Lehmusvirta (FIN)	threw.	Mariano Ciai (ITA)	7	11 July
Kalle Leivonen (FIN)	threw.	Percy Cockings (GBR)	12	9 July
Bruno Åkesson (SWE)	dec.	Alfred Taylor (GBR)	1-00	
Erik Öberg (SWE)	dec.	Mikael Hestdahl (NOR)	1-00	9 July
Josef Beránek (BOH)	wo.	Karl Karlsson (SWE)		9 July
Pavel Pavlovich (RUS)	dec.	Kristian Arnesen (NOR)	12	9 July
Arvid Beckman (SWE)	threw.	Ragnvald Gullaksen (NOR)	6	9 July
Otto Lasanen (FIN)	threw.	Ewald Persson (SWE)	10	9 July
Harry Larsson (SWE)	dec.	Arvo Kangas (FIN)	1-30	9 July
Aleksandr Ankondinov (RUS)	threw.	Conrad Stein (GER)	9	9 July
József Pongrácz (HUN)	threw.	Georg "Jonny" Andersen (GER)	6½	9 July

Hugo Johansson (SWE)	threw.	William Lyshon (USA)	7	9 July
Georg Gerstacker (GER)	threw.	Risto Mustonen (FIN)	43	9 July
Lauri Haapanen (FIN)	threw.	András Szoszky (HUN)	17	11 July
Verner Hetmar (DEN)	threw.	Aleksanders Meesits (RUS)	11	11 July
António Pereira (POR)	wo.	George MacKenzie (GBR)		11 July
Kaarlo Koskelo (FIN)	threw.	Carl Hansen (DEN)	7½	11 July
Friedrich Schärer (AUT)	threw.	Carl-Georg Andersson (SWE)	17	11 July
Hans Heinrich Rauss (AUT)	wo.	George Retzer (USA)		11 July

Round Three — Match Time — Date

H. Vilhelm Lehmusvirta (FIN)	threw.	Mikael Hestdahl (NOR)	5	11 July
Kalle Leivonen (FIN)	dec.	Erik Öberg (SWE)	1-00	11 July
Josef Beránek (BOH)	dec.	Pavel Pavlovich (RUS)	1-00	11 July
Arvid Beckman (SWE)	threw.	Kristian Arnesen (NOR)	2	11 July
Otto Lasanen (FIN)	threw.	Ragnvald Gullaksen (NOR)	15	11 July
Arvo Kangas (FIN)	threw.	József Pongrácz (HUN)	4	11 July
Harry Larsson (SWE)	threw.	Aleksandr Ankondinov (RUS)	31	11 July
Georg Gerstacker (GER)	dec.	Hugo Johansson (SWE)	1-00	11 July
Lauri Haapanen (FIN)	threw.	Verner Hetmar (DEN)	20	11 July
Carl-Georg Andersson (SWE)	threw.	António Pereira (POR)	2	11 July
Kaarlo Koskelo (FIN)	dec.	Friedrich Schärer (AUT)	1-00	11 July
Hans Heinrich Rauss (AUT)	bye			

Round Four — Match Time — Date

H. Vilhelm Lehmusvirta (FIN)	dec.	Hans Heinrich Rauss (AUT)	1-00	12 July
Kalle Leivonen (FIN)	threw.	Josef Beránek (BOH)	1½	12 July
Erik Öberg (SWE)	wo.	Pavel Pavlovich (RUS)		12 July
Arvo Kangas (FIN)	wo.	Arvid Beckman (SWE)		12 July
Otto Lasanen (FIN)	threw.[7]	Harry Larsson (SWE)	45	12 July
Hugo Johansson (SWE)	wo.	József Pongrácz (HUN)		12 July
Georg Gerstacker (GER)	threw.	Lauri Haapanen (FIN)	1	12 July
Verner Hetmar (DEN)	threw.	Friedrich Schärer (AUT)	45	
Kaarlo Koskelo (FIN)	threw.	Carl-Georg Andersson (SWE)	22[8]	12 July

Round Five — Match Time — Date

Erik Öberg (SWE)	dec.	H. Vilhelm Lehmusvirta (FIN)	1-00	12 July
Kalle Leivonen (FIN)	threw.	Harry Larsson (SWE)	49	12 July
Otto Lasanen (FIN)	dq2.[9]	Hugo Johansson (SWE)	1-00	12 July
Arvo Kangas (FIN)	threw.	Georg Gerstacker (GER)	18	12 July
Kaarlo Koskelo (FIN)	threw.	Verner Hetmar (DEN)	12	12 July
Lauri Haapanen (FIN)	bye			

Round Six — Match Time — Date

Erik Öberg (SWE)	dec.	Lauri Haapanen (FIN)	1-30	13 July
Georg Gerstacker (GER)	threw.	H. Vilhelm Lehmusvirta (FIN)	57	13 July
Otto Lasanen (FIN)	threw.	Kalle Leivonen (FIN)	3	13 July
Kaarlo Koskelo (FIN)	threw.	Arvo Kangas (FIN)	6	13 July

Round Seven			*Match Time*	*Date*
Georg Gerstacker (GER)	dec.	Kalle Leivonen (FIN)	1-00	13 July
Otto Lasanen (FIN)	threw.	Erik Öberg (SWE)	50	13 July
Kaarlo Koskelo (FIN)	bye			

Final Round One			*Match Time*	*Date*
Georg Gerstacker (GER)	threw.	Otto Lasanen (FIN)	2:13	13 July
Kaarlo Koskelo (FIN)	bye			

Final Round Two			*Match Time*	*Date*
Kaarlo Koskelo (FIN)	dec.	Otto Lasanen (FIN)		15 July
Georg Gerstacker (GER)	bye			

Final Round Three			*Match Time*	*Date*
Kaarlo Koskelo (FIN)	threw.	Georg Gerstacker (GER)	24	15 July

Lightweight 67½ kg. [148½ lbs.]) Class

A: 48; C: 13; D: 6, 8–9, 11, 13–15 July. Weigh-in and drawing of lots on 6 July; F: Double-elimination tournament.

Emil Väre (Vilén) of Finland was the likely favorite. In 1911 he had won one of four international championships which were contested that year, and in 1912 he also won the European championship. In the competition, he threw all six of his opponents, although the final against Gustaf Malmström (SWE) was a closely fought match, which took Väre a full hour to win. Väre returned in 1920 to defend his Olympic gold medal at Antwerp.

1.	Emil Väre (Vilén)	FIN	
2.	Gustaf Malmström	SWE	
3.	Edvin Mathiasson	SWE	
AC.	Carl Erik Lund	SWE	eliminated round 7
	Ödön Radvány	HUN	eliminated round 7
	Jan Balej	BOH	eliminated round 6
	Johan Nilsson	SWE	eliminated round 6
	Oscar Kaplur	RUS	eliminated round 6
	David "Tatu" Kolehmainen	FIN	eliminated round 6
	Volmar Wikström	FIN	eliminated round 6
	J. Alfred Salonen	FIN	eliminated round 5
	Bruno Heckel	GER	eliminated round 5
	Frederik Hansen	DEN	eliminated round 5
	Herbrand Lofthus	NOR	eliminated round 5
	Adam Tanttu	FIN	withdrew round 5
	O. Armas Laitinen	FIN	disqualified round 4
	Desző Orosz	HUN	eliminated round 4
	Gottfrid Svensson	SWE	eliminated round 4

Ludwig Sauerhöfer	GER	eliminated round 4
Richard Frydenlund	NOR	eliminated round 4
Viktor Fischer	AUT	eliminated round 4
J. Viktor Urvikko	FIN	eliminated round 4
Alessandro Covre	ITA	eliminated round 3
Ernő Márkus	HUN	eliminated round 3
Hugo Björklund	SWE	eliminated round 3
József Sándor-Stemmer	HUN	eliminated round 3
Karel Halík	BOH	eliminated round 3
Vilho Pukkila	FIN	eliminated round 3
Bror Flygare	SWE	withdrew after round 2
Paul Tirkkonen	FIN	withdrew after round 2
Andreas Dumrauf	GER	eliminated round 2
August Kippasto	RUS	eliminated round 2
Eugène Lesieur	FRA	eliminated round 2
Georg Baumann	RUS	eliminated round 2
Josef Stejskal	AUT	eliminated round 2
Martin Jonsson	SWE	eliminated round 2
Johannes Eillebrecht	NED	eliminated round 2
Raymond Cabal	FRA	eliminated round 2
Richard Rydström	SWE	eliminated round 2
Thorvald Olsen	NOR	eliminated round 2
Árpád Szántó	HUN	withdrew round 2
Arthur Gould	GBR	withdrew round 2
Jean Bouffechoux	FRA	withdrew round 2
Thorbjørn Frydenlund	NOR	withdrew round 2
William Hayes	GBR	withdrew round 2
William Lupton	GBR	withdrew round 2
William Ruff	GBR	withdrew round 2
Robert Phelps	GBR	withdrew round 2

10

Diplomas of Merit

Carl Erik Lund (SWE), Ödön Radvány (HUN), Jan Balej (BOH), Johan Nilsson (SWE), Oscar Kaplur (RUS), David "Tatu" Kolehmainen (FIN), Volmar Wikström (FIN)

Tournament Summary

Round One

			Match Time	Date
József Sándor-Stemmer (HUN)	threw.	Martin Jonsson (SWE)	29	6 July
Johan Nilsson (SWE)	threw.	Ludwig Sauerhöfer (GER)	47½	6 July
Herbrand Lofthus (NOR)	threw.	Raymond Cabal (FRA)	4½	6 July
Edvin Mathiasson (SWE)	dec.	Andreas Dumrauf (GER)	30	6 July
Volmar Wikström (FIN)	threw.	Eugène Lesieur (FRA)	8	8 July
Desző Orosz (HUN)	threw.	Richard Rydström (SWE)	5	8 July
Paul Tirkkonen (FIN)	threw.	Josef Stejskal (AUT)	12	8 July
Gustaf Malmström (SWE)	threw.	J. Viktor Urvikko (FIN)	31	8 July
Ernő Márkus (HUN)	threw.	Arthur Gould (GBR)	8	8 July
Frederik Hansen (DEN)	threw.	Árpád Szántó (HUN)	34	8 July

Viktor Fischer (AUT)	threw.	Thorbjørn Frydenlund (NOR)	48	8 July
O. Armas Laitinen (FIN)	threw.	Gottfrid Svensson (SWE)	35	8 July
Bror Flygare (SWE)	threw.	Karel Halík (BOH)	20	8 July
Ödön Radvány (HUN)	threw.	August Kippasto (RUS)	4	8 July
Jan Balej (BOH)	threw.	William Ruff (GBR)	21	8 July
Richard Frydenlund (NOR)	threw.	William Lupton (GBR)	11	8 July
J. Alfred Salonen (FIN)	threw.	Jean Bouffechoux (FRA)	9	8 July
Emil Väre (Vilén) (FIN)	threw.	Georg Baumann (RUS)	37	8 July
Oscar Kaplur (RUS)	threw.	William Hayes (GBR)	24	8 July
Alessandro Covre (ITA)	dec.	Vilho Pukkila (FIN)	1-00	8 July
David "Tatu" Kolehmainen (FIN)	threw.	Thorvald Olsen (NOR)	12	8 July
Aatami Tanttu (FIN)	threw.	Johannes Eillebrecht (NED)	16	8 July
Hugo Björklund (SWE)	threw.	Robert Phelps (GBR)	14	8 July
Carl Erik Lund (SWE)	threw.	Bruno Heckel (GER)	8	8 July

11

Round Two   *Match Time*   *Date*

Johan Nilsson (SWE)	threw.	József Sándor-Stemmer (HUN)	36	
Ludwig Sauerhöfer (GER)	threw.	Martin Jonsson (SWE)	5	9 July
Edvin Mathiasson (SWE)	threw.	Raymond Cabal (FRA)	37	9 July
Herbrand Lofthus (NOR)	threw.	Andreas Dumrauf (GER)	13	9 July
Desző Orosz (HUN)	threw.	Eugène Lesieur (FRA)	3½	9 July
Volmar Wikström (FIN)	threw.	Richard Rydström (SWE)	8	9 July
J. Viktor Urvikko (FIN)	threw.	Josef Stejskal (AUT)	4	9 July
Gustaf Malmström (SWE)	dec.	Paul Tirkkonen (FIN)	1-00	9 July
Frederik Hansen (DEN)	threw.	Ernő Márkus (HUN)	23	9 July
O. Armas Laitinen (FIN)	dec.	Viktor Fischer (AUT)	1-00	9 July
Gottfrid Svensson (SWE)	wo.	Thorbjørn Frydenlund (NOR)		
Karel Halík (BOH)	threw.	August Kippasto (RUS)	2	9 July
Ödön Radvány (HUN)	threw.	Bror Flygare (SWE)	33	9 July
Jan Balej (BOH)	wo.	William Lupton (GBR)		
Richard Frydenlund (NOR)	wo.	William Ruff (GBR)		
J. Alfred Salonen (FIN)	threw.	Georg Baumann (RUS)	4	9 July
Emil Väre (Vilén) (FIN)	wo.	Jean Bouffechoux (FRA)		
Oscar Kaplur (RUS)	threw.	Alessandro Covre (ITA)	5	9 July
Vilho Pukkila (FIN)	wo.	William Hayes (GBR)		
Adam Tanttu (FIN)	threw.	Thorvald Olsen (NOR)	13	9 July
David "Tatu" Kolehmainen (FIN)	threw.	Johannes Eillebrecht (NED)	52	9 July
Carl Erik Lund (SWE)	wo.	Robert Phelps (GBR)		
Bruno Heckel (GER)	threw.	Hugo Björklund (SWE)	5	9 July

12

Round Three   *Match Time*   *Date*

Ludwig Sauerhöfer (GER)	threw.	József Sándor-Stemmer (HUN)	52	11 July
Johan Nilsson (SWE)	threw.	Herbrand Lofthus (NOR)	22	11 July
Volmar Wikström (FIN)	threw.	Edvin Mathiasson (SWE)	10	11 July
J. Viktor Urvikko (FIN)	threw.	Desző Orosz (HUN)	54	11 July
Gustaf Malmström (SWE)	threw.	Ernő Márkus (HUN)	20	11 July

Viktor Fischer (AUT)	threw.	Frederik Hansen (DEN)	24	11 July
O. Armas Laitinen (FIN)	threw.	Karel Halík (BOH)	5	11 July
Gottfrid Svensson (SWE)	dec.	Ödön Radvány (HUN)	1-00	11 July
Jan Balej (BOH)	threw.	Richard Frydenlund (NOR)	8	11 July
Oscar Kaplur (RUS)	dec.	J. Alfred Salonen (FIN)	1-00	11 July
Emil Väre (Vilén) (FIN)	threw.	Alessandro Covre (ITA)	9	11 July
Bruno Heckel (GER)	threw.	Vilho Pukkila (FIN)	16	11 July
David "Tatu" Kolehmainen (FIN)	threw.	Hugo Björklund (SWE)	45	11 July
Adam Tanttu (FIN)	dec.	Carl Erik Lund (SWE)	1-00	11 July

Round Four   Match Time   Date

Volmar Wikström (FIN)	threw.	Johan Nilsson (SWE)	24	13 July
Herbrand Lofthus (NOR)	ret.	Ludwig Sauerhöfer (GER)	7	13 July
Edvin Mathiasson (SWE)	threw.	Desző Orosz (HUN)	13	
Frederik Hansen (DEN)	threw.	J. Viktor Urvikko (FIN)	34½	13 July
Gustaf Malmström (SWE)	threw.	Viktor Fischer (AUT)	7	13 July
Ödön Radvány (HUN)	dq.	O. Armas Laitinen (FIN)	12[13]	13 July
Jan Balej (BOH)	threw.	Gottfrid Svensson (SWE)	16	13 July
J. Alfred Salonen (FIN)	threw.	Richard Frydenlund (NOR)	23	13 July
Emil Väre (Vilén) (FIN)	dq2.[14]	Oscar Kaplur (RUS)	1-00	
Carl Erik Lund (SWE)	dec.	David "Tatu" Kolehmainen (FIN)	1-00	13 July
Bruno Heckel (GER)	threw.	Aatami Tanttu (FIN)	16	13 July

Round Five   Match Time   Date

Johan Nilsson (SWE)	dec.	J. Alfred Salonen (FIN)	1-00	14 July
Edvin Mathiasson (SWE)	threw.	Herbrand Lofthus (NOR)	9	13 July
Gustaf Malmström (SWE)	dec.	Volmar Wikström (FIN)	25	13 July
Ödön Radvány (HUN)	threw.	Frederik Hansen (DEN)	11	14 July
Emil Väre (Vilén) (FIN)	threw.	Jan Balej (BOH)	28	14 July
Oscar Kaplur (RUS)	wo.	Adam Tanttu (FIN)		14 July
David "Tatu" Kolehmainen (FIN)	threw.	Bruno Heckel (GER)	5	14 July
Carl Erik Lund (SWE)	bye.			

Round Six   Match Time   Date

Carl Erik Lund (SWE)	threw.	Volmar Wikström (FIN)	33[15]	14 July
Ödön Radvány (HUN)	threw.	Johan Nilsson (SWE)	17	14 July
Edvin Mathiasson (SWE)	dec.	Jan Balej (BOH)	1-00	14 July
Emil Väre (Vilén) (FIN)	threw.	Gustaf Malmström (SWE)	11	14 July
Oscar Kaplur (RUS)	dq2.[16]	David "Tatu" Kolehmainen (FIN)	1-00	14 July

Round Seven   Match Time   Date

Carl Erik Lund (SWE)	dq2.[17]	Ödön Radvány (HUN)	1-00	
Edvin Mathiasson (SWE)	bye.			
Gustaf Malmström (SWE)	bye.			
Emil Väre (Vilén) (FIN)	bye.			

Final Round One			*Match Time*	*Date*
Gustaf Malmström (SWE)	threw.	Edvin Mathiasson (SWE)		15 July
Emil Väre (Vilén) (FIN)	bye.			

Final Round Two			*Match Time*	*Date*
Emil Väre (Vilén) (FIN)	threw.	Edvin Mathiasson (SWE)		15 July
Gustaf Malmström (SWE)	bye.			

Final Round Three			*Match Time*	*Date*
Emil Väre (Vilén) (FIN)	threw.	Gustaf Malmström (SWE)		15 July

Middleweight A[18] (75 kg. [165 lbs.]) Class

A: 38; C: 14; D: 8, 10–11, 13, 15 July. Weigh-in and drawing of lots on 6 July; F: Double-elimination tournament.

Alois Totuschek of Austria had won two international championships in 1909 and 1910 in this weight class, while Alfred "Alppo" Asikainen (FIN) had triumphed at a 1911 meet in Helsinki. Totuschek lost his first round match against Sweden's Claes Johanson, and was eliminated after losing in the fourth round.

Asikainen fared better, advancing to the semifinals where he met Martin "Max" Klein, who was from Estonia but descended from the German minority in Russia, and who represented Russia in 1912. In the semis, Klein and Asikainen wrestled for 11 hours under a hot sun before Klein finally prevailed by pinning the Finn. But he was so exhausted from the effort that he could not continue and Johanson, who he was to have met in the final match, won the gold medal by default. Johanson later won the European championship, in 1913, and in 1920 at Antwerp, won another Olympic gold medal, this time wrestling as a light-heavyweight.

1.	Claes Johanson	SWE	
2.	Martin "Max" Klein[19]	RUS/EST	
3.	Alfred "Alppo" Asikainen	FIN	
AC.	August Jokinen	FIN	eliminated round 7
	K. Konrad Åberg	FIN	eliminated round 7
	Johannes Sint	NED	eliminated round 6
	Edvin Fältström	SWE	eliminated round 5
	Emil Westerlund	FIN	eliminated round 5
	Mikko Holm	FIN	eliminated round 5
	Fridolf Lundsten	FIN	withdrew round 5
	Alois Totuschek	AUT	eliminated round 4
	Andrea Gargano	ITA	eliminated round 4
	Árpád Miskey	HUN	eliminated round 4
	Fritz Johansson	SWE	eliminated round 4
	Josef Merkle	GER	eliminated round 4
	Peter Kotkovic	AUT	eliminated round 4
	Teodor Tirkkonen	FIN	eliminated round 4
	O. Mauritz Andersson	SWE	withdrew round 4

Axel Frank	SWE	eliminated round 3
Janis Polis	RUS	eliminated round 3
Joaquim Victal	POR	eliminated round 3
Zavirre Carcereri	ITA	eliminated round 3
Adolf Kurz	GER	withdrew round 3
Aleksandr Severov	RUS	withdrew round 3
Wilhelm Steputat	GER	withdrew round 3
Anastasios Antonopoulos	GRE	eliminated round 2
Anders Andersen	DEN	eliminated round 2
Hvitfeldt Hansen	DEN	eliminated round 2
Resző Somogyi-Steiner	HUN	eliminated round 2
Sven Ohlsson	SWE	eliminated round 2
A. Theodor Bergqvist	SWE	eliminated round 2
A. Theodor Dahlberg	SWE	eliminated round 2
Adrien Barrier	FRA	withdrew round 2
Edgar Bacon	GBR	withdrew round 2
Noel Rhys	GBR	withdrew round 2
Stanley Bacon	GBR	withdrew round 2
Alfred Gundersen	NOR	withdrew after round 1
Victor Melin	SWE	withdrew after round 1

[20]

Diplomas of Merit

August Jokinen (FIN), K. Konrad Åberg (FIN), Johannes Sint (NED)

Tournament Summary

Round One			*Match Time*	*Date*
Edvin Fältström (SWE)	threw.	Anastasios Antonopoulos (GRE)	5	6 July
Peter Kotkovic (AUT)	threw.	Andrea Gargano (ITA)	10	6 July
Janis Polis (RUS)	threw.	Stanley Bacon (GBR)	21:45	6 July
August Jokinen (FIN)	threw.	Alfred Gundersen (NOR)	2:55	6 July
Alfred "Alppo" Asikainen (FIN)	threw.	Edgar Bacon (GBR)	23:42	8 July
Fridolf Lundsten (FIN)	threw.	Victor Melin (SWE)	46:35	8 July
Zavirre Carcereri (ITA)	threw.	Joaquim Victal (POR)	4	8 July
O. Mauritz Andersson (SWE)	threw.	Adrien Barrier (FRA)	8:17	8 July
Axel Frank (SWE)	dec.	Aleksandr Severov (RUS)	1-00	8 July
Emil Westerlund (FIN)	dec.	A. Theodor Dahlberg (SWE)	1-00	8 July
Claes Johanson (SWE)	threw.	Alois Totuschek (AUT)	7:09[21]	8 July
Teodor Tirkkonen (FIN)	threw.	Noel Rhys (GBR)	5:06[22]	8 July
Johannes Sint (NED)	threw.	Sven Ohlsson (SWE)	44:06	8 July
Fritz Johansson (SWE)	threw.	Hvitfeldt Hansen (DEN)	43:05[23]	8 July
Árpád Miskey (HUN)	threw.	A. Theodor Bergqvist (SWE)	12:15	8 July
Martin "Max" Klein (RUS)	threw.	Resző Somogyi-Steiner (HUN)	4:21	8 July
Adolf Kurz (GER)	dec.	Anders Andersen (DEN)	1-00	
Josef Merkle (GER)	threw.	Mikko Holm (FIN)	6½	10 July
K. Konrad Åberg (FIN)	threw.	Wilhelm Steputat (GER)	8	10 July

Round Two | | | Match Time | Date

			Match Time	Date
Andrea Gargano (ITA)	threw.	Anastasios Antonopoulos (GRE)	1:04[24]	10 July
Edvin Fältström (SWE)	threw.	Peter Kotkovic (AUT)	17	10 July
August Jokinen (FIN)	threw.	Janis Polis (RUS)	6[25]	10 July
Alfred "Alppo" Asikainen (FIN)	wo.	Stanley Bacon (GBR)		10 July
Fridolf Lundsten (FIN)	wo.	Edgar Bacon (GBR)		10 July
O. Mauritz Andersson (SWE)	threw.	Zavirre Carcereri (ITA)	11	10 July
Joaquim Victal (POR)	wo.	Adrien Barrier (FRA)		10 July
Axel Frank (SWE)	dq2.[26]	Emil Westerlund (FIN) 1-00		10 July
Aleksandr Severov (RUS)	dec.	A. Theodor Dahlberg (SWE)	1-00	10 July
Claes Johanson (SWE)	dec.	Teodor Tirkkonen (FIN)	1-00	10 July
Alois Totuschek (AUT)	wo.	Noel Rhys (GBR)		10 July
Johannes Sint (NED)	threw.	Hvitfeldt Hansen (DEN)	4	10 July
Árpád Miskey (HUN)	dec.	Sven Ohlsson (SWE)	1-00	10 July
Fritz Johansson (SWE)	threw.	Resző Somogyi-Steiner (HUN)	1[27]	10 July
Martin "Max" Klein (RUS)	threw.	A. Theodor Bergqvist (SWE)	4	10 July
Mikko Holm (FIN)	threw.	Anders Andersen (DEN)	9	10 July
K. Konrad Åberg (FIN)	threw.	Adolf Kurz (GER)	3	10 July
Josef Merkle (GER)	bye			
Wilhelm Steputat (GER)	bye			

Round Three | | | Match Time | Date

			Match Time	Date
Josef Merkle (GER)	threw.	Edvin Fältström (SWE)	3	10 July
Andrea Gargano (ITA)	wo.	Wilhelm Steputat (GER)		10 July
Peter Kotkovic (AUT)	threw.	Janis Polis (RUS)	23	10 July
August Jokinen (FIN)	threw.	Zavirre Carcereri (ITA)	2½	10 July
Alfred "Alppo" Asikainen (FIN)	threw.	Joaquim Victal (POR)	3	10 July
Fridolf Lundsten (FIN)	dec.	O. Mauritz Andersson (SWE)	1-00	10 July
Alois Totuschek (AUT)	threw.	Axel Frank (SWE)	21:50	10 July
Claes Johanson (SWE)	wo.	Aleksandr Severov (RUS)		10 July
Emil Westerlund (FIN)	threw.	Johannes Sint (NED)	11	10 July
Teodor Tirkkonen (FIN)	threw.	Fritz Johansson (SWE)	43	10 July
Martin "Max" Klein (RUS)	threw.	Árpád Miskey (HUN)	11½[28]	10 July
Mikko Holm (FIN)	wo.	Adolf Kurz (GER)		10 July
K. Konrad Åberg (FIN)	threw.	Josef Merkle (GER)	7:42[29]	10 July

Round Four | | | Match Time | Date

			Match Time	Date
Edvin Fältström (SWE)	threw.	Andrea Gargano (ITA)	2[30]	10 July
August Jokinen (FIN)	threw.	Peter Kotkovic (AUT)	20:54	11 July
Alfred "Alppo" Asikainen (FIN)	wo.	O. Mauritz Andersson (SWE)		11 July
Claes Johanson (SWE)	dec.	Fridolf Lundsten (FIN)	30[31]	11 July
Emil Westerlund (FIN)	threw.	Alois Totuschek (AUT)	16:56	11 July
Johannes Sint (NED)	threw.	Teodor Tirkkonen (FIN)	20	11 July
Mikko Holm (FIN)	threw.	Fritz Johansson (SWE)	21[32]	11 July
K. Konrad Åberg (FIN)	dec.	Árpád Miskey (HUN)	12	11 July
Martin "Max" Klein (RUS)	dec.	Josef Merkle (GER)	1-00	11 July

Round Five   Match Time   Date

August Jokinen (FIN)	dec.	Edvin Fältström (SWE)	10	11 July
Alfred "Alppo" Asikainen (FIN)	dq2.[33]	Claes Johanson (SWE)	1-00	11 July
Johannes Sint (NED)	wo.	Fridolf Lundsten (FIN)		11 July
Martin "Max" Klein (RUS)	dq2.[34]	Emil Westerlund (FIN)	1-00	11 July
K. Konrad Åberg (FIN)	dec.	Mikko Holm (FIN)	6[35]	11 July

Round Six   Match Time   Date

Claes Johanson (SWE)	threw.	August Jokinen (FIN)	50	13 July
Alfred "Alppo" Asikainen (FIN)	threw.	Johannes Sint (NED)	4½	13 July
Martin "Max" Klein (RUS)	dec.	K. Konrad Åberg (FIN)	1-00	13 July

Round Seven   Match Time   Date

August Jokinen (FIN)	dec.	Martin "Max" Klein (RUS)	1-30	
Claes Johanson (SWE)	dec.	K. Konrad Åberg (FIN)	26	
Alfred "Alppo" Asikainen (FIN)	bye			

Final Round One   Match Time   Date

Martin "Max" Klein (RUS)	dec.	Alfred "Alppo" Asikainen (FIN)	11-40	15 July
Claes Johanson (SWE)	bye			

Final Round Two   Match Time   Date

Claes Johanson (SWE)	wo.	Alfred "Alppo" Asikainen (FIN)		15 July
Martin "Max" Klein (RUS)	bye			

Final Round Three   Match Time   Date

Claes Johanson (SWE)	wo.	Martin "Max" Klein (RUS)		15 July

Middleweight B[36] (82½ kg. [181½ lbs.]) class

A: 29; C: 12[37]; D: 7–8, 10, 12, 14–15 July. Weigh-in and drawing of lots on 7 July at 0800; F: Double-elimination tournament.

In the *Official Report*, this class was termed the "Middleweight B" class, which differentiated it from the 75 kg. class, which was called the "Middleweight A" class. In modern sources, it is usually called the light-heavyweight class.

Anders Ahlgren of Sweden had won medals at three international competitions in 1910 and 1911, while Finland's Ivar Böling was less well known. After eight rounds, Ahlgren had thrown four opponents, and received four byes or walkovers. Böling had been less impressive, advancing through eight rounds with two throws, two decisions, two wins by default, and two byes. But in the final match, which started at 0920 and continued until 2000, no decision was reached. With a short interval every 30th minute, they effectively wrestled for nine hours. The three judges then ruled the match a double loss, usually called, erroneously, a draw. As there was no winner, a gold medal was not awarded, so Ahlgren and Böling were declared cosilver medalists.

1.	not awarded		
=2.	Anders Ahlgren	SWE	
	Ivar Böling	FIN	
3.	Béla Varga	HUN	
AC.	A. August Rajala	FIN	eliminated round 6
	Fritz Lange	GER	eliminated round 6
	Harald Christiansen	DEN	eliminated round 5
	Johannes Eriksen	DEN	eliminated round 5
	Knut Lindberg	FIN	eliminated round 5
	Sigurjón Pétursson	ISL	eliminated round 5
	Ernst Nilsson	SWE	eliminated round 4
	Johan Andersson	SWE	eliminated round 4
	Peter Oehler	GER	eliminated round 4
	Renato Gardini	ITA	eliminated round 4
	Oscar Wiklund	FIN	withdrew round 4
	Oreste Arpe	ITA	withdrew round 4
	Johan Salila	FIN	eliminated round 3
	Karl Barl	AUT	eliminated round 3
	Karl Lind	FIN	eliminated round 3
	František Kopřiva	BOH	eliminated round 2
	Johann Trestler	AUT	eliminated round 2
	Karl Groß	GER	eliminated round 2
	Lennart Lind	FIN	eliminated round 2
	Otto Nagel	DEN	eliminated round 2
	Ragnar Fogelmark	SWE	eliminated round 2
	Augusts Pikker	RUS	eliminated round 2
	Ansgar Løvold	NOR	withdrew round 2
	Carl Ekman	SWE	withdrew round 2
	Edouard Martin	FRA	withdrew round 2
	Oskar Kumpu (Forssell)	FIN	withdrew round 2

38

Diploma of Merit

A. August Rajala (FIN)

Tournament Summary

Round One

			Match Time	Date
Ivar Böling (FIN)	ret.	Edouard Martin (FRA)	45	7 July
A. August Rajala (FIN)	dec.	Karl Groß (GER)	1-00	7 July
Peter Oehler (GER)	threw.	Otto Nagel (DEN)	35	7 July
Oreste Arpe (ITA)	threw.	Oskar Kumpu (Forssell) (FIN)	10	7 July
Sigurjón Pétursson (ISL)	threw.	Lennart Lind (FIN)	35	7 July
Johan Salila (FIN)	threw.	Ragnar Fogelmark (SWE)	40	7 July
Oscar Wiklund (FIN)	threw.	Johannes Eriksen (DEN)	11	7 July
Béla Varga (HUN)	threw.	Carl Ekman (SWE)	37½	8 July
Knut Lindberg (FIN)	threw.	Fritz Lange (GER)	13	8 July
Renato Gardini (ITA)	threw.	Johann Trestler (AUT)	2	8 July
Karl Lind (FIN)	threw.	Ansgar Løvold (NOR)	29	8 July

Augusts Pikker (RUS)	threw.	Karl Barl (AUT)	19	8 July
Johan Andersson (SWE)	threw.	František Kopřiva (BOH)	6½	8 July
Harald Christiansen (DEN)	threw.	Ernst Nilsson (SWE)	12½[39]	8 July
Anders Ahlgren (SWE)	bye			

Round Two

			Match Time	Date
Anders Ahlgren (SWE)	wo.	Edouard Martin (FRA)		
Ivar Böling (FIN)	threw.	Karl Groß (GER)	4	8 July
A. August Rajala (FIN)	dec.	Otto Nagel (DEN)	1-00	
Peter Oehler (GER)	wo.	Oskar Kumpu (Forssell) (FIN)		
Oreste Arpe (ITA)	threw.	Lennart Lind (FIN)	3[40]	8 July
Sigurjón Pétursson (ISL)	threw.	Johan Salila (FIN)	1	8 July
Johannes Eriksen (DEN)	threw.	Ragnar Fogelmark (SWE)	5½	8 July
Oscar Wiklund (FIN)	threw.	Béla Varga (HUN)	42	8 July
Knut Lindberg (FIN)	wo.	Carl Ekman (SWE)	32	8 July
Fritz Lange (GER)	threw.	Johann Trestler (AUT)	29	
Renato Gardini (ITA)	threw.	Karl Lind (FIN)	4½	
Karl Barl (AUT)	wo.	Ansgar Løvold (NOR)		
Johan Andersson (SWE)	dq.	Augusts Pikker (RUS)	8½	
Ernst Nilsson (SWE)	threw.	František Kopřiva (BOH)	53	
Anders Ahlgren (SWE)	threw.	Harald Christiansen (DEN)	20	

Round Three

			Match Time	Date
Ivar Böling (FIN)	threw.	Peter Oehler (GER)	43	8 July
A. August Rajala (FIN)	threw.	Oreste Arpe (ITA)	1	8 July
Johannes Eriksen (DEN)	threw.	Johan Salila (FIN)	10	8 July
Oscar Wiklund (FIN)	dec.	Sigurjón Pétursson (ISL)	1-30	8 July
Béla Varga (HUN)	threw.	Knut Lindberg (FIN)	55	8 July
Fritz Lange (GER)	threw.	Johan Andersson (SWE)	4	8 July
Ernst Nilsson (SWE)	threw.	Renato Gardini (ITA)	17	8 July
Anders Ahlgren (SWE)	threw.	Karl Lind (FIN)	3	8 July
Harald Christiansen (DEN)	threw.	Karl Barl (AUT)	10[41]	10 July

Round Four

			Match Time	Date
Ivar Böling (FIN)	wo.	Oreste Arpe (ITA)		10 July
Sigurjón Pétursson (ISL)	threw.	A. August Rajala (FIN)	2	10 July
Johannes Eriksen (DEN)	threw.	Peter Oehler (GER)	7	10 July
Fritz Lange (GER)	wo.	Oscar Wiklund (FIN)		10 July
Béla Varga (HUN)	threw.	Johan Andersson (SWE)	7	10 July
Knut Lindberg (FIN)	dec.	Ernst Nilsson (SWE)	1-00	10 July
Anders Ahlgren (SWE)	threw.	Renato Gardini (ITA)	4½	10 July
Harald Christiansen (DEN)	bye			

Round Five

			Match Time	Date
Ivar Böling (FIN)	dec.	Harald Christiansen (DEN)	1-00	12 July
A. August Rajala (FIN)	threw.	Johannes Eriksen (DEN)	29½	12 July
Béla Varga (HUN)	threw.	Sigurjón Pétursson (ISL)	4½	12 July

| Anders Ahlgren (SWE) | threw. | Knut Lindberg (FIN) | 35 | 12 July |
| Fritz Lange (GER) | bye | | | |

Round Six			Match Time	Date
Ivar Böling (FIN)	dec.	Fritz Lange (GER)	1-00	12 July
Béla Varga (HUN)	dec.	A. August Rajala (FIN)	1-00	12 July
Anders Ahlgren (SWE)	bye			

Final Round One			Match Time	Date
Anders Ahlgren (SWE)	threw.	Béla Varga (HUN)	2-5[42]	14 July
Ivar Böling (FIN)	bye			

Final Round Two			Match Time	Date
Ivar Böling (FIN)	wo.	Béla Varga (HUN)		14 July
Anders Ahlgren (SWE)	bye			

Final Round Three			Match Time	Date
Anders Ahlgren (SWE)	dq2.[43]	Ivar Böling (FIN)	9-00	15 July

Unlimited (Heavyweight) Class (> 82½ kg. [181½ lbs.])

A: 17[44]; C: 9; D: 9, 12, 14 July. No weigh-in. Drawing of lots on 7 July; F: Double-elimination tournament.

The deciding match came down to Yrjö Saarela of Finland and Søren Marinus Jensen of Denmark. Both were top international wrestlers. During his career, Jensen won eight medals at the Olympics, World Championships, and European Championships, including a gold medal in the heavyweight class at the 1906 Olympic Games. Saarela had won one of the World Championships held in 1911, this one in Helsinki. At Stockholm, Saarela prevailed, although only after three hours under a hot sun, when Jensen was forced to retire. Saarela had also won a silver medal at the 1908 Olympics in the light-heavyweight (73 kg.) class. In 1912, he earned, in addition to his gold medal, possession of the challenge trophy for the heavyweight Greco-Roman Wrestling, which had been donated in 1908 by the Gold and Silversmiths of Great Britain.

1.	Yrjö Saarela	FIN	
2.	Johan "John" Olin	FIN	
3.	Søren Marinus Jensen	DEN	
4.	Jakob Neser	GER	eliminated round 6
AC.	Emil Backenius	FIN	eliminated round 5
	Kalle Viljamaa	FIN	eliminated round 5
	Adolf Lindfors	FIN	eliminated round 4
	G. Uno Pelander	FIN	withdrew round 4
	Barend Bonneveld	NED	eliminated round 3
	F. Gustaf Lindstrand	SWE	eliminated round 3
	Edward Barrett	GBR	withdrew round 3

Alrik Sandberg	SWE	eliminated round 2
David Karlsson	SWE	eliminated round 2
Laurent Gerstmans	BEL	eliminated round 2
Jean Hauptmanns	GER	withdrew round 2
Nikolajs Farnest	RUS	withdrew round 2
Raoul Paoli	FRA	withdrew round 2

45

Tournament Summary

Round One

			Match Time	Date
Yrjö Saarela (FIN)	threw.	David Karlsson (SWE)	32:37	7 July
Kalle Viljamaa (FIN)	threw.	Jean Hauptmanns (GER)	1-18:53	7 July
John Olin (FIN)	threw.	Raoul Paoli (FRA)	30	7 July
F. Gustaf Lindstrand (SWE)	threw.	Laurent Gerstmans (BEL)	14:01	7 July
Barend Bonneveld (NED)	dec.	Emil Backenius (FIN)	1-30	7 July
Jakob Neser (GER)	dec.	Nikolajs Farnest (RUS)	1-00	9 July
Søren Marinus Jensen (DEN)	threw.	Edward Barrett (GBR)	46½	9 July
Adolf Lindfors (FIN)	threw.	Alrik Sandberg (SWE)	8:50[46]	9 July
G. Uno Pelander (FIN)	bye[47]			

Round Two

			Match Time	Date
G. Uno Pelander (FIN)	dec.	David Karlsson (SWE)	1-00	9 July
Yrjö Saarela (FIN)	wo.	Jean Hauptmanns (GER)		9 July
Kalle Viljamaa (FIN)	wo.	Raoul Paoli (FRA)		9 July
John Olin (FIN)	threw.	F. Gustaf Lindstrand (SWE)	44:45[48]	9 July
Emil Backenius (FIN)	threw.	Laurent Gerstmans (BEL)	20	9 July
Jakob Neser (GER)	threw.	Barend Bonneveld (NED)	25	9 July
Edward Barrett (GBR)	wo.	Nikolajs Farnest (RUS)		9 July
Søren Marinus Jensen (DEN)	dec.	Adolf Lindfors (FIN)	1-00	9 July
G. Uno Pelander (FIN)[49]	dec.	Alrik Sandberg (SWE)	1-00	9 July

Round Three

			Match Time	Date
Yrjö Saarela (FIN)	threw.	F. Gustaf Lindstrand (SWE)	6:12	12 July
Kalle Viljamaa (FIN)	dq2.[50]	Barend Bonneveld (NED)	1-00	12 July
John Olin (FIN)	threw.	Jakob Neser (GER)	32	12 July
Emil Backenius (FIN)	wo.	Edward Barrett (GBR)		12 July
Søren Marinus Jensen (DEN)	dec.	G. Uno Pelander (FIN)	1-00	12 July
Adolf Lindfors (FIN)	bye			

Round Four

			Match Time	Date
Jakob Neser (GER)	ret.	Adolf Lindfors (FIN)	2	12 July
Yrjö Saarela (FIN)	threw.	Søren Marinus Jensen (DEN)	3:36	12 July
Kalle Viljamaa (FIN)	threw.	John Olin (FIN)	0:27	12 July
Emil Backenius (FIN)	wo.	G. Uno Pelander (FIN)		12 July

Round Five

			Match Time	Date
John Olin (FIN)	ret.	Yrjö Saarela (FIN)	6	12 July

| Jakob Neser (GER) | dec. | Kalle Viljamaa (FIN) | 1-00 | 12 July |
| Søren Marinus Jensen (DEN) | dec. | Emil Backenius (FIN) | 1-30 | 12 July |

Round Six			*Match Time*	*Date*
Yrjö Saarela (FIN)	threw.	Jakob Neser (GER)	6	12 July
John Olin (FIN)	bye			
Søren Marinus Jensen (DEN)	bye			

Final Round One			*Match Time*	*Date*
Yrjö Saarela (FIN)	threw.	Søren Marinus Jensen (DEN)	3-16	14 July
John Olin (FIN)	bye			

Final Round Two			*Match Time*	*Date*
John Olin (FIN)	wo.	Søren Marinus Jensen (DEN)		14 July
Yrjö Saarela (FIN)	bye			

Final Round Three			*Match Time*	*Date*
Yrjö Saarela (FIN)	threw.	John Olin (FIN)	9	14 July

NOTES

1. Lyberg, p. 52.
2. Karlsson appears to have been a last-minute replacement for Gustaf Erik Julius Borg (SWE). There is no entry form for Karlsson but his name is in the official program. There is an entry form for Borg but he did not compete and is not listed in the official program.
3. Also entered in this event, but not competing, were Franz Beck (AUT), Ludwig Walter Huber (AUT), Leopold Glattauer (AUT), Franz Dobovisek (AUT), Hans Rauss (AUT), Hans Juratsch (AUT), Ferdinand Planegger (AUT), Franz Enichtmayer (AUT), Franz Andres (BOH), Rudolf Urban (BOH), Argirios Bairaktaris (GRE), Anastasios Antonopoulos (GRE), Frans Koucsek (HUN), Tivador Tóth (HUN), Emerich Kobor (HUN), Romildo Barlieri (ITA), Ugo Ghezzi (ITA), Valter Ranghieri (ITA), Sala Euster (ITA), Carlo Ponte (ITA), Anton van den Steen (NED), Eugen Larsen (NOR), Georg Baumann (RUS), Gustaf Erik Julius Borg (SWE), Carl Bernhard Larsson (SWE), Ira Alfred St. John (USA), Anthony Klinchoffski (USA), and Charles Goodwick (USA). Anastasios Antonopoulos (GRE) competed instead in the 75 kg. class. Georg Baumann (RUS) competed instead in the 67½ kg. class.
4. Match times are given in minutes. In a few instances, we have the time to the second, given as minute:second. In very prolonged matches, the time is given in hours-minutes.
5. Listed as 3½ minutes in SL.
6. Given as 59 minutes in 12OR, but as 57 minutes in ASZ.
7. This result is from ONews, but 12OR has it listed as a walkover.
8. Given as 22 minutes in 12OR, and 29 minutes in ONews.
9. dq2 indicates that both were declared losers because of lack of aggression (due to passivity).
10. Also entered in this event, but not competing, were Josef Vicher (AUT), Hugo Zelinek (AUT), Rudolf Arsenscheck (AUT), Josef Pospischil (AUT), Karl Steinfeld (AUT), Josef Hanisch (AUT), Leopold Glatzl (AUT), Josef Huml (BOH), Kustaa Kandelberg (FIN), Jean Bruce (FIN), Josef Papp (HUN), János Hajos (HUN), Károly Márton (HUN), Giovanni Aymar (ITA), Umberto Brigenthi (ITA), Enrico Dupont (ITA), Alcide Gubellini (ITA), Enrico Porro (ITA), Carlo Annoni (ITA), and Åke Odén (SWE).

11. ONews has two misprints for the round one results, noting that J. Viktor Urvikko (FIN) threw Vilho Pukkila (FIN) in 8:30, and that William Ruff (GBR) threw Raymond Cabal (FRA) in 20:00.

12. The match between Árpád Szántó (HUN) and Arthur Gould (GBR) did not take place.

13. Listed as 13 minutes in SL.

14. dq2 indicates that both were declared losers because of lack of aggression (due to passivity).

15. Given as 60 minutes in ONews, but 33 minutes in 12OR.

16. dq2 indicates that both were declared losers because of lack of aggression (due to passivity).

17. dq2 indicates that both were declared losers because of lack of aggression (due to passivity).

18. All 1912 official documents note that this class and the 82½ kg. class were termed "Middleweight A" and "Middleweight B." One often sees them listed as Middleweight (=A) and Light-Heavyweight (=B).

19. The name is listed as Martin Klein in most sources. But the 1912 entry form is clear that he entered as Martin "Max" Klein.

20. Also entered in this heat, but not competing, were Lorenz Kocandrle (AUT), Ludwig Hofer (AUT), Peter Hammerlock (AUT), Josef Sec (BOH), František Sec (BOH), František Čermak (BOH), Gyula Zolyomi (HUN), Jozsef Sugár (HUN), Gyula Ruzicska (HUN), Jozsef Maroti (HUN), Mihály Csapitzky (HUN), István Csontos (HUN), Ferencz Hegyesi (HUN), Béla Ormos (HUN), Emanuele Provaglio (ITA), Carlo Aldini (ITA), Bruto Manfredi (ITA), Umberto Semprebone (ITA), Alessandro Covre (ITA), Klaas de Boer (NED), Anton Simonsen (NOR), Jakob Rikheim (NOR), and Cesar de Melo (POR). Alessandro Covre (ITA) competed instead in the 67½ kg. class.

21. Listed as 1-19 in SL, which is probably a misprint for 79 minutes, from 7:9.

22. Listed as 56 in SL, which is probably a misprint for 56 minutes, from 5:6.

23. Listed as 4:35 in SL, which is probably a misprint for 43:05 minutes.

24. Listed as 15 minutes in SL.

25. Listed as 8 minutes in SL.

26. dq2 indicates that both were declared losers because of lack of aggression (due to passivity).

27. Listed as one hour in SL.

28. Listed as 32 minutes in SL.

29. Given as 7 minutes in 12OR, but as 2 minutes in ONews.

30. Given as 2 minutes in 12OR, but as 5 minutes in ONews.

31. Time listed in 12OR, but ONews lists this as a walkover.

32. Listed as 2:14 in SL and as 21 minutes in 12OR. It was likely 21:04 and SL misinterpreted the results.

33. dq2 indicates that both were declared losers because of lack of aggression (due to passivity).

34. dq2 indicates that both were declared losers because of lack of aggression (due to passivity).

35. Listed as 69 minutes (1-09) in SL.

36. All 1912 official documents note that this class and the 82½ kg. class were termed "Middleweight A" and "Middleweight B." One often sees them listed as Middleweight (=A) and Light-Heavyweight (=B).

37. DW, EK, and OSVK have 11.

38. Also entered in this event, but not competing, were Ferdinand Weissenberger (AUT), Josef Toso (AUT), Johan Preis (AUT), Alois Pudernick (AUT), Franz Josef Bachraty (AUT), Franz Mileder (AUT), Josef Dvorák (BOH), Josef Zácek (BOH), Nikolaus Orosz (HUN), Alexander Ujlaki (HUN), Pietro Piccizilli (ITA), Gino Manzatti (ITA), Vincenzi Neri (ITA), Vincenzo Ferrara (ITA), Bersaglio Pinco (ITA), Bruto Tectoni (ITA), Amadeo Altieri (ITA), Mario Mangiognagno (ITA), Gerri van der Bosch (NED), Johan Alfred Bark (SWE), and Emil Marshall (USA).

39. Listed as 6 minutes in SL.

40. Listed as 1½ minutes in SL.

41. Given as 10 minutes in 12OR but as 3 minutes in ONews.

42. Listed as 25 minutes in SL, which is likely a misinterpretation of 2-05.

43. dq2 indicates that both were declared losers because of lack of aggression (due to passivity).

44. DW, EK, FW, and OSVK have 18.

45. Also entered in this event, but not competing were Hubert Rodler (AUT), Karl Höltl (AUT), Karl Schönbauer (AUT), Franz Nawratil (AUT), Bernhardt Miksch (AUT), Josef Bechynê (BOH), Johan Viktor Salovaara (FIN), Frederick Humphreys (GBR), Otto Büren (GER), Richard Vertesi Weisz (HUN), Josef Elöd (HUN), and Tibor Halász (HUN).

46. Given as 8 minutes in 12OR and 9 minutes in ONews, but as 8:50 in SL.

47. Drawn against Frederick Humphreys (GBR), who had to withdraw with an illness shortly before the match.

48. Given as 44 minutes in 12OR and 45 minutes in ONews, but as 44:45 in SL.

49. Pelander had two matches in round two, one against David Karlsson (SWE), and one against Alrik Sandberg (SWE), and he won both. It is not known why he had to compete twice, but this does appear in all sources.

50. dq2 indicates that both were declared losers because of lack of aggression (due to passivity).

Yachting

The Olympic yacht races in 1912 were entrusted by the Swedish Olympic committee to Kungliga Svenska Segel Sällskapet, or the Royal Swedish Yacht Club. A series of international yacht races were held concurrent with the Olympic events at Nynäshamn, Kanholmsfjärden, and Sandhamm.

The Olympic events were conducted at Nynäshamn 20–22 July, and were for the best of two races. Scoring was by points, with seven points given to first place in each race, three points to second place, and one point to third place. The two main races for each class were held on 20 and 21 July, with the race-off of ties occurring on 22 July. The yachts sailed one lap of a triangular course, 15.5 nautical miles for the six- and eight-meter classes, 30.4 nautical miles for the ten- and 12-meter classes, plus a starting and finishing leg of 2.9 nautical miles. The total lengths of the races were 21.3 nautical miles for the six- and eight- meter classes, and 36.2 nautical miles for the ten- and 12-meter classes.

A nation could enter two yachts in each class. The gold medals were gilt-silver medals, as in nearly all team events in 1912, with two notable exceptions. The helmsmen on the winning yachts and the mate of the winning 12-meter yacht received solid gold medals. In addition to the Olympics medals, the owners of the winning yachts received commemorative plates to be placed on their yachts — gilt silver for the winning yacht, silver for second-place, and bronze for the third-place yacht.

The international events were held 20–21 July, and resumed on 23 July and continued after the Olympic events had been decided. International racing included a general international long-distance race from Nynäshamn to Sandhamn on 23 July; a general international race in Kanholmsfjärden on 25 July; and cup races and general international racing at Sandhamn on 26 July. In the international races, there were 111 starting yachts in 22 different classes of Finnish and Scandinavian boats.[1]* No sailing events of any sort took place near Stockholm on 24 July.

The sailing events were dominated by the Scandinavian nations as only France and Russia entered from outside Scandinavia. However, the classes were determined by the American rules for the measurement of yachts.

Site:	Nynäshamn
Dates:	20–22 July

*See Notes on pages 360–361.

	Competitors	Gold	Silver	Bronze	Medals
Events:	4 (4 Men — 0 Women)				
Competitors:	109 (109 Men — 0 Women)				
Nations:	6 (6 Men — 0 Women)				

Events: 4 (4 Men — 0 Women)
Competitors: 109 (109 Men — 0 Women)
Nations: 6 (6 Men — 0 Women)

	Competitors	*Gold*	*Silver*	*Bronze*	*Medals*
Denmark	3	–	1	–	1
Finland	27	–	1	2	3
France	3	1	–	–	1
Norway	18	2	–	–	2
Russia	17	–	–	1	1
Sweden	41	1	2	1	4
Totals	109	4	4	4	12
Nations	6	3	3	3	6

Committees for Yachting

President: Captain Oscar Holtermann, Gentleman of the Bedchamber
Secretary: Knut Boivin, Esquire
Members: Karl J. Ljungberg; Berndt August Hjorth; Sven Hydén; Hugo Andersson, Esquire
Finance Committee: Edward Cederlund, Jr.; Knut Boivin, Esquire; J. Sjödahl; Gustaf Steinwall, Esquire; Felix Nyberg; Hjalmar Andersson; C. F. Tranchell; Gunnar Setterwall; C. Frisk
Advertising Committee: Karl J. Ljungberg; Lieutenant Rolf Magnus von Heidenstam; Hugo Andersson, Esquire; Thore Blanche, Ch. Cahier
Traffic/Accommodation: Nynäshamn: G. Norström; E. A. af Ekenstam; E. Sterner; L. Widberg; Adolf Ljunggren; O. Lindeberg; Captain Erik Frestadius. *Sandhamn:* T. Öhlin; G. Eklund; Thore Sjöblom; Captain Erik Frestadius
Press Committee: Felix Nyberg; Henrik van Rijswijk; Alex Lilja, Esquire; Thore Blanche; Erik Pallin, Esquire
Reception/Entertainment: HRH Prince Wilhelm; Edward Cederlund, Jr.; Felix Nyberg; Captain Erik Frestadius; Lieutenant Rolf Magnus von Heidenstam; Admiral Jacob Hägg; Carl Henrik Granholm; Jean Jahnson (Consul General); G. Norström; Count C. Lagerberg; Professor Hjalmar Sjögren, Ch. Cahier; B. Clarino; H. Hansen; Gustaf Steinwall, Esquire; K. A. Lagergren; Henrik van Rijswijk; Nils Lundgren; Nils Lundgren; Captain Jacques Erik Tréport Lagerkrantz; E. Hallin

MIXED

6 Meter Class

A: 18; C: 5; D: 20–22 July; T: 1100 (each day); F: Points for first three places as follows: 1st — 7; 2nd — 3; 3rd —1; maximum of three sailors per boat. Distance: 21.3 nautical miles.

In the first race on 20 July, the Danish yacht "Nurdug II" and the French yacht "Mac Miche" fought closely throughout with "Nurdug II" winning by only 39 seconds. In the second race the next day, "Mac Miche" dominated, winning fairly easily. The two yachts tied with ten points and sailed off on 22 July. In the sail-off, "Mac Miche" again won easily to earn the gold medals. The French yacht, or presumably its owner and helmsman, Gaston Thubé, also was awarded possession of the challenge trophy for this class, which had been donated in 1908 by the French government.

		Race 1		Race 2		
		Time	Place	Time	Place	Points
1.	France [Mac Miche]	2-35:20	2	2-23:44	1	10[2]

(Gaston Thubé [helmsman], Amédée Thubé, Jacques Thubé) (Owners: Gaston Thubé, G. Fitau)

| 2. | Denmark [Nurdug II] | 2-34:41 | 1 | 2-26:07 | 2 | 10 |

(Hans Meulengracht Madsen [helmsman], Steen Herschend, Svenn Thomsen) (Owner: Otto Reedz-Thott)

| 3. | Sweden [Kerstin] | 2-44:54 | 6 | 2-26:44 | 3 | 1[3] |

(Harald Sandberg [helmsman], Eric Sandberg, Otto Aust) (Owner: Dan Broström)

| 4. | Sweden [Sass] | 2-37:01 | 3 | 2-30:24 | 4 | 1 |

(Olof Mark, Edvin Hagberg, E. Jonas Jansson) (Owner: Gustaf Cedergren)

| =5. | Finland [Finn II] | 2-39:33 | 4 | 2-31:02 | 6 | 0 |

(Ernst Estlander, Torsten Sandelin, Gunnar Stenbäck) (Owner: Ernst Krogius)

| | Norway [Sonja II] | 2-39:48 | 5 | 2-30:39 | 5 | 0 |

(Edvard Christensen, Hans Ferdinand Christiansen, Eigil Kragh Christiansen) (Owner: Edvard Christensen)

[4]

Diplomas of Merit

Sweden [Sass] (Olof Mark, Edvin Hagberg, E. Jonas Jansson) (Owner: Gustaf Cedergren)

8 Meter Class

A: 36[5]; C: 4; D: 20–22 July; T: 1100 (each day); F: Points for first three places as follows: 1st — 7; 2nd — 3; 3rd —1; maximum of five sailors per boat. Distance: 21.3 nautical miles.

The Norwegian yacht "Taifun" won this class easily, finishing first in both races. "Taifun" won the first race over the Swedish yacht "Sans Atout" by less than a minute, but in the second race, defeated the Finnish yacht "Lucky Girl" by almost two minutes. "Sans Atout" and "Lucky Girl" sailed off for the silver medals, with "Sans Atout" winning by almost one minute.

		Race 1		Race 2		
		Time	Place	Time	Place	Points
1.	Norway [Taifun]	2-15:59	1	2-12:59	1	14

(Thoralf Glad [helmsman], Thomas Valentin Aas, Andreas Brecke, Torleiv Corneliussen, Christian Jebe) (Owner: Thoralf Glad)

	Race 1		Race 2		
	Time	Place	Time	Place	Points

2. Sweden [Sans Atout]   2-16:40   2   2-16:04   4   3[6]
   (Bengt Heyman [helmsman], Emil Henriques, Herbert Westermark, Nils Westermark, Alvar Thiel) (Owner: Bengt Heyman)

3. Finland [Lucky Girl]   2-21:03   5   2-14:50   2   3
   (Bertil Tallberg [helmsman], Arthur Ahnger, Emil Lindh, Gunnar Tallberg, Georg West-ling) (Owners: Bertil Tallberg, Gunnar Tallberg)

4. Finland [Örn]   2-17:28   3   2-14:54   3   2
   (Axel Gustaf Estlander[7] [helmsman], Curt Andstén, Jarl Andstén, Carl-Oscar Girsén, Bertel Juslén) (Owner: Gustaf Estlander)

=5. Russia [Norman][8]   2-18:52   4   2-16:15   5   0
   (Ventseslav Kuzmichev, Yevgeny Kuhn, Pavel Pavlov, Viktor Markov, Yevgeny Lomach) (Owner: Ventseslav Kuzmichev)

   Sweden [K.S.S.S.[9] 1912]   2-23:46   6   2-16:33   6   0
   (Fritz Sjöqvist, Johan Sjöqvist, Ragnar Gripe, Thorsten Grönfors, Gunnar Månsson, Emil Hagström) (Owner: Kungliga Svenska Segel Sällskapet)

   Russia [Bylina]   2-27:59   7   2-21:43   7   0
   (Herman von Adlerberg, Johan Farber, Vladimir Ilyevich, Vladimir Lurasov, Nikolay Pod-gornov) (Owner: Herman von Adlerberg)

[10]

Diplomas of Merit

Finland [Örn] (Axel Gustaf Estlander [helmsman], Curt Andstén, Jarl Andstén, Carl-Oscar Girsén, Bertel Juslén) (Owner: Axel Gustaf Estlander)

10 Meter Class

A: 28[11]; C: 4; D: 20–22 July; T: 1100 (each day); F: Points for first three places as follows: 1st — 7; 2nd — 3; 3rd — 1; maximum of eight sailors per boat. Distance: 36.2 nautical miles.

This class was dominated by the Swedish yacht "Kitty" which won both races very easily. The Finnish yacht "Nina" and the Russian yacht "Gallia II" each had one second place and one third place, and thus tied for second. They sailed off on 22 July, with "Nina" winning by just under two minutes.

	Race 1		Race 2		
	Time	Place	Time	Place	Points

1. Sweden [Kitty]   3-46:04   1   3-43:51   1   14
   (Carl Hellström [helmsman], Erik Wallerius, Harald Wallerius, Humbert Lundén, Her-man Nyberg, Harry Rosenswärd, Paul Isberg, Filip Ericsson) (Owner: Nils Asp)

2. Finland [Nina]   3-59:07   2   3-50:09   3   4[12]
   (Harry Wahl [helmsman], Waldemar Björkstén, Jacob Carl Björnström, Bror Brenner, Allan Franck, Emil Lindh, Johan "Juho Aarne" Pekkalainen) (Owner: Harry Wahl)

| | Race 1 | | Race 2 | | |
	Time	*Place*	*Time*	*Place*	*Points*
3. Russia [Gallia II]	3-59:20	3	3-45:38	2	4

(Iossif Shomaker [helmsman], Yesper Beloselsky, Ernest Brasche, Karl Lindholm, Nikolay Pusnitsky, Aleksandr Rodionov, Filipp Strauch) (Owner: Aleksandr Vishnegradsky)

	Race 1		Race 2		
4. Sweden [Marga]	4-01:11	4	3-50:30	4	0

(Fred Wilhelm Forsberg, Björn Bothén, Bertil "Bo" Bothén, Erland Lindén, Erik Waller, K. Arvid Perslow) (Owner: Fred Wilhelm Forsberg)

12 Meter Class

A: 27[13]; C: 3; D: 20–21 July; T: 1100 (each day); F: Points for first three places as follows: 1st — 7; 2nd — 3; 3rd —1; maximum of ten sailors per boat. Distance: 36.2 nautical miles.

There were only three yachts in this class and they finished in the exact same positions in each race. Norway's "Magda X" won both races, with Sweden's "Erna Signe" second, and Finland's "Heatherbell" third. This was the only Olympic yachting class in 1912 in which no sail-off was required.

| | Race 1 | | Race 2 | | |
	Time	*Place*	*Time*	*Place*	*Points*
1. Norway [Magda IX]	3-17:17	1	3-32:00	1	14

(Alfred Larsen [helmsman], Johan Anker, Nils Berthelsen, Halfdan Hansen, Magnus Konow, Petter Andreas Larsen, Eilert Falch-Lund, Fritz Staib, Arnfinn Heje, Gustav Thaulow) (Owner: Alfred Larsen)

	Race 1		Race 2		
2. Sweden [Erna Signe]	3-24:13	2	3-48:06	2	6

(Hugo Clason [helmsman], Nils Persson, Richard Sällström, Nils Lamby, Kurt Bergström, Dick Bergström, Erik Lindqvist, Per Bergman, Sigurd Kander, Folke Johnson) (Owners: Nils Persson, Nils Asp)

	Race 1		Race 2		
3. Finland [Heatherbell]	3-25:45	3	3-48:55	3	2

(Ernst Krogius [helmsman], Max Alfthan, Erik "Pekka" Hartvall, Jarl Hulldén, Sigurd Juslén, Eino Sandelin, Johan Silen)[14] (Owner: Ernst Krogius)

NOTES

1. TF, 120, 27 July 1912, p. 200.
2. In the sail-off of the first place tie on 22 July, Mac Miche defeated Nurdug II, 2-38:48 to 2-41:40.
3. In the sail-off of the third-place tie on 22 July, Kerstin defeated Sass, 2-42:32 to 2-44:11.
4. Also entered in this class, but not competing, were the following yachts: Nurdug I (DEN; Waldemar Nielson, owner; W. Hansen, designer), Phoebe (FRA; M. Blanchy, owner; designer not known); and Schkitz (RUS; owner and designer not known).
5. EK and FW have 35. OSVK has 37.
6. In the sail-off of the second-place tie on 22 July, Sans Atout defeated Lucky Girl, 2-26:44 to 2-27:41.

7. In 1898, Axel Gustaf Estlander had been the first Finnish European Champion in speed skating.

8. Russia [Norman] was not listed as equal fifth in DW or in EK, both of which listed only two yachts tied for fifth — Russia [Bylina] and Sweden [KSSS 1912]. OSVK has both Russian yachts listed — Norman and Bylina. However, he has the rosters inverted from our listing. Specifically, our roster for Bylina is listed as crewing for Norman in OSVK and vice versa.

9. Kunglika Svenska Segel Sallskäpet.

10. Also entered in this class, but not competing, was the following yacht: Lucie IV (NOR; O. B. Nielsen, owner; Johan Anker, designer).

11. EK and FW have 27.

12. In the sail-off of the second-place tie on 22 July, Nina defeated Gallia II, 4-21:41 to 4-23:17.

13. FW has 28. OSVK has 29.

14. Some sources list Axel Krogius as a member of the Heatherbell (Finland) crew. Finnish sources do not list him but documents in 1912 Olympic archives indicate he was a crew member. Finnish Olympic historian Markku Siukonen believes he did not compete. He has spoken with Krogius's relatives, and they have no knowledge that he competed at the 1912 Olympic Games.

Art Competitions
(Concours d'Art)

The idea of holding art competitions in conjunction with the sporting events of the Olympic Games is entirely due to Baron Pierre de Coubertin, the founder of the modern Olympics. It is felt that Coubertin took the idea of Olympic art competitions from the British aesthetics theorist, John Ruskin, Slade Professor of Art Criticism at Oxford, and this is discussed in some detail by the German sports scholar, Arnd Krüger, in his article "Coubertin's Ruskianism."[1]* Norbert Müller has quoted Coubertin as follows: "Now the moment has come when we enter a phase and intend to reestablish the original beauty of the Olympic Games. In the high times of Olympia ... the fine arts were combined harmoniously with the Olympic Games to create their glory. This is to become reality once again."[2]

The main impetus for this to become a reality was the IVth Olympic Congress, held in Paris 23–25 May 1906. Coubertin announced the Congress in a circular letter sent to the IOC members on 2 April 1906, in which he noted the topic would be "to come and study to what extent and in what way art and literature could be included in the celebration of the modern Olympiads."[3]

The program of the conference was finally given as follows:

Programme de la Conférence

ARCHITECTURE.— Les conditions et les caractéristiques du gymnase moderne.— Architecture des cercles de plein air et des cercles urbains, des piscines, stands, manèges, clubs nautiques, salles d'armes — Palais des sports et parcs des sports.— Motifs architecturaux.— Utilisation du fer apparent et de la céramique — Dépenses et devis

ART DRAMATIQUE.— Représentations en plein air.— principes essentiels.— Essais récents.— Les sports sur la scène.

CHORÉGRAPHIE.— Cortèges, défilés, mouvements groupés et coordonnés — Danses.

*See Notes on pages 367–368.

DÉCORATION.— Tribunes et enceintes.— Màts, écussons, guirlandes, draperies, faisceaux.— Fêtes de nuit: les sports aux flambeaux.

LETTRES.— Possibilité d'établir des concours littéraires olympiques: conditions de ces concours — L'émotion sportive, source d'inspiration pour l'homme de lettres.

MUSIQUE.— Orchestres et choeurs de plein air.— Répertoire — Rythmes et alternances.— Fanfares.— Conditions d'un concours musical olympique.

PEINTURE.— Silhouettes individuelles et aspects d'ensemble.— Possibilité et conditions d'un concours de peinture olympique.— Aide apportée à l'artiste par la photographie instantanée.

SCULPTURE.— Attitudes et gestes athlétiques dans leurs rapports avec l'art.— Interprétation de l'effort.— Objets donnés en prix: statuettes et médailles.

Ordre des Séances

Le Mercredi 23 Mai, à 9 h. du matin et à 2 h. aprés-midi : Séances générales.
Le Jeudi 24 Mai : Séances de commissions.
Le Vendredi 25 Mai, à 9 h. du matin : Séances de commissions.
    "   à 2 h. aprés-midi : Séance générale.[4]

The final decision of the IVth Olympic Congress was to include competitions in five forms of the arts: architecture, literature, music, painting, and sculpture. It was intended that the Olympic art competitions would commence at the 1908 Olympic Games, originally scheduled for Rome. But when Rome had to withdraw from its obligation to celebrate the games of the IVth Olympiad, they were turned over to London in a decision made almost concurrent with the holding of the IVth Olympic Congress in Paris. London had to prepare very quickly for the 1908 Olympic Games and did not feel that it could host additional events in the form of art competitions.

But even before the 1912 Olympic Games, Coubertin made arrangements for an Olympic Art Competition. In October 1909 he announced that the IOC would sponsor an International Architecture Competition.[5] This was eventually held in Lausanne in 1911 with 21 entrants submitting plans for a modern Olympic city. The competition was won by Eugène-Edouard Monod and Alphonse Laverrière, for their design entitled "A Modern Olympia on the Right Bank of Lake Geneva."[6]

The Swedish Olympic committee made plans to conduct the first Olympic art competitions in 1912. They contacted the Swedish art institutions and associations, asking for their assistance. However, the competitions were controversial, as one might expect when planning "competition" among a relatively noncompetitive group such as artists, and the art institutions and associations had difficulty agreeing on the rules for such competitions.

Discussion in the IOC concerning the art competitions took place at the 11th IOC session in Luxembourg in 1910. Viktor Gustaf Balck was asked to present his report on the progress of the art competitions and noted that it was difficult to interest the Swedish institutions because they felt it was impossible to judge the contests fairly.[7]

Coubertin then asked Godefroy de Blonay (SUI) to chair the discussion of the art competitions. He stated that it had been decided in 1906 to make art competitions a mandatory portion of the Olympic program.[8] Further, he stated that art competitions were a part of the ancient Olympics[9] and that, if the 1912 Olympics did not include art competitions, Coubertin would show minimal interest in the games. As a result, the Swedes in attendance agreed to add art competitions to the 1912 Olympic program.[10]

The Swedish Olympic committee finally announced the rules for the art competitions as follows:[11]

> 1. The Fifth Olympiad will include competitions in Architecture, Sculpture, Painting, Music, and Literature.
> 2. The Jury can only consider subjects not previously published, exhibited or performed, and having some direct connection with sport.
> 3. The winner of each of the five competitions will be awarded the Gold Olympic Medal. The exhibits selected will, as far as possible, be published, exhibited or performed during the Olympic Games of 1912.
> 4. Competitors must notify their intention of entering for one or more of these competitions before the 15 January, 1912, and the exhibits themselves must be in the hands of the Jury before the 1 March, 1912.
> 5. No limitations as to size or form are laid down for manuscripts, plans, drawings or canvases, but sculptors are required to send in clay models, not exceeding 80 centimetres in height, length, or width.
> 6. For further information, application should be made to M. le Président du Comité International Olympique, 20, Rue Oudinot, Paris.

The jury decided the awards in the five categories, giving out five gold medals, and a lone silver medal in sculpture. But what or who constituted the jury? The Swedish Organizing committee gave 5,000 French francs to the IOC to carry out the arts contests. The works were sent to 20, Rue Oudinot in Paris, the address of Pierre de Coubertin. It is possible, perhaps likely, that he was the entire judge and jury for the arts contests, a fact made especially notable when one realizes he was awarded one of the gold medals (see below). After the decisions were made, all the prize-winning works were brought to Stockholm, where they were exhibited in a hall at Karlapan 10, two blocks away from the Olympic Stadium.

Two of the medalists stand out. The gold medal winner in sculpture was Walter Winans of the United States, who won for his bronze statuette of "An American Trotter." Winans also competed at Stockholm in shooting, appearing in six different events, and winning a silver medal in the running deer, team competition. Winans had also competed in shooting at London in 1908, where he had won a gold medal in the individual running deer (double shot) event.

Winans' sculpture was given to the Swedish Olympic committee, who added it to the Swedish Museum of Athletics that was planned for the Olympic Stadium. The nonmedal winning work by R. Tait McKenzie,[12] a bronze cast medallion, entitled "The Joy of Effort," was also given to the Swedish Olympic Committee, and inserted in the outer wall of the Olympic Stadium.

The *Official Report* notes that the gold medal for literature was awarded to "Georges Hohrod *et* M. Eschbach, Germany,"[13] for the work "Ode to Sport," which was submitted in three languages — French, English, and German. In reality, the poetic ode had been written by Baron Pierre de Coubertin, who entered it in the competitions under the dual pseudonym. Coubertin had used the name Georges Hohrod previously, publishing an autobiographical novel *Le Roman d'un rallié*, under that pseudonym in 1899. It is believed that M. Eschbach was his wife, Marie (née Rothan), who grew up partly in Germany, and that she translated the work into German.

What of the names Hohrod and Eschbach? Until recently, the source of the names was not known. But a recent article by Jean Durry in *Olympic Review* has shed light on the mystery.[14] Durry attempted to find the home in Luttenbach that had once belonged to the Rothan family, Coubertin's in-laws. Driving in the Fecht Valley near Alsace, Durry came across the small town of Hohrodberg. Very near Hohrodberg, Durry also found the small town of Eschbach-au-Val.[15] Although he does not describe it in as much detail, this was noted earlier (1994) by Norbert Müller, who wrote in a footnote in his book on Olympic congresses, "The author of this book discovered that the pseudonyms Hohrod and Eschbach were the names of two neighboring villages of the native village of Coubertin's wife, Luttenbach, near Colmar."[16]

	Gold	Silver	Bronze	Medals
France	1	1	–	2
Italy	2	–	–	2
Switzerland	1	–	–	1
United States	1	–	–	1
Totals	5	1	–	6
Nations	4	1	–	4

Designs for Town Planning[17]

Gold Medal	Eugène-Edouard Monod/ Alphonse Laverrière	SUI	Building plan of a modern stadium
Silver Medal	no prize was awarded		
Bronze Medal	no prize was awarded		
Also Entered	Frantz Jourdain	FRA	
	André Collin	––	
	Konrad Hippenmeier	SUI	
	Gyula Skarba	––	
	Guillaume Fatio	SUI	
	Fritz Eccord	––	
	J. W. Rees	GBR	
	A. Laffen	––	

Sculpture

Gold Medal	Walter Winans	USA	An American Trotter
Silver Medal	Georges Dubois	FRA	Model of the entrance to a modern stadium
Bronze Medal	no prize was awarded		
Also entered	R. Tait McKenzie	CAN	The Joy of Effort
	Rembrandt Bugatti	ITA	
	Prince Pavel Truvetsky	RUS	
	Victor Segoffin	ITA	
	Otakar Spaniel	BOH	
	–– Vinulsky	––	

Paintings

Gold Medal	Carlo Pellegrini	ITA	Winter Sports
Silver Medal	no prize was awarded		

Bronze Medal   no prize was awarded
Also Entered   Ernest Townsend   IRL
                      Ferdinand Joseph Gueldry   FRA
                      Jean-François Rafaelli   FRA

Literature — All Kinds

Gold Medal   Pierre Frédi, Baron de Coubertin   FRA   Ode to Sport
                  [Georges Hohrod/Martin Eschbach (GER)]
Silver Medal   no prize was awarded
Bronze Medal   no prize was awarded
Also Entered   Marcel Boulenger   FRA
                  Gabriel Letainturier-Fradin FRA
                  Paul Adam   FRA
                  Maurice Pottecher   FRA
                  William --   --
                  René --   --

Music — All Kinds

Gold Medal   Riccardo Barthelemy   ITA   Olympic Triumphal March
Silver Medal   no prize was awarded
Bronze Medal   no prize was awarded
Also Entered   Max d'Ollone   SUI
                  Gustave Doret   SUI
                  Ebbel P. Barnard   GBR
                  Émile-Jacques Dalcroze   FRA
                  Christien de --   --

Ode to Sport[18]

by Georges Hohrod and Martin Eschbach
(Pierre de Coubertin)

I. O Sport, pleasure of the Gods, essence of life, you appeared suddenly in the midst of the grey clearing which writhes with the drudgery of modern existence, like the radiant messenger of a past age, when mankind still smiled. And the glimmer of dawn lit up the mountain tops and flecks of light dotted the ground in the gloomy forests.

II. O Sport, you are Beauty! You are the architect of that edifice which is the human body and which can become abject or sublime according to whether it is defiled by vile passions or improved through healthy exertion. There can be no beauty without balance and proportion, and you are the peerless master of both, for you create harmony, you give movements rhythm, you make strength graceful and you endow suppleness with power.

III. O Sport, you are Justice! The perfect equity for which men strive in vain in their social institutions is your constant companion. No one can jump a centimetre higher than the height he can jump, nor run a minute longer than the length he can run. The limits of his success are determined solely by his own physical and moral strength.

IV.   O Sport, you are Audacity! The meaning of all muscular effort can be summed up in the word "dare." What good are muscles, what is the point of feeling strong and agile, and why work to improve one's agility and strength, unless it is in order to dare? But the daring you inspire has nothing in common with the adventurer's recklessness in staking everything on chance. Yours is a prudent, well-considered audacity.

V.   O Sport, you are Honour! The laurels you bestow have no value unless they have been won in absolute fairness and with perfect impartiality. He who, with some shameful trick, manages to deceive his fellow competitors feels guilt to his very core and lives in fear of the ignominious epithet which shall forever be attached to his name should his trickery be discovered.

VI.   O Sport, you are Joy! At your behest, flesh dances and eyes smile; blood races abundantly through the arteries. Thoughts stretch out on a brighter, clearer horizon. To the sorrowful you can even bring salutary diversion from their distress, whilst the happy you enable fully to savour their *joie de vivre*.

VII.   O Sport, you are Fecundity! You strive directly and nobly towards perfection of the race, destroying unhealthy seed and correcting the flaws which threaten its essential purity. And you fill the athlete with a desire to see his sons grow up agile and strong around him to take his place in the arena and, in their turn, carry off the most glorious trophies.

VIII.   O Sport, you are Progress! To serve you, a man must improve himself both physically and spiritually. You force him to abide by a greater discipline; you demand that he avoid all excess. You teach him wise rules which allow him to exert himself with the maximum of intensity without compromising his good health.

IX.   O Sport, you are Peace! You promote happy relations between peoples, bringing them together in their shared devotion to a strength which is controlled, organized and self-disciplined. From you, the young world-wide learn self-respect, and thus the diversity of national qualities becomes the source of a generous and friendly rivalry.

NOTES

1. Krüger, Arnd. "Coubertin's Ruskianism," In: *Olympic Perspectives: Third International Symposium for Olympic Research*, London, Ontario, CAN: Centre for Olympic Studies, October 1996, pp. 31–43.

2. Müller, *One Hundred Years of Olympic Congresses*, p. 69. However, Arnd Krüger notes that this source is incorrect in his article "Coubertin's Ruskianism," *Olympic Perspectives: Third International Symposium for Olympic Research*, pp. 31–42, eds. RK Barney, SG Martyn, DA Brown, GH Mac-Donald. (London, Ontario: University of Western Ontario, 1996). Krüger attributes the quote to Coubertin's *Une Campagne de Vingt-et-Un Années*, and notes that Coubertin stated he had written this immediately after the 1904 IOC meeting for *Le Figaro*. However, Krüger could not find it in any of Coubertin's editorials in *Le Figaro* for 1904 through 1906.

3. Müller, p. 70. Much of what follows is from Müller's excellent work on the Olympic Congresses, *One Hundred Years of Olympic Congresses, 1894–1994*.

4. *Ibid.*, p. 73.

5. Lyberg, p. 48.

6. Lyberg, p. 48. Lyberg also notes, "There is nothing known about such a decision!"

7. There is no known justification for this statement of de Blonay's.

8. *Ibid.*

9. 12OR, p. 808.

10. McKenzie was Canadian, but in 1912 was a professor at the University of Pennsylvania in Philadelphia.

11. 12OR, p. 808.

12. Durry, Jean. "Hohrod and Eschbach. A mystery finally solved," *Olympic Review*, 32: 26–28, April-May 2000.

13. *Ibid.*, p. 28.

14. Müller, p. 79.

15. English text published most recently in *Olympic Review*, 32, 29, April-May 2000.

Other Sports and Events

Besides the official Olympic medal competitions there were several other sports conducted in concert with the 1912 Olympics. It is difficult to call them "demonstration sports," the term usually used for nonofficial Olympic sports in the post–World War II era. Most of them were more similar to exhibitions as there were no "true" competitions, with champions declared. The *Official Report* termed them "displays."[1]* The following sports were either conducted concurrent with the 1912 Olympic Games in Stockholm, or in the case of certain sports, were seriously discussed in terms of possible inclusion on the Olympic program.

Demonstration Sports

American Baseball

American baseball was the only sport which is considered by some to have been a demonstration sport at the 1912 Olympics. Many sources describe the competition as a single game between an American side and a Swedish one. But there was also a second game held that is not often mentioned.

The Swedish side was represented by the Västerås Bäsboll Klubb. The Americans were simply made up of athletes competing in the track & field events at the Olympics. Still, it was felt to be a lopsided match-up, so the Americans provided a battery (pitcher Ben Adams and catcher Wesley Oler) for the Swedish club. In addition to the starting battery, two other American relief pitchers were also loaned to the Swedes.

The original schedule called for two games to be played, beginning on the evening of July 10, during the track & field athletics competition. The first game was to be between two U.S. teams, East vs. West, with the winner then taking on Västerås Bäsboll Klubb. The original team lineups were as follows:

U.S. East Albert Gutterson (P), Edward Fitzgerald (C), Ben Adams (1B), Jervis Burdick (2B), Platt Adams (3B), Abel Kiviat (SS), Wesley Oler (LF), Lawrence Whitney (CF), Harry Worthington (RF).

*See Notes on pages 383–384.

U.S. West Carroll Haff (P), Michael McDermott (C), Perry McGillivray (1B), Francis Irons (2B), Frank Belote (3B), Ira Davenport (SS), George Horine (LF), Ira Courtney (CF), J. Austin Menaul (RF).

Västeras BK Yngve Larson (P), Joel Lönnqvist (C), –– Forstedt (1B), –– Landahl (2B), –– Wikman (3B), Elis Johannson (SS), –– Velin (LF), Carl Axell (CF), –– Petterson (RF).

The American Olympic Committee, however, forbade the U.S. players from taking part in any exhibition until they had finished competing in their primary events. The game date then shifted to the morning of Monday, 15 July, with Västeras playing a combined U.S team. The U.S. intersquad game was postponed to 16 July. It was held at the Östermalm Idrottsplats (Athletic Park).

The U.S.–Sweden game started at ten in the morning. The Americans got to Platt Adams, pitching for Västerås, early, scoring four runs in the first. The Americans scored again in their half of the second to go up by 5–0. The Swedes got on the scoreboard with a pair of runs in the fourth. The Yanks put the game out of reach with an eight-run fifth inning. The Västerås club managed a final tally in the sixth, aided by the fact that they were allowed six outs in the frame. The U.S. won by a 13–3 score. One of the big guns for the United States was Abel Kiviat, who played short and batted third in the order. Kiviat stole a base and had a pair of hits in four at bats, including a triple. All told, eight American Olympic medalists took part in the game.

The umpire of this game was the well-known American 19th century player George Wright. He also had an Olympic connection as his son, Beals Coleman Wright, had won the gold medal in the lawn tennis men's singles at the 1904 Olympic Games.

But what about the rarely mentioned second baseball game at the 1912 Olympics? ISOH Member Pete Cava described it in the first issue of *Citius, Altius, Fortius,*[2] in an article entitled simply, "Olympic Baseball."[3]

"Legend has it that Olympic great Jim Thorpe, a future major-leaguer, played in the [Olympic demonstration] game. Thorpe's name does not appear in the boxscore and with good reason. The USA-Sweden match took place on the last day of the decathlon competition. Competing in both events simultaneously would have been an incredible feat, even for Thorpe.

"The game received little press coverage in the states. The 17 July edition of the *New York Times*, however, describes a game held the day after the USA–Sweden game (16 July). In this contest, two teams of American players squared off with the East squad topping the West,[4] 6–3. 'Platt Adams, New York Athletic Club, and C. E. Brickley, Harvard University, composed the battery for the East,' notes the *Times*, 'while Walter McClure, Olympic [Club], San Francisco, R. L. Byrd, Adrian College, and Edward F. Lindberg, Chicago Athletic Association, were in the points for the West.'

"'The game was novelty to the Swedes, and a large crowd was present,' according to the *Times*. Ironically, the Official Report says the previous day's USA–Sweden match had 'no great crowd of spectators, and those that were present were mostly Americans or Swedish Americans.' Thorpe did manage to get into the second game, playing right field and ripping a double in two official trips to the plate."

In addition to his Olympic feats in the decathlon and pentathlon, and his position as America's greatest collegiate football running back of his time, Jim Thorpe also managed to play major-league baseball after the Olympics. He played for six years (1913–1915, 1917–1919) with the New York Giants, Cincinnati Reds, and Boston Braves, finishing with a career batting average of a rather mediocre .252.

Baseball has often been a demonstration sport at the Olympics. It again was demonstrated in 1936, 1956, 1964, 1984, and 1988. In 1992 it became an official Olympic sport, and has been contested as such at the 1992, 1996 and 2000 Olympic games.

| United States | | 13 | | *Sweden* | | 3 | |

United States	AB	R	H	PO	A	E
H. Drew, rf	1	1	0	0	0	0
L. Whitney, rf	1	1	0	0	0	0
J.I. Courtney, 3b	3	2	2	1	0	0
A. Kiviat, ss	4	2	2	2	0	0
J.P. Jones, 2b	3	1	1	1	2	0
F. Kelly, cf	3	1	1	0	0	1
J.N. Patterson, cf	1	0	0	0	0	0
I. Davenport, c	3	2	2	7	0	0
F. Irons, lf	2	0	1	1	0	0
G. Horine, lf	1	1	0	1	0	0
G. Bonhag, 1b	2	0	0	6	0	0
V. Blanchard, 1b	1	1	1	2	0	1
R.L. Byrd, p	0	0	0	0	1	0
C. Haff, p	2	0	0	0	1	0
W. McClure, p	0	1	0	0	0	0
Totals	27	13	10	21	4	2

Sweden	AB	R	H	PO	A	E
W. Oler, c	4	0	1	7	2	0
B. Adams, p	3	0	1	2	2	1
F. Nelson, p	1	0	0	0	1	0
H. Holden, p	0	0	0	0	0	0
-- Sapery, ss	4	0	0	0	0	0
-- Welin, 1b	3	0	0	2	0	1
-- Wikman, 3b	3	0	1	0	0	0
-- Landahl, 2b	3	0	1	3	0	2
Y. Larson, rf	3	1	1	0	0	0
-- Torsleff, lf	2	1	1	0	0	1
E. Johannson, lf	1	1	1	0	0	0
C. Axell, cf	3	0	0	1	0	0
Totals	30	3	7	15	5	5

Sweden	0	0	0	2	0	1	3
United States	4	1	0	0	8	x	13

Date — 15 July. Time — 1000. 2B — Courtney, Wikman. 3B — Kiviat. SB — Kiviat, Jones 2, Davenport 2, Johannson. BB — Off. B Adams 1, off Nelson 3. SO — By B. Adams 3, by Byrd 3, by Haff, by McClure 1, by Nelson 3, by Holden 1. DP — Byrd to Bonhag. WP — B. Adams, Nelson. HBP — Drew, Kelly. PB — Oler 2, Davenport 2. Umpire — George Wright (USA).

| US East "Olympics" | | 6 | | US West "Finlands" | | 3 | |

US East	AB	R	H	PO	A	E
H. Drew, rf	3	1	1	0	0	0
J. Thorpe, rf	2	0	1	0	0	0
A. Kiviat, ss	3	1	2	1	2	2
C. Brickley, c	3	0	0	14	2	0
E. Mercer, 3b	4	1	1	0	1	0
P. Adams, p	4	1	0	1	2	0
J.P. Jones, 2b	2	0	1	0	1	0
G. Bonhag, 1b	4	0	0	8	0	1
H. Holden, lf	4	1	0	2	0	1
B. Adams, cf	2	0	0	1	0	0
W. Oler, cf	2	1	1	0	0	0
Totals	33	6	7	27	8	4

US West	AB	R	H	PO	A	E
F. Irons, 2b	4	0	1	0	4	1
J.I. Courtney, ss	3	0	0	1	1	0
I. Davenport, lf	4	0	1	1	0	1
E. Lindberg, c	4	0	0	12	2	1
C. Haff, 1b	4	0	0	7	0	0
F. Kelly, 3b	3	2	2	2	1	3
G. Horine, cf	4	1	1	3	0	0
W. McClure, rf/p	4	0	2	0	1	0
R.L. Byrd, p/rf	3	0	0	1	1	0
Totals	33	3	7	27	10	6

Date — 16 July. 2B — Kelly, Kiviat, Thorpe. SB — Irons, Haff, McClure 3, Kelly 2, Drew, Kiviat, P. Adams, Jones 2, Oler 2. BB — Off McClure 1, off P. Adams 2. SO — By Byrd 6, by McClure 4, by P. Adams 11. HB — Byrd 2. PB — Lindberg 3. LOB — US West Finlands 6, US East Olympics 4. Umpires — Bonine, Sweeney.

Gotland Sports

Gotland is the largest island in the Baltic Sea, measuring 3,001 km.^{2} (1,158 mi.^{2}) in size. It is located 150 km. (93 miles) south of Stockholm and, with the exception of 1361–1645, it has been part of Svitjod/Sweden since at least the 8th century. The island is well known for its sporting contests. Each summer, Gotland hosts the Stånga Games, which comprises traditional Gotlandic sporting events. Among these are a team ball game (Pärk), a throwing contest (Varpastning) somewhat similar to quoits and horseshoes, but using a much heavier stone disc (Varpa), and an event resembling the Scottish caber toss (Stångstörtning).

On Sunday, 7 July 1912, at 7:30 in the evening (1930), displays of Gotland sports were given in the Olympic Stadium, consisting of all three of the above events. The first event was Pärkspel, played between 16 Gotlanders, who divided up into a Blue team, made of Visby men, and a Yellow team from the country districts of Gotland. In an hour-long contest, the Yellow team won both "pärks" and claimed victory.

Both Varpastning and Stångstörtning were also displayed in the stadium. The "varpa" can be of any size and shape, but is usually a flat, nearly round stone, measuring 15 centimeters (six inches) in diameter. It is now usually made with small cavities for the fingers to allow the thrower to obtain a better grip. The varpas are thrown at a pin, or "hob," set at a distance of about 20 meters. After each player throws towards the hob, the player whose varpa is closest to it wins a point. The winner of a match is the first to record 12 points.

Stångstörtning is almost identical in principle to the Scottish caber toss. The event uses a large timber pole with a length of about five meters (16 feet), measuring 13 centimeters (5½ inches) in bottom diameter, and seven centimeters (three inches) in top diameter. Holding the thicker, bottom end, the player takes a short run, and then attempts to throw the caber as far as possible, getting it to turn over and fall away from them. The winner is is the one who throws farthest and who gets his pole to turn over properly.

Icelandic Glíma Wrestling

While the Gotlanders were displaying their traditional sports, at the other end of the stadium an exhibition of Glíma wrestling was given (7 July at 1930 [7:30 P.M.]). This ancient form of wrestlng has survived since the Viking age, but is practiced almost exclusively in Iceland, where it has been popular for over 1,000 years. *Glíma* is derived from the two Icelandic words, *glitra* and *glampa*, which mean "something that flashes or sparkles." Its linguistic origin comes from the words *glaumur* (glamour) and *gly*, which mean amusement or gladness, implying a game of pleasure, as opposed to *illskufang*, a form of wrestling intended to maim or kill.

In Glíma wrestling, each wrestler wears straps around both thighs, which are linked to a harness by vertical straps on the outside of the thigh. The match begins with each wrestler placing his right arm over the top of his opponent's hip at the back while the left hand holds onto the strap on the outside of the thigh. Competitors must maintain contact with the harness or the match is stopped and restarted. There is no ground wrestling. The purpose is to throw the opponent to the ground in a fall, which wins the match. The wrestlers compete in two-minute rounds until one of them succeeds in throwing his opponent.

Although Glíma was exhibited in the evening of 7 July, the Glíma wrestlers held a more formal competition on Monday, 15 July, at 3:00 P.M. (1500), when they competed for the Glíma Cup, donated by Icelanders in Denmark. Six Icelandic wrestlers were entered as follows: Sigurjón Pétursson, Hallgrímur Benidiktsson, Magnús Tómasson Kjaran, Axel Kristjánsson, Gudmundur Kristinu Guðmundsson, and Kári Arngrímsson. Halldór Hansen (1889–1975) acted as the judge for the matches, along with two Swedish referees. Arngrímsson was sick and had to withdraw and he was replaced by Jón Halldórsson, who had competed as a sprinter in track & field athletics. The results of this tournament were as follows[5]:

			Points
1. Hallgrímur Benidiktsson	ISL		5
2. Sigurjón Pétursson	ISL		4
3. Axel Kristjánsson	ISL		3
4. Guðmundur Kristinu Gudmundsson	ISL		2
5. Magnús Tómasson Kjaran	ISL		1
6. Jón Halldórsson	ISL		0

Exhibitions

Boy Scout Exhibitions

The Boy Scout section of the 1912 Olympics did not consist of a true series of sports or exhibitions. Rather, the Boy Scouts lived near the Stadium in a large camp, and assisted during the Olympics as volunteers, selling programs, helping officials, and giving a mass display in the stadium. Each day in the stadium, there were two sections of Boy Scouts present — one in the morning, which stayed until 1 P.M. (1300), at which time it was relieved by the second or afternoon section.

An invitation was extended to all of the Boy Scout troops in Sweden, and similar invitations were sent to the national Boy Scout organizations of Denmark, France, Germany, Great Britain, and Norway. Three foreign Boy Scout troops came to assist at the Olympics, as follows: Denmark — Det Danske Spejdercorps; Germany — Jung-Deutschland; and Norway — Norske Gutters Spejdekorps.

The foreign Boy Scout troops joined a large number of Swedish troops which were as follows: Åmåls Riddarpojkar, Bodens Scoutförening, Borås Scoutkår, Djursholms Spanare, Enköpings Scoutkår, Eskilstuna Sörmlandspojkarna, Falköpings Riddargossar, Falu Scoutkår, Göteborg Ridarpojkar, Karlshamns Riddarpojkar, Karlskrona Scoutkår, K.F.U.M. (YMCA) Scoutkår, Kristiansrads Scoutkår, Leufstra Bruks Scoutkår, Linköpings Scoutkår, Luleå Scoutkår, Örebro Scoutkår, Östgötapojkarna Norrköping, Sala Scoutkår, Skara Scoutkår, Sköfde Scoutkår, Stockholms Scoutkår, Strömstads Riddarpojkar, Uddevalla Riddarpojkar, Umeå Scoutförening, Vallentuna Spanarkår, Varbergs Scoutförening, Visby Scoutkår, Västerås Arospojkarna, and Vänersborgs Spejarkår.

The Boy Scouts gave their own display on Friday, 12 July, in the stadium. It began with a gymnastics display by all the Swedish scout troops, led by Captain Bernhard Erik Littorin. This was followed by exhibitions of special Boy Scout exercises, a tug-of-war event, relay racing, and finally by demonstrations of first aid practices.

After the Swedish scouts finished their display, the Danish Boy Scout troop gave an exhibition of "staff play," known in Denmark as *stokkeslag*. This was followed by some gymnastics exercises which the Danes also demonstrated and which were concluded by them spelling out "SVEA L,EVE" ("Long live Sweden").

At the close of the Boy Scout demonstration, all the scouts formed long lines of columns. Captain Littorin thanked the spectators, after which the Scouts sang the Swedish National Anthem, "Du Gamla, du Fria." After a cheer was given for Sweden, the Boy Scouts marched out, led by the band of the Göteborg Riddarpojkar.

Gymnastic Exhibitions

In addition to the formal Olympic competitions, there were several gymnastic exhibitions conducted in the stadium during the 1912 Olympic Games. They were as follows:

Date	Times	Teams
6 July	1200–1330	Display by 192 Swedish men gymnasts. Leader: Ebbe Lieberath
6 July	1200–1330	Display by 48 Swedish women gymnasts. Leader: Marrit Hallström
8 July	0930–1100	Display by 150 Danish men gymnasts. Leader: Miss –– Bentzen
8 July	0930–1100	Display by 320 Danish women gymnasts. Leader: Wilhelm Kristensen Skaarup
8 July	1100–1145	Display by 22 Norwegian women gymnasts. Leader: Reidar Fabritius
8 July	1145–1230	Display by 24 Finnish women gymnasts. Leader: Elli Björkstén
10 July	1600–1645	Display by 16 Hungarian men gymnasts. Leader: Rezsö Bábel
11 July	1600–1645	Display by 18 Russian men gymnasts. Leader: Captain –– Fock

Swimming Exhibitions

Several swimming exhibitions were given during the Olympics. On Sunday, 7 July, at 7:00 P.M. (1900), a display was given by Swedish swimmers. Another display, this one by female swimmers, was given on Tuesday evening, 9 July. On the next to last night of swimming competition, 14 July (Sunday), the program listed an exhibition as a "Grand General Display of Swimming."

On the evening of 15 July, at 8:00 P.M. (2000), the last night on which swimming events were held, Fanny Durack (AUS), who had easily won the 100 meter freestyle for women, gave an exhibition swim in which she tried to break the women's world record for 300 meters. She succeeded, setting a world record, being timed at 4:43.6, surpassing the previous record of 4:56.2 by 12.6 seconds, with splits of 1:24.0 at 100 meters, and 3:05.0 at 200 meters.

A friendly water polo match between Sweden and Great Britain was also planned for that night, but as Sweden was to play for second place in the consolation tournament the next morning, the Swedes declined to compete. Instead a friendly was played between two mixed Swedish/British teams, the Blacks defeating the Whites, 3–2 (1–1 at the half).

After the water polo game, there was an "Aquatic Festival" arranged by the Stockholms Kappsimningsklubb (the Stockholm Swimming Club), the Swedish Amateur Swimming Association and the Committee for the Barnens Dag Fund (Children's Summer Holiday Fund), with displays of high diving by Swedish male and female divers. The evening ended with illuminations, including fireworks. The Aquatic Festival was repeated the following evening, 16 July.

Other Sports

Boxing

No boxing events were held at the 1912 Olympic Games, although boxing had figured on the Olympic program in 1904 and 1908. This was a controversial decision that was discussed in detail at the 12th IOC session in Budapest (23–27 May 1911). The British IOC member, Robert de Courcy Laffan, requested that boxing competitions be placed on the program, but he was informed by Viktor Gustaf Balck that this was impossible as boxing was illegal in Sweden, and that public opinion against the sport was so strong that protest demonstrations were possible if boxing took place at the Olympics. The IOC session actually voted to place boxing on the program, but de Courcy Laffan graciously withdrew his proposal. The IOC noted, however, that boxing should be placed on the Olympic program in the future.[6]

The real reason that there was no boxing was that there was no national boxing federation in Sweden at the time and, consequently, there was no group to organize a boxing tournament. Balck's argument that boxing was prohibited in Sweden was not technically correct. Special police permits were required for boxing matches to take place but these were difficult to obtain. With his close contacts with the royal family and several government ministers, Balck would probably have had no difficulty in obtaining the necessary permits.

Game Shooting

Responding to a request by Baron Pierre de Coubertin, the Swedish Olympic Committee decided to give an Olympic gold medal for the best game shooting feat accomplished during the period 1908–1911. The jury which was assigned the task of deciding this award was as follows: President — Count Claes Lewenhaupt, Lord of the Bedchamber; Fredrik Björkenstam, Esquire, Master of the Hounds; E. von Eckermann, Esquire, Master of the Hounds; Professor Einar Lönnberg; and Professor A. G. Nathorst.[7]

However, the jury was unable to come up with an acceptable definition of what constituted the best game shooting feat. On 15 June 1912, they sent a memorandum to the Swedish Olympic committee recommending that the gold medal for game shooting not be awarded. This recommendation was accepted.[8]

Horse Races

A series of trotting horse races were held at Lindarängen on Tuesday, 9 July, from 4:30–6:30 P.M. (1630–1830), and on Thursday, 11 July and Friday, 12 July, during the same hours. In addition, on Wednesday, 10 July, horse racing, presumably thoroughbreds, was held at Lindarängen from 3–6 P.M. (1500–1800). The equestrian events started on 13 July, with the start of the endurance test, the 55 km. long-distance race of the military riding event held at Lindarängen.

Mountain Climbing

It is interesting to note that the very first *Bulletin du Comité International des Jeux Olympiques* mentioned a prize for alpinism. Published in 1894, this bulletin contained a list of 13 items concerning the first Olympic Games in Athens in 1896. Item #12 noted, "At the occasion of the Olympic games, an alpinism prize should be awarded to the most interesting climb accomplished since the last edition of the Games."[9]

The Swedish Olympic committee proposed that a prize be given for "the finest performance in mountain ascents during the years 1908–1911."[10] In September 1911 the committee sent out a circular letter to various Alpine clubs and organizations, asking them to propose candidates for the mountain climbing prize. In January 1912, Erik Ullén was given the assignment to choose among the replies from the clubs.

However, the prize was not a popular idea among the alpinism clubs, who thought that it would not be possible to choose the "finest performance." After receiving many replies to that effect, on 31 May 1912, Ullén issued a memorandum to the Swedish Olympic committee in which he proposed that the prize for mountain climbing should not be awarded. On 2 July 1912, the committee accepted this recommendation and withdrew the prize.

This was not the last the Olympic Games at which a prize for mountain climbing was considered or given. In 1924, 1932, and 1936 medals were awarded for "Merit for Alpinism."

Winter Olympic Sports

There were no winter Olympic sports conducted at the 1912 Olympic Games, despite Sweden being a very Northern country with a long history of winter sports competition. This was a controversial decision. In 1908 at London, figure skating was on the Olympic program and in 1920 at Antwerp both figure skating and ice hockey were contested as part of the "Summer" Olympics. But because of the politics of international winter sports, this did not occur at Stockholm.

In 1899, Professor E. Johan Widmark made the suggestion to begin a series of Nordic Games in Sweden.[11] The first ones were held in 1901 and thereafter in 1905, 1909, 1913, 1917, 1922, and 1926, usually in February in Stockholm.[12] The Nordic Games were organized by the Sveriges Centralförening för Idrottens Främjande (Swedish Central Association for Sports Promotion [SCIF]).[13] They usually lasted one week.

The SCIF was led by Colonel Viktor Gustaf Balck, the leading figure in the early Swedish sports movement. In 1897, Balck, Sven Hermelin, and Clarence von Rosen, all high-ranking Swedish military officers and well-known right-wing political nationalists, had founded the SCIF. Balck spoke of the reason for establishing the Nordic Games. "Above all we placed the national goal of rendering a service to the fatherland and bringing honor to our country. The Nordic Games have now become a national concern for our entire people."[14] In 1901, the Swedish sporting paper *Ny tidning för idrott*, wrote, "It is in the winter season that Scandinavians are able to achieve a sport week as no other people in Europe, and we should hold our banner high where we are able; we should make the Swedish name known and respected. That has thus been a fundamental idea with the arrangement of the Nordic Games."[15]

Some people think that the purpose of the Nordic Games was to establish an early Olympic Winter festival. Lindroth has written, "The goal was to thus create something for winter sports to correspond with the Olympic Games for summer sports."[16] But others differ, pointing to the more nationalistic aspects of the Nordic Games. According to *Ny tidning för idrott*, "The most fundamental implications of the Nordic Games have been, in addition to the fostering of a hardy species, the rallying of the Swedes around something really national. It had long been a weakness among us that we have not had something acceptably national, which could assemble the entire people."[17]

The Nordic Games included the usual popular winter sports, notably ski jumping, cross-country skiing, nordic combined, skeleton races, ice yachting, skate sailing, speed skating, figure skating, curling, bandy, sled-dog racing, and in the 1920, ice hockey. But nonwinter sports were also contested, such as fencing, swimming, and long-distance equestrian races through the snow. In addition, very unusual sports were contested, including skeleton sleighing behind horses, hunting with horses, skiing behind reindeers, kick-sledding, and pulka racing.[18, 19]

The Nordic Games were not purely sports events, however. They also including theater, gala performances at the Opera and Grand Theater, excursions to the archipelago, parades, celebrations, and visits to Skansen — an open air museum in central Stockholm which was inaugurated in 1891 for the purpose of preserving the Swedish countryside farms, houses, churches, and schools. The Nordic Games were meant to promote Skansen as a microcosm of Sweden.[20]

With this background, one can see that the Nordic Games were critically important to Sweden. They were also very important to their founder, Viktor Gustaf Balck, the first real sports administrator in Sweden. Balck (1844–1928) was a charter member of the International Olympic Committee, serving from 1894 to 1921. He was the second President of the International Skating

Union (ISU), manning that post from 1894 to 1925. He was also the President of the 1912 Stockholm organizing committee, which called itself the "Swedish Olympic Committee for the Olympic Games of Stockholm, 1912."[21]

When Coubertin succeeded in re-establishing the Olympic Games at the 1894 Sorbonne Congress, he produced a 14-point protocol which was to loosely govern the early Olympic Games. In point XII, he listed the sports which should be included and one of these was skating.[22] On 18 May 1899, at a meeting which established the Czech Olympic committee, a Czech sportsman and sports official, Jiří Rössler-Ořovský, suggested that skiing competitions be conducted in the Czech Giant Mountains as part of the 1900 Olympic games. Correspondence on this issue between Rössler-Ořovský, Coubertin, and Dr. Jiří Guth-Jarkovský then ensued, but these events did not occur.[23]

Figure skating was held as an Olympic sport at the 1908 Olympic Games in London. It was first discussed by the IOC at its 8th session at the Hague in 1907. Originally it was planned to be held in February but eventually the figure skating was conducted in late October 1908. The 1908 *Official Report* notes that the ISU was notified and the competitions conducted according to their rules. This is surprising, as Balck was ISU president. It is surprising because he raised no objection and, as will be seen, he later raised strenuous objections to winter sports at the 1912 Olympics.

At the 1909 10th IOC Session in Berlin (28 May–1 June 1909), a commission including the two members from Sweden (Balck and von Rosen) had prepared a provisional standard program for future Olympic Games. Balck presented the report and among the sports deleted was skating.[24]

At the 11th IOC session (Luxembourg, 11–13 June 1910), Reverend Robert de Courcy Laffan (GBR) asked Balck whether winter sports were on the 1912 Olympic Program, but was told that none were planned because the Nordic Games were scheduled for early 1913. After harsh protests, Balck declared that if the IOC desired, he could prepare a winter sports program for 1912 and present it at the following session.[25]

However, at the 12th IOC Session in Budapest (23–27 May 1911), when Count Brunetta d'Usseaux (ITA) asked Balck if the committee had planned a winter sports program, Colonel Balck answered curtly, "An Olympic winter sports program could not be considered, as the Nordic Games had already been scheduled for 1913." Brunetta d'Usseaux was not satisfied by Balck's statement and asked that the 1913 Nordic Games be changed into Olympic Winter Games and that the IOC fix the Olympic year as from 1 June 1912 to 31 May 1913. This would mean that the Summer Games preceded the Winter Games. This motion prompted a lively debate between Brunneta d'Usseaux, Balck, Lord Desborough (GBR), Count Clarence von Rosen (SWE), and William Milligan Sloane (USA). No agreement was reached and the motion was tabled until the next day.[26]

The next day (27 May) Brunetta d'Usseaux repeated his motion to "annex" the Nordic Games of 1913 to the Games of the Vth Olympiad. Another lengthy discussion ensued, which was now joined by de Courcy Laffan (GBR), Jiří Guth-Jarkovský (Bohemia), Count Adalbert von Francken-Sierstorpff (GER), and Prince Lev Urusov (RUS). Balck remained adamantly opposed to this motion, however, and as one of the most influential members of the IOC as well as chairman of the organizing committee for the Stockholm Olympics, his influence swayed the day. Balck's opposition to Brunetta d'Usseaux's plan to include the Nordic Games in the Olympic Games was understandable as it would likely have seen the end of his beloved Nordic Games. On 27 May 1911, it was decided that the Nordic Games could not be annexed to the Olympiad and no winter sports would be on the 1912 Olympic program. The Swedish Olympic Committee, led by Balck, rejected the idea on the theoretical basis that all events could not be held in the same place at the same time.[27]

There would be Olympic Winter Games, starting in 1924 at Chamonix, France, but several years of political maneuvering had to occur for this to materialize. The Olympic Winter Games had to overcome the objections of the skating federations, the skiing federations, and the Scandinavian sporting federations. As Balck likely realized, it meant the end of the Nordic Games, which were last held in 1926. Tentative plans for Nordic Games in 1930 and 1934 were made, but they were never contested.

Thus in 1912 at Stockholm, primarily because of the Nordic Games and the objections of their founder, Colonel Viktor Gustaf Balck, no winter sports appeared on the program of the Games of the Vth Olympiad.

Festivals and Entertainments

Date	Time	Site	Event
12 May		Hasselbacken	Closing banquet for players and officials in the covered court tennis tournament.
28 June		Drottningholm Castle	Reception by the Crown Prince and Crown Princess for the English, German, and Hungarian football teams.
28 June		Strand Hotel	Reception arranged by the football committee for those taking part in the football events.
30 June			Football committee Dinner for "honoraratiores."
3 July	1930	Catania Yacht	Dinner aboard his yacht (Catania) by Colonel Robert M. Thompson, President of the American Olympic Committee, for members of the IOC and presidents of the national Olympic committees.
4 July	1100	Riksdagshuset	Opening of the IOC session, with the opening declared by Crown Prince Gustaf Adolf.
4 July	1300	Hasselbacken	Swedish Olympic committee luncheon for the IOC with ladies.
4 July		Finlandia Yacht	Reception by the American team officials for athletes and officials.
5 July			Colonel Viktor Gustaf Balck's dinner for the IOC.
5 July		Hasselbacken	Farewell festivities arranged by the shooting committee.
5 July	2000	Grand Hotel Royal	Royal reception by the cycling committee for the officials and honoraries.
6 July	1100	Olympic Stadium	Opening ceremony of the Games of the Vth Olympiad.
6 July	1615	Logården Palace	Garden Party by HM King Gustav V.
6 July	2000	Olympic Stadium	Grand military concert by the Swedish Musicians' Association.
7 July	2000	Grand Hotel Royal	Official dinner given by the Swedish Olympic committee for officials and honoraries.

Date	Time	Site	Event
7 July	2000	Royal Opera House	First performance by the Folkdansens Vänner (Club for the promotion of Swedish national dances).
8 July	1600	Hasselbacken	Dinner given by the Svenska Simförbundet (Swedish Swimming Association) for the participants in the FINA Congress.
8 July		Hasselbacken	Awards ceremony in cycling and farewell festivities by the cycling committee for competitors and officials.
8 July	2130	Utrikeministerhotellet	Reception by His Excellency the Minister for Foreign Affairs at his hotel.
9 July	1930	Olympic Stadium	Concert
9 July		The Royal Palace	Dinner given by HRH the Crown Prince.
9 July	2000– 2330	Skansen	Skansen's Olympic festivities for Olympic competitors.
10 July			Reception given by Colonel Viktor Gustaf Balck.
10 July		Saltsjöbaden	Banquet given by the "Publicistklubben" (Swedish Journalism Institute) for the representatives of the foreign press.
11 July		The Royal Palace	Dinner given by HRH the Crown Prince.
11 July	1800	Choir Hall	Children's concert, arranged by the Swedish Choral Society, at the Choir Hall of the Östermalm Primary School.
11 July		Hasselbacken	Banquet given by the fencing committee.
11 July	2100	Royal Opera House	Gala performance.
12 July	1700		Five o'clock tea given by Baron Pierre de Coubertin.
12 July	1800– 2000	Östermalms 1° School	First Concert by the Svenska Såmgarförbundet (Swedish Choral Society), given at the Choir Hall of the Östermalm Primary School.
13 July	1830– 2000	Olympic Stadium	Grand choral festival arranged by the Swedish Choral Society.
13 July	2030	Hasselbacken	Reception given by the committee for the horse riding competitions.
14 July	1730	Hasselbacken	Banquet for competitors in the modern pentathlon.
14 July	2000	Royal Opera House	Second performance by the Folkdansens Vänner (Club for the promotion of Swedish national dances).
14 July	2000	Östermalms 1° School	Second concert by the Swedish Choral Society, at the Choir Hall of the Östermalm Primary School.
14 July	2100	Olympic Stadium	Farewell festivities for the assembled athletes, and the lady officials and competitors in gymnastics and swimming. After the banquet, entertainment with music, singers, and fireworks.

Date	Time	Site	Event
15 July	1700	Olympic Stadium	Presentation of prizes
15 July	2000	Djurgårdsbrunnsviken	Aquatic festival (illuminations, fireworks, and so on) arranged by the Stockholms Kappsimnings-klubb (the Stockholm Swimming Club), the Swedish Amateur Swimming Association and the Committee for the "Barnens Dag" Fund (Children's Summer Holiday Fund).
16 July		The Royal Palace	Dinner given by Their Majesties the King and Queen of Sweden.
16 July	1000	Stockholm-Sandhamn	Steamboat excursion and farewell festivities for all the foreign swimmers and officials, arranged by the swimming committee.
17 July		Saltsjöbaden	Farewell festivities, arranged by the officers of the Garrison of Stockholm.
17 July		Hasselbacken	Reception by the rowing committee.
17 July	2000	Hasselbacken	Banquet given by the Svenska Idrottsförbundet (Swedish Athletic Association) for the participants in the congress to found an international amateur athletic federation.
17 July	2130	Olympic Stadium	Fireworks and illumination.
18 July		Prince Wilhelm Palace	Dinner given by HRH Prince Wilhelm, Duke of Södernmanland (the King's second son).
18 July		Hasselbacken	Subscription ball arranged by Fältridtklubben (Stockholm Cross-Country Riding Club).
19 July		Nynäshamn	Reception given by the Kungliga Svenska Segel Sällskapet (Royal Swedish Yacht Club).
19 July		Hasselbacken	Farewell festivities given by the rowing committee.
20 July		Nynäshamn	Dinner given by Captain Oscar Holtermann, Gentleman of the Bedchamber, President of Kungliga Svenska Segel Sällskapet (the Royal Swedish Yachting Society).
27 July		Prince Wilhelm Palace	Garden party for yachtsmen given by HRH Prince Wilhelm, Duke of Södermanland.
27 July	1900	Hasselbacken	Awards ceremony for yachting, and farewell banquet given by the Kungligen Svenska Segel Sällskapet (Royal Swedish Yacht Club), and the closing ceremony of the Games of the Vth Olympiad.

The 13th Session of the International Olympic Committee[28]

The International Olympic Committee held its 13th Session in Stockholm during the Games of the Vth Olympiad. The session took place during six separate meetings of the membership, all held at the House of Parliament in Stockholm. The meetings were held as follows: 4 July — 1000–1030 (opening) and 1100–1130; 8 July —0930–1200; 9 July—0930–1145; 10 July—0930– 1130; and 17 July—0930–1130.[29] Thirty-one of the 44 IOC members were present at the Session.

The session was opened on 4 July at 1000 with speeches by Viktor Gustaf Balck (SWE), IOC President Baron Pierre de Coubertin (FRA), and Sweden's Prince Royal, Gustaf Adolf, who served as the Honorary President of the Swedish Olympic committee in 1912.

The session discussed a number of items. Switzerland's Godefroy de Blonay made a proposal to have the 13th Session in 1914 held in Lausanne, which was accepted. For the Games of the VIth Olympiad in 1916, candidatures were received and discussed from Alexandria (EGY), Berlin (GER), and Budapest (HUN). Alexandria and Budapest graciously withdrew their bids to allow Berlin to be elected unanimously as the host city for 1916. For the 1920 Olympic Games, bids were received from Amsterdam, Brussels, and Budapest.

A subcommittee of the IOC had met at Basel (SUI) earlier in 1912. Its report was discussed and accepted. It made decisions concerning the number of delegates the NOCs could send to the Olympics. It also discussed principles of the Olympic movement, including: 1) who can participate, 2) sports divided into three groups — essential, desirable, and possible; 3) sports must be practiced in at least six countries with IOC members to be considered for the Olympic program; 4) only one team from each nation could start in team events; 5) no age limits would be set; and 6) four to 12 athletes from each nation could start in each event, depending on the sport.

Three proposals concerning the opening ceremonies were made. Hungary's Gyula de Muzsa proposed that teams should march in alphabetical order at the opening ceremony. Pierre de Coubertin proposed the athletes should march in their sporting uniforms rather than team uniforms. Evert Jansen Wendell (USA) and Theodore Andrea Cook (GBR) proposed that confirmation of entries sent by cable must be confirmed by letter. These proposals were tabled for discussion at the 14th session in 1913.

Challenge trophies were discussed. Clarence von Rosen, a Swedish IOC member, noted that nine more trophies had been donated, which were from the following: the Emperor of Austria, the Emperor of Germany, the Emperor of Russia, the King of Italy, the King of Sweden, the City of Budapest, Countess Casa Miranda, Count Géza Andrassy, and the Swedish Cavalry.

Some details of protocol were also discussed. William Milligan Sloane (USA) proposed that the organizing committees should provide each NOC with an Olympic attaché. Germany and Hungary made proposals that the international jury members should be summoned promptly when their services were required. The IOC members also had some complaints about their parking arrangements in Stockholm, which were determined by the Stockholm chief of police.

The matter of the Chilean delegation to the 1912 Olympics was then brought before the session. Two different groups of athletes representing Chile appeared in Stockholm, expecting to compete in the Olympics. Eventually, both groups were allowed to compete, but the matter was to be discussed at the Olympic Congress of 1914.

The death of the Portuguese marathoner Francisco Lázaro was mentioned. After the Games a special benefit was held in his honor, which produced a benefit of 14,000 Kronors (SWE) (equivalent to £770 or $3,850 [US] in 1912 finances) for Lazaro's family.

Two groups were proposed to receive the Olympic Cup of 1913 — Amateur Athletic Union (AAU) of the United States, and the Magyar Athletikai Club in Budapest, Hungary. Sloane, an American member, proposed the Hungarian club should receive the cup and this was accepted with applause.

Finally, a number of medals were awarded. On 4 July, President de Coubertin handed over the gold medal for the re-establishment of the games to the City of Stockholm. Jiří Guth-

Jarkovský presented the Silver Medal of the City of Prague to President de Coubertin on 9 July. Finally, Madame Wersäll, a Swedish woman who had all six of her sons engaged in the Olympics in some way, as athletes, officials, or in the Boy Scout exhibition, was given an Olympic medal by the IOC.

Other International Sporting Meetings During the 1912 Olympic Games

Date	Time	Site	Meeting[30]
30 June	Morning	Riksdagshuset	The 9th Congress of FIFA (Fédération Internationale de Football Association), first day.
1 July	Morning	Riksdagshuset	The 9th Congress of FIFA (Fédération Internationale de Football Association), second day.
6 July		National Association	Congress of the Northern Bandy Federation, with Denmark, Finland, Russia, and Sweden attending.
8 July	0930	Riksdagshuset	Congress of FINA, the International Swimming Federation.
9 July	0930	Riksdagshuset	Congress of FINA, the International Swimming Federation.
15 July		Hotel Continental[31]	Founding Congress of the Internationaler Weltverband für Schwerathletik (International World Federation for Heavy Athletics [weightlifting and wrestling]).
17 July	1700	Riksdagshuset	Congress of the Svenska Idrottsförbundet (Swedish Athletic Association), for the formation of the International Amateur Athletic Federation.
18 July		Riksdagshuset	Meeting of the Northern Skating Congess.
21 July	1300	Riksdagshuset	Congress of the Northern Rowing Association.

International Federations

Two new international sporting federations were formed out of the 1912 Olympic Games — track & field athletics, and heavy athletics (weightlifting and wrestling). At London in 1908, Leopold Englund, President of Svenska Idrottsförbundet (the Swedish Amateur Athletic Association), had already tried to persuade the Amateur Athletic Association (AAA) to call a meeting with the aim of founding an international track & field athletics federation, but the AAA representatives declined. They told Englund that they were too preoccupied with the Olympic Games.

With the 1912 Olympic Games in Sweden, Englund saw his best opportunity to found an international federation for track & field athletics. In May 1911, Svenska Idrottsförbundet issued invitations to a congress scheduled for 5:00 P.M. (1700) on 16 July 1912, to be held at the Restaurant Hasselbacken "for the purpose of forming an INTERNATIONAL AMATEUR ATHLETIC FEDERATION." The invitation was signed by Leopold Englund and Hugo Levin, President and Secretary, respectively, of Svenska Idrottsförbundet.

When the final invitation was sent out the date had been changed to 17 July and the site to Riksdagshuset — the Parliament Building. Representatives of 17 nations attended, and sought to found the federation on that date, but the United States' James Sullivan opposed the idea. He said that the AAU delegates had no authority to take part in the founding of an international federation, and he wanted the decision to be deferred until the next year. A provisional committee for the purpose of forming an International Amateur Athletic Federation was elected with Sigfrid Edström as President and Kristian Hellström as Secretary. The other members of the committee were Pierre Roy (FRA), Carl Diem (GER), Percy Longhurst Fisher (GBR), Szilárd Stankovits (HUN), and James Sullivan (USA). The provisional committee was charged with proposing statutes and rules that were approved at a meeting in Berlin the following year. The International Amateur Athletic Federation (IAAF) was thus founded in Berlin 20–23 August 1913.

Sigfrid Edström is usually given credit for calling the meeting that led to the founding of the IAAF, but the credit belongs to Leopold Englund, who unsuccessfully launched the idea in 1908, and called the historic meeting as early as May 1911.

Sigfrid Edström was the Swedish sports leader who made his name known internationally because of the 1912 Olympic Games, especially when he attended IOC meetings as a representative of the Organizing Committee. He was elected the first President of the IAAF, and in 1921, he succeeded Viktor Balck as an IOC member in Sweden. He was immediately elected to the newly created Executive Committee of the IOC, and in 1937, was elected Vice-President of the IOC. When IOC President Henri de Baillet-Latour (BEL) died in 1942, Edström took over as Acting President of the IOC. After the war ended, Sigfrid Edström was elected the fourth President of the IOC in 1946, at which time he resigned as President of the IAAF. He served as IOC President until 15 August 1952, when he was succeeded by Avery Brundage (USA).

At the suggestion of Arnold Richard Nielsen of Denmark, in May 1912 the Svenska Atletikförbundet (Swedish Amateur Heavy Athletics Association) issued invitations for a meeting whose purpose was to found an international heavy athletics federation. The meeting was called for 15 July at the Hotel Continental. An earlier-formed international federation had ceased operations. Representatives of 12 nations attended the meeting. It was unanimously decided to provisionally found a new international sporting federation, the Internationaler Weltverband für Schwerathletik (International World Federation for Heavy Athletics) and Péter Tatics of Hungary was elected the first President. Four working groups were formed to work out proposals for statutes and rules. The proposals were to be forwarded to Péter Tatics by 31 December 1912, and to be considered at a meeting in Berlin in 1913. That meeting took place 6–7 July in the German capital, at which the proposed statutes and rules were accepted and a full board was elected.

While the IAAF was in Swedish hands, with a Swedish president and secretary, the IAWS was in Hungarian hands, with a Hungarian President and Secretary, Móritz Csanády of Hungary. The Vice-President was Richard Preuß of Germany. After World War I, this situation was not popular with the victorious allied nations, so the IAWS was decommissioned and several new international federations were considered, and some formed, to govern "heavy athletics" at the 1920 Olympic Games in Antwerp. The section of IAWS that governed Greco-Roman wrestling formed a wrestling federation and in 1921, the International Federation for Catch-as-Catch-Can Wrestling was formed. In 1922, these two federations merged to form the International Amateur Wrestling Federation. By 1926, weightlifting had formed the Fédération Internationale Haltérophile to govern that sport.

NOTES

1. 12OR, p. 812.
2. The journal is now called the *Journal of Olympic History*.

3. Cava P. "Olympic Baseball," *Citius, Altius, Fortius*, 1(1): 7–15, Summer 1992.

4. The teams called themselves the "Olympics" (East) and the "Finlands" (West).

5. We are indebted to Icelandic sports historian Þorstein Einarsson, who provided these results and the full names and dates of birth and death for the Glíma competitors.

6. Lyberg, pp. 51–52.

7. 12OR, p. 804.

8. *Ibid.*

9. *Bulletin du Comité International des Jeux Olympiques*, 1(1): 4, July 1894.

10. 12OR, p. 800.

11. Lindroth, Jan; Ljunggren, Jens; and Yttergren, Leif. "The Nordic Games," in: *1994 Swedish Media Guide for the Lillehammer Olympics*. Based on papers presented at the ISHPES Seminar in Lillehammer 25–30 January 1993.

12. Edgeworth, Ron (pseudonym for Bill Mallon). "The Nordic Games and the Origins of the Olympic Winter Games," in *Citius, Altius, Fortius* (now *Journal of Olympic History*), 2(2): 29–36, May 1994.

13. *Ibid.*

14. *Nordiskt idrottsliv*, Festnummer II 1909. Referenced in Yttergren, Leif. "The Nordic Games: Visions of Olympic Winter Games of a Festival?" Presented at the ISHPES Seminar in Lillehammer 25–30 1993.

15. *Ny tdining för idrott*, 1901/7,8. Referenced in Yttergren, Leif. "The Nordic Games: Visions of Olympic Winter Games of a Festival?" Presented at the ISHPES Seminar in Lillehammer 25–30 1993.

16. Lindroth, Jan. *Idrott mellan krigen. Organisationer, ledare och idéer i den svenska indrottsrörelsen 1919–1939*. Stockholm: 1987.

17. *Ny tdining för idrott*, 1901/7,8. Referenced in Yttergren, Leif. "The Nordic Games: Visions of Olympic Winter Games of a Festival?" Presented at the ISHPES Seminar in Lillehammer 25–30 1993.

18. Lindroth, Jan; Ljunggren, Jens; and Yttergren, Leif. "The Nordic Games," in: *1994 Swedish Media Guide for the Lillehammer Olympics*. Based on papers presented at the ISHPES Seminar in Lillehammer 25–30 January 1993.

19. Yttergren, Leif. "The Nordic Games: Visions of Olympic Winter Games of a Festival?" Presented at the ISHPES Seminar in Lillehammer 25–30 January 1993.

20. Ljunggren, Jens. "The Nordic Games, Nationalism, Sports, and Cultural Conflicts." Presented at the ISHPES Seminar in Lillehammer 25–30 January 1993.

21. More information on Balck can be found in the opening section of this book, under "Viktor Gustaf Balck and the Organization of Swedish Sports."

22. It never said if this was speed skating or figure skating, but it is assumed that it was figure skating.

23. *Czech Olympic Team Media Guide: XVII Olympic Winter Games. Lillehammer '94*. Prague: Czech Olympic Committee, 1994.

24. Lyberg, p. 45.

25. *Ibid.*

26. *Ibid.*

27. *Ibid.*

28. These notes on the 13th IOC session are derived almost completely from Lyberg, pp. 57–60.

29. Of note, the *Official Report* lists the scheduled meetings of the IOC as follows: 12 July at Riksdag House — the third meeting of the IOC; 18 July at Riksdag House — the fourth meeting of the IOC; and 23 July at Riksdag House — the fifth meeting of the IOC. No description of the first and second meetings of the IOC is given in the *Official Report*. It is unclear why this discrepancy exists, although it is likely the scheduled dates were eventually changed.

30. In addition to the following, the 12OR (p. 74) also notes that the International Football Federation (FIFA), held an athletic congress in Stockholm. I cannot find the dates of this congress.

31. This meeting was adjourned after three hours, and then resumed at the Olympic Stadium.

Appendix I
The 1912 Olympic Program

Date	Site	Time	Event
5 May	Royal Tennis Pavilion		Covered-court tennis events
6 May	Royal Tennis Pavilion		Covered-court tennis events
7 May	Royal Tennis Pavilion		Covered-court tennis events
8 May	Royal Tennis Pavilion		Covered-court tennis events
9 May	Royal Tennis Pavilion		Covered-court tennis events
10 May	Royal Tennis Pavilion		Covered-court tennis events
11 May	Royal Tennis Pavilion		Covered-court tennis events
12 May	Royal Tennis Pavilion		Covered-court tennis events
	Hasselbacken		Closing banquet for players and official in the covered-court tennis events
28 June	Östermalm Idrottsplats	0900	Lawn tennis events
	Drottningholm Castle		Reception by the Crown Prince and Crown Princess for the English, German, and Hungarian football teams
	Strand Hotel		Reception arranged by the football committee for those taking part in the football events
29 June	Östermalm Idrottsplats	0900	Lawn tennis events
	Kaknäs	0900	Dueling pistol, 30 meters
	Råsunda	0900–1200	Clay trap shooting, teams, first stage
	Kaknäs	1000	Military rifle, 200/400/500/600 meters, teams
	Råsunda	1000–1200	Running deer, single shot, individual
	Tranebergs Idrottsplats	1100	Football — FIN v. ITA
	Råsunda	1330	Clay trap shooting, teams, first stage
	Råsunda	1330–1800	Running deer, single shot, individual
	Kaknäs	1500	Dueling pistol, 30 meters, teams
	Råsunda Idrottsplats	1500	Football — AUT v. GER
	Olympic Stadium	1900	Football — NED v. SWE

Date	*Site*	*Time*	*Event*
30 June	Östermalm Idrottsplats	0900	Lawn tennis events
	Tranebergs Idrottsplats	1000	Football — FIN v. RUS
	Råsunda	1000–1200	Running deer, single shot, individual
	Riksdagshuset	Morning	The 9th Congress of FIFA (Fédération Internationale de Football Association), first day
	Råsunda	1330–1800	Running deer, single shot, individual
	Råsunda Idrottsplats	1330	Football — GBR v. HUN
	Råsunda Idrottsplats	1630	Football — DEN v. NOR
	Råsunda Idrottsplats	1900	Football — NED v. AUT
			Football Committee Dinner for "honoraratiores"
1 July	Östermalm Idrottsplats	0900	Lawn tennis events
	Råsunda	0900–1200	Clay trap shooting, teams, second stage
	Kaknäs	0900–1400	Military rifle, 300 meters, three-positions
	Råsunda	1000–1200	Running deer, single shot, individual
	Tranebergs Idrottsplats	1100	Football — AUT v. NOR
	Riksdagshuset	Morning	The 9th Congress of FIFA (Fédération Internationale de Football Association), second day
	Kaknäs	1200	Free pistol, 50 meters
	Råsunda	1330	Clay trap shooting, teams, second stage
	Råsunda	1330–1800	Running deer, single shot, individual
	Kaknäs	1500–1800	Military rifle, 600 meters, any position
	Råsunda Idrottsplats	1700	Football — GER v. RUS
	Råsunda Idrottsplats	1900	Football — ITA v. SWE
2 July	Östermalm Idrottsplats	0900	Lawn tennis events
	Råsunda	0900	Clay trap shooting, individual
	Kaknäs	1100–1400	Free rifle, 300 meters, three-positions, morning session
	Kaknäs	1200	Military pistol, 50 meters, teams
	Olympic Stadium	1500	Football — GBR v. FIN
	Kaknäs	1600–1900	Free rifle, 300 meters, three-positions, morning session
	Olympic Stadium	1900	Football — DEN v. NED
3 July	Östermalm Idrottsplats	0900	Lawn tennis events
	Råsunda	0900	Clay trap shooting, individual
	Råsunda	0900–1200	Running deer, double shot, individual
	Kaknäs	1200	Small-bore rifle, 50 meters, prone, teams
	Råsunda	1330	Running deer, double shot, individual
	Kaknäs	1500	Dueling pistol, 30 meters, teams
	Råsunda Idrottsplats	1500	Football — HUN v. GER
	Djurgården Stadium	1900	Football — AUT v. ITA
	Catania Yacht Club	1930	Dinner aboard his yacht (Catania) by Colonel Robert M. Thompson, President of the American Olympic Committee, for members of the IOC and presidents of the national Olympic committees

Date	Site	Time	Event
4 July	Östermalm Idrottsplats	0900	Lawn tennis events
	Råsunda	0900	Clay trap shooting, individual
	House of Parliament	1000	Opening of the 13th IOC Session
	Råsunda	1000–1200	Running deer, single shot, teams
	Riksdagshuset	1100	Second meeting of the 13th IOC Session, with the opening declared by Crown Prince Gustaf Adolf
	Kaknäs	1100–1400	Free rifle, 300 meters, three positions, teams
	Kaknäs	1200–1900	Small-bore rifle, prone position, 50 meters
	Råsunda	1330	Running deer, single shot, teams
	Hasselbacken	1300	Swedish Olympic committee luncheon for the IOC with ladies
	Råsunda Idrottsplats	1500	Football — NED v. FIN
	Olympic Stadium	1900	Football — GBR v. DEN
	Finlandia Yacht		Reception by the American team officials for athletes and officials
5 July	Östermalm Idrottsplats	0900	Lawn tennis events
	Kaknäs	1000	Small-bore rifle, 25 meters, disappearing target
	Kaknäs	1500	Small-bore rifle, 25 meters, disappearing target, teams
	Råsunda Idrottsplats	1900	Football — HUN v. AUT
			Colonel Viktor Gustaf Balck's dinner for the IOC
	Hasselbacken		Farewell festivities arranged by the shooting committee
	Grand Hotel Royal	2000	Royal reception by the cycling committee for the officials and honoraries
6 July	Östermalm Tennis Pavilion	0800–1030	Foil, individual; round one pools, pools 1–4
	Olympic Stadium	0800–0900	Wrestling — featherweight and lightweight classes
	Olympic Stadium	1100	Opening ceremony of the Games of the Vth Olympiad
	Olympic Stadium	1200	Display by Swedish men and women gymnasts
	Olympic Stadium	c. 1300	Athletics; javelin throw, qualifying round
	Östermalm Tennis Pavilion	1300–1600	Foil, individual; round one pools, pools 5–8
	Olympic Stadium	1330–1415	Athletics; 100 meters, round one
	Olympic Stadium	1445	Athletics; 800 meters, semifinals, round one
	Olympic Stadium	c. 1500	Athletics; javelin throw, final
	Olympic Stadium	1515	Wrestling — featherweight and lightweight classes
	Olympic Stadium	1545	Athletics; 100 meters, semifinals
	Östermalm Tennis Pavilion	1600–1900	Foil, individual; round-one pools, pools 9–12
	Logården Palace	1615	Garden party by HM King Gustav V
	Djurgårdsbrunnsviken Swim Stadium	1900	Men's 100 freestyle swimming, round one

Date	Site	Time	Event
	Djurgårdsbrunnsviken Swim Stadium	1930	Diving — men's plain high diving qualifying (heats 1–2)
	Djurgårdsbrunnsviken Swim Stadium	1940	Men's 1,500 freestyle swimming, round one, heat one
	Olympic Stadium	2000	Grand military concert by the Swedish Musicians' Association
	Djurgårdsbrunnsviken Swim Stadium	2030	Men's 1,500 freestyle swimming, round one, heat two
	Djurgårdsbrunnsviken Swim Stadium	2115	Men's 1,500 freestyle swimming, round one, heat three
	National Association		Congress of the Northern Bandy Federation, with Denmark, Finland, Russia, and Sweden attending
7 July	Around Lake Mälaren	0200	Cycling — road race
	Östermalm Tennis Pavilion	0800–1100	Foil, individual; round-one pools, pools 13–16
	Olympic Stadium	0800–0900	Wrestling — featherweight and middleweight B classes
	Kaknäs	0900	Modern Pentathlon — shooting
	Olympic Stadium	0900	Athletics; high jump, qualifying round
	Olympic Stadium	0900	Athletics; 10,000 meters, round one, heat one
	Olympic Stadium	0945	Athletics; 10,000 meters, round one, heat two
	Östermalm Tennis Pavilion	1300–1600	Foil, individual; quarterfinal pools, pools 1–4
	Olympic Stadium	1330	Athletics; pentathlon
	Olympic Stadium	1330	Athletics; 10,000 meters, round one, heat three
	Djurgårdsbrunnsviken Swim Stadium	1330	Men's 100 freestyle swimming, quarterfinals
	Djurgårdsbrunnsviken Swim Stadium	1330	Diving — men's plain high diving qualifying (heats three to four)
	Djurgårdsbrunnsviken Swim Stadium	1350	Men's 200 breaststroke swimming, round one, heats 1, 2 and 4
	Djurgårdsbrunnsviken Swim Stadium	1350	Men's 200 breaststroke swimming, round one, heats 5, 6 and extra
	Djurgårdsbrunnsviken Swim Stadium	1415	Men's 1,500 freestyle swimming, round one, heat four
	Olympic Stadium	1445	Athletics; 100 meters, final
	Olympic Stadium	1515	Wrestling — featherweight and middleweight B classes
	Olympic Stadium	1515	Athletics; 800 meters, semifinals, heat one
	Djurgårdsbrunnsviken Swim Stadium	1515	Water polo — GBR v. BEL
	Olympic Stadium	1530	Athletics; 800 meters, semifinals, heat two
	Östermalm Tennis Pavilion	1600–1900	Foil, individual; quarterfinal pools, pools 5–8
	Djurgårdsbrunnsviken Swim Stadium	1900	Display by Swedish swimmers

Date	Site	Time	Event
	Olympic Stadium	1930	Display of Gotland sports
	Olympic Stadium	1930	Icelandic *Glíma* wrestling exhibition
	Djurgårdsbrunnsviken Swim Stadium	2000	Men's 100 freestyle swimming, semifinals, heats 1–2
	Grand Hotel Royal	2000	Official dinner given by the Swedish Olympic Committee for officials and honoraries
	Royal Opera House	2000	First performance by the Folkdansens Vänner (Club for the promotion of Swedish national dances)
	Djurgårdsbrunnsviken Swim Stadium	2020	Men's 1,500 freestyle swimming, round one, heat five
8 July	Östermalm Tennis Pavilion	0900 –1200	Foil, individual; semifinal pools
	Riksdagshuset	0930	Congress of FINA, the International Swimming Federation
	Olympic Stadium	0930	Display by Danish men and women gymnasts
	House of Parliament	0930	Third meeting of the 13th IOC Session
	Olympic Stadium	0930	Athletics; ten-kilometer walk, round one
	Olympic Stadium	1030	Athletics; standing long jump, qualifying round
	Olympic Stadium	1100	Display by Norwegian women gymnasts
	Djurgårdsbrunnsviken Swim Stadium	1100	Modern pentathlon — swimming
	Olympic Stadium	1145	Display by Finnish women gymnasts
	Olympic Stadium	1200	Athletics; 4 × 100 meter relay, round one
	Olympic Stadium	c. 1200	Athletics; standing long jump, final
	Östermalm Tennis Pavilion	1300–1600	Foil, individual; final pool
	Djurgårdsbrunnsviken Swim Stadium	1330	Water polo — SWE v. FRA
	Olympic Stadium	1400	Gymnastics — all-around, Swedish system, teams
	Olympic Stadium	1400–1700	Wrestling — featherweight, lightweight and middleweight A and B classes
	Olympic Stadium	1500	Athletics; high jump, final
	Olympic Stadium	1530	Athletics; 4 × 100 meter relay, semifinals
	Hasselbacken	1600	Dinner given by the Svenska Simförbundet (Swedish Swimming Association) for the participants in the FINA Congress
	Olympic Stadium	1615	Athletics; 10,000 meters, final
	Olympic Stadium	1700	Athletics; 800 meters, final
	Djurgårdsbrunnsviken Swim Stadium	1900	Diving — springboard diving qualifying
	Djurgårdsbrunnsviken Swim Stadium	1930	Women's 100 freestyle swimming, round one, heat one
	Djurgårdsbrunnsviken Swim Stadium	1935	Women's 100 freestyle swimming, round one, heat two
	Djurgårdsbrunnsviken Swim Stadium	1930	Men's 400 breaststroke swimming, round one

Date	Site	Time	Event
	Utrikeministerhotellet	2130	Reception by His Excellency the Minister for Foreign Affairs at his hotel
	Hasselbacken		Awards ceremoy in cycling and farewell festivities by the cycling committee for competitors and officials
9 July	Östermalm Idrottsplats	0900	Modern pentathlon — fencing
	Östermalm Tennis Pavilion	0900–1330	Épée, team; round-one pools
	Olympic Stadium	0930	Athletics; 5,000 meters, round one, heat one
	Olympic Stadium	0930–1230	Wrestling — featherweight, lightweight, and heavyweight classes
	Riksdagshuset	0930	Congress of FINA, the International Swimming Federation
	House of Parliament	0930	Fourth meeting of the 13th IOC Session
	Olympic Stadium	c. 1000	Athletics; 5,000 meters, round one, heat two
	Olympic Stadium	c. 1030	Athletics; 5,000 meters, round one, heat three
	Djurgårdsbrunnsviken Swim Stadium	1200	Women's 100 freestyle swimming, round one, heat three
	Djurgårdsbrunnsviken Swim Stadium	1205	Women's 100 freestyle swimming, round one, heat four
	Djurgårdsbrunnsviken Swim Stadium	1210	Women's 100 freestyle swimming, round one, heat five
	Djurgårdsbrunnsviken Swim Stadium	1215	Men's 100 backstroke swimming, round one, heat one
	Djurgårdsbrunnsviken Swim Stadium	1225	Men's 100 backstroke swimming, round one, heat two
	Djurgårdsbrunnsviken Swim Stadium	1230	Men's 100 backstroke swimming, round one, heat three
	Djurgårdsbrunnsviken Swim Stadium	1335	Water polo — AUT v. HUN
	Djurgårdsbrunnsviken Swim Stadium		Men's 100 freestyle swimming, semifinals, heat 3
	Olympic Stadium	1400	Athletics; Javelin throw, both hands, qualifying round
	Olympic Stadium	1400–1700	Wrestling — featherweight, lightweight, and heavyweight classes
	Östermalm Tennis Pavilion	1400–1830	Épée, team; semifinal pools
	Olympic Stadium	1430	Athletics; 1,500 meters, round one
	Olympic Stadium	1600	Athletics; 4 × 100 meter relay, final
	Olympic Stadium	1615	Athletics; 5,000 meters, round one, heat four
	Olympic Stadium	c. 1645	Athletics; 5,000 meters, round one, heat five
	Olympic Stadium	1930	Concert
	Djurgårdsbrunnsviken Swim Stadium	1940	Men's 1,500 freestyle swimming, semifinals
	Djurgårdsbrunnsviken Swim Stadium	1940	Diving — springboard diving final

Date	Site	Time	Event
	Skansen	2000–2330	Skansen's Olympic festivities for Olympic competitors
	Djurgårdsbrunnsviken Swim Stadium	2015	Men's 200 breaststroke swimming, semifinals
	Djurgårdsbrunnsviken Swim Stadium	Evening	Display by female swimmers
	The Royal Palace		Dinner given by HRH the Crown Prince
	Hasselbacken	0800	Awards banquet for cycling competitors and officials
10 July	Östermalm Idrottsplats	0900	Modern Pentathlon — fencing
	Östermalm Tennis Pavilion	0900–1500	Épée, team; final pool
	Olympic Stadium	0930	Athletics; shot put, qualifying round
	Olympic Stadium	0930–1230	Wrestling — middleweight A and middleweight B classes
	Olympic Stadium	0930	Gymnastics — all-around, free system, teams (first session)
	House of Parliament	0930	Fifth Meeting of the 13th IOC Session
	Olympic Stadium	1030	Athletics; 200 meters, round one
	Olympic Stadium	c. 1100	Athletics; shot put, final
	Djurgårdsbrunnsviken Swim Stadium	1300	Men's 100 backstroke swimming, round one, heat four
	Djurgårdsbrunnsviken Swim Stadium	1305	Men's 100 backstroke swimming, round one, heat five
	Olympic Stadium	1400	Gymnastics — all-around, free system, teams (second session)
	Olympic Stadium	1400	Athletics; 5,000 meters, final
	Olympic Stadium	1400–1600	Wrestling — middleweight A and middleweight B classes
	Olympic Stadium	1415	Athletics; pole vault, qualifying round
	Djurgårdsbrunnsviken Swim Stadium	1430	Water polo — BEL v. HUN
	Olympic Stadium	1600	Athletics; 200 meters, semifinals
	Olympic Stadium	1530	Athletics; 1,500 meters, final
	Olympic Stadium	1600	Display by Hungarian men gymnasts
	Djurgårdsbrunnsviken Swim Stadium	1900	Diving — women's plain high diving qualifying
	Djurgårdsbrunnsviken Swim Stadium	1900	Men's 100 backstroke swimming, semifinal, heat one
	Djurgårdsbrunnsviken Swim Stadium	1905	Men's 100 backstroke swimming, semifinal, heat two
	Djurgårdsbrunnsviken Swim Stadium	1915	Men's 100 freestyle swimming, final
	Djurgårdsbrunnsviken Swim Stadium	1305	Men's 100 backstroke swimming, round one, heat five
	Djurgårdsbrunnsviken Swim Stadium	1930	Men's 200 breaststroke swimming, final

Date	Site	Time	Event
	Saltsjöbaden		Reception given by Colonel Viktor Gustaf Balck Banquet given by the "Publicistklubben" (Swedish Journalism Institute) for the representatives of the foreign press
11 July	Östermalm Tennis Pavilion	0900–1200	Épée, individual; round-one pools, pools 1–4
	Olympic Stadium	0930	Gymnastics — combined all-around, teams (first session)
	Olympic Stadium	0930	Athletics; 110 meter hurdles, round one
	Olympic Stadium	0930–1230	Wrestling — featherweight, lightweight, and middleweight A classes
	Olympic Stadium	1115	Athletics; 10-kilometer walk, final
	Djurgårdsbrunnsviken Swim Stadium	1130	Water polo — BEL v. FRA
	Djurgårdsbrunnsviken Swim Stadium	1200	Women's 100 freestyle swimming, semifinals
	Östermalm Tennis Pavilion	1200–1500	Épée, individual; round-one pools, pools 5–8
	Djurgårdsbrunnsviken Swim Stadium	1210	Men's 400 freestyle swimming, round one
	Barkaby	1215	Modern pentathlon — riding
	Olympic Stadium	1400	Athletics; shot put, both hands, qualifying round
	Olympic Stadium	1400	Gymnastics — combined all-around, teams (second session)
	Olympic Stadium	1400–1600	Wrestling — featherweight, middleweight B, and heavyweight classes
	Olympic Stadium	1500	Athletics; 200 meters, final
	Östermalm Tennis Pavilion	1500–1800	Épée, individual; round-one pools, pools 9–12
	Olympic Stadium	1515	Athletics; pole vault, final
	Olympic Stadium	c. 1530	Athletics; shot put, both hands, final
	Olympic Stadium	1600	Display by Russian men gymnasts
	Olympic Stadium	1615	Athletics; 110 meter hurdles, semifinals
	Choir Hall	1800	Children's concert, arranged by the Swedish Choral Society, at the Choir Hall of the Östermalm Primary School
	Djurgårdsbrunnsviken Swim Stadium	1930	Men's 400 breaststroke swimming, semifinals
	Djurgårdsbrunnsviken Swim Stadium	1930	Diving — men's plain high diving final
	Djurgårdsbrunnsviken Swim Stadium	2000	Water polo — GBR v. SWE
	Royal Opera House	2100	Gala performance
	The Royal Palace		Dinner given by HRH the Crown Prince
	Hasselbacken		Banquet given by the fencing committee

Date	Site	Time	Event
12 July	Östermalm Tennis Pavilion	0900–1200	Épée, individual; round-one pools, pools 13–16
	Olympic Stadium	0930	Gymnastics — combined all-around, individual (first session)
	Olympic Stadium	0930	Athletics; discus throw, qualifying round
	Olympic Stadium	0930–1230	Wrestling — featherweight, middleweight B, and heavyweight classes
	Olympic Stadium	1100	Athletics; 400 meters, round one
	Olympic Stadium (start/finish)	1100	Modern pentathlon — cross-country run
	Östermalm Tennis Pavilion	1200–1500	Épée, individual; quarterfinal pools, pools 1–4
	Olympic Stadium	c. 1200	Athletics; discus throw, final
	Djurgårdsbrunnsviken Swim Stadium	1240	Diving — plain and fancy diving qualifying
	Olympic Stadium	1400	Gymnastics — combined all-around, individual (second session)
	Olympic Stadium	1400	Athletics; broad (long) jump, final
	Olympic Stadium	1400	Athletics; broad (long) jump, qualifying round
	Olympic Stadium	1400–1700	Wrestling — featherweight, middleweight B, and heavyweight classes
	Olympic Stadium	1500	Athletics; 110 meter hurdles, final
	Olympic Stadium	1500	Athletics; 3,000 meter team race, round one
	Östermalm Tennis Pavilion	1500–1800	Épée, individual; quarterfinal pools, pools 5–8
	Olympic Stadium	1615	Athletics; 400 meters, semifinals
		1700	Five o'clock tea given by Baron Pierre de Coubertin
	Östermalms Folkskola	1800	First concert by the Swedish Choral Society, given at the Choir Hall of the Östermalm Primary School
	Djurgårdsbrunnsviken Swim Stadium	1900	Women's 100 freestyle swimming, final
	Djurgårdsbrunnsviken Swim Stadium	1900	Men's 4 × 200 freestyle relay swimming, round one
13 July	Field Riding Club Stadium	0800	Equestrian — 3-day event — cross-country ride
	Östermalm Tennis Pavilion	0900–1200	Épée, individual; semifinal pools
	Olympic Stadium	0930	Athletics; standing high jump, qualifying round
	Olympic Stadium	0930–1230	Wrestling — featherweight, lightweight, and middleweight A classes
	Olympic Stadium	1000	Athletics; decathlon
	Olympic Stadium	1400	Athletics; discus throw, both hands, qualifying round
	Olympic Stadium	1400–1700	Wrestling — featherweight, lightweight, and middleweight A classes

Date	Site	Time	Event
	Östermalm Tennis Pavilion	1400–1700	Épée, individual; final pool
	Olympic Stadium	1500	Athletics; 400 meters, finals
	Olympic Stadium	1530	Athletics; 3,000 meter team race, final
	Olympic Stadium	1600	Athletics; standing high jump, final
	Olympic Stadium	c. 1600	Athletics; discus throw, both hands, final
	Olympic Stadium	1830	Grand choral festival arranged by the Swedish Choral Society
	Djurgårdsbrunnsviken Swim Stadium	1900	Men's 400 freestyle swimming, semifinals
	Djurgårdsbrunnsviken Swim Stadium	1915	Diving — women's plain high diving final
	Djurgårdsbrunnsviken Swim Stadium	2105	Men's 1,500 freestyle swimming, round one, heat five
	Djurgårdsbrunnsviken Swim Stadium	1940	Men's 100 backstroke swimming, final
	Hasselbacken	2030	Reception given by the committee for the horse riding competitions
14 July	Östermalm Tennis Pavilion	0800–1100	Sabre, team; round-one pools, first stage
	Olympic Stadium	0830–1030	Wrestling — lightweight, middleweight B, and heavyweight classes
	Olympic Stadium	1000	Athletics; decathlon
	Östermalm Tennis Pavilion	1300–1330	Sabre, team; round-one pools, second stage
	Olympic Stadium	1330	Athletics; hammer throw, qualifying round
	Olympic Stadium	1330–1630	Wrestling — lightweight, middleweight B, and heavyweight classes
	Olympic Stadium	1348	Athletics; marathon
	Olympic Stadium	1445	Athletics; 4 × 400 meter relay, round one
	Östermalm Tennis Pavilion	1500–1930	Sabre, team; semifinal pools
	Olympic Stadium	c. 1530	Athletics; hammer throw, final
	Hasselbacken	1730	Banquet for competitors in the modern pentathlon
	Djurgårdsbrunnsviken Swim Stadium	1900	Men's 400 freestyle swimming, final
	Djurgårdsbrunnsviken Swim Stadium	2000	Water polo — SWE v. AUT
	Royal Opera House	2000	Second performance by the Folkdansens Vänner (Club for the promotion of Swedish national dances)
	Östermalm Primary School	2000	Second concert by the Swedish Choral Society, at the Choir Hall of the Östermalm Primary School

Date	Site	Time	Event
	Olympic Stadium	2100	Farewell Festivities for the assembled athletes, and the lady officials and competitors in gymnastics and swimming. After the banquet, entertainment with music, singers, and fireworks
	Djurgårdsbrunnsviken Swim Stadium	Evening	Grand display of swimming
15 July	Olympic Stadium	0800	Equestrian — dressage
	Östermalm Tennis Pavilion	0900–1500	Sabre, team; final pool
	Östermalm Idrottsplats	1000	American baseball exhibition
	Olympic Stadium	1000	Athletics; decathlon
	Lindarängen	1100	Equestrian — three-day event — steeplechase
	Olympic Stadium	1200	Equestrian — dressage
	Djurgårdsbrunnsviken Swim Stadium	1200	Women's 4 × 100 freestyle relay swimming, final
	Djurgårdsbrunnsviken Swim Stadium	1215	Diving — plain and fancy diving final
	Djurgårdsbrunnsviken Swim Stadium	1245	Men's 4 × 200 freestyle relay swimming, final
	Djurgårdsbrunnsviken Swim Stadium	1300	Water polo — BEL v. AUT
	Olympic Stadium	Afternoon	Wrestling — featherweight, lightweight, middleweight A, and middleweight B classes
	Olympic Stadium	1400	Athletics; hop, step, and jump (triple jump), qualifying round
	Olympic Stadium	1415	Athletics; cross-country race, individual and team
	Olympic Stadium	1430	Athletics; 4 × 400 meter relay, final
	Olympic Stadium	1500	Icelandic *Glíma* wrestling demonstration competition
	Olympic Stadium	c. 1600	Athletics; hop, step, and jump (triple jump), final
	Olympic Stadium	1700	Presentation of prizes
	Djurgårdsbrunnsviken Swim Stadium	Evening	Exhibition 300 meter swim by Sarah "Fanny" Durack (AUS)
	Djurgårdsbrunnsviken Swim Stadium	2000	Aquatic festival (illuminations, fireworks, and so on) arranged by the Stockholms Kapp-simningsklubb (the Stockholm Swimming Club), the Swedish Amateur Swimming Association and the Committee for the "Barnens Dag" Fund (Children's Summer Holiday Fund)
	Hotel Continental*		Founding Congress of the Internationaler Weltverband für Schwerathletik (Interna-

*This meeting was adjourned after three hours, and then resumed at the Olympic Stadium.

Date	Site	Time	Event
			tional World Federation for Heavy Athletics [weightlifting and wrestling])
16 July	Olympic Stadium	0900	Equestrian — 3-day event — jumping
	Djurgårdsbrunnsviken Swim Stadium	0900	Water polo — SWE v. BEL
	Östermalm Tennis Pavilion	0900–1200	Sabre, individual; round-one pools, pools 11–4
	Stockholm-Sandhamn	1000	Steamboat excursion and farewell festivities for all the foreign swimmers and officials, arranged by the swimming committee
	Östermalm Idrottsplats	Morning	American baseball exhibition
	Östermalm Tennis Pavilion	1200–1500	Sabre, individual; round-one pools, pools 5–8
	Olympic Stadium	1400	Equestrian — individual jumping
	Östermalm Tennis Pavilion	1500–1800	Sabre, individual; round-one pools, pools 9–12
	Djurgårdsbrunnsviken Swim Stadium	2000	Aquatic festival (illuminations, and so on) arranged by the Stockholms Kappsimn-ingsklubb (the Stockholm Swimming Club), the Swedish Amateur Swimming Association and the Committee for the "Barnens Dag" Fund (Children's Summer Holiday Fund)
	The Royal Palace		Dinner given by Their Majesties the King and Queen of Sweden
17 July	Olympic Stadium	0700	Equestrian — 3-day event — dressage
	Östermalm Tennis Pavilion	0900–1200	Sabre, individual; round-one pools, pools 13–16
	House of Parliament	0930	Sixth Meeting of the 13th IOC Session
	Djurgårdsbrunnsviken	1100	Rowing; coxed fours inriggers, round one, heat 1
	Djurgårdsbrunnsviken	1120	Rowing; coxed fours inriggers, round one, heat 2
	Djurgårdsbrunnsviken	1140	Rowing; coxed fours inriggers, round one, heat 3
	Djurgårdsbrunnsviken	1200	Rowing; coxed eights, round one, heat 1
	Östermalm Tennis Pavilion	1200–1500	Sabre, individual; quarterfinal pools, pools 1–4
	Djurgårdsbrunnsviken	1220	Rowing; coxed eights, round one, heat 2
	Djurgårdsbrunnsviken	1240	Rowing; coxed eights, round one, heat 3
	Djurgårdsbrunnsviken	1300	Rowing; coxed eights, round one, heat 4
	Olympic Stadium	1300	Equestrian — team jumping
	Djurgårdsbrunnsviken	1320	Rowing; coxed eights, round one, heat 5
	Djurgårdsbrunnsviken	1340	Rowing; coxed eights, round one, heat 6
	Djurgårdsbrunnsviken	1500	Rowing; single sculls, round one, heat 1
	Östermalm Tennis Pavilion	1500–1800	Sabre, individual; quarterfinal pools, pools 5–8

Date	Site	Time	Event
	Djurgårdsbrunnsviken	1520	Rowing; single sculls, round one, heat 2
	Djurgårdsbrunnsviken	1540	Rowing; single sculls, round one, heat 3
	Djurgårdsbrunnsviken	1600	Rowing; single sculls, round one, heat 4
	Djurgårdsbrunnsviken	1620	Rowing; single sculls, round one, heat 5
	Djurgårdsbrunnsviken	1640	Rowing; single sculls, round one, heat 6
	Djurgårdsbrunnsviken	1700	Rowing; single sculls, round one, heat 7
	Riksdagshuset	1700	Congress of the Svenska Idrottsförbundet (Swedish Athletic Association), for the formation of the International Amateur Athletic Federation
	Djurgårdsbrunnsviken	1720	Rowing; single sculls, round one, heat 8
	Djurgårdsbrunnsviken	1740	Rowing; coxed fours inriggers, semifinals, heat 1
	Djurgårdsbrunnsviken	1800	Rowing; coxed fours inriggers, semifinals, heat 2
	Djurgårdsbrunnsviken	1820	Rowing; coxed fours outriggers, round one, heat 1
	Djurgårdsbrunnsviken	1840	Rowing; coxed fours outriggers, round one, heat 2
	Djurgårdsbrunnsviken	1900	Rowing; coxed fours outriggers, round one, heat 3
	Djurgårdsbrunnsviken	1920	Rowing; coxed fours outriggers, round one, heat 4
	Djurgårdsbrunnsviken	1940	Rowing; coxed fours outriggers, round one, heat 5
	Djurgårdsbrunnsviken	2000	Rowing; coxed fours outriggers, round one, heat 6
	Hasselbacken	2000	Banquet given by the Svenska Idrottsförbundet (Swedish Athletic Association) for the participants in the congress to found an international amateur athletic federation
	Djurgårdsbrunnsviken	2020	Rowing; coxed fours outriggers, round one, heat 7
	Olympic Stadium	2130	Fireworks and illumination
	Saltsjöbaden		Farewell festivities, arranged by the officers of the Garrison of Stockholm
	Hasselbacken		Reception by the rowing committee
18 July	Östermalm Tennis Pavilion	0900–1200	Sabre, individual; semifinal pools
	Djurgårdsbrunnsviken	1100	Rowing; single sculls, quarterfinal, heat 1
	Djurgårdsbrunnsviken	1120	Rowing; single sculls, quarterfinal, heat 2
	Djurgårdsbrunnsviken	1140	Rowing; single sculls, round one, heat 1 rerace
	Djurgårdsbrunnsviken	1200	Rowing; single sculls, quarterfinal, heat 3
	Djurgårdsbrunnsviken	1210	Rowing; single sculls, quarterfinal, heat 4
	Djurgårdsbrunnsviken	1220	Rowing; coxed fours outriggers, quarterfinals, heat 1
	Djurgårdsbrunnsviken	1240	Rowing; coxed fours outriggers, quarterfinals, heat 2

Date	Site	Time	Event
	Djurgårdsbrunnsviken	1300	Rowing; coxed fours outriggers, quarterfinals, heat 3
	Djurgårdsbrunnsviken	1320	Rowing; coxed fours outriggers, quarterfinals, heat 4
	Östermalm Tennis Pavilion	1400–1700	Sabre, individual; final pool
	Djurgårdsbrunnsviken	1540	Rowing; coxed eights, quarterfinals, heat 1
	Djurgårdsbrunnsviken	1600	Rowing; coxed eights, quarterfinals, heat 2
	Djurgårdsbrunnsviken	1620	Rowing; coxed eights, quarterfinals, heat 3
	Djurgårdsbrunnsviken	1930	Rowing; single sculls, quarterfinal, heat 1 rerace
	Prince Wilhelm Palace		Dinner given by HRH Prince Wilhelm, Duke of Södernmanland (the King's second son)
	Hasselbacken		Subscription ball arranged by Fältridtklubben (Stockholm Cross-Country Riding Club)
	Riksdagshuset		Meeting of the Northern Skating Congess
19 July	Djurgårdsbrunnsviken	1130	Rowing; coxed eights, semifinals, heat 1
	Djurgårdsbrunnsviken	1200	Rowing; coxed eights, semifinals, heat 2
	Djurgårdsbrunnsviken	1230	Rowing; single sculls, semifinal heat 1
	Djurgårdsbrunnsviken	1300	Rowing; single sculls, semifinal heat 2
	Djurgårdsbrunnsviken	1330	Rowing; coxed fours outriggers, semifinals, heat 1
	Djurgårdsbrunnsviken	1400	Rowing; coxed fours outriggers, semifinals, heat 2
	Djurgårdsbrunnsviken	1700	Rowing; single sculls, final
	Djurgårdsbrunnsviken	1730	Rowing; coxed fours outriggers, final
	Djurgårdsbrunnsviken	1800	Rowing; coxed eights, final
	Nynäshamn		Reception given by the Kungliga Svenska Segel Sällskapet (Royal Swedish Yacht Club)
	Hasselbacken		Farewell festivities given by the Rowing Committee
20 July	Nynäshamn	1100	Yachting—first race in each class
	Nynäshamn		Dinner given by Captain Oscar Holtermann, Gentleman of the Bedchamber, President of Kungliga Svenska Segel Sällskapet (the Royal Swedish Yachting Society)
21 July	Nynäshamn	1100	Yachting—second race in each class
	Riksdagshuset	1300	Congress of the Northern Rowing Association
22 July	Nynäshamn	1100	Yachting—sail-off races in 6-, 8-, and 10-meter classes
27 July	Prince Wilhelm Palace		Garden party for yachtsmen given by HRH Prince Wilhelm, Duke of Södermanland
	Hasselbacken	1900	Awards ceremony for yachting, and farewell banquet given by the Kungliga Svenska Segel Sällskapet (Royal Swedish Yacht Club), and the closing ceremony of the Games of the Vth Olympiad

Appendix II
In the Matter of
Jacobus Franciscus Thorpe

Jim Thorpe is considered by many sports historians as the greatest all-around athlete of all time, and that appellation is based mostly on his performances in the decathlon and pentathlon at the 1912 Olympic Games. In 1950 the Associated Press voted him the greatest American athlete of the half-century. By 2000, time had dulled the memory of his feats somewhat, as ESPN, in their poll of North American athletes, voted him only the seventh greatest athlete of the century. But for an athlete of such acclaim, it is surprising how much mystery surrounds Thorpe, and how much apocrypha has been written about him. It was once said of him, "In the interest of scholarship you will no doubt carefully analyze all stories that come to your attention. Some ridiculous stories concerning Thorpe have been published in magazines and books and have been solemnly repeated by reliable writers such as Grantland Rice and Arthur Daley. I repeat, watch carefully what you write because more lies have been written about Jim Thorpe than about any player in football history."[1]*

There have basically been four biographies of Jim Thorpe. Two of them — *The Jim Thorpe Story: America's Greatest Athlete* by Gene Schoor, and *Jim Thorpe: The Story of an American Indian* by Robert Reising — are primarily children's books. A better effort is *The Best of the Athletic Boys: The White Man's Impact on Jim Thorpe* by Jack Newcombe. The most complete biography is that by Robert W. Wheeler, *Jim Thorpe: World's Greatest Athlete*, which was based on research Wheeler conducted while doing his masters thesis at Syracuse University on Thorpe. Wheeler, and his wife, Florence Ridlon, were later instrumental in helping convince the International Olympic Committee to restore Thorpe's Olympic status.

Despite Wheeler and Newcombe's careful research, however, there are still holes in the story of Thorpe's life. In this short appendix, we will primarily address some of the controversies, and attempt to resolve some of them. Further, Wheeler's book came out prior to the restoration of Thorpe's medals, so we will address that controversy, the events of 1913, and the many attempts to restore Thorpe's amateur status. Finally, details of Thorpe's track & field career and baseball

*See Notes on pages 414–415.

career, primarily in minor-league baseball, have not previously been published, and we will look at his sports career in more detail.

The controversy begins with his tribal status, his proper name, and when he was born. Thorpe is usually described as a Sauk and Fox Indian, but his ancestry is far more complex than that simple description. Jim Thorpe was born to Hiram P. Thorp,[2] the son of Hiram G. Thorp, an Irish immigrant trapper, and No-ten-o-quah, a member of the Thunder Clan of Chief Black Hawk of the Sauk and Fox[3] Tribe. Jim Thorpe's mother was Charlotte Vieux,[4] who had been brought up as a Potawatomi Indian, but she was the daughter of a Frenchman and an Indian woman, Elizabeth Goslin, who had both Potawatomi and Kickapoo blood.[5] Charlotte Vieux was Hiram Thorp's third wife and she bore him 11 children.[6]

It is well known that Jim Thorpe's Indian name was "Wa-tho-huck," a Sauk and Fox name meaning "Bright Path." He is known to the modern world as Jim Thorpe, and it is often written that his full name was James Francis Thorpe, but that may not be precisely correct. No birth certificate exists for Jim Thorpe, which is not surprising when one realizes that he was born on an Indian reservation in Oklahoma, near the town of Bellemont.[7] Further, he was not actually born an American citizen as Indians were not accorded that status at the time. The state of Oklahoma has no birth certificate for Jim Thorpe.

A christening certificate does exist, however. And on the certificate, the name is Jacobus Franciscus Thorpe.[8] These are probably only Latinized versions of James Francis Thorpe, but still no official certificate exists to label him as such. It is unlikely that his parents, with their background, ever gave him formal names other than those by which he was christened. Thus his formal birth names are probably either Wa-tho-huck or Jacobus Franciscus Thorpe.

When was he born? The date is established — it was 28 May, and Wheeler notes that it was at 6:30 in the morning.[9] But was it 1886, 1887, or 1888, or even possibly 1889? All four dates are seen in various sources. Wheeler lists the year as 1888, and Olympic and track & field statisticians have usually used this date. The Society for American Baseball Research (SABR) lists the year as 1887, and this is the date listed in *Total Baseball*, the definitive statistical tome on baseball, and in Newcombe's book. However, we have also seen both 1886 and 1889, but these are certainly wrong. The Thorpe family claims that the year of birth was 1887. Further the year on the christening certificate also gives 1887, so he was certainly not born in 1888. Thus it appears that the correct date of birth is 28 May 1887.[10]

From birth, he was not alone. Jim Thorpe was one of twin brothers, the other being Charles Thorpe. Charlie died young, when he was only eight. By then the boys were enrolled in the Sauk and Fox Indian Agency School near Tecumseh, Oklahoma. In 1898, at age 11, Jim Thorpe was sent to the Haskell Indian Junior College in Lawrence, Kansas, one of the two Indian schools that had been set up by the U.S. government and military. He remained there until 1904. In June 1904, Jim Thorpe entered the second Indian school, Carlisle Indian School in Carlisle, Pennsylvania. There he became a legend as both a football player and track & field athlete.

Thorpe's football career at Carlisle has been well documented. He is considered the greatest American football player pre–World War I. He primarily played running back, but apparently could do everything on the football field. Very little has been written about his track & field career, except for his performances at Stockholm in the 1912 Olympics.

How good was he in track & field? While his records in football and baseball are relatively well-documented, almost nothing factual has ever been written about his track & field career. No other great track & field athlete has earned such a reputation based on only one meet and two events.

Thorpe was undefeated in the decathlon — he competed in only one, that being in the 1912 Olympics. It must be remembered that the decathlon was a new event, having been invented by the Swedes around 1910. The first decathlons in the United States were the 1912 Olympic

Trials, but Thorpe did not compete. There were only two entrants in the decathlon in the eastern Olympic trials, so Thorpe was added to the team based on the strength of his performance in the pentathlon trial the week previously. The committee was certainly influenced by the strength of Thorpe's record in the few years prior.

Jim Thorpe's track & field career actually began in 1907 at Carlisle, when he was 18 years old. At that time he stood 5-8 (173 cm.) and weighed about 120 lbs. (55 kg.) and his early performances reflected the immaturity of his young body. In the Carlisle School Spring Games he won the high hurdles and the high jump, but with very average marks — 19.0 and 5-3. He would compete that year for the track team in only one dual meet, that against Bucknell College. At Bucknell's field, he finished second in both the hurdles and the high jump, the two events which would remain his favorites throughout his career.

In 1908, Thorpe began to develop his reputation based in part on the fact that he had grown to 5-10 (178 cm.) and 150 lbs. (68 kg.) His first meet of the year was at the Penn Relays where he tied for first with Lynn Miller of Indiana. Thorpe won the trophy via a coin toss. Later, in dual and tri meets against Syracuse and then Swarthmore/Dickinson, Thorpe entered the same five events — high hurdles, low hurdles, high jump, long jump, and shot put — winning three at each meet. On 30 May he entered four events at the State Intercollegiate Meet, winning the high jump, finishing second in the low hurdles and shot put, but failing to qualify in the high hurdles. It is a very little known fact that Thorpe competed in the 1908 Eastern Olympic Trials in the high jump, but failed to qualify for the team.

In 1909 Thorpe, by then his full-grown 5-11 (180 cm.) and 185 lbs. (84 kg.), began to convince the world that he was something special in track & field as well as football. He routinely entered five or more events at dual meets, usually winning most of the events. On 6 May, against Syracuse, he entered eight events, winning five, finishing second in one and third in two. One of those wins was in the shot put, in which he defeated Bill Horr, who had finished sixth in the 1908 Olympics in the event. At the Middle Atlantic AAU Meet in Philadelphia, Thorpe entered five events. The score read — Thorpe 5, Field 0. In the State Intercollegiate Championships the score was exactly the same.

That was it for his track & field career for several years. In the summers of 1909 and 1910, Thorpe left school to work on farms and also play some semipro baseball in North Carolina, the job that would eventually keep him from ever again seeing his gold medals. In 1912 he returned to Carlisle, and the track & field world has possibly never since seen such a year.

Early in the season, Thorpe entered three indoor meets with only moderate success. It was apparently a case of his working into shape, for on 9 March he won four events at the Pittsburgh AC Indoor Meet and on 25 March he took four of five events at the Middle Atlantic AAU Indoor. He did not compete a lot outdoors for Carlisle in 1912. Early on, his best performance was in a dual against mighty Penn, where he entered seven events and won four.

On 18 May, Thorpe took part in the pentathlon Olympic trials. He won three of the five events and finished second in the other two, to win the trials with a score of 7 points. The results of all three American trials in the pentathlon are given below. The next week, on 25 May, were the aforementioned decathlon trials. Since they were canceled, Thorpe won a dual meet for Carlisle against Lafayette, by himself. He entered and won the high hurdles, low hurdles, high jump, long jump, shot put, and discus throw.

1912 American Pentathlon Olympic Trials:

16 May 1912 (Thursday) at Northwestern U Field, Evanston — Central Trials

	Points	1912A Table	1985 Table
1. Avery Brundage	7	3,379.525	3,098
(651 4192 23.6 3716 5:45.8)			
2. J. Austin Menaul	8	3,517.520	3,297
(638 4175 22.8 3050 4:51.2)			

18 May 1912 (Saturday) at Celtic Park, NY — Eastern Trials

	Points	1912A Table	1985 Table
1. Jim Thorpe	7	3,656.98	3,372
(661 4165 23.6 3517 4:49.8)			
2. Ths. A. McLaughlin	13	--	--
(564 NM 26.0 est 3268 4:49.0)			
3. Henry C. Klages	15	--	--
(561 3273 24.2 est 3498 5:14.2)			
4. Bruno Brodd	15	--	--
(628 4800 24.3 est 2842 5:45.8)			

21 May 1912 (Tuesday) at Berkeley, CA — Western Trials

	Points	1912A Table	1985 Table
1. James Donahue	--		
(668 4178 23.3 2718 5:00.0)			

Overall Scores

	Points	1912A Table	1985 Table
1. Jim Thorpe	7	3,656.98	3,372
(661 4165 23.6 3517 4:49.8)			
2. J. Austin Menaul	8	3,517.520	3,297
(638 4175 22.8 3050 4:51.2)			
3. Avery Brundage	7	3,379.525	3,098
(651 4192 23.6 3716 5:45.8)			
4. James Donahue	--		
(668 4178 23.3 2718 5:00.0)			

On 12 June the US Olympic team gathered for a meet at the Polo Grounds in New York to raise money for their trip to Stockholm. Thorpe competed in one event, the high jump, and won. But more important is his mark and the men he defeated. Thorpe jumped 6-5 (196 cm.), which would eventually be the second best performance in the high jump for 1912. He defeated Alma Richards (second), who would win the 1912 Olympic gold medal in the event; George Horine (third), who would win the bronze medal at Stockholm and had earlier set two world records in the high jump; and Harry Grumpelt (fourth), another American Olympic high jumper.

His work finished in America, he went to Stockholm and first won the pentathlon on 7 July, winning four of the five events and taking third in the javelin to win easily with only seven points. The next day he competed in the Olympic high jump but on that day cleared only 6-1¾ (187 cm.) to finish equal fourth. Four days later he took seventh in the long jump. On 13

July, he started the decathlon, in that year a three-day affair. His performance there is well known as he set a world record which would have stood until 1926, had it not been struck from the books.

After the Olympics Thorpe competed in three meets in Europe. At one of these he again demonstrated his amazing ability in individual events. On 24 July, in Reims, France, he ran the 110 meter high hurdles in 15.6 seconds, a world-class time and he defeated Fred Kelly, who was fresh from winning the gold medal in the event at Stockholm.[11]

Thorpe's track & field career was almost over. He returned to a hero's welcome in America and partied a bit much. In late August he was briefly hospitalized but was released on 1 September to compete in the AAU All-Around Championship the next day. The All-Around was the early American forerunner of the decathlon. It had been a national championship since the 1880s and was called by Avery Brundage a much greater test than the decathlon. It also had ten events, slightly different from the decathlon, but all of these were held in a single day. September 2, 1912, dawned cold and rainy in New York. Conditions, however, and his recent illness, could not hamper Jim Thorpe. He won the All-Around title, breaking Martin Sheridan's world record in the process. He scored 7,476 points and won by over 3,000 points. But his track & field career was over.

What of Jim Thorpe's baseball career? It has been written that he was a poor excuse for a major-league player, but this is probably unwarranted denigration. He was no star, but he was an adequate major-leaguer. In his final major-league year, 1919, he batted .327 for 62 games. But most of his baseball career was spent in the minor leagues and via Ray Nemec, a member of the Society for American Baseball Research (SABR), we have been able to obtain details of Thorpe's almost complete record in organized baseball. Details are missing only for 1908, when he probably played some minor-league ball in Anardako, Oklahoma in the Oklahoma-Kansas Leagues. The record is as follows:[12]

Jim Thorpe's Organized Baseball Record

Batting

Year	Club	League	Pos	G	AB	R	H	TB	2B	3B	HR	RBI	SB	PCT
1908	Anardako	Okla-Kansas	[13]											
1909	Rocky Mount	East. Carol.	P-OF	44	138	11	35	42	4	0	1		6	.253
1910	Rocky Mount	East. Carol.	P-OF	29	76	11	18	22	2	1	0		4	.236
	Fayetteville	East. Carol.	1B	16	52	6	13	15	0	1	0		7	.250
	Year total	East. Carol.		45	128	17	31	37	2	2	0		11	.242
1911	out of organized baseball													
1912	out of organized baseball													
1913	New York	National	OF	19	35	6	5	8	0	0	1	2	2	.143
1914	New York	National	OF	30	31	5	6	7	1	0	0	2	1	.194
1915	New York	National	OF	17	52	8	12	17	3	1	0	1	4	.231
	Jersey C/Harris.	International	OF	96	370	51	112	145	13	7	2		22	.303
1916	Milwaukee	Amer. Assoc.	OF	143	573	85	157	240	25	14	10		48*	.274
1917	Cincinnati	National	OF	77	251	29	62	92	2	8	4	36	11	.247
	New York	National	OF	26	57	12	11	18	3	2	0	4	1	.193
	Year total	National		103	308	41	73	110	5	10	4	40	12	.237
1918	New York	National	OF	58	113	15	28	43	4	4	1	11	3	.248
1919	New York	National	OF	2	3	0	1	1	0	0	0	1	0	.333
	Boston	National	OF-1B	60	156	16	51	67	7	3	1	25	7	.327

Year	Club	League	Pos	G	AB	R	H	TB	2B	3B	HR	RBI	SB	PCT
	Year total	National		62	159	16	52	68	7	3	1	26	7	.327
1920	Akron	International	OF	128	522	102	188	294	28	15	16		22	.360
1921	Toledo	Amer. Assoc.	OF	133	505	79	181	270	36	13	9	112	34	.358
1922	Portland	Pacific Coast	OF	35	120	13	37	47	3	2	1	14	5	.308
	Hartford/Worces.	Eastern	OF	96	381	59	131	207	23	13	9		19	.344
	Year total	Pac. Co/East		131	501	72	168	254	26	15	10		24	.335
Career Major Leagues				289	698	91	176	253	20	18	7	82	29	.252

Pitching

Year	Club	League	W	L	Pct
1909	Rocky Mount	Eastern Carolina	9	10	.474
1910	Rocky Mount	Eastern Carolina	10	10	.500

Team Names

Akron Buckeyes; Fayetteville Highlanders; Harrisburg Senators; Hartford Senators; Jersey City Skeeters; Milwaukee Brewers; Portland Beavers; Rocky Mount Railroaders; Toledo Mud Hens; Worcester Boosters

Jim Thorpe later played professional football, but by then he was definitely in the twilight of his athletic brilliance. When Thorpe starred for Carlisle on the gridiron, there was no true professional football league, although there were scattered barnstorming teams. While still playing major-league baseball, Thorpe signed with one of those teams in 1915, the Canton Bulldogs. He was paid the then astronomical sum of $250.00 (US) per game. He played for the Bulldogs from 1915 through 1919 while they were still an independent team. By then he was 32 years old, but still the most feared runner in the game.

On 20 August 1920, the National Football League (NFL) was established among four barnstorming professional teams from Ohio — Akron, Canton, Cleveland, and Dayton. Because of his name and prominence, Thorpe was appointed as the first president of the National Football League. He continued to play as well, since he was the biggest drawing card in the nascent league, and would remain so until Red Grange finished his college career at the University of Illinois in 1925 and joined the Chicago Bears. Jim Thorpe played in the NFL from 1920 to 26 and again in 1928. By then he was 41 years old, ancient for a football player, and was but a shadow of his former greatness.

Thorpe's professional football career in the NFL is poorly documented but can be summarized as follows:[14]

Jim Thorpe's Organized Professional Football Record

1920	Canton Bulldogs	9 Games
1921	Cleveland	5 Games, 1 Rushing TD, 1 Passing TD, 1 FG, 11 Points
1922	Oorang Indians	5 Games, 3 Rushing TD, 1 Passing TD, 18 Points
1923	Oorang Indians	9 Games, 1 Passing TD, 1 FG, 3 Points
1924	Rock Island Independents	9 Games, 1 Passing TD, 2 FG, 1 XP, 7 Points
1925	New York Giants/Rock Island	5 Games (3 Games New York Giants; 2 Games Rock Island)
1926	Canton Bulldogs	9 Games, 2 Rushing TD, 12 Points
1928	Chicago Cardinals	1 Game
Total		*52 Games, 6 Rushing TD, 4 Passing TD, 4 FG, 3 XP, 51 Points*

How good was he as a football player? As did many other magazines, *Football Digest* produced an end of century special in June 1999, listing the Top 100 football players of all time. Thorpe was ranked 17th. This is especially significant when one notices that few old-timers made the list. The only other player from the 1920s was Red Grange, who was ranked 93rd. The only other primarily pre–WWII players were: Don Hutson (11th, 1935–45); Bronko Nagurski (33rd, 1930–43); George Musso (85th, 1933–44); and Mel Hein (87th, 1931–45).

In early 1913, it was revealed that Thorpe had played minor-league baseball in the United States, as described above. For this he was retroactively declared a professional by the AAU (Amateur Athletic Union) and the IOC and his records at the 1912 Olympics were declared void. He had to return his gold medals, and his challenge trophies.[15] What is not so well known is that Thorpe should never have been disqualified in the first place.

In 1982, when Bob Wheeler and Florence Ridlon and the Thorpe family succeeded in their long struggle to have Jim Thorpe's medals restored by the International Olympic Committee, it was revealed in *Sports Illustrated* that a key factor in this decision was a discovery by Ridlon, who found a pamphlet in the Library of Congress which gave the rules and regulations for the 1912 Olympic Games. It stated that the statute of limitations for a claim against any Olympic athlete's eligibility in 1912 had to have been made within 30 days after the awarding of the prizes. The announcement of Thorpe's professional baseball career occurred in January 1913, almost six months after the end of the Olympics. Thus his disqualification was completely unwarranted.

Ms. Ridlon is to be commended for this find, but she actually need not have looked so hard. The exact same phrase is easily found in the 1912 *Official Report*. In the report, the Swedish organizing committee defined amateur status and also defined the rules concerning the qualifications of the athletes, as follows:

Amateur Definitions

This general amateur rule, which was the same for *Athletics*, the *Tug-of-War* and *Wrestling*, was as follows:

The competition shall be confined to amateurs according to the following definition:—

An amateur is one who has never

a) competed for a money prize or for monetary consideration, or in any way drawn pecuniary gain from the exercise of his sport;

b) competed against a professional;

c) taught in any branch of sport for payment;

d) sold, pawned, hired out or exhibited for payment, any prize won in a competition.

General Rules for the Olympic Games

Rule #13 — Objections to the qualification of a competitor must be made in writing, and be forwarded without delay to the Swedish Olympic Committee.

No such objection shall be entertained unless accompanied by a deposit of 20 Swedish Kronor and received by the Swedish Olympic Committee before the lapse of 30 days from the distribution of the prizes.

The Swedish Olympic Committee shall decide on such objections after having obtained all necessary information, and its decision shall be final.

The deposit shall be forfeited if the objection shall appear to have been made on unreasonable grounds. If, on the other hand, the objection is upheld or appears to have been made on reasonable grounds, the deposit will be returned.[16]

The pamphlet found by Ridlon was the *Fifth Olympiad. Olympic Games of Stockholm, Sweden. 1912. (June 29th—July 22nd)—Programme and General Regulations.* It contained the exact same wording as the above Rule #13. It is unfortunate that nobody in 1912 realized that Rule #13 meant that Thorpe should not have been disqualified. Or was it so unfortunate?

To examine this question, we need to look a bit at the events of January 1913, during the few days in which Thorpe's amateur status was the subject of multiple newspaper articles. It is usually stated that the story of Thorpe's professional baseball status was revealed in a story in the *Worcester Telegram* on 23 January 1913.[17] This may be true, but if so, it is very obscure. We have searched throughout the *Worcester Telegram* at the Library of Congress and have not found the article. Further, longtime *Worcester Telegram* sportswriter Henry Landress also searched the archives at his newspaper at our request and was unable to find the article.[18]

Wheeler also states that the story was repeated five days later, 28 January 1913, in the *New York Times*. The earliest evidence we can find for the revelation is an article in the *Providence Times*, dated 24 January 1913. The story notes that Charles Clancy, former manager of the Rocky Mount Railroaders, for whom Thorpe played minor league baseball, was interviewed in his office. He stated:

> Thorpe played under his own name on the Rocky Mount team of the Eastern Carolina Association, of which I am manager for two years. The amateur athletic authorities simply never heard of his professional baseball career. I was pleased to see him get along so well in the Indian school and never said much about his playing on my team for two years. I signed him up as a pitcher but I thought he had a yellow streak at times. He would go along well for seven innings and then he would develop a lame arm. The arm would be all right the next day. A few things of that kind decided me to switch him to first base, where he broke in pretty well.
>
> He wasn't a wonderful hitter, but when he met the ball square on the nose it was usually good for a home run. He was mighty fast on the bases, that was his best point. If he got on he usually scored if there was any kind of chance.[19]

It is somewhat surprising that it took this long for Thorpe's professional identity to be revealed. In fact, only three days after the end of the 1912 Olympic decathlon (15 July), the *Charlotte Observer* ran the following story in its sports pages:

> Jim Thorp [*sic*], who, in the Olympic games at Stockholm proved himself the greatest all-round athlete in the world, was once traded for Pete Boyle, whom *The Observer* calls the best all-round baseball player in the Carolina League. Boyle was playing with the Fayetteville Highlanders under Clancy in 1910, the last year of the Eastern Carolina League, and had pitched fifteen games during the first half of the season without losing a single battle.
>
> Thorp was playing for Jim Connor, an old friend of Clancy's, at Rocky Mount, and was not doing much on the slab but was keeping up his stick work, which is a way he has, when a four-cornered deal that startled the little circuit was announced. Clancy had traded Peartree, a light-hitting outfielder, for Schumann, a veteran, who had led the league in batting the year before, while Connor was to give him Thorp for Boyle. After joining Rocky Mount, Boyle continued his brilliant work, while Peartree started burning a streak up the paths and at the bat, and up went the cry that Clancy had been "stung." But the big silent Indian proved the very man Clancy needed. He pitched but one game and asked to be relieved in the early stages at that, and was placed in the outfield for his stick work. Dobson had been sold to

Richmond and Schumaker to Columbia and Old Man Tim Dwyer, a third-sacker, was filling in at first. Clancy conceived the idea of trying Thorp at the first sack, and he put him there. The Big Chief proved a sensation at the bag. His great height and reach enabled him to take almost anything without shifting his feet; his work was heady and his throwing a revelation.

Thorp, despite his mountainous size, was the swiftest man who ever played ball in this section. He possesses tremendous strength, and many are the tales still told of his prowess in these regions. The longest hit ever made here was his. The big Indian is also, perhaps, the best all-round football player in America.[20]

The article was presumably not noticed at the time. But shortly after the January revelations about Thorpe, the *New York Times* ran an article, with the headline, "KNEW THORPE WAS A 'PRO': North Carolinians Surprised That He Had Been Classed as an Amateur."[21] The story then discussed the above article that had run in the *Charlotte Observer* six months previously.

After the 24 January 1913 story ran in the *Providence Times*, the newspapers were filled with stories concerning Thorpe's professional status. On Saturday, 25 January 1913, *The New York Times* ran a denial from Glenn "Pop" Warner, who had been Thorpe's football coach at Carlisle.

All I know about the charges against Thorpe have been gleaned from newspaper reports to the effect that a Mr. Clancy, Manager of a Southern ball team, had been quoted as saying that Thorpe played professional baseball with the Winston-Salem team under his management. I am in receipt of a letter from Mr. Clancy to-day in which he incloses [sic] a newspaper clipping, in which he had formally denied ever making the statement attributed to him in an alleged interview published in The Worcester Telegram. Mr. Clancy says: "I never made the statement that I signed Thorpe to pitch for my club, nor did I in any way question his amateur standing. I intend writing to President [James Edward] Sullivan of the Amateur Athletic Union to-day inclosing [sic] the article and explaining to him that it was absolutely all wrong.

In Mr. Clancy's letter to me, he further stated: "As a matter of fact and record, Mr. Thorpe has never pitched a game at all for the Winston-Salem team or played in any other position in that club, or in the Carolina League, and I have never paid Thorpe any money for any purpose. The article in the Worcester paper is not founded in facts, and was published without any authority."[22]

Warner also added, "I am further assured by Thorpe that there is nothing in the story." Charlie Clancy was certainly lying in the above quotes, in an attempt to help Jim Thorpe. Wheeler quoted an interview with Ernie Shore, a former major-league pitcher, who noted Clancy's obvious concern that he had exposed Thorpe's minor-league career. "Charlie was the highest type of gentleman and the conversation in question was a friendly one. If he had known how it would turn out, he wouldn't have told for the world. I talked to him after it had happened and he felt awfully bad."[23]

It took only a few days for Thorpe's Olympic career to be forever stained. On 26 January 1913, the *New York Times* ran quotes from several minor-league baseball players who remembered having played with Thorpe. One was B. C. Stewart, who stated he had played with "the Indian on the Winston-Salem team."[24] More damning were the quotes from the aforementioned Pete Boyle. He noted that he had played with Thorpe on the Fayetteville team in the Eastern Carolina league in 1910, and stated that he could identify him from old photographs. Boyle was described as having a reputation as "somewhat of a sprinter" but noted that he had been soundly beatened by Thorpe in a 100-yard race.[25]

On 27 January 1913, AAU Secretary James E. Sullivan began his formal investigation into the matter. Glenn "Pop" Warner was to come to New York and bring all the information he had on the matter. Sullivan had the following comments:

> If Thorpe is guilty, we want to find it out as soon as possible. We have no desire to cover up the doings of any one connected with the A.A.U. who may be charged with having broken the laws of amateur competition. This is a matter in which a delay is dangerous to the best interests of the union, and because Thorpe chances to be the accredited greatest athlete in America is no reason why prompt action should not be taken.
>
> It has been said that sustained charges against Thorpe would not be acted upon with the speed that would prevail in the case of an ordinary athlete. In reply to this I will say that we will act with greater dispatch than would prevail with the action in regard to any other athlete in America.
>
> If he is found to have broken the rules, as stated, he will be stripped of all his records; his name will be taken from athletic annuals, and he will be compelled to return all the prizes he has won since his infraction of the rules.
>
> While it has never been shown that he has broken the amateur law in any form of track and field competition over which the Amateur Athletic Union has jurisdiction, the fact that he signed a registration blank attesting that he had never in any manner transgressed the amateur rule makes him amenable to discipline by the Amateur Athletic Union, the Board of Managers of which, however distasteful to it to have an athlete of such status break the rules, will legislate as in the case of an athlete of minor importance.
>
> The remarkable feature of the case is that the baseball sharps of the country have not intimated this reputed wrong-doing long before this. It is known that the Pittsburgh league team managers had their eyes on Thorpe several years ago, and yet aside from rumors that Thorpe was slated to join that team nothing else was known of his intended professional tendencies until last week.
>
> In regard to his signing up with the Pirates, at Glenn Warner's instigation, I wrote Thorpe last year advising him to give up any such intention, and was rewarded with a note from Thorpe to the effect that such was the furthest thing from his intentions.
>
> The whole affair is probably the worst blow which could be struck to American athletics, but I am convinced that those who are aware of the interests of the Governors of the A.A.U. in the conservation of the purity of sport under their dominion will admit that it is something over which they had next to no control.
>
> At any rate, their position will be directly opposite to the condition which prevailed across the water several years ago when, upon the haling up of a champion before the tribunal which was to inquire into his amateur standing, stated that he was dumfounded [*sic*] to find that his judges were the very men who had paid him to transgress the amateur laws.
>
> No such a state of affairs can be ascribed to this case. Every phase in connection the charges have emanated from men mixed up in professional baseball, of whom I will say that they were probably unaware of the infringement of the amateur laws in connection with the supposed wrongdoing. It may cost the A.A.U. plenty of money to get at the facts in this case, but aside from those at present known, the Union will delve into it until it is cleared up, no matter what the expense.

Of course one thing which must be taken into consideration in the criticism which American athletics will have to stand for in this case is that no such conditions exist in any other part of the world. Here we have the Indian youth taken from environments that to say the least for them are peculiar, put in an institution controlled by the United States Government, and from reports emanating from these institutions from time to time we are prone to feel proud of the way we are bringing up the heretofore benighted red man.

It has been the custom to make pets of the crack Indian athletes, and because of their strange origin nothing back of their Government school careers has ever been delved into. It probably came natural before these lads came into contact with the registration feature of the A.A.U. to go out in their free times like Summer vacations and play baseball. If they got money for it it wouldn't serve as a saving grace for any one who did such a thing and then afterward desired to compete in amateur events, but in the case of the Indian whose life is laid out in grooves altogether different from ours there is something to be said that can't be brought to bear on the case of the boy whose upbringing has been on the best and most approved lines.[26]

This complete and thorough investigation to which Sullivan alluded, accompanied by the compassion he described in the last paragraph above, took all of one day. On 28 January 1913, the headlines read "OLYMPIC PRIZES LOST; THORPE NO AMATEUR Carlisle School Indian Admits He Once Played Professional Baseball in the South." Thorpe was required to return the gold medals he had won in Stockholm and the challenge trophies that had been awarded to him for winning the decathlon and pentathlon.

In reply to the AAU charges, Thorpe wrote the following somewhat poignant letter:

Carlisle, Penn., Jan. 26, 1913

James E. Sullivan, New York, N.Y.

Dear Sir —

When the interview with Mr. Clancy, stating that I had played baseball on the Winston-Salem team was shown me I told Mr. Warner that it was not true, and in fact I did not play on that team. But so much has been said in the papers since then that I went to the school authorities this morning and told them just what there was in the stories,

I played baseball at Rocky Mount and Fayetteville, N.C., in the summer of 1909 and 1910, under my own name. On the same teams I played with were several college men from the North who were earning money by ball-playing during their vacations and who were regarded as amateurs at home. I did not play for the money there was in it, because my property brings me in enough money to live on, but because I liked to play ball. I was not very wise to the ways of the world and did not realize that this was wrong, and it would make me a professional in track sports, altho I learned from the other players that it would be better for me not to let any one know that I was playing, and for that reason I never told any one at the school about it until to-day.

In the fall of 1911, I applied for re-admission to this school and came back to continue my studies and take part in school sports, and, of course, I wanted to get on the Olympic team and take the trip to Stockholm. I had Mr. Warner send in my application for registering in the A.A.U., after I had answered the questions and signed it, and I received my card allowing me to compete in the winter meets and other track sports. I never realized until now what a big mistake I made by keeping it a secret about my ball-playing, and I am sorry I did so. I hope I will be partly excused by the fact that I was simply an Indian schoolboy and did not know all about such things. In fact, I did not know that I was doing wrong, because I was doing what I knew several other college men had done, except that they did not use their own names.

I have always liked sport and only played or ran races for the fun of the thing and never to earn money. I have received offers amounting to thousands of dollars since my victories last summer, but I have turned them all down because I did not care to make money from my athletic skill. I am very sorry, Mr. Sullivan, to have it all spoiled in this way, and I hope the Amateur Athletic Union and the people will not be too hard in judging me.

(Signed) JAMES THORPE[27]

The AAU committee judging the Thorpe case comprised of James E. Sullivan, Chairman of the Registration Committee and Secretary of the AAU and American Olympic Committee; Gustavus T. Kirby, President of the AAU and Vice-President of the American Olympic Committee; and Bartow S. Weeks, Chairman of the Legislation Committee of the AAU and Vice-President of the American Olympic Committee. They issued a press release on the same day that Thorpe's letter was revealed.

The Team Selection Committee of the American Olympic Committee selected James Thorpe as one of the members of the Americans Olympic team, and did so without the least suspicion as to there having ever been any act of professionalism on Thorpe's part.

For the past several years Thorpe has been a member of the Carlisle Indian School, which is conducted by the Government of the United States at Carlisle, Pa., through the Indian Department of the Department of the Interior.

Mr. Glenn Warner, formerly of Cornell, a man whose reputation is of the highest and whose accuracy of statement has never been doubted, has been in charge of the athletic activities of the institution. During the period of Mr. Thorpe's membership at Carlisle he competed on its football, baseball, and track and field teams, and represented it in intercollegiate and other contests, all of which were open only to amateurs, as neither Carlisle nor any of the institutions with which it competes has other than amateur teams.

Thorpe's standing as an amateur had never been questioned, nor was any protest ever made against him or any statement ever made as to his even having practised with professionals, let alone having played with or as one of them.

The widest possible publicity was given the team selected by the American Olympic Committee, and it seems strange that men having knowledge of Mr. Thorpe's professional conduct did not at such time, for the honor of their country, come forward and place in the hands of the American committee such information as they had.

No such information was given, nor was a suggestion even made as to Thorpe's being other than the amateur which he was supposed to be. This country is of such tremendous territorial expanse, and the athletes taking part therein are so numerous, that it is sometimes extremely difficult to ascertain the history of an athlete's past. In the selection of the American team the committee endeavored to use every possible precaution, and where there was the slightest doubt as to a man's amateur standing, his entry was not considered.

Thorpe's act of professionalism was in a sport over which the Amateur Athletic Union has no direct control; it was as a member of a baseball team in a minor league, and in games which were not reported in the important papers of the country. That he played under his own name would give no direct notice to any one concerned, as there are many of his name. The reason why he himself did not give notice of his acts is explained by him on the ground of ignorance. In some justification of this position, it should be noted that Mr. Thorpe is an Indian of limited experience and education in the ways of other than his own people.

The American Olympic Committee and the Amateur Athletic Union feel that while Mr. Thorpe is deserving of the severest condemnation for concealing the fact that he had professionalized himself by receiving money for playing baseball, they also feel that those who knew of his professional acts are deserving of still greater censure for their silence.

The American Olympic Committee and the Amateur Athletic Union tender to the Swedish Olympic Committee and through the International Olympic Committee to the nations of the world, their apology for having entered Mr. Thorpe and having permitted him to compete at the Olympic games of 1912.

The Amateur Athletic Union regrets that it permitted Mr. Thorpe to compete in amateur contests during the past several years, and will do everything in its power to secure the return of prizes and the re-adjustment of points won by him, and will immediately eliminate his records from the books.[28]

Obviously the decision was clear. Thorpe had violated the rules of amateur status and his victories had to be declared invalid. Or was it so clear? What about Rule #13, stating that protests had to be made within the 30 days after the end of the awarding of prizes at the 1912 Olympic Games? Did Sullivan's committee not know of this rule? However, even if they did, Sullivan et al. make the case that ignorance was no excuse for Thorpe. What of their own ignorance of the rule about the statute of limitations to protest the results? Perhaps they were not so ignorant.

In fact, within one day of the above statements running in the *New York Times*, the *New York Herald* ran the following story:

Swedes Don't Want Thorpe's Trophies

STOCKHOLM, Jan. 29.—Swedish newspapers, commenting on the disclosure that James Thorpe was a professional athlete when he competed in the Olympic games, held here last summer, commend the honesty displayed by the Americans in making the fact known.

Leading authorities in the field of sport express the opinion that Thorpe is entitled to retain the prizes he won in the pentathlon and decathlon events, *as his status as an amateur had been raised too late.*[29]

The same article ran on 29 January 1913 in the *New York Times*.[30] Further, in the 8 February 1913 issue of the *Literary Digest*, only 11 days after the Thorpe-Sullivan announcements, the following item ran:

All the leading men in athletic circles think it will be impossible to cancel the prizes won by Thorpe, as the rules for the Olympic games in Stockholm clearly prescribe that protests against the amateur standing of participants must be made within thirty days after the distribution of the prizes. They consider that the only way of revoking the awards will be for the Amateur Athletic Union to demand it at the Olympic meeting at Lausanne, Switzerland, next summer.[31]

So obviously, James Sullivan and his vaunted AAU had to know within days of their disqualification of Thorpe, that they were themselves violating the rules of the 1912 Olympic organizing committee. Did they make any efforts to comment on this? There is nothing in the newspapers of any kind.

One must realize that James Sullivan wanted to control all sports in the United States and probably throughout the world. He had once called for the dissolution of the International Olympic Committee, and he feuded openly with Baron Pierre de Coubertin. Sullivan was likely irked that Coubertin never placed him on the IOC. Perhaps this was nothing but a power play by Sullivan to demonstrate to Coubertin, the British sports authorities, with whom he openly feuded during the 1908 Olympics in London, and all sports associations in the United States, that he was the man in control, and nobody should attempt to violate his glorifed "amateur laws." How else to explain Sullivan ignoring the statute of limitations, of which he had to be aware? But this is speculation. Sullivan's archives were later lost in a fire, and there is nothing in the records to suggest that Sullivan ever commented on the matter of the statute of limitations regarding the Thorpe case.[32]

Other things also do not fit. Wheeler notes that questions concerning Thorpe's amateur status had been raised in the autumn of 1911.[33] He speculates that the United States needed a top all-around athlete for the decathlon and pentathlon and chose Thorpe, knowing him to be their best, rumors or no rumors. Thus, it is possible that Sullivan, the AAU, and the American Olympic committee, knew that Thorpe was no simon pure amateur, but used him for their own purposes. Then, when he was found out, they used him again, to support their own goals in sports administration.

Further support for this theory comes from a Wheeler interview with Joe Libby, a teammate of Thorpe's at Carlisle Indian School. Glenn "Pop" Warner pleaded that he had no knowledge of Thorpe's minor-league baseball efforts. But Libby told Wheeler that he, Thorpe, and Jesse Youngdeer were sent to Rocky Mount *by* Warner. Wheeler noted, "Libby said he told the three he had arranged for them to go there and play baseball in the summer to keep in shape. When the scandal broke, Warner disclaimed any knowledge of it. But as it turned out, he was behind the entire situation. They were young Indian kids, unaware of the amateur rules and regulations, but Warner certainly wasn't."[34]

Within days of the announcement of his disqualification, Thorpe was being courted by major-league baseball teams and quickly signed a contract with the New York Giants. He then began his career as a professional baseball player, playing through 1922, as noted above. He began playing professional football as well, ending that career in 1928. He later worked as an extra and stuntman in movies in Hollywood. But the controversy of his disqualification haunted him throughout his life and it never really died. His son later commented, "He was always kind of bitter that it happened…. It wasn't the kind of thing he talked about continually. He didn't always bring it up. But I know that all his life he wanted to be vindicated."[35]

What of the aforementioned IOC Session in the summer of 1913? Wolf Lyberg's description is as follows: "The main item of the Session was the so called Thorpe Affaire from the Games 1912. After a very long discussion it was unanimously decided (and in complete accordance with the wish of the US IOC-members) to revise the results of the decathlon and pentathlon and to hand over the medals [and] the Challenges 'to the rightful and legal winner of them.'

"The Duke of Somerset and de Courcy-Laffan suggested that a special note should be added to the minutes in which 'the firm and very sporting attitude of the American IOC-members' should be mentioned. This proposal was carried unanimously."[36]

Over the years numerous attempts were made to get the IOC to reverse the decision, mostly started by Thorpe's children. Marty Hurney of the *Washington Times*, described the various attempts. "Damon Runyan made the first effort in 1914. Others (Franklin D. Roosevelt, Branch Rickey and Gerald R. Ford to name only three) followed and failed. But a few, if any, offered as much time and intensity as Robert Wheeler and Florence Ridlon."[37]

Some efforts succeeded gradually. In 1973, the AAU restored Thorpe's amateur status for the years 1909 through 1912. This was followed in 1975 by the United States Olympic Committee making a similar restoration. The next time Thorpe is mentioned in the IOC minutes is in those of the 1976 session in Montreal. It was noted, "It was unanimously considered to be out of the question to return the medals of Jim Thorpe to the relatives who had claimed them. Much too many years had passed since 1912!!"[38]

In 1979–80, the U.S. Jaycees started a petition campaign and gathered over 200,000 signatures requesting that Thorpe's victories and medals in Stockholm be restored. This occurred almost concurrently with U.S. Senate Resolution No. 29 to the same effect, introduced in the United States Senate by Sen. Alan Cranston (D-CA), and cosponsored in the United States House of Representatives by the Hon. Victor Fazio (D-CA). It passed unanimously in both houses of Congress and was forwarded to the U.S. Olympic Committee, but nothing came of it.[39]

On 27 February 1982, Wheeler and Ridlon founded the Jim Thorpe Foundation, expressly for the purpose of having his medals and honors restored. One of the members of the council of advisors to the foundation was the Hon. James J. Howard (D-NJ) of the U.S. House of Representatives. On 21 June 1982, Rep. Howard sponsored legislation in that house aimed at achieving restoration of Thorpe's medals. A portion of his statement is as follows:

> Mr. Speaker, I have introduced legislation to correct an injustice to an American of the highest caliber, Jim Thorpe.... These allegations were ruled incorrect by the U.S. Amateur Athletic Union in 1975 [*sic*].[40] This decision was endorsed by the U.S. Olympic Committee later in the same year. Nevertheless the International Olympic Committee has refused the overtures of these respected bodies
>
> I have introduced a concurrent resolution supporting the return of those medals and awards taken from Jim Thorpe by the International Olympic Committee. House Concurrent Resolution 364 seeks the return of Jim Thorpe's medals for presentation to his famiy at the 1984 Olympics in Los Angeles, Calif.

House Concurrent Resolution 364 was approved on 15 September 1982 by the House Foreign Affairs subcommittee.

Armed with the "new" information concerning the statute of limitations, and with stronger backing of the United States sports authorities and Congress, the IOC began to pay attention. Finally, all the efforts paid off. On 13 October 1982, only eight months after the formation of the Jim Thorpe Foundation, but fully 70 years too late, the IOC Executive Board approved, in a sense, the restoration of Jim Thorpe's medals. Strangely, Lyberg's notes on the IOC session for March 1983 do not mention the decision, which seems to have been taken solely by the Executive Board. By that time, the Thorpe family had finally been honored. At another meeting of the IOC Executive Board, this time on 18 January 1983 in Los Angeles, commemorative medals were presented to Bill and Gail Thorpe, two of Thorpe's children. It seemed that the matter was finally over.

But not fully. The IOC, in a very strange ruling, decreed that Thorpe would only be declared cowinner with Hugo Wieslander (decathlon) and Ferdinand Bie (pentathlon). This angered the Thorpe family and Wheeler and Ridlon. Further, only commemorative medals were given to the Thorpe family. What of the original medals?

It is well known that both Wieslander and Bie did not consider themselves the winners of the decathlon and pentathlon, respectively, at the 1912 Olympics. Both commented several times that Thorpe was the true champion. Apparently both offered to return the medals to Thorpe, but nothing came of it. Hugo Wieslander was presented the decathlon gold medal at a ceremony in the Olympic Stadium in 1913. In 1951, he donated it to the Swedish Sports Museum. Jim Thorpe died in March 1953. One year later, the Thorpe-Wieslander medal was stolen from the Swedish Sports Museum and has not been seen since.

Ferdinand Bie later commented that the disqualification of Thorpe was unfair and that he had always had mixed feelings about receiving the gold medal.[41] Similarly, Ferdinand Bie's medal was donated to a Norwegian sports museum, but it was also stolen and its whereabouts are unknown.

Thus the original medals could not be returned to the Thorpe family. What about the challenge trophies, which were still in the possession of the IOC? Fortunately for the IOC, competitors at the 1912 Olympic Games had to sign a pledge promising to return the challenge trophies before the opening of the next Olympic Games. Sleuthing through the Riksarkivet in Stockholm (the Swedish National Archives), Lyberg was able to find this pledge, signed by Thorpe, for the IOC, and they did not have to return the trophies.

Why were commemorative medals presented to the Thorpe family and not duplicates of the originals? This is unknown. Perhaps the original dies no longer exist?[42] But all these inconsistencies puzzled and angered the Thorpe family and supporters of Jim Thorpe.

Nonetheless, at least some closure has taken place. Finally, the IOC saw and admitted what the world had always known. Jim Thorpe was the winner of the decathlon and the pentathlon at the 1912 Olympic Games in Stockholm, and despite all the century-ending polls to the contrary, still, 88 years later, "You, sir, are the greatest athlete in the world."

NOTES

1. Letter from Col. Alexander M. Weyand, former U.S. wrestling Olympian and sports and football historian, in a letter to Robert Wheeler dated 24 October 1967. Quoted by Wheeler in the frontispiece to his biography of Thorpe, *Jim Thorpe: World's Greatest Athlete*, Norman, OK: Univ. of Oklahoma Press, 1975.

2. Hiram's last name, and even Jim's, was variously spelled Thorp and Thorpe. Newcombe describes the spelling of the last name as follows: "The spelling of the name, with or without an 'e,' became increasingly inconsistent as it appeared on annuity rolls, legal papers, letters signed by family members through the years. In the earliest Sac and Fox records and on allotment patent deeds it was usually Thorp; when Jim and his twin brother Charles first entered the Indian Agency School in 1893 they were Thorpes on the class rolls. After that, each teacher chose her own spelling."

3. Alternatively spelled Sac and Fox. We use Sauk for the following reason. The American coauthor of this book's wife (Karen Mallon) is originally from Rock Fall, Illinois, a small town on the Rock River. The Sauk and Fox tribe settled on the Rock River and that town is in Sauk County. The two-year college in the town is the Sauk Valley Community College.

4. Also spelled View in an Anglicized form.

5. Newcombe, p. 29.

6. *Ibid*. Newcombe notes that Hiram Thorpe fathered at least 19 known children by five different wives.

7. Some sources say Prague, Oklahoma, but this is based on Wheeler.

8. We have not actually seen the christening certificate. See the later footnote concerning the date on it.

9. *Ibid.*, p. 3.

10. Again, we have not seen the christening certificate. This is based on information from Thorpe's family to John Mallon, father of one of the coauthors of this book. John Mallon, in his later years, became an expert genealogist, and was researching the details of Thorpe's birth in an

attempt to get this precisely correct. He was the one who corresponded with the authorities in Oklahoma to confirm that no birth certificate existed. He also wrote to the church where Thorpe was christened. He corresponded with Grace Thorpe, who told him of the details of the christening certificate — notably the year of 1887 and the name of Jacobus Franciscus Thorpe. John Mallon wrote Grace Thorpe, requesting a copy of the certificate, but none was ever sent. The church also never responded to requests for copies of the certificate. Further, one author of this book, Bill Mallon, wrote to the Thorpe family requesting copies of the certificate, with no response. On 13 July 2000, John Mallon, an Olympian of a Dad to Bill Mallon, died from pneumonia, aged 85. Unfortunately, details of the correspondence between John Mallon and Grace Thorpe cannot be found.

11. The time has actually been described as 15.0, but this has been shown to be incorrect and the correct time was 15.6.

12. His major-league career is highlighted in bold.

13. Statistics are unavailable but Thorpe is purported to have played semipro baseball in the Oklahoma-Kansas league in the summer of 1908 as well.

14. Pietrusza, David, managing editor. *Total Football*, p. 1236.

15. And presumably his diploma of merit from the high jump, although this has never been confirmed.

16. 12OR, pp. 93–94; and Prog, pp. 5–6.

17. Wheeler, p. 142.

18. There are numerous quotes stating that the article first appeared in the *Worcester Telegram*, but it is never footnoted or referenced directly. Research at the Library of Congress was performed by Bill Mallon, and his late father, John Mallon. We were unable to find the article, but it is possible it does exist, as the story is so often repeated.

19. *Providence Times*, 25 January 1913, p. 7.

20. *Charlotte Observer*, 18 July 1912, p. 8.

21. *New York Times*, 28 January 1913, p. 12.

22. *New York Times*, 25 January 1913, p. 8.

23. Wheeler, p. 142.

24. Note above that Thorpe never actually played for a minor-league team in Winston-Salem.

25. *Ibid.*

26. *New York Times*, 27 January 1913, p. 10.

27. *New York Times*, 28 January 1913, p. 1.

28. *New York Times*, 28 January 1913, p. 3.

29. The italics are the authors.

30. *New York Times*, 29 January 1913, p. 9.

31. *Literary Digest*, 8 February 1913, p. 306.

32. Much of this background can be found in the article by John A. Lucas, "Early Olympic antagonists: Pierre de Coubertin and James E. Sullivan," *Stadion*, 3: 258–272, 1977. In addition, Lucas combed his own files on Sullivan in an attempt to find something concerning this new revelation that Sullivan had to know about the statute of limitations. He was not able to find any mention of it.

33. Wheeler, p. 152, quoting an interview with Ralph Craig, sprint champion at the 1912 Olympics.

34. Wheeler-Thorpe Archives. News clipping from Canton *Repository Sports*, 24 October 1982, p. 52.

35. Lyberg, Vol. 3, 46.

36. Lyberg, Vol. 1, p. 64.

37. Wheeler-Thorpe Archives.

38. Lyberg, Vol. 3, 46.

39. Lyberg, Vol. 3, 46.

40. Correctly, in 1973.

41. Bjørnsen, Knut and Jorsett, Per. *Store norske sportsbragder*. Oslo: 1995.

42. We discussed this with Jim Greensfelder and Jim Lally, who were two coauthors of the definitive book on Olympic medals. They are uncertain if the 1912 dies are still available.

Appendix III
"Smiling Hannes," the First of the Flying Finns

Johan Pietari Kolehmainen, known to the sports world as Hannes Kolehmainen, was the first great distance runner of the Olympic Games. His fame is primarily based on his performances at the 1912 Olympics at which he won the gold medal in the 5,000 meters, the 10,000 meters, the individual cross-country race, and set an individual world record for 3,000 meters in the 3,000 meter team race. A joyous spirit with a seeming perpetual smile on his face, he was known as "Smiling Hannes," in stark contrast to the later seemingly ever-suffering distance running legend, Emil Zátopek of Czechoslovakia. Hannes Kolehmainen was also the first great Finnish distance runner, setting the stage for many to follow him, including Paavo Nurmi, Ville Ritola, Albin Stenroos, Lauri Lehtinen, Volmari Iso-Hollo, and Lasse Virén.

Kolehmainen was born on 9 December 1889 in Kuopio, near Lake Lalki. He was but one of four well-known distance running brothers. The others were August Wiljami (Willie), Kalle, and Taavetti Heikki (Tatu). His older brother, Willie, was the first to achieve international acclaim. Running as a professional, he set a world best for the marathon on 20 October 1912, in Vailsburg, New Jersey. Tatu Kolehmainen also competed in marathons, and led, or was near the lead, of the 1912 Olympic marathon past the halfway mark. The brothers had trained together growing up. In addition to running, they trained with cross-country skiing and several times skiied to Iisalmi, a town about 100 kilometers away, and returned the next day.

Like his brothers, Hannes Kolehmainen began his running career competing in marathons. He ran his first marathon on 16 June 1907, finishing third in a race in Viipuri, Finland. Through 1909, he ran eight marathons, winning his final one on the track in Hankö, Finland, on 19 September 1909. His best time was 2-42:59, run on a track in Göteburg only two weeks earlier. But after 1909, Kolehmainen stopped running marathons, at least for several years. He then turned his attention to the track.

Originally a member of the Kuopion Riento Club, Hannes Kolehmainen moved to Helsinki in 1909 and joined the well-known sports club Helsingin Kisa-Veikot. He ran for that club for several years, but switched to Helsingin Jyry, a workers' association club, in early 1912. He was by then a renowned runner in his native Finland. In 1911 he had won 22 of 22 races, including

417

the British AAA title over four miles, which was his first major international victory. In early 1912 he trained diligently, recording a solo time trial over three miles in 14:31.2 on 10 June, proving his fitness for Stockholm.

In Stockholm, Kolehmainen became the first great Olympic distance runner. His Olympic efforts began on 7 July, when he won heat one of the 10,000 meters trial to qualify for the final. The next day, he won the 10,000 meters in 31:20.8, a new world record for the distance, and the first world record recognized by the IAAF for 10,000 meters. He won the race by 46 seconds over Lewis Tewanima (USA).

The following day, Kolehmainen raced again, winning the fourth heat of round one of the 5,000 meters. On 10 July, Kolehmainen ran in the 5,000 final, in what was to become one of the greatest races in Olympic history. His main rival was the Frenchman, Jean Bouin. Together they set out at a fairly slow pace, but at 1,500 meters, Bouin took over the lead, and pushed the pace. Kolehmainen responded and ran on Bouin's shoulder for the next several kilometers. At the beginning of the last lap, Kolehmainen made several attempts to pass Bouin, all to no avail until the final straightaway. Less than 50 meters from the line, Kolehmainen edged ahead briefly, but Bouin spurted, catching, but never passing him. At the line, Kolehmainen won by less than half a meter. His time was 14:36.6, with Bouin running 14:36.7. Together they shattered the 15-minute barrier, and Kolehmainen's new world record was almost 25 seconds faster than the previously recorded best (15:01.2 by Arthur Robertson [GBR] in 1908). Philip Noel-Baker later wrote, "Kolehmainen was happy and smiling, a generous competitor and a modest winner. Perhaps my personal affection for Kolehmainen makes me remember that 5,000 meters as the most exciting race I ever saw."[1]*

Kolehmainen was far from finished in Stockholm, however. He had a day of rest, and then on 12 July, ran in the heats of the 3,000 meter team race. In heat one, there were only two teams, Finland and the United States. In an upset, the United States won the team contest and Finland did not qualify for the final. But it was hardly Kolchmainen's fault — he won the race individually in 8:36.9, setting another world record for the distance.

Three days later, the cross-country race was run, with medals awarded to both individuals and teams. Kolehmainen won again, covering the 12 kilometer course 33 seconds ahead of Hjalmar Andersson of the host country. Finland finished second as a team, allowing Kolehmainen to finish his Olympic efforts with three gold medals, one silver medal, and three world records.

After the 1912 Olympic Games, Hannes Kolehmainen moved to the United States. There he competed for both the Irish-American Athletic Club, the Kaleva Athletic Club, and as an honorary member of the Finnish-American Athletic Club. In 1912, 1913, and 1915, he won AAU title over five miles. He also became a naturalized American citizen.

In 1917, Hannes Kolehmainen returned to his first event, the marathon, running the Boston Marathon, but finishing only fourth. In 1920, Kolehmainen won the New York Marathon in 2-47:49.4. This was an Olympic qualifying race for the Americans, but three Finns living in the United States (Kolehmainen, Juho Tuomikoski, and Villie Kyrönen) used the race as their own qualifying race.

The 1920 Olympic marathon course in Antwerp was the longest in Olympic history at 42.75 km. At 20 km. the lead pack consisted of Christopher Gitsham (RSA), Auguste Broos (BEL), Kolehmainen, and Italy's Ettore Blasi, with Estonia's Jüri Lossmann and another Finn, Juho Tuomikoski, close behind. Kolehmainen took the lead at the midpoint of the race and he and Gitsham ran together for almost 15 kilometers. Gitsham, however, was having problems with a leg injury and withdrew shortly thereafter. Kolehmainen by then was pulling away for what would be an easy victory. His time of 2-32:25.8 was a world's best mark for amateur runners.

See Notes on page 419.

After Antwerp, Kolehmainens continued to compete as a runner, but mostly at longer distances, at which he set several world records. He returned to Finland and thereafter represented the Turun Urheiluliitto Club. On 10 October 1920, he set a world record for the 25 kilometer distance, running 1-26:29.8 in Tampere, Finland. He bettered that time with 1-25:20.0, also in Tampere, on 22 June 1922. Later that year, he broke the world record for 30 kilometers, running 1-47:13.4 in Viipuri on 1 October.

Hannes Kolehmainen ran no marathons between 1920 and 1924. He did not run any of the Finnish Olympic marathon trials for 1924, but he ran a 27 kilometer solo trial in 1-35:00 shortly before the Olympics and convinced the Finnish selectors of his fitness. He was chosen to run the marathon in Paris, but did not finish the race. He ran one more marathon in his career. On 17 June 1928, he entered the Finnish Olympic trial in Kauhava, but again failed to finish. It was his last competition.

Hannes Kolehmainen settled again in Finland, where he was revered. He made his living with various careers, including as an inspector, a clerk, a farmer, a mason, and finally, as a businessman. In 1952, when the Olympic Games were held in Helsinki, the Olympic torch was brought into the stadium by Paavo Nurmi, the man who succeeded Kolehmainen as the greatest Finnish distance runner. Nurmi ran once around the track and then handed the torch to Hannes Kolehmainen, who lit the Olympic flame in the stadium. Kolehmainen died in Helsinki on 11 January 1966. To the end, he was known as "Smiling Hannes," the first of the Flying Finns.

NOTES

1. Hannus, Matti. *The Flying Finns*. Helsinki: Tietosanoma Oy, 1990.

Appendix IV
Philip Baker, Avery Brundage, and George Patton

The 1912 Olympic Games are often known as the Olympics of Jim Thorpe and Hannes Kolehmainen, for obvious reasons. In Appendix II, we devote considerable time to the story of Thorpe as an athlete, his performance at Stockholm, and the subsequent disqualification and reinstatement. Appendix III contains a short biography of Kolehmainen.

However, there were three other competing athletes in Stockholm who later achieved a great deal of fame in other fields of their life. These were Philip Baker, Avery Brundage, and George Patton. Brundage and Patton were Americans while Baker was British. Below we give details of the athletic careers of these gentlemen and brief summaries of their lives, especially the reasons for their fame.

Philip John Baker (Noel-Baker)

Philip John Baker was born in London on 1 November 1889, one of seven children of Canadian-born parents. He was raised in a Quaker home. His parents moved to England when his father, Joseph Allen Baker, was asked to establish a British branch of his father's engineering business. In London, Joseph Baker became a member of the London County Council and later served in the House of Commons on the Liberal ticket, beginning in 1905. Thus, Philip Baker's upbringing gave him exposure to both politics and peaceful ways.

Baker attended the Bootham School in York, after which he spent several years at a Quaker school in Philadelphia — Haverford College. He returned to England to earn his degrees from King's College, Cambridge, receiving honors in history (1910) and economics (1912). He earned an M.A. with honors from Cambridge in 1913.

Baker ran for Cambridge and joined the Cambridge Athletic Club, but little is known of his athletic career, outside of the Olympics. He represented Haverford in the IC4A championships in 1907, finishing fifth in the 880 yards. For Cambridge he won the 880 yards against Oxford in 1910, 1911, and 1912, and the mile in 1909 and 1911. At the Cambridge University AC sports days, he won the mile in 1910, and both the half-mile and mile in 1911 and 1912. He ran three times at the AAA Championships, finishing fifth in the 1910 mile, fourth in the 1911 mile, and participating on the winning medley relay team in 1920.

Baker eventually ran for Great Britain at the 1912 and 1920 Olympic Games. At Stockholm, he failed to survive the first round of the 800 meters. In the 1,500 meters, he qualified for the final, but sacrificed his own chances to pace his teammate, Arnold Jackson. Jackson won the gold medal, and Baker finished sixth.

At Antwerp in 1920, Baker again ran in the 800 meters. He qualified for the semifinals, but did not start in that round. In the 1,500 meters, he ran well, but was narrowly beaten by his teammate, Albert Hill, and earned a silver medal.

Baker's fame came from his career after sports. As a Quaker pacifist, he rejected combat service in World War I, but commanded the Friends' Ambulance Corps, serving at the front in France, and earning decorations for valor. He was later an adjutant in a British ambulance unit in Italy, and earned the British Silver Medal for Military Valor, and the Italian War Cross.

In 1915, Philip Baker married Irene Noel, and took her name in addition to his own, therafter being known as Philip Noel-Baker. They eventually had one child, Francis, a son born in 1920.

After the war, Noel-Baker was an assistant to Robert Cecil at the Paris Peace Conference and he helped draft the Covenant of the League of Nations. He was later named chief assistant to the Secretary-General of the League, Eric Drummond, until 1922. During this time, he became associated with Fridtjof Nansen, the Norwegian explorer and humanitarian who became known for his work on behalf of war refugees.

In 1924, Noel-Baker became Sir Ernest Cassell Professor of international relations at the University of London. He was elected to Parliament from Coventry in 1929, serving two years. In 1926 he wrote two books, *The League of Nations at Work*, and *Disarmament*, which earned him a reputation as an expert on disarmament. He was later (1932) appointed the parliamentary private secretary to Arthur Henderson, chairman of the World Disarmament Conference convened in Geneva in 1932. He was re-elected to Parliament in 1936 and held a seat representing Derby until 1970.

During World War II, Noel-Baker served as official spokesman for the War Ministry in the House of Commons. In 1945, when the Labour Party returned to power, he was made Minister of State, a noncabinet position under the Foreign Secretary. In that capacity, he headed the British delegation to the United Nations Preparatory Commission, and later served on the subcommittee that drew up the preliminary agenda for the United Nations General Assembly.

Noel-Baker was a forceful advocate of arms control, and later served on the U.N. Economic and Social Council. His final book was published in 1958, *The Arms Race: A Programme for World Disarmament*. It was a comprehensive analysis of the history of disarmament with practical suggestions for the future course of the policy, and in 1960 was awarded the Albert Schweitzer Book Prize.

In 1959, for his work with the League of Nations, the United Nations, his lifetime commitment to peace, his work on behalf of war refugees, and his vast knowledge of disarmament, Philip John Noel-Baker was awarded the Nobel Prize for Peace. During his Nobel Prize lecture, he spoke of the threat posed by nuclear weapons and the arms race. He declared that the solution lay, not in partial measures, but in a comprehensive and complete program of disarmament under the United Nations. "Disarmament is ... for every nation," he stated, "the safest and most practicable system of defense."

Noel-Baker retired from the House of Commons at age 80, declaring, "While I have the health and strength, I shall give all my time to the work of breaking the dogmatic sleep of those who allow the nuclear, chemical, biological, and conventional arms race to go on." In 1977, John Noel-Baker was made a life peer as Baron Noel-Baker of Derby. He died in London on 8 October 1982.

Avery Brundage

Avery Brundage was born in Detroit on 28 September 1887, the son of British immigrant parents, Charles and Minnie Lloyd Brundage. In 1893, the family moved to Chicago, but after his parents separated, Avery lived with his mother and several other relatives.

Brundage studied at R. T. Crane Manual Training School, where he first began participating in track & field athletics. There he competed in the high jump, the long jump, and the throwing events. After high school, he matriculated at the University of Illinois in December 1908. While at Illinois, Brundage played on the basketball team, although as a reserve, and he saw little playing time. His major athletic efforts were again reserved for the track. At Illinois, he competed in all the throwing events, and the high jump when needed. In his final year at Illinois (1909), he won the conference championship in the discus throw.

After college, Brundage continued competing in track & field athletics, but he concentrated his efforts on the all-around championship. The all-around was an American and Irish forerunner of the decathlon, consisting of ten events: 100 yards, shot put, high jump, 880 yards, hammer throw, pole vault, 120 yard hurdles, 56 lb. weight throw, long jump and one mile run. With heavy emphasis on the throwing events, the event was well-suited to Brundage's talents.

In 1910, Brundage competed in the AAU All-Around, finishing third with 6,083½ points, well behind the winner, Fred Thompson, who scored 6,991. In 1911, he slipped back a bit, scoring 5,863 and placed fourth, again behind Thompson, who won with 6,709 points.

In late May 1912, Brundage competed in the western Olympic trials in both the pentathlon and decathlon. He finished second in the decathlon trial behind Eugene Schobinger, but won the pentathlon trial, defeating his only opponent, J. Austin Menaul. All three were selected to represent the United States in Stockholm.

In Stockholm, Brundage competed in the decathlon, but did not finish, withdrawing after the pole vault. In the pentathlon, he finished sixth, far behind his teammate, Jim Thorpe. There is some controversy here, concerning whether or not Brundage finished the final event, the 1,500 meter run. He definitely started, and one American source gives him a time, but most sources do not have him finishing. He also competed in Stockholm in his best event, the discus throw, but did not advance beyond the qualifying rounds.

Brundage did not stop competing in track & field after the 1912 Olympics. In 1914, he won his first national title in the All-Around on 19 September, scoring 6,999 points in Birmingham, Alabama. He defeated Gilbert Ritchie, a local favorite, by over 200 points. Brundage eventually won three AAU titles in the all-around. In 1916 he won in Newark, New Jersey, and in 1918, he triumphed at Great Lakes, Illinois.

Track & field athletics was Brundage's first sport, but he also excelled at the American version of handball. He competed in handball from the 1910s into the 1930s, and was ranked for a time in the top ten in the United States. In 1933, aged 46, he played a two-game match against the defending national champion, Angelo Trulio, losing the first game 21–16, but defeating Trulio in the second, 21–19.

After college, using borrowed money, Brundage was able to start his own construction company in 1915, an enterprise at which he was eminently successful and that made him a wealthy man. By the mid–1920s, he had already made a fortune in construction, allowing him the freedom to pursue sports administration, and handball was the sport with which his avocation began. After working for several years with the Central Association of the AAU (Amateur Athletic Union), he served as chairman of the national handball committee of the AAU from 1925 to 1927. In 1928 he was elected President of both the AAU (serving until the fall of 1935, except for 1933) and the American Olympic Association (AOA), the forerunner of the United States

Olympic Committee (USOC). He continued as President of the American Olympic Association, and its successor organizations, until 1952.

Avery Brundage was elected to the International Olympic Committee in July 1936. He replaced Ernest Lee Jahncke, who was ousted because he spoke in favor of boycotting the 1936 Olympics. Within one year of his membership, Brundage was named to the IOC Executive Board.

When IOC President Henri de Baillot-Latour died in 1942, the Swede, Sigfrid Edström, stood in as de facto President until the end of World War II. He then appointed Brundage Second Vice-President. In 1946, at the first postwar IOC Session, Edström was chosen as IOC President by acclamation, and he appointed Brundage as First Vice-President. In 1952, when Edström stepped down as President, Avery Brundage was elected President of the IOC in a very close vote over David, Lord Burghley, of Great Britain, a former Olympic gold medalist in the 400 meter hurdles.

Brundage's term as President was a difficult one politically for the IOC. It was faced by the question of the two Germanies, the two Koreas, the two Chinas, the apartheid problem in sport in South Africa and Rhodesia, rising problems with professional encroachment on the Olympic movement, political demonstrations by American blacks, and finally, in the last days of his term, by the horrible massacre of 11 Israeli athletes and coaches in Munich at the 1972 Olympics.

South Africa vexed Brundage and the IOC throughout his term of office. South Africa was eventually evicted from the IOC and the Olympic movement in the 1960s because of apartheid and, in particular, its use of apartheid in choosing its Olympic teams. Similar problems confronted Brundage in regard to Rhodesia, the inclusion of which led to a small boycott of the 1972 Munich Olympics. Brundage was enraged by this and it later led him, during the memorial ceremony for the Israeli hostages in Munich, to compare the African boycott of Munich to the Israeli massacres, a comment so inappropriate that it evoked outrage from many and brought only contempt for Brundage from even his closest allies, including Lord Killanin, who was to succeed him as President in just six days.

Brundage believed in amateurism, pure and simple, with no possible compromise allowed. He was especially bothered by the Olympic Winter Games, in which the alpine skiiers openly flaunted advertising on their skis; many of them were known to be closet professionals. Brundage even proposed canceling the Olympic Winter Games because of the creeping professionalism, or at least canceling the alpine skiing events, often considered the highlight of the Olympic Winter program.

Avery Brundage stepped down as IOC President after the Munich Olympics in 1972. After retirement from the IOC, he lived only a few more years, dying in Garmisch-Partenkirchen, Germany, on 7 May 1975.

George Smith Patton, Jr.

George Smith Patton, Jr. was one the greatest military generals ever produced in the United States. Born in San Gabriel, California on 11 November 1885, he was from a wealthy family. He eventually married into more wealth, his wife, Beatrice Ayer, being the daughter of a Massachusetts textile magnate.

After attending school in Pasadena, Patton enrolled at the Virginia Military Institute, and from there went to the United States Military Academy at West Point. He graduated from that institution in 1909, and was commissioned as a second lieutenant.

Efforts to find information on Patton's athletic career have yielded little. At West Point he went out for football, but broke both his arms and never played. He ran on the track team and apparently set a school record in the hurdles in his senior year. He competed in the broadswords, and earned letters in his senior year in track & field, fencing, and sharpshooting (rifle and pistol). He never competed nationally in track & field or in fencing.

In addition to those three sports, Patton was an accomplished horseman. In his family, he had grown up with horses, and became a well-known polo player. With his ability in running, fencing, shooting, and riding, Patton was a natural to represent the United States in the first Olympic modern pentathlon event at the Stockholm Olympics. Still, almost nothing is known about how he was selected for the team, as he had little national reputation.

After graduation from the USMA, Patton served in the cavalry in Fort Sheridan, Illinois until December 1911. He kept a whole stable of polo ponies with him at his own expense. He was then transferred to Fort Myer, Virginia, where he was stationed when selected for the 1912 Olympic team. At Fort Myer, he competed in polo with the elite and wealthy, and Wilson notes that he hobnobbed with the influential and powerful.[1]* It is possible that Patton's new circle of friends had some influence in helping him be selected to the 1912 U.S. Olympic team.

At Stockholm, Patton finished fifth in the modern pentathlon. It is commonly stated that he also competed in fencing at the 1912 Olympics. While he was entered in that sport (in individual épée), there is no evidence that he competed.

The first event of the 1912 modern pentathlon was shooting, and Patton performed poorly, finishing only 21st. It cost him a chance at a gold medal, as he performed well in the last four contests. In swimming, probably the sport at which he had the least experience, he was seventh. He placed fourth in fencing and sixth in cross-country riding. He had moved up to sixth place with only the 4,000 meter run remaining. He did well there, placing third in the run, and moving up to fifth spot. But the deficit he had built for himself in the shooting was too much for him to overcome.

As a military officer on assignment, Patton was required to write a report on his experience at the 1912 Olympics, and he did so on 19 September 1912 in *Report on the Modern Pentathlon* addressed to the Adjutant General of the U.S. Army. Harold "Rusty" Wilson has written of this report in his article on Patton,[2] and details Patton's penchant for exaggerating his own achievements.

There is no record that George Patton ever again competed in organized sports after the Stockholm Olympics. Thus, he has one of the shortest athletic careers of any well-known American Olympian. His "career," as it were, consisted mostly of military training while at West Point, and then the 1912 Olympics.

Nonetheless, George Smith Patton was destined for far greater fame than he would achieve on the playing fields. During World War I, he served as a member of General John Pershing's staff. In November 1917 he was assigned to the Tank Corps, and attended a course at the French Tank School. He eventually became known, among many other things, for his brilliance in commanding tanks in battle.

Between World Wars, Patton had various assignments in many different locations, as is common with military personnel. But the bulk of his fame rests on his performance as a commanding general during World War II.

On 19 April 1941, Patton was assigned as the Commanding Officer of the Second Armored Division at Fort Benning, Georgia. He later became Commanding General of the Armored Corps. When American forces landed in North Africa on 3 November 1942, Patton commanded the units landing on the west coast. In February 1943, he became Commanding General of the Western Task Force and later assumed command of all American ground forces in the Tunisian Combat Area.

Patton was given command of the American Seventh Army in Sicily in July 1943. There

See Notes on pages 426.

he led a controversial charge across the island, probably disobeying orders from headquarters to only support British Field Marshal Sir Bernard Law Montgomery. In March 1944, he was put in charge of the Third Army in France. Commanding that force, he was instrumental in helping the Americans win the Battle of the Bulge, when his troops marched over two days and nights through terrible weather, to relieve and support beleaguered Americans who were meeting significant German resistance in Bastogne.

Patton is probably best remembered today in the United States because of a major 1970 movie of his life, entitled simply "Patton," which starred George C. Scott in the Academy Award–winning title role. The movie detailed his controversial command during World War II. Known as "Blood and Guts," his command style was tyrannical and swashbuckling. He was also known for his predilection for attacking, stating many times in his fluent French, "L'attaque, l'attaque, toujours l'attaque." He was vilified by the American press after the war because he refused to support the Soviets, but in retrospect many of his comments seem to have been prescient. As for public service, Patton himself stated that he had no political ambitions, or acumen.

The awards for his military career were numerous and included the following: Distinguished-Service Cross with one Oak-Leaf Cluster, Distinguished-Service Medal with two Oak-Leaf Clusters, Distinguished Service Medal (Navy), the Legion of Merit, the Silver Star, the Congressional Life Saving Medal of Honor, the Bronze Star Medal, the Purple Heart, the Mexican Service Badge, and the Victory Medal with four stars. He was also awarded the following foreign decorations: Medal Commemorative of the Volymored (Sweden), Order of the British Empire (Great Britain), Most Honorable Order of the Bath (Great Britain), Grand Cross of Ouissan Alaouite (Morocco), Grand Officer of the Order of Leopold with Palm (Belgium), Croix de Guerre (Belgium), Order of Adolphe of Nassau, Grand Croix (Luxembourg), Croix de Guerre (Luxembourg), Order of Kutusov (Soviet Union), and he was given the rank of Commander in the Legion of Honor (France).

After the war ended, Patton was placed in charge of the 15th Army in American-Occupied Germany. Sadly, he was involved in an automobile accident on the Frankfurt-Mannheim Highway and was rendered a quadriplegic. He died a few weeks later in Heidelberg on 21 December 1945.

NOTES

1. Wilson, Harold E., Jr. "A legend in his own mind: the Olympic experience of General George S. Patton, Jr." *Olympika* 6: 99–114, 1997, p. 101.
2. *Ibid.*

Appendix V
The 1912 Russian Olympic Team

The Russian Olympic team of 1912 was hardly a conglomerate of 159 Russian athletes. In fact, only a small percentage of the "Russians" competing in 1912 could be called native Russians. The exact states of origin for these athletes is complex and not fully known, but below we try to shed light on this, by listing the athletes by sports, and then by their best-known state of origin. In many cases, even this is somewhat controversial.

The spelling of the Russian names is also very complex and no consensus exists. The pure Russian names were certainly spelled in the Cyrillic alphabet and likely transliterated into the Latin alphabet for the entry forms. But it is unknown if the people doing that transliteration understood modern rules for transliteration into the Latin alphabet. In addition, transliteration differs from language to language. For example, the Russian name pronounced "Yur-ee" is spelled variably in English transliteration as Yury, Yuri, or Yuriy, but in French transliteration as Iouri, and in German transliteration often as Jurij. Further complicating matters is that many of the Russian entrants in 1912 were not native Russians. Many were from the Baltic states of Estonia, Latvia, and Lithuania, which do not use the Russian language, or the Cyrillic alphabet. If Russian authorities filled out the entry forms, they likely transliterated from the Baltic languages into Russian Cyrillic and then back again into some form of a Latin alphabet for the entry forms. Further, several of the Russian entrants in 1912 were actually of Finnish, Polish, or German descent.

We have made a spreadsheet of the various spellings seen for the Russian entrants in 1912. From this, we have tried to draw a consensus for the "best" spelling, using the *Encyclopædia Brittanica* system for transliteration into English. For the Baltic names, we have again attempted to form a consensus for the "best" spelling, again using rules for the Baltic languages and naming patterns. Although it may seem pedantic, we have listed all the variant spellings for the names, and their sources, to the right of each name. The first name listed is always what we consider the "best" spelling and is the one we use throughout this book in the results.

Finally, at the end of this listing, a short spreadsheet gives our "best guess" of the national origins of the 1912 Russian Olympic team, by sport. It should be cautioned that these are merely "best guesses" as there is certainly no consensus as to the national origin of some of the athletes.

Hymans   =   *USSR Athletics Statistics*
Lyberg   =   *The Athletes of the Summer Olympic Games 1896–1996*
EzM   =   *The Olympic Century*
Marichev   =   *Who is Who at the Olympic Games 1896–1992*
Uggla   =   *Olympiska Spelen i Stockholm 1912*

Athletics (Track & Field) [33]

Estonia [4]
    Hermann, Eduard   Hermann, Eduard (all sources)
    Lukk, Kaarel   Lukk, Karl (EzM; Uggla; Marichev); Lukk, Kaarel
                                     (Lyberg)
    Martin, Johannes   Martin, Johannes (EzM); Martin, Johan (Uggla); Martin,
                                     Johann (Lyberg; Marichev)
    Reimann, Elmar   Reimann, Elmar (EzM; Uggla; Marichev); Reiman/
                                     Reimann, Elmar (Lyberg)

Finland [1]
    Neklepayev, Nikolay   Neklepayev, N (Hymans); Neklepayev, Nikolay (EzM);
                                     Neklepaieff, Nicolas (Uggla; Marichev); Neklepajev,
                                     Nikolai (Lyberg)

Germany [3]
    Baasch, Ulrich   Baash, U (Hymans); Baasch, Ulrich (EzM; Uggla);
                                     Baasch, Ulrik (Lyberg); Baasch, Ulrich (Marichev)
    Schwarz, Alfred   Schwarz, Alfred (all sources)
    Schwarz, Richard   Schwarz, Richard (all sources)

Germany/Russia [2]
    Shtiglits, Pavel   Shtiglits, N (Hymans); de Stieglitz, Pavel (EzM); de
                                     Stieglitz, Paul (Uggla; Marichev); de Stieglitz, Pawel
                                     (Lyberg)
    Schultz, Aleksandr   Shults, A (Hymans); Schulz, Alexander (EzM); Choultz,
                                     Alexandre (Uggla; Marichev); Schults, Aleksandr
                                     (Lyberg)

Latvia [16]
    Alslebens, Alfreds   Alsleben, A. (Hymans); Alslebens, Alfreds (EzM;
                                   Marichev); Alsleben, Alfred (Uggla); Alsleben, Alfreds
                                   (Lyberg)
    Ayde, Aleksis   Aide, Aleksis (EzM; Uggla); Ayede, Aleksei (Lyberg);
                                   Aide/Ayde, Aleksis (Marichev)
    Baumanis, Herberts   Baumann, Herbert (EzM; Uggla); Baumanis, Herberts
                                   (Lyberg); Baumann/Baumanis, Herberts (Marichev)
    Hahne, Haralds   Hahne, Harald (EzM; Uggla); Hahne, Haralds (Lyberg);
                                   Hahne/Hans, Haralds (Marichev)
    Indriksons, Arnolds   Indriksons, Arnolds (EzM); Indrikson, Arnold (Uggla);
                                   Indrikson, Arnolds (Lyberg); Indrikson/Indriksons,
                                   Arnolds (Marichev)

Kapmals, Andrejs	Kapmals, Andrejs (EzM; Lyberg); Kapmal, Andrei (Uggla); Kapmal/Kapmals, Andrejs (Marichev)
Kruklins, Andrejs	Kruklins, Andrejs (EzM; Lyberg); Kruklin, Andreas (Uggla); Kruklin/Kruklins, Andrejs/Andreas (Marichev)
Levensteins, Leopolds	Löwenstein, Leopold (EzM; Uggla); Levensteins, Leopolds (Lyberg); Loewenstein/Levensteins, Leopolds (Marichev)
Ozols-Berne, Arvids	Ohsol-Berne, Arved (EzM); Ohsol-Berné, Arved (Uggla); Ohsola-Berne, Arvids (Lyberg); Ohsol-Berne/Ozols-Berne, Arvids (Marichev)
Rasso, Nikolajs	Rasso, Nikolajs (EzM; Lyberg; Marichev); Rasso, Nicolai (Uggla)
Ruks, Alfreds	Rukks, Alfreds (EzM); Rucks, Alfred (Uggla); Rukss, Alfreds (Lyberg); Rucks/Ruks, Alfreds (Marichev)
Svedrevits, Nikolajs	Shvedrevits, N (Hymans); Schwedrewitz, Nikolay (EzM — German); Svedrevits, Nikolajs (EzM — Latvian); Schwedrevitz, Nicolai (Uggla); Svedrevics, Niklajs (Lyberg); Schewdrewitz/ Svedrevics, Nikolajs (Marichev)
Upmals, Aleksandrs	Upmals, Aleksandrs (EzM; Lyberg); Upmal, Alexander (Uggla); Upmal/Upmals, Alexander/Aleksandrs (Marichev)
Villemson, Johannes Leopolds	Vilemson, J (Hymans); Villemson, Johannes (EzM); Wilhelmsohn, Leopold (Uggla); Willemsons, Johannes Leopolds (Lyberg); Wilhelmson, Leopold (Marichev)
Vitols, Rudolfs	Vitols, Rudolfs (EzM); Wihtol, Rudolf (Uggla); Wihtols, Rudolfs (Lyberg); Withol/Vitols, Rudolf (Marichev)
Vanags, Eriks	Wannag, Erich (EzM); Wannag, Erich (Uggla); Wanags, Eriks (Lyberg); Wannag/Vanags, Erich/Eriks (Marichev)

Russia [7]

Gayevsky, Pyotr	Gayevskiy, P (Hymans); Gayevskiy, Pyotr (EzM); Gajeffsky, Pierre (Uggla); Gajevskij, Petr (Lyberg); Gajeffsky/Gajewski, Pierre (Marichev)
Kharkov, Nikolay	Kharkov, N (Hymans); Kharkov, Nikolay (EzM); Charkof, Nicolas (Uggla; Marichev)
Molokanov, Vasily	Molokanov, Vasily (EzM); Molokanof, Basile (Uggla); Molokanov, Vasile (Lyberg); Molokanoff, Basile (Marichev)
Nazarov, Dmitry	Nazarov, D (Hymans); Nazarov, Dmitriy (EzM); Nazarof, Demetrius (Uggla); Nasarov, Dimitri (Lyberg); Nazarof, Demetrius (Marichev)
Nikolsky, Mikhail	Nikolskiy, M (Hymans); Nikolskiy, Mikhail (EzM); Nicolsky, Michel (Uggla; Marichev); Nikolski, Mikhail (Lyberg)
Petrov, Yevgeny	Petrov, Yevgeniy (EzM); Petroff, Eugène (Uggla); Petrov, Evgeni (Lyberg); Petroff, Eugene (Marichev)

Yelizarov, Aleksandr   Yelizarov, Aleksandr (EzM); Elizarof, Alexandre (Uggla); Jelisarov, Aleksandr (Lyberg); Elizarof, Alexandre (Marichev)

Cycling [10]

Germany [1]

Bosch, Friedrich   Bosch, Friedrich (Uggla); Bosch, Fricis (Lyberg); Bosch, Friedrich/Fricis (Marichev)

Latvia [7]

Apsits, Andrejs   Apsits, Andrejs (per Latvian OC); Apsit, Andzei (Uggla; Marichev); Apsit, Andrejs (Lyberg)

Bukse, Jakob   Bukse, Jacob (Uggla; Marichev); Bukse, Jakaps (Lyberg)

Köpke, Augusts   Koepke, August (Uggla; Marichev); Köpke, Augusts (Lyberg)

Köpke, Karlis   Koepke, Carl (Uggla); Köpke, Karlis (Lyberg); Koepke, Carl/Karlis (Marichev)

Lieven, Janis   Lieven, Johann (Uggla); Liewen, Janis (Lyberg); Lieven, Johann/Janis (Marichev)

Pratneek, Janis   Pratneek, Jahn (Uggla); Pratneek, Janis (Lyberg); Pratneek, Jahn/Janis (Marichev)

Richters, Edgars   Richter, Edgar (Uggla; Marichev); Richters, Edgars (Lyberg)

Russia [2]

Borisov, Fyodor   Borrisow, Fedor (Uggla; Marichev); Borisov, Fedor (Lyberg)

Pesteryev, Sergey   Pesteriff, Sergei (Uggla; Marichev); Pesterev, Sergei Petrovitch (Lyberg)

Diving [1]

Russia [1]

Baranov, Viktor   Baranoff, Wictor (Uggla; Marichev); Baranov, Wiidu (Viktor) (Lyberg)

Equestrian Events [7]

Poland [1]

Rómmel, Karol   Rómmel, Karol (Polish Olympic Book); de Rommel, Karel (Lyberg); von Rommel, Charl/Karol (Marichev/Poland)

Russia [6]

Plechkov, Mikhail   Pleskov, Mikail (Lyberg); Plechkoff, Michel (Marichev)

Rodzhianko, Aleksandr   Rodzianko, Aleksandr (Lyberg); Rodzianko, Alexander (Marichev)

Romanov, Dmitry Pavlovich	Dimitrij, Pavlovitch (Lyberg); Dimitri Paulowitsch, Kaiser Hoheit (Marichev)
Selikhov, Aleksey	Selikov, Aleksei (Lyberg); Selikhoff, Alexis (Marichev)
Yekimov, Mikhail	Jekimov, Mikail (Lyberg); Ekimoff, Michel (Marichev)
Zagorsky, Sergey	Zagorski, Sergei (Lyberg); Zagorsky, Serge (Marichev)

Fencing [24]

Germany [1]

Guiber von Greifenfels, Apollon	Guiber von Greifenfels, Apollon (Uggla; Marichev); Guber von Greifenfels, Apollon (Lyberg)

Russia [23]

Andreyev, Vladimir	Andreeff, Wladimir (Uggla; Marichev); Andrejev, Vladimir (Lyberg)
Arsenyev, Boris	Arsenieff, Boris (Uggla; Marichev); Arseniev, Boris (Lyberg)
Bertrain, Gavril	Bertrain, Gabriel (Uggla; Marichev); Betrain, Gavril (Lyberg)
Danich, Vladimir	Danitch, Wladimir (Uggla; Marichev); Danitch, Vladimir (Lyberg)
Filatov, Pavel	Filatoff, Paul (Uggla; Marichev); Filatove, Pavel (Lyberg)
Gorodetzky, Nikolay	Gorodetzky, Nicolas (Uggla; Marichev); Gorodetski, Nikolai (Lyberg)
Grinev, Leonid	Grineff, Leon (Uggla; Marichev); Grinev, Leonid (Lyberg)
Guvorsky, Pavel	Guoworsky, Paul (Uggla; Marichev); Guvorski, Pavel (Lyberg)
Keyser, Vladimir	Keiser, Vladimir (Uggla; Marichev); Kejser, Vladimir (Lyberg)
Knyazhevich, Dmitry	de Kniajévitsch, Dmitry (Uggla); Kniajevitch, Dimitri (Lyberg); De Kniajevitsch, Dmitry (Marichev)
Kuznyetsov, Nikolay	Kousnetzof, Nicolas (Uggla; Marichev); Kusnetsov, Nikolai (Lyberg)
Leparsky, Feliks	Leparsky, Felix (Uggla; Marichev); Leparski, Feliks (Lyberg)
Martuchev, Leonid	Martucheff, Leon (Uggla; Marichev); Martusjev, Leonid (Lyberg)
Mordovin, Aleksandr	Mordovine, Alexandre (Uggla; Marichev); Mordovin, Aleksandr (Lyberg)
Nepokupnoy, Boris	Nepokoupnoi, Boris (Uggla; Marichev); Nepokupnoj, Boris (Lyberg)
Samoylov, Vladimir	Samoilow, Wladimir (Uggla; Marichev); Samoilov, Vladimir (Lyberg)
Sarnavsky, Vladimir	de Sarnawsky, Wladimir (Uggla); Sarnavski, Vladimir (Lyberg); De Sarnawsky, Wladimir (Marichev)
Shkylev, Aleksandr	Chikleff, Alexandre (Uggla; Marichev); Kilev, Aleksandr (Lyberg)
Soldatenkov, Aleksandr	Soldatenkow, Alexandre (Uggla; Marichev); Soldatenkov, Aleksandr (Lyberg)

Timofeyev, Anatoly   Timoféen, Anatole (Uggla); Timofejev, Anatoli (Lyberg); Timofeev, Anatole (Marichev)

Vaterkampf, Konstantin   Watercampf, Constantin (Uggla; Marichev); Waterkampf, Konstantin (Lyberg)

Zakyrich, Georgy   Sakaritch, Georges (Uggla); Sakaritch, Georgi (Lyberg); Sakaritch/Sakiritch, Georges (Marichev)

Zhakovlev, Anatoly   de Jakovleff, Anatole (Uggla); Jakovlev, Anatoli (Lyberg); De Jakovleff, Anatole (Marichev)

Football (Association Football Soccer) [15]

Russia [15]

Akimov, Andrey   Akimow, André (Uggla); Akimov, Andrei (Lyberg); Akimow, Andre (Marichev)

Butusov, Vladimir Pavlovich   Boutoussoff, W. Pawlowitch (Uggla; Marichev); Butusov, Vladimir Pavlovitj (Lyberg)

Favorsky, Leonid   Faworski, Léon (Uggla); Favorski, Leonid (Lyberg); Faworski, Leon (Marichev)

Filipov, Aleksandr Pavlovich   Filippoff, Alexandre (Uggla; Marichev); Filipov, Aleksandr (Lyberg)

Filipov, Sergey Pavlovich   Filipoff, S. Pawlowitch (Uggla); Filipov, Sergei Pavlovitj (Lyberg); Filippoff, Sergei (Marichev)

Khromov, Nikita Akimovich   Chromoff, Nikita Akimowitch (Uggla); Kromov, Nikita Akimovitch (Lyberg); Chromoff, Nikita (Marichev)

Kynin, Nikolas   Kynin, Nicolas (Uggla; Marichev); Kynin, Nikolai (Lyberg)

Markov, Vladimir Anatolyevich   Markoff, W. Anatoliewitch (Uggla; Marichev); Markov, Vladimir Anatol (Lyberg)

Nikitin, Grigory Mikhailovich   Nikitin, G. Mikhailowitch (Uggla; Marichev)

Rimsha, Fyödor   de Rimsha, Frédéric (Uggla); de Rimscha, Frédéric (Lyberg); De Rimscha, Frederic (Marichev)

Smirnov, Mikhail   Smirnoff, Michel (Uggla; Marichev); Smirnov, Mikail (Lyberg)

Sokolov, Pyotr Petrovich   Sokoloff, P. Petrowitch (Uggla; Marichev); Sokolov, Petr Petrovitch (Lyberg)

Uversky, Aleksey   Ouwersky, Alexis (Uggla; Marichev); Uversky, Alexis (Lyberg)

Yakovlev, Mikhail Vasilyevich   Yakowleff, M. Wassiliewitsch (Uggla; Marichev)

Zhitaryev, Vasily   Gitareff, Basile (Uggla; Marichev)

Gymnastics [4]

Russia [4]

Akhyun, Aleksandr   Achum, Alexandre (Uggla); Akum, Aleksandr (Lyberg); Achun, Alexandre (Marichev)

Kushnikov, Pavel   Kouchnikoff, Paul (Uggla; Marichev); Kusnikov, Pavel (Lyberg)

Kulikov, Semyon   Kulikoff, Semen (Uggla; Marichev); Kulikov, Semen (Lyberg)

Zabelyn, Fyodor   Zabeline, Théodore (Uggla); Zabelin, Fedor (Lyberg); Zabeline, Theodore (Marichev)

Modern Pentathlon [4]

Finland [4]

Aejemelaeus, Carl Bror Emil "Kalle"[1]*   Ajmelans, Carl Bror Emil (Lyberg); Aejmelaens, Carl Bror Emil (Marichev)

Almqvist, Arno Aksel[2]   Almkvist, Arno Axel (Lyberg); Almquist, Arno Axel (Marichev)

von Hohenthal, Veli Gunnar   von Hohenthal, Veli Gunnar (Lyberg); Von Hohenthal, Veli Gunnar (Marichev)

Wilkman, Oskar Alfred[3]   Wilkman, Oskar (Lyberg; Marichev)

Russia [1]

Nepokupnoy, Boris   Nepokoupnoi, Boris (Uggla; Marichev); Nepokupnoj, Boris (Lyberg)

Rowing & Sculling [1]

Estonia [1]

Kusick, Hugo Maksimilian   Kusik, Mikail Maksimilian (Lyberg); Kusick, Mikhail (Marichev)

Shooting [26]

Germany [1]

Blau, Harry   Blau, Harry (Uggla; Lyberg; Marichev)

Latvia [1]

Weiss, Davids   de Weysse, Davide (Uggla); Weiss, Davids (Lyberg); De Weysse, Davide (Marichev)

Lithuania [1]

Syttin, Leonardus   Syltine, Leon (Uggla); Sittin, Leonardas (Lyberg); Syttine, Leon (Marichev)

Russia [23]

Barkov, Dmitry   de Barkoff, Dimitry (Uggla); Barkov, Dimitri (Lyberg); De Barkoff, Dimitry (Marichev)

Belinsky, Boris   de Belinsky, Boris (Uggla); Belinski, Boris (Lyberg); De Belinsky, Boris (Marichev)

Bodneck, Walter   Bodneck, Walter (all sources)

*See Notes on pages 436.

Davidov, Georgy	de Davidoff, George (Uggla); Davidov, Georgi (Lyberg); De Davidoff, George (Marichev)
Dobrzhansky, Aleksandr	de Dobrjansky, Alexandre (Uggla); Dorbianski, Aleksandr (Lyberg); De Dobrjansky, Alexandre (Marichev)
Kache, Amosse	de Kache, Amosse (Uggla); Kasj, Amos (Lyberg); De Kache, Amosse (Marichev)
Kalinin, Konstantin	de Kalinine, Constantin (Uggla); Kalinin, Konstantin (Lyberg); De Kalinine, Constantin (Marichev)
Kuskov, Dmitry	de Kouskoff, Dimitry (Uggla); Kuskov, Dimitri (Lyberg); De Kouskoff, Dimitry (Marichev)
Lebedev, Teotan	de Lebedoff, Thothan (Uggla); Lebedev, Teotan (Lyberg); De Lebedeff (Marichev)
Leche, Pavel	de Lesche, Paul (Uggla); Lesiev, Pavel (Lyberg); De Lesche, Paul (Marichev)
Lieth, Pavel	Lieth, Paul (Uggla; Marichev); Liet, Pavel (Lyberg)
Melnitsky, Nikolay	de Melnitsky, Nicolas (Uggla); Melnitski, Nikolai (Lyberg); De Melnitsky, Nicolas (Marichev)
Panin (Kolomenkin), Nikolay Aleks'vich	Kolomenkin, Nicolas Alexandrowitch (Uggla); Kolomenkin, Nikolai (Lyberg); Kolomenkin, Nicolas (Marichev)
Panteleymonov, Georgy	de Panteleymonoff, George (Uggla); Panteleimonov, Georgi (Lyberg); De Panteleymonoff (Marichev)
Pertel, Boris	Pertel, Boris (all sources)
Potekin, Vladimir	de Potékine, Wladimir (Uggla); Potekin, Vladimir (Lyberg); De Potekine, Wladimir (Marichev)
Rechke, Osvald	de Rechké, Oswalde (Uggla); Resjkev, Osvald (Lyberg); De Rechke, Oswalde (Marichev)
Shesterikov, Grigory	de Schestrikoff, Grigory (Uggla); Sjesterikov, Grigori (Lyberg); De Schesterikoff, Grigory (Marichev)
Skrotsky, Vasily	de Skrotsky, Basile (Uggla); Skrotski, Vasili (Lyberg); De Skrotsky, Basile (Marichev)
Tillo, Aleksandr	de Tillo, Alexandre (Uggla); Tillo, Aleksandr (Lyberg); De Tillo, Alexandre (Marichev)
Valdayne, Pavel	de Waldeine, Paul (Uggla); Waldein, Pavel (Lyberg); De Waldeine/Waldaine, Paul (Marichev)
Vishnyakov, Georgy	de Wischniakoff, George (Uggla); Wisinjakov, Georgi (Lyberg); De Wischnidakoff, George (Marichev)
Voyloshnikov, Pavel	de Woylochnikoff, Paul (Uggla); Vojlotchnikov, Pavel (Lyberg); De Woylochnikoff, Paul (Marichev)

Swimming [4]

Germany [1]

von Kuhlberg, Herbert	von Kuhlberg, Herbert (Uggla); von Kuhlberg, Herberts (Lyberg); Von Kuhlber, Herbert (Marichev)

Russia [3]

Avksentyev, Pavel	Awksentjeff, Parell (Uggla); Aksentjev, Parell (Lyberg); Awksentjeff, Pavel (Marichev)

Baymakov, Georgy   Bajmakoff, George (Uggla; Marichev); Bajmakov, Georgi (Lyberg)

Voronkov, Nikolay   Woronkoff, Nicolas (Uggla; Marichev); Voronkov, Nikolas (Lyberg)

Tennis [2]

Russia [2]

Alenitzyn, Aleksandr   Alenitzyn, Alexandre (Marichev); Aleinitsin, Aleksandr (Lyberg)

Sumarokov-Elston, Mikhail   Soumarokoff-Elston, Michel (Marichev); Sumarakov-Elston, Mikail (Lyberg)

Wrestling [11]

Estonia [2]

Kaplur, Oscar   Kaplur, Oscar (all sources)

Klein, Martin "Max"   Klein, Max (Uggla); Klein, Max/Martin (Marichev); Klein, Martin (Lyberg)

Germany [1]

Baumann, Georg   Baumann, Georg (Uggla; Marichev); Baumann, Georgi (Lyberg)

Latvia [5]

Farnest, Nikolajs   Farnest, Nicolai (Uggla; Marichev); Farnest, Niklavs (Lyberg)

Kippasto, August   Kippasto, August (Uggla; Marichev); Lippasto, Augusts (Lyberg)

Meesits, Aleksanders   Meesit, Alexandre (Uggla; Marichev); Meesits, Aleksanders (Lyberg)

Pikker, August   Pikker, August (Uggla; Marichev; Lyberg)

Polis, Janis   Polis, Jean (Uggla); Pohlis, Jean (Marichev); Polis, Janis (Lyberg)

Russia [3]

Ankondinov, Aleksandr   Ankondinoff, Alexandre (Uggla; Marichev); Ankondinov, Aleksandr (Lyberg)

Pavlovich, Pavel   Pawlowitch, Paul (Uggla; Marichev); Pavlovitch, Pavel (Lyberg)

Severov, Aleksandr   Seweroff, Alexandre (Uggla; Marichev); Severov, Aleksandr (Lyberg)

Yachting [17]

Germany [2]

Brasche, Ernest   Brasj, Ernest (Lyberg); Brasche, Ernest (Marichev)

von Adlerberg, Herman   von Adlerberg, Herman (Lyberg); von Adleberg, Herman (Marichev)

Russia [15]

Beloselsky, Yesper	Beloselski, Jesper (Lyberg); Belvselvsky, Esper (Marichev)
Farber, Johan	Färber, Johan (Lyberg); Farber, Johan (Marichev)
Ilyevich, Vladimir	Jilevitch, Vladimir (Lyberg); Jilewitch, Wladimir (Marichev)
Kuhn, Yevgeny	Kuhn, Evgeni (Lyberg; Marichev)
Kuzmichev, Ventseslav	Kusmitchev, Ventseslav (Lyberg); Kusmitscheff, Ventseslav (Marichev)
Lindholm, Karl	Lindholm, Karl (Lyberg; Marichev)
Lomach, Yevgeny	Lommatch, Evgeni (Lyberg); Lommatsch, Evgeni (Marichev)
Lurasov, Vladimir	Lurasov, Vladimir (Lyberg); Lourasoff, Vladimir (Marichev)
Markov, Viktor	Markov, Viktor (Lyberg); Markow, Wiktor (Marichev)
Pavlov, Pavel	Pavlov, Pavel (Lyberg); Pawlow, Pavel (Marichev)
Podgornov, Nikolay	Podgornov, Nikolai (Lyberg); Podgornoff, Nikolai (Marichev)
Pusnitsky, Nikolay	Pusnitski, Nikolai (Lyberg); Puschnitsky, A. (Marichev)
Rodionov, Aleksandr	Rodionov, Aleksandr (Lyberg); Rodionow, Aleksandr (Marichev)
Shomaker, Iossif	Sjomaker, Josif (Lyberg); Schomaker, Jossif (Marichev)
Strauch, Filipp	Strauch, Filip (Lyberg); Strauch, Filipp (Marichev)

Russian 1912 Olympic Team — National Origins by Sport

	Ath	Cyc	Div	Equ	Fen	Ftb	Gym	Mop	Row	Sho	Swi	Ten	Wre	Yac	Sub-Total	Multi	Totals
Estonia	4	–	–	–	–	–	–	–	1	–	–	–	2	–	7	–	7
Finland	1	–	–	–	–	–	–	4	–	–	–	–	–	–	5	–	5
Germany	3	1	–	–	1	–	–	–	–	1	1	–	1	2	10	–	10
Germany/Russia	2	–	–	–	–	–	–	–	–	–	–	–	–	–	2	–	2
Latvia	16	7	–	–	–	–	–	–	–	1	–	–	5	–	29	–	29
Lithuania	–	–	–	–	–	–	–	–	–	1	–	–	–	–	1	–	1
Poland	–	–	–	1	–	–	–	–	–	–	–	–	–	–	1	–	1
Russia	7	2	1	6	23	15	4	1	–	23	3	2	3	15	105	1	104
Totals	33	10	1	7	24	15	4	5	1	26	4	2	11	17	160	1	159

NOTES

1. Name source *Urheilutieto: Olympiaurheilu: 100 vuotta 10 Atlanta 1996 Paralympia.*
2. Name source *Urheilutieto: Olympiaurheilu: 100 vuotta 10 Atlanta 1996 Paralympia.*
3. Name source *Urheilutieto: Olympiaurheilu: 100 vuotta 10 Atlanta 1996 Paralympia.*

Appendix VI
Competitors (by Country)

In the following we have tried to give precise biographical information including full, complete names, complete date of birth and death (where known), and club affiliations (where known). Also given are all events in which the competitors competed and their placement. In events where competitors were eliminated prior to a final, the following notations serve as examples to explain the results:

4h3r1/2 = 4th in heat 3, round 1 of 2.
ach4r1/3 = also competed in heat 4, round 1 of 3.
dnfp1r2/4 = did not finish, pool 1, round 2 of 4.
=13 = tied for 13th

Australasia (Australia and New Zealand)[1]* (Total: 25; Men: 23; Women: 2. Australia: Total: 22; Men: 20; Women: 2. New Zealand: Total: 3; Men: 3; Women: 0)

Athletics (Track & Field) (Total: 5; Men: 5; Women: 0)
Hill, George Neville. (New Zealand) (b.26 February 1891) 5,000 meters [4h1r1/2]; 10,000 meters [7h3r1/2].
Murray, William M. (Australia) (b.17 April 1882) 10 kilometer walk [ac/h2r1/2].
Poulter, Stuart Henry. (Australia) (b.20 January 1889) Marathon [dnf].
Ross, Claude Murray. (Australia) (b.13 May 1883) 400 meters [dnf-h1r1/3].
Stewart, William Allan. (Australia) (b.22 October 1889) 100 meters [3h4r2/3]; 200 meters [dnf-h2r2/3].

Rowing & Sculling (Total: 10; Men: 10; Women: 0)
Fitzhardinge, Roger Berkely. (Australia) (b.23 March 1879) Coxed Eights [2h3r2/4].
Fraser, Simon. (Australia) (b.25 August 1884) Coxed Eights [2h3r2/4].

*See Notes on pages 527–530.

Hauenstein, Henry. (Australia) (b.3 May 1881) Coxed Eights [2h3r2/4].

McVilly, Cecil. (Australia) (b.20 August 1890) Single Sculls [ac/dq-h2r1/4].

Middleton, Sydney Albert. (Australia) (b.24 February 1884–d.1945) Coxed Eights [2h3r2/4].

Parker, Thomas Charles. (Australia) (b.20 August 1883) Coxed Eights [2h3r2/4].

Ross-Boden, Harry. (Australia) (b.17 May 1886) Coxed Eights [2h3r2/4].

Ryrie, John Alexander. (Australia) (b.21 December 1886) Coxed Eights [2h3r2/4].

Waley, Robert George K. (Australia) (b.26 November 1889) Coxed Eights [2h3r2/4].

Ward, Hugh Kingsley. (Australia) (b.17 September 1889) Coxed Eights [2h3r2/4].

Swimming (Total: 9; Men: 7; Women: 2)

Women

Durack, Sarah "Fanny." (Australia) (b.27 October 1889–d.20 March 1956) 100 meter freestyle [1].

Wylie, Wilhelmina "Mina." (Australia) (b.1892) 100 meter freestyle [2].

Men

Boardman, Leslie. (Australia) (b.2 August 1889) 100 meter freestyle [4h3r2/4]; 4 × 200 meter freestyle relay [1].

Champion, Malcolm. (New Zealand) (b.12 November 1883) 400 meter freestyle [4h2r2/3]; 1,500 meter freestyle [dnf-final]; 4 × 200 meter freestyle relay [1].

Hardwick, Harold Hampton. (Australia) (b.17 March 1889–d.1959) 100 meter freestyle [3h1r2/4]; 400 meter freestyle [3]; 1,500 meter freestyle [3]; 4 × 200 meter freestyle relay [1].

Healy, Cecil Patrick. (Australia) (b.28 November 1881–d.29 August 1918) 100 meter freestyle [2]; 400 meter freestyle [4]; 4 × 200 meter freestyle relay [1].

Longworth, William. (Australia) (b.26 September 1892) 100 meter freestyle [dns-final]; 1,500 meter freestyle [dns-h2r2/3].

Schryver, Frank. (Australia) (b.31 October 1891) 200 meter breaststroke [4h1r1/3]; 400 meter breaststroke [4h3r1/3].

Tartakover, Theodore B. (Australia) 100 meter freestyle [3h2r1/4]; 400 meter freestyle [dnf-h3r1/3].

Tennis (Total: 1; Men: 1; Women: 0)

Men

Wilding, Anthony Frederick. (New Zealand) (b.31 October 1883–d.9 May 1915) Men's Singles (Covered Court) [3].

Austria (Total: 86; Men: 80; Women: 6)

Athletics (Track & Field) (Total: 12; Men: 12; Women: 0)

Ehrenreich, Philipp. (b.15 July 1892) Broad Jump [23/9g2-3/qr].

Fleischer, Fritz. (b.2 March 1894) 100 meters [ach13r1/3]; 4 × 100 meter relay [2h5r1/3].

Franzl, Viktor. (b.27 July 1892) Pole Vault [=10g2qr]; Broad Jump [18/8g2-3/qr].

Hack, Karl. (b.15 June 1892) Marathon [dnf-].

Krojer, Gustav. (b.30 June 1885) 4 × 100 meter relay [2h5r1/3]; Hop, step, and jump [16/6g2qr]; Pentathlon [21].

Lixl-Kwieton, Felix. (b.16 November 1877–d.19 December 1958) Marathon [20].

Ponurski, Wladyslaw. (b.23 April 1891) 200 meters [4h15r1/3]; 400 meters [3h1r1/3].

Rath, Emmerich. (b.5 November 1883–d.21 December 1962) Marathon [33]; Cross-country, Individual [dnf-].

Rauch, Rudolf. (b.16 April 1893) 100 meters [3h2r1/3]; 200 meters [3h6r1/3]; 4 × 100 meter relay [2h5r1/3].

Schäffer, Josef. (b.2 July 1891) Shot Put [13/3g3qr]; Discus Throw [29/5g4qr]; Discus Throw, both hands [16/4g3qr]; Decathlon [10].

Tronner, Hans. (b.25 June 1883–d.7 October 1951) Discus Throw [5/2g1qr]; Discus Throw, both hands [13/7g1qr].

Weinzinger, Fritz. (b.14 July 1890) 100 meters [3h12r1/3]; 4 × 100 meter relay [2h5r1/3].

Cycling (Total: 6; Men: 6; Women: 0)

Hellensteiner, Josef. (b.13 April 1890) Road Race, Individual [45]; Road Race, Team [7].

Kofler, Adolf. (b.12 January 1892) Road Race, Individual [31]; Road Race, Team [7].

Kramer, Rudolf. (b.17 January 1886) Road Race, Individual [43]; Road Race, Team [7].

Rammer, Robert. (b.14 April 1890) Road Race, Individual [23]; Road Race, Team [7].

Wacha, Alois. (b.10 June 1888) Road Race, Individual [52]; Road Race, Team [7/ns].

Zilker, Josef. (b.19 March 1891) Road Race, Individual [46]; Road Race, Team [7/ns].

Diving (Total: 1; Men: 0; Women: 1)

Kellner, Hanny. (b.31 October 1892) Plain High Diving [ac/dnf-h2r1/2].

Fencing (Total: 12; Men: 12; Women: 0)

Bogen, Albert. (b.8 April 1882–d.14 July 1961) Sabre, Individual [dnc-p2r2/4]; Sabre, Team [2].

Cvetko, Rudolf.[2] (b.17 November 1880–d.15 December 1977) Foil, Individual (5p15r1/4); Sabre, Team (2).

Dereani, Franz. (b.10 September 1875) Foil, Individual (5p9r1/4); Sabre, Individual (dnc-p5r2/4).

Golling, Friedrich. (b.11 November 1883–d.11 October 1974) Foil, Individual (=5p6r2/4); Sabre, Individual (4p2r1/4); Sabre, Team (2).

Griez von Ronse, Arthur Dillon. Épée, Individual (=4p4r2/4).

Herschmann, Otto. (b.4 January 1877–d.14 June 1942) Sabre, Team (2).

Hohenlohe Schillingfürst, Ernest, Prince zu. (b.5 August 1891) Sabre, Individual (4p3r2/4).

Münich, Karl. (b.27 August 1848) Sabre, Individual (dnc-p4r2/4).

Puhm, Josef. (b.10 March 1877) Foil, Individual (=4p10r1/4); Sabre, Individual (dnc-p7r2/4).

Suttner, Andreas. (b.25 September 1876–d.5 July 1953) Foil, Individual (=4p1r1/4); Sabre, Team (2).

Trampler, Reinhold. (b.26 July 1877–d.21 December 1964) Foil, Individual (=6p13r1/4); Sabre, Team (2).

Verderber, Richard. (b.21 January 1884–d.8 September 1955) Foil, Individual (3); Sabre, Team (2).

Football (Association Football [Soccer]) (Total: 15; Men: 15; Women: 0)

Blaha, Gustav. [6].

Brandstätter, Josef. (b.29 December 1890) [6].

Braunsteiner, Karl. (b.27 October 1891) [6].

Cimera, Robert. (b.17 September 1887) [6].

Graubart, Bernhard. (b.22 December 1888) [6].

Grundwald, Leopold "Grundi." (b.28 October 1891) [6].
Hussak, Ludwig. (b.31 July 1883) [6].
Kaltenbrunner, Josef. (b.22 January 1888) [6].
Kurpiel, Ladislavs. (b.13 November 1883) [6].
Merz, Robert. (b.25 November 1887) [6].
Müller, Alois. (b.7 June 1890) [6].
Neubauer, Leopold. (b.15 October 1889) [6].
Noll, Otto. (b.24 July 1882) [6].
Studnicka, Johann. (b.7 October 1883) [6].
Weber, Franz. (b.3 July 1888) [6].

Modern Pentathlon (Total: 1; Men: 1; Women: 0)
Bernhardt, Ing. Edmond. (b.20 April 1885) Individual [8]. [See also Shooting.]

Rowing & Sculling (Total: 6; Men: 6; Women: 0)
Cuzna, Hugo. (b.16 February 1891) Coxed Fours, Outriggers [2h3r1/4].
Heinrich, Alfred. (b.10 February 1880) Single Sculls [2h1r1/4].
Jand, Emil. (b.24 September 1890) Coxed Fours, Outriggers [2h3r1/4].
Kröder, Georg. (b.17 January 1890) Coxed Fours, Outriggers [2h3r1/4].
Kromholz, Fritz. (b.24 March 1878) Coxed Fours, Outriggers [2h3r1/4].
Mayer, Richard. (b.23 March 1892) Coxed Fours, Outriggers [2h3r1/4].

Shooting (Total: 7; Men: 7; Women: 0)
Bernhardt, Ing. Edmond. (b.20 April 1885) Free Pistol, 50 meters [53]; Dueling Pistol, 30 meters [40]. [See also Modern Pentathlon.]
Dulnig, Johann. (b.13 September 1878) Military Rifle, 300 meters, 3-positions [32]; Military Rifle, 600 meters, any position [81].
Elbogen, Heinrich. (b.18 June 1872) Running Deer, Single Shot, Individual [7]; Running Deer, Double Shot, Individual [16]; Running Deer, Single Shot, Teams [4].
Michel, Adolf. (b.12 February 1878) Running Deer, Single Shot, Individual [10]; Running Deer, Single Shot, Teams [4].
Paternelli, Peter. (b.10 March 1856) Running Deer, Single Shot, Individual [=15]; Running Deer, Single Shot, Teams [4].
Schmal, Adolf, Jr. (b.12 January 1885) Free Pistol, 50 meters [39]; Dueling Pistol, 30 meters [20].
Steinböck, Eberhard. (b.30 November 1882) Running Deer, Single Shot, Individual [=31]; Running Deer, Single Shot, Teams [4].

Swimming (Total: 8; Men: 3; Women: 5)

Women
Adler, Margarete "Grete." (b.13 February 1896) 100 meter freestyle [4h4r1/3]; 4 × 100 meter freestyle relay [3].
Kellner, Josefa "Pepi." (b.12 March 1891) 100 meter freestyle [4h2r1/3].
Milch, Klara. (b.24 May 1891) 100 meter freestyle [3h1r1/3]; 4 × 100 meter freestyle relay [3].
Sticker, Josefine. (b.7 July 1894) 4 × 100 meter freestyle relay [3]; 100 meter freestyle [4h3r1/3].
Zahourek, Berta. (b.3 January 1896–d.14 June 1967) 100 meter freestyle [3h2r1/3]; 4 × 100 meter freestyle relay [3].

Men

Schuh, Franz. (b.15 March 1891) 400 meter freestyle [3h5r1/3]; 1,500 meter freestyle [dns-h1r2/3].

von Singalewicz, Zeno. (b.14 August 1875) 400 meter breaststroke [dnf-h1r2/3].

Wastl, Josef. (b.4 December 1892) 200 meter breaststroke [4h2r1/3]; 400 meter breaststroke [dnf-h1r1/3].

Tennis (Total: 3; Men: 3; Women: 0)

Piepes, Fritz Felix. (b.15 April 1887) Men's Doubles (Lawn) [2]; Men's Singles (Lawn) [=31].

von Salm-Hoogstraeten, Ludwig, Count. (b.24 February 1885) Men's Singles (Lawn) [=5].

Zborzil, Arthur. (b.15 July 1885–d.15 October 1937) Men's Doubles (Lawn) [2]; Men's Singles (Lawn) [=5].

Water Polo (Total: 7; Men: 7; Women: 0)

Buchfelder, Hermann. (b.21 December 1889) [4].

Buchfelder, Rudolf. (b.6 February 1884) [4].

Kovács, Ernst. (b.11 November 1884) [4].

Manuel, Richard. (b.1 October 1888) [4].

Schachlitz, Walter. (b.3 October 1887) [4].

Scheff, Otto.[3] (b.12 December 1889–d.26 October 1956) [4].

Wagner, Josef. (b.17 March 1886) [4].

Wrestling (Total: 8; Men: 8; Women: 0)

Barl, Karl. (b.3 March 1881) 82½ kg. Class (Greco-Roman) [AC].

Fischer, Viktor. (b.9 October 1892) 67½ kg. Class (Greco-Roman) [AC].

Kotkovic, Peter. (b.8 October 1890) 75 kg. Class (Greco-Roman) [AC].

Rauss, Hans Heinrich. (b.2 August 1890) 60 kg. Class (Greco-Roman) [AC].

Schärer, Friedrich. (b.27 May 1891) 60 kg. Class (Greco-Roman) [AC].

Stejskal, Josef. (b.26 August 1889) 67½ kg. Class (Greco-Roman) [AC].

Totuschek, Alois. (b.2 February 1885) 75 kg. Class (Greco-Roman) [AC].

Trestler, Johann. (b.27 October 1887) 82½ kg. Class (Greco-Roman) [AC].

Belgium[4] (Total: 35; Men: 34; Women: 1)

Athletics (Track & Field) (Total: 2; Men: 2; Women: 0)

Aelter(-Freddy), Léon Joseph. (b.6 January 1890) 100 meters [ach2r2/3]; 200 meters [3h3r1/3].

Delloye, François. (b.16 September 1888–d.1958) 1,500 meters [ach3r1/3].

Cycling (Total: 1; Men: 1; Women: 0)

Patou, Jean. (b.28 December 1878) Road Race, Individual [ac/dnf].

Equestrian Events (Total: 4; Men: 4; Women: 0)

Covert, Paul. Jumping, Team [6]; Three-day event, Individual [ac/dnf]; Three-day event, Team [dnf-] (La Sioute).

de Blommaert de Soye, Emanuel Hadelin, Colonel. (b.15 June 1875) Dressage, Individual [21]; Three-day event, Individual [ac/dnf]; Three-day event, Team [dnf-]; Jumping, Individual [3]; Jumping, Team [6] (Clonmore).

de Trannoy, Gaston Edouard François, Commandant. (b.18 October 1880–d.24 December 1960) Dressage, Individual [17]; Jumping, Team [6]; Three-day event, Individual [ac/dnf] (Capricieux); Three-day event, Team [ac/dnf] (Capricieux).

Reyntiens, Guy Nicolas. (b.26 August 1880–d.24 June 1932) Jumping, Individual [30]; Three-day event, Individual [ac/dnf]; Three-day event, Team [dnf-] (Beau Soleil).

Fencing (Total: 11; Men: 11; Women: 0)

Anspach, Henri. (b.10 July 1882–d.29 March 1979) Foil, Individual (=4p3r3/4); Épée, Individual (3p3r3/4); Épée, Team (1); Sabre, Team (=5).

Anspach, Paul. (b.1 April 1882–d.28 August 1981) Foil, Individual (=3p2r3/4); Épée, Individual (1); Épée, Team (1).

Berré, Marcel Louis. (b.12 November 1882–d.1953) Foil, Individual (=4p3r2/4); Épée, Individual (6p13r1/4); Sabre, Team (=5).

Boin, Victor C. (b.28 February 1886–d.31 March 1974) Épée, Individual (4). [See also Water Polo.]

de Montigny, Orphile Fernand. (b.5 January 1885–d.2 January 1974) Foil, Individual (=4p4r2/4); Épée, Individual (=4p1r2/4).

Hennet, Robert. (b.22 January 1886–d.1930) Foil, Individual (5p1r3/4); Épée, Team (1); Sabre, Team (=5).

Le Hardy de Beaulieu, Philippe. (b.1887) Épée, Individual (3); Sabre, Team (=5).

Ochs, Jacques. (b.1883–d.1971) Foil, Individual (=4p8r2/4); Épée, Individual (=4p3r2/4); Épée, Team (1).

Salmon, Gaston J. M. (b.1878–d.1917) Foil, Individual (=4p5r1/4); Épée, Individual (4p10r1/4); Épée, Team (1).

Tom, Léon. (b.1888) Foil, Individual (=5p1r2/4); Épée, Individual (7); Sabre, Team (=5).

Willems, Victor. (b.1877–d.1918) Foil, Individual (4p4r3/4); Épée, Individual (4p1r1/4); Épée, Team (1).

Rowing & Sculling (Total: 6; Men: 6; Women: 0)

Nuytens, Leonard. (b.7 Sepetmber 1892) Coxed Fours, Outriggers [2h3r2/4].

Van den Bossche, Georges. (b.15 July 1892) Coxed Fours, Outriggers [2h3r2/4].

Van Waes, Edmond. (b.7 April 1889) Coxed Fours, Outriggers [2h3r2/4].

Veirman, Polydore. (b.23 February 1881–d.1951) Single Sculls [2].

Visser, Guillaume. (b.20 April 1880–d.1952) Coxed Fours, Outriggers [2h3r2/4].

Willems, Georges. (b.5 September 1888) Coxed Fours, Outriggers [2h3r2/4].

Swimming (Total: 5; Men: 4; Women: 1)

Women

Guttenstein, Claire. (née Claire Frick) (b.26 March 1888–d.1948) 100 meter freestyle [5h3r1/3].

Men

Courbet, Félicien. (b.25 February 1888–d.1967) 200 meter breaststroke [5h2r2/3]; 400 meter breaststroke [4h1r2/3]. [See also Water Polo.]

Grégoire, Oscar, Jr. (b.27 March 1877–d.1947) 100 meter backstroke [dns-h1r1/3 and dq/h3r1/3[5]]. [See also Water Polo.]

Meyboom, Herman. (b.23 August 1889) 100 meter freestyle [3h6r1/4]. [See also Water Polo.]

Wuyts, Jules. (b.8 February 1886) 100 meter freestyle [4h2r1/4].

Water Polo (Total: 9; Men: 9; Women: 0)
  Boin, Victor C. (b.28 February 1886–d.31 March 1974) [3]. [See also Fencing.]
  Courbet, Félicien. (b.25 February 1888–d.1967) [3]. [See also Swimming.]
  Donners, Herman. (b.5 August 1888–d.1915) [3].
  Durant, Albert Paul. (b.1 July 1892) [3].
  Grégoire, Oscar, Jr. (b.27 March 1877–d.1947) [3]. [See also Swimming.]
  Hoffman, Jean. (b.29 September 1893) [3].
  Meyboom, Herman. (b.23 August 1889) [3]. [See also Swimming.]
  Nijs, Léon Pierre. (b.4 January 1890–d.1939) [3].
  Pletinckx, Joseph. (b.13 June 1888–d.1971) [3].

Wrestling (Total: 1; Men: 1; Women: 0)
  Gerstmans, Laurent. (b.26 February 1885) Unlimited Class (Greco-Roman) [AC].

Bohemia[6] (Total: 42; Men: 42; Women: 0)

Athletics (Track & Field) (Total: 11; Men: 11; Women: 0)
  Honzátko, Bohumil "Boris." (b.30 December 1875) Marathon [dnf-]. [See also Gymnastics.]
  Janda-Suk, František. (b.25 March 1878–d.23 June 1955) Shot Put [15/8g1-2/qr]; Discus Throw [17/4g3qr].
  Jiránek-Strana, Ladislav. (b.26 February 1883) 100 meters [ach3r1/3].
  Jirsák, Jindřich. (b.27 February 1885–d.1938) Pole Vault [=13g2qr].
  Labík-Gregan, Václav. (b.11 September 1893) 100 meters [ach10r1/3]; 200 meters [4h1r1/3]; 400 meters [4h9r1/3].
  Městecký, Zdeněk. (b.16 August 1881–d.15 May 1935) 800 meters [dnf-h5r1/3].
  Penc, Vladimír. (b.10 October 1893) 10,000 meters [9h1r1/2]; Marathon [dnf-].
  Richter, Rudolf. (b.7 April 1883–d.13 January 1962) 10 kilometer walk [dnf-h1r1/2].
  Slavík, František. (b.25 September 1888–d.2 October 1926) Marathon [dnf-].
  Šustera, Miroslav. (b.15 March 1878–d.15 December 1961) Discus Throw [38/8g3qr].
  Vygoda, Bedřich. (b.29 May 1894) 100 meters [3h5r2/3].

Cycling (Total: 5; Men: 5; Women: 0)
  Kubrycht, Bohumil. (b.27 July 1886) Road Race, Individual [88]; Road Race, Team [tm-dnf/[88]].
  Kundert, František. (b.28 July 1891) Road Race, Individual [ac/dnf]; Road Race, Team [tm-dnf/dnf].
  Rameš, Bohumil. (b.4 March 1895) Road Race, Individual [63]; Road Race, Team [tm-dnf/[63].
  Tintěra, Václav. (b.20 March 1893) Road Race, Individual [87]; Road Race, Team [tm-dnf/[87]].
  Vokoun, Jan. (b.2 August 1887) Road Race, Individual [ac/dnf]; Road Race, Team [tm-dnf/dnf].

Fencing (Total: 13; Men: 13; Women: 0)
  Bárta, Zdeněk. (b.15 May 1891–d.1 April 1987) Épée, Individual (=5p8r2/4); Sabre, Individual (=4p4r1/4).
  Čipera, Josef. (b.1888) Sabre, Team (4).

Goppold z Lobsdorfu, Karel. (b.1894) Épée, Individual (=5p7r2/4).

Goppold z Lobsdorfu, Vilém, Jr. (b.1893) Foil, Individual (=4p7r2/4); Épée, Individual (6p4r3/4); Épée, Team (=7).

Goppold z Lobsdorfu, Vilém, Sr. (b.28 May 1869–d.12 June 1943) Épée, Team (=7); Sabre, Team (4).

Javůrek, Josef. (b.1876) Foil, Individual (4p9r1/4); Épée, Individual (=5p7r1/4); Sabre, Individual (dnc-p6r2/4).

Klika, Miroslav. (b.1890) Foil, Individual (4p4r1/4); Épée, Individual (5p2r3/4);

Kříž, František. (b.18 May 1884–d.30 July 1966) Foil, Individual (6p15r1/4); Épée, Individual (6p3r3/4); Épée, Team (=7).

Pfeiffer, Josef. (b.1884) Foil, Individual (6p3r2/4); Épée, Individual (=5p10r1/4); Épée, Team (=7); Sabre, Team (4).

Schejbal, Bedřich. (b.1874) Sabre, Team (4).

Švorčík, Otakar. (b.7 December 1886–d.18 September 1955) Sabre, Team (4).

Tvrzský, Vilém. (b.1880) Foil, Individual (6p1r3/4); Épée, Individual (acp3r1/4);

Vávra, Zdeněk. (b.1891) Foil, Individual (6p10r1/4); Épée, Individual (6p1r3/4).

Gymnastics (Total: 1; Men: 1; Women: 0)

Honzátko, Bohumil "Boris." (b.30 December 1875) Combined All-Around, Individual [36]. [See also Athletics (Track & Field).]

Rowing & Sculling (Total: 1; Men: 1; Women: 0)[7]

Šourek, Jan. (b.2 September 1887) Single Sculls [ac/dnf-h6r1/4].

Tennis (Total: 8; Men: 8; Women: 0)

Hainz, Jaroslav. (b.17 September 1883) Men's Singles (Covered Court) [=16].

Hykš, Bohuslav "Černý." (b.7 May 1889) Men's Singles (Lawn) [=31]; Men's Doubles (Lawn) [=15].

Just, Jaroslav. (b.6 February 1883–d.5 August 1928) Men's Singles (Lawn) [=31]; Men's Doubles (Lawn) [4].

Kodl, Jiří. (b.3 April 1889) Men's Singles (Lawn) [=48].

Robětín (Fuchs), Karel "Sláva." (b.25 January 1889) Men's Singles (Lawn) [=17]; Men's Singles (Covered Court) [=5]; Men's Doubles (Lawn) [=15].

Šebek, Josef. (b.18 March 1888) Men's Singles (Lawn) [=9]; Men's Doubles (Lawn) [=15].

Zeman, Jaromír. (b.12 August 1886) Men's Singles (Lawn) [=31]; Men's Doubles (Lawn) [=15].

Žemla, Ladislav "Razný." (b.6 November 1887–d.17 June 1955) Men's Singles (Lawn) [4]; Men's Doubles (Lawn) [4].

Wrestling (Total: 4; Men: 4; Women: 0]

Balej, Jan. (b.20 May 1893) 67½ kg. Class (Greco-Roman) [AC].

Beránek, Josef. (b.6 December 1891–d.6 July 1959) 60 kg. Class (Greco-Roman) [AC].

Halík, Karel. (b.21 December 1883) 67½ kg. Class (Greco-Roman) [AC].

Kopřiva, František. (b.30 July 1892) 82½ kg. Class (Greco-Roman) [AC].

Canada (Total: 36; Men: 36; Women: 0)

Athletics (Track & Field) (Total: 18; Men: 18; Women: 0)

Beasley, Harry B. (b.14 March 1892–d.1972) 100 meters [4h11r1/3]; 200 meters [ach7r1/3]; 4 × 100 meter relay [2h3r2/3].

Bricker, Calvin David. (b.3 November 1885–d.24 April 1963) Broad Jump [2]; Hop, step, and jump [18/8g2qr].

Brock, George Melville. (b.3 February 1892–d.4 October 1956) 400 meters [3h11r1/3]; 800 meters [5]; 4 × 400 meter relay [2h1r1/2].

Corkery, James Joseph. (b.27 June 1889) Marathon [dnf-].

Decoteau, Alexander. (b.19 November 1887) 5,000 meters [6].

Duffy, James. (b.1 May 1890–d.23 April 1915) Marathon [5].

Fabre, Edouard. (b.21 August 1889–d.1 July 1939) Marathon [11].

Forsyth, William Charles. (b.20 January 1891) Marathon [15].

Gallon, Thomas Heaton. (b.28 November 1886) 400 meters [3h12r1/3]; 4 × 400 meter relay [2h1r1/2].

Gillis, Duncan. (b.3 January 1883–d.1965) Discus Throw [14/3g3qr]; Hammer Throw [2].

Goulding, George Henry. (b.16 November 1884–d.31 January 1966) 10 Kilometer Walk [1].

Happenny, William. (b.23 May 1885–d.1957) Pole Vault [=3].

Howard, John Armstrong "Army." (b.6 October 1888–d.1937) 100 meters [ach5r2/3]; 200 meters [3h4r2/3]; 4 × 100 meter relay [2h3r2/3]; 4 × 400 meter relay [2h1r1/2].

Keeper, Benjamin Joseph "Joe." (b.21 January 1888–d.9 September 1971) 5,000 meters [ac-final]; 10,000 meters [4].

Lukeman, Frank L. (b.1887) 110 meter hurdles [3h11r1/3]; 100 meters [3h3r2/3]; 4 × 100 meter relay [2h3r2/3]; Decathlon [ac/dnf]; Pentathlon [4].

Maranda, Arthur. (b.16 May 1887) Broad Jump [28/11g2-3/qr]; Standing Long Jump [17/4g2qr]; Hop, step, and jump [20/9g2qr].

McConnell, Frank Duncan. (b.17 January 1887) 100 meters [3h14r1/3]; 200 meters [3h14r1/3]; 4 × 100 meter relay [2h3r2/3].

Tait, John Lindsay. (b.25 September 1889–d.July 1971) 4 × 400 meter relay [2h1r1/2]; 800 meters [5h1r2/3]; 1,500 meters [4h3r1/3].

Cycling (Total: 2; Men: 2; Women: 0)
Brown, Frank Ruthers. (b.1890) Road Race, Individual [5].
Watson, George. (b.1891) Road Race, Individual [78].

Diving (Total: 2; Men: 2; Women: 0)
Lyons, John P. (b.8 August 1876) Plain and Fancy High Diving [ac/dnf-h3r1/2]; Plain High Diving [8h3r1/2].
Zimmerman, Robert M. (b.2 December 1881) Springboard Diving [6].

Rowing & Sculling (Total: 10; Men: 10; Women: 0)
Boyd, Philip Ewing. (b.1876) Coxed Eights [2h5r1/4].
Butler, Everard Burnside. (b.28 December 1885) Single Sculls [2h2r3/4].
Gale, Becher Robert. (b.14 April 1887) Coxed Eights [2h5r1/4].
Gregory, B. Richard John. (b.1890) Coxed Eights [2h5r1/4].
Kent, Albert Hilton E. (b.4 November 1877) Coxed Eights [2h5r1/4].
McCleary, Winslow Ogden. (b.1886) Coxed Eights [2h5r1/4].
Murphy, William Ewart G. (b.9 February 1889) Coxed Eights [2h5r1/4].
Riddy, Charles. (b.3 March 1885) Coxed Eights [2h5r1/4].
Sinclair, Alexander. (b.27 July 1882) Coxed Eights [2h5r1/4].
Taylor, Geoffrey Barron. (b.4 February 1890) Coxed Eights [2h5r1/4].

Shooting (Total: 3; Men: 3; Women: 0)
Davies, William Richard. (b.19 March 1881) Clay Trap Shooting, Individual [=45].

Hutcheson, Robert Bennett. (b.9 May 1870) Clay Trap Shooting, Individual [=17].
Kenyon, James H. (b.23 June 1876) Clay Trap Shooting, Individual [=45].

Swimming (Total: 1; Men: 1; Women: 0)
Hodgson, George Ritchie. (b.12 October 1893–d.1 May 1983) 400 meter freestyle [1]; 1,500 meter freestyle [1].

Chile[8] (Total: 14; Men: 14; Women: 0)

Athletics (Track & Field) (Total: 6; Men: 6; Women: 0)
Eitel, Pablo. (b.11 April 1888) 100 meters [ach3r1/3]; 200 meters [5h11r1/3]; 110 meter hurdles [4h1r2/3].
Hammersley, Rodolfo. (b.10 June 1889) High Jump [=11g1/qr]; Standing High Jump [=3g1qr].
Mueller, Federico A. (b.9 September 1888) 800 meters [ach6r1/3].
Palma, Leopoldo E. (b.13 March 1891) 200 meters [ach15r1/3]; 800 meters [dnf-h2r1/3].
Salinas, Rolando. (b.1 November 1889) 10 Kilometer Walk [7h2r1/2].
Sanchez Rodriguez, Alfonso. (b.29 August 1891) 5,000 meters [dnf-h5r1/2]; 10,000 meters [8h2r1/2].

Cycling (Total: 4; Men: 4; Women: 0)
Downey V., Alberto. (b.2 October 1890) Road Race, Individual [42]; Road Race, Team [9].
Friedemann, Arturo. (b.1 January 1893) Road Race, Individual [69]; Road Race, Team [9].
Koller V., Cárlos. (b.1 November 1890) Road Race, Individual [58]; Road Race, Team [9].
Torres P., José. (b.16 July 1889) Road Race, Individual [74]; Road Race, Team [9].

Equestrian Events (Total: 2; Men: 2; Women: 0)
Deichler, Enrique. Jumping, Individual [=16] (Chile).
Yanes, Elias. Jumping, Individual [25] (Patria).

Shooting (Total: 2; Men: 2; Women: 0)
Alegria, Felix. (b.20 November 1876) Military Rifle, 300 meters, 3-Positions [48]; Military Rifle, 600 meters, any position [72]; Free Pistol, 50 meters [38]; Dueling Pistol, 30 meters [25].
Ekwall, Harald Kurt. (b.14 December 1873) Military Rifle, 300 meters, 3-Positions [43]; Military Rifle, 600 meters, any position [67]; Free Pistol, 50 meters [23]; Dueling Pistol, 30 meters [38].

Denmark[9] (Total: 152; Men: 151; Women: 1)

Athletics (Track & Field) (Total: 14; Men: 14; Women: 0)
Baden, Holger Jakob. (b.18 January 1892–d.31 January 1966) Cross-Country, Individual [dnf-]; Cross-Country, Team [5/ns].
Christensen, Johannes Laurs (later Granholm). (b.14 February 1889–d.23 April 1957) Marathon [29].
Christiansen, Karl Lauritz. (b.27 December 1892–d.4 October 1976) Cross-Country, Individual [14]; Cross-Country, Team [5].

Danild, Fritz Johan. (b.18 August 1893–d.10 March 1951) Cross-Country, Individual [dnf-]; Cross-Country, Team [5/ns].

Gylche, Vilhelm Emanuael Jakob. (b.6 January 1888–d.18 December 1952) 10 Kilometer Walk [dnf-final].

Jensen, Karl Julius. (b.1 January 1888–d.31 October 1965) Cross-Country, Individual [dnf-]; Cross-Country, Team [5/ns].

Langkjær, Svend. (b.23 August 1886–d.2 May 1948) Decathlon [ac/dnf].

Lodal, Olaf. (b.6 July 1885) Marathon [30].

Pedersen, Niels. (b.5 August 1888–d.4 January 1968) 10 Kilometer Walk [ac/h2r1/2].

Pedersen, Viggo Christoffer. (b.22 April 1889–d.16 April 1965) Cross-Country, Individual [23]; Cross-Country, Team [5].

Rasmussen, Aage (later Remfeldt). (b.4 September 1889–d.29 November 1983) 10 Kilometer Walk [4].

Rasmussen, Steen. (b.1 December 1888) Cross-Country, Individual [28]; Cross-Country, Team [5/ns].

Topp, Gerhard August. (b.16 April 1893–d.17 January 1977) Cross-Country, Individual [26]; Cross-Country, Team [5].

Vikke, Fritz Bøchen. (b.14 February 1884–d.23 August 1955) Pole Vault [=8g2qr].

Cycling (Total: 8; Men: 8; Women: 0)

Hansen, Charles Carl Han. (b.23 April 1891) Road Race, Individual [32]; Road Race, Team [8].

Jensen, Otto Thomas. (b.1 January 1893–d.25 December 1972) Road Race, Individual [ac/dnf]; Road Race, Team [8/ns/dnf].

Nielsen, Valdemar. (b.21 June 1879–d.3 June 1954) Road Race, Individual [72]; Road Race, Team [8].

Nielsen, Valdemar Christoffer. (b.21 September 1893–d.16 May 1974) Road Race, Individual [dnf-]; Road Race, Team [8/ns/dnf].

Olsen, Godtfred Hegelund. (b.22 July 1883–d.21 June 1954) Road Race, Individual [53]; Road Race, Team [8].

Olsen, Hans Christian Hegelund. (b.1 January 1885–d.4 December 1959) Road Race, Individual [ac/dnf]; Road Race, Team [8/ns/dnf].

Reinwaldt, Johannes Ferdinand. (b.14 May 1890–d.28 June 1958) Road Race, Individual [48]; Road Race, Team [8].

Smith, Olaf Meyland (later Olaf Meyland-Smith). (b.23 July 1882–d.26 November 1924) Road Race, Individual [25]; Road Race, Team [8].

Equestrian Events (Total: 4; Men: 4; Women: 0)

Keyper, Rudolf Jakob Poul. (b.25 October 1880–d.28 February 1973) Dressage, Individual [16] (Kinley Princess).

Kirkebjerg, Frode Rasmussen. (b.10 May 1888–d.12 January 1975) Three-Day Event, Individual [ac/dnf]; Three-Day Event, Team [dnf-] (Dibbe-Libbe).

Kraft, Carl Adolph. (b.7 February 1876–d.13 February 1964) Three-Day Event, Individual [ac/dnf]; Three-Day Event, Team [dnf-] (Gorm).

Saunte, Carl Høst. (b.31 October 1872–d.27 February 1955) Dressage, Individual [18]; Three-Day Event, Individual [ac/dnf]; Three-Day Event, Team [dnf-] (Streg).

Fencing (Total: 6; Men: 6; Women: 0)

Berntsen, Oluf Christian. (b.5 November 1891–d.c.26 June 1987) Foil, Individual (=4p13r1/4); Épée, Individual (=5p15r1/4); Sabre, Individual (6p4r3/4).

Berthelsen, Jens Ole Holdorff. (b.17 December 1890–d.28 October 1961) Foil, Individual (4p2r2/4); Épée, Individual (6p6r2/4); Sabre, Individual (4p6r2/4); Sabre, Team (=9).

Levison, Ejnar Herman. (b.15 May 1880–d.3 August 1970) Foil, Individual (=4p8r2/4); Épée, Individual (=4p4r3/4); Épée, Team (=5); Sabre, Individual (=5p1r2/4); Sabre, Team (=9).

Olsen, Hans Knud Valdemar (later Frender). (b.21 January 1886–d.13 September 1976) Foil, Individual (=6p7r1/4); Épée, Individual (8p13r1/4); Épée, Team (=5); Sabre, Team (=9).

Osiier, Ivan Joseph Martin. (b.16 December 1888–d.23 September 1965) Foil, Individual (5p2r3/4); Épée, Individual (2); Épée, Team (=5); Sabre, Team (=9).

Østrup, Lauritz Christian. (b.6 June 1881–d.21 May 1940) Foil, Individual (=4p7r2/4); Épée, Individual (4p16r1/4); Épée, Team (=5); Sabre, Team (=9).

Football (Association Football [Soccer]) (Total: 15; Men: 15; Women: 0)

Berth, Paul Ludvig Laurits. (b.7 April 1890–d.9 November 1969) [2].

Christoffersen, Hjalmar Johan. (b.1 December 1889–d.28 December 1966) [2].

Hansen, Harald. (b.14 March 1884–d.10 May 1927) [2].

Hansen, Sofus Peter. (b.16 November 1889–d.19 February 1962) [2].

Jørgensen, Emil Ludvig Peter. (b.7 February 1882–d.23 March 1947) [2].

Middelboe, Nils. (b.5 October 1887–d.21 September 1976) [2].

Nielsen, Niels Christian Oscar. (b.4 October 1882–d.18 May 1941) [2]. (Later Niels Christian Oscar Nielsen-Nørlund [1914].)

Nielsen, Niels Poul. (b.25 December 1891–d.9 August 1962) [2].

Nielsen, Sofus Erhard. (b.15 March 1888–d.6 August 1963) [2].

Olsen, Ole Anton. (b.14 September 1889–d.17 March 1972) [2].

Petersen, Axel Karl. (b.10 December 1887–d.20 December 1968) [2].

Seidelin-Nielsen, Ivar-Lykke. (b.7 March 1889–d.9 January 1955) [2].

Tufvesson, Martin Axel. (b.11 November 1889–d.25 December 1962) [2].

von Buchwald, Charles. (b.22 October 1880–d.19 November 1951) [2].

Wolfhagen, Vilhelm. (b.11 November 1889–d.5 July 1958) [2].

Gymnastics (Total: 49; Men: 49; Women: 0)

Andersen, Axel Sigurd. (b.20 December 1891–d.15 May 1931) Combined All-Around, Individual [33]; Combined All-Around, Free System, Team [3].

Andersen, Hjalmart Nørregaard "Hjallis." (b.11 October 1889–d.23 January 1974) Combined All-Around, Free System, Team [3]. (Later Hjalmart Andersen-Eering [1918].)

Andersen, Peter Villemoes. (b.9 April 1884–d.25 September 1956) Combined All-Around, Swedish System [2].

Birch, Halvor. (b.21 February 1885–d.5 July 1962) Combined All-Around, Free System, Team [3].

Bøggild, Valdemar Jensen. (b.30 September 1893–d.2 July 1943) Combined All-Around, Swedish System [2].

Christensen, Søren Peter. (b.30 October 1884–d.12 October 1927) Combined All-Around, Swedish System [2].

Eriksen, Ingvald. (b.3 September 1884–d.28 January 1961) Combined All-Around, Swedish System [2].

Falcke, George. (b.2 March 1891–d.1 February 1979) Combined All-Around, Swedish System [2].

Garp, Torkild. (b.31 January 1883–d.16 February 1976) Combined All-Around, Swedish System [2].

Grimmelmann, Hermann Johann Wilhelm. (b.15 January 1893) Combined All-Around, Free System, Team [3].

Hansen, Aage Marius. (b.27 September 1880–d.5 May 1980) Combined All-Around, Free System, Team [3].

Hansen, Arvor. (b.5 November 1886–d.19 June 1962) Combined All-Around, Free System, Team [3]; Combined All-Around, Individual [26].

Hansen, Christian Marius. (b.24 September 1891–d.13 June 1961) Combined All-Around, Free System, Team [3].

Hansen, Hans Trier. (b.15 May 1893–d.12 September 1980) Combined All-Around, Swedish System [2].

Hansen, Johannes "Hanne." (b.6 December 1882–d.20 October 1959) Combined All-Around, Swedish System [2].

Hansen, Rasmus. (b.13 January 1885–d.3 July 1967) Combined All-Around, Swedish System [2].

Jensen, Charles Kristoffer Peter. (b.24 December 1885–d.5 June 1920) Combined All-Around, Free System, Team [3]; Combined All-Around, Individual [30].

Jensen, Jens Kristian (later Byge). (b.22 March 1885–d.27 March 1956) Combined All-Around, Swedish System [2].

Jensen, Søren Alfred. (b.22 May 1891–d.16 May 1978) Combined All-Around, Swedish System [2].

Johansen, Hjalmar Peter Martin. (b.1 November 1892–d.9 December 1979) Combined All-Around, Free System, Team [3].

Jørgensen, Poul Preben. (b.17 February 1892–d.6 October 1973) Combined All-Around, Free System, Team [3].

Kirk, Karl. (b.5 April 1890–d.6 March 1955) Combined All-Around, Swedish System [2].

Kirkegaard, Jens. (b.1 June 1889–d.20 April 1966) Combined All-Around, Swedish System [2].

Kjems, Olaf Nielsen. (b.31 May 1880–d.11 April 1952) Combined All-Around, Swedish System [2].

Krebs, Carl Immanuel. (b.11 February 1889–d.15 May 1971) Combined All-Around, Free System, Team [3].

Larsen, Carl Otto Laurits.[10] (b.3 June 1886–d.4 December 1962) Combined All-Around, Swedish System [2].

Laursen, Jens Peter Martinus. (b.1 January 1888–d.23 May 1967) Combined All-Around, Swedish System [2].

Lefevre, Marius Ludvig. (b.4 May 1875–d.14 March 1958) Combined All-Around, Swedish System [2].

Madsen, Vigo Meulengracht. (b.13 November 1889–d.17 June 1979) Combined All-Around, Free System, Team [3]. (Later Vigo Meulengracht-Madsen [1941].)

Mark, Povl Sørensen. (b.19 June 1889–d.18 January 1957) Combined All-Around, Swedish System [2].

Møbius, Ejnar August. (b.6 August 1891–d.22 November 1981) Combined All-Around, Individual [40].

Nielsen, Lukas Frederik Christian. (b.23 December 1884–d.29 September 1964) Combined All-Around, Free System, Team [3].

Nordstrøm, Rikard Hannibal. (b.23 April 1893–d.7 February 1955) Combined All-Around, Free System, Team [3].

Olsen, Peter Einar. (b.11 March 1893–d.3 June 1949) Combined All-Around, Swedish System [2].

Olsen, Steen Lerche. (b.17 June 1886–d.5 May 1960) Combined All-Around, Free System, Team [3]. (Later Steen Lerkentorp [1926].)

Olsson, Oluf. (b.30 May 1873–d.25 June 1947) Combined All-Around, Free System, Team [3].

Pedersen, Carl Julius. (b.25 July 1883–d.18 August 1971) Combined All-Around, Individual [=34]; Combined All-Around, Free System, Team [3].

Pedersen, Hans. (b.5 November 1887–d.22 September 1943) Combined All-Around, Swedish System [2].

Pedersen, Hans Eiler. (b.18 October 1890–d.1 December 1971) Combined All-Around, Swedish System [2].

Pedersen, Jens Olaf. (b.6 July 1884–d.6 April 1972) Combined All-Around, Swedish System [2].

Pedersen, Oluf Kristian Edvin. (b.14 March 1878–d.8 March 1917) Combined All-Around, Free System, Team [3].

Pedersen, Peder Larsen. (b.30 November 1880–d.20 January 1966) Combined All-Around, Swedish System [2].

Petersen, Niels Knudsen. (b.12 July 1885–d.29 April 1961) Combined All-Around, Free System, Team [3]; Combined All-Around, Individual [=34].

Ravn, Jørgen Christian Jensen. (b.22 February 1892–d.24 October 1976) Combined All-Around, Swedish System [2].

Svendsen, Christian Valdemar. (b.13 July 1890–d.28 June 1959) Combined All-Around, Free System, Team [3]. (Later Christian Valdemar Hauer [1919].)

Sørensen, Aksel. (b.5 October 1891–d.15 May 1955) Combined All-Around, Swedish System [2].

Thorborg, Søren Frederik. (b.10 March 1889–d.31 July 1978) Combined All-Around, Swedish System [2].

Vadgaard, Kristen Møller. (b.2 June 1886–d.16 February 1979) Combined All-Around, Swedish System [2].

Vinther, Johannes Larsen. (b.5 January 1893–d.24 May 1968) Combined All-Around, Swedish System [2].

Modern Pentathlon (Total: 4; Men: 4; Women: 0)

Jølver, Kai Albert Wognsen. (b.11 July 1889–d.24 July 1940) Individual [22].

Laybourn, Vilhelm Carl. (b.3 August 1885–d.4 April 1955) Individual [ac/dnf].

Ussing, Johannes Blom. (b.2 December 1883–d.13 March 1929) Individual [ac/dnf].

Zeilau, Theodor Cizeck. (b.1 February 1884–d.5 May 1970) Individual [ac/dnf].

Rowing & Sculling (Total: 15; Men: 15; Women: 0)

Allert, Ejler Arild Emil. (b.27 November 1881–d.25 March 1959) Coxed Fours, Inriggers [1].

Bisgaard, Erik. (b.25 January 1890–d.21 June 1987) Coxed Fours, Outriggers [2h1r3/4].

Clemmensen, Ejgil Becker. (b.21 June 1890–d.24 October 1932) Coxed Fours, Outriggers [2h1r3/4].

Eyrich, Theodor Hans Christian. (b.29 May 1893–d.9 October 1979) Coxed Fours, Outriggers [2h5r1/4].

Frandsen, Rasmus Peter. (b.17 April 1886–d.5 December 1974) Coxed Fours, Outriggers [2h1r3/4].

Gøtke, Knud Christian. (b.16 August 1886–d.28 May 1963) Coxed Fours, Outriggers [2h5r1/4].

Hansen, Jørgen Christian. (b.14 August 1890–d.10 September 1953) Coxed Fours, Inriggers [1].

Hartmann, Poul Richard. (b.1 May 1878–d.29 June 1969) Coxed Fours, Inriggers [1].

Jørgensen, Marius Hans. (b.25 December 1889–d.22 April 1955) Coxed Fours, Outriggers [2h5r1/4].

Møller, Carl Martin August. (b.24 August 1887) Coxed Fours, Inriggers [1].

Pedersen, Carl Frederik. (b.30 September 1884–d.3 September 1968) Coxed Fours, Inriggers [1].

Praem, Johan Vilhelm Thorolf. (b.13 October 1889–d.12 January 1967) Coxed Fours, Outriggers [2h5r1/4].

Simonsen, Mikael. (b.20 November 1882–d.29 March 1950) Single Sculls [dns-r2/4]; Coxed Fours, Outriggers [2h1r3/4].

Smedberg, Silva Constantin. (b.10 July 1891–d.22 August 1967) Coxed Fours, Outriggers [2h5r1/4].

Thymann, Poul. (b.10 May 1888–d.12 October 1971) Coxed Fours, Outriggers [2h1r3/4].

Shooting (Total: 14; Men: 14; Women: 0)

Andersen, Niels. (b.14 May 1867–d.9 October 1930) Free Rifle, 300 meters, 3-Positions, Teams [3]; Military Rifle, 200, 400, 500, and 600 meters, Teams [8].

Denver, Hans Peter Christian. (b.28 October 1876–d.18 September 1961) Free Rifle, 300 meters, 3-Positions [ac/dnf]; Small-Bore Rifle, 50 meters, Teams [=5].

Friis, Rasmus. (b.19 November 1871) Military Rifle, 600 meters, any position [48]; Military Rifle, 200, 400, 500, and 600 meters, Teams [8].

Gerlow, Povl. (b.18 August 1881–d.1 June 1959) Free Rifle, 300 meters, 3-Positions [60]; Military Rifle, 300 meters, 3-Positions [74]; Small-Bore Rifle, prone position, 50 meters [38]; Small-Bore Rifle, 25 meters, Disappearing Target [31]; Small-Bore Rifle, 50 meters, Teams [=5].

Hajslund, Jens Madsen. (b.29 May 1877–d.28 August 1964) Free Rifle, 300 meters, 3-Positions [ac/dnf]; Free Rifle, 300 meters, 3-Positions, Teams [3]; Military Rifle, 200, 400, 500, and 600 meters, Teams [8].

Larsen, Laurits Theodor Christian. (b.8 April 1872–d.28 June 1949) Free Rifle, 300 meters, 3-Positions [33]; Free Rifle, 300 meters, 3-Positions, Teams [3]; Free Pistol, 50 meters [21].

Larsen, Niels Hansen Ditlev. (b.21 November 1889–d.15 November 1969) Free Rifle, 300 meters, 3-Positions [3]; Military Rifle, 300 meters, 3-Positions [63]; Free Rifle, 300 meters, 3-Positions, Teams [3]; Military Rifle, 200, 400, 500, and 600 meters, Teams [8]; Free Pistol, 50 meters [41].

Madsen, Lars Jørgen. (b.19 July 1871–d.1 April 1925) Free Rifle, 300 meters, 3-Positions [2]; Free Rifle, 300 meters, 3-Positions, Teams [3]; Military Rifle, 200, 400, 500, and 600 meters, Teams [8]; Small-Bore Rifle, 50 meters, Teams [=5]; Free Pistol, 50 meters [14].

Nielsen, Anders Peter. (b.25 May 1867–d.16 April 1950) Free Rifle, 300 meters, 3-Positions [47]; Free Pistol, 50 meters [50].

Nielsen, Frants. (b.22 January 1874–d.6 June 1961) Free Rifle, 300 meters, 3-Positions [46]; Small-Bore Rifle, prone position, 50 meters [26]; Small-Bore Rifle, 50 meters, Teams [=5]; Free Pistol, 50 meters [40].

Nielsen, Peter Sofus. (b.22 January 1890–d.26 January 1972) Free Pistol, 50 meters [43].

Olsen, Ole. (b.7 June 1869–d.7 September 1944) Free Rifle, 300 meters, 3-Positions [12]; Free Rifle, 300 meters, 3-Positions, Teams [3].

Schultz, Hans Christian. (b.23 March 1864–d.26 June 1937) Free Rifle, 300 meters, 3-Positions [52]; Military Rifle, 300 meters, 3-Positions [36]; Military Rifle, 600 meters, any position [44]; Military Rifle, 200, 400, 500, and 600 meters, Teams [8].

Tauson, Hans Christian. (b.21 February 1885–d.24 November 1974) Free Rifle, 300 meters, 3-Positions [52].

Swimming (Total: 1; Men: 1; Women: 0)

Hedegaard, Harry Christian. (b.7 November 1894–d.19 July 1939) 400 meter freestyle [5h6r1/3]; 1,500 meter freestyle [3h3r1/3].

Tennis (Total: 10; Men: 9; Women: 1)

Women

Castenschiold, Thora Gerda Sofie. (b.1 February 1882–d.30 January 1979) Ladies' Singles (Covered Court) [2]; Mixed Doubles (Covered Court) [=5]. (Later Thorda Gerda Sofie Carlheim-Gyllenskøld [1912].)

Men

Arenholt, Jørgen. (b.14 December 1876–d.27 July 1953) Men's Doubles (Lawn) [=15]; Men's Singles (Lawn) [=31].

Frederiksen, Ove Kamphøwener. (b.22 August 1884–d.24 May 1966) Men's Doubles (Lawn) [=9]; Men's Singles (Lawn) [=31].

Frigast, Ernst Peter Lütken. (b.13 December 1889–d.29 November 1968) Men's Doubles (Lawn) [=9]; Men's Singles (Lawn) [=31].

Hansen, Victor Georg. (b.29 August 1889–d.6 March 1974) Men's Doubles (Lawn) [=9]; Men's Singles (Lawn) [=17].

Ingerslev, Vagn. (b.23 March 1885–d.28 December 1952) Men's Doubles (Lawn) [=15]; Men's Singles (Lawn) [=9].

Larsen, Erik Øckenholt. (b.23 August 1880) Men's Singles (Covered Court) [=16]; Mixed Doubles (Covered Court) [=5].

Madsen, Aage Sigfried. (b.25 May 1883–d.9 April 1937) Men's Doubles (Lawn) [=9]; Men's Singles (Lawn) [=31].

Rovsing, Ludvig Leif Sadi. (b.27 July 1887–d.17 June 1977) Men's Doubles (Lawn) [=9]; Men's Singles (Lawn) [=17].

Thayssen, Axel. (b.22 February 1885–d.31 January 1952) Men's Doubles (Lawn) [=9]; Men's Singles (Lawn) [=17].

Wrestling (Total: 9; Men: 9; Women: 0)

Andersen, Anders Peter. (b.26 October 1881–d.19 February 1961) 75 kg. Class (Greco-Roman) [AC].

Christensen, Jens Harald. (b.4 January 1884–d.1959) 82½ kg. Class (Greco-Roman) [AC].

Eriksen, Johannes Thorvald. (b.12 June 1889–d.25 June 1963) 82½ kg. Class (Greco-Roman) [AC].

Hansen, Carl Christian (later Bømervang). (b.21 January 1887–d.16 July 1953) 60 kg. Class (Greco-Roman) [AC].

Hansen, Frederik Oluf. (b.11 September 1885–d.23 January 1981) 67½ kg. Class (Greco-Roman) [AC].

Hansen, Hvitfeldt. (b.30 July 1890–d.15 October 1964) 75 kg. Class (Greco-Roman) [AC].

Hetmar, Verner Edmund Reimer. (b.27 October 1890–d.28 May 1962) 60 kg. Class (Greco-Roman) [AC].

Jensen, Søren Marinus. (b.5 May 1879–d.6 January 1965) Unlimited Class (Greco-Roman) [3].

Nagel, Otto Walter Dannemann. (b.23 February 1889–d.2 September 1947) 82½ kg. Class (Greco-Roman) [AC].

Yachting (Total: 3; Men: 3; Women: 0)

Herschend, Steen Steensen. (b.12 November 1888–d.3 August 1976) 6-meter class [2] (Nurdug II).

Madsen, Hans Meulengracht. (b.9 September 1885–d.7 October 1966) 6-meter class [2] (Nurdug II). (Later Hans Meulengracht-Madsen [1941].)

Thomsen, Svenn Bernth. (b.7 September 1884–d.14 November 1968) 6-meter class [2] (Nurdug II).

Finland[11] (Total: 164; Men: 162; Women: 2)

Athletics (Track & Field) (Total: 23; Men: 23; Women: 0)

Aho, Paavo. (b.21 December 1891–d.4 March 1918) Shot Put [10/5g1-2/qr]; Shot Put, both hands [6/3g1qr].

Eskola, Jalmari Johannes "Lauri." (b.16 November 1886–d.7 January 1958) Cross-Country, Individual [4]; Cross-Country, Team [2].

Halme, Johan "Juho" Waldemar. (b.24 May 1888–d.1 February 1918) Hop, step, and jump [11/4g1qr]; Javelin Throw [4/3g1qr]; Javelin Throw, both hands [9/4g1qr].

Harju, Matti Efferi "Efraim." (b.4 June 1889–d.17 July 1977) 1,500 meters [4h7r1/3]; Cross-Country, Individual [dnf-]; Cross-Country, Team [2/ns]; 3,000 Meter Team Race [2h1r1/2-ns].

Heikkilä (later Rauvola), Väinö Selim. (b.25 April 1888–d.5 May 1943) Cross-Country, Individual [25]; Cross-Country, Team [2/ns].

Järvinen, Venne "Verner." (b.4 March 1870–d.31 January 1941) Discus Throw [15/3g2qr]; Discus Throw, both hands [12/4g2qr].

Johansson, Franz William "Viljam." (b.18 April 1887–d.8 August 1931) 3,000 Meter Team Race [2h1r1/2]; 5,000 meters [dns-final]; Cross-Country, Individual [11]; Cross-Country, Team [2/ns].

Kallberg, Aarne Erik. (b.27 July 1891–d.2 April 1945) Marathon [dnf-].

Kolehmainen, Johan Pietari "Hannes." (b.9 December 1889–d.11 January 1966) 5,000 meters [1]; 10,000 meters [1]; Cross-Country, Individual [1]; Cross-Country, Team [2]; 3,000 Meter Team Race [2h1r1/2].

Kolehmainen, Taavetti Heikki "Tatu." (b.21 April 1885–d.15 June 1967) 10,000 meters [dnf-final]; Marathon [dnf].

Kukko (later Skarra), Emil. (b.14 May 1888–d.1963) Broad Jump [24/9g1qr]; Javelin Throw [18/3g2qr]; Pentathlon [12].

Kyrönen, Wilhelm "Ville." (b.14 January 1891–d.24 May 1959) Cross-Country, Individual [7]; Cross-Country, Team [2/ns].

Laine, Arvo Anselm. (b.8 August 1887–d.24 April 1938) High Jump [=7g2qr].

Lindholm (later Linnolahti), Karl Aarne. (b.12 February 1889–d.19 July 1972) 5,000 meters [dnf-h3r1/2]; Cross-Country, Individual [dnf-]; Cross-Country, Team [2/ns]; 3,000 Meter Team Race [2h1r1/2-ns].

Myyrä, Joonas "Jonni." (b.13 July 1892–d.22 January 1955) Javelin Throw [8/1g2qr].

Niklander, Elmer Konstantin. (b.19 January 1890–d.12 November 1942) Shot Put [4/2g3qr]; Shot Put, both hands [3]; Discus Throw [4/1g3qr]; Discus Throw, both hands [2].

Peltonen, Urho Pellervo. (b.15 January 1893–d.4 May 1950) Javelin Throw [9/4g1qr]; Javelin Throw, both hands [3/1g2qr].

Pihkala (later Gummerus), Lauri "Tahko." (b.5 January 1888–d.20 May 1981) 800 meters [dnf-h9r1/3].

Saaristo, Juho Julius. (b.21 July 1891–d.12 October 1969) Javelin Throw [2]; Javelin Throw, both hands [1/1g1qr].

Siikaniemi (Siegberg), Väinö Villiam. (b.27 March 1887–d.24 August 1932) Javelin Throw [5/1g4qr]; Javelin Throw, both hands [2/1g3qr].

Stenroos, Oskar Albinus "Albin." (b.25 February 1889–d.30 April 1971) 10,000 meters [3]; Cross-Country, Team [2]; Cross-Country, Individual [6]; 3,000 Meter Team Race [2h1r1/2].

Taipale, Armas Rudolf. (b.27 July 1890–d.9 November 1976) Discus Throw [1]; Discus Throw, both hands [1].

Wickholm, Julius Valdemar. (b.7 November 1890–d.20 July 1970) 110 meter hurdles [2h5r2/3]; Decathlon [7].

Cycling (Total: 5; Men: 5; Women: 0)

Jaakonaho, Johannes "Juho." (b.1 September 1882–d.21 January 1964) Road Race, Individual [ac/dnf]; Road Race, Team [5/ns/dnf].

Kankkonen, Johan Werner. (b.11 July 1886–d.3 February 1955) Road Race, Individual [34]; Road Race, Team [5].

Raita, Anders August "Antti." (b.15 November 1883–d.1968) Road Race, Individual [6]; Road Race, Team [5].

Tilkanen, Wilho Oskari. (b.14 April 1885–d.1 August 1945) Road Race, Individual [21]; Road Race, Team [5].

Väre, Frans Albert Hjalmar. (b.22 July 1879–d.20 March 1952) Road Race, Individual [66]; Road Race, Team [5].

Diving (Total: 6; Men: 6; Women: 0)

Aro (later Ahlstedt), Toivo Nestori. (b.9 February 1887–d.8 October 1962) Plain and Fancy High Diving [8]; Plain High Diving [5].

Ilmoniemi (later Granit), Tauno. (b.16 May 1893–d.21 September 1934) Plain High Diving [3h1r1/2]. (See also Gymnastics.)

Kainuvaara (later Ingberg), Kalle. (b.19 March 1891–d.1943) Plain and Fancy High Diving [7h2r1/2]; Plain High Diving [3h4r1/2].

Nyman, Albert Mikael. (b.22 November 1872–d.9 March 1924) Plain High Diving [4h4r1/2].

Suni, Leo Olavi. (b.18 May 1891–d.1942) Plain and Fancy High Diving [9h1r1/2]; Plain High Diving [5h4r1/2].

Wetzell, Oskar Wilhelm. (b.5 December 1888–d.28 November 1928) Springboard Diving [7h1r1/2]; Plain and Fancy High Diving [6h2r1/2]; Plain High Diving [2h4r1/2].

Football (Association Football [Soccer]) (Total: 14; Men: 14; Women: 0)

Holopainen, Hjalmar "Jalmari." (b.29 June 1892–d.3 April 1954) [4].

Lietola, Viljo. (b.9 October 1888–d.1955) [4].

Löfgren, Gösta Bernhard. (b.10 September 1891–d.21 February 1932) [4].

Lund, Knut Ernfrid. (b.17 July 1891–d.14 January 1974) [4].

Niska, Algoth Johannes. (b.5 December 1888–d.28 May 1954) [4].

Nyssönen, Artur Harald "Artturi." (b.1 May 1892–d.1973) [4].

Öhman, Jari "Lali." (b.24 November 1891–d.20 January 1936) [4].

Soinio (né Salin), Eino Aleksi. (b.12 November 1894–d.7 December 1973) [4].

Soinio (né Salin), Kaarlo Kyösti (Gustaf). (b.28 January 1888–d.24 October 1960) [4].

Syrjäläinen, August Matias. (b.24 April 1891–d.18 May 1960) [4].

Tanner, Lauri Arvo. (b.20 November 1890–d.11 July 1950) [4]. (See also Gymnastics.)

Wiberg, Bror Axel Rudolf. (b.14 June 1890–d.1935) [4].
Wickström, August Ragnar. (b.12 November 1892–d.1950) [4].

Gymnastics (Total: 24; Men: 24; Women: 0)

Ekholm, Kaarle Wäinö "Kalle." (b.7 December 1884–d.13 May 1946) Combined All-Around, Free System, Team [2]; Combined All-Around, Individual [ac/dnf].

Forsström, Eino Vilho. (b.10 April 1889–d.26 July 1961) Combined All-Around, Free System, Team [2].

Hyvärinen, Eero Juho. (b.27 April 1890–d.27 May 1973) Combined All-Around, Free System, Team [2].

Hyvärinen, Johannes Mikael "Mikko." (b.8 January 1889–d.6 June 1973) Combined All-Around, Free System, Team [2].

Ilmoniemi (later Granit), Tauno. (b.16 May 1893–d.21 September 1934) Combined All-Around, Free System, Team [2]. (See also Diving.)

Jansson, Karl Edvard. (b.18 September 1888–d.1929) Combined All-Around, Individual [31].

Keinänen, Ilmari. (b.5 November 1887–d.8 November 1934) Combined All-Around, Free System, Team [2].

Kivenheimo (later Stenvall), Viktor Jalmar "Jalmari." (b.25 September 1889–d.29 October 1994) Combined All-Around, Free System, Team [2].

Lund, Karl Fredrik Leonard. (b.31 July 1888–d.11 December 1942) Combined All-Around, Free System, Team [2].

Nieminen, Villiam Arvid "Viljami." (b.22 February 1888–d.13 April 1972) Combined All-Around, Individual [27].

Pelkonen, Aarne Eliel Tellervo. (b.24 November 1891–d.6 November 1949) Combined All-Around, Free System, Team [2].

Pernaja, Kustaa Ilmari. (b.10 February 1892–d.20 July 1963) Combined All-Around, Free System, Team [2].

Rydman, Arvid. (b.25 June 1884–d.14 May 1953) Combined All-Around, Free System, Team [2].

Saastamoinen, Kaarlo Eino. (b.9 October 1887–d.4 December 1946) Combined All-Around, Free System, Team [2].

Salovaara (later Nylenius), Aarne (Arne) Ihamo. (b.25 February 1887–d.11 September 1945) Combined All-Around, Free System, Team [2].

Sammallahti (Lundahl), Heikki Albert "Henry." (b.20 January 1886–d.17 October 1954) Combined All-Around, Free System, Team [2].

Sirola (later Sirén), Hannes Juho Rikhard. (b.18 April 1890–d.4 April 1985) Combined All-Around, Free System, Team [2].

Suomela (Lindholm), Klaus Uuno. (b.10 November 1888–d.4 April 1962) Combined All-Around, Free System, Team [2].

Tamminen, Anders Fredrik "Antti." (b.17 July 1886) Combined All-Around, Individual [37].

Tanner, Lauri Arvo. (b.20 November 1890–d.11 July 1950) Combined All-Around, Free System, Team [2]. (See also Football [Association Football/Soccer].)

Tiiri, Väinö Edward. (b.31 January 1886–d.30 July 1966) Combined All-Around, Free System, Team [2].

Vähämäki, Karl Gustaf "Kaarlo." (b.30 May 1892–d.1 January 1984) Combined All-Around, Free System, Team [2].

Vasama, Kaarlo Hjalmar "Kalle." (b.20 November 1885–d.12 November 1926) Combined All-Around, Free System, Team [2].

Vuolio, Yrjö Villiam. (b.8 December 1888–d.2 September 1948) Combined All-Around, Individual [ac/dnf].

Rowing & Sculling (Total: 6; Men: 6; Women: 0)

Forsman, Oskar Edvin. (b.13 August 1878–d.19 December 1957) Coxed Fours, Outriggers [2h1r2/4].

Haglund, Axel Matias. (b.16 December 1884–d.21 February 1948) Single Sculls [2h3r1/4].

Henriksson, Valdemar. (b.18 July 1884–d.17 February 1929) Coxed Fours, Outriggers [2h1r2/4].

Lönnberg, Karl Edvin. (b.13 March 1885–d.5 January 1934) Coxed Fours, Outriggers [2h1r2/4].

Nyholm, Johan Valdemar. (b.3 February 1881–d.8 April 1935) Coxed Fours, Outriggers [2h1r2/4].

Nylund, Emil. (b.23 November 1881–d.30 January 1926) Coxed Fours, Outriggers [2h1r2/4].

Shooting (Total: 19; Men: 19; Women: 0)

Autonen, Jalo Urho. (b.4 May 1883–d.15 June 1959) Free Rifle, 300 meters, 3-Positions [59].

Bacher, Carl Edvard. (b.16 October 1875– d.22 March 1961) Clay Trap Shooting, Individual [=45]; Clay Trap Shooting, Teams [5].

Collan, Emil Johannes. (b.21 May 1882–d.22 December 1948) Clay Trap Shooting, Individual [=29]; Clay Trap Shooting, Teams [5].

Fabritius, Emil Ernst. (b.23 December 1874–d.15 June 1949) Clay Trap Shooting, Individual [=53].

Fazer, Karl Otto. (b.16 August 1866–d.9 October 1932) Clay Trap Shooting, Individual [=12]; Clay Trap Shooting, Teams [5].

Holm, Emil. (b.2 September 1877–d.1 January 1968) Free Rifle, 300 meters, 3-Positions [49]; Free Rifle, 300 meters, 3-Positions, Teams [5].

Huber, Robert Waldemar. (b.30 March 1878–d.25 November 1946) Clay Trap Shooting, Individual [=29]; Clay Trap Shooting, Teams [5].

Huttunen, Heikki. (b.26 September 1880–d.21 September 1947) Free Rifle, 300 meters, 3-Positions [25]; Free Rifle, 300 meters, 3-Positions, Teams [5]; Free Pistol, 50 meters [28].

Kolho (later Saxberg), Lauri. (b.7 September 1886–d.17 September 1940) Free Rifle, 300 meters, 3-Positions [57].

Kolho (later Saxberg), Voitto Valdemar. (b.6 February 1885–d.4 October 1963) Free Rifle, 300 meters, 3-Positions [13]; Free Rifle, 300 meters, 3-Positions, Teams [5].

Londen, Axel Fredrik. (b.5 August 1859–d.8 September 1928) Running Deer, Single Shot, Individual [=15]; Running Deer, Single Shot, Teams [3]; Clay Trap Shooting, Teams [5].

Nyman, Gustav Rikhard "Kustaa." (b.12 October 1874–d.14 May 1952) Free Rifle, 300 meters, 3-Positions [19]; Free Rifle, 300 meters, 3-Positions, Teams [5].

Reilin, Karl Henrik Lorentz. (b.15 March 1874–d.18 January 1962) Running Deer, Single Shot, Individual [=26].

Rosenqvist, Ernst Edvard. (b.24 August 1869–d.27 May 1932) Running Deer, Single Shot, Individual [14]; Running Deer, Single Shot, Teams [3].

Schnitt, Gustaf Adolf "Aadolf." (b.17 April 1858–d.4 December 1924) Clay Trap Shooting, Individual [=4]; Clay Trap Shooting, Teams [5].

Toivonen, Nestor Kallenpoika. (b.25 March 1865–d.6 April 1927) Free Rifle, 300 meters, 3-Positions [ac/dnf]; Running Deer, Single Shot, Individual [3]; Running Deer, Single Shot, Teams [3].

Tuiskunen, Huvi Hjalmar. (b.22 July 1872–d.31 March 1930) Free Rifle, 300 meters, 3-Positions [39]; Free Rifle, 300 meters, 3-Positions, Teams [5]; Running Deer, Single Shot, Individual [=21].

Väänänen, Iivar "Iivo." (b.17 September 1877–d.13 April 1959) Running Deer, Single Shot, Individual [=21]; Running Deer, Single Shot, Teams [3].

Vauhkonen, Vilhelm "Vilho/Ville." (b.6 February 1877–d.1 February 1957) Free Rifle, 300 meters, 3-Positions [41]; Free Rifle, 300 meters, 3-Positions, Teams [5].

Swimming (Total: 6; Men: 4; Women: 2)

Women

Järvi, Tyyne Maria (later Tyyne Maria Järvi-Sjöblad). (b.4 February 1891–d.4 April 1929) 100 meter freestyle [5h1r1/3].

Kari, Regina (later Regina Kari-Harjula). (b.18 June 1892–d.24 May 1970) 100 meter freestyle [6h4r1/3].

Men

Aaltonen, Arvo Ossian. (b.2 December 1892–d.17 June 1949) 200 meter breaststroke [6h1r2/3]; 400 meter breaststroke [3h2r2/3].

Cederberg, Herman Edvard. (b.7 September 1883–d.30 January 1969) 200 meter breaststroke [3h6r1/3].

Lindgrén (later Lietkari), Fredrik Vilhelm. (b.3 July 1895–d.26 July 1960) 200 meter breast-stroke [4h6r1/3]; 400 meter breaststroke [3h4r1/3].

Lindroos, Karl Gustaf Lennart. (b.23 February 1886) 200 meter breaststroke [4h1r2/3]; 400 meter breaststroke [4h2r2/3].

Wrestling (Total: 37; Men: 37; Women: 0)

Åberg, Karl Konrad. (b.18 January 1890–d.4 November 1950) 75 kg. Class (Greco-Roman) [AC].

Asikainen, Alfred Johan "Alpo." (b.2 November 1888–d.January 1942) 75 kg. Class (Greco-Roman) [3].

Backenius (Palasmaa), Emil Isidor. (b.16 December 1884–d.6 November 1968) Unlimited Class (Greco-Roman) [AC].

Böling, Ivar Theodor. (b.10 September 1889–d.12 January 1929) 82½ kg. Class (Greco-Roman) [2].

Haapanen, Lauri Johannes. (b.9 August 1889–d.24 April 1947) 60 kg. Class (Greco-Roman) [AC].

Holm, Mikko. (b.2 February 1889–d.17 March 1975) 75 kg. Class (Greco-Roman) [AC].

Jokinen, August. (b.11 December 1887–d.3 August 1970) 75 kg. Class (Greco-Roman) [AC].

Kangas (later Huhtala), Karl Arvo Johannes. (b.13 June 1886–d.8 February 1966) 60 kg. Class (Greco-Roman) [AC].

Kolehmainen, David "Tatu." (b.10 September 1885–d.1918) 67½ kg. Class (Greco-Roman) [AC].

Koskelo (later Ääpälä), Kaarlo "Kalle." (b.12 April 1888–d.21 December 1953) 60 kg. Class (Greco-Roman) [1].

Kumpu (né Forssell), Oskar Wiljam "Oskari." (b.29 January 1889–d.25 June 1935) 82½ kg. Class (Greco-Roman) [AC].

Laitinen, Otto Armas. (b.20 November 1891–d.1969) 67½ kg. Class (Greco-Roman) [AC].

Lasanen, Otto Abraham. (b.14 April 1891–d.25 July 1958) 60 kg. Class (Greco-Roman) [3].

Lehmusvirta, Hjalmar Vilhelm "Jalmari Ville." (b.20 November 1889–d.17 April 1952) 60 kg. Class (Greco-Roman) [AC].

Leivonen (later Vilenius), Kaarle Herman "Kalle." (b.17 September 1886–d.1 January 1978) 60 kg. Class (Greco-Roman) [AC].

Lind, Gustaf Lennart. (b.24 June 1893–d.6 August 1961) 82½ kg. Class (Greco-Roman) [AC].

Lind, Karl Gustaf. (b.13 February 1880–d.1957) 82½ kg. Class (Greco-Roman) [AC].

Lindberg, Knut Ferninand. (b.5 January 1880–d.1928) 82½ kg. Class (Greco-Roman) [AC].

Lindfors, Adolf Valentin. (b.8 February 1879–d.6 May 1959) Unlimited Class (Greco-Roman) [AC].

Lundsten, Fridolf Vilhelm. (b.26 July 1883–d.5 January 1947) 75 kg. Class (Greco-Roman) [AC].

Mustonen, Risto. (b.24 April 1875–d.3 March 1941) 60 kg. Class (Greco-Roman) [AC].

Olin, Johan Fredrik "John." (b.30 June 1883–d.3 December 1928) Unlimited Class (Greco-Roman) [2].

Pelander, Gustaf Uno "Uuno." (b.13 August 1887–d.9 August 1964) Unlimited Class (Greco-Roman) [AC].

Pukkila, Tuomas Vilho "Ville." (b.10 August 1890–d.7 December 1968) 67½ kg. Class (Greco-Roman) [AC].

Rajala, Anders August. (b.30 November 1891–d.7 March 1957) 82½ kg. Class (Greco-Roman) [AC].

Saarela, Yrjö Erik Mikael. (b.13 July 1884–d.30 June 1951) Unlimited Class (Greco-Roman) [1].

Salila, Johan Kustaa "Jussi." (b.28 July 1884–d.12 August 1932) 82½ kg. Class (Greco-Roman) [AC].

Salonen, Johan Alfred. (b.9 March 1884–d.1938) 67½ kg. Class (Greco-Roman) [AC].

Tanttu, Adam Richard "Aatami." (b.24 December 1887–d.26 December 1939) 67½ kg. Class (Greco-Roman) [AC].

Tirkkonen, Paul Ernst Wilhelm. (b.9 October 1884–d.31 August 1968) 67½ kg. Class (Greco-Roman) [AC].

Tirkkonen, Teodor Alexander. (b.21 January 1883–d.24 April 1951) 75 kg. Class (Greco-Roman) [AC].

Urvikko (later Wiren), Johan Viktor "Vihtori." (b.21 April 1889–d.2 April 1961) 67½ kg. Class (Greco-Roman) [AC].

Väre (later Vilén), Emil Ernst. (b.28 September 1885–d.31 January 1974) 67½ kg. Class (Greco-Roman) [1].

Viljamaa (né Sillman), Kalle Albinus. (b.15 February 1885–d.28 March 1918) Unlimited Class (Greco-Roman) [AC].

Westerlund, Emil Aleksander. (b.6 February 1887–d.18 February 1964) 75 kg. Class (Greco-Roman) [AC].

Wiklund, Oscar Wilhelm. (b.31 October 1888–d.1942) 82½ kg. Class (Greco-Roman) [AC].

Wikström, Volmar Valdemar. (b.27 December 1889–d.10 June 1957) 67½ kg. Class (Greco-Roman) [AC].

Yachting (Total: 27; Men: 27; Women: 0)

Ahnger, Arthur. (b.27 February 1886–d.7 December 1940) 8-meter class [3] (Lucky Girl).

Alfthan, Max Ferdinand. (b.11 February 1892–d.30 May 1960) 12-meter class [3] (Heatherbell).

Andstén, Curt Magnus Wilhelm. (b.12 September 1881–d.1 June 1926) 8-meter class [4] (Örn).

Andstén, Jarl Oskar Wilhelm. (b.7 December 1884–d.2 July 1943) 8-meter class [4] (Örn).

Björkstén, Waldemar. (b.12 August 1873–d.31 May 1933) 10-meter class [2] (Nina).

Björnström, Jacob Carl Gustaf Herman. (b.14 December 1881–d.17 July 1935) 10-meter class [2] (Nina).

Brenner, Bror Benediktus Bernhard. (b.17 July 1885–d.17 April 1923) 10-meter class [2] (Nina).

Estlander, Ernst Henrik. (b.18 September 1870–d.6 February 1949) 6-meter class [=5] (Finn II).

Estlander, Axel Gustaf. (b.18 September 1876–d.1 December 1930) 8-meter class [4] (Örn).

Franck, Allan Gunthard. (b.17 September 1888–d.28 May 1963) 10-meter class [2] (Nina).

Girsén, Carl-Oscar. (b.16 February 1889–d.22 April 1930) 8-meter class [4] (Örn).

Hartvall, Knut Erik "Pekka." (b.18 February 1875–d.18 February 1939) 12-meter class [3] (Heatherbell).

Hulldén, Jarl. (b.26 February 1885–d.1913) 12-meter class [3] (Heatherbell).

Juslén, Bertel. (b.13 August 1880–d.19 June 1951) 8-meter class [4] (Örn).

Juslén, Sigurd Ludvig. (b.25 November 1885–d.4 April 1954) 12-meter class [3] (Heatherbell).

Krogius, Ernst Edvard. (b.6 June 1865–d.21 September 1955) 12-meter class [3] (Heatherbell).

Lindh, Emil Alexander.[12] (b.15 April 1867–d.3 September 1937) 10-meter class [2] (Nina).

Lindh, Erik Aleksander. (b.1 May 1865–d.1 December 1914) 8-meter class [3] (Lucky Girl).

Pekkalainen, Johan Anders "Juho Aarne." (b.20 May 1895–d.19 March 1958) 10-meter class [2] (Nina).

Sandelin, Eino Kauno. (b.16 December 1864–d.15 October 1937) 12-meter class [3] (Heatherbell).

Sandelin, Karl Viktor Torsten. (b.28 September 1887–d.8 May 1950) 6-meter class [=5] (Finn II).

Silen, Johan Fredrik. (b.19 June 1869–d.3 October 1949) 12-meter class [3] (Heatherbell).

Stenbäck, Gunnar Ludvig. (b.31 October 1880–d.2 February 1947) 6-meter class [=5] (Finn II).

Tallberg, Bertil. (b.17 September 1883–d.20 April 1963) 8-meter class [3] (Lucky Girl).

Tallberg, Gunnar. (b.23 December 1881–d.27 August 1931) 8-meter class [3] (Lucky Girl).

Wahl, Harry August. (b.17 July 1869–d.1941) 10-meter class [2] (Nina).

Westling, Georg Gustaf. (b.24 August 1879–d.14 November 1930) 8-meter class [3] (Lucky Girl).

France (Total: 109; Men: 108; Women: 1)

Athletics (Track & Field) (Total: 25; Men: 25; Women: 0)

André, Georges Ivan. (b.13 August 1889–d.4 May 1943) 110 meter hurdles [3h6r2/3]; High Jump [7g3qr]; Standing High Jump [=2g3qr]; Standing Long Jump [16/5g4qr]; Decathlon [ac/dnf]; Pentathlon [22].

Arnaud, Henri Auguste. (b.16 April 1891) 1,500 meters [ac-final].

Boissière, Jean. (b.9 April 1893) Marathon [13].

Bouin, Jean. (b.28 December 1888–d.29 September 1914) 5,000 meters [2]; Cross-Country, Individual [dnf-].

Boullery, Julien. (b.4 October 1886) 100 meters [3h15r1/3].

Campana, Andre. (b.21 May 1886) Broad Jump [16/6g1qr].

Caulle, Joseph. (b.3 May 1885–d.c.1914–18) 800 meters [5h1r1/3].

Delaby, Marius François Louis. (b.13 June 1890) 100 meters [ach10r1/3]; 110 meter hurdles [3h2r2/3]; High Jump [nh/g1qr].

Estang, Armand. (b.10 December 1886) High Jump [nh/g1qr].

Failliot, Pierre. (b.25 February 1887–d.1 January 1936) 100 meters [3h3r1/3]; 200 meters [3h11r1/3]; 4 × 100 meter relay [2h6r1/3]; 4 × 400 meter relay [2]; Decathlon [ac/dnf]; Pentathlon [17].

Gonder, Fernand. (b.12 June 1883–d.12 March 1969) Pole Vault [8g1qr].

Heuet, Gaston. (b.11 November 1892–d.1979) 5,000 meters [dnf-h5r1/2]; 10,000 meters [dns-final].

Labat, André.[13] (b.19 February 1889) High Jump [=4g3qr].

Lagarde, Charles. (b.13 September 1878) Shot Put [22/6g4qr]; Discus Throw [36/8g5qr].

Lelong, Charles Louis. (b.18 March 1891) 200 meters [3h9r1/3]; 400 meters [3h2r2/3]; 4 × 100 meter relay [2h6r1/3]; 4 × 400 meter relay [2]; 100 meters [ach7r1/3].

Malfait, Georges W. (b.9 December 1878) 200 meters [ach7r1/3]; 400 meters [3h8r1/3].

Meerz, Michel Henri. High Jump [=11/g1qr]

Motte, Alfred. (b.2 June 1887) Standing Long Jump [10/2g1qr].

Mourlon, René. (b.12 May 1893–d.19 October 1977) 100 meters [ach4r2/3]; 4 × 100 meter relay [2h6r1/3].

Paoli, Raoul Lucien. (b.24 November 1887) Shot Put [16/4g3qr]. (See also Wrestling.)

Pauteux, Louis. (b.18 April 1883) Marathon [dnf-].

Poulenard, Charles Alexander Casimir. (b.30 March 1885–d.10 November 1958) 200 meters [3h2r1/3]; 400 meters [5h1r2/3]; 800 meters [3h4r1/3]; 4 × 400 meter relay [2].

Rolot, Georges Jean Baptiste. (b.10 May 1889) 100 meters [ach9r1/3]; 200 meters [4h3r2/3]; 400 meters [5h12r1/3]; 4 × 100 meter relay [2h6r1/3].

Schurrer, Robert. (b.24 March 1890) 100 meters [ach6r1/3]; 200 meters [5h6r2/3]; 400 meters [5h15r1/3]; 4 × 400 meter relay [2].

Tison, André. (b.26 February 1885) Shot Put [9/3g4qr]; Discus Throw [30/6g5qr].

Cycling (Total: 12; Men: 12; Women: 0)

Alancourt, Gaston. (b.10 February 1888) Road Race, Individual [91]; Road Race, Team [10/ns].

Bes, Louis. (b.25 December 1891) Road Race, Individual [ac/dnf]; Road Race, Team [10/ns/dnf].

Capelle, André. (b.13 November 1892) Road Race, Individual [50]; Road Race, Team [10].

Cheret, Étienne. (b.26 July 1886) Road Race, Individual [89]; Road Race, Team [10/ns].

Gagnet, René. (b.5 February 1891) Road Race, Individual [64]; Road Race, Team [10].

Lepère, André. (b.1878) Road Race, Individual [93]; Road Race, Team [10/ns].

Marcault, Jacques. (b.7 December 1883) Road Race, Individual [ac/dnf]; Road Race, Team [10/ns/dnf].

Michiels, Alexis. (b.13 December 1883) Road Race, Individual [94]; Road Race, Team [10/ns].

Peinaud, Pierre. (b.9 February 1888) Road Race, Individual [92]; Road Race, Team [10/ns].

Racine, Joseph. (b.18 July 1891) Road Race, Individual [40]; Road Race, Team [10].

Rillon, René. (b.9 May 1892) Road Race, Individual [ac/dnf]; Road Race, Team [10/ns/dnf].

Valentin, Georges. (b.24 January 1892) Road Race, Individual [83]; Road Race, Team [10].

Equestrian Events (Total: 4; Men: 4; Women: 0)

Cariou, Jean. Dressage, Individual [14] (Mignon); Jumping, Individual [1] (Mignon); Jumping, Team [2] (Mignon); Three-Day Event, Individual [3] (Cocotte); Three-Day Event, Team [4] (Cocotte).

Dufort d'Astafort, Michel. Jumping, Team [2] (Amazone); Jumping, Individual [=13] (Amazone); Dressage, Individual [19] (Castibalza); Three-Day Event, Individual [ac/dnf] (Castibalza); Three-Day Event, Team [4] (Castibalza).

Meyer, Bernard. Jumping, Individual [ac/dnf] (Ursule); Jumping, Team [2] (Allons-y); Three-Day Event, Individual [=12] (Allons-y); Three-Day Event, Team [4] (Allons-y).

Seigner, Albert. Dressage, Individual [10]; Three-Day Event, Individual [14]; Three-Day Event, Team [4] (Dignité); Jumping, Team [2] (Cocotte).

Gymnastics (Total: 6; Men: 6; Women: 0)

Costa, Antoine. (b.23 October 1884) Combined All-Around, Individual [10].

Lalue, Marcel. (b.24 March 1882) Combined All-Around, Individual [=7].

Marty, Louis-Charles. (b.30 December 1891) Combined All-Around, Individual [11].

Pompogne, Auguste. (b.5 December 1882) Combined All-Around, Individual [14].

Ségura, B. Louis. (b.23 July 1889) Combined All-Around, Individual [2].

Torrès, Marco. (b.22 January 1888) Combined All-Around, Individual [=7].

Modern Pentathlon (Total: 2; Men: 2; Women: 0)

Brulé, Georges, Commandant. (b.23 October 1876) Individual [19].

de Mas Latrie, Jean, Count. (b.23 November 1879) Individual [16].

Rowing & Sculling (Total: 17; Men: 17; Women: 0)

Allibert, Pierre. (b.26 June 1892) Coxed Fours, Outriggers [2h2r1/4].

Alvarez, Pierre. (b.7 August 1887) Coxed Eights [2h1r1/4].

Arné, Jean. (b.26 February 1891) Coxed Eights [2h1r1/4].

Campot, Joseph. (b.2 November 1886) Coxed Eights [2h1r1/4].

Elichagaray, François. (b.3 September 1895) Coxed Fours, Inriggers [2h3r1/3]; Coxed Fours, Outriggers [2h2r1/4]; Coxed Eights [2h1r1/4].

Elichagaray, Jean. (b.3 September 1886) Coxed Eights [2h1r1/4].

Garnier, Charles. (b.9 October 1887) Coxed Fours, Inriggers [2h3r1/3].

Lafitte, Louis. (b.2 June 1886) Coxed Eights [2h1r1/4].

Lenjeune, Marius. (b.2 November 1882) Coxed Eights [2h1r1/4].

Lesbats, Etienne. (b.7 August 1887) Coxed Eights [2h1r1/4].

Meignant, Alphonse. (b.27 March 1882) Coxed Fours, Inriggers [2h3r1/3].

Mirambeau, André. (b.8 November 1879) Coxed Fours, Outriggers [2h2r1/4].

Poix, Gabriel. (b.8 November 1888) Coxed Fours, Inriggers [2h3r1/3].

Richard, Auguste. (b.14 February 1883) Coxed Fours, Inriggers [2h3r1/3].

Saintongey, René Pierre. (b.22 February 1886) Coxed Fours, Outriggers [2h2r1/4].

St. Laurent, Gabriel. (b.4 August 1888) Coxed Eights [2h1r1/4].

Thomaturgé, Louis Stanislas. (b.25 November 1878) Coxed Fours, Outriggers [2h2r1/4].

Shooting (Total: 19; Men: 19; Women: 0)

Colas, Paul René. (b.6 May 1880) Free Rifle, 300 meters, 3-Positions [1]; Free Rifle, 300 meters, 3-Positions, Teams [4]; Military Rifle, 300 meters, 3-Positions [22]; Military Rifle, 600 meters, any position [1]; Military Rifle, 200, 400, 500, and 600 meters, Teams [5].

Creuzé de Lesser, Edouard. (b.12 February 1883) Clay Trap Shooting, Individual [=41]; Clay Trap Shooting, Teams [6].

de Boigne, Raoul, Count. (b.25 December 1862) Free Rifle, 300 meters, 3-Positions [53]; Military Rifle, 300 meters, 3-Positions [58]; Military Rifle, 600 meters, any position [50]; Free Rifle, 300 meters, 3-Positions, Teams [4]; Military Rifle, 200, 400, 500, and 600 meters, Teams [5].

de Castex, Henri, Baron. (b.13 July 1854) Dueling Pistol, 30 meters [42]; Clay Trap Shooting, Individual [=29]; Clay Trap Shooting, Teams [6].

de Crequi-Montfort de Courtivron, Georges, Marquis. (b.27 July 1877) Dueling Pistol, 30 meters [26]; Dueling Pistol, 30 meters, Teams [6]; Clay Trap Shooting, Individual [=35]; Clay Trap Shooting, Teams [6].

de Jaubert, Charles, Baron. (b.18 April 1864) Dueling Pistol, 30 meters [36]; Dueling Pistol,

30 meters, Teams [6]; Running Deer, Double Shot, Individual [10]; Clay Trap Shooting, Individual [=25]; Clay Trap Shooting, Teams [6].

Fauré, Maurice. (b.26 June 1859) Dueling Pistol, 30 meters [31]; Dueling Pistol, 30 meters, Teams [6].

Fleury, André. (b.30 March 1882) Clay Trap Shooting, Individual [=27]; Clay Trap Shooting, Teams [6].

Gentil, Pierre. (b.12 October 1881) Free Rifle, 300 meters, 3-Positions [ac/dnf]; Military Rifle, 300 meters, 3-Positions [61]; Military Rifle, 600 meters, any position [69]; Free Rifle, 300 meters, 3-Positions, Teams [4]; Military Rifle, 200, 400, 500, and 600 meters, Teams [5]; Small-Bore Rifle, 25 meters, Disappearing Target [27]; Small-Bore Rifle, 50 meters, Teams [4].

Johnson, Léon. (b.28 February 1876–d.1943) Free Rifle, 300 meters, 3-Positions [24]; Free Rifle, 300 meters, 3-Positions, Teams [4]; Military Rifle, 200, 400, 500, and 600 meters, Teams [5]; Small-Bore Rifle, 25 meters, Disappearing Target [19]; Small-Bore Rifle, 50 meters, Teams [4]; Free Pistol, 50 meters [10].

Landin, Maxime. (b.24 April 1855) Military Rifle, 300 meters, 3-Positions [70]; Military Rifle, 200, 400, 500, and 600 meters, Teams [5]; Small-Bore Rifle, 50 meters, Teams [4].

le Marié, Henri Auguste. (b.28 October 1882) Clay Trap Shooting, Individual [=51].

Marion, Auguste. (b.11 July 1876) Free Rifle, 300 meters, 3-Positions [45]; Military Rifle, 600 meters, any position [63]; Free Rifle, 300 meters, 3-Positions, Teams [4].

Mérillon, Daniel. (b.29 June 1852) Military Rifle, 300 meters, 3-Positions [78]; Military Rifle, 600 meters, any position [64].

Percy, Louis. (b.15 September 1872) Free Rifle, 300 meters, 3-Positions [44]; Military Rifle, 300 meters, 3-Positions [23]; Military Rifle, 600 meters, any position [20]; Free Rifle, 300 meters, 3-Positions, Teams [4]; Military Rifle, 200, 400, 500, and 600 meters, Teams [5].

Regaud, André. (b.13 February 1868) Small-Bore Rifle, 50 meters, Teams [4]; Small-Bore Rifle, prone position, 50 meters [41]; Free Pistol, 50 meters [15].

Sandoz, Edmond. (b.8 July 1872) Dueling Pistol, 30 meters [12]; Dueling Pistol, 30 meters, Teams [6].

Sartori, Athanase. (b.10 May 1852) Free Rifle, 300 meters, 3-Positions [63]; Military Rifle, 300 meters, 3-Positions [90]; Military Rifle, 600 meters, any position [84].

Texier, René. (b.28 October 1882) Clay Trap Shooting, Individual [=45]; Clay Trap Shooting, Teams [6].

Swimming (Total: 3; Men: 3; Women: 0)

Caby, Auguste. (b.6 October 1887) 1,500 meter freestyle [dnf-h2r1/3].

Meister, Gérard. (b.4 September 1889) 100 meter freestyle [4h5r1/4].

Rigal, Georges. (b.6 January 1890–d.25 March 1974) 100 meter freestyle [dns-r2/4]. (See also Water Polo.)

Tennis (Total: 6; Men: 5; Women: 1)

Women

Broquedis, Marguerite-Marie. (b.17 April 1893–d.23 April 1983) Ladies' Singles (Lawn) [1]; Mixed Doubles (Lawn) [3].

Men

Blanchy, François Joseph. (b.12 December 1886) Men's Singles (Lawn) [=17].

Canet, Albert. (b.17 April 1878) Men's Singles (Lawn) [=17]; Men's Doubles (Lawn) [3]; Mixed Doubles (Lawn) [3].

Germot, Maurice. (b.17 November 1882–d.6 August 1958) Men's Singles (Covered Court) [=9]; Men's Doubles (Covered Court) [1].

Gobert, André Henri. (b.30 September 1890–d.6 December 1951) Men's Singles (Covered Court) [1]; Men's Doubles (Covered Court) [1].

Mény de Marangue, Edouard Marie Marc. (b.30 November 1882–d.23 January 1960) Men's Singles (Lawn) [=31]; Men's Doubles (Lawn) [3].

Water Polo (Total: 8; Men: 8; Women: 0)
  Beulque, Paul Louis. (b.29 April 1877) [=5].
  Decoin, Henri. (b.18 March 1890) [=5].
  Prouvost, Gustave. (b.25 March 1887) [=5].
  Rigal, Georges. (b.6 January 1890–d.25 March 1974) [=5]. (See also Swimming.)
  Rodier, Jean. (b.4 July 1891) [=5].
  Thorailles, Jean. (b.7 January 1888) [=5].
  Vanlaere, Gaston. (b.6 December 1887) [=5].
  Vasseur, Paul. (b.10 October 1884–d.12 October 1971) [=5].

Wrestling (Total: 6; Men: 6; Women: 0)
  Barrier, Adrien. (b.7 March 1891) 75 kg. Class (Greco-Roman) [AC].
  Bouffechoux, Jean. (b.19 January 1891) 67½ kg. Class (Greco-Roman) [AC].
  Cabal, Raymond. (b.16 January 1888) 67½ kg. Class (Greco-Roman) [AC].
  Lesieur, Eugène. (b.24 March 1890) 67½ kg. Class (Greco-Roman) [AC].
  Martin, Edouard. (b.22 September 1889) 82½ kg. Class (Greco-Roman) [AC].
  Paoli, Raoul Lucien. (b.24 November 1887) Unlimited Class (Greco-Roman) [AC]. (See also Athletics [Track & Field].)

Yachting (Total: 3; Men: 3; Women: 0)
  Thubé, Amédée. (b.8 December 1884–d.29 January 1941) 6-meter class [1] (Mac Miche).
  Thubé, Gaston. (b.16 October 1876–d.22 June 1974) 6-meter class [1] (Mac Miche).
  Thubé, Jacques. (b.22 June 1882–d.14 May 1969) 6-meter class [1] (Mac Miche).

Germany[14] (Total: 183; Men: 178; Women: 5)

Athletics (Track & Field) (Total: 24; Men: 24; Women: 0)
  Abraham, Alexander. (b.17 January 1886–d.February 1949) Decathlon [ac/dnf].
  Amberger, Georg Wilhelm. (b.31 July 1890–d.6 February 1947) 1,500 meters [3h2r1/3]; 3,000 Meter Team Race [2h2r1/2].
  Bäurle, Otto. (b.3 February 1887–d.26 April 1951) Hop, step, and jump [14/5g3qr]; Pentathlon [13].
  Braun, Hanns. (b.26 October 1886–d.9 October 1918) 400 meters [2]; 800 meters [6]; 4 × 400 meter relay [2h2r1/2].
  Burkowitz, Hermann Heinrich. (b.31 January 1892–d.November 1914) 400 meters [3h9r1/3]; 4 × 400 meter relay [2h2r1/2].
  Herrmann, Max. (b.17 March 1885–d.29 January 1915) 100 meters [3h16r1/3]; 200 meters [3h3r2/3]; 400 meters [3h7r1/3]; 4 × 100 meter relay [dq/final]; 4 × 400 meter relay [2h2r1/2].
  Jahn, Richard "Willi." (b.27 February 1889) 800 meters [4h4r1/3].

Kern, Erwin. (b.23 August 1888–d.20 March 1963) 100 meters [4h1r2/3]; 4 × 100 meter relay [dq/final].

Ketterer, Emil. (b.6 August 1883–d.23 December 1959) 100 meters [dnf-h13r1/3].

Lehmann, Erich. (b.12 September 1890–d.c.1914-18) 400 meters [4h12r1/3]; 800 meters [3h7r1/3]; 4 × 400 meter relay [2h2r1/2].

Liesche, Hans. (b.11 October 1891–d.30 March 1979) High Jump [2].

Mickler, Alfred Georg. (b.7 September 1892–d.14 June 1915) 1,500 meters [5h5r1/3]; 3,000 Meter Team Race [2h2r1/2-ns/dnf].

Pasemann, Robert. (b.14 December 1886–d.17 October 1968) Pole Vault [11]; Broad Jump [8/4g1qr].

Person, Julius. (b.1 May 1889- d.c.1914-18) 400 meters [dnf-h2r2/3]; 800 meters [4h5r1/3].

Rau, Richard. (b.26 August 1889–d.6 November 1945) 100 meters [2h4r2/3]; 200 meters [4]; 4 × 100 meter relay [dq/final].

Röhr, Franz Hermann Otto. (b.22 November 1891–d.8 January 1972) 4 × 100 meter relay [dq/final]; High Jump [=7g2qr]; Decathlon [dnf-].

Vietz, Gregor. (b.26 July 1890) 5,000 meters [dnf-h4r1/2]; 10,000 meters [11h2r1/2]; Cross-Country, Individual [27]; 3,000 Meter Team Race [2h2r1/2].

von Bönninghausen, Hermann "Menzi." (b.24 July 1888–d.26 January 1919) 110 meter hurdles [2h3r2/3].

von Halt, Karl Ferdinand.[15] (b.2 June 1891–d.5 August 1964) 4 × 100 meter relay [1/rd. one only]; Shot Put [14/7g1-2/qr]; Javelin Throw [22/5g2qr]; Decathlon [9]; Pentathlon [ac/dnf].

von Sigel, Erwin. (b.14 August 1884–d.2 January 1967) 1,500 meters [ac-final]; 3,000 Meter Team Race [2h2r1/2].

Waitzer, Josef. (b.1 May 1884–d.28 March 1966) Discus Throw [16/6g1qr]; Javelin Throw [19/9g1qr]; Pentathlon [ac/dnf].

Welz, Emil. (b.5 April 1879) Discus Throw [24/4g4qr].

Wenseler, Heinrich. (b.26 March 1891) 200 meters [ach13r1/3]; 400 meters [3h15r1/3].

Willführ, Paul. (b.30 October 1885–d.22 April 1922) Shot Put [18/6g3qr]; Discus Throw [nm/q3qr]; Javelin Throw [23/6g2qr].

Cycling (Total: 11; Men: 11; Women: 0)

Baier, P. Rudolf. (b.22 March 1892) Road Race, Individual [27]; Road Race, Team [6].

Birker, Robert. (b.21 February 1885) Road Race, Individual [62]; Road Race, Team [6/ns].

Koch, Martin. (b.4 September 1887) Road Race, Individual [61]; Road Race, Team [6/ns].

Lemnitz, Franz. (b.11 July 1890) Road Race, Individual [26]; Road Race, Team [6].

Lüthje, Carl. (b.22 January 1883) Road Race, Individual [79]; Road Race, Team [6/ns].

Männel, Otto. (b.27 June 1887) Road Race, Individual [44]; Road Race, Team [6/ns].

Rabe, Wilhelm. (b.16 May 1876) Road Race, Individual [55]; Road Race, Team [6/ns].

Rathmann, Oswald. (b.21 July 1891) Road Race, Individual [33]; Road Race, Team [6].

Rieder, Josef. (b.26 December 1893) Road Race, Individual [57]; Road Race, Team [6/ns].

Smiel, Hermann. (b.31 July 1880) Road Race, Individual [76]; Road Race, Team [6/ns].

Warsow, Georg. (b.22 September 1877) Road Race, Individual [36]; Road Race, Team [6].

Diving (Total: 4; Men: 4; Women: 0)

Behrens, Kurt. (b.26 November 1884–d.5 February 1928) Springboard Diving [1]; Plain and Fancy High Diving [8h1r1/2]; Plain High Diving [7h3r1/2].

Günther, Paul. (b.24 October 1882–d.1945) Springboard Diving [2]; Plain High Diving [ac/dnf-final].

Luber, Hans. (b.15 October 1893–d.15 October 1940) Springboard Diving [5]; Plain and Fancy High Diving [3h1r1/2]; Plain High Diving [6h3r1/2].

Zürner, Albert. (b.30 January 1890–d.18 July 1920) Springboard Diving [4]; Plain and Fancy High Diving [2]; Plain High Diving [6h4r1/2].

Equestrian Events (Total: 13; Men: 13; Women: 0)

Bürkner, Felix. (b.15 May 1883) Dressage, Individual [7] (King).

Deloch, Ernst Hubertus. (b.17 May 1886) Jumping, Individual [=9]; Jumping, Team [3] (Hubertus).

Freyer, Sigismund. (b.22 January 1881) Jumping, Individual [5]; Jumping, Team [3] (Ultimus).

von Flotow, Andreas. (b.6 June 1876) Dressage, Individual [11] (Senta).

von Grote, Friedrich Ernst August, Count. (b.22 April 1885) Jumping, Individual [=18] (Polyphem).

von Hohenau, Wilhelm, Count. (b.27 November 1884–d.11 April 1957) Jumping, Individual [=6]; Jumping, Team [3] (Pretty Girl).

von Kröcher, Rabod Wilhelm. (b.30 June 1880–d.25 December 1945) Jumping, Individual [2] (Dohna).

von Lütcken, Eduard. (b.26 October 1882–d.15 September 1914) Three-Day Event, Individual [8]; Three-Day Event, Team [2] (Blue Boy).

von Moers, Carl. (b.9 December 1871) Dressage, Individual [12] (New Bank); Three-Day Event, Individual [15] (May-Queen); Three-Day Event, Team [2] (May-Queen).

von Osterley, Friedrich Karl. (b.5 April 1871) Dressage, Individual [4] (Condor).

von Preußen, Friedrich Karl, Prince. (b.6 April 1893–d.1917) Jumping, Individual [=18]; Jumping, Team [3] (Gibson Boy).

von Rochow, Friedrich Leopold Harry, Lieutenant-Colonel. (b.12 August 1881–d.17 August 1945) Three-Day Event, Individual [2]; Three-Day Event, Team [2] (Idealist).

von Schaesberg-Tannheim, Rudolf, Count. (b.7 January 1884–d.20 September 1953) Three-Day Event, Individual [=5]; Three-Day Event, Team [2] (Grundsee).

Fencing (Total: 16; Men: 16; Women: 0)

Adam, Johannes. (b.1871) Foil, Individual (=4p2r1/4); Sabre, Team (=7).

Davids, Adolf. (b.1867) Foil, Individual (=4p4r2/4).

Erckrath de Bary, Jakob. (b.10 March 1864–d.14 August 1938) Sabre, Team (=7).

Jack, Friedrich "Fritz." (b.24 December 1879–d.15 May 1960) Sabre, Team (=7).

Lichtenfels, Julius. (b.19 May 1884–d.29 June 1968) Foil, Individual (=4p3r3/4); Épée, Individual (5p1r1/4); Sabre, Individual (dnc-p2r3/4); Sabre, Team (=7).

Löffler, Wilhelm. (b.7 February 1886) Foil, Individual (=4p5r2/4).

Meienreis, Walther. (b.1877) Épée, Individual (5p16r1/4); Sabre, Team (=7).

Naumann, Albert. (b.1875) Foil, Individual (=5p12r1/4).

Plaskuda, Hermann. (b.1879) Foil, Individual (6p7r2/4); Épée, Individual (=4p13r1/4); Épée, Team (=7); Sabre, Team (=7).

Schön, Emil. (b.4 August 1872–d.29 January 1945) Foil, Individual (=3p2r3/4); Épée, Individual (6p5r2/4); Épée, Team (=7); Sabre, Team (=7).

Schrader, Heinrich. (b.1878) Épée, Individual (6p8r1/4).

Schwarz, Friedrich. (b.1876) Épée, Individual (4p2r1/4); Épée, Team (=7); Sabre, Individual (5p1r3/4); Sabre, Team (=7).

Stöhr, Georg. (b.21 May 1885–d.31 March 1977) Sabre, Individual (=5p1r2/4); Sabre, Team (=7).

Thomson, Hans. (b.14 June 1888) Épée, Individual (=4p3r2/4); Sabre, Individual (4p5r2/4).

Thomson, Julius. (b.14 June 1888) Foil, Individual (7p4r1/4).

Ziegler, Heinrich. (b.1891) Foil, Individual (4p15r1/4); Épée, Team (=7).

Football (Association Football [Soccer]) (Total: 22; Men: 22; Women: 0)

Bosch, Hermann. (b.10 March 1891) [=7].

Breunig, Max. (b.12 November 1888) [=7].

Burger, Karl. (b.26 December 1883) [=7].

Förderer, Friedrich "Fritz." (b.5 January 1888) [=7].

Fuchs, Gottfried Fritz. (b.3 March 1889–d.1972) [=7].

Glaser, Josef. (b.11 May 1887) [=7].

Hempel, Walter. (b.12 August 1887) [=7].

Hirsch, Julius. (b.7 April 1892–d.6 May 1941) [=7].

Hollstein, Ernst. (b.9 December 1886) [=7].

Jäger, Adolf. (b.31 March 1889–d.21 November 1944) [=7].

Kipp, Eugen. (b.26 February 1885) [=7].

Krogmann, Georg. (b.4 September 1886) [=7].

Oberle, Emil. (b.16 November 1889) [=7].

Reese, Hans Heinrich. (b.17 September 1891) [=7].

Röpnack, Helmuth. (b.23 September 1884) [=7].

Thiel, Otto. (b.23 November 1891) [=7].

Ugi, Camillo. (b.21 December 1884) [=7].

Uhle, Heinrich Karl. (b.16 July 1887) [=7].

Weber, Albert. (b.21 November 1888) [=7].

Wegele, Karl. (b.27 September 1887) [=7].

Werner, Adolf Friedrich August. (b.19 October 1886) [=7].

Worpitzky, Willi. (b.25 August 1886) [=7].

Gymnastics (Total: 18; Men: 18; Women: 0)

Brülle, Wilhelm. (b.17 February 1891) Combined All-Around, Free System, Team [4]; Combined All-Around, European System, Team [5].

Buder, Johannes Erwin. (b.22 July 1885) Combined All-Around, Free System, Team [4]; Combined All-Around, European System, Team [5].

Engelmann, Walter Otto. (b.5 August 1888) Combined All-Around, Free System, Team [4]; Combined All-Around, European System, Team [5].

Glockauer, Arno. (b.31 July 1888) Combined All-Around, Free System, Team [4]; Combined All-Around, European System, Team [5].

Jesinghaus, Walter. (b.10 October 1887–d.1918) Combined All-Around, Free System, Team [4]; Combined All-Around, European System, Team [5].

Jordan, Karl. (b.23 March 1888–d.1972) Combined All-Around, Free System, Team [4]; Combined All-Around, European System, Team [5].

Körner, Rudolf. (b.8 January 1892) Combined All-Around, Free System, Team [4]; Combined All-Around, European System, Team [5].

Pahner, Heinrich. (b.16 December 1891) Combined All-Around, Free System, Team [4]; Combined All-Around, European System, Team [5].

Reichenbach, Kurt. (b.18 January 1890) Combined All-Around, Free System, Team [4]; Combined All-Around, European System, Team [5].

Reuschle, Johannes. (b.23 June 1890) Combined All-Around, Free System, Team [4]; Combined All-Around, European System, Team [5].

Richter, Karl Wilhelm. (b.23 September 1887) Combined All-Around, Free System, Team [4]; Combined All-Around, European System, Team [5].

Roth, Hans. (b.17 March 1890) Combined All-Around, Free System, Team [4]; Combined All-Around, European System, Team [5].

Seebaß, Adolf. (b.22 February 1890) Combined All-Around, Free System, Team [4]; Combined All-Around, European System, Team [5].

Sorge, Hans Eberhard. (b.27 May 1892) Combined All-Around, Free System, Team [4]; Combined All-Around, European System, Team [5].

Sperling, Alexander. (b.19 April 1890) Combined All-Around, Free System, Team [4]; Combined All-Around, European System, Team [5].

Staats, Alfred. (b.2 November 1891) Combined All-Around, Free System, Team [4]; Combined All-Around, European System, Team [5].

Werner, Hans. (b.11 October 1891) Combined All-Around, Free System, Team [4]; Combined All-Around, European System, Team [5].

Worm, Martin Erich. (b.11 May 1887) Combined All-Around, Free System, Team [4]; Combined All-Around, European System, Team [5].

Modern Pentathlon (Total: 1; Men: 1; Women: 0)
Pauen, Carl. (b.7 April 1859) Individual [ac/dnf].

Rowing & Sculling (Total: 25; Men: 25; Women: 0)
Arnheiter, Albert. (b.20 July 1890–d.26 April 1945) Coxed Fours, Outriggers [1].
Bartholomae, Fritz. (b.29 October 1886–d.1915) Coxed Eights [2h2r3/4].
Bartholomae, Willi. (b.31 January 1885) Coxed Eights [2h2r3/4].
Bröske, Max. (b.25 July 1882) Coxed Eights [2h2r3/4].
Charlet, Otto. (b.22 March 1885) Coxed Eights [2h2r2/4].
Dehn, Werner. (b.17 September 1889–d.1960) Coxed Eights [2h2r3/4].
Eggebrecht, Fritz. (b.15 January 1883) Coxed Eights [2h2r2/4].
Eichhorn, Carl. (b.16 March 1886) Coxed Eights [2h2r2/4].
Fickeisen, Otto. (b.24 December 1879–d.14 December 1963) Coxed Fours, Outriggers [1].
Fickeisen, Rudolf. (b.15 May 1885–d.21 August 1943) Coxed Fours, Outriggers [1].
Friesicke, Richard. (b.10 April 1892) Coxed Eights [2h2r2/4].
Gelfort, Gottfried. (b.6 April 1885) Coxed Eights [2h2r2/4].
Hoffmann, Kurt Georg. (b.11 November 1890) Single Sculls [2h4r1/4].
Landrock, Heinrich. (b.26 December 1890) Coxed Eights [2h2r2/4].
Liebing, Otto. (b.31 March 1891–d.7 November 1967) Coxed Eights [2h2r3/4].
Maier, Otto. (b.23 December 1887–d.29 May 1957) Coxed Fours, Outriggers [1].
Matthiae, Hans. (b.22 December 1884) Coxed Eights [2h2r3/4].
Reichelt, Rudolf. (b.24 March 1890) Coxed Eights [2h2r3/4].
Reinsfeld, Egbert. (b.2 March 1890) Coxed Eights [2h2r2/4].
Runge, Kurt. (b.13 September 1887–d.6 November 1959) Coxed Eights [2h2r3/4].
Stahnke, Martin. (b.11 November 1888) Single Sculls [2h3r2/4].
Vetter, Max. (b.17 March 1892) Coxed Eights [2h2r3/4].
Wegener, Andreas. (b.25 August 1878) Coxed Eights [2h2r2/4].
Weihnacht, Ludwig. (b.17 February 1888) Coxed Eights [2h2r2/4].
Wilker, Hermann. (b.24 July 1874–d.28 December 1941) Coxed Fours, Outriggers [1].

Shooting (Total: 11; Men: 11; Women: 0)
Bock, Gerhard. (b.5 March 1879) Free Pistol, 50 meters [44]; Dueling Pistol, 30 meters, Teams [7].
Goeldel-Bronikoven, Alfred. (b.12 March 1882) Clay Trap Shooting, Individual [2]; Clay Trap Shooting, Teams [3].

Goeldel-Bronikoven, Horst. (b.7 June 1883) Running Deer, Single Shot, Individual [=24]; Clay Trap Shooting, Teams [3]; Clay Trap Shooting, Individual [=12].

Hoffmann, Heinrich. (b.20 February 1869) Free Pistol, 50 meters [54]; Dueling Pistol, 30 meters, Teams [7].

Koch, Erland. (b.3 January 1867–d.29 April 1945) Running Deer, Single Shot, Individual [13]; Running Deer, Double Shot, Individual [=17]; Clay Trap Shooting, Individual [=12]; Clay Trap Shooting, Teams [3].

Lüttich, Hans Joachim. (b.11 January 1884) Clay Trap Shooting, Individual [=25].

Meyer, Georg Hermann. (b.24 December 1868) Dueling Pistol, 30 meters [39]; Dueling Pistol, 30 meters, Teams [7].

Preuß, Albert. (b.29 January 1864) Running Deer, Single Shot, Individual [=21]; Running Deer, Double Shot, Individual [=17]; Clay Trap Shooting, Individual [=4]; Clay Trap Shooting, Teams [3].

von Bernstorff-Gyldensteen, Erich, Count. (b.26 June 1883–d.6 October 1968) Clay Trap Shooting, Individual [=17]; Clay Trap Shooting, Teams [3].

von Zedlitz und Leipe, Franz, Baron. (b.21 April 1876–d.29 March 1944) Clay Trap Shooting, Individual [=4]; Clay Trap Shooting, Teams [3].

Wandolleck, Bernhard. (b.18 April 1864) Dueling Pistol, 30 meters, Teams [7].

Swimming (Total: 17; Men: 13; Women: 4)

Women

Dressel, Wally. (b.3 June 1893) 100 meter freestyle [4h2r2/3]; 4 × 100 meter freestyle relay [2].

Otto, Louise. (b.30 August 1896) 100 meter freestyle [6h1r2/3]; 4 × 100 meter freestyle relay [2].

Rosenberg, Margarete "Grete." (b.7 October 1896–d.5 February 1979) 100 meter freestyle [4]; 4 × 100 meter freestyle relay [2].

Stindt, Hermine. (b.3 January 1888–d.19 February 1974) 100 meter freestyle [3h3r1/3]; 4 × 100 meter freestyle relay [2].

Men

Bathe, Walter. (b.1 December 1892–d.21 September 1959) 200 meter breaststroke [1]; 400 meter breaststroke [1].

Binner, Walther. (b.28 January 1891–d.1971) 100 meter freestyle [ac/puk-3h3r1/4].

Bretting, Kurt. (b.8 June 1892–30 May 1918) 100 meter freestyle [4]; 4 × 200 meter freestyle relay [4].

Fahr, Otto. (b.19 August 1892–d.28 February 1969) 100 meter backstroke [2].

Groß, Otto. (b.1 January 1890) 100 meter backstroke [5].

Kellner, Paul. (b.6 June 1890–d.1972) 100 meter backstroke [3].

Kunisch, Georg. (b.21 April 1892) 100 meter freestyle [5h4r1/4]; 4 × 200 meter freestyle relay [4].

Lützow, Wilhelm "Willy." (b.19 May 1892–d.1916) 200 meter breaststroke [2]; 400 meter breaststroke [dnf-].

Malisch, Kurt Paul. (b.15 June 1881–d.9 April 1970) 200 meter breaststroke [3]; 400 meter breaststroke [4].

Ramme, Walter. (b.28 January 1895) 100 meter freestyle [5].

Ritter, Richard Max. (b.7 November 1886–d.24 May 1974) 100 meter freestyle [=3h2r2/4]; 400 meter freestyle [dns-r2/3]; 4 × 200 meter freestyle relay [4].

Schiele, Oskar. (b.14 April 1889–d.1 July 1950) 400 meter freestyle [3h6r1/3]; 100 meter backstroke [dqh1r1/3]; 4 × 200 meter freestyle relay [4].

Schultze, Erich. (b.22 May 1890) 100 meter backstroke [5h1r2/3].

Tennis (Total: 7; Men: 6; Women: 1)

Women

Köring, Dorothea "Dora." (b.11 July 1880–d.13 February 1945) Ladies' Singles (Lawn) [2]; Mixed Doubles (Lawn) [1].

Men

Heyden, Ludwig Maria. (b.17 November 1893) Men's Singles (Lawn) [=5]; Men's Doubles (Lawn) [=5].

Kreuzer, Oscar. (b.14 June 1887–d.3 May 1968) Men's Singles (Lawn) [3].

Lindpaintner, Otto Paul. (b.22 May 1883) Men's Singles (Lawn) [=48].

Schomburgk, Heinrich. (b.30 June 1885–d.29 March 1965) Men's Singles (Lawn) [=9]; Men's Doubles (Lawn) [=9]; Mixed Doubles (Lawn) [1].

Spies, Robert Cleon. (b.17 February 1891–d.22 October 1982) Men's Singles (Lawn) [=17]; Men's Doubles (Lawn) [=5].

von Müller, Otto. (b.17 October 1875–d.2 April 1976) Men's Singles (Lawn) [=5]; Men's Doubles (Lawn) [=9].

Wrestling (Total: 14; Men: 14; Women: 0)

Andersen, Georg "Jonny." (b.5 July 1887) 60 kg. Class (Greco-Roman) [AC].

Dumrauf, Andreas. (b.29 December 1888) 67½ kg. Class (Greco-Roman) [AC].

Gerstacker, Georg. (b.3 June 1889–d.21 December 1949) 60 kg. Class (Greco-Roman) [2].

Groß, Karl. (b.30 January 1884) 82½ kg. Class (Greco-Roman) [AC].

Hauptmanns, Jean. (b.24 January 1886) Unlimited Class (Greco-Roman) [AC].

Heckel, Bruno. (b.10 April 1887) 67½ kg. Class (Greco-Roman) [AC].

Kurz, Adolf. (b.22 April 1888) 75 kg. Class (Greco-Roman) [AC].

Lange, Fritz. (b.22 January 1885) 82½ kg. Class (Greco-Roman) [AC].

Merkle, Josef. (b.16 August 1882) 75 kg. Class (Greco-Roman) [AC].

Neser, Jakob. (b.30 December 1883) Unlimited Class (Greco-Roman) [AC].

Oehler, Peter. (b.23 June 1883) 82½ kg. Class (Greco-Roman) [AC].

Sauerhöfer, Ludwig. (b.5 March 1883) 67½ kg. Class (Greco-Roman) [AC].

Stein, Conrad. (b.26 March 1892) 60 kg. Class (Greco-Roman) [AC].

Steputat, Wilhelm. (b.28 October 1888) 75 kg. Class (Greco-Roman) [AC].

Great Britain[16] (Total: 271; Men: 261; Women: 10)

Athletics (Track & Field) (Total: 61; Men: 61; Women: 0)

Abrahams, Sidney Solomon. (b.11 February 1885–d.14 May 1967) Broad Jump [12/5g2-3/qr].

Anderson, Arthur Emilius David. (b.30 September 1886–d.21 October 1967) 100 meters [5h6r2/3]; 200 meters [dnf-h1r2/3].

Anderson, Gerard Rupert Leslie. (b.15 March 1889–d.9 November 1914) 110 meter hurdles [dnf-h4r2/3].

Applegarth, William Reuben. (b.11 May 1890–d.5 December 1958) 100 meters [2h5r2/3]; 200 meters [3]; 4 × 100 meter relay [1].

Ashington, Henry Sherard Osborn. (b.25 September 1891–d.31 January 1917) Broad Jump [10/3g2-3/qr]; Standing Long Jump [15/4g3qr].

Baker, Benjamin Howard. (b.15 February 1892–d.10 September 1987) High Jump [11]; Standing High Jump [5g1qr].

Baker, Philip John. (b.1 November 1889–d.9 October 1982) 800 meters [dnf-h5r1/3]; 1,500 meters [6]. (Later Philip John Noel-Baker).

Barker, James J. (b.6 November 1892) 100 meters [dnf-h15r1/3].

Barrett, Henry Frederick, "Harry." (b.30 December 1879–d.18 December 1927) Marathon [dnf-].

Beale, James George. (b.7 February 1881) Marathon [dnf-].

Blakeney, Henry Edward Hugh. (b.6 October 1890–d.12 February 1958) 100 meters [4h3r1/3]; 110 meter hurdles [3h5r2/3].

Bridge, Robert. (b.16 April 1883–d.1953) 800 meters [dnf-h4r1/3]; 10 Kilometer Walk [ac/h2r1/2].

Burton, Robert. (b.11 April 1885–d.14 June 1950) 800 meters [dnf-h4r1/3].

Carey, Denis. (b.6 August 1872) Hammer Throw [6/4g1qr].

Carroll, Timothy J. [Ireland] (b.8 July 1888) High Jump [=9]; Hop, step, and jump [19/5g1qr].

Cottrill, William. (b.14 October 1889–d.26 October 1972) 1,500 meters [3h7r1/3]; Cross-Country, Individual [dnf-]; Cross-Country, Team [3/ns]; 3,000 Meter Team Race [3].

d'Arcy, Victor Henry Augustus. (b.30 June 1887–d.12 March 1961) 100 meters [ach5r2/3]; 200 meters [2h6r2/3]; 4 × 100 meter relay [1].

Dumbill, Thomas Henry. (b.23 September 1884) 10 Kilometer Walk [dq-final].

Duncan, Robert Cochran. (b.4 October 1887) 100 meters [ach9r1/3]; 200 meters [dnf-h6r2/3].

Francom, Septimus. (b.14 September 1882–d.15 March 1965) Marathon [dnf-].

Glover, Ernest. (b.19 February 1891) 5,000 meters [dns-final]; 10,000 meters [dns-final]; Cross-Country, Individual [16]; Cross-Country, Team [3].

Green, Henry Harold. (b.15 July 1886–d.12 March 1934) Marathon [14].

Haley, Ernest William. (b.3 January 1885–d.20 February 1975) 200 meters [4h11r1/3]; 400 meters [dnf-h4r2/3].

Hare, Albert. (b.12 May 1887–d.23 December 1969) 1,500 meters [3h1r1/3].

Henderson, Walter Edward Bonhôte. (b.21 June 1880–d.2 September 1944) Discus Throw [32/7g5qr].

Henley, Ernest John. (b.31 March 1889–d.14 March 1962) 400 meters [dnf-h3r2/3]; 800 meters [ach2r2/3]; 4 × 400 meter relay [3].

Hibbins, Frederick Newton. (b.23 March 1890) 5,000 meters [ac-final]; 10,000 meters [10h2r1/2]; Cross-Country, Individual [15]; Cross-Country, Team [3].

Hulford, Frederick Henry. (b.6 February 1883–d.23 January 1876) 800 meters [dnf-h1r2/3]; 1,500 meters [ach6r1/3].

Humphreys, Thomas Frederick. (b.8 September 1890–d.9 April 1967) 10,000 meters [9h2r1/2]; Cross-Country, Individual [18]; Cross-Country, Team [3].

Hutson, George William. (b.22 December 1889–d.14 September 1914) 5,000 meters [3]; 3,000 Meter Team Race [3].

Jackson, Arnold Nugent Strode. (b.5 April 1891–d.13 November 1972) 1,500 meters [1].

Jacobs, David Henry. (b.30 April 1888–d.5 June 1976) 100 meters [2h3r2/3]; 200 meters [2h1r2/3]; 4 × 100 meter relay [1].

Kellaway, Henry George "Tim." (b.7 October 1891–d.31 December 1952) Marathon [dnf-].

Kingsford, Philip Cave. (b.10 August 1891) Broad Jump [15/4g4qr]; Standing Long Jump [19/6g4qr].

Lee, George. (b.28 December 1886) 5,000 meters [4h4r1/2]; 10,000 meters [7h1r1/2].

Lloyd, Edgar William. (b.31 July 1884–d.3 January 1972) Marathon [25].

Lord, Frederick Thomas. (b.11 February 1879) Marathon [21].

Macintosh, Henry Maitland. (b.10 June 1892–d.26 July 1918) 100 meters [3h11r1/3]; 200 meters [dns-r2/3]; 4 × 100 meter relay [1].

Macmillan, Duncan. (b.1 June 1890–d.15 September 1963) 100 meters [ach12r1/3]; 200 meters [5h4r2/3].

Mann, Percy Edward. (b.12 May 1888–d.23 September 1974) 800 meters [6h1r2/3].

Moore, William Craig. (b.5 April 1890–d.12 May 1956) 1,500 meters [3h6r1/3]; 3,000 Meter Team Race [3-ns/dnf].

Nicol, George. (b.28 December 1886–d.28 January 1967) 400 meters [3h1r2/3]; 4 × 400 meter relay [3].

O'Donahue, Thomas. [Ireland] (b.12 December 1887) High Jump [=7g1qr].

Owen, Edward. (b.6 November 1886–d.24 September 1949) 1,500 meters [dnf-h3r1/3]; 3,000 Meter Team Race [3-ns/dnf].

Palmer, William James. (b.19 April 1882–d.21 December 1967) 10 Kilometer Walk [dnf-final].

Patterson, Alan. (b.12 March 1886–d.14 March 1916) 400 meters [4h15r1/3]; 800 meters [dnf-h8r1/3].

Porter, Cyril Henry Atwell. (b.12 January 1890–d.25 June 1977) 5,000 meters [ac-final]; 3,000 Meter Team Race [3].

Powell, Kenneth. (b.8 April 1885–d.18 February 1915) 110 meter hurdles [5].

Quinn, Patrick. [Ireland] (b.10 December 1885) Shot Put [8/4g1-2qr].

Rice, Richard Goodenough. (b.19 March 1886–d.15 October 1939) 100 meters [3h2r2/3]; 200 meters [dnf-h5r2/3].

Ruffell, Charles Henry. (b.16 September 1888–d.9 November 1923) 1,500 meters [dnf-h5r1/3]; 5,000 meters [dnf-h2r1/2]; 10,000 meters [8h1r1/2].

Scott, William. (b.23 March 1886) 10,000 meters [dnf-final]; Cross-Country, Individual [dnf-]; Cross-Country, Team [3/ns].

Seedhouse, Cyril Norman. (b.10 April 1892–d.21 January 1966) 200 meters [4h2r2/3]; 400 meters [dnf-h2r2/3]; 4 × 400 meter relay [3].

Soutter, James Tindal. (b.1 January 1885–d.8 August 1966) 400 meters [ach5r2/3]; 800 meters [dnf-h1r2/3]; 4 × 400 meter relay [3].

Townsend, Arthur Henry. (b.7 April 1883) Marathon [19].

Treble, Arnold Leonard. (b.8 October 1889–d.1966) 5,000 meters [dnf-h5r1/2].

Wallach, George Curtis Locke. (b.20 March 1883–d.2 April 1980) 10,000 meters [6h3r1/2].

Webb, Ernest James. (b.25 April 1874–d.24 February 1937) 10 Kilometer Walk [2].

Wells, Joseph Algernon. (b.9 September 1885–d.20 October 1946) 200 meters [ach7r1/3]; 400 meters [dnf-h2r2/3].

Yates, William George. (b.5 August 1880–d.27 December 1967) 10 Kilometer Walk [dq-final].

Yorke, Richard Francis Charles. (b.28 July 1885–d.22 December 1914) 800 meters [3h6r1/3]; 1,500 meters [4h5r1/3].

Cycling (Total: 26; Men: 26; Women: 0)

England (Total: 12; Men: 12; Women: 0)

Davey, Charles Frederick. (b.27 August 1886) Road Race, Individual [39]; Road Race, Team [2/ns].

Gayler, Herbert Henry. (b.3 December 1881) Road Race, Individual [30]; Road Race, Team [2/ns].

Gibbon, Arthur William John. (b.1884) Road Race, Individual [38]; Road Race, Team [2/ns].

Grubb, Frederick Henry. (b.27 May 1887–d.6 March 1949) Road Race, Individual [2]; Road Race, Team [2].

Hammond, William Robert. (b.1 July 1886) Road Race, Individual [22]; Road Race, Team [2].

Higgins, Francis Cecil. (b.29 January 1882–d.19 April 1948) Road Race, Individual [37]; Road Race, Team [2/ns].

Jones, Stanley Lawrence. (b.24 March 1888) Road Race, Individual [29]; Road Race, Team [2/ns].

Kirk, John William. (b.20 November 1890) Road Race, Individual [ac/dnf]; Road Race, Team [2/ns/dnf].

Meredith, Leon Lewis. (b.2 February 1882–d.27 January 1930) Road Race, Individual [4]; Road Race, Team [2].

Merlin, Ernest Alfred. (b.5 September 1886) Road Race, Individual [59]; Road Race, Team [2/ns].

Moss, Charles. (b.6 March 1882) Road Race, Individual [18]; Road Race, Team [2].

Stokes, Arthur Joseph. (b.13 November 1875) Road Race, Individual [ac/dnf]; Road Race, Team [2/ns/dnf].

Ireland (Total: 6; Men: 6; Women: 0)

Doyle, Bernhard Joseph. (b.9 April 1888) Road Race, Individual [85]; Road Race, Team [11/ns].

Guy, Francis. (b.1885) Road Race, Individual [71]; Road Race, Team [11].

Mecredy, Ralph, Jr. (b.12 July 1888) Road Race, Individual [80]; Road Race, Team [11].

Walker, John. (b.23 December 1888) Road Race, Individual [81]; Road Race, Team [11].

Walker, Michael. (b.31 August 1886) Road Race, Individual [67]; Road Race, Team [11].

Walsh, Matthew. (b.4 July 1887) Road Race, Individual [82]; Road Race, Team [11/ns].

Scotland (Total: 8; Men: 8; Women: 0)

Corsar, George. (b.7 February 1881) Road Race, Individual [86]; Road Race, Team [4/ns].

Griffiths, Arthur J. (b.30 November 1881) Road Race, Individual [90]; Road Race, Team [4/ns].

Hill, Charles. (b.15 August 1886) Road Race, Individual [49]; Road Race, Team [4/ns].

Miller, John. (b.27 February 1882) Road Race, Individual [35]; Road Race, Team [4].

Stevenson, James. (b.1 February 1887) Road Race, Individual [68]; Road Race, Team [4/ns].

Stevenson, David M. (b.17 January 1882) Road Race, Individual [41]; Road Race, Team [4].

Thompson, Robert. (b.28 April 1884) Road Race, Individual [24]; Road Race, Team [4].

Wilson, John. (b.17 November 1876–d.24 November 1957) Road Race, Individual [16]; Road Race, Team [4].

Diving (Total: 3; Men: 2; Women: 1)

Women

White, Isabelle Mary "Belle." (b.1 September 1894–d.7 July 1972) Plain High Diving [3].

Men

Pott, Herbert Ernest. (b.15 January 1883) Springboard Diving [8].

Yvon, George. (b.15 February 1887–d.20 November 1957) Plain and Fancy High Diving [5]; Plain High Diving [3h2r1/2].

Equestrian Events (Total: 4; Men: 4; Women: 0)

Kenna, Paul Alyoysius. (b.16 August 1862–d.30 August 1915) Jumping, Individual [27]; Three-Day Event, Individual [ac/dnf]; Three-Day Event, Team [dnf-] (Harmony).

Lawrence, Bryan Turner Thomas. (b.9 November 1873–d.6 June 1949) Three-Day Event, Individual [ac/dnf]; Three-Day Event, Team [dnf-] (Patrick).

Radcliffe-Nash, Edward. (b.9 June 1888) Jumping, Individual [29]; Three-Day Event, Individual [ac/dnf]; Three-Day Event, Team [dnf-] (The Flea).

Scott, Herbert Stuart Lauriston. (b.29 December 1885–d.3 June 1966) Jumping, Individual [4] (Shamrock); Three-Day Event, Individual [ac/dnf] (Whisper II); Three-Day Event, Team [dnf-] (Whisper II).

Fencing (Total: 22; Men: 22; Women: 0)

Alexander, Gordon Reuben. (b.1888–d.24 April 1917) Foil, Individual (4p1r2/4); Épée, Individual (=7p1r1/4).

Ames, Gerald R. (b.1880) Épée, Individual (=4p2r3/4).

Amphlett, Edgar Montague. (b.1 September 1867–d.9 January 1931) Foil, Individual (acp2r3/4); Épée, Individual (5p1r3/4).

Blake, John Percy. (b.1874–d.19 December 1950) Épée, Individual (=5p15r1/4).

Brookfield, Edward Williams Hamilton. (b.1880) Sabre, Individual (5p5r2/4); Sabre, Team (=7).

Butterworth, Harry Robert. (b.1867) Sabre, Individual (=4p2r2/4); Sabre, Team (=7).

Cooke, Stenson. (b.5 October 1874–d.19 November 1942) Foil, Individual (=4p6r1/4); Épée, Individual (4p12r1/4).

Corble, Archibald Harrison. (b.23 May 1883–d.22 January 1944) Sabre, Individual (4p14r1/4); Sabre, Team (=7).

Crawshay, Richard Oakes. (b.1881) Sabre, Team (=7).

Davson, Percival May. (b.30 September 1887–d.5 December 1959) Foil, Individual (=5p4r1/4); Épée, Individual (=5p10r1/4); Épée, Team (2).

Everitt, Arthur Francis Graham. (b.27 August 1872–d.10 January 1952) Épée, Individual (=5p2r2/4); Épée, Team (2).

Fagan, Arthur William. (b.10 December 1890) Foil, Individual (=5p6r2/4).

Godfree, Douglas William. (b.16 October 1881–d.5 August 1929) Sabre, Individual (=4p8r1/4). (See also Modern Pentathlon.)

Holt, Martin Drummond Vesey. (b.13 January 1881–d.2 November 1956) Épée, Individual (8); Épée, Team (2).

Keene, Alfred Valentine. Sabre, Individual (4p7r2/4).

Marsh, William Walter. (b.29 March 1877–d.12 February 1959) Sabre, Individual (5p4r3/4); Sabre, Team (=7).

Martin, Alfred Ridley. (b.9 May 1881–d.6 May 1970) Sabre, Individual (5p8r2/4); Sabre, Team (=7).

Martineau, Sydney. (b.6 January 1863) Foil, Individual (=4p7r1/4); Épée, Individual (=4p13r1/4); Épée, Team (2).

Montgomerie, Robert Cecil Lindsay. (b.15 February 1880–d.24 August 1939) Foil, Individual (8); Épée, Individual (=4p3r3/4); Épée, Team (2).

Seligman, Edgar Isaac. (b.14 April 1867–d.27 September 1958) Foil, Individual (6); Épée, Individual (6); Épée, Team (2).

Syson, Alfred Edward. Sabre, Individual (3p2r3/4).

Vander Byl, Charles Fennelly. (b.5 April 1874–d.9 February 1956) Épée, Individual (5p6r2/4); Sabre, Individual (4p3r3/4).

Football (Association Football [Soccer]) (Total: 14; Men: 14; Women: 0)

Berry, Arthur. (b.3 January 1888–d.15 March 1953) [1].

Brebner, Ronald Gilchrist. (b.23 September 1881–d.11 November 1914) [1].

Burn, Thomas Christopher. (b.29 November 1888)[17] [1].

Dines, Joseph. (b.12 April 1886–d.27 September 1918) [1].

Hanney, Edward Terrance. (b.19 January 1889) [1].

Hoare, Gordon Rahere. (b.18 April 1884–d.27 October 1973) [1].
Knight, Arthur Egerton. (b.7 September 1887–d.10 March 1956) [1].
Littlewort, Henry Charles. (b.7 July 1882–d.21 November 1934) [1].
McWhirter, Douglas. (b.13 August 1886–d.14 October 1966) [1].
Sharpe, Ivor Gordon. (b.15 June 1889–d.9 February 1968) [1].
Stamper, Harold. (b.6 October 1889) [1].
Walden, Harold Adrian. (b.10 October 1889–d.2 December 1955) [1].
Woodward, Vivian John. (b.3 June 1879–d.31 January 1954) [1].
Wright, Edward Gordon Dundas. (b.3 October 1884–d.5 June 1947) [1].

Gymnastics (Total: 23; Men: 23; Women: 0)
Betts, Albert Edward. (b.8 February 1888) Combined All-Around, European System, Team [3].
Cowhig, William. (b.5 April 1887) Combined All-Around, Individual [29]; Combined All-Around, European System, Team [3].
Cross, Sidney. (b.5 January 1891) Combined All-Around, European System, Team [3].
Dickason, Harold. (b.16 April 1890) Combined All-Around, European System, Team [3].
Drury, Herbert James. (b.5 January 1883–d.11 July 1936) Combined All-Around, European System, Team [3].
Franklin, Bernard Wallis. (b.10 November 1889) Combined All-Around, European System, Team [3].
Hanson, Leonard. (b.1 November 1887) Combined All-Around, Individual [12]; Combined All-Around, European System, Team [3].
Hodgetts, Samuel. (b.28 October 1887) Combined All-Around, Individual [25]; Combined All-Around, European System, Team [3].
Luck, Charles James. (b.19 November 1886) Combined All-Around, European System, Team [3].
MacKune, William. (b.6 August 1882) Combined All-Around, European System, Team [3].
McLean, Ronald Gordon. (b.26 March 1881) Combined All-Around, European System, Team [3].
Messenger, Alfred William. (b.4 December 1887) Combined All-Around, European System, Team [3].
Oberholzer, Henry Arthur. (b.12 April 1893) Combined All-Around, European System, Team [3].
Pepper, Edward Ernest. (b.12 November 1879) Combined All-Around, European System, Team [3].
Potts, Edward William. (b.12 July 1881) Combined All-Around, European System, Team [3].
Potts, Reginald Hubert. (b.3 January 1892) Combined All-Around, Individual [32]; Combined All-Around, European System, Team [3].
Ross, George James. (b.1 December 1887) Combined All-Around, European System, Team [3].
Simmons, Charles.[18] (b.24 December 1885) Combined All-Around, Individual [28]; Combined All-Around, European System, Team [3].
Southern, Arthur George Heron. (b.26 March 1883) Combined All-Around, European System, Team [3].
Titt, William. (b.8 February 1881) Combined All-Around, European System, Team [3].
Vigurs, Charles Alfred. (b.11 July 1888–d.22 February 1917) Combined All-Around, European System, Team [3].
Walker, Samuel John. (b.5 October 1883) Combined All-Around, European System, Team [3].
Whitaker, John T. (b.9 April 1886) Combined All-Around, Individual [21]; Combined All-Around, European System, Team [3].

Modern Pentathlon (Total: 3; Men: 3; Women: 0)

Clilverd, Ralph Egerton. (b.30 July 1887) Individual [11].

Durant, Hugh. (b.23 February 1887) Individual [18]. (See also Shooting.)

Godfree, Douglas William. (b.16 October 1881–d.5 August 1929) Individual [10]. (See also Fencing.)

Rowing & Sculling (Total: 24; Men: 24; Women: 0)

Beresford, Julius (né Julius Wisniewski). (b.29 June 1868–d.29 September 1959) Coxed Fours, Outriggers [2].

Bourne, Robert Croft. (b.15 July 1888–d.7 August 1938) Coxed Eights [2].

Burdekin, Beaufort. (b.27 December 1891–d.15 May 1963) Coxed Eights [2].

Burgess, Edgar Richard. (b.23 September 1891–d.23 April 1952) Coxed Eights [1].

Carr, Geoffrey. (b.22 January 1886) Coxed Fours, Outriggers [2].

Fison, William Guy. (b.25 October 1890–d.6 December 1924) Coxed Eights [2].

Fleming, Philip. (b.15 August 1889–d.13 October 1971) Coxed Eights [1].

Garton, Arthur Stanley. (b.31 March 1889–d.20 October 1960) Coxed Eights [1].

Gillan, James Angus. (b.11 October 1885–d.23 April 1981) Coxed Eights [1].

Gillespie, Thomas Cunningham. (b.14 December 1892–d.10 October 1914) Coxed Eights [2].

Horsfall, Ewart Douglas. (b.24 May 1892–d.1 February 1974) Coxed Eights [1].

Kinnear, William Duthie. (b.3 December 1880–d.5 March 1974) Single Sculls [1].

Kirby, Alister Graham. (b.14 April 1886–d.29 March 1917) Coxed Eights [1].

Littlejohn, Charles William Berry. (b.4 January 1889–d.August 1960) Coxed Eights [2].

Logan, Hubert Bruce. (b.2 March 1886–d.24 November 1965) Coxed Fours, Outriggers [2].

Parker, William Lorenzo, Sir. (b.9 January 1889–d.27 October 1971) Coxed Eights [2].

Pitman, Frederick Archibald Hugo. (b.1 June 1892–d.25 July 1963) Coxed Eights [2].

Rought, Charles Gardner. (b.16 October 1884–d.31 January 1918) Coxed Fours, Outriggers [2].

Swann, Sidney Ernest. (b.24 June 1890–d.19 September 1976) Coxed Eights [1].

Vernon, Karl. (b.19 June 1880–d.11 July 1973) Coxed Fours, Outriggers [2].

Walker, John Drummond. (b.4 January 1891–d.22 July 1952) Coxed Eights [2].

Wells, Henry Bensley. (b.12 January 1891–d.4 July 1967) Coxed Eights [1].

Wiggins, Arthur Frederick Reginald. (b.4 December 1891) Coxed Eights [2].

Wormwald, Leslie Graham. (b.19 August 1890–d.10 July 1965) Coxed Eights [1].

Shooting (Total: 38; Men: 38; Women: 0)

Black, Alfred William. (b.17 November 1856–d.12 December 1912) Clay Trap Shooting, Individual [=53].

Burr, Henry George. (b.21 March 1872) Military Rifle, 600 meters, any position [10]; Military Rifle, 200, 400, 500, and 600 meters, Teams [2].

Burt, Harold. (b.6 May 1876) Small-Bore Rifle, prone position, 50 meters [3]; Small-Bore Rifle, 25 meters, Disappearing Target [9].

Butt, John Hurst. (b.30 October 1852–d.1939) Clay Trap Shooting, Individual [=17]; Clay Trap Shooting, Teams [2].

Davies, Robert M. Finden. (b.10 December 1876–d.9 September 1916) Military Rifle, 300 meters, 3-Positions [39]; Military Rifle, 600 meters, any position [37].

Durant, Hugh. (b.23 February 1887) Free Pistol, 50 meters [20]; Dueling Pistol, 30 meters, Teams [3]; Military Pistol, 50 meters, Teams [3]. (See also Modern Pentathlon.)

Fulton, Arthur George. (b.16 September 1877–d.26 January 1972) Military Rifle, 300 meters, 3-Positions [6]; Military Rifle, 600 meters, any position [9]; Military Rifle, 200, 400, 500, and 600 meters, Teams [2].

Goodwin, John Morris. (b.14 March 1859) Clay Trap Shooting, Individual [=56].

Griffiths, David James. (b.31 March 1874) Small-Bore Rifle, prone position, 50 meters [24]; Small-Bore Rifle, 25 meters, Disappearing Target [29].

Grosvenor, William Percy. (b.18 July 1869) Clay Trap Shooting, Individual [16]; Clay Trap Shooting, Teams [2].

Humby, Harold Robinson. (b.8 April 1879–d.23 February 1923) Clay Trap Shooting, Individual [=4]; Clay Trap Shooting, Teams [2].

Jones, Peter H. (b.3 September 1879) Free Pistol, 50 meters [32].

Kemp, Francis William. (b.1 July 1891) Small-Bore Rifle, prone position, 50 meters [5]; Small-Bore Rifle, 25 meters, Disappearing Target [23].

Kempster, Albert Joseph. (b.23 August 1875) Free Pistol, 50 meters [24]; Dueling Pistol, 30 meters, Teams [3]; Military Pistol, 50 meters, Teams [3].

Lessimore, Edward John. (b.20 January 1881–d.7 March 1960) Small-Bore Rifle, prone position, 50 meters [4]; Small-Bore Rifle, 25 meters, Disappearing Target [12]; Small-Bore Rifle, 50 meters, Teams [1].

Lloyd, Langford Newnan. (b.28 December 1873–d.20 April 1956) Military Rifle, 300 meters, 3-Positions [57].

Maunder, Alexander Elsdon. (b.21 January 1895–d.2 February 1932) Clay Trap Shooting, Individual [=45]; Clay Trap Shooting, Teams [2].

McClure, William. (b.20 May 1883) Military Rifle, 300 meters, 3-Positions [69]; Free Pistol, 50 meters [35]; Dueling Pistol, 30 meters [41].

Milne, William. (b.23 March 1852) Small-Bore Rifle, prone position, 50 meters [2]; Small-Bore Rifle, 25 meters, Disappearing Target [22]; Small-Bore Rifle, 25 meters, Disappearing Target, Teams [2].

Murray, Robert Cook. (b.18 February 1870–d.28 April 1948) Small-Bore Rifle, prone position, 50 meters [6]; Small-Bore Rifle, 25 meters, Disappearing Target [5]; Small-Bore Rifle, 50 meters, Teams [1].

Ommundsen, Harcourt. (b.23 November 1878–d.1915) Military Rifle, 600 meters, any position [7]; Military Rifle, 200, 400, 500, and 600 meters, Teams [2].

Palmer, Charles. (b.18 August 1869) Clay Trap Shooting, Individual [=21]; Clay Trap Shooting, Teams [2].

Parnell, Edward Louis. (b.21 June 1875–d.15 February 1941) Military Rifle, 300 meters, 3-Positions [56]; Military Rifle, 600 meters, any position [18]; Military Rifle, 200, 400, 500, and 600 meters, Teams [2].

Pepé, Joseph. (b.5 March 1881) Small-Bore Rifle, prone position, 50 meters [14]; Small-Bore Rifle, 25 meters, Disappearing Target [4]; Small-Bore Rifle, 25 meters, Disappearing Target, Teams [2]; Small-Bore Rifle, 50 meters, Teams [1].

Pimm, William Edwin. (b.10 December 1864–d.1952) Small-Bore Rifle, prone position, 50 meters [10]; Small-Bore Rifle, 25 meters, Disappearing Target [7]; Small-Bore Rifle, 25 meters, Disappearing Target, Teams [2]; Small-Bore Rifle, 50 meters, Teams [1].

Pinchard, George Ernest. (b.17 June 1871) Clay Trap Shooting, Individual [39].

Plater, Philip Edward. (b.6 June 1866) Military Rifle, 300 meters, 3-Positions [86]; Military Rifle, 600 meters, any position [5].

Poulter, Horatio Orlando. (b.29 October 1877) Free Pistol, 50 meters [6]; Dueling Pistol, 30 meters, Teams [3]; Military Pistol, 50 meters, Teams [3].

Reid, James. (b.8 March 1875) Military Rifle, 600 meters, any position [13]; Military Rifle, 200, 400, 500, and 600 meters, Teams [2].

Richardson, Philip Wigham. (b.26 January 1865–d.23 November 1953) Military Rifle, 300 meters, 3-Positions [65]; Military Rifle, 600 meters, any position [33].

Sedgewick, John. (b.12 August 1873) Military Rifle, 300 meters, 3-Positions [38]; Military Rifle, 600 meters, any position [31].

Skilton, Edward. (b.26 September 1863) Military Rifle, 600 meters, any position [16]; Military Rifle, 200, 400, 500, and 600 meters, Teams [2].

Somers, John Percy. (b.12 July 1874) Military Rifle, 300 meters, 3-Positions [54]; Military Rifle, 600 meters, any position [46].

Stewart, Charles Edward. (b.1881) Free Pistol, 50 meters [3]; Dueling Pistol, 30 meters, Teams [3]; Military Pistol, 50 meters, Teams [3].

Styles, William Kensett. (b.11 October 1874–d.8 April 1940) Small-Bore Rifle, prone position, 50 meters [27]; Small-Bore Rifle, 25 meters, Disappearing Target [13]; Small-Bore Rifle, 25 meters, Disappearing Target, Teams [2].

Tickell, Edward James. (b.9 February 1861–d.4 January 1942) Free Pistol, 50 meters [45].

Varley, Fleetwood Ernest. (b.12 July 1862–d.26 March 1936) Military Rifle, 300 meters, 3-Positions [50]; Military Rifle, 600 meters, any position [27].

Whitaker, George. (b.25 August 1864) Clay Trap Shooting, Individual [=29]; Clay Trap Shooting, Teams [2].

Swimming (Total: 18; Men: 12; Women: 6)

Women

Curwen, Daisy. (b.6 December 1889) 100 meter freestyle [dns-final].

Fletcher, Jennie. (b.19 March 1890–d.1968) 100 meter freestyle [3]; 4 × 100 meter freestyle relay [1].

Langford, Mary Ada. (b.23 November 1894) 100 meter freestyle [5h1r2/3].

Moore, Isabella "Belle." (b.23 October 1894–d.7 March 1975) 100 meter freestyle [4h1r2/3]; 4 × 100 meter freestyle relay [1].

Speirs, Annie. (b.14 July 1889–d.October 1926) 100 meter freestyle [5]; 4 × 100 meter freestyle relay [1].

Steer, Irene. (b.10 August 1889–d.18 April 1977) 100 meter freestyle [dqh2r2/3]; 4 × 100 meter freestyle relay [1].

Men

Atkinson, Carlyle. (b.4 December 1892) 200 meter breaststroke [5h1r2/3].

Battersby, Thomas Sydney. (b.18 November 1887) 400 meter freestyle [5h1r2/3]; 1,500 meter freestyle [4h2r2/3]; 4 × 200 meter freestyle relay [3].

Courtman, Percy. (b.14 May 1888–d.2 June 1917) 200 meter breaststroke [4]; 400 meter breaststroke [3].

Derbyshire, John Henry. (b.29 November 1878–d.30 July 1938) 100 meter freestyle [3h3r1/4].

Foster, William. (b.10 July 1890–d.17 December 1963) 400 meter freestyle [3h1r2/3]; 1,500 meter freestyle [3h2r2/3]; 4 × 200 meter freestyle relay [3].

Haresnape, Herbert Nickall. (b.2 July 1880–d.1968) 100 meter backstroke [3h2r2/3].

Hatfield, John Gatenby. (b.15 August 1893–d.30 March 1965) 400 meter freestyle [2]; 1,500 meter freestyle [2]; 4 × 200 meter freestyle relay [3].

Innocent, George. (b.13 May 1885–d.4 April 1957) 200 meter breaststroke [dqh5r1/3]; 400 meter breaststroke [dnf-h2r2/3].

Radmilovic, Paul. (b.5 March 1886–d.29 September 1968) 100 meter freestyle [5h342/4]. (See also Water Polo.)

Sandon, Frank. (b.3 June 1890–d.29 May 1979) 100 meter backstroke [4h2r2/3].

Taylor, Henry. (b.17 March 1885–d.28 February 1951) 400 meter freestyle [5h2r2/3]; 1,500 meter freestyle [dnf-h1r2/3]; 4 × 200 meter freestyle relay [3].

Webster, George Henry. (b.31 July 1875) 100 meter backstroke [6h1r2/3].

Tennis (Total: 11; Men: 8; Women: 3)

Women

Aitchison, Francis Helen. (b.1881) Ladies' Singles (Covered Court) [=5]; Mixed Doubles (Covered Court) [2].

Hannam, Edith Margaret Boucher. (b.28 November 1878–d.16 January 1951) Ladies' Singles (Covered Court) [1]; Mixed Doubles (Covered Court) [1].

Parton, Mabel Bramwell. (b.22 July 1881) Ladies' Singles (Covered Court) [3]; Mixed Doubles (Covered Court) [=5].

Men

Barrett, Herbert Roper. (b.24 November 1873–d.27 July 1943) Men's Singles (Covered Court) [=9]; Men's Doubles (Covered Court) [4]; Mixed Doubles (Covered Court) [2].

Beamish, Alfred Ernest. (b.6 August 1879–d.28 February 1944) Men's Singles (Covered Court) [=16]; Men's Doubles (Covered Court) [3].

Caridia, George Aristides. (b.20 February 1869) Men's Singles (Covered Court) [=5]; Men's Doubles (Covered Court) [=7].

Dixon, Charles Percy. (b.7 February 1873–d.29 April 1939) Men's Singles (Covered Court) [2]; Men's Doubles (Covered Court) [3]; Mixed Doubles (Covered Court) [1].

Gore, Arthur William Charles "Wentworth." (b.2 January 1868–d.1 December 1928) Men's Singles (Covered Court) [=9]; Men's Doubles (Covered Court) [4].

Lowe, Arthur Holden. (b.29 January 1886–d.22 October 1958) Men's Singles (Covered Court) [=5]; Men's Doubles (Covered Court) [=5].

Lowe, Francis Gordon. (b.21 June 1884–d.17 May 1972) Men's Singles (Covered Court) [4]; Men's Doubles (Covered Court) [=5].

Mavrogordato, Theodore Michel. (b.31 July 1883–d.29 August 1941) Men's Singles (Covered Court) [=9]; Men's Doubles (Covered Court) [–7]; Mixed Doubles (Covered Court) [=5].

Tug-of-War (Total: 8; Men: 8; Women: 0)

Chaffe, Walter. (b.2 April 1870–d.22 April 1918) [2].

Dowler, Joseph. (b.1 February 1879–d.13 February 1931) [2].

Humphreys, Frederick Harkness. (b.28 January 1878–d.10 September 1954) [2].

Hynes, Mathias. [Ireland] (b.21 January 1883–d.9 March 1926) [2].

Mills, Edwin Archer. (b.17 May 1878–d.12 November 1946) [2].

Munro, Alexander. (b.30 November 1870) [2].

Sewell, John. (b.23 April 1882–d.18 July 1947) [2].

Shepherd, John James. (b.2 June 1884–d.9 July 1954) [2].

Water Polo (Total: 7; Men: 7; Women: 0)

Bentham, Isaac. (b.27 October 1886–d.c.1914-1918) [1].

Bugbee, Charles. (b.29 August 1887–d.18 October 1959) [1].

Cornet, George Thomson. (b.15 July 1877–d.22 November 1952) [1].

Hill, Arthur Edwin. (b.9 January 1888) [1].

Radmilovic, Paul. (b.5 March 1886–d.29 September 1968) [1]. (See also Swimming.)

Smith, Charles Sydney. (b.26 January 1879–d.6 April 1951) [1].

Wilkinson, George. (b.3 March 1879–d.7 August 1946) [1].

Wrestling (Total: 12; Men: 12; Women: 0)

Bacon, Edgar Hugh. (b.9 October 1887) 75 kg. Class (Greco-Roman) [AC].

Bacon, Stanley Vivian. (b.13 August 1885–d.13 October 1952) 75 kg. Class (Greco-Roman) [AC].

Barrett, Edward. (b.3 November 1880) Unlimited Class (Greco-Roman) [AC].

Cockings, Percy Horatius. (b.19 December 1885) 60 kg. Class (Greco-Roman) [AC].

Gould, Arthur Edwin. (b.31 January 1892) 67½ kg. Class (Greco-Roman) [AC].

Hayes, William Ernest. (b.20 April 1891) 67½ kg. Class (Greco-Roman) [AC].

Lupton, William Thomas. (b.14 June 1884) 67½ kg. Class (Greco-Roman) [AC].

MacKenzie, George. (b.21 November 1888–d.1957) 60 kg. Class (Greco-Roman) [AC].

Phelps, Robert Edward. (b.21 July 1890) 67½ kg. Class (Greco-Roman) [AC].

Rhys, Noel Raymond. (b.23 February 1888) 75 kg. Class (Greco-Roman) [AC].

Ruff, William. (b.30 January 1883) 67½ kg. Class (Greco-Roman) [AC].

Taylor, Alfred William. (b.8 February 1889) 60 kg. Class (Greco-Roman) [AC].

Greece[19] (Total: 21; Men: 21; Women: 0)

Athletics (Track & Field) (Total: 5; Men: 5; Women: 0)

Banikas, Georgios. (b.19 May 1888–d.9 April 1956) Pole Vault [=9g1qr].

Dorizas, Mikhail M. (b.16 April 1888–d.21 October 1957) Shot Put [11/6g1-2/qr]; Discus Throw [13/5g1qr].

Sakellaropoulos, Iraklis P. (b.1 March 1888) Marathon [26].

Triantafyllakos, Dimitrios. (b.3 April 1890–d.22 May 1966) 100 meters [ach6r1/3].

Tsiklitiras, Konstantinos. (b.30 October 1888–d.10 February 1913) Standing High Jump

Fencing (Total: 6; Men: 6; Women: 0)

Kotzias, Konstantinos. (b.1890) Épée, Individual (4p7r2/4); Épée, Team (=5).

Manos, Petros. (b.1871) Épée, Individual (=3p1r3/4); Épée, Team (=5).

Notaris, Sotirios. (b.1879–d.1924) Foil, Individual (=4p5r2/4); Épée, Individual (4p2r2/4).

Petropoulos, Georgios. (b.23 May 1872) Épée, Individual (3p4r3/4); Épée, Team (=5). (See also Shooting.)

Triantafyllakos, Trifon. (b.1891) Épée, Individual (4p6r2/4); Épée, Team (=5).

Versis, Georgios.[20] (b.1894) Épée, Individual (4p8r2/4); Épée, Team (=5).

Shooting (Total: 9; Men: 9; Women: 0)

Levidis, Nikolaos M. (b.25 May 1868) Military Rifle, 300 meters, 3-Positions [4]; Military Rifle, 600 meters, any position [52]; Military Rifle, 200, 400, 500, and 600 meters, Teams [7]; Small-Bore Rifle, 25 meters, Disappearing Target [30]; Small-Bore Rifle, prone position, 50 meters [25]; Small-Bore Rifle, 25 meters, Disappearing Target, Teams [4]; Small-Bore Rifle, 50 meters, Teams [=5]; Running Deer, Single Shot, Individual [=15]; Dueling Pistol, 30 meters [34].

Maurommatis, Frangiskos D. (b.13 January 1870) Military Rifle, 300 meters, 3-Positions [17]; Military Rifle, 600 meters, any position [22]; Military Rifle, 200, 400, 500, and 600 meters, Teams [7]; Small-Bore Rifle, prone position, 50 meters [34]; Small-Bore Rifle, 25 meters, Disappearing Target [18]; Small-Bore Rifle, 25 meters, Disappearing Target, Teams [4]; Small-Bore Rifle, 50 meters, Teams [=5]; Free Pistol, 50 meters [26]; Dueling Pistol, 30 meters [29]; Dueling Pistol, 30 meters, Teams [5]; Military Pistol, 50 meters, Teams [5].

Metaxas, Anastasios. (b.27 February 1862–d.1937) Dueling Pistol, 30 meters [35]; Clay Trap Shooting, Individual [=4].

Mostras, Spyridon D. (b.23 October 1890) Military Rifle, 300 meters, 3-Positions [88]; Military Rifle, 200, 400, 500, and 600 meters, Teams [7].

Petropoulos, Georgios. (b.23 May 1872) Dueling Pistol, 30 meters, Teams [5]. (See also Fencing.)

Skarlatos, Konstantinos. (b.27 March 1877–d.1969) Free Pistol, 50 meters [30]; Dueling Pistol, 30 meters [27]; Dueling Pistol, 30 meters, Teams [5]; Military Pistol, 50 meters, Teams [5].

Theofilakis, Alexandros. (b.1877) Free Pistol, 50 meters [47]; Dueling Pistol, 30 meters [33]; Military Pistol, 50 meters, Teams [5]; Military Rifle, 300 meters, 3-Positions [67]; Military Rifle, 600 meters, any position [68]; Military Rifle, 200, 400, 500, and 600 meters, Teams [7].

Theofilakis, Ioannis. (b.1879) Military Rifle, 300 meters, 3-Positions [75]; Military Rifle, 600 meters, any position [34]; Military Rifle, 200, 400, 500, and 600 meters, Teams [7]; Small-Bore Rifle, prone position, 50 meters [32]; Small-Bore Rifle, 25 meters, Disappearing Target [21]; Small-Bore Rifle, 25 meters, Disappearing Target, Teams [4]; Small-Bore Rifle, 50 meters, Teams [=5]; Dueling Pistol, 30 meters [23]; Dueling Pistol, 30 meters, Teams [5]; Free Pistol, 50 meters [18]; Military Pistol, 50 meters, Teams [5]; Running Deer, Single Shot, Individual [=29].

Theofilas, Iakovos. (b.22 October 1861) Military Rifle, 300 meters, 3-Positions [72]; Military Rifle, 600 meters, any position [85]; Military Rifle, 200, 400, 500, and 600 meters, Teams [7]; Small-Bore Rifle, prone position, 50 meters [37]; Small-Bore Rifle, 25 meters, Disappearing Target [36]; Small-Bore Rifle, 25 meters, Disappearing Target, Teams [4]; Small-Bore Rifle, 50 meters, Teams [=5].

Swimming (Total: 1; Men: 1; Women: 0)
Asimakopoulos, Andreas. (b.14 January 1889) 100 meter freestyle [3h1r1/4].

Wrestling (Total: 1; Men: 1; Women: 0)
Antonopoulos, Anastasios. (b.1893) 75 kg. Class (Greco-Roman) [AC].

Hungary[21] (Total: 123; Men: 123; Women: 0)

Athletics (Track & Field) (Total: 27; Men: 27; Women: 0)
Antal, Janos. (b.7 October 1888) 800 meters [dnf-h7r1/3].

Baronyi, András. (b.13 September 1892–d.6 June 1944) Standing Long Jump [7/3g4qr]. (See also Swimming.)

Bodor, Ödön. (b.24 October 1882–d.22 January 1927) 400 meters [6h12r1/3]; 800 meters [3h5r1/3]; 4 × 400 meter relay [3h3r1/2].

Déván, István. (b. 4 October 1890–d.20 July 1977) 200 meters [4h6r2/3]; 400 meters [3h5r1/3]; 4 × 400 meter relay [3h3r1/2].

Drubina, István.[22] (b.17 August 1884) 10 Kilometer Walk [ac/h2r1/2].

Forgács-Faczinek, Ferenc.[23] (b.25 September 1891) 800 meters [ach6r1/3]; 1,500 meters [5h3r1/3].

Fóti, Samu. (b.6 November 1884–d.17 June 1916) Discus Throw [25/5g2qr]. (See also Gymnastics.)

Horvag, Andor. Standing High Jump [nm/g3qr].

Jankovich, István.[24] (b.17 October 1889) 100 meters [ach4r2/3]; 4 × 100 meter relay [2h2r2/3].

Kárpáti Kraml, Ödön. (b.2 January 1892) Marathon [31].

Kobulszky, Károly.[25] (b.28 September 1887) Discus Throw [19/7g1qr]; Discus Throw, both hands [18/8g1qr].

Kóczán-Kovács, Miklós "Móric".[26] (b.8 January 1885–d.30 July 1972) Discus Throw [33/6g3qr]; Javelin Throw [3]; Javelin Throw, both hands [12/4g2qr].

Kováts, Nándor. (b.18 May 1881–d.4 January 1972) Broad Jump [26/10g2-3qr].

Ludinszky, Lajos. (b.9 October 1889) High Jump [=11g1qr].

Luntzer, György "Juraj".[27] (b.23 August 1882) Discus Throw [21/3g5qr]; Discus Throw, both hands [nm/g3qr].

Mezei Wiesner, Frigyes. (b.26 September 1887–d.27 March 1938) 200 meters [4h1r2/3]; 400 meters [4h1r2/3]; 4 × 400 meter relay [3h3r1/2].

Mudin, Imre. (b.8 November 1887–d.23 October 1918) Shot Put [6/2g1-2qr].

Rácz, Vilmos.[28] (b.31 March 1889–d.18 July 1976) 100 meters [6h1r2/3]; 4 × 100 meter relay [2h2r2/3].

Radóczy, Károly. (31 August 1885) 800 meters [dnf-h9r1/3].

Ripszám, Henrik, Jr. (b.1 February 1889) 10 Kilometer Walk [8h2r1/2]; Marathon [dnf-].

Savniki-Marschalko, Teofil. (b.19 May 1894–d.23 January 1966) 1,500 meters [ach2r1/3].

Solymár Stollmár, Károly. (b.23 December 1894) 110 meter hurdles [dnf-h2r2/3].

Szalay, Pál.[29] (b.30 June 1892) 4 × 100 meter relay [2h2r2/3]; 100 meters [4h3r2/3]; Broad Jump [25/10g1qr].

Szerelemhegyi, Ervin. (b.23 March 1891–d.13 October 1969) 100 meters [ach16r1/3]; 200 meters [4h14r1/3]; 400 meters [3h4r2/3]; 4 × 400 meter relay [3h3r1/2].

Szobota, Ferenc.[30] (b.30 August 1891) 100 meters [ach4r2/3]; 4 × 100 meter relay [2h2r2/3].

Ujlaki, Resző. (b.13 January 1892–d.5 January 1927) Discus Throw [9/3g4qr]; Discus Throw, both hands [14/3g3qr].

Wardener, Iván, Baron.[31] (b.1 December 1889) High Jump [=9].

Cycling (Total: 5; Men: 5; Women: 0)

Henzsely, János. (b.19 August 1881) Road Race, Individual [75]; Road Race, Team [12].

Mazur, Gyula. (b.9 April 1888) Road Race, Individual [77]; Road Race, Team [12].

Müller, István. (b.3 June 1883) Road Race, Individual [73]; Road Race, Team [12].

Teiszenberger, Ignác. (b.11 December 1880) Road Race, Individual [84]; Road Race, Team [12].

Teppert, Károly. (b.20 July 1891) Road Race, Individual [ac/dnf]; Road Race, Team [12/ns/dnf].

Fencing (Total: 13; Men: 13; Women: 0)

Békessy, Béla. (b.16 November 1875–d.6 July 1916) Foil, Individual (7); Épée, Individual (=7p15r1/4); Sabre, Individual (2).

Berty, László. (b.23 June 1875–d.22 June 1952) Foil, Individual (4); Sabre, Individual (3p4r3/4); Sabre, Team (1).

Dunay, Bertalan. (b.29 October 1882) Foil, Individual (4p3r1/4); Sabre, Individual (4p1r3/4).

Földes, Dezső. (b.30 December 1880–d.27 March 1950) Foil, Individual (acp4r3/4); Sabre, Individual (8); Sabre, Team (1).

Fuchs, Jenő. (b.29 October 1882–d.14 March 1955) Sabre, Individual (1); Sabre, Team (1).

Gerde, Oszkár. (b.8 July 1883–d.8 October 1944) Sabre, Individual (dnc-p2r3/4); Sabre, Team (1).

Mészáros, Ervin. (b.2 April 1877–d.21 May 1940) Sabre, Individual (3); Sabre, Team (1).

Pajzs, Pál. (b.1886) Foil, Individual (=3p1r3/4); Sabre, Individual (3p3r3/4).

Rosty, Pál. (b.1885) Épée, Individual (=4p2r3/4).

Schenker, Zoltán. (b.13 October 1880–d.25 August 1966) Foil, Individual (=3p1r3/4); Sabre, Individual (4); Sabre, Team (1).

Tóth, Péter. (b.12 July 1882–d.28 February 1967) Foil, Individual (3p3r3/4); Sabre, Individual (6); Sabre, Team (1).

Werkner, Lajos. (b.23 October 1883–d.12 November 1943) Sabre, Individual (7); Sabre, Team (1).

Zulavszky, Béla. (b.23 October 1869–d.24 October 1914) Foil, Individual (=4p3r3/4); Sabre, Individual (3p1r3/4).

Football (Association Football [Soccer]) (Total: 14; Men: 14; Women: 0)
Biró, Gyula. (b.10 May 1890) [5].
Blum, Zoltán. (b.3 January 1892) [5].
Bodnár, Sándor. (b.16 June 1890) [5].
Borbás, Gáspár. (b.5 December 1884) [5].
Domonkos, László. (b.10 October 1887) [5].
Fekete, Miklóz. (b.10 February 1892) [5].
Károly, Jenő. [5].
Pataky, Mihály. (b.7 December 1893) [5].
Payer, Imre. (b.1 June 1888) [5].
Rumbold, Gyula. (b.6 February 1887) [5].
Schlosser, Imre. (b.11 October 1889) [5].
Sebestyén, Béla. (b.23 January 1886) [5].
Szury, Kálmán. (b.4 February 1889) [5].
Vágó, Antal. (b.9 August 1891) [5].

Gymnastics (Total: 17; Men: 17; Women: 0)
Bittenbinder, József. (b.31 December 1890–d.25 November 1963) Combined All-Around, European System, Team [2].
Erdődy, Imre. (b.26 March 1889–d.11 January 1973) Combined All-Around, European System, Team [2].
Fóti, Samu. (b.6 November 1884–d.17 June 1916) Combined All-Around, European System, Team [2]. (See also Athletics [Track & Field].)
Gellért, Imre. (b.24 July 1888–d.1981) Combined All-Around, Individual [17]; Combined All-Around, European System, Team [2].
Haberfeld, Győző. (b.13 June 1889–d.1945) Combined All-Around, European System, Team [2].
Hellmich, Ottó. (b.6 April 1874–d.4 July 1937) Combined All-Around, European System, Team [2].
Herczeg, István. (b.7 December 1887–d.3 July 1949) Combined All-Around, European System, Team [2].
Keresztessy, József. (b.19 September 1885–d.29 December 1962) Combined All-Around, European System, Team [2].
Kmetykó, Lajos. (b.22 March 1884–d.4 January 1952) Combined All-Around, European System, Team [2].
Krizmanich, János. (b.6 December 1889–d.26 July 1944) Combined All-Around, Individual [19]; Combined All-Around, European System, Team [2].
Pászti, Elemér. (b.20 December 1889–d.27 October 1965) Combined All-Around, Individual [13]; Combined All-Around, European System, Team [2].

Pédery, Árpád. (b.1 February 1891–d.21 October 1914) Combined All-Around, European System, Team [2].

Rittich, Jenő. (b.13 January 1889) Combined All-Around, European System, Team [2].

Szalai, József. (b.18 December 1892) Combined All-Around, Individual [=15].

Szűts, Ferenc. (b.16 December 1891–d.28 November 1966) Combined All-Around, European System, Team [2].

Téry, Ödön. (b.8 July 1890–d.7 June 1981) Combined All-Around, European System, Team [2].

Tuli, Géza. (b.4 January 1888–d.30 January 1966) Combined All-Around, European System, Team [2].

Rowing & Sculling (Total: 11; Men: 11; Women: 0)

Baján, Artúr. (b.4 April 1888) Coxed Eights [2h3r1/4].

Gráf, Lájos. (b.28 May 1893) Coxed Eights [2h3r1/4].

Jenei, István. (b.27 February 1887) Coxed Eights [2h3r1/4].

Levitzky, Károly. (b.1 May 1885–d.23 August 1978) Single Sculls [2h4r2/4].

Manno, Miltiades. (b.3 March 1880–d.February 1935) Coxed Eights [2h3r1/4].

Mészáros, József. (b.27 September 1884) Single Sculls [2h1r2/4].

Szebeny, Antal. (b.6 April 1886) Coxed Eights [2h3r1/4].

Szebeny, Georg. (b.18 November 1887) Coxed Eights [2h3r1/4].

Szebeny, Miklós. (b.18 November 1887) Coxed Eights [2h3r1/4].

Szebeny, István. (b.22 November 1890) Coxed Eights [2h3r1/4].

Vasko, Kálmán. (b.23 November 1874) Coxed Eights [2h3r1/4].

Shooting (Total: 10; Men: 10; Women: 0)

Bömches von Boor, Emil, Ritter. (b.9 July 1879) Free Rifle, 300 meters, 3-Positions [50]; Military Rifle, 300 meters, 3-Positions [66]; Military Rifle, 600 meters, any position [80]; Military Rifle, 200, 400, 500, and 600 meters, Teams [10].

Hauler, László. (b.26 June 1884) Free Rifle, 300 meters, 3-Positions [74]; Military Rifle, 300 meters, 3-Positions [27]; Military Rifle, 600 meters, any position [83]; Military Rifle, 200, 400, 500, and 600 meters, Teams [10]; Small-Bore Rifle, prone position, 50 meters [29].

Jelenffy-Tóth von Csejthe, Zoltán. (b.26 October 1876) Free Rifle, 300 meters, 3-Positions [69]; Military Rifle, 300 meters, 3-Positions [87]; Military Rifle, 600 meters, any position [78]; Free Pistol, 50 meters [52].

Mészöly von Sárbogárd, Géza. (b.8 September 1876) Free Rifle, 300 meters, 3-Positions [ac/dnf]; Military Rifle, 300 meters, 3-Positions [29]; Military Rifle, 600 meters, any position [79]; Military Rifle, 200, 400, 500, and 600 meters, Teams [10].

Prihoda, István. (b.15 November 1891) Free Rifle, 300 meters, 3-Positions [ac/dnf]; Military Rifle, 300 meters, 3-Positions [85]; Military Rifle, 200, 400, 500, and 600 meters, Teams [10].

Prokopp, Sándor. (b.7 May 1887–d.4 November 1964) Military Rifle, 300 meters, 3-Positions [1].

Török von Mura, Sándor, Count. (b.14 February 1881) Small-Bore Rifle, prone position, 50 meters [31]; Small-Bore Rifle, 25 meters, Disappearing Target [33]; Free Pistol, 50 meters [27]; Dueling Pistol, 30 meters [9].

Velez, Rezső. (b.31 August 1887) Free Rifle, 300 meters, 3-Positions [72]; Military Rifle, 300 meters, 3-Positions [7]; Military Rifle, 600 meters, any position [73] Military Rifle, 200, 400, 500, and 600 meters, Teams [10].

von Darányi, Béla. (b.22 April 1894) Military Rifle, 300 meters, 3-Positions [91].

von Farkas, Aladár. (b.20 October 1874) Free Rifle, 300 meters, 3-Positions [75]; Military Rifle, 300 meters, 3-Positions [24]; Military Rifle, 600 meters, any position [76]; Military Rifle, 200, 400, 500, and 600 meters, Teams [10].

Swimming (Total: 8; Men: 8; Women: 0)

Baronyi, András. (b.13 September 1892–d.6 June 1944) 100 meter backstroke [4]. (See also Athletics [Track & Field].)

Beleznai, László. (b.16 October 1892) 100 meter freestyle [dns-r2/4]; 4 × 200 meter freestyle relay [dns-final]. (See also Water Polo.)

Demján, Oszkár. (b.28 December 1891) 200 meter breaststroke [4h2r2/3]; 400 meter breast-stroke [dqh1r1/3].

Kenyery, Alajos Ferenc. (b.21 September 1892) 100 meter freestyle [ac/puk-3h3r1/4]; 400 meter freestyle [dns-r2/3]; 4 × 200 meter freestyle relay [dns-final].

Szentgróti, László. (b.11 October 1891) 100 meter freestyle [3h8r1/4]; 100 meter backstroke [4h1r2/3].

von Las-Torres, Béla. (b.20 April 1890–d.13 October 1915) 400 meter freestyle [5]; 1,500 meter freestyle [dnf-final]; 4 × 200 meter freestyle relay [dns-final].

Wenk, János. (b.17 January 1892) 100 meter backstroke [dqh2r1/3]. (See also Water Polo.)

Zachár, Imre. (b.11 May 1890–d.7 April 1954) 4 × 200 meter freestyle relay [dns-final]. (See also Water Polo.)

Tennis (Total: 6; Men: 6; Women: 0)

Segner, Paul. (b.2 January 1876) Men's Doubles (Lawn) [=15].

Tóth, Ede. (b.11 March 1884) Men's Doubles (Lawn) [=15].

von Baráth, Leó. (b.9 June 1891) Men's Singles (Lawn) [=31]; Men's Doubles (Lawn) [=15].

von Kehrling, Béla. (b.25 January 1891) Men's Singles (Lawn) [=9]; Men's Doubles (Lawn) [=9].

von Kelemen, Aurél. (b.20 April 1888) Men's Singles (Lawn) [=17]; Men's Doubles (Lawn) [=15].

von Zsigmondy, Jenő. (b.4 July 1888) Men's Singles (Lawn) [=17]; Men's Doubles (Lawn) [=9].

Water Polo (Total: 7; Men: 7; Women: 0)

Ádám, Sándor. (b.1 February 1889) [=5].

Beleznai, László. (b.16 October 1892) [=5]. (See also Swimming.)

Fazekas, Tibor. (b.1892) [=5].

Rémi, Károly. (b.1 May 1891) [=5].

Tóth, Jenő Hégner. (b.17 April 1892) [=5].

Wenk, János. (b.17 January 1892) [=5]. (See also Swimming.)

Zachár, Imre. (b.11 May 1890–d.7 April 1954) [=5]. (See also Swimming.)

Wrestling (Total: 10; Men: 10; Women: 0)

Márkus, Ernő. (b.15 April 1890) 67½ kg. Class (Greco-Roman) [AC].

Miskey, Árpád. (b.27 September 1886) 75 kg. Class (Greco-Roman) [AC].

Orosz, Desző. (b.11 April 1887) 67½ kg. Class (Greco-Roman) [AC].

Pongrácz, József. (b.10 September 1881) 60 kg. Class (Greco-Roman) [AC].

Radvány, Ödön. (b.27 December 1888) 67½ kg. Class (Greco-Roman) [AC].

Sándor-Stemmer, József. (b.6 August 1892) 67½ kg. Class (Greco-Roman) [AC].

Somogyi-Steiner, Resző. (b.27 July 1887) 75 kg. Class (Greco-Roman) [AC].

Szántó, Árpád. (b.10 October 1889) 67½ kg. Class (Greco-Roman) [AC].

Szoszky, András. (b.9 January 1889) 60 kg. Class (Greco-Roman) [AC].
Varga, Béla. (b.2 June 1888–d.4 April 1969) 82½ kg. Class (Greco-Roman) [3].

Iceland[32] (Total: 2; Men: 2; Women: 0) (Demonstration Sports: Total: 6; Men: 6; Women: 0)

Athletics (Track & Field) (Total: 1; Men: 1; Women: 0)
Halldórsson, Jón. (b.2 November 1889–d.7 July 1984) 100 meters [ach8r1/3]. (See also Demonstration Sport–Glíma Wrestling.)

Wrestling (Total: 1; Men: 0; Women: 0)
Pétursson, Sigurjón. (b.9 March 1888–d.3 May 1955) 82½ kg. Class (Greco-Roman) [AC].

Demonstration Sport–Glíma Wrestling (Total: 6; Men: 0; Women: 0)
Benediktsson, Hallgrímur. (b.1885–d.1954) Glíma [1].
Gudmundsson, Guðmundur Kristinu. (b.1892–d.1955) Glíma [4].
Halldórsson, Jón. (b.2 November 1889–d.7 July 1984) Glíma [6].
Kristjánsson, Axel. (b.1892–d.1942) Glíma [3].
Pétursson, Sigurjón. (b.9 March 1888–d.3 May 1955) Glíma [2].
Tómasson Kjaran, Magnús. (b.1890–d.1962) Glíma [5].

Italy[33] (Total: 62; Men: 62; Women: 0)

Athletics (Track & Field) (Total: 12; Men: 12; Women: 0)
Altimani, Fernando. (b.8 December 1892–d.2 January 1963) 10 Kilometer Walk [3].
Calvi, Guido. (b.1 May 1893–d.6 September 1958) 800 meters [ach3r1/3]; 1,500 meters [dnf-h6r1/3].
Colbacchini, Daciano. (b.31 October 1893) 110 meter hurdles [2h2r2/3].
Giongo, Franco. (b.7 July 1891–d.28 December 1981) 100 meters [ach2r2/3]; 200 meters [4h5r2/3]; 400 meters [3h10r1/3].
Legat, Manlio. (b.30 August 1889–d.18 September 1915) Pole Vault [=13g2qr]; Broad Jump [29/8g4qr]; Decathlon [ac/dnf].
Lenzi, Aurelio. (b.19 June 1891–d.23 December 1967) Shot Put [12/4g4qr]; Discus Throw [18/2g5qr].
Lunghi, Emilio. (b.16 March 1887–d.26 September 1925) 400 meters [2h4r2/3]; 800 meters [5h2r2/3].
Orlando, Alfonso. (b.17 May 1892–d.29 August 1969) 5,000 meters [dnf-h5r1/2]; 10,000 meters [5].
Pagani, Alfredo. (b.6 September 1887) 110 meter hurdles [3h6r1/3]; High Jump [8g3qr]; Broad Jump [27/7g4qr]; Decathlon [ac/dnf]; Pentathlon [24].
Ruggero, Francesco. (b.22 November 1892) Marathon [dnf-].
Speroni, Carlo. (b.13 July 1895–d.12 October 1969) Marathon [dnf-].
Tonini, Angelo. (b.26 November 1888) High Jump [acg1qr]; Broad Jump [19/7g1qr].

Diving (Total: 1; Men: 1; Women: 0)
Bonfanti, Carlo. (b.7 July 1875) Springboard Diving [4h2r1/2]; Plain High Diving [6h2r1/2].

Fencing (Total: 9; Men: 9; Women: 0)

Alaimo, Edoardo. (b.1893) Foil, Individual (5); Sabre, Individual (dnc-p3r2/4); Sabre, Team (=5).

Belloni, Gino. (b.1884) Sabre, Team (=5).

Benfratello, Giovanni. (b.1888) Sabre, Individual (4p1r2/4); Sabre, Team (=5).

Cavallini, Fernando. (b.1893) Foil, Individual (acp4r3/4); Sabre, Team (=5).

Di Nola, Ugo. Sabre, Team (=5).

Nadi, Nedo. (b.9 June 1894–d.29 January 1940) Foil, Individual (1); Sabre, Individual (5); Sabre, Team (=5).

Pietrasanta, Francesco. Foil, Individual (5p2r2/4); Sabre, Individual (4p8r2/4); Sabre, Team (=5).

Pontenani, Aristide, Baron. Sabre, Individual (=4p4r2/4).

Speciale, Pietro. (b.29 September 1876–d.9 November 1945) Foil, Individual (2); Sabre, Team (=5).

Football (Association Football [Soccer]) (Total: 14; Men: 14; Women: 0)

Barbesino, Luigi. (b.1 May 1894–d.1942) [=7].

Berardo, Felice. (b.6 July 1888–d.1956) [=7].

Binaschi, Angelo. (b.15 January 1889–d.1973) [=7].

Bontadini, Franco. (b.3 January 1893–d.1943) [=7].

Campelli, Piero. (b.20 December 1893–d.1946) [=7].

De Marchi, Carlo. (b.25 March 1890–d.1972) [=7].

De Vecchi, Renzo. (b.3 February 1894–d.1967) [=7].

Leone, Pietro. (b.31 January 1888–d.1958) [=7].

Mariani, Edoardo "Dino." (b.5 March 1893–d.1956) [=7].

Milano, Giuseppe. (b.26 September 1887–d.1971) [=7].

Morelli di Popolo, Vittorio. (b.11 May 1888–d.1963) [=7].

Sardi, Enrico. (b.1 April 1891–d.1969) [=7].

Valle, Modesto. (b.16 March 1893) [=7].

Zuffi, Enea. (b.27 February 1891–d.1969) [=7].

Gymnastics (Total: 18; Men: 18; Women: 0)

Bianchi, Pietro. (b.5 March 1883–d.1 July 1965) Combined All-Around, Individual [6]; Combined All-Around, European System, Team [1].

Boni, Guido. (b.7 February 1892–d.15 December 1956) Combined All-Around, Individual [=4]; Combined All-Around, European System, Team [1].

Braglia, Alberto. (b.23 April 1883–d.5 February 1954) Combined All-Around, Individual [1]; Combined All-Around, European System, Team [1].

Domenichelli, Giuseppe. (b.31 July 1887–d.13 March 1955) Combined All-Around, European System, Team [1].

Fregosi, Carlo. (b.15 October 1890–d.13 November 1968) Combined All-Around, European System, Team [1].

Gollini, Alfredo. (b.24 December 1881–d.22 April 1957) Combined All-Around, European System, Team [1].

Loy, Francesco. (b.21 February 1891–d.9 March 1977) Combined All-Around, European System, Team [1].

Maiocco, Luigi. (b.11 October 1892–d.11 December 1965) Combined All-Around, European System, Team [1].

Mangiante, Giovanni. (b.28 August 1893–d.6 December 1957) Combined All-Around, European System, Team [1].

Mangiante, Lorenzo. (b.14 March 1891–d.16 June 1936) Combined All-Around, European System, Team [1].

Mazzarocchi, Serafino. (b.2 February 1890–d.21 April 1961) Combined All-Around, European System, Team [1].

Romano, Guido. (b.31 January 1887–d.18 June 1916) Combined All-Around, Individual [9]; Combined All-Around, European System, Team [1].

Salvi, Paolo. (b.22 November 1891–d.12 January 1945) Combined All-Around, European System, Team [1].

Savorini, Luciano. (b.3 October 1885–d.30 October 1964) Combined All-Around, European System, Team [1].

Tunesi, Adolfo. (b.27 August 1887–d.29 November 1964) Combined All-Around, Individual [3]; Combined All-Around, European System, Team [1].

Zampori, Giorgio. (b.4 January 1887–d.7 December 1965) Combined All-Around, Individual [=4]; Combined All-Around, European System, Team [1].

Zanolini, Umberto. (b.31 March 1887–d.12 February 1973) Combined All-Around, European System, Team [1].

Zorzi, Angelo. (b.4 May 1890–d.28 December 1974) Combined All-Around, European System, Team [1].

Swimming (Total: 2; Men: 2; Women: 0)

Baiardo, Davide. (b.13 February 1888–d.28 November 1977) 100 meter freestyle [ac/puk-3h3r1/4]; 400 meter freestyle [5h1r1/3].

Massa, Mario. (b.29 May 1892–d.16 February 1956) 100 meter freestyle [dnf-h3r3/4]; 400 meter freestyle [dnf-h1r1/3]; 1,500 meter freestyle [dnf-h4r1/3].

Wrestling (Total: 6; Men: 6; Women: 0)

Arpe, Oreste. (b.18 June 1889) 82½ kg. Class (Greco-Roman) [AC].

Carcereri, Zavirre. 75 kg. Class (Greco-Roman) [AC].

Ciai, Mariano. 60 kg. Class (Greco-Roman) [AC].

Covre, Alessandro. 67½ kg. Class (Greco-Roman) [AC].

Gardini, Renato. (b.10 March 1889) 82½ kg. Class (Greco-Roman) [AC].

Gargano, Amedeo Andrea. (b.1887) 75 kg. Class (Greco-Roman) [AC].

Japan[34] (Total: 2; Men: 2; Women: 0)

Athletics (Track & Field) (Total: 2; Men: 2; Women: 0)

Kanaguri, Shizo. (b.20 August 1891–d.13 November 1983) Marathon [dnf-].

Mishima, Yahiko. (b.23 February 1886–d.1 February 1954) 100 meters [ach16r1/3]; 200 meters [ach13r1/3]; 400 meters [dns-r2/3].

Luxembourg (Total: 21; Men: 21; Women: 0)

Athletics (Track & Field) (Total: 2; Men: 2; Women: 0)

Fournelle, Paul. Broad Jump [nm/qr].

Pelletier, Marcel. (b.26 February 1886) Discus Throw [7g4qr]; Shot Put [5g2qr].

Gymnastics (Total: 19; Men: 19; Women: 0)

Adam, Nicolas Dominique. (b.12 February 1881) Combined All-Around, Free System, Team [5]; Combined All-Around, European System, Team [4].

Behm, Charles. (b.17 January 1883) Combined All-Around, Free System, Team [5]; Combined All-Around, European System, Team [4].

Bordang, André. (b.8 August 1875) Combined All-Around, Free System, Team [5]; Combined All-Around, European System, Team [4].

Frantzen, Jean-Pierre. (b.9 May 1890) Combined All-Around, Free System, Team [5].

Hemmerling, Michal. (b.9 November 1870) Combined All-Around, Free System, Team [5]; Combined All-Around, European System, Team [4].

Hentges, François. (b.11 June 1885) Combined All-Around, Individual [23]; Combined All-Around, Free System, Team [5]; Combined All-Around, European System, Team [4].

Hentges, Pierre. (b.4 September 1890) Combined All-Around, Individual [18]; Combined All-Around, Free System, Team [5]; Combined All-Around, European System, Team [4].

Horn, Jean-Baptiste. (b.7 April 1886) Combined All-Around, Free System, Team [5]; Combined All-Around, European System, Team [4].

Kanive, Nicolas. (b.23 November 1887) Combined All-Around, Individual [20]; Combined All-Around, Free System, Team [5]; Combined All-Around, European System, Team [4].

Knepper, Émile. (b.21 August 1892) Combined All-Around, Free System, Team [5].

Kummer, Nicolas. (b.4 August 1882) Combined All-Around, Free System, Team [5]; Combined All-Around, European System, Team [4].

Langsam, Marcel. (b.21 November 1891) Combined All-Around, Free System, Team [5]; Combined All-Around, European System, Team [4].

Lanners, Emile. (b.13 April 1888) Combined All-Around, Individual [24]; Combined All-Around, Free System, Team [5]; Combined All-Around, European System, Team [4].

Palgen, Maurice. (b.13 May 1893) Combined All-Around, Free System, Team [5].

Thommes, Jean-Pierre. (b.28 July 1890) Combined All-Around, Individual [22]; Combined All-Around, Free System, Team [5]; Combined All-Around, European System, Team [4].

Wagner, François. (b.16 November 1890) Combined All-Around, Free System, Team [5]; Combined All-Around, European System, Team [4].

Wehrer, Antoine. (b.2 February 1890) Combined All-Around, Individual [=15]; Combined All-Around, Free System, Team [5]; Combined All-Around, European System, Team [4].

Wirtz, Ferdinand. (b.26 November 1885) Combined All-Around, Free System, Team [5]; Combined All-Around, European System, Team [4].

Zuang, Joseph. (b.15 March 1891) Combined All-Around, Free System, Team [5]; Combined All-Around, European System, Team [4].

The Netherlands[35, 36] (Total: 33; Men: 33; Women: 0)

Athletics (Track & Field) (Total: 1; Men: 1; Women: 0)

Grijseels, Johannes Antonius Constantius Marie "Jan." (b.6 October 1890–d.10 May 1961) 100 meters [ach7r1/3]; 200 meters [6h4r2/3].

Fencing (Total: 12; Men: 12; Women: 0)

Beaufort, Jan Daniël Hendrik de, Jonkheer. (b.2 December 1880–d.2 April 1946) Épée, Individual (=4p4r2/4).

Doorman, Jetze. (b.2 July 1881–d.28 February 1931) Épée, Team (3); Sabre, Team (3). (See also Modern Pentathlon.)

Geuns, Jacob Eliza Catrinus van. (b.15 November 1872–d.12 November 1952) Épée, Individual (5p9r1/4).

Hubert van Blijenburgh, Willem Peter. (b.11 July 1881–d.14 October 1936) Épée, Individual (4p15r1/4); Épée, Team (3); Sabre, Team (3).

Iongh, Hendrik de. (b.4 August 1877–d.9 August 1962) Épée, Individual (6p1r2/4); Sabre, Individual (dnc-p6r2/4); Sabre, Team (3).

Jong, Adrianus Egbertus Willem de. (b.21 June 1882–d.23 December 1966) Foil, Individual (4p14r1/4); Épée, Individual (3p2r3/4); Épée, Team (3); Sabre, Team (3).

Kolling, Johannes Cornelis. (b.25 March 1887–d.1 February 1969) Sabre, Individual (4p6r1/4).

Molijn, Willem Hendrik. (b.20 July 1874–d.9 June 1957) Épée, Individual (6p16r1/4).

Nardus, Leonardus (né Leonardus Salomon). (b.5 May 1868–d.*ddi*) Épée, Team (3).

Perk, Albertus Cornelis. (b.16 September 1887–d.14 May 1919) Épée, Individual (=5p7r1/4).

Rossem, George van. (b.30 May 1882–d.14 January 1955) Épée, Individual (=4p4r1/4); Épée, Team (3); Sabre, Team (3).

Scalongne, Dirk. (b.12 December 1879–d.1 April 1973) Sabre, Team (3).

Football (Association Football [Soccer]) (Total: 15; Men: 15; Women: 0)
Bouman, Pieter. (b.14 October 1892–d.20 July 1980) [3].
Boutmij, Johannes Wouter "Jaap." (b.29 April 1884–d.26 July 1972) [3].
Bouvy, Nicolaas Jan Jerôme. (b.11 July 1892–d.14 June 1957) [3].
Breda Kolff, Jan Gualtherus van. (b.8 January 1894–d.February 1976) [3].
Cate, Caesar Herman ten. (b.20 August 1890–d.9 June 1972) [3].
Feith, Constant Willem, Jonkheer. (b.3 August 1884–d.15 September 1958) [3].
Fortgens, Gerardus. (b.10 July 1887–d.4 May 1957) [3].
Göbel, Marius Just. (b.21 November 1891–d.5 March 1984) [3].
Groot, Henri Franciscus de "Huug." (b.7 May 1890–d.18 April 1957) [3].
Korver, Johannes Marius de "Bok." (b.27 January 1883–d.22 October 1957) [3].
Lotsij, Dirk Nicolaas. (b.3 July 1882–d.27 March 1965) [3].
Sluis, Jan van der. (b.29 April 1889–d.19 October 1952) [3].
Vos, Jan. (b.17 April 1888–d.25 August 1939) [3].
Wijnveldt, David. (b.15 December 1891–d.28 March 1962) [3].
Wolf, Nicolaas de. (b.27 October 1887–d.18 July 1967) [3].

Modern Pentathlon (Total: 1; Men: 1; Women: 0)
Doorman, Jetze. (b.2 July 1881–d.28 February 1931) Individual [ac/dnf]. (See also Fencing.)

Shooting (Total: 1; Men: 1; Women: 0)
Jurgens, Emile Wilhelmus Johannes. (b.30 September 1878–d.8 July 1929) Clay Trap Shooting, Individual [=9].

Tennis (Total: 1; Men: 1; Women: 0)
Blom, Otte Pierre Nicolas. (b.9 March 1887–d.22 July 1972) Men's Singles (Lawn) [=31].

Wrestling (Total: 3; Men: 3; Women: 0)
Bonneveld, Barend. (b.27 November 1887–d.9 February 1978) Unlimited Class (Greco-Roman) [AC].
Eillebrecht, Johannes Petrus. (b.3 November 1888–d.7 June 1954) 67½ kg. Class (Greco-Roman) [AC].
Sint, Jan. (b.30 March 1887–d.8 February 1941) 75 kg. Class (Greco-Roman) [AC].

Norway[37] (Total: 190; Men: 188; Women: 2)

Athletics (Track & Field) (Total: 21; Men: 21; Women: 0)

Aarnes, Ole Augunsen. (b.27 May 1888–d.3 February 1992) High Jump [=4g3qr].

Andersen, Johannes E. H. (b.29 September 1888–d.2 December 1967) Cross-Country, Individual [22]; Cross-Country, Team [4].

Bie, Ferdinand Reinhardt. (b.16 February 1888–d.9 November 1961) 110 meter hurdles [3h1r2/3]; Broad Jump [11/4g2-3/qr]; Decathlon [ac/dnf]; Pentathlon [2].

Brodtkorb, Birger. (b.3 July 1891–d.24 July 1935) Standing High Jump [=3g1qr]; Standing Long Jump [12/3g1qr].

Dahl, Nils. (b.12 November 1882–d.17 July 1966) Cross-Country, Individual [dnf-]; Cross-Country, Team [4/ns].

Finnerud, Parelius N. (b.20 October 1888–d.9 December 1969) Cross-Country, Individual [20]; Cross-Country, Team [4].

Fixdal, Nils. (b.20 November 1889–d.11 October 1971) Broad Jump [13/6g2-3/qr]; Hop, step, and jump [8/4g2qr].

Fonbæk, Oscar. (b.6 July 1887–d.6 September 1965) Marathon [dnf-].

Halse, Arne. (b.20 October 1887–d.3 July 1975) Javelin Throw [7/3g3qr]; Javelin Throw, both hands [5/2g3qr].

Hovdenak, Olaf Sigvart. (b.6 October 1891–d.12 September 1929) Cross-Country, Individual [19]; Cross-Country, Team [4].

Johansen (Sundsten), Daniel Victor. (b.2 April 1885–d.7 December 1967) Javelin Throw [12/2g4qr]; Javelin Throw, both hands [7/3g3qr].

Larsen, Edvard. (b.27 October 1881–d.11 September 1914) Hop, step, and jump [6/3g2qr].

Larsen, Oscar. (b.11 September 1887–d.16 April 1975) 800 meters [3h3r1/3]; 1,500 meters [5h4r1/3].

Meling (Olsen), Gerhard Tomin. (b.27 May 1882–d.1 July 1955) High Jump [=4g1qr].

Monsen, Otto. (b.19 August 1887–d.14 December 1979) High Jump [=4g1qr].

Osen, Otto. (b.4 July 1882–d.3 November 1950) Marathon [34].

Pedersen, Alexander. (b.4 February 1891–d.1955) 100 meters [4h12r1/3]; 400 meters [dqh14r1/3].

Pedersen, Ole Jacob. (b.29 April 1889–d.27 March 1961) 400 meters [5h3r2/3]; 800 meters [3h2r1/3]; 1,500 meters [ach3r1/3].

Simonsen, Axel G. (b.11 March 1887–d.3 April 1938) Marathon [23].

Sotaaen (Naess), Herman. (b.27 August 1888–d.27 August 1967) 100 meters [ach10r1/3]; 200 meters [3h15r1/3].

Vinne, Erling. (b.7 August 1892–d.7 June 1963) Hop, step, and jump [4/1g3qr].

Cycling (Total: 6; Men: 6; Women: 0)

Andreassen, Birger Marinus. (b.31 December 1891–d.25 March 1961) Road Race, Individual [14]; Road Race, Team [tm-dnf/(14)].

Guldbrandsen, Carl Johan. (b.22 May 1892–d.28 August 1973) Road Race, Individual [ac/dnf]; Road Race, Team [tm-dnf/dnf].

Hansen, Anton Ludvig. (b.26 November 1886) Road Race, Individual [65]; Road Race, Team [tm-dnf/(64)].

Henrichsen, Paul Gotthard. (b.2 March 1883–d.1962) Road Race, Individual [47]; Road Race, Team [tm-dnf/(47)].

Olsen, Carl Thorstein. (b.16 February 1893–d.13 February 1968) Road Race, Individual [ac/dnf]; Road Race, Team [tm-dnf/dnf].

Sæterhaug, Martin. (b.13 August 1882–d.23 August 1961) Road Race, Individual [dnf-]; Road Race, Team [tm-dnf/dnf].

Diving (Total: 3; Men: 3; Women: 0)

Andersen, Sigvard. (b.18 August 1893) Plain and Fancy High Diving [5h2r1/2]; Plain High Diving [7h1r1/2].

Engelsen, Alfred. (b.16 January 1893–d.13 September 1966) Plain High Diving [7h2r1/2]. (See also Gymnastics.)

Tvedt, Nils. (b.21 May 1883–d.25 May 1965) Plain High Diving [5h1r1/2].

Equestrian Events (Total: 3; Men: 3; Women: 0)

Falkenberg, Jens Christian Baltazar, Captain. (b.6 May 1875–d.26 March 1963) Dressage, Individual [15] (Hjørdis); Jumping, Individual [28] (Florida).

Jensen, Jørgen Martinius. (b.1 January 1878–d.31 March 1970) Jumping, Individual [26] (Jossy).

Kildal, Karl. (b.1 February 1881–d.14 November 1932) Jumping, Individual [24] (Garcia).

Fencing (Total: 7; Men: 7; Women: 0)

Aas, Lars Thorlaksøn. (b.26 February 1879–d.24 February 1964) Foil, Individual (=4p6r1/4); Épée, Individual (6p3r2/4); Épée, Team (=9).

Bergsland, Hans. (b.15 November 1878–d.9 June 1956) Épée, Individual (=4p3r1/4); Épée, Team (=9).

Eriksen, Bjarne Gottfred. (b.31 July 1886–d.13 November 1976) Foil, Individual (=4p8r2/4); Épée, Individual (4p6r1/4).

Finne, Severin. (b.12 March 1883–d.24 March 1953) Épée, Individual (6p4r2/4); Épée, Team (=9).

Mathiesen, Sigurd Wilhelm. (b.30 August 1873–d.4 January 1951) Épée, Individual (=4p5r2/4).

Platou, Harald Frederik Stoud. (b.29 October 1877–d.23 September 1946) Épée, Individual (=4p8r1/4).

von Tangen, Christopher Georges Johan. (b.29 June 1877–d.24 February 1964) Foil, Individual (=6p13r1/4); Épée, Individual (4p5r1/4); Épée, Team (=9).

Football (Association Football [Soccer]) (Total: 12; Men: 12; Women: 0)

Andersen, Gunnar. (b.18 March 1890–d.25 April 1968) [=9].

Baastad, Einar Friis. (b.8 May 1890–d.1968) [=9].

Endrerud, Hans O. Christian. (b.13 October 1885–d.24 October 1957) [=9].

Herlofsen, Charles Oluf. (b.15 June 1891–d.9 November 1968) [=9].

Jensen, Sverre. (b.22 January 1893–d.26 October 1963) [=9].

Johansen (Seiertun), Harald Andreas. (b.9 October 1887–d.11 July 1965) [=9].

Krefting, Kristian August. (b.9 February 1891–d.13 April 1964) [=9].

Maartmann, Erling. (b.3 November 1887–d.9 February 1944) [=9].

Maartmann, Rolf. (b.3 November 1887–d.8 July 1941) [=9].

Pedersen, Carl Ingolf. (b.7 December 1890–d.2 January 1964) [=9].

Reinholt, Henry. (b.16 January 1890–d.1 February 1980) [=9].

Skou, Per. (b.20 May 1891–d.24 February 1962) [=9].

Gymnastics (Total: 46; Men: 46; Women: 0)

Abrahamsen, Isak. (b.28 April 1891–d.29 April 1972) Combined All-Around, Free System, Team [1].

Amundsen, Arthur M. (b.22 March 1886–d.1936) Combined All-Around, Swedish System [3].

Andersen, Jørgen Marius. (b.20 February 1886–d.30 May 1973) Combined All-Around, Swedish System [3].

Beyer, Hans Anthon. (b.23 August 1889–d.15 May 1965) Combined All-Around, Free System, Team [1].

Bjørnson, Hartman Alfred. (b.2 February 1889–d.25 September 1974) Combined All-Around, Free System, Team [1].

Bøyesen, Trygve Carlsen. (b.15 February 1886–d.27 July 1963) Combined All-Around, Swedish System [3].

Brustad, Georg. (b.23 November 1892–d.17 March 1932) Combined All-Around, Swedish System [3].

Christensen, Conrad. (b.25 January 1882–d.1951) Combined All-Around, Swedish System [3].

Engelsen, Alfred. (b.16 January 1893–d.13 September 1966) Combined All-Around, Free System, Team [1]. (See also Diving.)

Engelstad, Oscar. (b.2 November 1882–d.17 July 1972) Combined All-Around, Swedish System [3].

Eriksen, Marius. (b.9 December 1886–d.14 September 1950) Combined All-Around, Swedish System [3].

Hansen, Aksel Henry. (b.25 June 1887–d.4 January 1980) Combined All-Around, Swedish System [3].

Hol, Peter. (b.19 March 1883–d.22 June 1981) Combined All-Around, Swedish System [3].

Ingebretsen, Eugen. (b.30 December 1884–d.1949) Combined All-Around, Swedish System [3].

Ingebretsen, Olaf. (b.24 May 1892–d.20 July 1971) Combined All-Around, Swedish System [3].

Jacobsen, Olof. (b.24 March 1888) Combined All-Around, Swedish System [3].

Jensen, Erling. (b.3 July 1891 d.20 September 1973) Combined All-Around, Swedish System [3].

Jensen, Thor. (b.4 June 1889–d.19 June 1950) Combined All-Around, Swedish System [3].

Johnsen, Bjarne. (b.27 April 1892–d.4 September 1984) Combined All-Around, Free System, Team [1].

Jørgensen, Sigurd. (b.15 February 1887–d.14 December 1929) Combined All-Around, Free System, Team [1].

Knudsen, Knud Leonard. (b.6 September 1879–d.28 April 1954) Combined All-Around, Free System, Team [1].

Lie, Alf. (b.10 April 1887–d.22 March 1969) Combined All-Around, Free System, Team [1].

Lie, Rolf. (b.20 May 1889–d.18 June 1959) Combined All-Around, Free System, Team [1].

Lund, Tor. (b.20 January 1888–d.1 September 1972) Combined All-Around, Free System, Team [1].

Martinsen, Petter. (b.14 May 1887–d.27 December 1972) Combined All-Around, Free System, Team [1].

Mathiesen, Per Anton. (b.11 March 1885–d.2 June 1971) Combined All-Around, Free System, Team [1].

Olsen, Frithjof. (b.30 November 1882–d.22 February 1922) Combined All-Around, Swedish System [3].

Olstad, Oscar. (b.22 June 1887–d.2 April 1957) Combined All-Around, Swedish System [3].

Opdahl, Jacob. (b.15 January 1894–d.21 March 1938) Combined All-Around, Free System, Team [1].

Opdahl, Nils. (b.16 November 1882–d.28 December 1951) Combined All-Around, Free System, Team [1].

Paulsen, Edvin. (b.3 December 1889–d.13 March 1963) Combined All-Around, Swedish System [3].

Pedersen, Carl Alfred. (b.5 May 1882–d.25 June 1960) Combined All-Around, Swedish System [3].

Pedersen, Paul Andreas. (b.18 September 1886–d.16 August 1948) Combined All-Around, Swedish System [3].

Pettersen, Bjarne Viktor. (b.8 June 1891–d.14 December 1983) Combined All-Around, Free System, Team [1].

Robach, Rolf "Realf." (b.6 December 1885–d.10 June 1963) Combined All-Around, Swedish System [3].

Sælen, Frithjof. (b.5 August 1892–d.9 October 1975) Combined All-Around, Free System, Team [1].

Schirmer, Øistein. (b.11 April 1879–d.24 May 1947) Combined All-Around, Free System, Team [1].

Selenius, Georg. (b.18 October 1884–d.7 May 1924) Combined All-Around, Free System, Team [1].

Sivertsen, Sigvard I. (b.27 February 1881–d.27 December 1963) Combined All-Around, Free System, Team [1].

Sjursen Rafto, Robert. (b.8 March 1891–d.21 July 1965) Combined All-Around, Free System, Team [1].

Smebye, Sigurd. (b.16 March 1886–d.7 June 1954) Combined All-Around, Swedish System [3].

Strøm, Einar. (b.17 March 1885–d.26 September 1964) Combined All-Around, Free System, Team [1].

Thorstensen, Gabriel. (b.1 September 1888–d.14 June 1974) Combined All-Around, Free System, Team [1].

Torkildsen, Torleif. (b.12 May 1892–d.14 October 1944) Combined All-Around, Swedish System [3].

Torstensen, Thomas. (b.18 May 1880–d.18 June 1953) Combined All-Around, Free System, Team [1].

Voss (Repål), Nils Knutsen. (b.22 February 1886–d.7 October 1969) Combined All-Around, Free System, Team [1].

Modern Pentathlon (Total: 2; Men: 2; Women: 0)
Norby, Henrik Calmeyer. (b.18 March 1889–d.28 October 1964) Individual [ac/dnf].
Paaske, Carl. (b.29 July 1890–d.7 July 1970) Individual [13].

Rowing & Sculling (Total: 24; Men: 24; Women: 0)
Bjørnstad, John Wilhelm. (b.9 March 1888–d.3 June 1968) Coxed Fours, Inriggers [2h1r1/3]; Coxed Eights [2h4r1/4].
Bjørnstad, Olav T. (b.16 December 1882–d.13 June 1963) Coxed Fours, Inriggers [2h1r2/3].
Dahll, Olaf Ottesen. (b.19 December 1889–d.27 February 1968) Coxed Fours, Outriggers [2h2r2/4].
Davidsen, Øivin. (b.1 September 1891–d.6 June 1976) Coxed Fours, Outriggers [2h2r2/4].
Eriksen, Einar. (b.3 March 1880–d.15 July 1965) Coxed Fours, Outriggers [2h2r2/4].
Fegth, Ole Hannibal Sommerfeldt. (b.27 August 1879–d.15 September 1967) Coxed Fours, Inriggers [2h1r1/3]; Coxed Eights [2h4r1/4].
Grantz, Gunnar H. (b.27 January 1885–d.1916) Coxed Fours, Inriggers [2h1r1/3]; Coxed Eights [2h4r1/4].

Hæhre, Gustav. (b.5 September 1878–d.25 September 1950) Coxed Fours, Inriggers [2h1r1/3]; Coxed Eights [2h4r1/4].

Herlofson, Harald. (b.18 February 1887–d.17 November 1957) Coxed Eights [2h4r1/4].

Herseth, Magnus. (b.25 April 1892–d.29 October 1976) Coxed Fours, Inriggers [2h1r2/3].

Høie, Thomas. (b.28 April 1883–d.30 August 1948) Coxed Eights [2h4r1/4].

Holter, Reidar Durie. (b.28 December 1892) Coxed Fours, Inriggers [2h1r2/3].

Høyer, Claus. (b.17 March 1891–d.13 July 1923) Coxed Fours, Inriggers [2h1r2/3].

Klem, Theodor "Thea." (b.20 January 1889–d.15 July 1963) Coxed Fours, Outriggers [2h2r3/4].

Krogh, Otto Theodor. (b.29 February 1880–d.3 March 1952) Coxed Eights [2h4r1/4].

Larsen, Henry Ludvig. (b.16 August 1891–d.20 January 1969) Coxed Fours, Outriggers [2h2r3/4].

Olstad, Frithjof. (b.23 November 1890–d.16 December 1956) Coxed Fours, Inriggers [2h1r2/3].

Rode, Leif Sundt. (b.23 January 1885–d.2 November 1967) Coxed Fours, Outriggers [2h2r2/4].

Schjøth, Theodor Hammer Schlytter "Tommy." (b.16 April 1890–d.7 November 1932) Coxed Fours, Outriggers [2h2r2/4].

Solberg, Olaf. (b.10 May 1885–d.31 July 1968) Coxed Fours, Inriggers [2h1r1/3]; Coxed Eights [2h4r1/4].

Sommerfeldt, Einar. (b.16 September 1889–d.29 April 1976) Coxed Eights [2h4r1/4].

Torstensen, Mathias Abraham. (b.1 November 1890–d.9 July 1975) Coxed Fours, Outriggers [2h2r3/4].

Tønsager, Ejnar. (b.12 April 1888–d.15 October 1967) Coxed Fours, Outriggers [2h2r3/4].

Tønsager, Haakon. (b.31 July 1890–d.15 January 1975) Coxed Fours, Outriggers [2h2r3/4].

Shooting (Total: 28; Men: 28; Women: 0)

Bjerke, Ole G. (b.13 April 1881–d.15 April 1959) Military Rifle, 300 meters, 3-Positions [80].

Bough, Søren Christian. (b.9 June 1873–d.November 1939) Military Rifle, 600 meters, any position [82].

Braathe, Julius "Jul." (b.4 May 1876–8 July 1914) Free Rifle, 300 meters, 3-Positions [29]; Military Rifle, 300 meters, 3-Positions [15].

Bruun, Carsten Henrik. (b.7 November 1868–d.16 July 1951) Clay Trap Shooting, Individual [=27].

Degnes, Ole Christian. (b.29 June 1877–d.27 May 1943) Military Rifle, 600 meters, any position [17]; Military Rifle, 200, 400, 500, and 600 meters, Teams [6].

Espelund, Johannes "Johs." (b.20 February 1885–d.20 April 1952) Military Rifle, 300 meters, 3-Positions [81].

Glomnes, Mathias. (b.2 February 1869–d.6 June 1956) Military Rifle, 300 meters, 3-Positions [35]; Military Rifle, 200, 400, 500, and 600 meters, Teams [6].

Helgerud, Albert. (b.16 September 1876–27 June 1954) Free Rifle, 300 meters, 3-Positions [7]; Military Rifle, 300 meters, 3-Positions [55]; Military Rifle, 600 meters, any position [47]; Free Rifle, 300 meters, 3-Positions, Teams [2].

Husby, Olaf. (b.17 January 1878–d.30 June 1948) Free Rifle, 300 meters, 3-Positions [27]; Military Rifle, 200, 400, 500, and 600 meters, Teams [6].

Jensen, Ole Hviid. (b.21 December 1879) Military Rifle, 600 meters, any position [56]; Military Rifle, 200, 400, 500, and 600 meters, Teams [6].

Jordell, Johannes O. (b.24 June 1879–d.23 August 1958) Military Rifle, 300 meters, 3-Positions [41]; Small-Bore Rifle, prone position, 50 meters [35].

Liberg, Einar. (b.16 October 1873–11 September 1955) Free Rifle, 300 meters, 3-Positions [15]; Free Rifle, 300 meters, 3-Positions, Teams [2].

Lie, Birger. (b.20 October 1891–d.22 September 1970) Military Rifle, 300 meters, 3-Positions [82].

Maseng, Ragnvald. (b.21 October 1891–d.4 July 1920) Military Rifle, 600 meters, any position [55]; Small-Bore Rifle, prone position, 50 meters [40].

Nordvik, Hans. (b.1 August 1880–d.1960) Military Rifle, 600 meters, any position [35]; Military Rifle, 200, 400, 500, and 600 meters, Teams [6].

Østensen, Østen. (b.12 August 1878–22 December 1939) Free Rifle, 300 meters, 3-Positions [23]; Free Rifle, 300 meters, 3-Positions, Teams [2].

Refsum, Thomas. (b.18 February 1878–d.1957) Free Rifle, 300 meters, 3-Positions [26]; Military Rifle, 600 meters, any position [41].

Rosenberg, Frantz Munch. (b.27 January 1883–d.1956) Clay Trap Shooting, Individual [=23].

Sæter, Olaf. (b.1 July 1872–1 November 1945) Free Rifle, 300 meters, 3-Positions [18]; Free Rifle, 300 meters, 3-Positions, Teams [2].

Sæther, Ole Andreas. (b.23 January 1870–13 October 1946) Free Rifle, 300 meters, 3-Positions [9]; Free Rifle, 300 meters, 3-Positions, Teams [2]; Military Rifle, 600 meters, any position [60].

Skatteboe, Gudbrand Gudbrandsen. (b.18 July 1875–3 April 1965) Free Rifle, 300 meters, 3-Positions [5]; Military Rifle, 600 meters, any position [40]; Free Rifle, 300 meters, 3-Positions, Teams [2].

Skjerven, Herman Nilsen. (b.28 August 1872–d.14 March 1952) Military Rifle, 300 meters, 3-Positions [62].

Skogen, Engebret E. "Embret." (b.20 August 1887–d.4 September 1968) Free Rifle, 300 meters, 3-Positions [31]; Military Rifle, 300 meters, 3-Positions [3].

Stabell, Alfred. (b.30 January 1862–d.25 March 1942) Clay Trap Shooting, Individual [61].

Sunde, Arne Torolf. (b.6 February 1883–d.30 July 1972) Free Rifle, 300 meters, 3-Positions [30]; Military Rifle, 300 meters, 3-Positions [44]; Military Rifle, 600 meters, any position [30]; Military Rifle, 200, 400, 500, and 600 meters, Teams [6]; Small-Bore Rifle, prone position, 50 meters [30].

Thielemann, Alfred Ludvig Ferdinand. (b.25 March 1869–d.20 December 1954) Military Rifle, 300 meters, 3-Positions [76]; Military Rifle, 600 meters, any position [75].

Vighals, Paul. (b.31 March 1886–d.1 September 1962) Free Rifle, 300 meters, 3-Positions [22]; Military Rifle, 600 meters, any position [57].

Weydahl, Carl. (b.6 March 1879–d.27 July 1974) Military Rifle, 300 meters, 3-Positions [89].

Swimming (Total: 5; Men: 4; Women: 1)

Women

Normann, Aagot. (b.29 July 1892–d.22 February 1979) 100 meter freestyle [dnf-h1r1/3].

Men

Johnsen, John Haakon. (b.5 January 1892–d.24 August 1984) 100 meter freestyle [4h7r1/4]; 400 meter freestyle [6h1r2/3]; 1,500 meter freestyle [3h5r1/3]; 100 meter backstroke [4h4r1/3].

Rusten, Audun. (b.11 June 1894–d.14 December 1957) 200 meter breaststroke [dqh5r1/3].

Svendsen (Aspestrand), Harry. (b.2 January 1895–d.20 January 1960) 100 meter backstroke [4h3r1/3].

Wetter, Herbert Mauritz. (b.15 March 1891–d.5 September 1966) 1,500 meter freestyle [dnf-h1r1/3].

Tennis (Total: 7; Men: 6; Women: 1)[38]

Women
Bjurstedt, Anna Margrethe "Molla." (b.6 March 1884–22 November 1959) Ladies' Singles (Lawn) [3]; Mixed Doubles (Lawn) [=5].

Men
Angell, Bjarne. (b.24 August 1888–d.12 December 1938) Men's Doubles (Lawn) [=15].

Bjørklund, Herman. (b.29 April 1883–d.15 March 1960) Men's Singles (Lawn) [=31]; Men's Doubles (Lawn) [=15].

Langaard, Conrad. (b.6 August 1890–24 December 1950) Men's Singles (Lawn) [=31]; Men's Doubles (Lawn) [=9]; Mixed Doubles (Lawn) [=5].

Petersen, Richard Momme. (b.9 March 1884–d.2 April 1967) Men's Singles (Lawn) [=31]; Men's Doubles (Lawn) [=9].

Smith, Trygve. (b.20 September 1880–d.10 November 1948) Men's Singles (Lawn) [=31]; Men's Doubles (Lawn) [=15].

Stibolt, Willem Noble. (b.9 June 1890–d.4 April 1964) Men's Singles (Lawn) [=17]; Men's Doubles (Lawn) [=15].

Wrestling (Total: 9; Men: 9; Women: 0)

Arnesen, Kristian. (b.26 July 1890–d.18 November 1956) 60 kg. Class (Greco-Roman) [AC].

Frydenlund, Richard. (b.1 May 1891–d.20 January 1981) 67½ kg. Class (Greco-Roman) [AC].

Frydenlund, Thorbjørn. (b.15 November 1892–d.13 February 1989) 67½ kg. Class (Greco-Roman) [AC].

Gullaksen, Ragnvald. (b.27 March 1891–d.1935) 60 kg. Class (Greco-Roman) [AC].

Gundersen, Alfred. (b.11 May 1892–d.8 January 1958) 75 kg. Class (Greco-Roman) [AC].

Hestdahl, Mikael. (b.13 November 1890–d.11 November 1918) 60 kg. Class (Greco-Roman) [AC].

Lofthus, Herbrand. (b.10 December 1889–d.1 January 1972) 67½ kg. Class (Greco-Roman) [AC].

Løvold, Ansgar. (b.19 November 1888–d.13 November 1961) 82½ kg. Class (Greco-Roman) [AC].

Olsen, Thorvald. (b.30 July 1889–d.3 November 1938) 67½ kg. Class (Greco-Roman) [AC].

Yachting (Total: 18; Men: 18; Women: 0)

Aas, Thomas Valentin. (b.28 April 1887–d.14 August 1961) 8-meter class [1] (Taifun).

Anker, Johan August. (b.26 June 1871–d.2 October 1940) 12-meter class [1] (Magda IX).

Berthelsen, Nils. (b.29 September 1879–d.5 October 1958) 12-meter class [1] (Magda IX).

Brecke, Andreas Bang. (b.14 September 1879–d.13 June 1952) 8-meter class [1] (Taifun).

Christensen, Edvard G. (b.21 February 1867–d.13 August 1922) 6-meter class [=5] (Sonja II).

Christiansen, Hans Ferdinand. (b.16 October 1867–d.20 July 1938) 6-meter class [=5] (Sonja II).

Corneliussen, Torleiv Schibsted. (b.25 July 1890–d.29 April 1975) 8-meter class [1] (Taifun).

Falch-Lund, Eilert Dietrichson. (b.27 January 1875–d.1960) 12-meter class [1] (Magda IX).

Glad, Thoralf. (b.1 February 1878–d.17 July 1969) 8-meter class [1] (Taifun).

Hansen, Halfdan Nicolai. (b.16 October 1883–d.2 April 1953) 12-meter class [1] (Magda IX).

Heje, Arnfinn Kolbjørn. (b.26 October 1887–d.29 January 1958) 12-meter class [1] (Magda IX).

Jebe, Christian Fredrik. (b.23 June 1876–d.24 March 1946) 8-meter class [1] (Taifun).

Konow, Magnus Andreas Thulstrup Clasen. (b.1 September 1887–d.25 August 1972) 12-meter class [1] (Magda IX).

Kragh Christiansen, Eigil. (b.16 May 1894–d.11 June 1943) 6-meter class [=5] (Sonja II).

Larsen, Alfred Waldemar Garmann. (b.24 November 1863–d.10 September 1950) 12-meter class [1] (Magda IX).

Larsen, Petter Andreas. (d.1959) 12-meter class [1] (Magda IX).

Staib, Christian Fredrik Maximillian "Fritz." (b.10 February 1892–d.16 May 1956) 12-meter class [1] (Magda IX).

Thaulow, Carl Gustav. (b.23 October 1875–d.30 May 1942) 12-meter class [1] (Magda IX).

Portugal (Total: 6; Men: 6; Women: 0)

Athletics (Track & Field) (Total: 3; Men: 3; Women: 0)

Luzarte-Cortesão, Armando Z. (b.30 January 1891) 400 meters [3h3r1/3]; 800 meters [ach2r2/3].

Lázaro, Francisco. (b.8 January 1891–d.15 July 1912) Marathon [dnf-].

Stromp, António. (b.2 June 1894) 100 meters [3h5r1/3]; 200 meters [3h18r1/3].

Fencing (Total: 1; Men: 1; Women: 0)

Correia, Fernando. (b.1880) Épée, Individual [acp3r1/4].

Wrestling (Total: 2; Men: 2; Women: 0)

Pereira, António. (b.4 April 1888) 60 kg. Class (Greco-Roman) [AC].

Victal, Joaquim. (b.24 August 1884) 75 kg. Class (Greco-Roman) [AC].

Russia[39] (Total: 159; Men: 159; Women: 0)

Athletics (Track & Field) (Total: 33; Men: 33; Women: 0)

Alslebens, Alfreds. [Latvia] (b.12 July 1892) Decathlon [12].

Ayde, Aleksis. [Latvia] (b.3 December 1888) 10 Kilometer Walk [9h2r1/2].

Baasch, Ulrich. (b.23 February 1890) Pole Vault [=8g2qr].

Baumanis, Herberts. [Latvia] (b.5 January 1889) 200 meters [dnf-h3r1/3].

Gayevsky, Pyotr. (b.5 February 1888) 400 meters [4h11r1/3].

Hahne, Haralds. [Latvia] (b.8 June 1893) 200 meters [4h3r1/3].

Hermann, Eduard. [Estonia] (b.28 July 1887–d.8 February 1960)–10 Kilometer Walk [dnf-h1r1/2].

Indriksons, Arnolds. [Latvia] (b.20 August 1893) 1,500 meters [6h4r1/3].

Kapmals, Andrejs. [Latvia] (b.5 November 1889–d.21 January 1994) Marathon [dnf-].

Kharkov, Nikolay. (b.1890) 1,500 meters [ach5r1/3].

Kruklins, Andrejs. [Latvia] (b.10 January 1891) 1,500 meters [ach6r1/3]; Marathon [dnf-].

Levensteins, Leopolds. [Latvia] (b.13 December 1893) 100 meters [ach6r1/3].

Lukk, Kaarel. [Estonia] (b.24 November 1887–d.17 November 1970) 10 Kilometer Walk [dnf-h1r1/2].

Martin, Johannes. [Estonia] (b.2 January 1893–21 December 1959) Pole Vault [nh/g1qr].

Molokanov, Vasily. (b.1888) Discus Throw, both hands [19/9g1qr].

Nazarov, Dmitry. (b.1890) 800 meters [5h5r1/3]; 1,500 meters [dnf-h2r1/3].

Neklepayev, Nikolay. (b.1888) Discus Throw [35/7g2qr]; Javelin Throw [17/2g2qr].
Nikolsky, Mikhail. (b.1891) 5,000 meters [4h3r1/2]; 10,000 meters [11h1r1/2].
Ozols-Berne, Arvids. [Latvia] (b.25 June 1888) Shot Put [21/8g3qr].
Petrov, Yevgeny. (b.5 January 1888) 1,500 meters [5h7r1/3].
Rasso, Nikolajs. [Latvia] (b.18 October 1890) Marathon [dnf-].
Reimann, Elmar. [Estonia] (b.2 January 1893–d.21 April 1963) Marathon [dnf-].
Ruks, Alfreds. [Latvia] (b.28 October 1890–d.30 November 1941) 1,500 meters [7h4r1/3].
Schwarz, Alfred. (b.16 November 1887) Standing High Jump [8g2qr].
Schwarz, Richard. (b.8 January 1890) 100 meters [ach7r1/3].
Shtiglits, Pavel. (b.1892) 100 meters [4h13r1/3].
Schultz, Aleksandr. (b.26 June 1892) Broad Jump [22/8g1qr]; Decathlon [11].
Svedrevits, Nikolajs. [Latvia] (b.18 January 1891) Javelin Throw [20/4g2qr].
Upmals, Aleksandrs. [Latvia] (b.1 September 1892) Marathon [dnf-].
Villemson, Johannes Leopolds. [Latvia] (b.25 March 1893–d.22 March 1971) 800 meters [dnf-h7r1/3].
Vitols, Rudolfs. [Latvia] (b.15 April 1892) 1,500 meters [ach2r1/3].
Vanags, Eriks. [Latvia] (b.20 January 1893) Shot Put [20/5g4qr]; Discus Throw [39/10g5qr].
Yelizarov, Aleksandr. (b.1892) 800 meters [ach6r1/3]; 1,500 meters [ach5r1/3].

Cycling (Total: 10; Men: 10; Women: 0)
Apsits, Andrejs. [Latvia] (b.7 February 1888) Road Race, Individual [60]; Road Race, Team [tm-dnf/(60)].
Borisov, Fyodor. (b.5 February 1892) Road Race, Individual [ac/dnf]; Road Race, Team [tm-dnf/dnf].
Bosch, Friedrich. [Latvia] (b.7 February 1887) Road Race, Individual [ac/dnf]; Road Race, Team [tm-dnf/dnf].
Bukse, Jakob. [Latvia] (b.2 June 1879) Road Race, Individual [ac/dnf]; Road Race, Team [tm-dnf/dnf].
Köpke, Augusts. [Latvia] (b.6 January 1886) Road Race, Individual [ac/dnf]; Road Race, Team [tm-dnf/dnf].
Köpke, Karlis. [Latvia] (b.6 November 1890) Road Race, Individual [ac/dnf]; Road Race, Team [tm-dnf/dnf].
Lieven, Janis. [Latvia] (b.16 April 1884) Road Race, Individual [ac/dnf]; Road Race, Team [tm-dnf/dnf].
Pesteryev, Sergey. (b.12 January 1888) Road Race, Individual [ac/dnf]; Road Race, Team [tm-dnf/dnf].
Pratneek, Janis. [Latvia] (b.29 July 1887) Road Race, Individual [ac/dnf]; Road Race, Team [tm-dnf/dnf].
Richters, Edgars. [Latvia] (b.6 June 1887) Road Race, Individual [ac/dnf]; Road Race, Team [tm-dnf/dnf].

Diving (Total: 1; Men: 1; Women: 0)
Baranov, Viktor. (b.1893) Plain High Diving [ac/dnf-h1r1/2].

Equestrian Events (Total: 7; Men: 7; Women: 0)
Plechkov, Mikhail. Jumping, Individual [21]; Jumping, Team [5] (Eveta).
Rodzhianko, Aleksandr. Jumping, Individual [=16]; Jumping, Team [5] (Eros).
Romanov, Dmitry Pavlovich.[40] (b.6 September 1891) Jumping, Individual [=9]; Jumping, Team [5] (Unité).

Rómmel, Karol.[41] (b.23 May 1888–d.7 March 1967) Jumping, Individual [15] (Siablik).

Selikhov, Aleksey. Jumping, Individual [=22]; Jumping, Team [5] (Tugela).

Yekimov, Mikhail. Dressage, Individual [9] (Tritonich).

Zagorsky, Sergey. Jumping, Individual [=18] (Bandoura).

Fencing (Total: 24; Men: 24; Women: 0)

Andreyev, Vladimir. (b.1878) Sabre, Individual (dnc-p2r3/4); Sabre, Team (=9).

Arsenyev, Boris. (b.1888) Sabre, Individual (5p3r3/4).

Bertrain, Gavril. (b.1869) Foil, Individual (4p11r1/4); Épée, Individual (=5p2r2/4); Épée, Team (=9).

Danich, Vladimir. (b.1886) Sabre, Individual (dnc-p3r2/4); Sabre, Team (=9).

Filatov, Pavel. (b.1887) Sabre, Individual (4p12r1/4).

Gorodetsky, Nikolay. (b.1888) Foil, Individual (7p6r1/4).

Grinev, Leonid. (b.1888) Foil, Individual (5p16r1/4).

Guiber von Greifenfels, Apollon. (b.1887) Sabre, Individual (4p4r3/4); Sabre, Team (=9).

Guvorsky, Pavel. (b.1884) Foil, Individual (5p3r1/4); Épée, Individual (=7p1r1/4); Épée, Team (=9).

Keyser, Vladimir. (b.1878) Foil, Individual (7p5r1/4); Épée, Individual (=4p3r1/4); Épée, Team (=9).

Knyazhevich, Dmitry. (b.1874) Foil, Individual (=4p1r1/4); Épée, Team (=9).

Kuznyetsov, Nikolay. (b.1882) Sabre, Individual (=4p4r2/4); Sabre, Team (=9).

Leparsky, Feliks. (b.1875) Foil, Individual (=4p2r1/4).

Martuchev, Leonid. (b.1880) Foil, Individual (=4p13r1/4); Épée, Individual (5p6r1/4); Épée, Team (=9).

Mordovin, Aleksandr. (b.1873) Foil, Individual (=4p7r1/4); Sabre, Individual (=4p8r1/4); Sabre, Team (=9).

Nepokupnoy, Boris.[42] (b.1887) Sabre, Individual (4p3r1/4). (See also Modern Pentathlon.)

Samoylov, Vladimir. (b.1876) Foil, Individual (5p8r1/4).

Sarnavsky, Vladimir. (b.1875) Foil, Individual (=5p12r1/4); Épée, Individual (=4p4r1/4); Épée, Team (=9).

Shkylev, Aleksandr. (b.1889) Sabre, Individual (=4p4r1/4); Sabre, Team (=9).

Soldatenkov, Aleksandr. (b.1887) Épée, Individual (=5p2r1/4); Épée, Team (=9).

Timofeyev, Anatoly. (b.1887) Sabre, Individual (dnc-p1r3/4); Sabre, Team (=9).

Vaterkampf, Konstantin. (b.1888) Sabre, Individual (4p7r1/4).

Zakyrich, Georgy. (b.1884) Sabre, Individual (=4p5r1/4); Sabre, Team (=9).

Zhakovlev, Anatoly. (b.1884) Foil, Individual (5p14r1/4).

Football (Association Football [Soccer]) (Total: 15; Men: 15; Women: 0)

Akimov, Andrey. (b.12 October 1890) [=9].

Butusov, Vladimir Pavlovich. (b.25 January 1892) [=9].

Favorsky, Leonid. (b.1893) [=9].

Filipov, Aleksandr Pavlovich. (b.1888) [=9].

Filipov, Sergey Pavlovich. (b.2 July 1893) [=9].

Khromov, Nikita Akimovich. (b.1 May 1888) [=9].

Kynin, Nikolas. (b.1892) [=9].

Markov, Vladimir Anatolyevich. (b.1899) [=9].

Nikitin, Grigory Mikhailovich. [=9].

Rimsha, Fyodor. [=9].

Smirnov, Mikhail. (b.1892) [=9].

Sokolov, Pyotr Petrovich. (b.1 December 1891) [=9].
Uversky, Aleksey. [=9].
Yakovlev, Mikhail Vasilyevich. [=9].
Zhitaryev, Vasily. (b.1892) [=9].

Gymnastics (Total: 4; Men: 4; Women: 0)
Akhyun, Aleksandr. (b.24 June 1892) Combined All-Around, Individual [39].
Kushnikov, Pavel. (b.24 August 1893) Combined All-Around, Individual [38].
Kulikov, Semyon. (b.8 July 1891) Combined All-Around, Individual [41].
Zabelyn, Fyodor. (b.27 May 1888) Combined All-Around, Individual [42].

Modern Pentathlon[43] (Total: 5; Men: 5; Women: 0)
Aejemelaeus, Carl Bror Emil "Kalle."[44] [Finland] (b.20 May 1882–d.13 July 1935) Individual [ac/dnf] (later Aejemelaeus-Áimä, Carl Bror Emil "Kalle").
Almqvist, Aarno Aksel "Arno."[45] [Finland] (b.23 September 1881–d.5 March 1940) Individual [20].
Hohenthal, Weli Gunnar Bogislaus.[46] [Finland] (b.15 November 1880) Individual [21].
Nepokupnoy, Boris. [Finland] (b.1887) Individual [ac/dnf]. (See also Fencing.)
Wilkman, Oskar Alfred. [Finland] (b.7 April 1880–d.28 June 1953) Individual [15]. (later [1918] Vilkama, Oskar Alfred)

Rowing & Sculling (Total: 1; Men: 1; Women: 0)
Kusick, Hugo Maksimilian. [Estonia] (b.9 December 1877–d.24 August 1965) Single Sculls [2h1r3/4].

Shooting (Total: 26; Men: 26; Women: 0)
Barkov, Dmitry. (b.28 October 1880) Running Deer, Single Shot, Individual [=31]; Running Deer, Double Shot, Individual [19]; Running Deer, Single Shot, Teams [5].
Belinsky, Boris. (b.28 March 1885) Free Rifle, 300 meters, 3-Positions [65]; Military Rifle, 300 meters, 3-Positions [46]; Military Rifle, 600 meters, any position [65].
Blau, Harry. (b.24 December 1885) Running Deer, Single Shot, Individual [20]; Running Deer, Single Shot, Teams [5]; Clay Trap Shooting, Individual [3].
Bodneck, Walter. (b.17 December 1885) Clay Trap Shooting, Individual [=35].
Davidov, Georgy. (b.25 March 1874) Free Rifle, 300 meters, 3-Positions [76]; Military Rifle, 300 meters, 3-Positions [68]; Military Rifle, 600 meters, any position [61]; Military Rifle, 200, 400, 500, and 600 meters, Teams [9].
Dobrzhansky, Aleksandr. (b.19 August 1874) Free Rifle, 300 meters, 3-Positions [78]; Military Rifle, 300 meters, 3-Positions [71]; Military Rifle, 600 meters, any position [71]; Small-Bore Rifle, prone position, 50 meters [33]; Small-Bore Rifle, 25 meters, Disappearing Target [26]; Running Deer, Single Shot, Individual [33]; Running Deer, Single Shot, Teams [5].
Kache, Amosse. (b.15 June 1868) Free Pistol, 50 meters [46]; Dueling Pistol, 30 meters [28]; Dueling Pistol, 30 meters, Teams [2].
Kalinin, Konstantin. (b.12 August 1885) Free Rifle, 300 meters, 3-Positions [68]; Military Rifle, 300 meters, 3-Positions [79]; Military Rifle, 600 meters, any position [39]; Free Rifle, 300 meters, 3-Positions, Teams [7].
Kuskov, Dmitry. (b.1 December 1876) Free Rifle, 300 meters, 3-Positions [58]; Military Rifle, 300 meters, 3-Positions [49]; Military Rifle, 600 meters, any position [59]; Free Rifle, 300

meters, 3-Positions, Teams [7]; Military Rifle, 200, 400, 500, and 600 meters, Teams [9]; Free Pistol, 50 meters [19].

Lebedev, Teotan. (b.2 November 1871) Free Rifle, 300 meters, 3-Positions [54]; Military Rifle, 300 meters, 3-Positions [42]; Military Rifle, 600 meters, any position [74]; Free Rifle, 300 meters, 3-Positions, Teams [7]; Military Rifle, 200, 400, 500, and 600 meters, Teams [9].

Leche, Pavel. (b.7 May 1887) Free Rifle, 300 meters, 3-Positions [71]; Military Rifle, 300 meters, 3-Positions [30]; Military Rifle, 600 meters, any position [70]; Free Rifle, 300 meters, 3-Positions, Teams [7].

Lieth, Pavel. (b.28 December 1883) Running Deer, Single Shot, Individual [34]; Clay Trap Shooting, Individual [=51].

Melnitsky, Nikolay. (b.9 May 1887) Free Pistol, 50 meters [33]; Dueling Pistol, 30 meters [22]; Dueling Pistol, 30 meters, Teams [2]; Military Pistol, 50 meters, Teams [4].

Panin (Kolomenkin), Nikolay Aleksandrovich. (b.1 January 1874–d.19 January 1956) Free Pistol, 50 meters [8]; Military Pistol, 50 meters, Teams [4].

Panteleymonov, Georgy. (b.30 December 1887) Free Pistol, 50 meters [17]; Dueling Pistol, 30 meters [14]; Dueling Pistol, 30 meters, Teams [2].

Pertel, Boris. (b.21 April 1888) Clay Trap Shooting, Individual [=53].

Potekin, Vladimir. (b.10 December 1875) Small-Bore Rifle, prone position, 50 meters [36]; Small-Bore Rifle, 25 meters, Disappearing Target [32].

Rechke, Osvald. (b.27 September 1883) Free Rifle, 300 meters, 3-Positions [73]; Military Rifle, 300 meters, 3-Positions [47]; Military Rifle, 600 meters, any position [58].

Shesterikov, Grigory. (b.10 January 1877) Free Pistol, 50 meters [31]; Dueling Pistol, 30 meters [32]; Military Pistol, 50 meters, Teams [4].

Skrotsky, Vasily. (b.1 January 1878) Running Deer, Single Shot, Individual [=15]; Running Deer, Double Shot, Individual [20]; Running Deer, Single Shot, Teams [5].

Syttin, Leonardus. [Lithuania] (b.3 December 1892) Clay Trap Shooting, Individual [=23].

Tillo, Aleksandr. (b.11 July 1870) Free Rifle, 300 meters, 3-Positions [66]; Military Rifle, 300 meters, 3-Positions [51]; Military Rifle, 600 meters, any position [62]; Free Rifle, 300 meters, 3-Positions, Teams [7]; Military Rifle, 200, 400, 500, and 600 meters, Teams [9].

Valdayne, Pavel. (b.3 August 1887) Free Rifle, 300 meters, 3-Positions [62]; Military Rifle, 300 meters, 3-Positions [11]; Military Rifle, 600 meters, any position [45]; Free Rifle, 300 meters, 3-Positions, Teams [7]; Military Rifle, 200, 400, 500, and 600 meters, Teams [9].

Vishnyakov, Georgy. (b.1 April 1871) Military Rifle, 300 meters, 3-Positions [26]; Military Rifle, 600 meters, any position [77].

Voyloshnikov, Pavel. (b.10 January 1879) Free Pistol, 50 meters [34]; Dueling Pistol, 30 meters [24]; Dueling Pistol, 30 meters, Teams [2]; Military Pistol, 50 meters, Teams [4].

Weiss, Davids. [Latvia] (b.22 September 1879) Free Rifle, 300 meters, 3-Positions [77]; Military Rifle, 300 meters, 3-Positions [60]; Military Rifle, 600 meters, any position [51]; Military Rifle, 200, 400, 500, and 600 meters, Teams [9].

Swimming (Total: 4; Men: 4; Women: 0)

Avksentyev, Pavel. (b.1890) 400 meter freestyle [dnf-h2r1/3]; 1,500 meter freestyle [dnf-h5r1/3].

Baymakov, Georgy. (b.1 June 1894) 200 meter breaststroke [5h2r1/3]; 400 meter breaststroke [dns-r2/3].

von Kuhlberg, Herbert. (b.22 November 1893) 100 meter freestyle [4h1r1/4].

Voronkov, Nikolay. (b.1883) 400 meter freestyle [dnf-h4r/13].

Tennis (Total: 2; Men: 2; Women: 0)

Alenitsyn, Aleksandr. (b.29 November 1884) Men's Doubles (Lawn) [=5].

Sumarokov-Elston, Mikhail. (b.2 January 1893) Men's Singles (Lawn) [=9]; Men's Doubles (Lawn) [=5].

Wrestling (Total: 11; Men: 11; Women: 0)
　Ankondinov, Aleksandr. (b.30 August 1891) 60 kg. Class (Greco-Roman) [AC].
　Baumann, Georg. (b.1 September 1892) 67½ kg. Class (Greco-Roman) [AC].
　Farnest, Nikolajs. [Latvia] (b.1 October 1885) Unlimited Class (Greco-Roman) [AC].
　Kaplur, Oscar. [Estonia] (b.8 September 1889) 67½ kg. Class (Greco-Roman) [AC].
　Kippasto, August. [Latvia] (b.28 August 1887) 67½ kg. Class (Greco-Roman) [AC].
　Klein, Martin "Max."[47] [Estonia] (b.12 September 1884–d.11 February 1947) 75 kg. Class (Greco-Roman) [2].
　Meesits, Aleksanders. [Latvia] (b.1890) 60 kg. Class (Greco-Roman) [AC].
　Pavlovich, Pavel. (b.14 February 1893) 60 kg. Class (Greco-Roman) [AC].
　Pikker, Augusts. [Latvia] (b.24 January 1887) 82½ kg. Class (Greco-Roman) [AC].
　Polis, Janis. [Latvia] (b.1892) 75 kg. Class (Greco-Roman) [AC].
　Severov, Aleksandr. (b.24 February 1889) 75 kg. Class (Greco-Roman) [AC].

Yachting (Total: 17; Men: 17; Women: 0)
　Beloselsky, Yesper. 10-meter class [3] (Gallia II).
　Brasche, Ernest. 10-meter class [3] (Gallia II).
　Färber, Johan. 8-meter class [=5] (Bylina).
　Ilyevich, Vladimir. 8-meter class [=5] (Bylina).
　Kuhn, Yevgeny. 8-meter class [=5] (Norman).
　Kuzmichev, Ventseslav. 8-meter class [=5] (Norman).
　Lindholm, Karl. 10-meter class [3] (Gallia II).
　Lomach, Yevgeny. 8-meter class [=5] (Norman).
　Lurasov, Vladimir. 8-meter class [=5] (Bylina).
　Markov, Viktor. 8-meter class [=5] (Norman).
　Pavlov, Pavel. 8-meter class [=5] (Norman).
　Podgornov, Nikolay. 8-meter class [=5] (Bylina).
　Pusnitsky, Nikolay. 10-meter class [3] (Gallia II).
　Rodionov, Aleksandr. 10-meter class [3] (Gallia II).
　Shomaker, Iossif. 10-meter class [3] (Gallia II).
　Strauch, Filipp. 10-meter class [3] (Gallia II).
　von Adlerberg, Herman. 8-meter class [=5] (Bylina).

Serbia (Total: 2; Men: 2; Women: 0)

Athletics (Track & Field) (Total: 2; Men: 2; Women: 0)
　Milošević, Dušan. (b.1 June 1894–d.19 May 1967) 100 meters [ach8r1/3].
　Tomašević, Dragutin. (b.17 January 1891–d. *ca*1915) Marathon [dnf-].

South Africa[48] (Total 421; Men: 21; Women: 0)

Athletics (Track & Field) (Total: 7; Men: 7; Women: 0)
　Gitsham, Christopher William. (b.15 October 1888–d.16 June 1956) Marathon [2].
　McArthur, Kennedy Kane. (b.10 February 1880–d.13 June 1960) Marathon [1].

Patching, George Herbert. (b.15 September 1886) 100 meters [4]; 200 meters [dnf-h3r2/3]; 400 meters [3h3r2/3].

Povey, Reuben. (b.2 July 1889) 100 meters [2h6r2/3]; 200 meters [5h5r2/3].

Richardson, Leonard William Walter. (b.13 July 1882–d.1955) 10,000 meters [dnf-final]; Cross-Country, Individual [8].

St. Norman, Arthur Claude Champion. (b.20 October 1882–d.18 May 1956) Marathon [dnf-]; 10 Kilometer Walk [dq-final].

Victor, Joachim Jan Hendrik "John." (b.15 April 1892–d.22 September 1935) 800 meters [3h8r1/3]; 1,500 meters [3h4r1/3].

Cycling (Total: 1; Men: 1; Women: 0)

Lewis, Rudolph. (b.12 July 1887–d.29 October 1933) Road Race, Individual [1].

Fencing (Total: 1; Men: 1; Women: 0)

Gates, Walter Percy. (b.1874) Foil, Individual (=5p4r1/4); Épée, Individual (7p7r1/4); Sabre, Individual (4p13r1/4).

Shooting (Total: 8; Men: 8; Women: 0)

Bodley, Robert. (b.31 July 1878–d.6 November 1956) Free Rifle, 300 meters, 3-Positions [55]; Free Rifle, 300 meters, 3-Positions, Teams [6]; Military Rifle, 300 meters, 3-Positions [45]; Military Rifle, 600 meters, any position [54]; Military Rifle, 200, 400, 500, and 600 meters, Teams [4].

Harvey, George Henry. (b.9 January 1878–d.1958) Free Rifle, 300 meters, 3-Positions [40]; Military Rifle, 300 meters, 3-Positions [10]; Military Rifle, 600 meters, any position [21]; Free Rifle, 300 meters, 3-Positions, Teams [6]; Military Rifle, 200, 400, 500, and 600 meters, Teams [4].

Jeffreys, Charles Alfred. (b.7 December 1877) Free Rifle, 300 meters, 3-Positions [70]; Military Rifle, 300 meters, 3-Positions [34]; Military Rifle, 600 meters, any position [42]; Military Rifle, 200, 400, 500, and 600 meters, Teams [4].

Johnstone, Albert Edward. (b.7 September 1878–d.23 July 1918) Free Rifle, 300 meters, 3-Positions [67]; Military Rifle, 300 meters, 3-Positions [77]; Military Rifle, 600 meters, any position [43].

Keeley, Ernest James. (b.26 May 1890) Free Rifle, 300 meters, 3-Positions [56]; Military Rifle, 300 meters, 3-Positions [13]; Free Rifle, 300 meters, 3-Positions, Teams [6]; Military Rifle, 200, 400, 500, and 600 meters, Teams [4].

Patterson, Robert. (b.8 March 1875) Free Rifle, 300 meters, 3-Positions [51]; Military Rifle, 300 meters, 3-Positions [59]; Military Rifle, 600 meters, any position [53]; Free Rifle, 300 meters, 3-Positions, Teams [6]; Military Rifle, 200, 400, 500, and 600 meters, Teams [4].

Smith, Arthur Athelstan. (b.24 July 1883–d.23 October 1958) Free Rifle, 300 meters, 3-Positions [64]; Military Rifle, 300 meters, 3-Positions [84]; Free Rifle, 300 meters, 3-Positions, Teams [6]; Military Rifle, 200, 400, 500, and 600 meters, Teams [4].

Whelan, George William. (b.6 May 1859–d.12 November 1938) Free Rifle, 300 meters, 3-Positions [61]; Military Rifle, 300 meters, 3-Positions [73]; Free Rifle, 300 meters, 3-Positions, Teams [6].

Swimming (Total: 1; Men: 1; Women: 0)

Godfrey, George Albert. (b.26 July 1888–d.22 May 1965) 400 meter freestyle [4h6r1/3].

Tennis (Total: 3; Men: 3; Women: 0)

    Kitson, Harry Austin. (b.17 June 1874–d.30 November 1951) Men's Singles (Lawn) [2]; Men's Doubles (Lawn) [1].

    Tapscott, Lionel Eric. (b.18 March 1894–d.7 July 1934) Men's Singles (Lawn) [=9].

    Winslow, Charles Lyndhurst. (b.1 August 1888–d.15 September 1963) Men's Singles (Lawn) [1]; Men's Doubles (Lawn) [1].

Sweden (Total: 444; Men: 421; Women: 23)

Athletics (Track & Field) (Total: 108; Men: 108; Women: 0)

    Åberg, Arvid. (b.14 June 1885–d.8 November 1950) Hammer Throw [10/6g1qr].

    Åberg, Georg. (b.20 January 1893–d.18 August 1946) Broad Jump [3]; Hop, step, and jump [2].

    Åbrink, Richard. (b.1 January 1889–d.9 October 1973) Javelin Throw [6/2g3qr]; Javelin Throw, both hands [6/2g2qr].

    Ahlgren, Alexis. (b.14 July 1887) Marathon [dnf-].

    Almlöf, Erik. (b.20 December 1891–d.18 January 1971) Hop, step, and jump [3].

    Andersson, Carl Nicanor. (b.3 January 1877–d.4 January 1956) Marathon [24].

    Andersson, Hjalmar J. (b.13 July 1889–d.2 November 1971) Cross-Country, Individual [2]; Cross-Country, Team [1].

    Bergh, Karl. (b.9 March 1883–d.9 May 1954) Standing High Jump [2g1qr]; Standing Long Jump [18/5g1qr].

    Bergvall, Johan Thure. (b.23 November 1887–d.20 September 1950) Marathon [dnf-].

    Betzén, Gustav. (b.14 January 1886–d.13 November 1978) Broad Jump [21/6g4qr].

    Björn, Evert. (b.21 January 1888–d.21 December 1974) 800 meters [ach2r2/3]; 1,500 meters [ac-final].

    Bolander, Gunnar. (b.20 July 1889–d.19 December 1964) Discus Throw [26/4g5qr].

    Brauer, Thage. High Jump [=11g1/qr].

    Carlén, Gustav "Gusten." (b.29 December 1890–d.8 January 1975) Cross-Country, Individual [21]; Cross-Country, Team [1/ns].

    Carlsson, Gustaf Mauritz "Sörle." (b.5 January 1890) 5,000 meters [7]; 10,000 meters [dnf-final].

    Dahl, Janne. (b.28 December 1882–d.18 December 1961) Javelin Throw [15/3g3qr].

    Dahlberg, Hjalmar Alexius. (b.4 November 1886–d.5 March 1962) Marathon [27].

    Dahlin, John. (b.11 January 1886) 400 meters [dns-r2/3]; 4 × 400 meter relay [2h3r1/2].

    Ekberg, Olle Ragnar B. (b.12 August 1886) 100 meters [3h17r1/3]; Standing Long Jump [13/4g4qr].

    Eke, John Wicktor. (b.12 March 1886–d.November 1964) 10,000 meters [dns-final]; Cross-Country, Individual [3]; Cross-Country, Team [1].

    Ekman, Leif. (b.16 January 1893) Standing High Jump [=2g3qr].

    Ericson, Hugo. (b.10 March 1886–d.2 February 1945) Pentathlon [18].

    Falk, Eskil Adolf. (b.4 February 1889) Javelin Throw [nm/g4qr].

    Fjästad, Nils. (b.26 February 1890–d.13 July 1964) Pentathlon [11].

    Fleetwood, Folke Fredrik. (b.15 November 1890–d.4 February 1949) Discus Throw [28/5g5qr]; Discus Throw, both hands [7/2g3qr].

    Fock, Bror Karl. (b.29 March 1888–d.4 September 1964) 10,000 meters [6h2r1/2]; Cross-Country, Individual [17]; Cross-Country, Team [1/ns]; 3,000 Meter Team Race [2].

    Frisell, Erik. (b.3 May 1889–d. December 1964) 800 meters [=3h9r1/3].

Frykberg, Nils. (b.13 March 1888–d.13 December 1966) 1,500 meters [4h6r1/3]; 3,000 Meter Team Race [2-ns].

Gille, Clas Thorulf. (b.1 May 1888–d.26 August 1952) Pole Vault [=6g2qr].

Grandell, Emil. (b.5 December 1889–d.20 May 1963) 200 meters [dnf-h14r1/3].

Grüner, Karl Wilhelm Kristian "William." (b.6 May 1888–d.15 February 1961) Marathon [dnf-].

Guttman, David Abraham. (b.24 July 1883–d.9 December 1940) Marathon [dnf-].

Hackberg, Wiktor Engelbrekt. (b.13 August 1891–d.5 November 1968) Hammer Throw [13/5g2qr]; Decathlon [ac/dnf].

Hagander, Sten. (b.22 November 1891) Javelin Throw, both hands [11/3g2qr].

Haglund, Karl. (b.24 September 1890–d.5 November 1971) 800 meters [ach6r1/3].

Hallberg, Gösta. (b.4 August 1891) High Jump [=4g1qr].

Hårleman, Carl. (b.23 June 1886–d.20 August 1948) Pole Vault [7g1qr].

Hellgren, Erik Edvin. (b.11 May 1888–d.25 February 1919) Cross-Country, Individual [dnf-]; Cross-Country, Team [1/ns].

Holmér, Gustaf Richard Mikael "Gösta." (b.23 September 1891–d.22 April 1983) High Jump [=11g1/qr]; Decathlon [4]; Pentathlon [8].

Jacobsson, Sigfrid "Sigge." (b.4 June 1883–d.20 July 1961) Marathon [6].

Jacobsson, Skotte. (b.24 February 1888–d.8 October 1964) 100 meters [4h14r1/3]; 200 meters [5h2r2/3]; Hop, step, and jump [17/7g2qr]; Decathlon [ac/dnf].

Jahnzon, Carl. (b.29 April 1881–d.25 June 1955) Hammer Throw [=8/5g1qr].

Johnson, Gunnar. (b.3 July 1889–d.19 June 1926) Hammer Throw [11/7g1qr].

Klintberg, John. (b.6 February 1885–d.16 December 1955) Cross-Country, Individual [dnf-]; Cross-Country, Team [1/ns].

Krigsman, Anders Wilhelm. (b.25 October 1886–d.5 March 1947) Javelin Throw [14/4g3qr]; Javelin Throw, both hands [13/4g3qr].

Kugelberg, Erik. (b.9 March 1891–d.15 October 1975) Decathlon [8]; Pentathlon [15].

Kullerstrand, Karl-Axel. (b.1 March 1892–d.14 May 1981) High Jump [8].

Larsson, Algot. (b.29 November 1889–d.12 November 1967) Javelin Throw [21/5g3qr].

Larsson, Erik Brynolf. (b.20 June 1885) 10,000 meters [7h2r1/2]; Cross-Country, Individual [9]; Cross-Country, Team [1/ns].

Lemming, Eric Valdemar. (b.22 February 1880–d.5 June 1930) Discus Throw, both hands [11/6g1qr]; Javelin Throw [1]; Javelin Throw, both hands [4/2g1qr].

Lemming, Oscar Runo. (b.11 October 1886–d.30 August 1979) Pentathlon [10].

Lind, Carl Johan "Masse." (b.25 May 1883–d.2 February 1965) Discus Throw [27/6g2qr]; Discus Throw, both hands [8/5g1qr]; Hammer Throw [5/3g1qr].

Lindahl, Alexander Leander "Axel." (b.8 December 1885) Cross-Country, Individual [dnf]; Cross-Country, Team [1/ns].

Lindberg, Knut "Knatten." (b.2 February 1882–d.6 April 1961) 100 meters [2h2r2/3]; 200 meters [3h6r2/3]; 4 × 100 meter relay [2].

Lindblom, Gustaf "Topsy." (b.3 December 1891–d.26 April 1960) Hop, step, and jump [1].

Lindblom, Karl. (b.7 June 1892–d.10 January 1969) 200 meters [4h2r1/3].

Linde, Nils Harald. (b.18 July 1890–d.17 August 1962) Discus Throw, both hands [9/2g2qr]; Hammer Throw [7/3g2qr].

Lindholm, Eric Evert. (b.22 August 1890) 400 meters [2h2r2/3]; 800 meters [4h1r1/3]; 4 × 400 meter relay [2h3r1/2].

Lindholm, Inge. (b.22 June 1892–d.24 May 1932) Hop, step, and jump [12/3g3qr]; Pentathlon [9].

Ljunggren, Sven Gustav. (b.6 February 1893) Standing Long Jump [11/3g2qr].

Appendix VI

Lomberg, Charles Georg. (b.4 December 1886–d.5 March 1966) Broad Jump [17/7g2-3qr]; Decathlon [3]; Pentathlon [16].

Lönnberg, Ivan. (b.12 November 1891–d.26 April 1918) Marathon [dnf-].

Lundberg, Ivar Gustaf. (b.11 November 1878–d.31 July 1952) Marathon [28].

Lundström, Klas Julius. (b.19 February 1889–d.26 March 1951) 5,000 meters [dnf-h1r1/2]; Cross-Country, Individual [13]; Cross-Country, Team [1/ns].

Luther, Karl August "Charles." (b.8 August 1885–d.24 January 1962) 100 meters [5h1r2/3]; 200 meters [3h5r2/3]; 4 × 100 meter relay [2].

Magnusson, Emil. (b.23 November 1887–d.26 July 1933) Discus Throw [8/3g1qr]; Discus Throw, both hands [3].

Måhl, Helmer. (b.22 May 1888) Standing High Jump [4g3qr].

Malmsten, Gustaf. (b.4 December 1889) Standing Long Jump [4/1g4qr].

Mattson, Ragnar. (b.5 January 1892) High Jump [=7g1qr].

Melin, Douglas Edvard. (b.4 October 1895–d.29 March 1946) Standing Long Jump [14/4g1qr].

Modigh, Bror Oscar Anders. (b.10 February 1891–d.22 February 1956) 5,000 meters [4h2r1/2].

Möller, Carl Edvin. (b.13 February 1888–d.23 June 1920) Standing High Jump [=4]; Standing Long Jump [=5/2g4qr].

Möller, Gustav "Gösta." (b.15 June 1887–d.23 September 1983) 200 meters [3h10r1/3]; 400 meters [4h5r1/3].

Möller, Henning. (b.21 June 1885–d.7 February 1968) Discus Throw [37/9g5qr].

Möller, Ivan. (b.12 February 1884–d.31 July 1972) 100 meters [4h6r2/3]; 200 meters [4h4r2/3]; 4 × 100 meter relay [2].

Nilsson, Carl Johan "Calle." (b.18 May 1888–d.23 June 1915) Marathon [32].

Nilsson, E. Gunnar. (b.19 August 1889–d.8 March 1948) Discus Throw [23/5g3qr]; Discus Throw, both hands [10/3g2qr].

Nilsson, Einar. (b.8 June 1891–d.February 1937) Shot Put [7/3g1-2/qr]; Shot Put, both hands [5/2g1qr]; Discus Throw [10/4g1qr]; Discus Throw, both hands [4/3g1qr]; Decathlon [ac/dnf]; Pentathlon [14].

Nilsson, Magnus Teodard "Manne." (b.2 June 1888–d.18 November 1958) Pole Vault [=9g1qr].

Nilsson, Sven Otto. (b.26 June 1879–d.10 November 1960) Discus Throw [40/9g1qr]; Javelin Throw [10/5g1qr]; Javelin Throw, both hands [8/3g1qr].

Nordén, Gustaf. (b.23 October 1884–d.14 December 1947) Hop, step, and jump [10/5g2qr].

Nordström, Johan Henrik. (b.30 April 1891) 5,000 meters [dns-final]; Cross-Country, Individual [dnf-]; Cross-Country, Team [1/ns].

Öberg, Bror Albert. (b.24 August 1888) 10,000 meters [6h1r1/2].

Ohlsson, Hjalmar. (b.9 October 1891–d.27 February 1975) Hop, step, and jump [7/3g1qr].

Ohlsson, Patrik. (b.28 October 1889) Broad Jump [20/5g4qr]; Hop, step, and jump [15/6g3qr].

Ohrling, Arvid. (b.1 February 1877–d.11 April 1972) Javelin Throw [16/8g1qr]; Javelin Throw, both hands [10/5g1qr].

Olsson, Bror (later Bror Ryde). (b.20 May 1893) Javelin Throw [13/7g1qr].

Olsson, Carl Robert. (b.14 March 1883–d.21 July 1954) Hammer Throw [4/2g1qr].

Olsson, Thorild. (b.26 November 1886–d.20 March 1934) 5,000 meters [dns-final]; 3,000 Meter Team Race [2].

Person, Ture. (b.23 November 1892–d.14 November 1956) 100 meters [3h6r1/3]; 200 meters [5h1r2/3]; 4 × 100 meter relay [2].

Persson, Martin. (b.13 October 1886–d.13 February 1918) 5,000 meters [dnf-h2r1/2]; 10,000 meters [dns-final].

Rönström, Gunnar V. (b.25 January 1884–d.5 July 1941) Decathlon [ac/dnf].

Santesson, Carl Sander. (b.6 April 1887–d.22 May 1967) Pole Vault [=10g2qr].

Sjöberg, Richard Gustafsson. (b.20 September 1890–d.14 September 1960) High Jump [=7g2qr]; Pole Vault [=6g2qr].

Smedmark, Rudolf. (b.1 January 1886–d.29 April 1951) 100 meters [dnf-h3r2/3]; Standing High Jump [=5g2qr].

Sonne, Karl Hilding. (b.8 April 1890–d.20 April 1938) Javelin Throw [11/6g1qr]; Javelin Throw, both hands [14/6g1qr].

Stenborg, Knut. (b.25 March 1890) 200 meters [3h1r1/3]; 400 meters [4h3r2/3]; 4 × 400 meter relay [2h3r1/2].

Sundkvist, Johan. (b.22 June 1889) Cross-Country, Individual [10]; Cross-Country, Team [1/ns].

Svensson, Hugo. (b.6 January 1891–d.23 April 1960) Pole Vault [=10g2qr].

Ternström, Josef Irving. (b.4 December 1888–d.2 May 1953) Cross-Country, Individual [5]; Cross-Country, Team [1].

Törnros, Gustaf. (b.18 March 1887–d.2 April 1941) Marathon [dnf-].

Uggla, Bertil Gustafsson. (b.19 August 1890–d.29 September 1945) Pole Vault [=3].

af Uhr, Paulus. (b.25 January 1892–d.28 April 1972) High Jump [=7g1qr].

Westberg, Jacob. (b.15 December 1885) Marathon [22].

Wide, Ernst. (b.9 November 1888–d.8 April 1950) 1,500 meters [5]; 3,000 Meter Team Race [2].

Wieslander, Karl Hugo. (b.11 June 1889–d.24 May 1976) Decathlon [2]; Pentathlon [7].

Zander, John Adolf Fredrik. (b.31 January 1890–d.9 June 1967) 1,500 meters [7]; 3,000 Meter Team Race [2-ns].

Zerling, Paul G. (b.7 April 1890–d.17 May 1972) 400 meters [ach5r2/3]; 4 × 400 meter relay [2h3r1/2].

Cycling (Total: 12; Men: 12; Women: 0)

Björk, Ernst Gunnar. (b.21 January 1891) Road Race, Individual [51]; Road Race, Team [1/ns].

Ekström, Alexis. (b.4 October 1883–d.25 February 1958) Road Race, Individual [12]; Road Race, Team [1/ns].

Friborg, Erik. (b.24 January 1893–d.22 May 1968) Road Race, Individual [7]; Road Race, Team [1].

Karlsson, Werner. (b.8 July 1887) Road Race, Individual [19]; Road Race, Team [1/ns].

Landsberg, Karl Josef. (b.13 May 1890–d.4 August 1964) Road Race, Individual [ac/dnf]; Road Race, Team [1/ns/dnf].

Levin, John Gustafsson Hjalmar. (b.14 June 1884) Road Race, Individual [ac/dnf]; Road Race, Team [1/ns/dnf].

Lönn, Karl Algot. (b.18 December 1887–d.3 April 1953) Road Race, Individual [10]; Road Race, Team [1].

individual [ac/dnf]; Road Race, Team [1/ns/dnf].

Malm, Karl Oscar Ragnar. (b.14 May 1893–d.1 March 1959) Road Race, Individual [8]; Road Race, Team [1].

Morén, Henrik Hjalmar Simon. (b.5 January 1877–d.31 January 1956) Road Race, Individual [15]; Road Race, Team [1/ns].

Persson, Axel Wilhelm. (b.23 January 1888–d.2 September 1955) Road Race, Individual [9]; Road Race, Team [1].

Pettersson, Johan Arvid Josef. (b.31 March 1893) Road Race, Individual [ac/dnf]; Road Race, Team [1/ns/dnf].

Diving (Total: 34; Men: 22; Women: 12)

Women

Adlerz, Märta Elvira. (b.3 April 1897) Plain High Diving [8h1r1/2].

Andersson, Elsa Helena. (b.19 August 1894) Plain High Diving [6].

Andersson, Selma Augusta Maria. (b.21 October 1894) Plain High Diving [7].

Edström, Ester Märta. (b.5 September 1891) Plain High Diving [5h2r1/2].

Eklund, Ella Dorotea. (b.6 February 1894) Plain High Diving [5].

Johansson, Anna Theresia Margareta "Greta." (b.9 January 1895–d.28 January 1978) Plain
    High Diving [1]. (See also Swimming.)

Johansson, Gerda Matilda Eleonora. (b.14 March 1891) Plain High Diving [3h2r1/2].

Larsson, Alma Viktoria "Tora." (b.12 March 1891) Plain High Diving [8].

Nilsson, Dagmar. (b.29 January 1894) Plain High Diving [4h2r1/2].

Regnell, Elsa Albertina. (b.29 May 1889) Plain High Diving [4].

Regnell, Lisa Teresia. (b.3 February 1887–d.5 November 1979) Plain High Diving [2].

Thulin, Wilhelmina Elvira "Willy." (b.26 October 1889) Plain High Diving [7h1r1/2].

Men

Adlerz, William Eric. (b.23 July 1892–d.8 September 1975) Plain and Fancy High Diving [1];
    Plain High Diving [1].

Andersson, Robert Theodor. (b.18 October 1886–d.2 March 1972) Plain and Fancy High Div-
    ing [4h3r1/2]. (See also Swimming and Water Polo.)

Appelqvist, Ernst Oscar Ernfred. (b.15 June 1888) Springboard Diving [5h3r1/2].

Arbin, Harald (né Andersson). (b.4 August 1867–d.31 July 1944) Plain and Fancy High Div-
    ing [6].

Blomgren, Gustaf. (b.24 December 1887–d.1956) Plain and Fancy High Diving [3].

Brandsten, Ernst Magnus. (b.13 June 1883–d.15 May 1965) Springboard Diving [4h1r1/2];
    Plain and Fancy High Diving [5h1r1/2]; Plain High Diving [7].

Brodd, Eskil Augustus. (b.28 August 1885–d.22 October 1969) Springboard Diving [6h1r1/2].

Carlsson, Alvin. (b.25 September 1891) Plain and Fancy High Diving [7].

Crondahl, Viktor Gustaf. (b.5 April 1887) Plain High Diving [4].

Eklund, Ernst Rudolf. (b.24 July 1894) Springboard Diving [3h2r1/2]; Plain and Fancy High
    Diving [4h2r1/2].

Ekstrand, Gunnar. (b.19 January 1892–d.15 June 1966) Plain High Diving [4h2r1/2].

Eriksson, Torsten Julius. (b.20 February 1891) Plain High Diving [2h1r1/2].

Holmer, Sven Elis. (b.1 December 1893) Plain High Diving [6h1r1/2].

Jansson, Karl Johan Erik. (b.18 July 1892–d.10 October 1943) Springboard Diving [3]; Plain
    and Fancy High Diving [7h1r1/2]; Plain High Diving [3].

Johansson, Alfred John Emannuel. (b.8 May 1876–d.28 March 1941) Plain High Diving
    [4h1r1/2].

Johansson, Carl Hjalmar August. (b.20 January 1874–d.30 September 1957) Plain and Fancy
    High Diving [4]; Plain High Diving [2].

Montan, Sven Magnus. (b.22 July 1887) Plain High Diving [7h4r1/2].

Nylund, Sven Tore. (b.5 October 1894) Springboard Diving [5h1r1/2].

Runström, Axel Vilhelm. (b.15 October 1883–d.10 August 1943) Springboard Diving [6h3r1/2];
    Plain High Diving [6].

Sjöberg, Gösta Gabriel. (b.6 March 1896) Plain and Fancy High Diving [4h1r1/2].

Stefenson, Jens Harald. (b.1 February 1895–d.1 March 1986) Plain and Fancy High Diving
    [5h3r1/2]; Plain High Diving [9h3r1/2].

Tjäder, Erik. (b.18 May 1863–d.9 April 1949) Springboard Diving [7h3r1/2].

Equestrian Events (Total: 17; Men: 17; Women: 0)

Adlercreutz, Nils August Domingo. (b.8 July 1866–d.27 September 1955) Jumping, Individual [=6] (Ilex); Three-Day Event, Individual [4] (Atout); Three-Day Event, Team [1] (Atout).

von Blixen-Finecke, Hans Gustaf, Sr. (b.25 July 1886–d.26 September 1917) Dressage, Individual [3] (Maggie).

Boltenstern, Gustaf Adolf, Sr. (b.1 April 1861–d.9 October 1935) Dressage, Individual [2] (Neptun).

Bonde, Carl Gustaf. (b.28 April 1872–d.13 June 1957) Dressage, Individual [1] (Emperor).

Casparsson, Ernst Gustaf. (b.15 November 1886–d.7 September 1973) Jumping, Individual [=6] (Kiriki); Three-Day Event, Individual [=5] (Irmelin); Three-Day Event, Team [1] (Irmelin).

Hök, Åke Karl Wilhelm. (b.17 June 1889–d.2 May 1963) Jumping, Individual [=22] (Mona).

Horn af Åminne, Henric Arvid Bengt Christer. (b.12 March 1880–d.6 December 1947) Three-Day Event, Individual [10]; Three-Day Event, Team [1] (Omen).

Kilman, Gustaf Olof Falhem. (b.9 July 1882–d.21 February 1946) Jumping, Team [1] (Gatan).

Kruckenberg, Carl Wilhelm. (b.27 October 1881–d.7 November 1940) Dressage, Individual [8] (Kartusch).

Lewenhaupt, Carl Gustaf Sixtensson. (b.20 August 1879–d.7 August 1962) Jumping, Individual [=9]; Jumping, Team [1] (Medusa). (See also Modern Pentathlon.)

Lewenhaupt, Charles Auguste Sixtensson. (b.25 February 1881–d.23 April 1936) Jumping, Individual [=9] (Arno).

Nordlander, Axel. (b.21 September 1879–d.30 April 1962) Three-Day Event, Individual [1]; Three-Day Event, Team [1] (Lady Artist).

von Rosen, Hans Robert. (b.8 August 1888–d.2 September 1952) Jumping, Team [1] (Lord Iron).

Rosenblad, Carl Axel Eberhart. (b.25 August 1886–d.24 January 1953) Dressage, Individual [5] (Miss Hastings).

Rosencrantz, Fredrik Jakob Tage Ulfstand. (b.26 October 1879–d.15 April 1957) Jumping, Team [1] (Drabant).

af Ström, Oscar Adolf Richard. (b.8 July 1867–d.13 March 1952) Dressage, Individual [6] (Irish Lass).

Torén, Carl-Axel Oscar. (b.8 March 1887–d.21 October 1961) Jumping, Individual [=13] (Falken).

Fencing (Total: 18; Men: 18; Women: 0)

Armgarth, Gustaf. (b.1 February 1879–d. March 1930) Foil, Individual (6p5r1/4); Sabre, Individual (4p1r1/4).

Böös, Gunnar Mac Erik. (b.30 May 1894–d.4 February 1987) Foil, Individual (6p16r1/4).

Branting, Georg. (b.21 September 1887–d.6 July 1965) Épée, Individual (=4p4r3/4); Épée, Team (4).

Carlberg, Gustaf Eric. (b.5 April 1880–d.14 August 1963). Épée, Team (4). (See also Modern Pentathlon and Shooting.)

Enell, Knut Hugo Adolf. (b.19 March 1887–d.9 November 1985) Épée, Individual (=5p2r1/4).

Grönhagen, Åke Edvard. (b.24 January 1885–d.25 December 1974) Épée, Individual (6p1r1/4). (See also Modern Pentathlon.)

Grönwall, Nils Ragnar Johannes. (b.15 May 1894) Foil, Individual (4p8r1/4).

Hjorth, Carl Hjalmar Reinhold. (b.15 July 1875–d.26 April 1949) Foil, Individual (4p6r2/4).

Jöhncke, Axel. (b.16 January 1878–d.29 September 1953) Foil, Individual (=4p4r2/4); Sabre, Team (=9).

Klerck, Carl-Gustaf. (b.28 December 1885–d.29 March 1976) Sabre, Individual (=4p5r1/4); Sabre, Team (=9).

Lindblom, Gustaf Thorbjörn. (b.19 August 1883–d.16 March 1976) Épée, Individual (=4p3r3/4); Épée, Team (4).

Lindholm, Gunnar Wilhelm Melcher. (b.28 December 1887) Sabre, Individual (4p16r1/4).

Nordenström, Sven Alvar Martin. (b.9 December 1888–d.2 May 1945) Sabre, Individual (5p7r2/4).

Personne, Carl Birger. (b.11 May 1888–d.4 October 1976) Foil, Individual (=6p7r1/4); Sabre, Individual (6p3r3/4); Sabre, Team (=9).

von Rosen, Pontus Robert Conrad. (b.21 November 1881–d.11 January 1951) Épée, Team (4).

Sörensen, Einar Folke. (b.26 July 1875–d.23 August 1941) Épée, Individual (5); Épée, Team (4).

Sparre, Per Louis. (b.3 August 1863–d.19 October 1964) Épée, Individual (=5p7r2/4); Épée, Team (4).

Werner, Helge. (b.23 October 1883–d.6 February 1953) Sabre, Individual (5p2r1/4); Sabre, Team (=9).

Football (Association Football [Soccer]) (Total: 14; Men: 14; Women: 0)

Ansén, Karl Anshelm. (b.26 July 1887–d.20 July 1959) [=9].

Bergström, Erik. (b.6 January 1886–d.30 January 1966) [=9].

Börjesson, Erik Oskar. (b.1 December 1888–d.18 July 1983) [=9].

Börjesson, Josef Alfred. (b.15 April 1891) [=9].

Dahlström, Erik. (b.26 June 1894–d.30 October 1953) [=9].

Ekroth, August Helge "Ekis." (b.26 February 1892–d.29 November 1950) [=9].

Frykman, Götrik Wilhelm Adolf. (b.1 December 1891–d.7 April 1944) [=9].

Gustafsson, Karl. (b.16 September 1888–d.20 February 1960) [=9].

Lewin, Jacob. (b.22 November 1880) [=9].

Myhrberg, Herman. (b.29 December 1889–d. August 1919) [=9].

Sandberg, Gustaf. (b.29 July 1888) [=9].

Svensson, Ivar Samuel. (b.7 November 1893–d.18 June 1934) [=9].

Törnquist, Konrad. (b.17 July 1888–d.12 July 1952) [=9].

Wicksell, Ragnar. (b.26 September 1892) [=9].

Gymnastics (Total: 24; Men: 24; Women: 0)

Bertilsson, Per Daniel. (b.4 December 1892–d.18 September 1972) Combined All-Around, Swedish System [1].

Carlberg, Carl Ehrenfried. (b.24 February 1889–d.22 January 1962) Combined All-Around, Swedish System [1].

Granfelt, Nils Daniel. (b.17 February 1887–d.21 July 1959) Combined All-Around, Swedish System [1].

Hartzell, Curt. (b.3 September 1891–d.17 January 1975) Combined All-Around, Swedish System [1].

Holmberg, Torsten Oswald Magnus. (b.17 July 1882–d.11 February 1969) Combined All-Around, Swedish System [1].

Hylander, Anders. (b.6 November 1883–d.10 February 1967) Combined All-Around, Swedish System [1].

Janse, Axel Johan. (b.18 March 1888–d.25 August 1973) Combined All-Around, Swedish System [1].

Kullberg, Anders Boo Georg. (b.23 May 1889–d.4 May 1962) Combined All-Around, Swedish System [1].

Landberg, Sven Axel Richard. (b.6 December 1888–d.11 April 1962) Combined All-Around, Swedish System [1].

Nilsson, Per Elis Albert. (b.4 January 1890–d.18 June 1964) Combined All-Around, Swedish System [1].

Norelius, Benkt Rudolf. (b.26 April 1886–d.30 November 1974) Combined All-Around, Swedish System [1].

Norling, Axel. (b.16 April 1884–d.7 May 1964) Combined All-Around, Swedish System [1].

Norling, Lars Daniel. (b.16 January 1888–d.28 August 1958) Combined All-Around, Swedish System [1].

Rosén, Sven Axel Ariga. (b.10 March 1887–d.22 June 1963) Combined All-Around, Swedish System [1].

Silfverskiöld, Nils Otto. (b.3 January 1888–d.8 August 1957) Combined All-Around, Swedish System [1].

Silfverstrand, Carl Johan. (b.9 October 1885–d.2 January 1975) Combined All-Around, Swedish System [1].

Sörenson, John Emil. (b.15 September 1889–d.25 October 1976) All-Around, Swedish System, Teams [1].

Stiernspetz, Yngve. (b.27 April 1887–d.4 April 1945) Combined All-Around, Swedish System [1].

Svensson, Carl-Erik. (b.20 February 1891) Combined All-Around, Swedish System [1].

Svensson (Sarland), Karl-Johan. (b.12 March 1887–d.20 January 1964) Combined All-Around, Swedish System [1].

Torell, Knut Emanuel. (b.1 May 1885–d.24 December 1966) Combined All-Around, Swedish System [1].

Wennerholm, Oscar Edward. (b.22 January 1890–d.13 March 1943) Combined All-Around, Swedish System [1].

Wersäll, Claës Axel. (b.26 June 1888–d.12 February 1951) Combined All-Around, Swedish System [1].

Wiman, David Leopold. (b.6 June 1884–d.6 October 1950) Combined All-Around, Swedish System [1].

Modern Pentathlon (Total: 12; Men: 12; Women: 0)

Åsbrink, Karl Gösta. (b.18 November 1881–d.19 April 1966) Individual [2].

Carlberg, Gustaf Eric. (b.5 April 1880–d.14 August 1963) Individual [ac/dnf]. (See also Fencing and Shooting.)

Grönhagen, Åke Edvard. (b.24 January 1885–d.25 December 1974) Individual [4]. (See also Fencing.)

Hæggström, Nils Ivarson. (b.4 October 1885–d.15 March 1974) Individual [12].

de Laval, Claude Patrik Gustaf. (b.14 October 1886–d.29 October 1974) Individual [14]. (See also Shooting.)

de Laval, Erik Patrik Honoré. (b.28 April 1888–d.9 November 1973) Individual [ac/dnf].

de Laval, Patrik Georg Fabian. (b.16 April 1883–d.10 March 1970) Individual [3]. (See also Shooting.)

Lewenhaupt, Carl Gustaf Sixtensson. (b.20 August 1879–d.7 August 1962) Individual [17]. (See also Equestrian Events.)

Lilliehöök, Gustaf Malcolm "Gösta." (b.25 May 1884–d.18 November 1974) Individual [1].

Mannström, Bror Karl Anton. (b.26 October 1884–d.19 July 1916) Individual [7].

Stranne, James Sidney Mathias. (b.8 February 1886–d.3 August 1957) Individual [6].

Wersäll, Erik Gustaf. (b.14 January 1887–d.24 March 1973) Individual [9].

512   *Appendix VI*

Rowing & Sculling (Total: 28; Men: 28; Women: 0)
Ahlberg, Gillis. (b.8 November 1892–d.6 November 1930) Coxed Eights [2h2r1/4].
Almqvist, Anders. (b.1885–d.30 November 1915) Coxed Eights [2h2r1/4].
Amundén, Einar. (b.1882) Coxed Eights [2h2r1/4].
Bergstedt, Ragnar. (b.1889) Coxed Eights [2h2r1/4].
Brandes, Wilhelm. (b.1879–d.4 February 1944) Coxed Fours, Inriggers [2h2r1/3].
Brunkman, Gustaf. (b.2 September 1888–d.26 November 1959) Coxed Eights [2h1r2/4].
Broberg, Gustaf. (b.18 October 1885) Coxed Eights [2h2r1/4].
Bruhn-Möller, William. (b.11 February 1887–d.13 August 1964) Coxed Fours, Inriggers [2];
    Coxed Eights [2h1r2/4].
Brunkman, Conrad. (b.20 January 1887–d.27 May 1925) Coxed Fours, Inriggers [2]; Coxed
    Eights [2h1r2/4].
Dahlbäck, Herman. (b.7 March 1891–d.20 July 1968) Coxed Fours, Inriggers [2]; Coxed Eights
    [2h1r2/4].
Ericsson, Simon. (b.1886) Coxed Eights [2h2r1/4].
Eriksson, Axel. (b.10 March 1884) Coxed Fours, Outriggers [2h6r1/4].
Gabrielsson, Axel. (b.20 September 1886–d.1 June 1975) Coxed Fours, Inriggers [2h2r1/3].
Gabrielsson, Charles. (b.7 October 1884–d.16 April 1976) Coxed Fours, Inriggers [2h2r1/3].
Johansson, Axel. (b.1885) Coxed Fours, Inriggers [2h2r1/3].
Johnson, Tage. (b.1878) Coxed Fours, Inriggers [2h2r1/3].
Lager, Gunnar. (b.3 September 1888–d.30 October 1960) Coxed Fours, Outriggers [2h6r1/4].
Lager, John. (b.1 March 1887–d.24 June 1954) Coxed Fours, Outriggers [2h6r1/4].
Mattson, Per. Coxed Eights [2h1r2/4].
Rosvall, Ture. (b.6 July 1891–d.10 October 1977) Coxed Fours, Inriggers [2]; Coxed Eights
    [2h1r2/4].
Rydberg, Ivar. (b.1885) Coxed Eights [2h2r1/4].
Sörvik, Leif. (b.28 August 1889–d.23 October 1963) Coxed Eights [2h2r1/4].
Sundholm, Karl. (b.20 March 1885–d.11 March 1955) Coxed Fours, Outriggers [2h6r1/4].
Svendel, Arvid. (b.13 January 1888–d.23 August 1962) Coxed Eights [2h2r1/4].
Tamm, Sebastian. (b.1 December 1889–d.26 September 1962) Coxed Eights [2h1r2/4].
Wachtmeister, Schering "Ted." (b.14 July 1892–d.18 December 1975) Coxed Eights [2h1r2/4].
Wetterstrand, Ernst. (b.9 October 1887–d.21 August 1971) Coxed Fours, Outriggers [2h6r1/4].
Wilkens, Wilhelm "Willie." (b.1893–d. January 1967) Coxed Fours, Inriggers [2]; Coxed Eights
    [2h1r2/4].

Shooting (Total: 62; Men: 62; Women: 0)
Arvidsson, Per-Olof. (b.18 December 1864–d.30 August 1947) Free Rifle, 300 meters, 3-Posi-
    tions [48]; Military Rifle, 300 meters, 3-Positions [18]; Running Deer, Single Shot, Indi-
    vidual [=26]; Running Deer, Double Shot, Individual [=4]; Running Deer, Single Shot,
    Teams [1].
Benedicks, Edward. (b.9 February 1879–d.24 August 1960) Running Deer, Single Shot, Indi-
    vidual [=26]; Running Deer, Double Shot, Individual [2]; Clay Trap Shooting, Individual
    [38].
Björkman, Carl. (b.31 December 1869–d.4 February 1960) Free Rifle, 300 meters, 3-Positions
    [34]; Free Rifle, 300 meters, 3-Positions, Teams [1]; Military Rifle, 200, 400, 500, and 600
    meters, Teams [3].
Björkman, Tönnes. (b.25 March 1888–d.21 November 1959) Free Rifle, 300 meters, 3-Posi-
    tions [8]; Military Rifle, 300 meters, 3-Positions [14]; Military Rifle, 600 meters, any posi-
    tion [25]; Military Rifle, 200, 400, 500, and 600 meters, Teams [3].

Blomqvist, Erik Gustaf. (b.5 January 1879–d.17 September 1956) Free Rifle, 300 meters, 3-Positions [10]; Free Rifle, 300 meters, 3-Positions, Teams [1].

Boivie, Gustaf Carl Fredrik. (b.27 November 1864–d.12 January 1951) Free Pistol, 50 meters [42]; Dueling Pistol, 30 meters [11]; Small-Bore Rifle, 25 meters, Disappearing Target [15]; Small-Bore Rifle, 25 meters, Disappearing Target, Teams [1].

Bökman, Otto. (b.3 May 1874–d.22 November 1938) Clay Trap Shooting, Individual [=56].

Boström, Erik. (b.23 August 1869–d.1930) Free Pistol, 50 meters [5]; Dueling Pistol, 30 meters [17]; Military Pistol, 50 meters, Teams [2]; Small-Bore Rifle, prone position, 50 meters [8].

Carlberg, Gustaf Eric. (b.5 April 1880–d.14 August 1963) Free Pistol, 50 meters [12]; Dueling Pistol, 30 meters [6]; Dueling Pistol, 30 meters, Teams [1]; Military Pistol, 50 meters, Teams [2]; Small-Bore Rifle, 25 meters, Disappearing Target [20]; Small-Bore Rifle, prone position, 50 meters [17]; Small-Bore Rifle, 25 meters, Disappearing Target, Teams [1]; Small-Bore Rifle, 50 meters, Teams [2]. (See also Fencing and Modern Pentathlon.)

Carlberg, Gustaf Wilhelm. (b.5 April 1880–d.1 October 1970) Free Pistol, 50 meters [16]; Dueling Pistol, 30 meters [15]; Dueling Pistol, 30 meters, Teams [1]; Military Pistol, 50 meters, Teams [2]; Small-Bore Rifle, prone position, 50 meters [21]; Small-Bore Rifle, 25 meters, Disappearing Target [1]; Small-Bore Rifle, 25 meters, Disappearing Target, Teams [1]; Small-Bore Rifle, 50 meters, Teams [2].

Cederschiöld, Hugo Montgomery. (b.25 September 1878–d.17 March 1968) Free Pistol, 50 meters [51]; Dueling Pistol, 30 meters [37].

Cederström, Adolf Fredrik Ture. (b.25 October 1886–d.7 September 1982) Running Deer, Single Shot, Individual [=8].

Dybäck, C. Wilhelm. (b.11 May 1877–d.22 September 1933) Running Deer, Double Shot, Individual [14].

Ekman, Johann Olof. (b.10 October 1854) Running Deer, Single Shot, Individual [=11]; Running Deer, Double Shot, Individual [=12]; Clay Trap Shooting, Individual [40]; Clay Trap Shooting, Teams [4].

Ericsson, Gideon Levi. (b.2 March 1871–d.27 January 1936) Free Pistol, 50 meters [37]; Small-Bore Rifle, prone position, 50 meters [39]; Small-Bore Rifle, 25 meters, Disappearing Target [3].

Eriksson, Herman A. (b.8 May 1872) Clay Trap Shooting, Individual [=41].

Eriksson, Mauritz. (b.18 December 1888–d.14 February 1947) Free Rifle, 300 meters, 3-Positions [14]; Military Rifle, 600 meters, any position [38]; Free Rifle, 300 meters, 3-Positions, Teams [1]; Military Rifle, 200, 400, 500, and 600 meters, Teams [3].

Flodström, Carl E. (b.12 August 1863–d.27 January 1953) Military Rifle, 300 meters, 3-Positions [8].

Frisell, Erik Hjalmar. (b.27 August 1880–d.27 May 1967) Running Deer, Double Shot, Individual [=12]; Clay Trap Shooting, Individual [=29]; Clay Trap Shooting, Teams [4].

Gustafsson, Erik. (b.10 April 1884) Military Rifle, 600 meters, any position [15].

Gyllenkrok, Axel Walfrid Carl. (b.9 August 1888–d.8 August 1946) Dueling Pistol, 30 meters [30]; Small-Bore Rifle, 25 meters, Disappearing Target [6].

Hoflund, J. Arvid. (b.12 June 1883–d.15 September 1952) Military Rifle, 300 meters, 3-Positions [64].

Hübner von Holst, Johan. (b.22 August 1881–d.13 June 1945) Dueling Pistol, 30 meters [3]; Dueling Pistol, 30 meters, Teams [1]; Small-Bore Rifle, 25 meters, Disappearing Target [2]; Small-Bore Rifle, prone position, 50 meters [9]; Small-Bore Rifle, 25 meters, Disappearing Target, Teams [1].

Jernström, Verner. (b.5 January 1883–d.29 April 1930) Free Rifle, 300 meters, 3-Positions

[20]; Military Rifle, 300 meters, 3-Positions [53]; Military Rifle, 600 meters, any position [6]; Military Rifle, 200, 400, 500, and 600 meters, Teams [3].

Johansson, Carl Hugo. (b.16 June 1887–d.23 February 1977) Free Rifle, 300 meters, 3-Positions [4]; Military Rifle, 600 meters, any position [23]; Free Rifle, 300 meters, 3-Positions, Teams [1]; Military Rifle, 200, 400, 500, and 600 meters, Teams [3].

Johansson, Ernst Alfred. (b.11 March 1876) Small-Bore Rifle, prone position, 50 meters [20].

Jonsson, Gustaf Adolf. (b.26 June 1879–d.30 April 1949) Free Rifle, 300 meters, 3-Positions [11]; Military Rifle, 300 meters, 3-Positions [16]; Free Rifle, 300 meters, 3-Positions, Teams [1].

Jonsson, Sven Robert. (b.6 December 1886–d.20 May 1921) Free Rifle, 300 meters, 3-Positions [37]; Military Rifle, 300 meters, 3-Positions [19]; Military Rifle, 600 meters, any position [36]; Small-Bore Rifle, 25 meters, Disappearing Target [35].

Klein, Nils F. H. (b.14 July 1878) Clay Trap Shooting, Individual [60].

Lagerlöf, John Leonard. (b.8 April 1870–d.30 November 1951) Military Rifle, 600 meters, any position [29].

Larsson, Bernhard. (b.14 August 1879–d.1 August 1947) Free Rifle, 300 meters, 3-Positions [6]; Free Rifle, 300 meters, 3-Positions, Teams [1]; Military Rifle, 200, 400, 500, and 600 meters, Teams [3].

Larsson, Karl. (b.8 July 1865) Running Deer, Single Shot, Individual [=4].

de Laval, Claude Patrik Gustaf. (b.14 October 1886–d.29 October 1974) Dueling Pistol, 30 meters [13]. (See also Modern Pentathlon.)

de Laval, Patrik Georg Fabian. (b.16 April 1883–d.10 March 1970) Dueling Pistol, 30 meters [7]; Free Pistol, 50 meters [4]; Military Pistol, 50 meters, Teams [2]. (See also Modern Pentathlon.)

Lindewald, Emil W. (b.14 September 1858) Running Deer, Single Shot, Individual [25]; Running Deer, Double Shot, Individual [8].

Lindskog, Sven August. (b.16 January 1875) Running Deer, Single Shot, Individual [=4]; Running Deer, Double Shot, Individual [6].

Löfman, Robert Wilhelm. (b.22 July 1875–d.8 January 1940) Free Pistol, 50 meters [29]; Small-Bore Rifle, prone position, 50 meters [22]; Small-Bore Rifle, 25 meters, Disappearing Target [10].

Lundeberg, Åke. (b.14 December 1888–d.29 May 1939) Running Deer, Single Shot, Individual [2]; Running Deer, Double Shot, Individual [1]; Running Deer, Single Shot, Teams [1]; Clay Trap Shooting, Individual [=17]; Clay Trap Shooting, Teams [4].

Lyman, Gustaf. (b.25 August 1880–d.14 August 1969) Running Deer, Single Shot, Individual [=15]; Running Deer, Double Shot, Individual [9].

Nordenswan, Arthur Georg. (b.27 January 1883–d.29 December 1970) Small-Bore Rifle, prone position, 50 meters [16]; Small-Bore Rifle, 25 meters, Disappearing Target [28]; Small-Bore Rifle, 50 meters, Teams [2].

Nyberg, C. E. Herman. (b.11 July 1863–d.12 February 1947) Clay Trap Shooting, Individual [=45].

Nyström, Jonas Fredrik. (b.17 July 1880–d.13 February 1967) Free Pistol, 50 meters [25]; Small-Bore Rifle, prone position, 50 meters [15].

Nyström, Torsten E. (b.11 July 1878–d.13 September 1953) Military Rifle, 300 meters, 3-Positions [40]; Military Rifle, 600 meters, any position [66].

Odelberg, Erik Albrekt. (b.13 March 1889–d.26 October 1938) Small-Bore Rifle, prone position, 50 meters [28]; Small-Bore Rifle, 25 meters, Disappearing Target [11].

Ohlsson, Erik. (b.20 November 1884–d.19 September 1980) Military Rifle, 300 meters, 3-Positions [21]; Military Rifle, 600 meters, any position [28].

Örtegren, Ruben. (b.13 October 1881–d.27 February 1965) Military Rifle, 600 meters, any position [49]; Small-Bore Rifle, prone position, 50 meters [19]; Small-Bore Rifle, 50 meters, Teams [2].

Palén, A. G. Paul. (b.4 April 1881–d.12 October 1944) Free Pistol, 50 meters [36]; Dueling Pistol, 30 meters [2]; Dueling Pistol, 30 meters, Teams [1].

Romander, Nils. (b.3 July 1893–d.1 October 1978) Military Rifle, 300 meters, 3-Positions [5].

Schartau, Frans-Albert Vaksal. (b.13 July 1877–d.6 June 1943) Dueling Pistol, 30 meters [18].

Skog, Nils J:son. (b.16 December 1877–d.28 April 1964) Free Rifle, 300 meters, 3-Positions [43].

Sökjer-Petersén, Erik. (b.4 December 1887–d.17 April 1967) Running Deer, Single Shot, Individual [=11]; Running Deer, Double Shot, Individual [7].

Stiernspetz, Gustaf Erik. (b.20 October 1889–d.25 March 1956) Free Pistol, 50 meters [48].

Stridfeldt, Per August. (b.7 March 1872–d.11 December 1942) Military Rifle, 300 meters, 3-Positions [20].

Sund, Carl-Johan. (b.6 December 1869–d.11 June 1956) Military Rifle, 600 meters, any position [24].

Swahn, Alfred Gomer Albert. (b.20 August 1879–d.16 March 1931) Running Deer, Single Shot, Individual [1]; Running Deer, Double Shot, Individual [=4]; Running Deer, Single Shot, Teams [1]; Clay Trap Shooting, Individual [=21]; Clay Trap Shooting, Teams [4].

Swahn, Oscar Gomer. (b.20 October 1847–d.1 May 1927) Running Deer, Single Shot, Individual [=4]; Running Deer, Double Shot, Individual [3]; Running Deer, Single Shot, Teams [1]; Clay Trap Shooting, Individual [=56].

Törnmarck, Curt Ivan. (b.25 January 1885–d.17 April 1963) Free Pistol, 50 meters [11]; Dueling Pistol, 30 meters [5].

Wahlstedt, Axel Johan Gabriel. (b.11 January 1867–d.15 December 1943) Small-Bore Rifle, prone position, 50 meters [11]; Small-Bore Rifle, 25 meters, Disappearing Target [25].

Wallenberg, Victor. (b.13 November 1875–d.3 November 1970) Clay Trap Shooting, Individual [34]; Clay Trap Shooting, Teams [4].

Wallenborg, Carl. (b.12 May 1875–d.16 January 1962) Military Rifle, 300 meters, 3-Positions [83]; Military Rifle, 600 meters, any position [11].

Wikström, O. August. (b.25 November 1874–d.16 August 1954) Free Rifle, 300 meters, 3-Positions [42].

Wollert, Carl. (b.11 March 1877–d.4 April 1953) Clay Trap Shooting, Individual [=56]; Clay Trap Shooting, Teams [4].

Swimming (Total: 24; Men: 18; Women: 6)

Women

Björklund, Elsa Margareta. (b.14 January 1895) 100 meter freestyle [6h3r1/3].

Carlsson, Greta Ingeborg. (b.7 July 1898) 100 meter freestyle [5h4r1/3]; 4 × 100 meter freestyle relay [4].

Johansson, Anna Theresia Margareta "Greta." (b.9 January 1895–d.28 January 1978) 100 meter freestyle [4h1r1/3]; 4 × 100 meter freestyle relay [4]. (See also Diving.)

Jonsson, Sonja Sofia Valfrida. (b.7 August 1895) 100 meter freestyle [6h2r1/3]; 4 × 100 meter freestyle relay [4].

Lundgren, Karin. (b.4 January 1895–d.16 September 1977) 100 meter freestyle [5h2r1/3].

Thulin, Vera Julia. (b.7 June 1893) 100 meter freestyle [3h5r1/3]; 4 × 100 meter freestyle relay [4].

Men

Andersson, Eric Cletus Thule. (b.14 March 1893–d.12 July 1971) 100 meter freestyle [4h4r1/4].

Andersson, Nils Gustaf. (b.24 October 1889) 200 meter breaststroke [3h2r1/3]; 400 meter breaststroke [3h2r1/3].

Andersson, Robert Theodor. (b.18 October 1886–d.2 March 1972) 100 meter freestyle [4h1r2/4]. (See also Diving and Water Polo.)

Andersson, Wilhelm. (b.11 March 1891–d.21 September 1933) 1,500 meter freestyle [4h1r2/3]. (See also Water Polo.)

Bergman, Åke Herman Gottfrid. (b.26 April 1896) 100 meter backstroke [3h1r1/3].

Bergqvist, Erik Gustaf. (b.20 June 1891–d.17 February 1954) 100 meter freestyle [dns-r2/4]. (See also Water Polo.)

Collin, Karl Gustaf Adolf. (b.23 May 1890–d.25 October 1966) 1,500 meter freestyle [4h5r1/3].

Haglund, Nils-Erik. (b.19 June 1893–d.19 March 1921) 400 meter freestyle [4h1r1/3].

Hamrén, Oscar Bror Emanuel. (b.19 September 1891) 200 meter breaststroke [6h6r1/3].

Hanson, Pontus. (b.24 May 1884–d.4 December 1962) 200 meter breaststroke [dnf-h2r2/3]. (See also Water Polo.)

Hanson, Sven. (b.22 February 1892–d.22 June 1972) 200 meter breaststroke [5h6r1/3].

Henning, Thor Bernhard. (b.13 September 1894–d.7 October 1967) 200 meter breaststroke [dnf-]; 400 meter breaststroke [2].

Julin, Harald Alexander Sigfrid. (b.27 March 1890–d.31 July 1967) 100 meter freestyle [dns-r2/4]; 200 meter breaststroke [3h1r2/3]. (See also Water Polo.)

Löwenadler, Fredrik Wilhelm. (b.12 September 1895) 200 meter breaststroke [3h4r1/3].

Lundevall, Knut Hugo Valfrid. (b.7 December 1892–d.16 January 1949) 100 meter backstroke [3h2r1/3].

Sundman, Gunnar Isidor. (b.15 April 1893) 100 meter backstroke [5h2r2/3].

Theander, Bror David. (b.19 March 1892–d.18 July 1985) 400 meter freestyle [dnf-h3r1/3].

Wedholm, Johan Eskil. (b.2 March 1891) 400 meter freestyle [3h2r1/3]; 1,500 meter freestyle [3h4r1/3].

Tennis (Total: 16; Men: 10; Women: 6)

Women

Arnheim Lasch, Edith. (b.21 February 1884–d.16 October 1964) Ladies' Singles (Lawn) [4]; Ladies' Singles (Covered Court) [=5]; Mixed Doubles (Lawn) [=5]; Mixed Doubles (Covered Court) [=7].

Brusewitz, Ellen. (b.10 November 1878–d.17 May 1952) Ladies' Singles (Lawn) [=8].

Cederschiöld, Margareta. (b.31 December 1879–d.29 July 1963) Ladies' Singles (Lawn) [=5]; Ladies' Singles (Covered Court) [8]; Mixed Doubles (Covered Court) [4].

Fick, Sigrid. (b.28 March 1887–d.4 June 1979) Ladies' Singles (Lawn) [=8]; Ladies' Singles (Covered Court) [4]; Mixed Doubles (Lawn) [2]; Mixed Doubles (Covered Court) [3].

Hay, Ebba. (b.11 December 1866–d.26 May 1954) Mixed Doubles (Covered Court) [=7].

Holmström, Annie. (b.22 February 1880–d.26 October 1953) Ladies' Singles (Lawn) [=5]; Ladies' Singles (Covered Court) [=5]; Mixed Doubles (Lawn) [4].

Men

Benckert, Curt Ragnar. (b.8 August 1887–d.28 November 1950) Men's Singles (Lawn) [=31]; Men's Doubles (Lawn) [=5]; Men's Doubles (Covered Court) [=5].

Boström, Wollmar Filip. (b.15 June 1878–d.7 November 1956) Men's Singles (Lawn) [=17]; Men's Singles (Covered Court) [=16]; Men's Doubles (Lawn) [=5]; Men's Doubles (Covered Court) [=5].

Grönfors, Thorsten G. M. H. (b.8 August 1888–d.28 May 1968) Men's Singles (Lawn) [=17]; Men's Singles (Covered Court) [=9]; Men's Doubles (Lawn) [=15]; Mixed Doubles (Lawn) [4]. (See also Yachting.)

Kempe, Johan Carl. (b.8 December 1884–d.8 July 1967) Men's Singles (Covered Court) [=9]; Men's Doubles (Covered Court) [2]; Mixed Doubles (Covered Court) [4].

Leffler, Hakon. (b.11 March 1887–d.31 July 1972) Men's Singles (Lawn) [=31]; Men's Singles (Covered Court) [=16].

Möller, Frans Julius. (b.19 May 1886–d.10 December 1954) Men's Singles (Lawn) [=17]; Men's Singles (Covered Court) [=16]; Men's Doubles (Lawn) [=15]; Mixed Doubles (Covered Court) [=7].

Nylén, Carl-Olof S. (b.30 June 1892–d.2 October 1978) Men's Doubles (Lawn) [=5]; Men's Doubles (Covered Court) [=7]; Mixed Doubles (Lawn) [=5]; Mixed Doubles (Covered Court) [=7].

Setterwall, Carl Gunnar Emanuel. (b.18 August 1881–d.26 February 1928) Men's Singles (Lawn) [=17]; Men's Singles (Covered Court) [=5]; Men's Doubles (Covered Court) [2]; Mixed Doubles (Lawn) [2]; Mixed Doubles (Covered Court) [3].

Silverstolpe, Lennart Mascoll. (b.27 June 1888–d.4 August 1969) Men's Singles (Covered Court) [=16].

Wennergren, Charles Sven Otto. (b.7 February 1889–d.3 January 1978) Men's Singles (Lawn) [=9]; Men's Singles (Covered Court) [=9]; Men's Doubles (Lawn) [=5]; Men's Doubles (Covered Court) [=7].

Tug-of-War (Total: 8; Men: 8; Women: 0)
Andersson, Arvid Leander. (b.9 July 1881–d.7 August 1956) [1].
Bergman, Adolf. (b.14 April 1879–d.14 May 1926) [1].
Edman, Johan Viktor. (b.29 March 1875–d.19 August 1927) [1].
Fredriksson, Erik Algot. (b.13 June 1885–d.14 May 1930) [1].
Gustafsson, Per August. (b.4 November 1875–d.31 October 1938) [1].
Jonsson, Carl. (b.16 July 1885–d.11 November 1966) [1].
Larsson, Erik Victor. (b.14 May 1888–d.23 August 1934) [1].
Lindström, Carl Herbert. (b.16 March 1886–d.26 November 1951) [1].

Water Polo (Total: 7; Men: 7; Women: 0)
Andersson, Robert Theodor. (b.18 October 1886–d.2 March 1972) [2]. (See also Diving and Swimming.)
Andersson, Wilhelm. (b.11 March 1891–d.21 September 1933) [2]. (See also Swimming.)
Bergqvist, Erik Gustaf. (b.20 June 1891–d.17 February 1954) [2]. (See also Swimming.)
Gumpel, Max. (b.23 April 1890–d.3 August 1965) [2].
Hanson, Pontus. (b.24 May 1884–d.4 December 1962) [2]. (See also Swimming.)
Julin, Harald Alexander Sigfrid. (b.27 March 1890–d.31 July 1967) [2]. (See also Swimming.)
Kumfeldt, Karl Torsten. (b.4 January 1886–d.2 May 1966) [2].

Wrestling (Total: 34; Men: 34; Women: 0)
Ahlgren, Anders Oscar. (b.12 February 1888–d.27 December 1976) 82_ kg. Class (Greco-Roman) [2].
Åkesson, Bruno Vincent. (b.22 January 1887) 60 kg. Class (Greco-Roman) [AC].
Andersson, Carl-Georg. (b.19 May 1885) 60 kg. Class (Greco-Roman) [AC].
Andersson, Johan Hilarius. (b.21 February 1889) 82½ kg. Class (Greco-Roman) [AC].

Andersson, Olof Mauritz. (b.22 September 1886–d.1 November 1997) 75 kg. Class (Greco-Roman) [AC].

Beckman, Arvid Magnus. (b.14 June 1889–d.10 September 1970) 60 kg. Class (Greco-Roman) [AC].

Bergqvist, Axel Theodor. (b.13 May 1885) 75 kg. Class (Greco-Roman) [AC].

Björklund, Hugo. 67½ kg. Class (Greco-Roman) [AC].

Dahlberg, Axel Theodor. (b.3 May 1884) 75 kg. Class (Greco-Roman) [AC].

Ekman, Carl Sanfrid. (b.1 January 1892) 82½ kg. Class (Greco-Roman) [AC].

Fältström, Carl Edvin Daniel. (b.30 December 1890–d.26 July 1965) 75 kg. Class (Greco-Roman) [AC].

Flygare, Bror Edvin. (b.29 November 1888) 67½ kg. Class (Greco-Roman) [AC].

Fogelmark, Ragnar. (b.15 March 1888–d.20 September 1914) 82½ kg. Class (Greco-Roman) [AC].

Frank, Axel Peter Rudolf. (b.17 December 1882) 75 kg. Class (Greco-Roman) [AC].

Johanson, Claes Edvin. (b.4 November 1884–d.9 March 1949) 75 kg. Class (Greco-Roman) [1].

Johansson, Fritz Rudolf. (b.27 May 1893) 75 kg. Class (Greco-Roman) [AC].

Johansson, Hugo Anders Sigfrid. (b.19 April 1888–d. May 1969) 60 kg. Class (Greco-Roman) [AC].

Jonsson, Martin. 67½ kg. Class (Greco-Roman) [AC].

Karlsson, David. (b.25 March 1881–d.17 December 1946) Unlimited Class (Greco-Roman) [AC].

Karlsson, Karl. 60 kg. Class (Greco-Roman) [AC].

Larsson, Harry. (b.12 December 1888) 60 kg. Class (Greco-Roman) [AC].

Lindstrand, Frans Gustaf. (b.11 February 1883–d. April 1961) Unlimited Class (Greco-Roman) [AC].

Lund, Carl Erik. (b.23 September 1884–d.1940) 67½ kg. Class (Greco-Roman) [AC].

Malmström, Gustaf Hjalmar. (b.4 July 1884–d.24 December 1970) 67½ kg. Class (Greco-Roman) [2].

Mathiasson, Edvin. (b.16 April 1890–d.15 March 1975) 67½ kg. Class (Greco-Roman) [3].

Melin, Victor. (b.18 April 1891) 75 kg. Class (Greco-Roman) [AC].

Nilsson, Ernst Hilding Waldemar. (b.10 May 1891–d. February 1937) 82½ kg. Class (Greco-Roman) [AC].

Nilsson, Johan Theodor. (b.2 December 1890) 67½ kg. Class (Greco-Roman) [AC].

Öberg, Erik. (b.9 March 1889–d.19 March 1924) 60 kg. Class (Greco-Roman) [AC].

Ohlsson, Sven. (b.25 February 1886–d.27 February 1961) 75 kg. Class (Greco-Roman) [AC].

Persson, Ewald Patrik Leopold. (b.3 September 1891) 60 kg. Class (Greco-Roman) [AC].

Rydström, Richard Rudolf. (b.11 April 1886) 67½ kg. Class (Greco-Roman) [AC].

Sandberg, Alrik. (b.3 April 1885) Unlimited Class (Greco-Roman) [AC].

Svensson, Gottfrid. (b.13 May 1889–d.19 August 1956) 67½ kg. Class (Greco-Roman) [AC].

Yachting (Total: 41; Men: 41; Women: 0)

Aust, Otto. (b.25 July 1892–d.12 October 1943) 6-meter class [3] (Kerstin).

Bergman, Per H. (b.15 May 1886–d.18 October 1950) 12-meter class [2] (Erna Signe).

Bergström, Dick. (b.15 February 1886–d.17 August 1952) 12-meter class [2] (Erna Signe).

Bergström, Kurt J. (b.23 July 1891–d.20 November 1955) 12-meter class [2] (Erna Signe).

Bothén, Bertil "Bo." (b.14 February 1892–d.31 March 1966) 10-meter class [4] (Marga).

Bothén, Björn. (b.26 April 1893–d.19 August 1955) 10-meter class [4] (Marga).

Clason, Hugo. (b.2 June 1865–d.21 January 1935) 12-meter class [2] (Erna Signe).

Ericsson, Filip. (b.25 May 1882–d.25 December 1951) 10-meter class [1] (Kitty).

Forsberg, Fred Wilhelm. (b.12 March 1862–d.25 December 1939) 10-meter class [4] (Marga).

Gripe, Ragnar. (b.9 September 1883–d.8 December 1942) 8-meter class [=5] (K.S.S.S. 1912).

Grönfors, Thorsten G. M. H. (b.8 August 1888–d.28 May 1968) 8-meter class [=5] (K.S.S.S. 1912). (See also Tennis [Lawn].)

Hagberg, Edvin. (b.31 July 1875–d.1 September 1947) 6-meter class [4] (Sass).

Hagström, Emil. (b.23 October 1883–d.19 March 1941) 8-meter class [=5] (K.S.S.S. 1912).

Hellström, Carl Ludvig. (b.10 December 1864–d.4 July 1962) 10-meter class [1] (Kitty).

Henriques, Emil. (b.19 December 1883–d.19 November 1957) 8-meter class [2] (Sans Atout).

Heyman, Bengt. (b.26 August 1883–d.3 June 1942) 8-meter class [2] (Sans Atout).

Isberg, Paul. (b.2 September 1882–d.5 March 1955) 10-meter class [1] (Kitty).

Jonsson, Ernst Jonas. (b.30 September 1873–d.14 March 1926) 6-meter class [4] (Sass).

Johnson, Folke. (b.15 June 1887–d.20 February 1960) 12-meter class [2] (Erna Signe).

Kander, Sigurd. (b.29 January 1890–d.30 April 1980) 12-meter class [2] (Erna Signe).

Lamby, Nils Iwan. (b.29 October 1885–d.15 January 1970) 12-meter class [2] (Erna Signe).

Lindén, Erland. (b.28 July 1880–d.16 September 1952) 10-meter class [4] (Marga).

Lindqvist, Erik J. (b.20 May 1886–d.17 September 1934) 12-meter class [2] (Erna Signe).

Lundén, Humbert. (b.7 January 1882–d.5 February 1961) 10-meter class [1] (Kitty).

Månsson, Gunnar. (b.1 March 1885) 8-meter class [=5] (K.S.S.S. 1912).

Mark, Knut Olof. (b.13 January 1873–d.15 May 1920) 6-meter class [4] (Sass).

Nyberg, Herman. (b.22 February 1880–d.6 July 1968) 10-meter class [1] (Kitty).

Perslow, Karl Arvid. (b.16 September 1880–d.1930) 10-meter class [4] (Marga).

Persson, Nils. (b.11 February 1879–d.4 February 1941) 12-meter class [2] (Erna Signe).

Rosenswärd, Harry. (b.20 April 1882–d.6 July 1955) 10-meter class [1] (Kitty).

Sällström, Richard. (b.15 December 1870–d.19 February 1951) 12-meter class [2] (Erna Signe).

Sandberg, Eric. (b.19 December 1884–d.8 December 1966) 6-meter class [3] (Kerstin).

Sandberg, Harald. (b.22 October 1883–d.28 November 1940) 6-meter class [3] (Kerstin).

Sjöqvist, Fritz H. (b.18 November 1884–d.26 April 1962) 8-meter class [=5] (K.S.S.S. 1912).

Sjöqvist, Johan Arvid. (b.18 November 1884–d.22 March 1960) 8-meter class [=5] (K.S.S.S. 1912).

Thiel, Alvar. (b.23 February 1893–d.1 October 1973) 8-meter class [2] (Sans Atout).

Waller, Erik. (b.24 March 1887–d.25 September 1958) 10-meter class [4] (Marga).

Wallerius, Erik. (b.16 April 1878–d.7 May 1967) 10-meter class [1] (Kitty).

Wallerius, Harald. (b.7 January 1882) 10-meter class [1] (Kitty).

Westermark, Nils. (b.9 September 1892–d.24 January 1980) 8-meter class [2] (Sans Atout).

Westmark, Herbert. (b.30 August 1891) 8-meter class [2] (Sans Atout).

Switzerland (Total: 1; Men: 1; Women: 0)

Athletics (Track & Field) (Total: 1; Men: 1; Women: 0)
Wagner, Julius. (b.10 October 1882–d.2 March 1952) Pentathlon [20].

Turkey (Total: 2; Men: 2; Women: 0)

Athletics (Track & Field) (Total: 2; Men: 2; Women: 0)
Mıgıryan, Mıgır[49]. (b.12 September 1892) Shot Put [19/7g3qr]; Shot Put, both hands [4/4g2qr]; Discus Throw [34/7g3qr]; Decathlon [ac/dnf]; Pentathlon [23].
Papazyan, Vahran Hepet. (b.12 September 1892) 1,500 meters [dnf-h7r1/3].

United States (Total: 174; Men: 174; Women: 0)

Athletics (Track & Field) (Total: 109; Men: 109; Women: 0)

Adams, Benjamin W. (b.31 March 1890–d.15 March 1961) Standing High Jump [2]; Standing Long Jump [3].

Adams, Platt. (b.23 March 1885–d.27 February 1961) High Jump [=7g1/qr]; Standing High Jump [1]; Standing Long Jump [2]; Hop, step, and jump [5/2g1qr].

Allen, Frederick Harold. (b.6 December 1890–d.16 January 1969) Broad Jump [6/3g1qr].

Anderson, Lewis Robbins. (b.15 March 1889–d.4 May 1958) 1,500 meters [4h4r1/3].

Babcock, Harold Stoddard. (b.15 December 1890–d.5 June 1965) Pole Vault [1]; Decathlon [ac/dnf].

Bellah, Samuel Harrison. (b.24 June 1887–d.January 1963) Pole Vault [7].

Belote, Frank V. (b.8 October 1883) 100 meters [5]; 4 × 100 meter relay [dqh1r2/3]; Standing High Jump [=5g2qr].

Berna, Tell Schirnding. (b.24 July 1891–d.5 April 1975) 5,000 meters [5]; Cross-Country, Individual [dnf-]; Cross-Country, Team [dnf-/ns]; 3,000 Meter Team Race [1].

Blanchard, Vaughn Seavy. (b.11 July 1889–d.26 November 1969) 110 meter hurdles [3h3r2/3].

Bonhag, George V. (b.31 January 1882–d.30 October 1960) 5,000 meters [4]; Cross-Country, Individual [dnf-]; Cross-Country, Team [dnf-]; 3,000 Meter Team Race [1].

Brickley, Charles Edward. (b.24 November 1891–d.28 December 1949) Hop, step, and jump [9/2g3qr].

Brundage, Avery. (b.28 September 1887–d.8 May 1975) Discus Throw [22/8g1qr]; Decathlon [ac/dnf]; Pentathlon [6].

Burdick, Jervis Watson. (b.8 March 1889–d.11 November 1962) High Jump [6g2qr].

Byrd, Richard Leslie. (b.16 May 1892–d.June 1953) Standing High Jump [=4]; Standing Long Jump [8/3g3qr]; Discus Throw [2]; Discus Throw, both hands [17/5g3qr].

Caldwell, David Story. (b.20 November 1890–d.6 January 1953) 800 meters [4].

Case, John Ruggles. (b.31 March 1889–d.20 January 1975) 110 meter hurdles [4].

Childs, Clarence Chester. (b.24 July 1884–d.16 September 1960) Hammer Throw [3].

Chisholm, George Alpin. (b.2 December 1887) 110 meter hurdles [2h4r2/3].

Cooke, Carl Clement. (b.25 August 1889–d.28 July 1971) 200 meters [2h3r2/3]; 4 × 100 meter relay [dqh1r2/3].

Courtney, J. Ira. (b.27 April 1890) 100 meters [2h1r2/3]; 200 meters [3h1r2/3]; 4 × 100 meter relay [dqh1r2/3].

Coyle, Frank James. (b.2 November 1886–d.February 1947) Pole Vault [=8].

Craig, Ralph Cook. (b.21 June 1889–d.24 July 1972) 100 meters [1]; 200 meters [1].

Davenport, Ira Nelson. (b.8 October 1887–d.17 July 1941) 400 meters [ach5r2/3]; 800 meters [3].

DeMar, Clarence Harrison. (b.7 June 1888–d.11 June 1958) Marathon [12].

Donahue, James Joseph. (b.20 April 1886–d.15 March 1966) Decathlon [5]; Pentathlon [3].

Drew, Howard Porter. (b.28 June 1890–d.20 February 1956) 100 meters [dns-final].

Dukes, Gordon Bennett. (b.23 December 1888–d.August 1966) Pole Vault [=8].

Duncan, James Henry. (b.25 September 1887) Discus Throw [3]; Discus Throw, both hands [5/1g3qr].

Edmundson, Clarence Sinclair "Hec." (b.3 August 1886–d.6 August 1964) 400 meters [2h1r2/3]; 800 meters [7].

Eller, John J., Jr. (b.15 October 1883–d.February 1967) 110 meter hurdles [2h1r2/3]; Pentathlon [19].

Enright, Harold Bradford. (b.28 April 1890–d.3 February 1946) High Jump [=7g2qr].

Erickson, Egon R. (b.4 July 1888–d.January 1973) High Jump [=4].

Erxleben, Joseph. (b.15 February 1889–d.August 1973) Marathon [8].

Farrell, Edward Leo. (b.14 June 1886–d.18 July 1958) Broad Jump [14/3g4qr]; Hop, step, and jump [13/4g3qr].

Fitzgerald, Edward John. (b.18 February 1888) 5,000 meters [dnf-h2r1/2].

Fletcher, Forest. (b.27 April 1888) Standing High Jump [=5g2qr]; Standing Long Jump [9/2g2qr].

Forshaw, Joseph, Jr. (b.13 May 1880–d.26 November 1964) Marathon [10].

Fritz, William Howard, Jr. (b.22 March 1892) Pole Vault [=8].

Gallagher, John James, Jr. (b.13 April 1890) Marathon [7].

Gerhardt, Peter C. (b.26 November 1876) 100 meters [3h1r2/3]; 200 meters [2h5r2/3].

Gillis, Simon. (b.6 April 1880–d.14 January 1964) Hammer Throw [nm/g2qr].

Goehring, Leo. (b.6 November 1891–d.February 1967) Standing High Jump [=4]; Standing Long Jump [=5/2g3qr].

Grumpelt, Henry John "Harry." (b.2 March 1885–d.3 November 1973) High Jump [=6].

Gutterson, Albert Lovejoy. (b.23 August 1887–d.7 April 1965) Broad Jump [1].

Haff, Carroll Barse. (b.19 February 1892–d.9 April 1947) 400 meters [5].

Halpin, Thomas J. (b.17 May 1892–d.10 December 1960) 800 meters [=3h9r1/3].

Hawkins, Martin William. (b.20 February 1888–d.27 October 1959) 110 meter hurdles [3].

Hedlund, Oscar Frederick. (b.26 August 1887–d.December 1971) 1,500 meters [ac-final].

Heiland, Harold William. (b.26 April 1890–d.April 1963) 100 meters [3h13r1/3]; 200 meters [3h2r2/3].

Hellawell, Harry Hallas. (b.6 November 1888–d.March 1968) 10,000 meters [12h1r1/2]; Cross-Country, Individual [12]; Cross-Country, Team [dnf-].

Holden, Harlan Ware. (b.31 March 1888) 800 meters [ach2r2/3].

Horine, George Leslie. (b.3 February 1890–d.28 November 1948) High Jump [3].

Irons, Francis C. (b.23 March 1886) Broad Jump [9/5g1qr].

Johnstone, John Oliver. (b.21 January 1892–d.February 1969) High Jump [=6].

Jones, John Paul. (b.15 October 1890–d.5 January 1970) 800 meters [dns-r2/3]; 1,500 meters [4].

Kaiser, Frederick Henry. (b.13 October 1889) 10 Kilometer Walk [dnf-final].

Kelly, Frederick Warren. (b.12 September 1891–d.7 May 1974) 110 meter hurdles [1].

Kiviat, Albert Richard "Abel." (b.23 June 1892–d.24 August 1991) 1,500 meters [2]; 3,000 Meter Team Race [1-ns/dnf].

Kramer, William J. (b.23 January 1884–d.29 February 1964) 10,000 meters [10h1r1/2]; Cross-Country, Individual [dnf-]; Cross-Country, Team [dnf-].

Lilley, Thomas H. (b.19 December 1887–d.18 September 1954) Marathon [18].

Lindberg, Edward Ferdinand Jacob. (b.9 November 1886–d.February 1978) 400 meters [3]; 4 × 400 meter relay [1].

Lippincott, Donald Fithian. (b.16 November 1893–d.9 January 1962) 100 meters [3]; 200 meters [2].

Madeira, Louis Childs, III. (b.5 February 1892–d.20 March 1943) 1,500 meters [13].

Maguire, Hugh Francis. (b.1 July 1887–d.February 1967) 10,000 meters [dnf-final].

McClure, Walter Rayburn. (b.24 August 1892–d.12 April 1959) 800 meters [3h1r1/3]; 1,500 meters [8].

McCurdy, Wallace Macafee. (b.23 October 1892–d.26 October 1970) 5,000 meters [dnf-h5r1/2].

McDonald, Patrick Joseph. (b.29 July 1878–d.16 May 1954) Shot Put [1]; Shot Put, both hands [2].

McGrath, Matthew John. (b.18 December 1878–d.29 January 1941) Hammer Throw [1].

Menaul, James Austin. (b.26 March 1888–d.17 October 1975) Pentathlon [5].

Mercer, Eugene Leroy. (b.30 October 1888–d.2 July 1957) Broad Jump [5/2g2-3/qr]; Decathlon [6].

Meredith, James Edwin "Ted." (b.14 November 1891–d.2 November 1957) 400 meters [4]; 800 meters [1]; 4 × 400 meter relay [1].

Meyer, Alvah T. (b.18 July 1888–d.1940) 100 meters [2]; 200 meters [2h4r2/3].

Mucks, Arlie Max. (b.10 December 1891–d.10 July 1967) Discus Throw [6/1g2qr]; Discus Throw, both hands [15/5g2qr].

Muller, Emil Joseph. (b.19 February 1891) Discus Throw [12/2g2qr]; Discus Throw, both hands [6/4g1qr].

Murphy, Frank Dwyer. (b.21 September 1889–d.11 June 1980) Pole Vault [=3].

Nelson, Frank Thayer. (b.22 May 1887–d.16 July 1970) Pole Vault [=2].

Nicholson, John Patrick. (b.30 July 1889–d.2 April 1970) 110 meter hurdles [dnf-final]; High Jump [nh/g1qr].

Oler, Wesley Marion, Jr. (b.15 December 1892–d.5 April 1980) High Jump [=4g3qr].

Patterson, James Norman Carlton. (b.4 July 1886–d.October 1971) 1,500 meters [3h3r1/3].

Philbrook, George Warren. (b.10 October 1886–d.25 March 1964) Shot Put [5/2g4qr]; Discus Throw [7/1g5qr]; Decathlon [ac/dnf].

Piggott, Richard Francis. (b.6 July 1888–d.November 1966) Marathon [9].

Pritchard, Edwin M. (b.17 May 1889–d.April 1976) 110 meter hurdles [2h6r2/3].

Putnam, Herbert Nathan. (b.7 May 1890–d.January 1967) 800 meters [8]; 1,500 meters [3h5r1/3].

Reidpath, Charles Decker. (b.20 September 1889–d.21 October 1975) 200 meters [5]; 400 meters [1]; 4 × 400 meter relay [1].

Renz, Edward. (b.13 October 1891–d.April 1976) 10 Kilometer Walk [7h1r1/2].

Reynolds, John James. (b.9 August 1889–d.June 1987) Marathon [dnf-].

Richards, Alma Wilford. (b.20 February 1890–d.3 April 1963) High Jump [1].

Rose, Ralph Waldo. (b.17 March 1885–d.16 October 1913) Shot Put [2]; Shot Put, both hands [1]; Discus Throw [11/2g3qr]; Hammer Throw [=8/4g2qr].

Rosenberger, James Maher. (b.6 April 1887) 400 meters [dnf-h4r2/3].

Ryan, Michael J. (b.1 January 1889–d.December 1971) Marathon [dnf-].

Schwartz, Samuel. (b.1 July 1882–d.January 1978) 10 Kilometer Walk [6h1r1/2].

Scott, Henry Louis. (b.16 November 1891) 5,000 meters [7]; 10,000 meters [dnf-final]; Cross-Country, Individual [24]; Cross-Country, Team [dnf-]; 3,000 Meter Team Race [1-ns/dnf].

Sheppard, Melvin Winfield. (b.5 September 1893–d.4 January 1942) 400 meters [2h3r2/3]; 800 meters [2]; 1,500 meters [ac-final]; 4 × 400 meter relay [1].

Sherman, Benjamin Franklin. (b.5 April 1881) Hammer Throw [12/8g1qr].

Smith, Harry J. (b.30 July 1888–d.20 January 1992) Marathon [17].

Sockalexis, Andrew. (b.11 January 1891) Marathon [4].

Strobino, Gaston M., "Gal." (b.23 August 1891–d.30 March 1969) Marathon [3].

Taber, Norman Stephen. (b.3 September 1891–d.15 July 1952) 1,500 meters [3]; 3,000 Meter Team Race [1].

Tewanima, Lewis. (b.1888–d.18 January 1969) 10,000 meters [2]; Marathon [16].

Thomas, Rupert Broas, Jr. (b.21 November 1890–d.28 February 1956) 100 meters [3h6r2/3].

Thorpe, James Francis (né Wa-Tho-Huck [Bright Path].) (b.28 May 1887–d.28 March 1953) High Jump [=4]; Broad Jump [7/2g4qr]; Decathlon [1]; Pentathlon [1].

Voellmeke, Alfred. (b.19 December 1874) 10 Kilometer Walk [6h2r1/2].

Wendell, James Isaac. (b.1 September 1890–d.22 November 1958) 110 meter hurdles [2].

Whitney, Lawrence Atwood. (b.2 February 1891–d.24 April 1941) Shot Put [3]; Shot Put, both hands [4/1g1qr]; Discus Throw [20/4g2qr].

Wikoff, Garnett Merrill. (b.12 November 1886–d.4 November 1959) 5,000 meters [dnf-h3r1/2].

Wilson, Clement Pierce. (b.1 February 1891–d.April 1983) 100 meters [ach5r2/3]; 200 meters [2h2r2/3]; 4 × 100 meter relay [dqh1r2/3].

Worthington, Harry Thomas. (b.25 December 1891–d.4 March 1990) Broad Jump [4/1g4qr].

Wright, Marc Snowell. (b.21 April 1890–d.5 August 1975) Pole Vault [=2].

Young, Donnell Brooks. (b.25 April 1888–d.28 July 1989) 200 meters [6]; 400 meters [dqh5r2/3].

Cycling (Total: 9; Men: 9; Women: 0)

Becht, John. (b.13 October 1886–d.September 1977) Road Race, Individual [28]; Road Race, Team [3/ns].

Kopsky, Joseph G. (b.4 November 1884–d.January 1974) Road Race, Individual [20]; Road Race, Team [3/ns].

Kruschel, Albert Michael. (b.21 October 1889) Road Race, Individual [13]; Road Race, Team [3].

Loftes, Alvin Hjalmar. (b.1 January 1891–d.July 1971) Road Race, Individual [11]; Road Race, Team [3].

Martin, Walter C. (b.28 September 1891) Road Race, Individual [17]; Road Race, Team [3].

Meissner, Frank August. (b.19 July 1895–d.14 May 1966) Road Race, Individual [70]; Road Race, Team [3/ns].

Pike, James R., "Jesse." (b.17 September 1890–d.October 1986) Road Race, Individual [54]; Road Race, Team [3/ns].

Schutte, Carl Otto. (b.5 October 1887) Road Race, Individual [3]; Road Race, Team [3].

Steinert, Jerome. (b.6 November 1883–d.October 1966) Road Race, Individual [56]; Road Race, Team [3/ns].

Diving (Total: 2; Men: 2; Women: 0)

Gaidzik, George William. (b.22 February 1885) Springboard Diving [7]; Plain and Fancy High Diving [6h1r1/2]; Plain High Diving [2h2r1/2].

McAleenan, Arthur, Jr. (b.15 October 1894–d.23 March 1947) Springboard Diving [3h1r1/2]; Plain and Fancy High Diving [ac/dnf-h2r1/2]; Plain High Diving [5h2r1/2].

Equestrian Events (Total: 4; Men: 4; Women: 0)

Graham, Ephraim Foster. (b.10 August 1881–d.23 December 1962) Three-Day Event, Individual [=12]; Three-Day Event, Team [3] (Connie).

Henry, Guy Vernor, Jr. (b.26 December 1875–d.29 November 1967) Dressage, Individual [13] (Chiswell); Jumping, Team [4] (Connie); Three-Day Event, Individual [11] (Chiswell); Three-Day Event, Team [3] (Chiswell).

Lear, Benjamin, Jr. (b.12 May 1879–d.1 November 1966) Jumping, Team [4]; Three-Day Event, Individual [7]; Three-Day Event, Team [3] (Poppy).

Montgomery, John Carter. (b.22 November 1881–d.7 June 1948) Dressage, Individual [20]; Jumping, Team [4]; Three-Day Event, Individual [9]; Three-Day Event, Team [3] (Deceive).

Fencing (Total: 13; Men: 13; Women: 0)

Bowman, William Lawrence. (b.3 December 1881–d.December 1964) Foil, Individual (=4p10r1/4); Épée, Individual (=3p1r3/4); Épée, Team (=9).

Breckinridge, Scott Dudley. (b.23 May 1882–d.1 August 1941) Foil, Individual (=4p3r2/4); Épée, Team (=9).

Breed, George Horace. (b.14 July 1876–d.24 June 1956) Foil, Individual (4p16r1/4); Épée, Individual (=4p5r2/4); Épée, Team (=9).

Gignoux, John Ernest. (b.26 August 1878) Foil, Individual (6p9r1/4); Épée, Individual (7p13r1/4).

Hall, Sherman. (b.1885) Foil, Individual (3p4r3/4); Épée, Individual (=4p4r1/4); Épée, Team (=9).

Hammond, Graeme Monroe. (b.1 February 1858–d.30 October 1944) Foil, Individual (=4p5r1/4); Épée, Individual (4p9r1/4).

Larimer, Marc Winthrop. (b.1890) Foil, Individual (=5p1r2/4); Épée, Individual (=4p8r1/4).

MacLaughlin, John Andrews. (b.1890) Foil, Individual (=4p6r1/4); Épée, Individual (7p10r1/4); Épée, Team (=9).

Moore, James Merriam. (b.1890) Épée, Individual (=7p15r1/4).

Rayner, Harold Marvin. (b.27 July 1888–d.8 December 1954) Foil, Individual (6p5r2/4).

Sauer, Alfred Ernest. (b.1880) Foil, Individual (4p12r1/4); Épée, Individual (4p7r1/4); Sabre, Individual (=4p2r2/4).

Schenck, Fredric. (b.23 October 1886–d.April 1969) Épée, Individual (=4p1r2/4).

Van Zo Post, Albertson. (b.1866–d.23 January 1938) Foil, Individual (dnc-p2r2/4); Épée, Individual (=5p8r2/4); Épée, Team (=9); Sabre, Individual (dnc-p8r2/4).

Modern Pentathlon (Total: 1; Men: 1; Women: 0)

Patton, George Smith, Jr. (b.11 November 1885–d.21 December 1945) Individual [5]. (See also Fencing.)

Shooting (Total: 26; Men: 26; Women: 0)

Adams, Harry Loren. (b.1 October 1880–d.16 February 1960) Free Rifle, 300 meters, 3-Positions [28]; Military Rifle, 300 meters, 3-Positions [12]; Military Rifle, 600 meters, any position [12]; Military Rifle, 200, 400, 500, and 600 meters, Teams [1].

Anderson, Edwin L. (b.26 November 1886) Small-Bore Rifle, prone position, 50 meters [23]; Small-Bore Rifle, 25 meters, Disappearing Target [16].

Bartlett, Harold Terry. (b.26 July 1887–d.14 September 1955) Free Rifle, 300 meters, 3-Positions [36]; Military Rifle, 300 meters, 3-Positions [9]; Military Rifle, 600 meters, any position [19].

Billings, Charles W. (b.26 November 1866–d.13 December 1928) Clay Trap Shooting, Individual [=41]; Clay Trap Shooting, Teams [1].

Briggs, Allan Lindsay. (b.14 February 1873) Free Rifle, 300 meters, 3-Positions [35]; Military Rifle, 300 meters, 3-Positions [25]; Military Rifle, 600 meters, any position [4]; Military Rifle, 200, 400, 500, and 600 meters, Teams [1].

Burdette, Cornelius L. (b.6 November 1878) Free Rifle, 300 meters, 3-Positions [21]; Military Rifle, 300 meters, 3-Positions [52]; Military Rifle, 600 meters, any position [8]; Military Rifle, 200, 400, 500, and 600 meters, Teams [1].

Dietz, John A. (b.24 November 1870–d.11 October 1939) Free Pistol, 50 meters [9]; Dueling Pistol, 30 meters [4]; Dueling Pistol, 30 meters, Teams [4]; Military Pistol, 50 meters, Teams [1].

Dolfen, Peter J. (b.21 May 1880) Free Pistol, 50 meters [2]; Dueling Pistol, 30 meters [16]; Military Pistol, 50 meters, Teams [1].

Gleason, Edward Francis. (b.9 November 1869–d.9 April 1944) Clay Trap Shooting, Individual [=9]; Clay Trap Shooting, Teams [1].

Graham, James R. (b.12 February 1873–d.18 February 1950) Clay Trap Shooting, Individual [1]; Clay Trap Shooting, Teams [1].

Hall, Frank. (b.8 July 1865) Clay Trap Shooting, Individual [=12]; Clay Trap Shooting, Teams [1].

Hendrickson, John H. (b.25 February 1871) Clay Trap Shooting, Individual [=41]; Clay Trap Shooting, Teams [1].

Hird, Frederick S. (b.6 December 1879–d.27 September 1952) Free Rifle, 300 meters, 3-Positions [38]; Military Rifle, 300 meters, 3-Positions [28]; Military Rifle, 600 meters, any position [26]; Small-Bore Rifle, prone position, 50 meters [1]; Small-Bore Rifle, 25 meters, Disappearing Target [8]; Small-Bore Rifle, 25 meters, Disappearing Target, Teams [3]; Small-Bore Rifle, 50 meters, Teams [3].

Jackson, John E. (b.14 February 1885–d.June 1971) Military Rifle, 300 meters, 3-Positions [33]; Military Rifle, 600 meters, any position [3]; Military Rifle, 200, 400, 500, and 600 meters, Teams [1].

Lane, Alfred P. (b.26 September 1891–d.October 1965) Free Pistol, 50 meters [1]; Dueling Pistol, 30 meters [1]; Dueling Pistol, 30 meters, Teams [4]; Military Pistol, 50 meters, Teams [1].

Leuschner, William D. F. (b.27 November 1863–d.25 October 1935) Small-Bore Rifle, prone position, 50 meters [7]; Small-Bore Rifle, 25 meters, Disappearing Target [24]; Small-Bore Rifle, 25 meters, Disappearing Target, Teams [3]; Small-Bore Rifle, 50 meters, Teams [3]; Running Deer, Single Shot, Individual [=8]; Running Deer, Double Shot, Individual [15]; Running Deer, Single Shot, Teams [2].

Libbey, William A. (b.27 March 1855) Running Deer, Single Shot, Teams [2].

McDonnell, William Neil. (b.15 July 1876) Military Rifle, 300 meters, 3-Positions [31]; Military Rifle, 600 meters, any position [32]; Small-Bore Rifle, prone position, 50 meters [18]; Small-Bore Rifle, 25 meters, Disappearing Target [14]; Small-Bore Rifle, 25 meters, Disappearing Target, Teams [3]; Running Deer, Single Shot, Teams [2].

McMahon, Daniel Francis. (b.16 February 1890–d.August 1975) Clay Trap Shooting, Individual [=35].

Osburn, Carl Townsend. (b.5 May 1884–d.28 December 1966) Free Rifle, 300 meters, 3-Positions [17]; Military Rifle, 300 meters, 3-Positions [2]; Military Rifle, 600 meters, any position [2]; Military Rifle, 200, 400, 500, and 600 meters, Teams [1]; Small-Bore Rifle, prone position, 50 meters [13]; Small-Bore Rifle, 25 meters, Disappearing Target [34]; Small-Bore Rifle, 50 meters, Teams [3].

Roedder, Hans. (b.12 March 1879–d.December 1966) Free Pistol, 50 meters [22]; Dueling Pistol, 30 meters [10].

Sayre, Reginald Hall. (b.18 October 1859–d.29 May 1929) Free Pistol, 50 meters [13]; Dueling Pistol, 30 meters [19]; Dueling Pistol, 30 meters, Teams [4].

Sears, Henry Francis. (b.8 January 1862–d.1 January 1942) Free Pistol, 50 meters [7]; Dueling Pistol, 30 meters [21]; Military Pistol, 50 meters, Teams [1].

Spotts, Ralph Lewis. (b.14 June 1875–d.17 April 1924) Clay Trap Shooting, Individual [=9]; Clay Trap Shooting, Teams [1].

Sprout, Warren A. (b.3 February 1874–d.23 August 1945) Free Rifle, 300 meters, 3-Positions [32]; Military Rifle, 300 meters, 3-Positions [37]; Military Rifle, 600 meters, any position [14]; Military Rifle, 200, 400, 500, and 600 meters, Teams [1]; Small-Bore Rifle, prone position, 50 meters [12]; Small-Bore Rifle, 25 meters, Disappearing Target [17]; Small-Bore Rifle, 25 meters, Disappearing Target, Teams [3]; Small-Bore Rifle, 50 meters, Teams [3].

Winans, Walter. (b.5 April 1852–d.12 August 1920) Free Pistol, 50 meters [49]; Dueling Pistol, 30 meters [8]; Dueling Pistol, 30 meters, Teams [4]; Running Deer, Single Shot, Individual [=29]; Running Deer, Double Shot, Individual [11]; Running Deer, Single Shot, Teams [2]. (See also Art Competition Entrants.)

Swimming (Total: 7; Men: 7; Women: 0)

Hebner, Harry J. (b.15 June 1891–d.12 October 1968) 100 meter freestyle [3h5r1/4]; 100 meter backstroke [1]; 4 × 200 meter freestyle relay [2].

Huszagh, Kenneth Arthur. (b.3 September 1891–d.11 January 1950) 100 meter freestyle [3]; 4 × 200 meter freestyle relay [2].

Kahanamoku, Duke Paoa Kahinu Makoe Hulikohoa. (b.24 August 1890–d.22 January 1968) 100 meter freestyle [1]; 4 × 200 meter freestyle relay [2].

McDermott, Michael J. (b.18 January 1893–d.October 1970) 200 meter breaststroke [dqh4r1/3]; 400 meter breaststroke [dqh2r1/3].

McGillivray, Perry. (b.5 August 1893–d.27 July 1944) 100 meter freestyle [3h3r3/4]; 4 × 200 meter freestyle relay [2].

Nerich, Nicholas J. (b.13 November 1893–d.September 1977) 100 meter freestyle [=3h2r2/4]; 400 meter freestyle [4h1r2/3].

Reilly, James H. (b.11 March 1890–d.3 March 1962) 100 meter freestyle [4h6r1/4]; 400 meter freestyle [3h1r1/3].

Tennis (Total: 1; Men: 1; Women: 0)

Pell, Theodore Roosevelt. (b.12 May 1878–d.18 August 1967) Men's Singles (Lawn) [=9].

Wrestling (Total: 2; Men: 2; Women: 0)

Lyshon, William Jones. (b.30 December 1887) 60 kg. Class (Greco-Roman) [AC].

Retzer, George Washington, Jr. (b.14 March 1883–d.October 1979) 60 kg. Class (Greco-Roman) [AC].

Art Competition Medalists

Bohemia

Spaniel, Otakar. (b.1881–d.1955) Sculpture.

Canada

McKenzie, Robert Tait. (b.1867–d.1938) Sculpture.

France

Adam, Paul. Literature.

Boulenger, Marcel. Literature.

Coubertin, Pierre Frédi, Baron de.[50] (b.1 January 1863–d.2 September 1937) Literature (1).

Dalcroze, Émile-Jacques. (b.1865–d.1950) Music.

Dubois, Georges. (d.1934) Sculpture (2).

Gueldry, Ferdinand Joseph.[51] Painting.

Jourdain, Frantz. (b.1847–d.1935) Designs for town planning.

Letainturier-Fradin, Gabriel. Literature.

Pottecher, Maurice. (b.1867–d.1960) Literature.

Rafaelli, Jean-François. Painting.

Great Britain

Barnard, Ebbel P. Music.

Ireland
Townsend, Ernest. (b.26 June 1893) Painting.

Italy
Barthelemy, Riccardo. Music (1).
Bugatti, Rembrandt.[52] (b.16 October 1884–d.8 January 1916) Sculpture.
d'Annunzio, Gabriele. (b.12 March 1863–d.1 March 1938) Literature.
Segoffin, Victor. Sculpture.
Pellegrini, Carlo. (b.1839–d.1917) Painting (1).

Russia
Truvetsky, Prince Pavel. (b.1866–d.1938) Sculpture.

Switzerland
d'Ollone, Max. (b.1875–d.1959) Music.
Doret, Gustave. (b.1863–d.1943) Music.
Fatio, Guillaume. (b.1860–d.1958) Designs for town planning.
Hippenmeier, Konrad. Designs for town planning.[53]
Laverrière, Alphonse. (b.16 May 1872–d.11 March 1954) Designs for town planning (1).
Monod, Eugène-Edouard. (b.16 June 1871–d.9 November 1929) Designs for town planning (1).

United States
Winans, Walter. (b.5 April 1852–d.12 August 1920) Sculpture (1). (See also Shooting under United States.)

Nation Not Identified
Collin, André. Designs for town planning.
Eccord, Fritz. Designs for town planning.
Laffen, A. Designs for town planning.
Rees, J. W. Designs for town planning.
Skarba, Gyula. Designs for town planning.

Full Name Not Identified[54]
Vinulsky, –– Sculpture.
––, Christian de. Music.
––, René. Literature.
––, William. Literature.

NOTES

1. Special thanks are due to Harry Gordon and Ron Palenski, Australian and New Zealand Olympic historians, respectively, who reviewed the entire Australasian index in great detail.

2. Cvetko was born in Senoze, near Kranj, in present day Slovenia. Though it was not a country at the time, Cvetko can be considered the first Slovenian to have competed in the Olympic Games.

3. Otto Scheff was from what is now the Polish portion of the Austro-Hungarian Empire. He was born Sheff-Sochaczewski, but changed his name to the more Germanlike Scheff. He won a bronze medal in swimming at the 1906 Intercalated Olympic Games.

4. Special thanks are due to Jos Luypaers, Belgian Olympic historian, who reviewed the entire Belgian index in great detail.

5. Grégoire was assigned to the original heat two, but did not appear in time for the redrawn heat one start. He appeared for the original heat four (this heat after the redraw), and was for some reason allowed to start in this heat. But the performance was eventually disallowed and his correct place in the results is DNS in heat one (which was the original heats one and two). Grégoire's time should have advanced him to the semifinals, as the fastest third-place finisher in round one was supposed to qualify for the semifinals, but it was not allowed.

6. Special thanks are due to Jiří Kössl and Jaroslav Pruner, Czechoslovak Olympic historians, who reviewed the entire Bohemian index in great detail.

7. Ivan Schweizer is usually listed as competing in the single sculls, but it appears he did not actually start. See the rowing section.

8. Ian Buchanan, British Olympic historian, and Wolf Lyberg, Swedish Olympic historian, are preparing a book on IOC members. From the entry on Oscar N. Garcia, they have given us the following information. There were actually two Chilean teams prepared to compete in Stockholm. The National Sports Federation nominated a team and Garcia told them that they had no right to do so, and he then nominated his own team. The Swedes eventually allowed members of both teams to compete. An excerpt from their forthcoming book explains this further "On 15 March 1912 the NSF (National Sporting Federation), with the backing of the Minister of Instruction, announced that they would be sending a team to the Stockholm Games and shortly thereafter the NSF advised all sporting bodies in the country that they had formed a Chilean Olympic Committee and elected Admiral Arthur Fernando Vidal as President. Garcia then had a meeting with the Minister of Instruction and pointed out that, because of his mandate from the IOC, he was the only person authorized to approve the participation of Chilean competitors at the Stockholm Games. Garcia then nominated his own choice as to who should represent Chile in Stockholm and the Swedish organizers were placed in the embarrassing position of having two separate sets of entries from Chile, the 'NSF' team and 'Garcia' team. Eventually the problem was resolved when it was decided to accept entries from both the Chilean committees."

9. Special thanks are due to Hans Agersnap Larsen, Danish Olympic historian, who reviewed the entire Danish index in great detail.

10. Larsen later changed his last name to Branning.

11. Special thanks are due to Markku Siukonen, Finnish Olympic historian, who reviewed the entire Finnish index in great detail.

12. It is listed in some sources that Emil Lindh and Erik Lindh were twin brothers, with the same birthdate. Finnish Olympic historian Markku Siukonen notes, "Erik A. Lindh was not a brother of Emil Lindh."

13. Sometimes listed as his brother, Jean René Labat, who was originally entered, but withdrew and was replaced by André.

14. Special thanks are due to Rupert Kaiser, German Olympic historian, who reviewed the entire German index in great detail.

15. Often seen as Karl Ritter von Halt, in 1912 he was Karl von Halt. On 24 February 1921 he received the "Max-Joseph-Order" which granted him the title of "Ritter" which he added to his name at that time. It was, in English, the effective equivalent of being knighted, or having sir added to one's name.

16. Special thanks are due to Ian Buchanan, British Olympic historian, who reviewed the entire Great Britain index in great detail.

17. Listed as deceased on 25 September 1916 in *British Olympians*. An identically named person was killed in action in World War I on that date but it was not the 1912 footballer. The 1912 footballer was known to be alive in South Africa circa 1937, but his further whereabouts are unknown.

18. Charles Simmons was the father of well-known actress, Jean Simmons.

19. Based primarily on the book, *Helliniki Simmetokhi Stis Sinkhrones Olympiades* (Athens: author, 1990) by Athanassios Tarasouleas.

20. There is some confusion over the this name. The two chroniclers of Olympian athletes, Wolf Lyberg, and Gennady Marichev, list him as Cambopoulos Versis (Lyberg) and Chambopoulos Versis (Marichev). Marichev actually lists two Versises competing in fencing in 1912 for Greece, with

no first name given for the other one. But the best source must be Tarasouleas, who in his book on Greek Olympians, *Helliniki Simmetokhi Stis Sinkhrones Olympiades,* lists only one such athlete competing in fencing at the 1912 Olympics for Greece—Georgios Versis. The only other similar name he lists is An. Kharalampopoulos.

21. Name spellings and information based primarily on the list of Hungarian Olympians published by the Hungarian Olympic Committee, *Az Olimpiai Játékokon Indult Magyar Versenyzők Névsora 1896–1980.*

22. Hungarian sources list Drubina by this name, but Czech sources list him as Slovakian and by the name István Drubina.

23. Hungarian sources list Forgács by this name, but Czech sources list him as Slovakian and by the name František Facínek-Forgács.

24. Hungarian sources list Jankovich by this name, but Czech sources list him as Slovakian and by the name Stefan Jankovich.

25. Also listed as Slovakian by Czech sources.

26. Also listed as Slovakian by Czech sources.

27. Hungarian sources list Luntzer by this name, but Czech sources list him as Slovakian and by the name Juraj Luntzer.

28. Also listed as Slovakian by Czech sources.

29. Hungarian sources list Szalay by this name, but Czech sources list him as Slovakian and by the name Szalav.

30. Hungarian sources list Szobota by this name, but Czech sources list him as Slovakian and by the name Frantisek Szobota.

31. Also listed as Slovakian by Czech sources.

32. Special thanks to Þorstein Einarsson, Icelandic sports historian, who provided much of the data on the *Glíma* wrestlers, and checked the spelling of the names for the Icelandic athletes.

33. Special thanks are due to Giuseppe Odello, Italian Olympic historian, who reviewed the entire Italian index in great detail.

34. Special thanks are due to Tsuyoshi "Bob" Miyakawa, Japanese Olympic historian, who reviewed the Japanese index in great detail.

35. Special thanks are due to Tony Bijkerk, Dutch Olympic historian, who reviewed the Netherlands index in great detail. It is also based to a great degree on his book (with Ruud Paauw), *Gouden Boek van de Nederlandse Olympiers* (Haarlem, NED: Uitgeverij de Vrieseborch, 1996.)

36. In keeping with Dutch custom, the alphabetization of the Dutch athletes is different from that of the athletes of other nations. Specifically, we have placed the particles (de, von, van der, and so on) after the name and disregarded them with respect to alphabetization.

37. Special thanks are due to Magne Teigen and Arild Gjerde, Norwegian Olympic historians, who reviewed the entire Norwegian index in great detail.

38. In ladies' singles, Valborg Bjurstedt (NOR), sister of Anna "Molla" Bjurstedt, is listed as winning in the first round. But the match was a walkover over Miken Rieck (NOR). In round two, Bjurstedt did not compete and lost by default to Dora Köring (GER). Thus she never actually competed. Norwegian Olympic historians Magne Teigen and Arild Gjerde have examined this situation and are also not certain what to do. It appears that Valborg Bjurstedt may not actually have been in Stockholm, and the first round walkover was merely a matter of record keeping by the officials. So we have not included her as a competitor.

39. See Appendix V for a more complete discussion of the Russian athletes in 1912, and also notes concerning the variant spellings of their names.

40. Dimitry Romanov was a member of the Russian Romanov family, who carried the title Kaiser Hoheit. Lyberg notes that he was the nephew of Csar Aleksandr III, and the son of the grandduke Pavel, and the brother of Maria Pavlovna. Dmitry Romanov participated in the murder of Rasputin and was then expelled from the Russian court. After the Bolshevik Revolution, he lived in exile in France, Germany, and Switzerland.

41. Also seen listed as Charles von Rommel, Karel de Rommel, and Karol von Rommel. He later lived in Poland and competed for Poland in the 1924 and 1928 Olympic Games. Polish Olympic

records list him as Karol Rómmel. It should be noted that these records were published before the 1991 fall of Communism, and that "von" and "de" are honorary titles, and were likely disregarded by Polish authorities.

42. Of Finnish descent.

43. Four of the five members of the Russian modern pentathlon team in 1912 were of Finnish origin, all save Nepokupnoy. At the time, they were serving as soldiers in the Russian army which is why they represented Russia in 1912 (according to Markku Siukonen, Finnish Olympic historian). As noted in other places in this text, in 1912 Finland was still a part of Russia.

44. Of Finnish descent. Served as an alternate for Finland in modern pentathlon at the 1920 Olympic Games.

45. Almqvist served in the Russian army as an officer from 1903 to 1917, and then in the Finnish army 1918 to 1924 and later at the outset of World War II. It is ironic that he competed for Russia in the 1912 Olympics, for he later died while fighting against the Russians as a Finnish military officer.

46. Often seen as Veli Gunnar von Hohenthal. This spelling of the name was found by Markku Siukonen in the archives of the Finnish church and the Army records.

47. The name is usually listed as Martin Klein in most sources. But the 1912 entry form is clear that he entered as Max Klein. It was likely a nickname, or a shortened form of Martin.

48. Special thanks are due to Lappe Laubscher, South African Olympic historian, who reviewed the entire South African index in great detail.

49. This is the modern Turkish spelling. Also seen spelled as Megherian, Megerdich.

Index